# THE ECONOMIC ASS
# MERGERS UNDER I
# COMPETITION LAW

This concise and practical guide to the most important economic techniques and evidence employed in modern merger control draws on the authors' extensive experience in advising on European merger cases. It offers an introduction to the relevant economic concepts and analytical tools, and stand-alone chapters provide an in-depth overview of the theoretical and practical issues related to market definition, unilateral effects, coordinated effects and non-horizontal mergers. Each form of economic evidence and analysis is illustrated with practical examples and an overview of key merger decisions.

DANIEL GORE is a principal with RBB Economics, a consultancy specialising in the economics of competition policy.

STEPHEN LEWIS is a principal with RBB Economics.

ANDREA LOFARO is a partner at RBB Economics.

FRANCES DETHMERS is a counsel economist with leading international law firm Clifford Chance LLP.

# THE ECONOMIC ASSESSMENT OF MERGERS UNDER EUROPEAN COMPETITION LAW

DANIEL GORE, STEPHEN LEWIS, ANDREA LOFARO
and FRANCES DETHMERS

CAMBRIDGE
UNIVERSITY PRESS

# CAMBRIDGE
## UNIVERSITY PRESS

University Printing House, Cambridge CB2 8BS, United Kingdom

Cambridge University Press is part of the University of Cambridge.

It furthers the University's mission by disseminating knowledge in the pursuit of education, learning and research at the highest international levels of excellence.

www.cambridge.org
Information on this title: www.cambridge.org/9781107596146

© Frances Dethmers, Daniel Gore, Stephen Lewis and Andrea Lofaro 2013

First published 2013
Reprinted 2013
First paperback edition 2015

*A catalogue record for this publication is available from the British Library*

*Library of Congress Cataloguing in Publication data*

Gore, Daniel.
The economic assessment of mergers under European competition law / Daniel Gore, Stephen Lewis, Andrea Lofaro and Frances Dethmers.
pages cm
ISBN 978-1-107-00772-7 (Hardback)
1. Consolidation and merger of corporations–Europe. 2. Competition–Law and legislation–Europe. I. Title.
HD2746.5.G667 2013
338.8′3094–dc23
2012046195

ISBN 978-1-107-00772-7 Hardback
ISBN 978-1-107-59614-6 Paperback

# CONTENTS

# TABLE OF MERGER DECISIONS

# ACKNOWLEDGMENTS

A number of people have assisted with the production of this book. Daniel Gore, Stephen Lewis and Andrea Lofaro are particularly indebted to their colleagues at RBB Economics for many of the materials drawn upon in its preparation. Special mention is deserved by Derek Ridyard, Simon Bishop and Simon Baker from whom we have learned a lot over the years – many of the insights into economic and policy issues contained in the book are due to them. Frances Dethmers is very grateful to her colleagues at Clifford Chance and, in particular Tony Reeves, Heleen Engelen and Adam Dawson for providing unconditional support. In addition, she would like to thank the 'wrecking crew' (Julianne O'Leary, Jürgen Schindler, Julia Holtz, Kylie Sturtz and Barbara Nijs) for making competition law that bit more exciting. Last but not least, thanks to Luc Peeperkorn (DG Comp) and Ali Nikpay (OFT) who were invaluable teachers at the beginning.

We also thank Adrian Majumdar, Iestyn Williams, Sam Brown, Alan Crawford, Chris Doyle, Paul Hutchinson, Daria Prigioni and Toby Watt for critically reviewing various chapters and for providing invaluable insights, comments and suggestions. Joan de Solà-Morales assisted with the research and exposition of a number of merger cases, while the many charts and figures contained in the book would have looked far less professional without the help of Stéphanie Bouchet, Ina Esser and Alicia Fecci. Florentin Genthon, Julie Lassebie, Louise Lee and Michael Lewis all have our gratitude for spotting typos and suggesting innumerable drafting improvements. Both Monica Michiels van Kessenich and Chantal Roosseleers at Clifford Chance worked incredibly hard to improve the overall layout, including all references.

Special thanks go to Nicholas Levy who agreed to write the foreword and to Simon Baxter, Fiona Carlin, Jeffrey Church, Claire Jeffs, Frédéric Louis and Frank Verboven for their encouraging feedback and kind endorsements.

We are also very grateful to Kim Hughes and her colleagues at Cambridge University Press for their enduring support throughout the project and for not losing patience despite countless missed deadlines over the last two years.

Finally, we would like to thank Katy, Daria, Jane and Hilde for tolerating our absence during many evenings and weekends and for providing support throughout this project.

We would like to dedicate this book to our parents.

# FOREWORD

It is difficult now to recall the sense of expectation, uncertainty, and excitement that greeted the entry into force of the Merger Regulation in 1990. Among the many unanswered questions was how the Commission would define markets and analyse the substantive issues raised by reportable concentrations. Notwithstanding the explicit emphasis placed on competition-based criteria in the original text of the Merger Regulation, the use of economics and economists was in its infancy in the EU: few Commission officials had a background in economics; outside counsel were for the most part unfamiliar with economic theory and concepts; and economics was at the time applied only rarely in antitrust cases. Fundamental issues concerning the role of economic evidence in EU merger control were therefore unresolved and very real.

Initially in respect of market definition and subsequently in connection with horizontal and non-horizontal effects, the Commission started to employ a more rigorous, quantitative, and economically orientated approach to the assessment of mergers and other forms of concentration, placing increasing reliance on firm evidence and solid investigative techniques that could be tested against what Joseph Schumpeter called 'the cold metal of economic theory'. When, in 2003 and 2004, as part of the package of measures implemented in response to a series of reversals before the EU Courts, the Commission adopted the Horizontal Mergers Guidelines and appointed its first Chief Economist, the central role of economics and economists in the application of the Merger Regulation was confirmed, and decisions since then have been increasingly grounded in hard data and sound economics.

This magnificent and comprehensive textbook introduces students, practitioners, economists, and regulators alike to the economic tools and methodologies used to assess concentrations under the Merger Regulation. The principal empirical techniques employed to define markets and to analyse unilateral effects, coordinated effects, vertical effects, and conglomerate effects are described with clarity and precision. Each chapter explains – clearly, concisely, and thoughtfully – the underlying economic concepts before describing the Commission's practice. Charts, tables, and graphs illustrate the applicable principles, and individual cases, including many of the leading decisions of the past decade – *Nokia/Navteq, Sony/BMG, Google/DoubleClick, Statoil/JET, ABF/GBI Business, Oracle/Sun Microsystems* and *Gas Natural/Endesa* – are given detailed analysis, drawing on the authors' considerable experience and insights. And, most importantly perhaps, authoritative guidance is provided on those quantitative techniques that have been employed most successfully to address the wide array of substantive issues that have arisen in practice.

No antitrust lawyer can aspire to practice EU merger control today without a sound knowledge of economics. This textbook provides that knowledge. It is a formidable achievement, a truly invaluable work. Daniel Gore, Stephen Lewis, Andrea Lofaro, and Frances Dethmers have authored a terrific antitrust reference book.

*Nicholas Levy*
*December 2012*

# A COMMENT ON THE TEXT BY PROFESSOR
JEFFREY CHURCH

This comprehensive and insightful volume is distinguished by its skillful and knowledgeable mix of relevant economic theory and practice of competition economics.

The authors have been at the forefront of the economic revolution that has transformed merger enforcement policy in Europe in the last decade and this book reflects their inside knowledge and experience.

In providing a comprehensive discussion of the economic concepts that underlie modern merger enforcement policy and in presenting and assessing the empirical techniques and methodologies used in practice to marshal and assess the evidence on competitive effects of a merger, whether horizontal, vertical, or conglomerate, the authors have provided a real and valuable service to the competition policy enforcement community worldwide. Their focus is clearly on the "what" of enforcement policy, with deft discussion of the actual use of the techniques in merger cases considered by the European Commission.

This is a foundational text destined to be the "go to" reference for those new to the intricacies of the practice of merger policy enforcement, as well as experienced hands.

*Professor Jeffrey Church*
*University of Calgary*
*December 2012*

# 1

# Introduction

## 1. Purpose and scope of this book

This book is intended to support and assist practitioners involved in the application of European competition law to mergers. Our principal intention is to provide lawyers who do not have a background in economics with an overview of the economic foundations of merger analysis, and of the analytical techniques and evidence used to appraise the competitive impact of mergers. We also hope that this book may be useful to economists who wish to gain an understanding of how economics is applied to merger assessment in practice. The goal is to assist readers to understand the economic concepts relevant to a particular case; to identify forms of economic analysis and evidence relevant to that case; to recognise what analyses and evidence would best be prepared by the merging parties and their advisers; and to evaluate critically economic evidence prepared on behalf of merging parties or by competition authorities.

In line with this goal, the book is structured according to the types of issue that particular merger notifications may raise. Each issue, and the relevant forms of evidence and analyses, is discussed on a stand-alone basis. This approach is intended to allow the text to be used as a reference, with the reader able to consult the relevant section for the type of merger or question faced.

Chapter 2 introduces the concept of **market definition**. Market definition is a conceptual framework for identifying the groups of firms, products and regions amongst which competitive interactions arise. As such, market definition is a central element of all antitrust investigations, including merger assessment, where market definition provides the starting point for investigating the impact of changes in firm ownership. Chapter 2 provides an overview of the evidence and analytical techniques used by the Commission to inform the assessment of market definition in merger investigations.

Chapter 3 discusses **unilateral effects**, a theory of harm that frequently arises in the context of **horizontal mergers**. Unilateral effects may lead to a lessening of competition where a merger brings together two firms whose products represent important substitutes for customers. Chapter 3 describes a range of considerations relevant to the assessment of unilateral effects, and surveys the various forms of evidence and analysis employed in practice to assess the scope for unilateral effects in horizontal mergers.

Chapter 4 discusses **coordinated effects**, a less common theory of harm that may apply in the case of horizontal mergers. Coordinated effects arise where a merger changes market conditions such that firms may be better able to restrict competition between themselves via a tacit understanding of their joint interest in higher prices. Chapter 4 reviews the factors that economic theory predicts might make coordinated effects more or less likely, discusses the framework established by the Commission for the practical assessment of coordinated effects, and describes the forms of evidence that have been considered by the Commission within that framework.

Finally, Chapter 5 considers **non-horizontal mergers**, which are distinguished from horizontal mergers by the fact that they do not concern products that customers would consider substitutes and therefore do not eliminate direct competitive constraints between firms. Non-horizontal mergers encompass **vertical mergers** between firms at different levels of a supply chain, and **conglomerate mergers** between firms active in different markets and different supply chains. While non-horizontal mergers will raise competition concerns less frequently than horizontal mergers, in some circumstances they may permit firms to engage in **foreclosure**, that is, behaviour that weakens rivals and consequently lessens competition. Chapter 5 discusses the various forms of foreclosure theory that may apply in non-horizontal mergers, the framework used by the Commission to assess these theories, and the types of evidence considered in such assessments.

In preparation for this material, this introduction provides an overview of the framework within which mergers are assessed in Europe, focusing on the role of economic evidence and analysis. Section 2 starts by setting out the regulatory standard for merger assessment in the European Union and the procedure by which the European Commission investigates and rules upon notified transactions. Section 3 goes on to provide an introductory discussion of the role of economics in European merger analysis, focusing on the increased usage and importance of economic analysis over the last five years.

Section 4 provides an introduction to the core economic principles that underpin merger control. It discusses the central concepts of industrial organisation, the academic field that provides the basis for economic analysis of firm behaviour and market structure. The practical application of industrial organisation theory to real-world firms and industries is the essence of the economic analysis of mergers.

Theory alone is usually not sufficient to reach a firm conclusion on the likely impact of a merger on competition. While economic theory will often provide an indication of the *direction* of relationships between variables (for instance the relationship between a product's price and demand for that product), it is generally not able to provide an indication of the *strength* of those relationships. The strength of relevant economic relationships must be assessed on an ad hoc basis for the industry and firms involved in each merger investigation using empirical evidence. This often requires the use of econometrics, a field concerned with the use of mathematics and statistics to connect economic theory with empirical data. This is the subject of Section 5, which provides a brief introduction to empirical economic evidence and its application to merger assessment.

## 2.   Legal framework and Commission procedure

### 2.1   The Merger Regulation

The legal basis for the regulatory supervision of corporate mergers and acquisitions in Europe is provided by the EC Merger Regulation (the '**Merger Regulation**').[1] The Merger Regulation applies to concentrations, defined as covering 'operations bringing about a lasting change in the control of the undertakings concerned and therefore in the structure of the market', a definition that encompasses joint ventures as well as mergers and acquisitions.[2]

The Merger Regulation acknowledges that such concentrations 'are to be welcomed to the extent that they are in line with the requirements of dynamic competition and capable of increasing the competitiveness of European industry, improving the conditions of growth and raising the standard of living in the Community'.[3] However, the Merger Regulation

---

[1] Council Regulation (EC) No. 139/2004 of 20 January 2004 on the control of concentrations between undertakings (the EC Merger Regulation), OJ L24/1, 29 January 2004.
[2] Merger Regulation, para. 20.     [3] Ibid., para. 4.

also notes that mergers should be permitted only in so far as they do not 'result in lasting damage to competition', and that the European Union asserts a legal basis for 'governing those concentrations which may significantly impede effective competition in the common market or in a substantial part of it'.[4]

The Merger Regulation affords the European Commission exclusive jurisdiction over transactions that bring about 'significant structural changes, the impact of which on the market goes beyond the national borders of any one Member State'.[5] Transactions affecting individual Member States fall within the purview of the applicable national competition authorities.[6]

The Merger Regulation limits assessment by the Commission to mergers that meet specified turnover thresholds, concentrations that meet these thresholds being referred to as having a '**Community dimension**'.[7] A concentration has a Community dimension if:[8]

> (a) the combined aggregate worldwide turnover of all the undertakings concerned is more than EUR 5 000 million; and (b) the aggregate Community-wide turnover of each of at least two of the undertakings concerned is more than EUR 250 million, unless each of the undertakings concerned achieves more than two-thirds of its aggregate Community-wide turnover within one and the same Member State.

From an economic perspective, the most important element of the Merger Regulation is that concerning the competitive assessment of mergers. The Merger Regulation establishes the concept of a **significant impediment to effective competition ('SIEC')** as the criterion against

---

[4] Merger Regulation, para. 5.     [5] Ibid., paras. 8 and 9.     [6] Ibid., para. 8.
[7] Ibid., paras. 9 and 10.
[8] Ibid., Art. 1, para. 2. Alternatively, a concentration has a Community dimension where:

> (a) the combined aggregate worldwide turnover of all the undertakings concerned is more than EUR 2 500 million; (b) in each of at least three Member States, the combined aggregate turnover of all the undertakings concerned is more than EUR 100 million; (c) in each of at least three Member States included for the purpose of point (b), the aggregate turnover of each of at least two of the undertakings concerned is more than EUR 25 million; and (d) the aggregate Community-wide turnover of each of at least two of the undertakings concerned is more than EUR 100 million, unless each of the undertakings concerned achieves more than two-thirds of its aggregate Community-wide turnover within one and the same Member State.

See ibid., Art. 1, para. 3.

which concentrations are to be assessed. It provides that 'any concentration which would significantly impede effective competition, in the common market or in a substantial part of it, should be declared incompatible with the common market'.[9]

The concept of an SIEC represented a departure from the standard set out in the previous regulation governing merger control in Europe ('the 1989 Merger Regulation').[10] The 1989 Merger Regulation prohibited any concentration which 'creates or strengthens a dominant position as a result of which effective competition in the common market or in a substantial part of it would be significantly impeded'.[11]

It should be apparent that the criterion for prohibition established in the Merger Regulation is a broadening of the equivalent condition in the 1989 Merger Regulation. Both refer to a significant or substantial impediment to effective competition, but the 1989 Regulation includes an additional requirement for prohibition that a dominant position be created or strengthened that is absent from the 2004 Merger Regulation.

The dominance provision in the 1989 Regulation was held by some commentators to give rise to a 'gap', whereby the Commission would be legally prevented from prohibiting mergers with the potential to harm consumers through a lessening of competition in oligopolistic industries in which no individual firm was dominant.[12] While the Commission had, via its case law, created the concept of collective dominance with which it prohibited mergers under the 1989 Merger Regulation in industries not characterised by a single dominant firm, this concept depended on establishing scope for firms to coordinate their actions via collusive behaviour.[13] The enforcement gap was held to arise in the case of mergers taking place in markets in which there was no realistic prospect of coordinated

---

[9] Merger Regulation, para. 25.     [10] Council Regulation (EEC) No. 4064/89.
[11] 1989 Merger Regulation, para. 24.
[12] An oligopolistic market is one characterised by a small number of competing suppliers, such that those firms are able to influence price and take into account the behaviour of rivals when determining their own strategies (as distinct from the textbook model of pure competition, in which individual firms have no such influence but must charge the price determined by the market or make zero sales). In practice, almost all markets of interest to competition law are oligopolies.
[13] For an articulation of the view that the Commission's decision to prohibit the *Airtours/ First Choice* merger on collective dominance grounds possibly represented an attempt to sidestep a lacuna in the 1989 Merger Regulation see M. Motta (1999) 'EC Merger Policy, and the Airtours case', available at http://people.exeter.ac.uk/maf206/motta_1999.pdf.

behaviour, and no single dominant firm, but nonetheless the prospect of a lessening of competition via unilateral effects.

The 2004 Merger Regulation was introduced to address this possible gap in enforcement, and comments on the concept in the following terms.[14]

> In view of the consequences that concentrations in oligopolistic market structures may have, it is all the more necessary to maintain effective competition in such markets. Many oligopolistic markets exhibit a healthy degree of competition. However, under certain circumstances, concentrations involving the elimination of important competitive constraints that the merging parties had exerted upon each other, as well as a reduction of competitive pressure on the remaining competitors, may, even in the absence of a likelihood of coordination between the members of the oligopoly, result in a significant impediment to effective competition ... The notion of 'significant impediment to effective competition' ... should be interpreted as extending, beyond the concept of dominance, only to the anti-competitive effects of a concentration resulting from the non-coordinated behaviour of undertakings which would not have a dominant position on the market concerned.

However, since the introduction of the new substantive test, the Commission's enforcement practice suggests that the alleged 'gap' in merger control under the dominance test was smaller than initially believed.[15] An article published in April 2006 by Lars-Hendrik Röller, former Chief Economist, and Miguel de la Mano, Deputy Chief Economist, found no horizontal merger in the sample they reviewed that was a clear cut 'gap case', although it was suggested that one vertical merger (*E.ON/MOL*)[16] might constitute a gap case that may not have been challenged under the 1989 Merger Regulation.[17]

Since then, gap features have emerged in only a very small number of cases. In particular, in *T-Mobile Austria/Tele.ring*,[18] which brought together the second and fourth largest network operators on the

---

[14] Merger Regulation, para. 25.

[15] See A. Lofaro and D. Ridyard, 'The Role of Economics in European Merger Control', published in N. Levy, *European Merger Control Review – A Guide to the Merger Regulation* (LexisNexis, 2011).

[16] Case COMP/M.3696 – *E.ON/MOL*, Commission decision of 21 December 2005.

[17] See L.-H. Röller and M. de la Mano, 'The Impact of the New Substantive Test in European Merger Control' (2006) 2(1) *European Competition Journal* 9.

[18] Case COMP/M.3916 – *T-Mobile Austria/Tele.ring*, Commission decision of 26 April 2006 (2007 OJ L88/44).

Austrian mobile telecommunications sector, the Commission concluded that anti-competitive effects would occur despite the fact that the merged entity would account for only one-third of the market. Similarly, in *EDF/Segebel*,[19] which involved EDF's acquisition of a majority stake in SPE, the second largest electricity operator in Belgium, the Commission required the parties to make significant divestments despite a combined share in the Belgian electricity wholesale market of only 10–20%. In both cases, the Commission considered that remedies were warranted since the proposed transactions as originally notified would have eliminated rivals whose competitive importance was significantly understated by their market shares.

## 2.2 Procedure for notification and assessment

It is beyond the scope of this book to give a complete description of merger notification and assessment under the Merger Regulation. In this section we instead seek to provide an overview of the various elements of the Commission procedure and timelines for those unfamiliar with the process.

Mergers falling under the Merger Regulation are assessed by the **Directorate-General for Competition ('DG COMP')**. The Merger Regulation establishes a system of mandatory notification for concentrations with a Community dimension, stating that:[20]

> undertakings should be obliged to give prior notification of concentrations with a Community dimension following the conclusion of the agreement, the announcement of the public bid or the acquisition of a controlling interest. Notification should also be possible where the undertakings concerned satisfy the Commission of their intention to enter into an agreement for a proposed concentration and demonstrate to the Commission that their plan for that proposed concentration is sufficiently concrete, for example on the basis of an agreement in principle, a memorandum of understanding, or a letter of intent signed by all undertakings concerned, or, in the case of a public bid, where they have publicly announced an intention to make such a bid, provided that the intended agreement or bid would result in a concentration with a Community dimension.

[19] Case COMP/M.5549 – *EDF/Segebel*, Commission decision of 12 November 2009.
[20] Merger Regulation, para. 34.

Mergers are normally notified to the Commission via a standard notification document template known as **Form CO**.[21] The purpose of the Form CO is to provide the Commission with the information concerning the transaction that it requires to conduct its competitive assessment. In particular, the Form CO calls for information about the parties and their ownership, details of the concentration, relevant internal documents, the definition of the relevant markets affected by the transaction, and the structure of and competitive conditions within those markets.

A merger notification becomes effective, setting the administrative timetable underway, on the date on which the Commission receives a Form CO that it accepts as complete. In principle, therefore, the Form CO may represent the first point of contact between the parties and the Commission. In practice, however, parties involved in transactions that may raise competition issues will often engage in **pre-notification** discussions with the Commission. During pre-notification the Commission will provide feedback on drafts of the Form CO, which allows the parties to identify areas in which further argumentation, evidence or analysis would assist in dispelling competition concerns.

Once a notification has become effective, the Commission commences a 25-working-day **Phase I** initial examination. This Phase I process may be extended to 35 days if the parties offer **commitments** (also known as remedies) aimed at addressing potential competition concerns. During this investigation the Commission must form a view on whether the transaction raises serious doubts as to its effect on competition. In order to reach such a view, the Commission will take account of information from the parties contained in the Form CO and responses to supplementary questionnaires issued during the course of the Phase I process. Importantly, the Commission will augment this material with its own **market investigation**, which will canvass the views of and collect evidence from third parties (particularly customers, but also rivals) active in the markets affected by the transaction.

Given the limited timescale, the Commission will typically not pursue detailed or sophisticated economic analyses during a Phase I investigation but instead focus on identifying and weighing the merits of potential concerns flagged by the information received from the parties and market participants. It will, nonetheless, engage with and consider detailed economic evidence and analyses put forward by the parties,

---

[21] The Form CO is provided as an annex to Commission Regulation (EC) No. 802/2004 implementing Council Regulation (EC) No. 139/2004.

particularly where such analyses have been discussed with the Commission during pre-notification. It is therefore feasible for parties to bring complex and sophisticated economic evidence into play during Phase I merger proceedings.

The Phase I investigation period ends in a decision under **Article 6** of the Merger Regulation. In the significant majority of cases, the Commission concludes that the transaction does not raise serious doubts, leading to an Article 6(1)(b) approval decision. Where such a finding depends on commitments offered by the parties, the Article 6(1)(b) decision will be issued in conjunction with Article 6(2), making the approval conditional on compliance with those commitments. An approval decision will close the merger assessment and permit the parties to complete the transaction.

Alternatively, if the Commission has serious doubts as to the impact of the transaction at the end of its Phase I investigation, it will issue an Article (6)(1)(c) decision, triggering a **Phase II** investigation. The basic timetable for the Phase II review is 90 working days, although this is extended to 105 working days where the parties offer commitments later than 55 days into the Phase II process, and/or may be extended by 20 working days with the agreement of the parties.

The Phase II process normally involves a detailed and evidence-intensive review of specific competition concerns identified during the Phase I process. The Phase II investigation provides sufficient time for the Commission to engage fully with detailed and sophisticated economic analyses and evidence provided by the parties, and for it to undertake its own economic analyses based on information both from the parties and its market investigation. Where third party information plays a part in the Commission's investigation there may be scope for the use of a **data room** process, whereby the parties' advisers, under suitable confidentiality conditions, are permitted to review and comment on data and analyses employed by the Commission's staff and/or provided by third parties.

The Phase II process ultimately leads to a decision as to the transaction's compatibility with competition law under **Article 8** of the Merger Regulation. Typically, the Commission will reach one of three decisions at the end of a Phase II investigation: unconditional clearance under Article 8(1); clearance subject to commitments addressing identified competition concerns under Article 8(2); or, in the case of a transaction deemed incompatible with the common market, prohibition under Article 8(3).

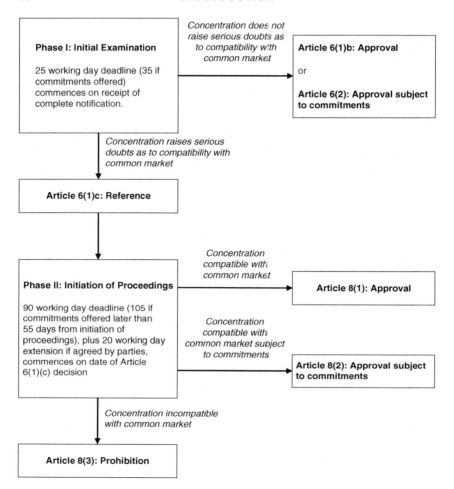

**Figure 1.1**    European merger review process under the Merger Regulation

Where the Commission intends to prohibit a transaction or clear it only subject to commitments, such a decision will be preceded by a **statement of objections** ('SO'), which sets out the Commission's basis for such a decision. The SO provides the parties with an opportunity to respond to the Commission's arguments prior to the decision, both in writing and at an **oral hearing**.

Figure 1.1 summarises the European merger review process under the Merger Regulation.

Table 1.1 *Conclusion of merger cases in which the Commission has reached a decision under Article 6 (from 2004 to 2011)*

|  | Number of cases | Proportion of Article 6 decisions (%) |
|---|---|---|
| Article 6 decisions, of which ... | 2,453 | |
| ... cleared unconditionally | 2,271 | 92.6 |
| ... cleared subject to commitments | 109 | 4.4 |
| ... Phase II proceedings initiated, of which... | 73 | 3.0 |
| ... withdrawn | 15 | 0.6 |
| ... cleared unconditionally | 27 | 1.1 |
| ... cleared subject to commitments | 28 | 1.1 |
| ... prohibited | 3 | 0.1 |

*Source:* European Commission statistics.

Table 1.1 summarises the conclusion of merger cases in which the Commission has reached a decision under Article 6 over the eight years from 2004 to 2011.

These data show that the vast majority of mergers investigated by the Commission are cleared at Phase I without commitments. Only around 7.5% of mergers that reach the end of the Phase I process require commitments or a more detailed investigation under Phase II. It is also notable that a sizeable proportion, around one-third, of cases that proceed to Phase II are ultimately cleared without conditions, demonstrating that serious doubts identified in the Phase I process may nevertheless be overcome by a more detailed review. Finally, the table shows that only a tiny fraction of the transactions notified to the Commission are ultimately prohibited on competition grounds.[22]

---

[22] In addition to the three prohibitions observed over the eight years shown in the table, it may be inferred that some fraction of the fifteen notifications withdrawn in Phase II may otherwise have resulted in a prohibition decision; similarly, some proportion of the fifty notifications withdrawn during Phase I (not shown in the table) may have ultimately led to prohibition. Nonetheless, the vast majority of transactions considered by the Commission are ultimately cleared, and most of these without commitments.

## 3.   The role of economics in EU merger control

Merger analysis in the EU has undergone a radical transformation in the last decade with an increased reliance on economics in all areas of EU competition law. This approach is often referred to as 'effects-based', whereby the focus is on the impact that particular market structures and conduct have on outcomes for consumers. This is contradistinct to a 'form-based' approach that regulates competition according to pre-scribed rules defining acceptable and unacceptable forms of firm behaviour and market structure.

An effects-based competition enforcement regime necessarily comes at a cost in terms of the legal certainty afforded by a form-based approach, whereby firms can immediately understand whether a particular act (e.g. offering loyalty rebates, merging with a supplier) will or will not risk intervention on competition grounds; the associated need for case specific investigation and analysis also places a greater burden on both firms and regulators. Nonetheless, it is now generally acknowledged that the application of insights provided by economics to a particular case is more likely to avoid both under- and over-intervention by competition regulators, and so produce outcomes that best serve consumers.

In the context of merger appraisal, this change in enforcement policy has most obviously been embodied in the shift away from market shares as a tool for the assessment of unilateral effects in horizontal mergers in favour of a greater focus on the economic concepts of substitutability and closeness of competition. Arguably, however, the move towards effects-based analysis has had its most significant impact in the assessment of non-horizontal and coordinated effect theories of harm. In both of these areas there has been a departure from the use of checklists and per se prohibitions over the past ten years.

From a practitioners' point of view, the move towards effects-based enforcement has led to increased reliance on economic analysis and evidence in European merger control, both on the part of the Commission and merging parties.

DG COMP created the post of **Chief Competition Economist (CCE)** in 2003 as part of a reform programme intended to address evidential and analytical failings highlighted by the General Court's annulments of the *Airtours/First Choice*,[23] *Tetra Laval/Sidel*[24] and

---

[23] Case COMP/M.1524 – *Airtours/First Choice*, Commission decision of 22 September 1999.
[24] Case COMP/M.2416 – *Tetra Laval/Sidel*, Commission decision of 30 October 2001.

*Schneider/Legrand*[25] prohibition decisions. The CCE heads a group of specialist competition economists, the **Chief Economist's Team (CET)**, that provides the Commission with in-house expertise in the application of economic theory and econometric techniques to antitrust enforcement. In merger control the CET supports investigation case teams via two primary functions. First, the CET provides independent internal review of proposed clearance, reference and prohibition decisions (the 'checks and balances' function). Second, the CET participates in and assists case teams with ongoing merger assessments (the 'support' function).[26]

Via the first of these roles the CET has been instrumental in improving the quality of Commission decision making in recent years, by subjecting case teams to internal scrutiny in terms of both the economic logic of their arguments and the strength of the supporting evidence. On a day-to-day basis, however, it is the second function that most directly affects merger practitioners. The support role encompasses the allocation of a CET member to join the case team on mergers that raise complex economic or evidential issues. Such allocations may be made at the request of either the case team or the CCE. As a result, CET economists typically play an important role in the most complex and contentious cases, particularly those under or likely to enter Phase II review.

## 4.   Basic economic concepts

Throughout this book we will introduce the particular economic concepts and theories that are relevant to each type of merger and theory of harm at the beginning of the applicable chapters. There are, however, a number of basic economic concepts that underpin all merger assessment. In this section we provide an overview of these concepts, focusing on the demand curve, the nature and role of firms' costs, rational profit-maximising behaviour, and the concept of market power.

Competition economics lies within the broader field of **industrial organisation ('IO')**, which is the branch of microeconomics that deals

---

[25] Case COMP/M.2283 – *Schneider/Legrand*, Commission decision of 10 October 2001.

[26] See L.-H. Röller and P. A. Buigues, 'The Office of the Chief Competition Economist at the European Commission' (Commission, May 2005).

with the behaviour of firms and the structure of markets. The fundamental topic of interest in industrial organisation is the analysis of how rational firms go about maximising their profits given the behaviour of consumers and other firms.

This question is addressed through consideration of firms' cost conditions, demand conditions and the nature of interaction between firms. Each firm is assumed to maximise its profits by reference to its own cost conditions and the demand it faces, taking account of other firms' profit-maximisation decisions.

Competition economics is built upon the analysis of individual firms' incentives and behaviour. In particular, merger analysis derives from the analysis of how firms' current incentives and behaviour, a result of current cost and demand conditions, might be expected to change following a consolidation of two or more separate firms under common control. As will be demonstrated below, the most significant change in incentives following a merger arises through changes in the demand curve facing firms involved with or affected by the merger.

The following sections provide a brief overview of the basic economic concepts relevant to competition analysis in general, and to merger analysis in particular.

### 4.1   The demand curve

The demand facing a firm derives from a wide range of factors. These include the price of the firm's goods, the characteristics of the product, the price and attributes of other suppliers' products, consumers' income and consumers' tastes and preferences. Economists summarise these factors in the concept of the demand curve. A demand curve is a description of the volume of sales that a firm will make for each price level it sets, holding other factors (such as product characteristics and competitors' prices) constant. Figure 1.2 plots an illustrative demand curve for WidgetCo, a firm producing widgets.

The x-axis shows the quantity (q) of widgets sold by WidgetCo, while the y-axis shows the price (p) charged by WidgetCo. The demand curve reflects the relationship between these two variables, illustrating the number of units that WidgetCo would sell at each price level; or, analogously, the price that would have to be set to sell a given number of widgets.

The demand curve is downward sloping, reflecting the fact that higher prices lead to lower volumes and vice versa. This negative relationship

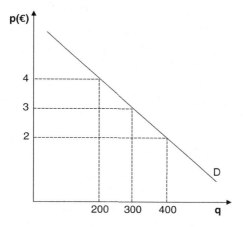

**Figure 1.2**   Illustrative demand curve

holds true for (practically) all demand curves.[27] The demand curve for WidgetCo is a 'linear' demand curve (i.e. a straight line), with every €1 change in price leading to a 100 unit change in sales.

We shall see in the discussion of profit maximisation below that firms combine this information on the relationship between price and sales volume with information on their own costs to decide on the level of price (and therefore output) to offer. Firms' behaviour thus depends on the characteristics of the demand curve faced.

---

[27] In theory, demand may be upward sloping for some goods, such that higher prices increase demand for the good. One (theoretical) class of such goods is known as 'Giffen goods'. These are a special case of so called 'inferior goods' (goods for which demand increases as income decreases). If an inferior good represents a sufficiently large part of a consumer's total expenditure, an increase in the price of such a good may reduce income available for expenditure to such an extent that it causes an *increase* in demand for the good itself (for which demand is inversely related to income). Giffen goods are of theoretical interest because, despite their apparent absurdity, they cannot be ruled out by the axioms of rational choice that underpin microeconomic theory. However, they are of little or no practical relevance. Another class of products that may appear to have upward sloping demand curves are known as 'Veblen goods'. These are goods that attract higher demand at higher prices because consumers associate higher prices with higher perceived quality. It has been conjectured that luxury goods such as perfume may represent Veblen goods. It could, however, be argued that, while a bottle of perfume sold at €100 may attract more demand than a chemically identical perfume sold at €10, the two are not the same product due to the extent to which the price is an element of the product's characteristics for such items. It is not clear, for instance, that a bottle of perfume normally retailing at €100 would lose customers if its price were to be reduced by 5% as a promotional offer.

A critical element of the demand curve for competition analysis is the **elasticity** of demand, normally represented by the Greek symbol ε. The own-price elasticity of demand measures the responsiveness of demand for a good to changes in its price, that is, how many sales the firm can expect to win (lose) as a result of a given reduction (increase) in price.[28] The own-price elasticity of demand is defined as the ratio of the percentage change in demand to the percentage change in price causing that change in demand. This can be expressed via the following formula, where $\Delta q$ is the change in the quantity demanded, q is the quantity originally demanded, $\Delta p$ is the change in price and p is the original price:

$$\varepsilon = (\Delta q/q)/(\Delta p/p)$$

Thus, to give an example, if a 10% increase in price would lead to a 5% reduction in sales, the elasticity would be −5%/10%, or −0.5. Note that, because demand is downward sloping, the own-price elasticity of demand will always be a negative number. By convention, however, elasticity is often expressed in absolute terms (i.e. the minus sign is omitted), such that the own-price elasticity of demand in this case would be described as 0.5.

It is important to note that elasticity will normally be different at different points along the demand curve.[29] Indeed, because elasticity is calculated on the basis of proportionate, rather than absolute, changes in price and volume, own-price elasticity will always differ at different points on a linear demand curve. This can be seen with the illustrative linear demand curve shown for WidgetCo above. At a price of €2, WidgetCo would be selling 400 units. A €1 price increase to €3 would lead to a 100 unit reduction in sales, to 300. The elasticity at this point is therefore −25%/50%, which is 0.5.

At a price of €3, WidgetCo would be able to sell 300 units. A €1 price increase at this price level would again lead to a 100 unit reduction in demand. However, the proportionate price increase is now 33%, while the proportionate volume change is −33%. The elasticity at this point is thus 1.

---

[28] In addition to own-price elasticity, the cross-price elasticity of demand, which measures the responsiveness of one good's demand to changes in another good's price, is also relevant to competition analysis. See the discussion of demand estimation in the context of market definition at Chapter 2.

[29] The exception is the constant elasticity, or isoelastic, demand curve, which is defined according to a specific shape such that elasticity does not change as one moves along the demand curve. The constant elasticity demand curve is discussed further at Appendix B.

Finally, at a price of €4, WidgetCo would sell 200 units. Given that the demand curve is a straight line, a €1 price increase will again lead to a 100 unit demand fall (from 200 to 100 units). The percentage increase in price is now 25%, whereas the percentage decrease in demand is now 50%, implying that the elasticity at this point is 2.

Thus, while the relationship between price and sales for WidgetCo is linear, each €1 change in price being associated with a 100 unit change in demand, the elasticity changes according to the starting point at which it is measured. WidgetCo will therefore face different demand elasticity depending upon the price that it is charging. Specifically, at prices lower than €3, it can be seen that WidgetCo has an elasticity of demand that is less than one in absolute terms, whereas at prices higher than €3, it has an elasticity of demand that is greater than one in absolute terms. At a price of €3 exactly, its elasticity of demand is equal to one in absolute terms.

Where elasticity is less than one in absolute value (i.e. less negative than −1), demand is referred to as being 'inelastic', or 'relatively inelastic'.[30] Demand will be relatively inelastic where a given percentage change in price will lead to a less than proportionate percentage change in volume.

Where elasticity is greater than one in absolute value (i.e. more negative than −1), demand is called 'elastic' or 'relatively elastic'.[31] In regions of relatively elastic demand, changes in price will lead to more than proportionate changes in volume. At the point between these two regions, demand elasticity of (minus) one is referred to as 'unitary elasticity'.

It is useful at this stage to introduce the concept of **marginal revenue**. Marginal revenue is the rate of change of revenue with respect to sales volumes. A decision by a firm to increase output by one unit will affect its revenues in two ways. The direct effect will be a boost to its revenue as it will earn extra revenue on the incremental unit it sells. However, as an indirect effect, it will suffer a loss in revenues as it will have to lower the price of *all* units it sells in order to make that incremental sale. Whether marginal revenue is positive or negative will depend on which of these two effects is larger.

---

[30] Perfectly inelastic demand ($\varepsilon = 0$) refers to a vertical demand curve, at which the same output is demanded irrespective of price.

[31] Perfectly elastic demand ($\varepsilon = \infty$) arises where the demand curve is horizontal, which implies that there exists a price at which the firm can sell any number of units, but that any price above this level will result in zero sales.

Recall that we noted that where demand elasticity is less than one in absolute terms, a given percentage change in price will lead to a smaller percentage change in volume. Therefore, a price reduction in the region where demand is inelastic will *reduce* total revenue, as the lower price will more than offset the increase in sales. We can therefore see that where demand is inelastic, the relationship between output and revenue is negative, meaning that marginal revenue is negative.

Conversely, where demand elasticity is greater than one in absolute terms, a given percentage change in price will lead to a larger percentage change in volume. Therefore, a price reduction in the region where demand is elastic will *increase* total revenue, as the increase in sales will more than outweigh the reduction in price. Thus, where demand is elastic, the relationship between output and revenue is positive, meaning that marginal revenue is positive.

Marginal revenue therefore falls as output increases. More specifically, the marginal revenue curve will lie above zero where demand is elastic, cross zero at the point where demand elasticity is unitary, and lie below zero where demand is inelastic.

Figure 1.3 illustrates the relationship between demand elasticity, marginal revenue and total revenue for a linear demand curve.

The chart shows that total revenue is maximised at the point of unitary elasticity, or where marginal revenue is equal to zero.[32] This does not imply, however, that firms will aim to operate at the point on their demand curve at which elasticity is equal to one. Profit-maximising firms must also take into account the costs of production associated with each price and output level.

Even without considering costs, however, it can be noted that a firm will always operate in the elastic portion of its demand curve, or, equivalently, where marginal revenue is positive. This can be seen by considering the choices available to a firm operating in the inelastic portion of its demand curve. Where demand is inelastic, revenue is unambiguously increasing with price because a given percentage increase in price will bring about a smaller percentage decrease in volume. Given that costs would not be expected to increase with reductions in output, it follows that increasing total revenue while reducing volume must increase profitability. As such, whenever a firm faces inelastic demand (or where marginal revenue is negative) it has an incentive to increase price, such

---

[32] The characteristic that revenue is maximised when marginal revenue is zero is not only the case for linear demand curves but holds more generally.

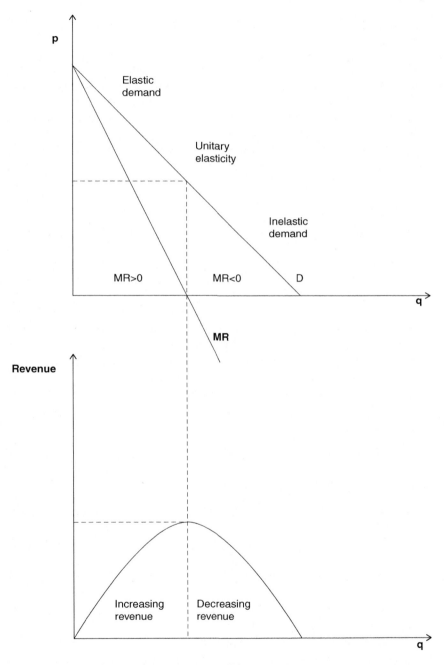

**Figure 1.3**   Relationship between demand elasticity, marginal revenue and total revenue

that it will only cease to increase price at some point after demand has become elastic (or where marginal revenue has become positive).

The particular point on the elastic portion of the demand curve at which the firm will choose to operate will depend on the trade-off between the revenue that is lost due to increases in price (recall that revenue is maximised at unitary elasticity) and the costs that are saved due to the accompanying reduction in output. The process by which the optimal trade-off between these effects is identified is discussed in the section on profit maximisation below. Before doing so, however, it is necessary to introduce the concept of the cost curve.

### 4.2   The cost curve

The cost curve is a tool for summarising the way in which a firm's costs change with the volume of output that it supplies. Cost curves can be expressed via a mathematical formula or on a graph, and provide a recipe for calculating the (minimum) costs associated with each potential level of output.

Economists distinguish between two fundamental types of cost: fixed and variable. **Fixed costs** are defined as expenditures that do not vary with the level of output. The types of cost that are fixed for a given firm will differ according to its activities and the relevant time horizon over which output decisions are considered, but examples of costs that are typically considered fixed include rent and managerial staff costs. **Variable costs** are defined as expenditures that vary according to the level of output. Variable costs normally comprise chiefly input costs associated with the production of each unit of output.

The distinction between fixed and variable costs is not always clear and many costs are, in practice, **semi-fixed**, meaning that they vary to some extent with output. Staff costs in particular tend to be semi-fixed. For small changes in output, a firm is unlikely to change its staff costs. A firm running five production lines at full capacity would still need to operate those five production lines and employ the associated staff if its output fell by 10%. If output were to fall by 20%, however, then the firm may choose to shut down one of the production lines, in which case it would require only sufficient staff to operate four production lines. In this example staff costs are fixed for a 10% reduction in output, but variable for a 20% reduction in output.

In competition economics we are often concerned with marginal cost. As discussed further below, marginal cost is the rate of change in cost as

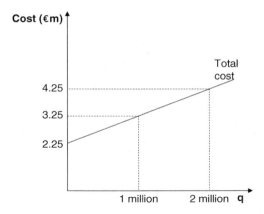

**Figure 1.4**  Illustrative total cost curve

output changes. Marginal cost is determined by those costs that vary with small changes in output. In many instances it is therefore relevant to focus on the most variable cost categories, and to treat semi-fixed costs as fixed.

These cost types can be illustrated by considering the costs facing a manufacturer of window blinds that operates a single production plant. Let us assume that rent on the production plant is €0.5 million per annum. Further assume that staff costs are €0.75 million per annum and that the firm spends €1.0 million per annum on advertising. These cost categories will not vary with the number of blinds produced and sold, and so a minimum of €2.25 million in costs will be incurred for any output level.

Let us also assume that the materials used to produce the blinds cost €1 per unit. This represents the variable cost that will depend on the level of blinds output. Combining the fixed and variable costs, the total cost incurred by the blind manufacturer will be equal to €2.25 million plus €1 multiplied by the number of blinds produced. This relationship is plotted in Figure 1.4.

The figure shows the total cost curve, which represents the total costs associated with each level of blind production. The total cost curve allows two further measures of cost, both relating to the cost per unit of production, to be derived. The first is **average cost**, which for each output level is defined as the total cost divided by the number of units produced. Where firms face fixed costs, average costs will normally decline with volume due to the spreading of the fixed costs across a greater number of sales. This phenomenon is often referred to as **economies of scale**, a reference to a situation in which a firm's costs fall as its sales volumes increase. As will be explained in the section on profit maximisation below, while such fixed cost spreading will affect a firm's profitability, it does not affect firms' behaviour.

The second cost concept is that of **marginal cost**. Marginal cost reflects, for any given output level, the additional cost incurred in the production of the final unit supplied. A marginal cost curve shows the relationship between marginal cost and output produced. Thus, in the example of the blind manufacturer set out above, the additional cost incurred on each unit sold is the €1 cost of materials. This marginal cost is constant for all levels of output; the incremental cost of supplying, for instance, the tenth unit is €1, the same as the incremental cost of supplying the ten thousandth or ten millionth unit.[33] As a result, the marginal cost curve would be represented graphically as a horizontal line at €1. As will be explained in the discussion of profit maximisation below, it is marginal costs that are relevant to firms' decisions of how much output to produce and at what price.

The preceding discussion has considered the description of costs faced by a firm operating in a given industry. Cost structures will also affect firms' decisions on whether to enter or exit a market. The central concept relevant to this decision is that of **sunk costs**. Sunk costs are a sub-set of fixed costs, defined as those fixed costs that cannot be recovered in the event of ceasing operations. Examples of sunk costs include expenditure on advertising, investments in staff training and specialised machinery that cannot be used for any other purposes and therefore has no resale value. Because these costs cannot be avoided or recovered in the event of shutdown, sunk costs may make entry into a particular market unattractive. All else being equal, the greater the extent of sunk costs associated with a particular industry, the less attractive entry to that industry will be, as firms will take into account the degree to which costs can be recovered in the event that entry is unsuccessful. The role of sunk costs in merger analysis is discussed further in Chapter 3.

---

[33] Note that, strictly speaking, the marginal cost of the first unit is €2,250,001, as the difference in total costs between supplying zero and one units will include the €2.25 million fixed costs.

## 4.3   Profit maximisation

The preceding sections have discussed how economists describe a firm's demand and cost conditions and explained the concepts of the marginal revenue curve and the marginal cost curve. In this section we consider how firms go about making pricing and output decisions based on the information contained in those curves.

The starting point for this analysis is the assumption that rational firms seek to maximise profits, where profits are defined as total revenues less total costs. Intuitively, it can be understood that each firm faces a trade-off between setting a high price that will generate high margins on a small number of sales and setting a low price that will allow a greater volume of sales to be made at lower margins. The optimal trade-off between these two approaches that will maximise profits will depend upon the production costs faced by the firm and the sensitivity of customers to price.

Without any assumptions other than that firms seek to maximise profits, it is possible to derive the central theoretical result regarding profit maximisation, which is that firms will organise their operations so as to set **marginal revenue equal to marginal cost**.

This result is derived from differential calculus, but can be readily understood using the concepts of marginal cost and revenue defined above. Marginal cost represents the cost of supplying the final unit of output for any given output level. Marginal revenue gives, for any given output level, the total change in the firm's revenue brought about by supplying the final unit. Figure 1.5 plots illustrative marginal cost (MC) and marginal revenue (MR) curves.

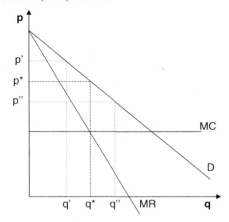

**Figure 1.5**   Cost, demand and profit maximisation

The marginal cost curve is constant, indicating that each additional unit generates as much additional cost to supply as every other unit. The marginal revenue curve slopes downwards more steeply than the demand curve, reflecting the fact that a reduction in price required to sell an additional unit reduces revenue generated from the sale of *all* units and not just the last unit.

To understand the principle of profit maximisation, consider the options facing a firm currently operating at volume q' and the associated price p'. At this output level, it can be seen that the marginal revenue is greater than the marginal cost curve (that is, following the dotted line upwards from the x-axis at q', the marginal revenue curve lies above the marginal cost curve). Thus, if the firm is operating at q', the additional cost of the final unit supplied is less than additional revenue generated by selling that unit. This implies that an increase in output would increase the firm's profitability, as the additional revenue of one more sale will be greater than the additional cost of making that sale. By this logic, it follows that, wherever the marginal revenue curve lies above the marginal cost curve, the firm can increase its profits by increasing its sales volumes.

By contrast, consider the options facing a firm operating at volume q" and the associated price p". At this output level marginal revenue is below marginal cost. The incremental revenue from the final unit sold at q" is therefore less than the incremental cost of making that sale. The firm would therefore be able to increase its profits by withdrawing that final sale, as the lost revenue would be outweighed by the saving in costs. By this logic, a firm will improve its profits by reducing output wherever marginal cost exceeds marginal revenue.

Combining these two results, it follows that, if a profit-maximising firm will have an incentive to increase volumes wherever marginal revenue exceeds marginal cost and to reduce volumes where marginal cost exceeds marginal revenue, then the optimum point at which to operate is the volume and price level at which marginal cost and marginal revenue are equated. This point, shown as p*, q* on the chart, represents the optimal trade-off between the increased margin that results from higher prices on the one hand and the reduced sales volume on the other.

## 4.4  Market power

The purpose of competition policy is to provide the conditions in which consumers can enjoy low prices, high quality, product innovation and other benefits resulting from rivalry between firms. In order to do so, competition enforcement aims to prevent the creation or exploitation of **market power**.

The term 'market power' is frequently used in a loose and informal sense, typically in relation to firms with large market shares. In industrial organisation, however, market power (or pricing power) is defined with reference to the mark-up over marginal cost that a profit-maximising firm earns. This mark-up, or **price–cost margin**, is defined as the difference between price and marginal cost divided by price. The price–cost margin thus reflects the extent to which a product's price exceeds the incremental cost to the producer of supplying that product. The greater this mark-up, the greater the degree of market power or pricing power the firm in question is said to have.

It is important to note that, according to this definition, almost all firms will, in reality, hold some degree of market power. Where firms face any degree of fixed costs, firms will choose to remain in the market in the long run only while they are able to earn a positive margin over average variable costs with which to fund those fixed costs.[34] Market power that may give rise to competition concerns is therefore a matter of degree and durability.[35]

The price–cost margin earned by each firm is determined by the elasticity of demand facing that firm. The less elastic is demand, the greater the price–cost mark-up that the firm can set and so the greater is the market power enjoyed. This follows because the less elastic is demand the lower is the reduction in quantity demanded when price rises. This implies that profit will be maximised at a higher price and lower output level when demand is less elastic. More intuitively, it is apparent that less elastic demand reflects a situation in which customers are less likely to switch away from the product in question, which will give its supplier greater latitude to raise price above marginal costs.

---

[34] Note that, as per the discussion in Section 4.3, firms price with reference only to their marginal cost, and without regard to fixed costs. Where firms' profit-maximising price is too low to produce a price–cost margin sufficient to cover fixed costs firms will be unable to earn a profit even at that profit-maximising price, in response to which some firms will exit the industry. This process will continue until the demand facing the remaining firms becomes sufficiently inelastic to produce a profit-maximising price that does allow the recovery of fixed costs.

[35] In particular, the concern may be that a firm can maintain prices significantly higher than average total cost in the long run.

For a single product firm, the relationship between price–cost margin and elasticity of demand is summarised by the **Lerner condition**. This is an observation, following from the mathematics of profit maximisation, that a firm's profit-maximising price–cost margin is related to the demand elasticity that it faces. This relationship takes the following form, where p is price, mc is marginal cost and ε is the elasticity of demand:

$$(p - mc)/p = -1/\varepsilon$$

The left hand side of the equation is the firm's price–cost margin; that is, the difference between the price at which a good is sold and its marginal cost of production, expressed as a proportion of the sale price. Recalling that the elasticity of demand is expressed as a negative number, it follows that less elastic demand (that is, a smaller absolute value of ε) is associated with greater values of the price–cost margin and therefore less favourable terms for customers. Equally, more elastic demand is associated with lower values of the price–cost margin and therefore more favourable outcomes for consumers.

The Lerner condition therefore provides a formal link between the market conditions faced by firms and their ability to raise price above marginal cost, demonstrating that market power is determined by the demand elasticity faced by firms.

In seeking to control the exercise of market power, competition enforcement is thus concerned with the demand elasticity faced by firms. It is through demand elasticity that the process of competition affects firms' behaviour. Merger control, which seeks to prevent increases in market power, is thus concerned with the analysis of the impact of supplier consolidation on firms' elasticities of demand.[36]

Having established the link between demand elasticity and market power, we can now consider the connection between competition and elasticity.

Demand elasticity is greater the more and better the alternative options available to customers – the better and closer the alternatives to a particular firm's products, the greater the demand loss that firm will suffer in response to a price increase. Where there are few substitutes for

---

[36] Note that mergers may also affect firm behaviour via the supply curve in so far as mergers generate synergies that affect marginal costs and therefore pricing incentives. The effect of mergers on prices via changes in firms' costs is discussed at Chapter 3.

a firm's products, customers will be less willing to switch in response to a price increase, meaning that demand will be less elastic.

The presence and closeness of competitors affects the range of alternatives available to customers, which in turn affects the elasticity of the demand curve perceived by each firm. This is reflected in the previous discussion of market power, which established that a firm will choose a higher price–cost margin where it faces less elastic demand.

It is important to note that, because merger control is assessed according to changes in competitive conditions, analysis must focus on changes in elasticity. Demand elasticity derives from consumers' willingness to substitute between alternatives. Where a merger brings together producers of close substitutes, that merger is likely to reduce the elasticity of the merged firm's demand, thereby producing an incentive to increase price. Where merging firms are not close substitutes, however, the impact of the transaction on each firm's demand curve, and therefore its behaviour, will be more limited.

## 5. Empirical economic evidence

While economic theory provides the framework within which the potential impact of a merger on competition is assessed, the Commission is an evidence-led body and will seek to reach merger decisions that are consistent with and supported by observations regarding the operation of the markets in question. Merger control is necessarily a forward-looking process, in which the impact of a change in the structure of markets must be inferred from observations gathered before that change has taken place.

As a very general statement, economists seek to make such inferences by using the observed reactions of economic agents (firms and consumers) to past events. This broad approach encompasses a wide range of techniques, the applicability and importance of which will vary according to the particular circumstances of each market and merger. There are no hard and fast rules regarding which techniques should be applied within a given investigation, and the evidential requirements of each merger analysis need to be assessed on a case-by-case basis. For this reason, the use of empirical economic evidence in merger investigations is as much an art as it is a science.

The range of evidence that might be collected and submitted within a merger investigation will run from the use of simple summary statistics through to the use of sophisticated econometric analyses.[37] The use of empirical evidence in competition enforcement has developed substantially in recent years, with techniques such as regression analysis, demand estimation and merger simulation being used in a number of European merger investigations.[38]

Due to the time and resource demands involved, however, complex econometric analyses remain the exception, rather than the norm, in European merger control. While cases involving advanced econometric analyses may attract disproportionate attention amongst competition practitioners, the majority of cases reviewed by the European Commission are decided on the basis of qualitative evidence and simpler quantitative techniques. Indeed, this may be true even for the most high-profile cases. Commenting on the *Deutsche Börse/NYSE Euronext* investigation, the Commission's Chief Economist noted that sophisticated econometric techniques seeking to establish firms' responses to changes in market conditions, can generally be applied only where those firms have previously been affected by some form of market shock.[39] In the absence of suitable data, as was the case in *Deutsche Börse/NYSE Euronext*[40] and also *Olympic/Aegean Airlines*,[41] the Commission will rely on qualitative evidence, internal documents and market questionnaires.

In line with the Commission's practice, the purpose of this book is to provide a non-technical introduction to the various forms of evidence and analytical techniques that are frequently employed in European merger control. In preparation for this material, we set out below a brief overview of empirical evidence as employed in merger investigations. At a high level, there are three ways in which economic evidence is typically employed in merger cases.

---

[37] Econometrics is a field concerned with the use of mathematics and statistics to connect economic theory with empirical facts. Over the past 50 years econometrics has developed into an extensive and highly complex specialised field, the vast majority of which is beyond the scope of this book. Appendix A gives an introduction to the principles and techniques of practical econometric analysis.

[38] For a discussion of econometric techniques recently employed in European merger analyses, see I. Small, 'Econometric Analyses of Unilateral Effects in Merger Cases', *Concurrences*, No. 2 (2009).

[39] K.-U. Kühn, speaking at Global Competition Law Centre Lunch Talk, 'The Commission Notice on the Definition of the Relevant Market', Brussels, 15 February 2012.

[40] Case COMP/M.6166 – *Deutsche Börse/NYSE Euronext*, Commission decision of 1 February 2012.

[41] Case COMP/M.5830 – *Olympic/Aegean Airlines*, Commission decision of 26 January 2011.

First, empirical evidence may comprise basic statistics. For example, a statistical test might be undertaken to assess whether and to what extent the prices of two products differ. Techniques such as price correlation analysis (discussed in Chapter 2, Section 3.6) and stationarity analysis (discussed in Chapter 2, Section 3.7) fall into this category. Such analyses can be considered 'statistical' rather than 'econometric' because they are not motivated by an underlying economic model that seeks to explain the determinants of the statistic(s) being measured. Once a statistical property of interest has been established (e.g. 'prices are equal' or 'prices are highly correlated'), it is then necessary to consider whether that property is economically meaningful.

Second, empirical evidence may derive from the use of 'reduced form' econometric models, which attempt to measure the direction and strength of relationships between economic variables without reference to a specific underlying theory concerning those relationships. Techniques such as price concentration analysis (discussed in Chapter 3, Section 3.3) and some bidding studies (discussed in Chapter 3, Section 3.7) fall into this category. Reduced form models differ from purely statistical methods in that, even though an explicit economic model concerning all relevant processes may not be specified, the influence of factors not formally incorporated within the analysis may be taken into account. It is in the context of reduced form models that econometricians often seek to find 'natural experiments' (discussed in Chapter 3, Section 3.5) that lay bare the actual relationships of interest, which might otherwise be obscured by absence of data to disentangle the various relevant factors.

Third, economic evidence may be provided by structural econometric models, which seek to use observed data to calibrate explicit theoretical models of the relevant economic relationships thought to give rise to those data. Techniques such as demand estimation (discussed in Chapter 2, Section 3.2) and merger simulation (discussed in Chapter 3, Section 3.6) fall into this category.

These methods are unified by the use of statistical inference to describe the precision of the results found. This inference normally takes the form of comparing the observed finding to the result that would be expected under some maintained assumption. If the realised result is very different (in a statistical sense) from the results that would be expected if the assumption were true, then this constitutes evidence that the assumption is false. Appendix A to this book describes a number of concepts from statistics in more detail.

The remainder of this book will consider in detail the various forms of empirical evidence that have previously been considered and relied upon by the Commission in the context of particular types of merger. Due to the case-specific nature of economic evidence, however, it is difficult to generalise what forms of economic analysis will prove decisive in particular cases. In practice, it is advisable to employ a range of complementary analyses that give rise to mutually supportive results since no single piece of analysis will likely be qualified as decisive on its own. The weight which the Commission will attach to particular pieces of economic evidence and analysis will depend on the extent to which they are consistent with the evidence gained by the Commission from other sources, including the Commission's market investigation and internal business documents.

# 2

## Market definition

### 1. Introduction

This chapter focuses on the principles and practice of market definition for the purpose of merger assessment. Market definition is a long-established element of merger analysis, although its importance in some merger control regimes has diminished in recent years due to the increasing use of analytical techniques and evidence that may to some extent bypass market definition.[1] Despite arguments that market definition may be a crude tool for economic analysis, in practice the topic remains centrally important to the assessment of most European merger investigations.

The Commission's approach to market definition is set out in its Notice on the definition of relevant market for the purposes of Community competition law (the 'Market Definition Notice').[2] The goal of market definition is to provide a context for the competitive assessment of a merger (or indeed any other competition issue being considered). It seeks to do so by identifying the **relevant antitrust market** (or relevant market) for the goods and services in question. The relevant market comprises the set of suppliers and products amongst which competitive interactions take place, such that changes in the control of those suppliers and products may potentially give rise to market power, and thereby adversely affect customers. The Market Definition Notice explains that:[3]

---

[1] Specifically, the US and UK merger control regimes have in recent years moved towards the use of upward pricing pressure and illustrative price rise methodologies respectively, which seek to use information on margins and sales diversion between the parties to identify directly changes in firms' pricing incentives resulting from a merger. Upward pricing pressure and illustrative price rise methodologies are discussed in Chapter 3.

[2] Notice on the definition of relevant market for the purposes of Community competition law (the 'Market Definition Notice'), OJ C372, 9.12.1997, pp. 5–13.

[3] Market Definition Notice, para. 2.

> Market definition is a tool to identify and define the boundaries of competition between firms. It serves to establish the framework within which competition policy is applied by the Commission. The main purpose of market definition is to identify in a systematic way the competitive constraints the undertakings involved [in a merger] face. The objective of defining a market ... is to identify those actual competitors of the undertakings involved that are capable of constraining those undertakings' behaviour and of preventing them from behaving independently of competitive pressure.

The identification of relevant markets takes place via the so-called hypothetical monopolist test, a thought experiment which asks whether a single firm controlling a particular group of assets would be able to raise prices above the level that would prevail if those assets were controlled by competing firms. If it is the case that sole control over those assets would create market power, that is, lead to prices above the competitive level, then that group must encompass the important competitive constraints on those assets, such that a competition authority is justified in investigating concentration in their ownership. If, on the other hand, even monopoly control of those assets would not bring about market power, then other assets and suppliers outside the group must be exerting an important competitive constraint, in which case they must be included in the relevant market.

Importantly, relevant markets for competition law purposes need not, and typically will not, correspond to the term 'market' as more generally understood, even by firms in the context of their own activities.[4] The 'markets' as perceived and understood by firms may be narrower than relevant antitrust markets, in the sense that suppliers may describe a market that does not include alternative suppliers that exert a competitive constraint on them; or, and more typically, may be broader than a relevant antitrust market, meaning that firms may pay regard to a broader set of rivals than the smallest set that could collectively constrain their behaviour.

We discuss the theoretical basis of market definition and the hypothetical monopolist test in Section 2 below. In Section 3 we then consider a number of quantitative techniques that the Commission has used for the purpose of assessing the definition of the relevant market in merger cases, highlighting for each technique both the circumstances in which it might be relevant and its potential shortcomings.

---

[4] See Market Definition Notice, para. 3.

## 2.   Conceptual framework

This section sets out the conceptual framework within which market definition is undertaken, the so-called **hypothetical monopolist** or **SSNIP** test.[4a] Section 2.1 introduces the logic and purpose of this test, while Section 2.2 discusses a number of issues and complications that can arise with practical application of the test.

### 2.1   The hypothetical monopolist/SSNIP test

The SSNIP test asks whether a hypothetical monopolist of a particular group of goods or services would be able profitably to implement a small but significant non-transitory increase in price (a 'SSNIP') over those goods or services.[5] A relevant market is the smallest set of products for which a hypothetical monopolist could profitably impose a SSNIP above the competitive price level.

The intuition underlying the SSNIP test is that if the hypothetical monopolist would not be able profitably to increase the price for the products under its control then those products must face an important competitive constraint from alternative goods outside the group controlled by the hypothetical monopolist. That competition should be taken into account in any competitive assessment involving those products, meaning that the relevant market must be widened to encompass those constraints. The SSNIP test is therefore typically applied sequentially to what are referred to as **candidate markets**, that is, groups of products and regions that may potentially represent relevant antitrust markets. The hypothetical monopolist test is applied to increasingly broad candidate markets surrounding the product or region of interest until the SSNIP condition is satisfied, and the smallest group of products that could profitably be monopolised is identified.

For example, in order to assess a potential merger between two suppliers of Golden Delicious cultivar apples, the market definition process would begin with the narrowest possible candidate market that

---

[4a]  The SSNIP test was first applied by the US Department of Justice and Federal Trade Commission, and set out in these bodies' 1992 Horizontal Merger Guidelines.

[5]  While the SSNIP test is normally phrased in terms of price increases, precisely the same logic applies to any worsening of supply terms, for instance in respect of product, quality, range or service. For the remainder of this chapter we will refer to the SSNIP test in terms of price, but the discussion should be understood as referring also to an equivalent worsening in other supply conditions.

encompasses the parties' operations, namely Golden Delicious apples. If a hypothetical monopolist of Golden Delicious apples would be unable profitably to impose a small but significant price increase, then this candidate market cannot represent a relevant antitrust market due to the existence of external competitive constraints affecting the hypothetical monopolist. The analysis would then proceed to a broader market definition including, for instance, all green apples. If this broader candidate market for green apples were also found to fail the SSNIP test then the analysis would proceed through broader candidate markets including all types of apples, fruits, snack foods etc., until a relevant market was found.

Conceptually, a candidate market may fail the SSNIP test (i.e. a price increase would be unprofitable) for two reasons. First, customers may respond to the hypothesised increase in price by switching to substitutable goods and services. If a sufficient proportion of existing customers switches away from the hypothetical monopolist, the resulting loss of turnover will exceed the increased margin enjoyed on retained customers, rendering the SSNIP unprofitable. This customer-led process is referred to as **demand-side substitution**. In the context of the above example, if Golden Delicious apples failed the SSNIP test due to customers switching from Golden Delicious to Granny Smith apples then this would be an example of demand-side substitution.

Alternatively, a SSNIP may be defeated by **supply-side substitution**. This term describes a situation in which a SSNIP implemented by a hypothetical monopolist would induce firms not currently active in the candidate market to begin producing the goods or services in question in response to the increased margins and higher profits being earned. This increased competition will reduce the hypothetical monopolist's margins, and may be sufficient to render the SSNIP unprofitable. If this is the case, the candidate market must be broadened to take account of the competition from those potential competitors.

In the above example, supply-side substitution may undermine a SSNIP by a hypothetical monopolist of an 'all apples' candidate market if a small but significant increase in the price of apples were sufficient to encourage orange growers to switch some of their land to the cultivation of apples. If supply-side substitution by orange growers would prevent a single firm controlling all apple-growing assets from profitably increasing price then the relevant market in which apple producers operate should be defined to include the land controlled by orange growers.

In practice, the Commission's focus in the assessment of market definition is on demand-side substitution. The Market Definition Notice notes that demand-side substitution 'constitutes the most immediate and effective disciplinary force on the suppliers of a given product, in particular in relation to their pricing decisions'.[6] By contrast, the Commission's view is that 'competitive constraints arising from supply side substitutability … and from potential competition are in general less immediate and in any case require an analysis of additional factors'.[7] In practice, the Commission will typically consider supply-side substitution to be feasible only where suppliers would find it very easy to redeploy their assets to a new activity in response to price changes. Where this is not the case the scope for supply-side substitution and potential entry will be assessed in the context of the overall competitive assessment, rather than at the point of defining relevant markets.[8]

An important concept that is often referred to in the assessment of demand-side substitution is the distinction between marginal and inframarginal consumers. In the preceding discussion, we have referred to 'sufficient' customer switching being required in order to conclude that a hypothetical monopolist is constrained by outside products. Section 3.1 below considers more explicitly what degree of switching is 'sufficient' in order to place two products in the same relevant market. At this stage, however, it is important to recognise that substitution from a given product in response to a SSNIP need not (and generally will not) include all customers but will normally only concern a sub-set of customers with the weakest preference for that product relative to alternatives. These are referred to as **marginal consumers**.

Returning to the apple example set out above, if the price of Golden Delicious apples were to be progressively increased, the first customers to switch to alternatives will be those with the weakest preference for Golden Delicious relative to other cultivars, that is, those customers that were, at the initial price, almost indifferent between choosing a Golden Delicious apple or a different apple. It is the preferences over alternatives of these marginal customers that determine the destination of switching in response to a small price increase and, ultimately, the boundaries of the relevant market.

By contrast, those customers that would not switch in response to a small price increase are referred to as **infra-marginal customers**.[9]

---

[6] Market Definition Notice, para. 13.    [7] Ibid., para. 14.    [8] Ibid., paras. 23 and 24.
[9] It should be clear that the categorisation of customers as marginal and infra-marginal will depend upon the magnitude of the price increase in question. Assume, for instance, that Golden Delicious apples are initially sold for €0.5 each. A customer that values Golden

The preferences over alternatives of these customers are not relevant for determining the boundaries of the relevant market. Infra-marginal customers are nonetheless relevant to the market definition exercise since the greater the proportion of infra-marginal customers in a candidate market, the more likely a hypothetical monopolist of that candidate market will find it profitable to increase price above the competitive level. It should be noted that, while they would not respond to a small but significant price increase for the products in question, infra-marginal customers nonetheless benefit from the behaviour of marginal customers, as the threat of marginal customers switching to alternatives provides the competitive constraint on suppliers' pricing that determines the price paid by all customers, both marginal and infra-marginal.

## 2.2   Issues and complications arising in market definition

### 2.2.1   Magnitude of the SSNIP and the 'binary fallacy'

The phrase 'small but significant' is usually held to mean a 5–10% change in price.[10] There is, however, no formal economic basis for this choice of level. Ultimately, it is a question of judgment as to how tight a constraint competition authorities regard as sufficient to delineate a relevant market for the purposes of framing competition analysis. Although 5–10% has become the established norm, and the de facto definition of a SSNIP in Europe (as well as the US and other jurisdictions around the world), there is no fundamental or objective reason why the SSNIP that defines the boundaries of a relevant market should be 5–10%.

In practice, competition authorities almost always use either 5% or 10% rather than a figure between the two to define the SSNIP. In many cases it is not possible to quantify the sensitivity of demand to price changes in a way that would allow one to answer the question posed by the hypothetical monopolist test sufficiently precisely for the choice of the level of the SSNIP to have a determinative impact on the results of the market definition exercise. Nevertheless, given that there are no fundamental economic grounds for adopting one of these figures over the

---

Delicious Apples at €0.04 more than his next preferred apple would be marginal for a 10% SSNIP in Golden Delicious, taking the price of Golden Delicious to €0.55, but infra-marginal for a SSNIP of 5%, taking the price of Golden Delicious apples to €0.525.

[10] Market Definition Notice, para. 17.

**Figure 2.1**   Hypothetical example of the binary fallacy

other, a pragmatic approach may be to investigate (where possible) the impact on the competition analysis of market definitions based on both figures. Where the two give qualitatively similar results this should provide reassurance that the conclusion is well founded on the economics of the industry in question. If, on the other hand, the result of the competitive analysis is sensitive to the definition of the SSNIP adopted, then this would suggest that care should be taken in relying heavily on the results of one approach to the exclusion of the other.

A related issue regarding the boundaries of relevant markets defined by the SSNIP test is the so-called **binary fallacy**.[11] This concept refers to the truism that a literal application of the SSNIP test as described above will necessarily identify a relevant market with a sharply defined boundary. Specifically, once the decision on the appropriate SSNIP (usually 5% or 10%) has been made, each potential substitute is either in that market or out of that market. Such dichotomous conclusions are clearly artificial, and in reality most markets will be characterised by a continuum of more and less substitutable products and regions. Figure 2.1 illustrates this situation, showing the relevant market defined by a 5% SSNIP for a hypothetical product A for which there are three potential substitutes of decreasing quality, products B, C and D.

Following an increase in the price of product A, some consumers would switch to the other products, and we assume for the purpose of this example that the lower the quality of the alternative products, the lower the proportion of switching customers that each product would be able to attract.

---

[11] Professor Sir John Vickers defines the binary fallacy as 'the tendency, once "the market" is defined, to think of all products within it as extremely substitutable for the products at the centre of concern, and those beyond the boundaries as irrelevant'. See J. Vickers, Director General of Fair Trading, 'Competition Economics and Policy – A Speech on the Occasion of the Launch of the New Social Sciences Building at Oxford University', 3 October 2002.

A rigid interpretation of the 5% SSNIP test would imply that products B and C are each part of the relevant market, and therefore of equal importance as competitive constraints to A, but that product D is not part of the market. Such an interpretation, however, would not accurately reflect the economic reality. In fact, in our stylised example product B is by far product A's closest substitute while there is no major difference between the degree of constraint offered by products C and D.

Thus, while a literal application of the SSNIP test might imply that A competes in a market with B and C but not D, the economic reality is that A is likely to be constrained to a large degree by B, while C and D each exert a less significant competitive constraint on A. It is worth noting that the use of a 10% SSNIP as a sensitivity test may well lead to the inclusion of product D in the relevant market. The lesson to be learnt from this example, however, is that the somewhat arbitrary binary nature of the SSNIP test means that the hypothetical monopolist framework should be used as the starting point for a pragmatic assessment of competitive interactions, and not applied in a dogmatic or mechanical fashion.

### 2.2.2   The relevant pre-SSNIP price and the 'cellophane fallacy'

A further issue associated with the practical application of the market definition exercise is that the hypothetical monopolist test is sensitive to the initial price level at which the SSNIP is applied. Strictly speaking, the hypothetical monopolist test concerns price increases in a candidate market relative to the 'competitive level'. If competition in the candidate market in question is not effective, however, then the observed price in that candidate market is likely to be above the competitive level. In the presence of inflated prices, the range of alternative products that consumers consider as substitutes will likely be wider, and potentially to a significant extent, than if the SSNIP test had been applied from the competitive price level.

Consequently, the application of a 5–10% SSNIP to the observed price, rather than the competitive price, may result in the identification of an overly broad market by overstating the importance of certain alternatives outside a candidate market in constraining competitive outcomes within that candidate market. This is the well-known **cellophane fallacy**, whereby distant substitutes appear to represent an effective constraint on a candidate market simply because prices in the candidate market have already been increased up to the level where the closest alternative, albeit one outside the appropriately defined relevant market, prevents further price increases.[12]

Importantly, while the cellophane fallacy is a potentially major issue in antitrust cases in which competition authorities are seeking to identify the extent to which observed outcomes reflect effective competition, it is not normally a concern in merger investigations. Indeed, mergers should be assessed against a *relative* benchmark, in the sense that the key question to address is whether the proposed transaction would result in a reduction in the intensity of competition relative to a counterfactual scenario in which the merger did not take place. In this context, the fact that pre-merger the absence of effective competitive constraints may have allowed firms to raise their prices to the point where further price increases would lead to customers switching to relatively distant competitors (i.e. to products that would not have been considered by customers as adequate substitutes if effective competition had kept prices at a lower level) is not a relevant consideration and should not affect the outcome of the investigation.

Consequently, market definition for merger analysis is almost always conducted from the starting point of prevailing prices. However, the cellophane fallacy does mean that care should be taken in transposing relevant markets defined for the purposes of antitrust cases to merger assessment (and vice versa).

### 2.2.3   Asymmetry in market definition

A further potential complication for market definition arises from the possibility of asymmetric competitive constraints. The fact that product A exerts a competitive constraint on suppliers of product B does not necessarily imply that product B exerts a constraint on suppliers of product A. Consequently, it is important to specify the appropriate starting point when applying the SSNIP test as the outcome may differ according to the order in which candidate relevant markets are assessed.

To give a simple example, consider an assessment of market definition for grocery retailers in a town where two large supermarkets and a

---

[12]   The term 'cellophane fallacy' derives from *United States* v. *E.I. du Pont de Nemours & Co.*, 351 U.S. 377, 76 S.Ct. 994, 100 L.Ed. 1264 (1956), in which it was found that the apparent constraint exerted on cellophane packaging by aluminium, foil, wax paper and polyethylene was due to DuPont's having raised the price of cellophane to the point at which customers began to switch to these alternatives, rather than their lying in the same relevant antitrust market as cellophane.

number of smaller stores are present. Each smaller store specialises in a particular product area. Specifically, suppose the town contains a number of greengrocers (specialising in the sale of fruit and vegetables), a number of butchers (specialising in the sale of meat) and a number of bakers (specialising in the sale of bread and pastries). On the other hand, the two large supermarkets sell each of these product categories. All the stores are located a few hundred metres from each other, implying that visitors experience negligible transport costs from visiting multiple stores.

When applying the hypothetical monopolist test in this context, the results may depend on what particular merger is being considered and, therefore, on what starting point is used to run the SSNIP test.

Considering first a merger between two greengrocers, the relevant question would be: starting from the greengrocers, should the relevant market be extended to include fruit and vegetables sold by the two large supermarkets?

The answer to this question depends on the competitive constraint exercised by the supermarkets on the greengrocers. To the extent that the vegetables sold by the two types of retailers are of a similar quality, it would seem plausible that a sufficient number of specialist greengrocers' customers would switch to the supermarkets in the event of a SSNIP, and therefore that the relevant market would comprise both greengrocers and supermarkets. To the extent that supermarkets account for the large majority of the total amount of vegetables sold in the town, the proposed merger between the two greengrocers may be considered unlikely to give rise to competition concerns.

Now consider a merger between the two supermarkets. In this case, the relevant question would be: starting from the supermarkets, should the relevant market be extended also to include some or all of the specialist retailers?

The answer in this case may be very different. If a hypothetical monopolist of supermarkets in the town were to impose a SSNIP across its products some customers would switch to combined use of specialist retailers (i.e. making separate visits to a greengrocer, a butcher and a baker). However, many consumers are likely to consider this approach too costly in terms of time and effort and will continue to purchase from the supermarkets, such that the hypothesised supermarket SSNIP would be profitable. As such, the relevant market in which supermarkets compete may not include specialist greengrocers, even if those greengrocers compete in a relevant market that does include the supermarkets.

## 2.2.4 Indirect constraints and chains of substitution

Another important feature to note in the context of market definition is that firms may exert an indirect competitive constraint on each other via **chains of substitution**. This term describes a situation in which, although certain products or regions do not directly impose a competitive constraint on another (in the sense that no customer would switch between them in response to changes in the prices of these products or regions), they may do so indirectly due to the presence of intermediate products or regions that do constrain the pricing of each of them. In this regard, the Market Definition Notice states that:[13]

> The existence of chains of substitution might lead to the definition of a relevant market where products or areas at the extreme of the market are not directly substitutable. An example might be provided by the geographic dimension of a product with significant transport costs. In such cases, deliveries from a given plant are limited to a certain area around each plant by the impact of transport costs. In principle, such an area could constitute the relevant geographic market. However, if the distribution of plants is such that there are considerable overlaps between the areas around different plants, it is possible that the pricing of those products will be constrained by a chain substitution effect, and lead to the definition of a broader geographic market.

As an illustration, consider the four products shown in Figure 2.2. The products are differentiated on the basis of one dimension and overlap in functionality terms according to the circles shown in the figure.

Assume that we are defining the market starting from product A and that prices charged for product A are constrained by prices for B. On this basis, A and B are likely to be part of the same relevant market. However, if B's prices are in turn constrained by C and D, prices of A will indirectly be constrained by C and D. If this is the case, it would thus be appropriate also to include C and D in the market due to a chain of substitution between A, B, C and D.

The Commission has stated that in practice 'the concept of chains of substitution has to be corroborated by actual evidence, for instance related to price interdependence at the extremes of the chains of substitution, in order to lead to an extension of the relevant market in an individual case'.[14] This position was reiterated in *Lufthansa/SN*

---

[13] Market Definition Notice, para. 57.
[14] Market Definition Notice, para. 58. The same paragraph goes on to suggest that price equality at each end of the chain is also a necessary condition to support a broad market

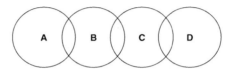

**Figure 2.2**   Hypothetical example of chain of substitution

*Airholding*,[15] where the Commission rejected the argument put forward by Lufthansa that time-sensitive and non-time-sensitive passengers should belong to the same market due to the existence of chains of substitution between different types of flexible and non-flexible tickets. Specifically, the Commission stated that:[16]

> It is very doubtful that there could be a chain of substitution between different types of tickets so as to justify the inclusion of all types of tickets in the same relevant market. The complicated pricing structures and sophisticated yield management systems aim at and allow the carriers to segment demand so as to extract high prices from time-sensitive passengers whose price elasticity is considerably lower than [*sic*] non time-sensitive passengers … [T]he price analysis conducted by the Commission … shows that prices at the extremes of the alleged chain of substitution (namely prices of business class tickets and prices of non flexible economy class tickets) have very different levels and are not interdependent.

A notable recent case where a wide market was defined on the grounds of the existence of chains of substitution between the various products is *Oracle/Sun Microsystems*.[17] Referring to the market definition reached in the first phase of the investigation of that case, which was retained in the second phase, the Commission noted that:[18]

> although the market investigation undertaken by the Commission in the first phase indicated that databases are differentiated products from the perspective of both suppliers and users, it did not identify a single appropriate approach to delineating the database market. On the contrary it pointed towards a continuum of database substitutability and hence competition.

---

on the basis of a chain of substitution. In line with the discussion at Section 3.5 of the inferences for market definition that can be drawn from price levels we would disagree with this position.

[15] Case COMP/M.5335 – *Lufthansa/SN Airholding*, Commission decision of 22 June 2009.

[16] Ibid., para. 33.

[17] Case COMP/M.5529 – *Oracle/Sun Microsystems*, Commission decision of 21 January 2010.

[18] Ibid., para. 87.

## 3.  Empirical techniques to assess market definition

In this section we consider various forms of evidence and analytical techniques that the Commission routinely relies on to inform the definition of relevant antitrust markets.

Economic agents' responses to changes in relative prices are the central concern of market definition and the hypothetical monopolist test. As the name suggests, the test requires inferences regarding the consequences of hypothetical changes in pricing patterns. These cannot be made directly via controlled experiments as in the natural sciences, and so must be drawn from the available evidence on current firm and consumer conduct.

There is a wide range of methods by which information on consumer and firm behaviour relevant to market definition may be gleaned, ranging from qualitative assessment of consumers' likely behaviour to quantitative econometric analysis. The appropriate approach for any given case will largely be driven by the way competition works in the industry in question and the available data. Similarly, the forms of analysis undertaken will also vary according to how critical market definition is to the competitive assessment of the case in question. As stated in the Market Definition Notice:[19]

> In individual cases, certain types of evidence will be determinant, depending very much on the characteristics and specificity of the industry and products or services that are being defined. The same type of evidence may be of no importance in other cases. In most cases, a decision will have to be based on the consideration of a number of criteria and different items of evidence. The Commission follows an open approach to empirical evidence, aimed at making an effective use of all available information which may be relevant in individual cases. The Commission does not follow a rigid hierarchy of different sources of information or types of evidence.

In what follows, we review the following eight forms of quantitative analyses that may provide evidence on market definition:

- Critical loss analysis
- Demand estimation
- Survey evidence
- Analysis of sales patterns
- Analysis of price levels

---

[19] Market Definition Notice, para. 25.

- Price correlation analysis
- Price stationarity analysis
- Shock analysis.

In addition to the abovementioned techniques, the Commission also draws on qualitative evidence to inform its view on market definition. Indeed, in many cases such qualitative evidence is held to be sufficient to allow a conclusion to be drawn without proceeding to detailed quantitative analysis.

Two forms of qualitative evidence are often employed in market definition analysis. The first of these approaches involves a review of the characteristics of products that might lie in the same relevant market in an attempt to predict whether customers would be willing to switch between those products in the event of changes in their relative prices. The Market Definition Notice states, however, that while 'an analysis of the product characteristics and its intended use allows the Commission, as a first step, to limit the field of investigation of possible substitutes … product characteristics and intended use are insufficient to show whether two products are demand substitutes'.[20]

The second qualitative technique often observed involves a review of company documents and operating practice. This is an improvement on the characteristics approach in the sense that, while it focuses on firms' behaviour rather than that of customers, firms' behaviour is ultimately a response to companies' perceptions of consumer behaviour. It is not unreasonable to believe that firms, at least those that have survived in the medium to long term, are well-informed about the industry in which they operate and so that their views will shed light on customers' behaviour patterns. Thus, the Commission will frequently cite examples of firms stating that they cannot compete in a particular region, that they face a competitive threat from a particular rival, or references to the markets in which they operate in its assessments of market definition.

While such statements can be informative as an insight into companies' internal perceptions, care should be taken in placing weight on comments that have not been prepared in the context of formal economic assessments of relevant markets for the purposes of competition law. Business people will frequently use the words 'market' and 'competition' in a looser sense than they carry in competition law analysis, and will not generally be aware of or think in terms of the hypothetical

---

[20] Market Definition Notice, para. 36.

monopolist test. In particular, firms' internal planning documents will normally assess the markets in which they operate from their own perspective only, rather than focusing on substitution from a broader group of firms representing a candidate market. Thus, a manufacturer of widgets will typically consider only potential substitution if it were to increase the price of its own widgets, rather than the consequences of a concerted increase in all widget manufacturers' prices.

The same observation can be made in respect of external market studies undertaken on behalf of the merging parties or more generally. These studies do not employ an antitrust market definition, but will typically deal with industry segmentations that may have little or no relevance to competition analysis for the purpose of merger review.

As such, while internal documents can provide a useful starting point for market definition analysis, where market definition is a non-trivial element of the assessment of a particular merger, this qualitative evidence should always be augmented by and confirmed against direct quantitative evidence collected and reviewed for the purposes of identifying the relevant market.

Finally, it should be noted that, while the various quantitative techniques discussed in this section have been used in numerous EU merger investigations, cases that involve such detailed analysis of market definition are nonetheless in the minority. In the majority of cases the Commission does not apply any detailed empirical analysis to define the relevant product and geographic markets, as the results of the competitive assessment may be similar regardless of whether a wide or a narrow definition of the market is adopted. As explained in the Market Definition Notice:[21]

> The Commission will usually be in a position to broadly establish the possible relevant markets within which ... a concentration ... has to be assessed. In general, and for all practical purposes when handling individual cases, the question will usually be to decide on a few alternative possible relevant markets. For instance, with respect to the product market, the issue will often be to establish whether product A and product B belong or do not belong to the same product market. It is often the case that the inclusion of product B would be enough to remove any competition concerns.
>
> In such situations it is not necessary to consider whether the market includes additional products, or to reach a definitive conclusion on the precise product market. If under the conceivable market definitions the operation in question does not raise competition concerns, the question of market definition will be left open, reducing thereby the burden on companies to supply information.

---

[21]  Ibid., paras. 26 and 27.

On the other hand, the Commission will devote significant resources to market definition, and parties would be well advised to do so too, where the definition of the relevant market is contentious and likely to have a significant bearing on the outcome of the competitive analysis. Table 2.1 summarises Phase II cases since 2004 in which the Commission has undertaken a detailed assessment of market definition, together with the key empirical techniques used in each case.

### 3.1    Critical loss analysis

### 3.1.1    Description of technique

We begin our discussion of empirical techniques in market definition with critical loss analysis. While critical loss analysis is not frequently applied explicitly in European merger assessment practice, it does provide a useful framework for analysing evidence on the substitution that lies at the heart of market definition. By clarifying the role and purpose of the types of evidence that are typically used for market definition, the technique provides context for the discussion of empirical techniques more frequently cited in European Commission market definition practice that makes up the remainder of this section.

Critical loss analysis was originally developed in the US, where it is considered to be one of the major elements of modern merger enforcement.[22] Critical loss analysis and its practical application has been the subject of considerable discussion and debate by competition economists and practitioners in the US.[23] While the technique has recently begun to gain traction in European enforcement, it remains rarely applied or referred to in EU merger cases.

**3.1.1.1    The SSNIP and pricing decisions**    Critical loss analysis addresses the central trade-off of firms' pricing decisions arising from the negative relationship between margins and sales volumes. An increase in price will allow a firm to achieve greater margins on the sales that it makes, but will also reduce the volume of sales that it will make (and vice versa). Rational firms will take into account these two

---

[22] See D. Scheffman, M. Coate and L. Silvia, 'Twenty Years of Merger Guidelines Enforcement at the FTC: An Economic Perspective' (2003) 71 *Antitrust Law Journal* 277–318.

[23] For an overview of this debate see: D. P. O'Brien and A. L. Wickelgren, 'A Critical Analysis of Critical Loss Analysis' (2003) 71 *Antitrust Law Journal* 161–84; J. Farrell and C. Shapiro, 'Improving Critical Loss Analysis' (2008) *The Antitrust Source*, February.

Table 2.1 Quantitative analysis of market definition in Phase II merger cases since 2004

| Case | Critical loss | Demand estimation | Sales patterns | Correlation | Stationarity | Shock analysis |
|---|---|---|---|---|---|---|
| Areva/Urenco/ETC JV[1] (2004) | | | | X | | |
| Bertelsmann/Springer/JV[2] (2005) | | | X | | | X |
| Blackstone/Acetex[3] (2005) | | | | X | | |
| Johnson&Johnson/Guidant[4] (2005) | | | | X | | |
| Inco/Falconbridge[5] (2006) | | | | X | | X |
| Omya/Huber PCC[6] (2006) | | | X | | | |
| JCI/VB /FIAMM[7] (2007) | | | | X | | |
| Kronospan/Constantia[8] (2007) | | | X | | | |
| Ryanair/Aer Lingus[9] (2007) | | | | X | | |
| ABF/GBI Business[10] (2008) | | | | X | | |
| Arjowiggins/M-real Zanders Reflex[11] (2008) | | | | X | X | X |
| StatoilHydro/ConocoPhillips[12] (2008) | | | X | X | | |
| Friesland Foods/Campina[13] (2008) | | | X | X | | |
| Ineos/Kerling[14] (2008) | X | | X | X | X | X |
| Arsenal/DSP[15] (2009) | | | X | X | X | X |
| Lufthansa/SN Airholding[16] (2009) | X | | | X | | |
| Unilver/Sara Lee Body Care[17] (2010) | | X | | X | | X |

Table 2.1 (cont.)

| Case | Critical loss | Demand estimation | Sales patterns | Correlation | Stationarity | Shock analysis |
|---|---|---|---|---|---|---|
| *Votorantim/Fischer/JV*[18] (2011) | | X | | X | X | X |
| *UPM/Myllykoski and Rhein Papier*[19] (2011) | | | | X | | |

1 Case COMP/M.3099 – *Areva/Urenco/ETC JV*, Commission decision of 6 October 2004.
2 Case COMP/M.3178 – *Bertelsmann/Springer/JV*, Commission decision of 3 May 2005.
3 Case COMP/M.3625 – *Blackstone/Acetex*, Commission decision of 13 July 2005.
4 Case COMP/M.3687 – *Johnson&Johnson/Guidant*, Commission decision of 25 August 2005.
5 Case COMP/M.4000 – *Inco/Falconbridge*, Commission decision of 4 July 2006.
6 Case COMP/M.3796 – *Omya/Huber PCC*, Commission decision of 19 July 2006.
7 Case COMP/M.4381 – *JCI/VB/FIAMM*, Commission decision of 10 May 2007.
8 Case COMP/M.4525 – *Kronospan/Constantia*, Commission decision of 19 September 2007.
9 Case COMP/M.4439 – *Ryanair/Aer Lingus*, Commission decision of 27 June 2007.
10 Case COMP/M.4980 – *ABF/GBI Business*, Commission decision of 23 September 2008.
11 Case COMP/M.4513 – *Arjowiggins/M-real Zanders Reflex*, Commission decision of 4 June 2008.
12 Case COMP/M.4919 – *StatoilHydro/ConocoPhillips*, Commission decision of 21 October 2008.
13 Case COMP/M.5046 – *Friesland Foods/Campina*, Commission decision of 17 December 2008.
14 Case COMP/M.4734 – *Ineos/Kerling*, Commission decision of 30 January 2008.
15 Case COMP/M.5153 – *Arsenal/DSP*, Commission decision of 9 January 2009.
16 Case COMP/M.5335 – *Lufthansa/SN Airholding*, Commission decision of 22 June 2009.
17 Case COMP/M.5658 – *Unilever/Sara Lee Body Care*, Commission decision of 17 November 2010.
18 Case COMP/M.5907 – *Votorantim/Fischer/JV*, Commission decision of 4 May 2011.
19 Case COMP/M.6101 – *UPM/Myllykoski and Rhein Papier*, Commission decision of 13 July 2011.

opposing factors in identifying an optimal profit-maximising price that balances margins and sales.

The logic of this price setting process feeds directly into the hypothetical monopolist test. The hypothetical monopolist test asks whether a firm controlling a given set of production assets would find it profitable to impose a small but significant increase in price relative to the level that would result from competition between independent firms controlling those assets. The SSNIP test thus turns on the question of the profitability of a small price increase above the competitive level for the hypothetical monopolist. The outcome of the SSNIP test for any given set of goods or regions thus depends on the extent to which an increase in margins following a SSNIP would be offset by a consequent loss in sales.

In determining whether an increase in price above the competitive level would be profitable, the hypothetical monopolist will compare the value of the extra margin it would earn as a result of the price increase across retained sales to the value of the sales that it could expect to lose. The former is equal to the increase in margin per unit multiplied by the number of units that it would continue to sell after the price increase. The latter is equal to the original margin per unit (i.e. the margin earned in the absence of the price increase) multiplied by the number of sales that would be lost due to the price increase.

If the former benefit is lower than the latter cost, then the price increase will generate incremental profits that are more than outweighed by the incremental losses. In this case, the price increase will be unprofitable, implying that substitution to other products or regions outside the hypothetical monopolist's control is sufficiently great to provide an external constraint on its behaviour, such that the SSNIP test is failed. Conversely, if the value of the greater margin on the retained sales is larger than the value of the lost sales then the price increase implemented by the hypothetical monopolist will be profitable. In this case, the SSNIP test is passed and the assets owned by the hypothetical monopolist represent a relevant antitrust market.

This can be illustrated with a simple numerical example. Table 2.2 sets out stylised price and cost data for a hypothetical monopolist of a particular product considering whether to implement a 5% SSNIP over the prevailing competitive price level. The table shows that the marginal production cost for the product in question is €80 per unit, the prevailing competitive price is €100 per unit and the total demand at that price is 100 units. Table 2.2 also shows that following a SSNIP demand would fall to 90 units.

Table 2.2 *Illustrative critical loss example*

|                  | Pre-SSNIP | Post-SSNIP |
| ---------------- | --------- | ---------- |
| Price            | 100       | 105        |
| Marginal cost    | 80        | 80         |
| Margin per unit  | 20        | 25         |
| Sales            | 100       | 90         |

This information alone is sufficient to calculate the profitability of a SSNIP. In line with the discussion above, we calculate the profitability of the SSNIP by comparing the incremental profit gain from the increase in margin over retained sales to the incremental profit loss resulting from lost sales.

The incremental gain from the SSNIP is given by the increase in the margin per unit multiplied by the number of units that will be retained after the price increase. On the basis of the above figures, this is given by the €5 increase in margin (i.e. the value of the SSNIP) multiplied by the 90 units sold after the SSNIP, which corresponds to an incremental profit gain of €450.

The incremental profit loss due to the reduction in demand is given by the €20 pre-SSNIP margin multiplied by the 10 units lost, which is equal to €200. Netting these two countervailing effects gives a total change in profitability of €250, meaning that the hypothetical monopolist would increase its profits by €250 if it were to impose a SSNIP.[24] This indicates that the set of assets assumed to be under the control of the hypothetical monopolist is sufficiently insulated from competitive constraints to represent a relevant antitrust market. It is thus competition from within, rather than outside, that group of assets that is constraining price to the pre-SSNIP level.

Conversely, if the volume of sales that would be made post-SSNIP is assumed to be 70 rather than 90, the profitability of the SSNIP reverses.

---

[24] This calculation follows the preceding discussion by separating the net change in profitability into two offsetting components representing increased margins and reduced sales. Alternatively, the gross profitability both pre- and post-SSNIP may be compared to assess the profitability of the SSNIP. In this case, the pre-SSNIP profitability is equal to a margin of €20 over 100 units, giving total profits of €2,000, while post-SSNIP profits are equal to a margin of €25 over 90 units, giving total profits of €2,250. The €250 difference in these two totals is identical to that calculated in the text on the basis of incremental gains and losses.

At post-SSNIP sales of 70 units, the increase in profits from a 5% increase in price is €350 (obtained by multiplying the incremental margin of €5 by the 70 remaining units). The profit loss meanwhile is €600 (obtained by multiplying the original margin of €20 by the 30 lost units). This gives a net change in profitability due to the SSNIP of − €250. Thus, with a larger demand response, the same 5% SSNIP becomes unprofitable, such that the assets controlled by the hypothetical monopolist do not represent a relevant antitrust market.

**3.1.1.2   The SSNIP test and critical loss analysis**   The above discussion explained how a hypothetical monopolist would assess the costs and benefits of a price increase, and therefore choose whether to impose a SSNIP, assuming that it had information on the degree of volume loss that would occur as a result of the SSNIP. Clearly, while this information is the crux of the SSNIP decision, it is also inherently uncertain, depending on the unknown aggregate response of customers and rival suppliers.

Critical loss analysis reverses this logic. Instead of asking how a hypothetical monopolist's profits would change if it increased price for a specified level of sales loss, critical loss analysis asks, for a specified change in price, what level of sales loss could be borne without rendering that price increase unprofitable.

This principle can be illustrated with the price and margin data set out in Table 2.2. Given pre-SSNIP margins of €20 per unit, and a 5% SSNIP, the loss of demand that would leave the hypothetical monopolist with unchanged profits can be shown to be 20 units.[25] If the loss of demand is greater than 20 units then the 5% SSNIP would result in a reduction in profits; conversely, if the loss of demand is less than 20 units then the SSNIP will be profitable and the candidate market represents a relevant antitrust market.

Critical loss analysis thus provides a benchmark for the maximum extent of consumer switching that would permit a hypothetical monopolist profitably to increase prices. In principle, as shown in the next section, calculation of the critical loss requires only information on sales margins.

---

[25] This figure is calculated by identifying the change in quantity that equalises the incremental profit gain and incremental profit loss resulting from the SSNIP. Specifically, for m pre-SSNIP margin, q pre-SSNIP quantity, $\Delta m$ change in margin and $\Delta q$ change in quantity, the SSNIP leaves profits unchanged for $\Delta m(q - \Delta q) = \Delta q m$. Rearranging, $\Delta q = (q\Delta m)/(m + \Delta m)$. Consequently, for the figures in the text, $\Delta q = (100 * 5)/(20 + 5) = 20$.

Clearly however, establishing the critical sales loss is only the starting point for an assessment of market definition. The critical loss provides context for the degree of sales loss that is consistent with a candidate market representing a relevant market, but does not provide any information on whether that degree of demand loss is likely to arise in practice. Estimating the degree of actual switching that could be expected to result from the hypothetical price increase remains the more onerous task.

**3.1.1.3 Calculation of the critical loss in practice** The preceding discussion set out a numerical example illustrating the concept of a critical demand loss that would leave a hypothetical monopolist indifferent between leaving prices unchanged and imposing a SSNIP. More generally, the critical demand change can be expressed by the following formula, which is specified in terms of *proportionate* changes in demand and prices and assumes that marginal costs are constant:

$$\text{Critical percentage loss of demand} = \frac{t}{(m+t)}$$

where $m$ is the pre-SSNIP margin and $t$ is the percentage change in price.

Thus, for a 5% SSNIP (that is, $t = 0.05$) and 20% prevailing margins (that is, $m = 0.2$), as in the example in Table 2.2 above, the critical demand change is $0.05/0.25 = 0.2$ (or 20%). Given the pre-SSNIP sales of 100 units, a 20% reduction in volumes corresponds to 20 units, as already identified above. If the expected total volume loss following a 5% SSNIP is greater than 20 units, then it follows that a SSNIP would be unprofitable and that the products/regions in question do not constitute a relevant antitrust market. If the expected loss of sales from the products/regions is less than 20 units, then a SSNIP by the hypothetical monopolist would be profitable, implying that a relevant market has been identified.

It can be seen that the only figure required to calculate the critical loss, once the level of the SSNIP has been decided (say 5%), is the pre-SSNIP margin for the candidate market. Importantly, as shown in Figure 2.3, the higher the pre-SSNIP margin, the lower the critical volume loss that is required to leave a hypothetical monopolist indifferent between raising prices or leaving them unchanged. The reason for the negative relationship between critical volume and margin is that higher margins on existing sales make the loss of any unit increasingly costly, thereby reducing the critical amount of sales loss that is required to render the hypothesised price increase unprofitable.

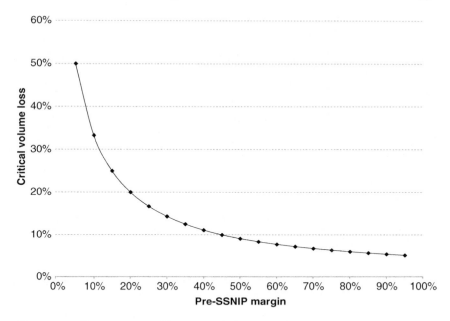

**Figure 2.3**    Illustrative critical loss example (5% SSNIP)

The preceding discussion has introduced the critical demand loss that would leave a hypothetical monopolist indifferent between maintaining the prevailing competitive price and increasing that price by 5–10%. This so called 'breakeven' critical loss test corresponds to the hypothetical monopolist test as it is generally applied in the EU, where the relevant question is whether a hypothetical monopolist could profitably increase price by a small but significant amount. An alternative version of the hypothetical monopolist test question (and the one that is employed in the US horizontal merger guidelines) is whether a hypothetical profit-maximising monopolist would choose to increase price by a small but significant amount.[26]

To the extent that one is interested in the latter rather than former SSNIP test question, it is necessary to employ an alternative version of the critical loss test often referred to as the 'profit-maximising' critical

---

[26] 'Specifically, the test requires that a hypothetical profit-maximizing firm, not subject to price regulation, that was the only present and future seller of those products ("hypothetical monopolist") likely would impose at least a small but significant and non-transitory increase in price ("SSNIP") …' See US Department of Justice and the Federal Trade Commission Horizontal Merger Guidelines, 19 August 2010, Section 4.1.1.

loss test. This test asks whether the profit-maximising decision of a hypothetical monopolist is to impose a price increase of at least 5–10%. Thus, while the breakeven critical loss identifies the proportionate decrease in quantity sold resulting from the price increase that is just large enough to cause the price increase to be unprofitable, the profit-maximising critical loss provides the proportionate decrease in quantity sold resulting from the price increase that is just large enough so that a hypothetical profit-maximising monopolist would not impose a price increase of *at least* the given amount.[27]

The Market Definition Notice is clearly phrased in terms of whether a SSNIP would be *profitable* rather than *profit maximising*.[28] Where the European Commission has undertaken critical loss analysis in recent cases, however, it has reported the results of both the breakeven and the profit maximising critical loss concepts.[29]

Generally, if a profit-maximising hypothetical monopolist would impose *at least* a SSNIP, then it is more profitable to impose a SSNIP than to maintain prices at prevailing levels.[30] Thus, if the profit-maximising price increase for a hypothetical monopolist were higher than 5% then a smaller price increase of 5% will normally increase profits.[31]

Consequently, the profit-maximising critical loss will normally be smaller than the breakeven critical loss, and therefore represents a more onerous condition for the definition of a relevant market (i.e. it will tend to suggest wider markets).[32] That is, a given actual demand loss may be insufficient to broaden the market beyond a given candidate market

---

[27] This definition of the profit-maximising critical loss is given by Gregory Werden: see G. J. Werden, 'Demand Elasticities in Antitrust Analysis' (1998) 66 *Antitrust Law Journal* 363, 370, 373–4 and n. 36.

[28] 'If substitution were enough to make the price increase unprofitable because of the resulting loss of sales, additional substitutes and areas are included in the relevant market.' See Market Definition Notice, para. 17.

[29] To date, the choice between the two has not been a critical factor in the assessment of the relevant market; the question of which approach the Commission would favour in the event that the choice affected the outcome of the analysis is therefore unresolved.

[30] The only condition required is that profit as a function of price has a single maximum.

[31] An exceptional circumstance in which this does not hold can arise if rivals outside the candidate market are capacity constrained. This may imply that a 5% increase in price is not profitable because many customers switch to rivals outside the candidate market, but that a larger, say, 15%, increase in price is profitable because further demand losses from the candidate market are small due to the fact that once rivals' capacity is filled no further customers are able to switch away.

[32] See J. Farrell and C. Shapiro, 'Improving Critical Loss Analysis' (2008) *The Antitrust Source*, February.

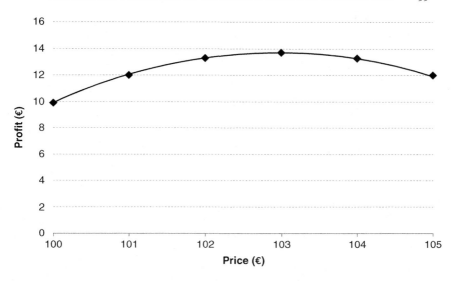

**Figure 2.4**   Illustrative relationship between profits and prices

under the breakeven critical loss standard but be sufficiently large to prevent the same candidate market from constituting a relevant antitrust market under the profit-maximising standard.

In principle, the profit-maximising critical loss standard is the more appropriate one. The profit-maximising critical loss will identify a relevant market only where the hypothetical monopolist would indeed choose to impose a SSNIP of at least the specified level (for instance 5%). The breakeven critical loss, by contrast, will identify a relevant market where a given SSNIP is profit improving (relative to the competitive price) even in circumstances where the hypothetical monopolist would in fact choose to impose a lower price increase. The fact that the hypothetical monopolist would choose not to impose the entirety of the specified SSNIP in this situation points to the existence of external constraints that suggest that the candidate market is not a relevant antitrust market. The breakeven critical loss test, however, would suggest that a relevant antitrust market exists so long as a profitable opportunity to impose the SSNIP exists.

A scenario in which the two versions of the critical loss test provide divergent results is illustrated in Figure 2.4, which shows how the profit of a hypothetical monopolist varies as prices are increased above the initial €100 level. It can be seen that if prices were increased by 5% to €105, profits would rise from €10 to €12, implying that the SSNIP test is passed. However, the figure also shows that a hypothetical monopolist

Table 2.3 *Critical loss formulae*

| | Critical loss |
|---|---|
| Breakeven | $\dfrac{t}{(m+t)}$ |
| Profit-maximising (linear demand) | $\dfrac{t}{(m+2t)}$ |
| Profit-maximising (isoelastic demand) | $1 - (1+t)^{-\frac{(1+t)}{(t+m)}}$ |

would not choose to increase prices by 5% since its profits would be even higher were a more modest 3% price increase to €103 to be implemented.

While the profit-maximising critical loss is the more appropriate concept for market definition, its implementation is more complex than the break-even critical loss. This is because the profit-maximising critical loss, which does not simply compare the profitability of the competitive price and the post-SSNIP price but seeks to establish the optimal price increase, requires an assumption regarding the shape of the demand curve faced by the hypothetical monopolist.

Two demand specifications tend to be typically used due to their mathematical tractability: **linear demand** and **isoelastic** demand. Table 2.3 summarises the profit-maximising critical demand formulae for these demand assumptions, together with the breakeven critical demand formula set out above (which does not depend upon, or therefore require an assumption regarding, the shape of the demand curve).[33] Each of these formulae assumes that the hypothetical monopolist charges a uniform price and faces a constant marginal cost.

**3.1.1.4 Data requirements** The relevant margin for the calculation of critical loss is often a source of considerable debate in practice. The formulae above are derived on the assumption that the hypothetical monopolist faces a constant marginal cost, such that each unit it sells at a given price generates the same incremental margin. This incremental margin is equal to the price of the last unit sold less the cost incurred in offering that unit for sale (or, equivalently, the costs that would be saved if that unit had not been sold). This raises two potential difficulties.

---

[33] For derivation of these formulae, see Annex A of G. J. Werden, 'Demand Elasticities in Antitrust Analysis' (1998) 66 *Antitrust Law Journal*.

The first is that this margin will not typically be reported in firms' accounts, which will generally include fixed costs that do not vary with the number of units sold, such as staff costs, administrative costs and asset depreciation. The major relevant incremental costs will typically comprise only the raw material and distribution costs for each unit. As such, the relevant margin for critical loss analysis may be higher than the margins calculated and reported in businesses' accounts.

Second, and more importantly, the assumption that margins are constant may not hold in some industries, either because price is not constant (see the European Commission's comments in *Lufthansa/SN Airholding*,[34] discussed below) or because of non-linearities in costs. Non-linear costs will be relevant to the extent that firms may be able to remove some portion of their fixed costs in the event of losing sales volumes as a result of a SSNIP. If, for instance, firms are able to shut down a production facility, decommission a piece of equipment or reduce the number of production shifts, an increase in price will potentially generate a cost saving that will, in addition to the margin increase, serve to offset the loss of demand.

Consequently, where non-marginal costs can be saved following a price increase, a SSNIP may be attractive at higher levels of demand loss than suggested by a critical loss analysis conducted on the assumption of constant margins. In such cases, the critical demand loss will be greater than the above formulae would imply, such that these formulae may wrongly imply that a given demand loss would be too great to permit a profitable SSNIP. This would lead to a conclusion that a candidate market does not represent a relevant antitrust market, when in fact a hypothetical monopolist might rationally choose to implement a price rise.

Where cost non-linearities are likely to be present, it may be possible to test the sensitivity of the results of the breakeven critical loss formula by manually calculating the change in volume that would leave the hypothetical monopolist indifferent with respect to a SSNIP, taking account of any non-linear changes in costs that might result from the lost volume, according to the methodology used to introduce the critical loss concept above.[35]

---

[34] Case COMP/M.5335 – *Lufthansa/SN Airholding*, Commission decision of 22 June 2009.

[35] Extending the derivation set out at footnote 25 above, assume that $\gamma$ is the average per unit fixed cost saving. The critical $\Delta q$ change in quantity then arises at $\Delta m(q - \Delta q) + \gamma\Delta q = m\Delta q$. Rearranging, $\Delta q = (q\Delta m)/(m + \Delta m - \gamma)$. This will give an approximation of the adjusted critical volume assuming that the non-linear cost element is linear.

### 3.1.2  An example

This illustrative example concerns the definition of the relevant geographic market for the manufacture of paper in Finland. The competing hypotheses are that the relevant market is national, such that the determinative constraint on Finnish paper manufacturers is represented by other Finnish paper manufacturers, and that the relevant market is European, such that Finnish paper manufacturers' pricing behaviour is constrained by the presence of European paper manufacturers located outside Finland.

Let us assume that there are four Finnish paper producers, each selling 5 million tonnes of paper per annum. Assume also that the profit margin on each unit is 10% of the sale price. Table 2.4 shows the breakeven and profit-maximising critical losses for the case of a 5% SSNIP.

The table illustrates the relationship between the breakeven and the profit-maximising critical loss concepts. In order for a 5% price rise to yield an increase in profits, the hypothetical monopolist's loss of sales (that is the loss of sales that all four Finnish producers would experience in aggregate following a concerted 5% SSNIP) can be no more than 33.33% of pre-SSNIP sales, equivalent to 6.67 million tonnes per annum. If the anticipated loss of sales due to a 5% SSNIP were more than 6.67 million tonnes, then such a price increase would serve to reduce the hypothetical Finnish paper monopolist's profits due to substitution to paper producers located outside Finland. Conversely, if the anticipated loss of sales following the 5% increase in the price of paper produced in Finland were less than 6.67 million tonnes, then the price rise would be profitable as the value of the increased margin would outweigh the value of the lost volumes.

Table 2.4 *Breakeven and profit-maximising critical loss calculations*

| | Formula | Calculation | Critical loss (tonnes per annum) |
|---|---|---|---|
| Breakeven | $\dfrac{t}{(m+t)}$ | $\dfrac{0.05}{(0.15)} = 33.33\%$ | 6.67 |
| Profit-maximising (linear demand) | $\dfrac{t}{(m+2t)}$ | $\dfrac{0.05}{(0.2)} = 25\%$ | 5 |
| Profit-maximising (isoelastic demand) | $1 - (1+t)^{-\frac{(1+t)}{(t+m)}}$ | $1 - (1.05)^{-\frac{(1.05)}{(0.15)}} = 28.93\%$ | 5.79 |

The profit-maximising critical loss calculation, by contrast, asks not whether a 5% SSNIP would *increase* the profits of a Finnish paper monopolist, but whether such a monopolist would choose to raise price by at least 5% above the prevailing competitive level. The figures in the table indicate that the profit-maximising critical loss is either 5 or 5.79 million tonnes per annum, depending upon the assumption made regarding the shape of the demand curve for paper. These figures are smaller than the breakeven critical loss, demonstrating that the hypothetical Finnish paper monopolist would need to face the loss of only 5 million tonnes per annum (for linear demand) or 5.79 million tonnes per annum (for isoelastic demand) for a 5% price increase to be greater than the price increase that maximises profits, even if such a price increase would serve to increase profits.[36]

This, however, is as far as critical loss analysis can, in and of itself, take the market definition analysis. The critical loss analysis simply tells us that if we believe that the total loss of sales that Finnish paper producers collectively would experience were they to raise prices by 5% is above 6.67 million then a hypothetical monopolist of Finnish paper production would experience a reduction in its profits following that price increase; and that if the demand loss were greater than 5 million tonnes per annum (or 5.79 million tonnes if isoelastic demand is assumed) then the hypothetical monopolist would prefer to raise its price by less than 5% even if the hypothesised 5% increase would improve profits from the competitive level.

The critical loss analysis therefore only provides the benchmark against which evidence on the likely actual loss resulting from a SSNIP can be assessed. In our hypothetical example it would therefore be necessary to go on to investigate the magnitude of demand substitution away from Finnish paper producers following a SSNIP via one or more of the techniques discussed in the remainder of this chapter in order to resolve the question of geographic market definition.

### 3.1.3    Use in EU merger control

Although critical loss analysis has seldom been applied in EU merger cases, the Commission has discussed this technique in at least three notable instances since 2004.

In *Lufthansa/SN Airholding*[37] the parties put forward a critical loss analysis that sought to demonstrate that flights from Antwerp Brussels

---

[36] As noted above, the price increase serves to increase profits so long as losses are no greater than 6.67 million tonnes per annum.

[37] Case COMP/M.5335 – *Lufthansa/SN Airholding*, Commission decision of 22 June 2009.

North are substitutes for flights from the main Brussels airport in Zaventem. The Commission, however, argued that a critical loss analysis was not appropriate in the airline industry for two reasons. The first of these related to the definition of the appropriate margin, the Commission arguing that, while the majority of costs in the airline industry are fixed in the short run (specifically, if the capacity on each route is held constant), following the imposition of a permanent price increase an airline might rearrange its flight schedules and frequency or aircraft sizes in order to reduce its capacity and, therefore, its costs to meet the lower demand that it would face. Thus, the Commission was concerned that the observable margin would not accurately represent the margin that would be considered by a hypothetical monopolist contemplating the implementation of a SSNIP. The Commission does not appear to have sought to produce an estimate of this long-term margin in order to undertake a more meaningful critical loss analysis.

The second concern related to the complex way in which prices are set in the airline industry which, according to the Commission, made it impossible meaningfully to apply the standard critical loss formulae. In this regard, the Commission argued that:[38]

> In an industry where price discrimination is as prominent as in the airline industry (the main purpose of yield management systems is to charge higher prices to high yield, less price-sensitive passengers), the application of critical loss analysis poses [a] number of additional problems. Indeed, the critical loss analysis assumes that a single price is charged to all customers. The use of an average price and a single price increase across the board to calculate the critical loss is not consistent with the way a hypothetical monopolist would price in this industry. It is possible that a 5–10% average price increase could profitably be achieved through a large price increase for high yield, less price-sensitive passengers and a very small (or even no) price increase for low yield, price sensitive passengers.

In dismissing the parties' critical loss analysis, the Commission noted that the high margins observed in the airline industry – notwithstanding its earlier comment that these high margins would, to some extent, be an artefact of viewing the industry on a short-term basis – might themselves provide information on the likely *actual loss* that would arise following a price rise. This argument is based on the observation that high margins point to the existence of a low price elasticity (the two being related via

[38] See ibid., para. 89.

the 'Lerner condition', as discussed in Chapter 1).[39] Such a low price elasticity would then suggest that the actual loss resulting from a 5–10% price increase would be relatively low, and therefore unlikely to exceed a given critical loss. Specifically, the Commission noted that:[40]

> In industries with very high fixed costs (and low variable costs), the gross margin will be high and hence, the critical loss will be low. This means that in markets where gross margins are high, markets tend to be defined as wide because a price increase would be unprofitable with few lost sales. However, high margins also tend to indicate that firms have a certain degree of market power and that in fact, price elasticity may be rather low. Not only would this suggest that actual loss would in fact be low as well but it would also suggest that markets may possibly be narrow (as firms can charge high prices, because customers would not switch). Indeed, firms are expected to set prices that maximise profits and price is inversely related with the demand elasticity faced by the firm. Hence, low price elasticity tends to lead to high prices (and high margins).

While this logic is correct, it is debatable whether this is an appropriate basis on which to dismiss critical loss analysis. On the one hand, the theoretical relationship between the critical loss and actual loss implies that in arguing for a broad market definition, it is not sufficient merely to point out that the critical loss is 'small' due to the fact that there are grounds for believing a priori that the actual loss in this circumstance will be 'small' as well. On the other hand, it seems unsatisfactory to use the observation that there is a theoretical relationship between the critical loss and the actual loss as a basis to rule out analysis that would seek to capture which of these is likely to be higher from the perspective of a hypothetical monopolist of any given candidate market.[41] Farrell and

---

[39] For further discussion of the link between margins and likely actual loss, see J. Farrell and C. Shapiro, 'Improving Critical Loss Analysis' (2008) *The Antitrust Source*, February.

[40] See Case COMP/M.5335 – *Lufthansa/SN Airholding*, Commission decision of 22 June 2009, para. 87.

[41] For an interesting series of articles in which both points of view are argued, see M. L. Katz and C. Shapiro, 'Critical Loss: Let's Tell the Whole Story' (2003) *Antitrust Magazine*, Spring, 49 and D. P. O'Brien & A. L. Wickelgren, 'A Critical Analysis of Critical Loss Analysis' (2003) 71 *Antitrust Law Journal* 161–84 (which present the view that critical loss analysis is prone to abuse and potentially highly misleading); D. T. Scheffman and J. I. Simons, 'The State of Critical Loss Analysis: Let's Make Sure We Understand the Whole Story' (2003) *The Antitrust Source*, November (which provides a defence of critical loss analysis); M. L. Katz and C. Shapiro, 'Further Thoughts on Critical Loss' (2004) *The Antitrust Source*, March, and D. P. O'Brien and A. L. Wickelgren, 'The State of Critical Loss Analysis: Reply to Scheffman and Simons' (2004) *The Antitrust Source*, March (which respond to the defence of critical loss presented by Scheffman and Simons

Shapiro have suggested that information on customer diversion patterns could be combined with margin data within the critical loss framework to identify relevant antitrust markets.[42]

In *Arsenal/DSP*[43], the merging parties put forward a critical loss analysis that suggested that a 5% SSNIP for benzoic acid in the EEA would be unprofitable in the event of an actual loss of more than 11.8% of the merged entity's sales volume. The Commission responded to this evidence by stating that:[44]

> The notifying party did not provide any elasticity estimates or any other evidence that would show how much sales would be lost as a result of a price increase of 5% to 10%. Instead, it only noted that … if the actual loss of sales from a 5% price increase in solid benzoic acid were greater than 11.8%, the market should be widened to include other regions … As a result, there is thus no direct evidence against which the notifying party's critical loss analysis can be assessed, and thus the Commission does not view this analysis as convincing. In this regard, it is noteworthy that although a large number of customers were unable to evaluate by how much prices in the EEA would have to rise in order for them to decide to switch to a Chinese or US supplier, the majority of the customers who replied indicated that prices of benzoic acid in the EEA would need to be increased by more than 15% for such a switch to be worth considering.

Ideally, the Commission or the parties would have sought to pursue this analysis by investigating whether the actual loss would indeed exceed the critical volume loss identified by the parties' critical loss analysis. In this regard, it should be noted that the Commission's reference to a 'majority of customers' being unwilling to switch even with a 15% price increase is not sufficient to rule out the possibility of a broad market by reference to the critical loss analysis, as only a small minority of customers (representing more than 11.8% of sales) would need to respond in order to render a 5% price increase unprofitable.

In the two cases discussed above, critical loss analyses were put forward by the parties but ultimately dismissed by the Commission.

---

(2003)); and J. Farrell and C. Shapiro (2008), 'Improving Critical Loss Analysis' (2008) *The Antitrust Source* (which proposes new tests to determine, using critical loss analysis, whether a candidate group of products contains enough substitutes to form a market, and that nonetheless extract information from firm's observed decisions).

[42] J. Farrell and C. Shapiro, 'Improving Critical Loss Analysis' (2008) *The Antitrust Source*, February.

[43] Case COMP/M.5153 – *Arsenal/DSP*, Commission decision of 9 January 2009.

[44] See ibid., para. 83.

*Ineos/Kerling*,[45] however, represents an example of the Commission undertaking its own critical loss analysis in order to investigate whether the relevant geographic market for the supply of S-PVC, an input for the manufacture of window frames, pipes and mouldings, was, as argued by the parties, wider than the UK.

The Commission estimated the critical loss for a hypothetical monopolist of S-PVC using both the breakeven and profit-maximising formulae, and assuming separately a 5% and a 10% price increase.[46] Due to some uncertainty regarding the appropriate cost measures, the Commission also calculated each critical loss estimate on the basis of two margin estimates.[47] These calculations produced a range of critical loss volume estimates, from 61 to 108 Kt and from 107 to 170 Kt for 5% and 10% SSNIP respectively.[48]

Having established a range of estimates for the critical volume loss that would render a price rise by a hypothetical UK monopolist of S-PVC unprofitable, the Commission sought to identify the actual loss that could be expected to arise as a result of a SSNIP. It initially attempted to quantify the actual loss directly via an econometric estimate of the aggregate elasticity of demand facing the UK producers, that is, the sensitivity of the sales volumes of UK producers to their prices.[49] This approach was unable to reliably identify this relationship, however, largely due to an absence of suitable instrumental variables with which to identify the impact of shifts in S-PVC supply and demand. (For further discussion of identification and instrumental variables see Section 3.2.1 and Appendix A.)

While the econometric estimation was not able to produce a reliable estimate of actual loss with which to compare the estimated critical loss, the Commission went on to use its critical loss estimate as a framework within which to review qualitative information on the likely response of imports to a SSNIP by UK S-PVC producers. The Commission has explained that such information could include 'surveys or other qualitative evidence, such as planned uncommitted capacity expansions, demand forecasts or the costs of switching'.[50] Specifically, a detailed

---

[45] Case COMP/M.4734 – *Ineos/Kerling*, Commission decision of 30 January 2008.
[46] Ibid., para. 98.    [47] Ibid.
[48] A. Amelio et al., '*Ineos/Kerling* Merger: An example of quantitative analysis in support of a clearance decision' (2008) 1 *Competition Policy Newsletter*.
[49] Ibid., 67.    [50] Ibid., 68.

analysis of production capacity in continental Europe led the Commission to conclude that:[51]

> The current spare capacity plus the expected capacity expansions in Western Europe ... would be more than enough to compensate the expected growth of the market of Western Europe as a whole, leaving a spare production capacity of around [100–150] kt to supply the United Kingdom in case prices were to increase in that country, which represents around [20–30]% of the expected United Kingdom market size by 2011.

This conclusion was further corroborated by evidence on price stationarity (discussed at Section 3.7) and demand and currency shocks (discussed at Section 3.8), which also suggested that imports exerted a competitive constraint on UK producers of S-PVC, leading the Commission to conclude that the relevant geographic market was broader than the UK.

## 3.2 Demand estimation

### 3.2.1 Description of technique

The previous section has explained how market definition ultimately turns on the relationship between the price of a set of goods and the quantity of those goods that will be sold. The SSNIP test requires that a hypothetical monopolist of a relevant market would be able to impose a profitable price increase over the products within that market. The profitability of such a SSNIP is determined by the volume of sales that the hypothetical monopolist would lose as a result of the price increase, together with the value of those sales as reflected by the margin.

Critical loss analysis links the volume loss resulting from a SSNIP to the sales margin in order to identify the maximum demand loss consistent with profitability. The critical loss methodology thus focuses the assessment of market definition on the measurement of the relationship between price and demand. The more responsive demand for a given set of products is to changes in price, or, put differently, the more sales will be lost in response to a SSNIP, the less likely that set of products is to represent a relevant market. Information on the sensitivity of sales to changes in price can therefore allow for determination of whether a particular candidate market represents a relevant antitrust market.

---

[51] See Case COMP/M.4734 – *Ineos/Kerling*, Commission decision of 30 January 2008, para. 135.

If historical data on sales figures and on the price and non-price factors that affect those sales exist, an econometric analysis can potentially be used to estimate the sensitivity of demand to a change in price. The utility of this approach is noted in the Market Definition Notice, which highlights econometric techniques as one of the key sources of quantitative evidence on market definition.[52]

Econometric demand estimation can be an extremely complex exercise and one that requires knowledge of advanced statistical and econometric techniques that are beyond the scope of this text. As such, the goal of this section is to provide the reader with a general overview of the technique and its relationship to practical market definition, of the data required for its implementation, and of the manner in which its findings should be interpreted.

### 3.2.1.1   Empirical demand estimation and identification   As explained in Chapter 1, a demand curve represents the relationship between price and sales volume for a given good or set of goods. For any given price, a demand curve will indicate the volume of the product in question that consumers will wish to purchase at that price. Consider the example of a linear demand curve defined by the following equation:

$$quantity = 200 - 4^*price$$

Figure 2.5 shows this demand curve graphically. The chart shows that at a price of 20 customers will be willing to purchase 100 units, while at a price of 25 customers will demand only 80 units. This tells us that, at a price of 20, a 25% price increase will reduce demand for the good in question by 20 units. More generally, knowing the mathematical equation that defines the demand curve allows us to infer the impact that any given change in price will have on sales of a product or group of products.

Demand estimation is the process of using observed price and quantity data to infer the demand curve for a given product or set of products. In effect, this process reverses the logic used in the illustrative example above; rather than starting with a description of the demand curve and using that information to predict combinations of price and volume that are consistent with that relationship, demand estimation uses price and volume observations to produce a mathematical expression for the demand curve that gave rise to those observations.

---

[52] Market Definition Notice, para. 39; see also para. 45.

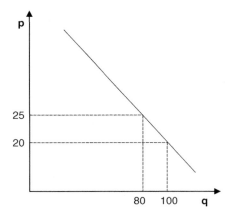

**Figure 2.5** Illustrative demand curve

This is normally done via regression analysis. Appendix A provides a further discussion of regression analysis and the challenges in identifying economically meaningful relationships, while Appendix B provides some further discussion of different forms of demand estimation.

For present purposes, however, the use of regression analysis to infer demand curves can be illustrated with a simple example. Consider a firm called Jaffa that sells still orange juice. Suppose, for the time being, that factors that affect the demand for orange juice, such as the price of substitute goods, do not change over a particular time period. Assume, however, that the marginal cost of producing orange juice varies over this time period, which causes variation in the price of orange juice and the output of orange juice produced by Jaffa. Figure 2.6 shows ten pairs of prices and volumes observed over time for Jaffa. Visual inspection shows that these combinations lie along an unobserved straight line. By drawing in this line (as in the right hand chart) the demand curve for this product is established. The demand curve can be shown to be described by the equation *quantity* $= 1500 - 10 * price.$

From this information the responsiveness of demand to a SSNIP for this product can be easily calculated. Assume that the current price is 100, at which level sales volume amounts to 500 units. Applying a 5% SSNIP would give a price of 105, at which point the sales volume would be 450. Consequently, the actual volume loss that this firm could expect to suffer as a result of a 5% price increase is 50 units, equal to 10%.

In the example above we assumed that the relationship between quantity demanded and price was fixed, and that the variation in price

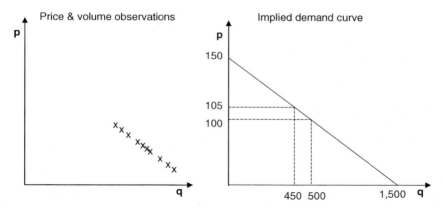

**Figure 2.6**    Illustrative demand curve for Jaffa orange juice

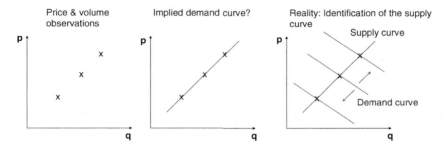

**Figure 2.7**    The problem of identifying the demand curve

and quantity observed was caused only by changes on the supply side over time. This enabled us to trace out the demand curve simply by drawing a line through each pair of prices and volumes. In practice, however, it will generally not be possible to isolate the demand curve in this way due to the problem of **identification**.[53]

The problem of identification can be illustrated by supposing that Jaffa's costs do not change over time, but that the demand curve that it

---

[53] The problem of identification has long been recognised in the empirical estimation of demand curves. See, for instance, the analysis of pig iron demand in H. L. Moore, *Economic Cycles: Their Law and Cause* (New York: Macmillan, 1914); and subsequent commentary in 'Economic Cycles: Their Law and Cause by H. L. Moore. Review by: Philip G. Wright' (1915) 29(3) *The Quarterly Journal of Economics*.

Price & volume observations

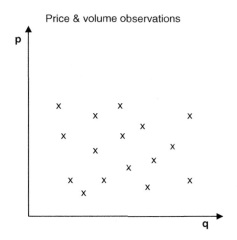

**Figure 2.8**   Prices and quantities produced by shifts in supply and demand

faces does shift. Figure 2.7 shows that, under these circumstances, a line through the observed pairs of prices and quantities would identify the supply curve (that is, the volume that Jaffa would choose to supply at each price), rather than the demand curve.

In practice, variation in observed prices and quantities may often be due both to factors causing shifts in demand and factors causing shifts in supply. This means that price/quantity pair data will resemble those displayed in Figure 2.8.

Under these circumstances drawing a 'line of best fit' through the observed pairs of prices and quantities will produce neither the demand curve nor the supply curve but a relationship between prices and quantities with no economic meaning (which could be either upward or downward sloping depending on the relative size of supply and demand shifts). There is no obvious method based on inspection of the chart alone for separating the supply and demand equations that are here acting simultaneously to produce the various price and quantity pairs reflected in the data.

Econometric techniques can be used to identify a demand curve that best explains the various combinations of price level and quantity purchased over time, taking account of the fact that the observed prices and quantities are determined by both supply and demand conditions. To achieve this identification requires the use of econometric techniques involving **instrumental variables**. These are variables that are correlated with price but not with anything else in the demand equation and which as a result may allow us to isolate the effect that price has on consumer demand.[54]

**3.2.1.2 Demand estimation and market definition** If the above methodology is applied to sales data for a particular firm, this will allow the demand curve facing that firm to be identified. Thus, in the simple illustrative example above it was found that a 5% price increase by the Jaffa orange juice manufacturer would result in a loss of 50 sales, equivalent to 10% of volume. Combined with a critical loss estimate based on margin data, this estimated loss from a SSNIP would allow an assessment of whether Jaffa's still orange juice represents a relevant market.

In practice, however, the issue of interest is not whether a single product supplied by a particular firm represents a relevant market but whether a group of products represents a market. For instance, we may be seeking to establish whether all still orange juice drinks constitute a relevant market. Estimating the demand curve for Jaffa orange juice does not give sufficient information to answer this question.

The elasticity facing Jaffa orange will reflect both the propensity of customers to switch away from still orange juice in the event of a change in Jaffa's prices, but also the extent of switching from Jaffa to other still orange juice brands. The demand curve facing an individual firm will thus reflect both substitution within and outside the candidate market in which that firm lies. Intuitively, due to the scope for intra-market switching, the demand faced by each firm within a market will always be more elastic than the demand facing the market as a whole.

Consequently, for the purposes of market definition demand estimation must be applied to all products that potentially constitute a candidate relevant market rather than to just one individual product. By applying regression techniques to data on the price and volume of groups of products representing candidate markets, the demand curve that would face a hypothetical monopolist of those candidate markets can be identified.

### 3.2.2 An example

There are a number of complex econometric techniques that can be used for the purpose of demand estimation. Regardless of the technique that is ultimately adopted, though, the exercise will result in an equation that

---

[54] For a good exposition of the classic problem of identifying demand and an explanation of more advanced techniques, see E. Rasmusen, 'The BLP Method of Demand Curve Estimation in Industrial Organization', Indiana University Working Paper, 2007.

describes the demand for a given product as a function of its own price, the price of other products, and various other factors. An example of such an equation is shown below, reflecting the weekly demand for instant coffee in the UK as a function of the price of instant coffee, filter coffee, tea and soft drinks, as well as the weekly average temperature. As a technical point, the regression equation has been estimated using the natural logarithms of each variable. As a result, the coefficients on each variable can be interpreted as elasticities.[55]

$$Volume\ instant\ coffee = -2.2 * price\ of\ instant\ coffee$$
$$+1.8 * price\ of\ filter\ coffee$$
$$+0.6 * price\ of\ tea + 0.1 * price\ of\ soft\ drinks$$
$$-0.1 * temperature.$$

These results indicate that the own price elasticity of demand for instant coffee is 2.2 at current prices, meaning that the demand for instant coffee is elastic. It is worth noting that if the coefficient had been less than one in absolute terms (that is, if demand had been inelastic), then this finding would have indicated that instant coffee represents a relevant market, since a hypothetical monopolist of instant coffee would be able profitably to raise prices above prevailing levels.[56]

However, the fact that demand is relatively elastic does not, in itself, permit a conclusion on the definition of the relevant market to be drawn. Even in the presence of elastic demand, a SSNIP may be profitable to the extent that the higher margins obtained on any retained sales more than offset the value of sales that would be lost as a result of the price increase.

As an illustration, let us assume that the margin on instant coffee is 45%. Applying the formula set out in Section 3.1.1, this implies that the critical loss for a hypothetical monopolist of instant coffee considering a 5% SSNIP is 0.05/0.5 = 10%. An instant coffee monopolist could therefore lose up to 10% of sales volume as a result of a 5% SSNIP without that price rise being unprofitable.

The estimated own-price elasticity of instant coffee is 2.2, which implies that a 5% SSNIP would result in a 5 * 2.2 = 11% volume reduction. Combined with the critical loss estimate, this implies that the loss of sales that would be suffered by a hypothetical monopolist of instant coffee in

---

[55] See Appendix B for more details.

[56] As explained in Chapter 1, it is a standard economic result that any profit-maximising firm will operate at a point where its demand is elastic, that is, greater than one in absolute.

response to a SSNIP would be sufficiently large as to render that price increase unprofitable. This in turn implies that, in our hypothetical example, instant coffee does not represent a relevant antitrust market.

The above demand estimation results also provide an indication of the competitive constraints on instant coffee suppliers that prevent instant coffee from being profitably monopolised. The cross-price elasticity to filter coffee is high, and higher than that in respect of tea and soft drinks. The value of 1.8 indicates that increases in the price of filter coffee lead to larger than proportionate increases in the sales of instant coffee. This implies that instant coffee is a constraint on suppliers of filter coffee, and may suggest that the converse is true; that is, that filter coffee may be a constraint on suppliers of instant coffee (although, as per the discussion of asymmetric competitive constraints at Section 2.2.3, this need not be the case). By contrast, the lower cross-price elasticities in respect of tea and soft drinks suggest that these products are more distant substitutes.

Based on this observation, the candidate market could be broadened to encompass both instant and filter coffee. On this hypothesis, the same data on UK prices and volumes can be used to estimate a demand function for the broader coffees group, resulting in the following equation.

$$Volume\ coffee = -0.8 * price\ of\ coffee + 1.5 * price\ of\ tea$$
$$+0.2 * price\ of\ soft\ drinks - 0.1 * temperature.$$

The most important element of this demand function is the fact that the own-price elasticity figure is, at $-0.8$, significantly lower (in absolute terms) than the equivalent figure for instant coffee. The broader group of all coffees thus faces significantly less sensitive demand than does the group of instant coffees, which is vulnerable to switching to filter coffees, amongst other products. Critically, the own-price elasticity for coffees is less than one in absolute terms, indicating that the UK demand curve for coffee is, in this hypothetical example, inelastic. This implies that a price increase for all coffees would result in a less than proportionate volume reduction, which in turn indicates that a hypothetical monopolist would choose to increase the price of coffee relative to prevailing levels. This finding implies that instant and filter coffees are likely to represent a relevant antitrust product market.

### 3.2.3    Use in EU merger control

Despite its direct applicability to the assessment of market definition, the Commission has seldom used demand elasticity estimation in merger analyses. This likely reflects the technical complexity of robust demand estimation techniques and the data required to apply those techniques.

Demand elasticity estimation for the purpose of market definition was employed or cited in a number of cases prior to 2004, including *Guinness/Grand Metropolitan*,[57] *Kimberly-Clark/Scott*[58] and *Procter&Gamble/ VP Schickedanz*.[59] In *Kimberly-Clark/Scott*, econometric analyses were submitted by the parties and by a competitor to investigate, on the basis of weekly Nielsen supermarket scanner data, the elasticity of demand for toilet tissue in the UK and Ireland. Both studies concluded that the own-price elasticity was less than one, and therefore that there existed a relevant market for toilet tissue in these countries.

These studies also attempted to address the issue of whether branded products were constrained by private label products by estimating cross-price elasticities. The study submitted by the competitor indicated that the private label segment did not exert a strong constraint on the branded segment. On the other hand, the study submitted by the parties indicated that significant competitive interaction existed between the two segments, a conclusion that was in line with the Commission's view on market definition, which ultimately included both branded and private label sales.

In *Procter&Gamble/VP Schickedanz*,[60] the parties sought to demonstrate that the high own-price elasticity (between -1 and -3) of *Always* sanitary towels in Germany, combined with evidence of high cross-price elasticities with respect to the leading tampon brand, indicated that sanitary towels did not represent a relevant product market. The Commission observed, however, that evidence on the elasticity facing one particular product within a candidate market (in this case, the *Always* towel) would not reflect, and would overstate, the elasticity facing a hypothetical monopolist of the candidate market as a whole. Thus, while a price rise limited to the *Always* brand may not be profitable due to the possibility of customers switching to other towels, a price rise applied simultaneously to all towels may nonetheless be profitable. Moreover, the Commission criticised the parties' econometric model on the grounds

---

[57] Case COMP/M.938 – *Guinness/Grand Metropolitan*, Commission decision of 15 October 1997.

[58] Case COMP/M.623 – *Kimberly-Clark/Scott*, Commission decision of 16 January 1996.

[59] Case COMP/M.430 – *Procter&Gamble/VP Schickedanz*, Commission decision of 21 June 1994.

[60] Ibid.

that it did not take into account potentially important explanatory variables, such as seasonal factors and changes in price in stores not included in the data used. The Commission emphasised that demand estimation should seek 'to estimate a model including as many relevant variables as possible, i.e., to use a multivariate rather than univariate approach. In this way it is possible to distinguish the various effects of the explanatory variables from each other.'[61]

The leading recent cases in which demand elasticity estimation has been used for the purpose of market definition are *Friesland Foods/ Campina*,[62] *Unilever/Sara Lee Body Care*[63] and *Votorantim/Fischer/JV*.[64]

In *Friesland Foods/Campina*,[65] the Commission used weekly retail scanner data to undertake an extensive demand estimation exercise for dairy products in the Netherlands. This analysis was used both to assess the definition of the relevant product markets and to investigate the closeness of competition between the parties' brands and private label products for the assessment of unilateral effects. As regards market definition, the Commission found inelastic demand for, and low cross-price elasticities between, the basic dairy products milk, yoghurt, buttermilk and custard, suggesting that these products each constituted separate relevant markets. The Commission also found that fresh health drinks represented a separate relevant market, based on this product group's inelastic demand, but that long-life chocolate dairy drinks and long-life fruit dairy drinks exhibited elastic demand and high cross-price elasticities in respect of one another, suggesting that neither represented a relevant product market.

A notable aspect of the *Friesland Foods/Campina*[66] decision is the Commission's recognition that it would be unsafe to rely solely on demand estimation analysis. The Commission noted that:[67]

> there are many crucial choices to be made in constructing, estimating, and simulating econometric models. These choices can only be evaluated in

---

[61] See ibid., para. 56.

[62] Case COMP/M.5046 – *Friesland Foods/Campina*, Commission decision of 17 December 2008.

[63] Case COMP/M.5658 – *Unilever/Sara Lee Body Care*, Commission decision of 17 November 2010.

[64] Case COMP/M.5907 – *Votorantim/Fischer/JV*, Commission decision of 4 May 2011.

[65] Case COMP/M.5046 – *Friesland Foods/Campina*, Commission decision of 17 December 2008.

[66] Case COMP/M.5046 – *Friesland Foods/Campina*, Commission decision of 17 December 2008.

[67] See ibid., Annex 1, para. 7.

the broader context of the specific case. With econometric and related qualitative materials, the whole is certainly greater than the sum of the parts.

In *Unilever/Sara Lee Body Care*,[68] the Commission conducted a merger simulation, which is discussed further in Chapter 3. As part of this merger simulation, the Commission estimated the relevant demand elasticities for male and non-male deodorants, and found that 'the profits of a hypothetical monopolist of the male (non-male) segment would increase if the prices of all male (non-male) deodorants increased by 5%'.[69] That is, the Commission's analysis found that a SSNIP would be profitable for each of the male and non-male deodorant segments. On the basis of this analysis, in combination with other more qualitative evidence (mainly related to the alleged price differences between male and non-male deodorants), the Commission held that male and non-male deodorants represented separate relevant markets.

In *Votorantim/Fischer/JV*[70] the notifying parties estimated own and cross-price elasticities for orange juice and other drinks using monthly retail data for France, Germany, the Netherlands and the UK.[71] The Commission criticised the parties' analysis on a number of technical grounds, noting in particular the small sample size and paucity of control variables, and noted that the results were subject to a wide margin of error (that is, the reported coefficients exhibited wide confidence intervals).[72] In any case, taking the parties' results at face value, the Commission noted that the own-price elasticity estimates found, combined with recent margins, indicated that a 5% SSNIP on orange juice would, contrary to the parties' contention, be profitable.[73]

## 3.3   Survey evidence

### 3.3.1   Description of technique

As well as analysing information and evidence provided by the merging parties, the Commission typically collects information from other

---

[68] Case COMP/M.5658 – *Unilever/Sara Lee Body Care*, Commission decision of 17 November 2010.

[69] See ibid., para. 94.

[70] Case COMP/M.5907 – *Votorantim/Fischer/JV*, Commission decision of 4 May 2011.

[71] Paragraphs 97 et seq.

[72] See paras. 99 and 100. The wide confidence intervals were particularly relevant for the purpose of market definition, which requires assessment not just of the direction but also the magnitude of the own-price elasticity.

[73] See para. 102.

industry participants during merger inquiries. In addition to providing basic information on the functioning of the markets affected by the proposed merger, the responses to the Commission's information gathering may inform the assessment of the relevant market. In this regard, the Market Definition Notice explains that:[74]

> When a precise market definition is deemed necessary, the Commission will often contact the main customers and the main companies in the industry to enquire into their views about the boundaries of product and geographic markets and to obtain the necessary factual evidence to reach a conclusion.

Such information gathering may fall within two broad categories. First, the Commission normally commences its merger assessments with a **market investigation** conducted via questionnaires sent to, and, in some cases, interviews with, market participants. These enquiries will usually be addressed to the parties' rivals and, where customers are businesses rather than end-consumers, to buyers. The general purpose is to assist the Commission in understanding the nature of the products in question and the composition of the supply and demand sides of the industry, although the Commission will often ask market participants' views on the definition of the relevant markets. The Commission has stated that market investigations in merger assessments are conducted as 'an on-going process, in the course of which the Commission usually refines and narrows down the issues it analyses and clarifies unclear and contradictory opinions with third parties'.[75]

Second, and less commonly, the Commission may undertake a formal **customer survey** aimed at assessing market definition by investigating customers' willingness to switch between alternatives. Such surveys may be particularly useful in cases where the merging parties supply end-consumers, permitting the use of samples sufficiently large to give statistically meaningful results. Parties may also choose to undertake their own consumer surveys as a form of evidence on market definition to submit to the Commission.

Customer surveys potentially provide a valuable and direct source of evidence on the behaviour of customers that underpins demand-side substitution. In principle, surveys allow customers directly to be asked how they would change their behaviour in response to a SSNIP over a

---

[74] Market Definition Notice, para. 33; see also para. 47.
[75] Case COMP/M.5830 – *Olympic/Aegean Airlines*, Commission decision of 26 January 2011, paragraph 27.

candidate geographic or product market, obviating the need to infer such behaviour from observations of historical market outcomes. In particular, survey evidence may provide a source of information on likely demand losses in the event of a SSNIP that can be assessed against critical loss calculations, or, as discussed further in Chapter 3 Section 3.1, may be used to assess the likelihood of unilateral effects directly.

There are, however, a number of potential problems raised by this approach to collecting information on the views and likely behaviour of market participants.

First, market investigation questions directly asking for opinions on the definition of the relevant market assume that respondents are familiar with the antitrust concept of a relevant market definition. This is frequently not the case. Even with questions on substitution, many respondents will not be familiar with the SSNIP test as a guide to the degree of substitutability required to place products and regions within the same antitrust market. Respondents may identify substitutes that are feasible but not economic in the context of a 5–10% SSNIP; or, conversely, may fail to mention economic substitutes that they currently have no need to consider at prevailing prices. In many cases the responses received from a particular company will depend upon the identity and views of the individual or individuals within that company set to deal with the questionnaire. This subjectivity is potentially problematic when using surveys to obtain meaningful market information on which to base merger assessment.

Second, in interpreting evidence from surveys, care must be taken to distinguish between marginal and infra-marginal customers, that is, between the customers that are most likely to switch in the event of a SSNIP and those that are less likely to do so. As explained in Section 2 above, it is the behaviour of the former that determines firms' price-setting behaviour, and the destinations to which those customers would switch that identify the competitive constraints on firms' behaviour. If the preferences over alternatives of these two customer types differ, then the aggregate responses from customers as a whole may not provide a meaningful guide to the likely behaviour of marginal customers that would switch in the event of a SSNIP.

In particular, the customers that switch away in response to a SSNIP in a candidate market, and that are therefore relevant to market definition, are more price sensitive than customers in general. As a result of this, their preferences may be systematically different from those of the average customer. For this reason, the question 'which product would you purchase if product x were not available?', which provides insights into the closest alternative for the 'average' customer, may give rise to a misleading view of the relative importance of alternatives from the perspective of market definition. One way of correcting for this issue is to consider only the responses of customers that indicated a willingness to switch in response to a SSNIP. For example, the pair of questions 'would you switch in response to a 5% increase in the price of product x?' and 'if so, to which products would you switch?' provides insights into the closest alternatives for the 'marginal' customers. Considering only the responses of marginal customers, however, can reduce survey sample sizes substantially, which may in itself give rise to concerns regarding reliability.

Third, the number of customers from which the Commission seeks views is often quite limited, both as a practical matter and due to the limited number of customers that business-to-business firms may serve. The sample sizes are therefore frequently small, which increases the sensitivity of the findings to the idiosyncrasies affecting individuals' responses.

Fourth, respondents may not be in a position to give, or may choose not to give, representative responses. Consumers may have limited industry knowledge and may give little thought to their response to hypothetical changes in market conditions. In particular, survey respondents faced with bald statements about hypothetical changes in prices may overstate their propensity to change their behaviour, although the scope for such bias can be limited by the way in which questions are phrased and presented. Where survey respondents are businesses, they are likely to have greater knowledge of a market, and to devote greater resources to responding to questions, but may have an incentive to behave strategically in the knowledge that their responses will influence the investigation outcome. For this reason, the Commission has stated that it will take care in considering the reported views of competitors.[76]

Finally, a related problem is that market questionnaire surveys undertaken by the Commission will frequently be subject to self-selection bias, which may potentially lead to unrepresentative and misleading results. Many recipients will incur the time required to produce detailed and comprehensive responses only if they have a strong view about the transaction. Where such strong views are held they are typically more

---

[76] Case COMP/M.5830 – *Olympic/Aegean Airlines*, Commission decision of 26 January 2011, footnote 20.

likely to be negative than positive ones. Thus, even if only a minority of customers have concerns about a transaction, those customers' views may be disproportionately represented amongst responses to a market questionnaire, potentially giving rise to an erroneous impression of market participants' views.

In view of the above, the Commission tends to use its customer surveys to provide qualitative insights into market definition, rather than as a basis for detailed quantitative analysis. This can result in somewhat anecdotal evidence in some cases, with the weight that should be attached to such evidence being questionable.

The scope exists for parties to commission and submit their own customer surveys that seek to provide an insight into customer behaviour while avoiding these flaws. Ideally, in order to be meaningful, these surveys should cover a large number (hundreds rather than tens) of randomly selected customers and employ questions that clearly distinguish those customers that would and would not switch in the event of a SSNIP, and the alternatives to which the former group would switch. The scope to operate large-scale surveys of this type is typically greatest in consumer facing retail industries in which a large sample of individual customers can readily be identified and surveyed.

Surveys commissioned by merging parties should be undertaken by, and in consultation with, independent market research companies in order to ensure that the results are accorded the desired weight and reliability by the Commission. Wherever possible, survey results should also be cross-checked against observed customer behaviour.[77]

### 3.3.2   Use in EU merger control

The Commission's market investigation proved decisive in its decision to prohibit the *Olympic/Aegean Airlines* merger. In the absence of suitable data with which to undertake empirical or econometric analyses, the Commission carried out an unusually extensive market investigation, which encompassed airlines, ferry and train operators, groundhandlers, travel agents, corporate customers, airports, slot coordination authorities, civil aviation authorities and consumer associations.[78] The Commission

---

[77] For further details see 'Best Practices on Submission of Economic Evidence' (DG COMP Staff Working Paper, 17 October 2011), paras. 30, 31 and 48.

[78] Case COMP/M.5830 – *Olympic/Aegean Airlines*, Commission decision of 26 January 2011, paras. 23, 30 and 31.

rejected the parties' criticisms of its reliance on qualitative evidence from the market investigation by pointing to the General Court's finding in *Ryanair/Aer Lingus* that there is no hierarchy between 'technical' and 'non-technical' evidence, and that the latter may be relied upon without support from the former.[79]

The Commission's assessment of market definition for the parties' supply of scheduled passenger airline transport derived primarily from information and views received during the market investigation, particularly from corporate customers and providers of other modes of transport. This information led the Commission to conclude, *inter alia*, that there existed separate relevant product markets for time-sensitive and non-time-sensitive passengers, and that, on most routes, sea and train transport did not lie in the same relevant market as the parties' airline services for time-sensitive passengers.[80]

In addition to the market investigation, the Commission considered the scope for a consumer survey to investigate market definition in *Olympic/Aegean Airlines*. The Commission concluded that it would not be possible to implement a representative consumer survey for a number of reasons.[81] While most of these reasons are not specified in the decision, the Commission did highlight the fact that any survey undertaken during the merger assessment would represent only a snapshot within the highly seasonal Greek travel industry, an issue that it felt could not be resolved by 'redressing' the data.[82]

The parties nonetheless commissioned two surveys concerning the degree of competition imposed on airlines by ferry operators.[83] The Commission criticised this evidence on a number of methodological grounds concerning sample selection and size. Most materially, however, the Commission noted that the parties' surveys did not concern customers' propensity to switch between airlines and ferries but instead investigated the extent to which customers using each service had also used the other. While the fact that some customers had in the past travelled by

[79] Case COMP/M.5830 – *Olympic/Aegean Airlines*, Commission decision of 26 January 2011, para. 33. See also Case T-342/07 *Ryanair Holdings plc* v. *Commission* [2011] 4 CMLR 245, para. 136.

[80] Case COMP/M.5830 – *Olympic/Aegean Airlines*, Commission decision of 26 January 2011, paras. 52–193.

[81] Case COMP/M.5830 – *Olympic/Aegean Airlines*, Commission decision of 26 January 2011, para. 35.

[82] Ibid., para. 35, footnote 31.      [83] Ibid., paras. 194–208.

both ferry and airline indicates that those customers are not inherently disinclined to use either mode, such parallel usage is not sufficient to imply that the two services are substitutable.[84] The surveys did not allow for ferry usage *in addition to* airline travel to be distinguished from ferry usage as a *substitute for* airline travel. As such, the Commission concluded that the parties' surveys fell short of providing information on the extent to which airline passengers might switch to ferries in the event of a SSNIP on airline travel.

In *Friesland Foods/Campina*,[85] the merging parties disputed the Commission's reliance on its market questionnaire, and argued that 'instead of relying on the majority of consumers, the Commission should have identified the set of marginal customers, that is those customers who discipline the pricing of sales of naturally matured Dutch-type cheese made in the Netherlands.'[86]

The Commission did not directly comment on this argument. It did, however, go on to suggest that the degree of likely substitution suggested by the market investigation may be overstated due to customers' lack of knowledge of and familiarity with the alternative products.[87] In effect, the Commission appears to have substituted the reported views of consumers regarding their own preferences with its own view of how those customers would in fact behave. While there is a risk that consumers may not respond accurately to hypothetical questions, this approach to survey evidence should give rise to concerns. Moreover, it should be clear that the Commission's argument would work in both directions; the Commission (or merging parties) could equally seek to argue that the level of substitutability identified by a customer survey is erroneously low due to customers' not being familiar with the alternatives which they have, at prevailing prices, had no cause to consider. The Commission's apparent disinclination to take its own survey evidence at face value raises questions over the weight that such evidence will be accorded when submitted by the parties.

---

[84] The parties' second survey asked respondents using one transport mode whether they intended to use the other in the future. Again, without reference to an airline SSNIP, such willingness to use ferries is not sufficient to demonstrate substitutability between the two.

[85] Case COMP/M.5046 – *Friesland Foods/Campina*, Commission decision of 17 December 2008.

[86] See ibid., para. 752.      [87] See ibid., para. 753.

### 3.4    Analysis of sales patterns

### 3.4.1    Description of technique

The European Commission frequently considers evidence on existing trade patterns to inform its assessment of market definition for merger analysis. This involves examining the origin of customers' purchases and the destination of suppliers' sales in order to draw inferences about the extent to which a hypothetical monopolist of a candidate group of goods or geographic region might be able profitably to raise prices.

The primary advantage of this approach is that the requisite information is normally readily available. Firms, whether operating in business-to-business or business-to-consumer industries, typically maintain comprehensive records of their sales, including the types of customers served and the associated volumes. Customers contacted in the course of a market investigation may also be able to provide such information, allowing competition authorities to cross-check evidence provided by the merging parties.

As we shall explain, however, the evidential value of information on supply patterns in the context of market definition may be somewhat limited. Supply patterns reflect prevailing industry conditions only, and as such do not necessarily convey any information on the likely behaviour of firms and customers in response to changes in supply terms, which is the determinative element of market definition. Nonetheless, a review of sales patterns may shed light on the way in which an industry functions, which in turn may provide useful context for more powerful analyses of market definition.

The analysis of data on sales patterns in market definition was proposed in a 1973 article by Kenneth Elzinga and Thomas Hogarty that considered the issue of geographic market definition for merger assessment.[88] In particular, the authors proposed a test based on observed shipment volumes and encompassing the concepts of 'little in from outside' (LIFO) and 'little out from inside' (LOFI), which concern the extent of shipments of a given product into and out of a candidate geographic market respectively. The application of the so-called Elzinga–Hogarty test (also known as the **LIFO/LOFI test**) for the purpose of geographic market definition is discussed in Section 3.4.1.1 below. The logic of the test can, however, be generalised to some extent to questions of product market definition, as explained in Section 3.4.1.2.

---

[88] K. G. Elzinga and T. F. Hogarty, 'The Problem of Geographic Market Definition in Antimerger Suits' (1973) 18 *Antitrust Bulletin*, 45–81.

**3.4.1.1 Geographic market definition** The Elzinga–Hogarty test states that a region represents a relevant geographic market if and only if:

- at least 75% of volumes purchased within the region are produced by suppliers located within the region (the LIFO condition); and
- at least 75% of production within the region is sold to customers located within the region (the LOFI condition).

The purpose of the Elzinga–Hogarty test is thus to identify a region that is, to a large extent, independent of other geographic areas, in which producers have little reliance on customers located in other areas and in which customers have little reliance on suppliers located in other areas. However, this test has a number of important flaws when considered in the context of the SSNIP test approach to market definition.

As an initial observation, the 75% benchmark is, as Elzinga and Hogarty themselves acknowledge, 'somewhat arbitrary'. Although the authors describe the 75% threshold as a conservative estimate of the 'shipments which encompass the primary demand and supply forces', this view is a subjective one. In practice, where the Commission has used evidence on sales patterns for market definition it has not cited any specific benchmark of what proportion constitutes 'little' from inside and outside a geographic region.

More substantively, it is not clear that the LOFI condition has any role at all to play in geographic market definition. The finding that suppliers within a particular region do not export significant volumes outside that region has no bearing on the question of whether that region constitutes a separate relevant geographic market. Suppliers within a particular region may be heavily constrained by imports even if suppliers within the region do not export any volumes outside that region at all.[89]

Finally, even the LIFO condition does not fully capture the economic processes that lie at the heart of the hypothetical monopolist test. The concept of market definition rests on the extent to which demand- and supply-side substitution would constrain pricing power over a particular group of goods or services. These phenomena depend on the responsiveness

---

[89] Consider a small beer brewery that is the only producer located in a particular region, which only sells in that region. A number of large breweries are located in other regions and make sales across the entire country. The finding that the small brewery does not make sales outside the region in which it is located clearly does not necessarily imply that that region is a relevant antitrust market. A monopoly supplier in that region may be heavily constrained by large breweries that compete on a national basis regardless of whether the supplier exports to other regions.

of customers and producers to changes in price. The Elzinga–Hogarty test, however, is a static one, in the sense that it measures only how customers and firms have chosen to behave under prevailing prices. The sales pattern data on which it relies cannot convey any information on how agents would respond to changes in prices.

By way of illustration, consider what conclusions can be drawn from an observation that more than 75% of widgets consumed in France are produced in France (further assume that 75% of widgets produced in France are consumed in France). Does this imply that France is a relevant geographic market? This is not necessarily the case, since sales pattern data do not provide any indication as to how suppliers and customers might respond to a price rise in France. It is perfectly possible that, notwithstanding the sales patterns described above, a 5–10% increase in French widget prices would induce French widget consumers and/or widget producers outside France to begin importing widgets from other countries into France. If such responses were sufficient to render the hypothesised SSNIP unprofitable, then France would not represent a relevant geographic market, despite meeting the conditions of the Elzinga–Hogarty test.

Importantly, this is not a contrived example but reflects a situation that will arise quite frequently. Even in the presence of broad geographic markets, sales patterns for a given product are likely to be relatively localised due to market participants' incentives to minimise transport costs. Thus, in the previous example, even if French, German and Spanish widgets each compete within the same relevant geographic market, French customers would seek to use French suppliers (and French suppliers seek to serve French customers) in order to minimise transportation costs. However, the knowledge that a price rise in any of these countries would be defeated by an increase in the level of imports implies that prices in each of France, Germany and Spain are competitively constrained by that possibility, despite a lack of significant cross-border trade at prevailing prices.

As such, evidence on trade flows can be regarded as a one-sided test for market definition, with current sales patterns delineating only the *minimum* extent of the relevant market. The observation that non-trivial amounts of products are being shipped between two regions is sufficient to conclude that it is possible to do so even at prevailing prices, and therefore that buyers and sellers could be expected to increase such shipments in response to a SSNIP in one region. Conversely, an observation that products are being shipped between two regions is not a necessary condition for the two to lie in the same relevant market.

**3.4.1.2 Product market definition – 'multi-sourcing'** The Elzinga–Hogarty test was originally defined in the context of geographic market definition, focusing on observed trade flows between geographic regions. In principle, however, the same logic concerning customers' exhibited choices between alternatives can be applied to product market definition.

The Elzinga–Hogarty test uses an observation that customers in one region are willing and able to purchase from suppliers in another region to infer that there is scope for competition between suppliers in those two regions. The equivalent observation for product market definition purposes would be that customers purchasing one product also purchase another product to fulfil the same need. This situation can be referred to as **multi-sourcing**.

In principle, multi-sourcing demonstrates an ability to use more than one supplier (and, therefore, potentially to switch between them) in the same way that importing demonstrates ability to source from other regions (and, therefore, potentially to switch between them). There are, however, two issues to be aware of when using such observations as evidence of broad product markets, and which limit the evidential value of multi-sourcing sales patterns.

The first is that care must be taken to distinguish between complementary and substitutable multi-sourcing. If a customer is using two products interchangeably to fulfil the same requirement, then this may represent evidence that the two are substitutable, and therefore part of the same relevant market. However, if the products in question are used in a complementary, rather than substitutable, way, then this inference is invalid. Clearly, if a newspaper publisher is purchasing paper and ink, it would not be correct to argue that these two inputs lie in the same relevant market, as a SSNIP for paper would not induce a publisher to switch to the use of ink instead. If, however, the publisher is purchasing both 45 $g/m^2$ and 50 $g/m^2$ paper, and is using both for the same purpose (that is, printing the same content, rather than, for example, using the former for printing newspapers and the latter for magazine supplements), this may be evidence that the two lie in the same product market.

The second theoretical difficulty with the application of the LIFO/LOFI logic to product market definition is the scope for differences in customer preferences over goods. In the context of geographic market definition, the potential obstacle to switching between alternatives is produced by distance and travel costs. This barrier to switching will be comparable for customer and supplier pairs in particular regions. Thus, if one customer in region A is willing and able to purchase from region B, then it is reasonable to assume that all customers (at least of a comparable size; see the discussion at Section 3.4.3 below) in region A would be similarly able to use suppliers in region B as they would face similar transport costs to do so.

In the case of product market definition, however, the barriers to switching between products are likely to be customer specific. The obstacles to switching between two products facing a given customer will be unobservable and cannot necessarily be generalised between individual customers or groups of customers. Thus, even if one newspaper publisher is willing and able to switch between different weights of paper, this does not imply that other newspaper publishers would be willing or able to do so. It cannot therefore be concluded from observations that one customer is multi-sourcing or switching between two products that the relevant product market would encompass both of those products for all customers.

Unfortunately, once these two drawbacks are recognised it becomes clear that multi-sourcing behaviour can carry little evidential weight in product market definition unless it is corroborated by other evidence on the substitutability of the products in question. Nonetheless, while the Commission has applied the LIFO/LOFI logic to questions of product market definition less frequently than it has to geographic market definition, it has on occasion used observations of product multi-sourcing as corroborative evidence for product market definition.

### 3.4.2    An example

Consider a proposed merger between two producers of printer cartridges, L'Équipe Copie, which operates a plant in France, and Ink International, which operates plants in France, Germany and Austria. Given that the immediate geographic overlap between the parties' operations arises in France, this can be considered the narrowest candidate market of interest, and so is the first region to be examined.

Table 2.5 summarises Ink International's shipments from its French plant during 2009. The table shows that the majority of shipments from Ink International's French plant were made to destinations in France, with virtually no deliveries being made to countries not immediately adjacent to France.

Suppose also that public national accounts data indicate that French imports in 2009 were 6 million units. Since Table 2.5 showed that Ink International's sales in France are in excess of 65 million units, even

Table 2.5 *Destination of Ink International France sales, 2009*

| Destination | Sales (million units) | Proportion of sales |
|---|---|---|
| France | 69.9 | 78% |
| Spain | 10.1 | 11% |
| Italy | 5.6 | 6% |
| UK | 1.2 | 1% |
| Others | 2.4 | 3% |
| Total | 89.2 | 100% |

without taking into account L'Équipe Copie's and other firms' sales, it is clear that imports must represent significantly less than 10% of French consumption and, as such, they are a relatively unimportant source of supply in France.

Together, these data might suggest that France represents a separate relevant market for printer cartridge production. We observe little of Ink International's French output being delivered to destinations outside France, and observe very little in the way of imports into France. Nonetheless, the possibility should not be excluded that, while French customers do not currently choose to purchase from plants in other countries, they could and would choose to do so in the event of a worsening of supply terms in France.

It should also be noted that Ink International's limited exports, and the relatively low distances over which they take place, may be a result of its international production profile. Ink International is unlikely to use its French plant to serve customers in Central and Eastern Europe given that its German and Austrian plants are closer to these destinations. The fact that Ink International's French plant does not export across Europe does not necessarily demonstrate that it is not possible for other firms economically to do so.

In order to assess the scope for international sales, it will therefore be instructive to consider whether other plants make sales over longer distances. The destination of the output of L'Équipe Copie's French plant is relevant in this regard. Table 2.6 shows the location of its customers over the year 2010, indicating that L'Équipe Copie is able to serve customers as distant as the Czech Republic, Austria and Hungary. The low volumes sold to the latter country, 300,000 units, might cast some doubt as to whether these are representative transactions, however. Further investigation of the circumstance of these transactions (for

Table 2.6 *Destination of L'Équipe Copie sales, 2010*

| Destination | Sales (million units) | Proportion of sales |
| --- | --- | --- |
| France | 7.4 | 23% |
| Germany | 5.7 | 17% |
| Spain | 4.5 | 14% |
| Italy | 4.3 | 13% |
| UK | 3.5 | 11% |
| Austria | 2.1 | 6% |
| Czech Republic | 1.7 | 5% |
| Benelux | 1.1 | 3% |
| Ireland | 1.1 | 3% |
| Portugal | 0.9 | 3% |
| Hungary | 0.3 | 1% |
| Croatia | 0.2 | 1% |
| Total | 32.8 | 100% |

instance, whether they constitute regular orders or a single shipment), may be prudent before relying on them as evidence that printer cartridges can be economically delivered over the circa 1,250 km between France and Hungary.

As a cross-check, Table 2.7 shows the delivery patterns of Ink International's German plant for 2009. These data show sizeable volumes being delivered to customers located significant distances from Germany, such as Russia, Belarus and Ukraine. While deliveries to these countries account for a relatively small portion of Ink International's production due to the plant's size, their absolute size does suggest regular shipments in the ordinary course of business across distances of 1,500 km or more. It is notable that the other countries served are mainly to the east of Germany, which is consistent with Ink International using its French plant to serve Western Europe and its German plant to serve Central and Eastern Europe.

In total, the evidence from the merging parties' sales records suggests that printer cartridges shipments can be made across significant distances. While Ink International and L'Équipe Copie's respective French plants do not make substantial exports over significant distances, this is likely due to the former's being part of a larger company with other production facilities and the latter being able to place its relatively small total output without recourse to more distant locations. Nonetheless, the

Table 2.7 *Destination of Ink International Germany sales, 2009*

| Destination | Sales (million units) | Proportion of sales |
|---|---|---|
| Germany | 75.4 | 39% |
| Austria | 24.3 | 13% |
| Poland | 24.2 | 13% |
| Italy | 17.8 | 9% |
| Denmark | 12.1 | 6% |
| Russia | 9.7 | 5% |
| Romania | 5.8 | 3% |
| Hungary | 5.4 | 3% |
| Ukraine | 5.4 | 3% |
| Belarus | 4.1 | 2% |
| Bulgaria | 3.8 | 2% |
| Greece | 2.3 | 1% |
| Switzerland | 1.3 | 1% |
| Total | 191.6 | 100% |

fact that Ink International's German plant is able to ship significant volumes to customers around 1,500 km away indicates that the economics of printer cartridge delivery allow such distances to be covered where necessary. The evidence in this hypothetical example therefore suggests that France should not be considered a relevant geographic market for the supply of ink cartridges.

### 3.4.3   Use in EU merger control

The Commission has undertaken analysis of sales patterns in several cases in the context of the definition of the relevant geographic market. In *Ineos/Kerling*,[90] the Commission examined in detail actual sourcing patterns of UK S-PVC customers so as to verify whether supplies from non-UK producers posed a competitive constraint. The Commission noted that imports of S-PVC consistently represented 30–45% of UK demand over the five years 2002 to 2006.[91] It also examined trade flows between Western and Eastern Europe. The Commission found that trade flows from Western Europe represented 30–40% of Eastern European

[90] Case COMP/M.4734 – *Ineos/Kerling*, Commission decision of 30 January 2008.
[91] Ibid., para. 107.

consumption, and that flows from Eastern Europe, although larger in absolute terms, represented only 5–10% of Western Europe consumption due to the latter's larger demand for S-PVC. Interestingly, these data suggest that Western Europe would meet the Elzinga–Hogarty LIFO condition for a separate relevant market.[92]

Nonetheless, the Commission concluded from these data that there were 'considerable trade flows between Eastern and Western Europe', and so that the parties' contention that the relevant market is EEA-wide was plausible.[93] In part the Commission's view appears to have been based on the recognition that the relative imbalance in trade flows between Western and Eastern Europe could be 'explained by the fact that the vast majority of demand in the S-PVC business is located in Western Europe'.[94] This suggests that the Commission accepted that the presence of significant trade flows between regions in one direction was sufficient to demonstrate the possibility of trade flows in the opposite direction in the event of a change in relative prices.

In *Kronospan/Constantia*,[95] the Commission requested volume data regarding all shipments of raw particle board and the distance to each customer in order to analyse the relevant geographic market. The results of this analysis demonstrated that the 'vast majority' of sales were made within a radius of 500 km.[96] Based on this finding, the Commission argued that the competitive assessment should focus on an affected area defined as suppliers located within a 500-km radius rather than the 1,000 km argued by the parties. This position was based on the observations that 'customers generally source within a range of well below 1000 km and in most cases not more than 500 km' and that 'the overwhelming majority of customers … source their raw particle board from plants located within 500 km of their own facilities.'[97]

Arguably, however, the presence of non-trivial deliveries over distances in excess of 1,000 km should have pointed to the possibility of shipments over such distances in response to a price rise, even if, at

---

[92] The destination of Western European production is not considered and so the LOFI condition cannot be assessed.

[93] See Case COMP/M.4734 – *Ineos/Kerling*, Commission decision of 30 January 2008, paras. 62 and 64.

[94] See ibid., para. 62.

[95] Case COMP/M.4525 – *Kronospan/Constantia*, Commission decision of 19 September 2007.

[96] Ibid., para. 25.      [97] Ibid., para. 26.

prevailing prices, the majority of customers were able to source their product requirements at competitive terms from within a 500-km radius.

The Commission followed a similar logic in *Sonoco/Ahlstrom*,[98] which combined the parties' coreboard and cores (paper tubes) activities. In this case, the Commission held that a figure of 80% of sales within a given radius was sufficient to delineate the extent of the geographic market, stating that 'The large majority of competitors have confirmed during the market investigation that 80% of their production is supplied within a radius of up to 250 km, which supports a market definition based on regional or even national markets.'[99]

A similar assumption provided the starting point for the Commission's analysis of geographic market definition in *Omya/Huber PCC*,[100] although the Commission went further during its review of sales pattern data. In this case, the Commission began its assessment by examining the distances that encompassed 80% of all calcium carbonate shipments for each mode of transportation. It then went on to augment these radii with data on the maximum distances over which the parties' plants actually delivered 'on a regular basis' via each transport mode (note that the Commission's decision does not provide a definition for 'regular basis' in this context).[101]

The Commission then considered the maximum of these two figures for each plant to represent a proxy for the radius within which each plant represented a credible supply alternative.[102] Implicitly within this approach, the Commission acknowledged that the radius containing 80% of deliveries represented only the minimum radius over which deliveries could potentially be made, stating that, where particular plants were not observed to make deliveries over such a radius it 'does not mean they cannot do it but simply, for example, that other plants already provide some significant competitive constraints, or that there are no such remote customers'.[103]

Again, however, the Commission's analysis may have failed to capture the potential full extent of the relevant geographic market by restricting the delivery radius of each plant to the maximum of the distance encompassing 80% of the parties' overall sales or that over which each plant 'regularly' made sales. The fact that these were the maximum observed delivery radii

---

[98]  Case COMP/M.3431 – *Sonoco/Ahlstrom*, Commission decision of 6 October 2004.
[99]  Ibid., para. 74.
[100]  Case COMP/M.3796 – *Omya/Huber PCC*, Commission decision of 19 July 2006.
[101]  Ibid., para. 255.     [102]  Ibid., para. 259.     [103]  Ibid., para. 256.

at prevailing prices does not rule out the possibility of greater delivery radii, but only rules out the possibility of narrower geographic markets.

In *Arsenal/DSP*,[104] the parties sought to extend the use of trade flows in the definition of the relevant geographic market by arguing that the existence of exports of benzoic acid out of Europe that could be redirected back into Europe in the event of a SSNIP implied that the relevant market was broader than Europe. The Commission argued that this evidence was not sufficient to demonstrate a broader geographic market:[105]

> The fact that the parties' competitors may export significant amounts of benzoic acid to regions other than the EEA is not relevant for assessing whether the relevant geographic market is wider than the EEA.
>
> Similarly, the notifying party's argument that DSP and Velsicol sell more than 50% of their benzoic acid production outside of the EEA cannot be used as evidence for markets that are wider than the EEA, as the issue is not whether benzoic acid can be exported outside of the EEA, but rather whether benzoic acid that is produced outside of the EEA can be imported into the EEA and thus whether the non-EEA competitors can pose a competitive constraint on the EEA producers.

This logic is correct as stated, in that the possibility of redirection of European production currently exported back to Europe does not necessarily mean that non-European production facilities and capacity represent a credible supply option for European customers, only that the entirety of European production is potentially available to serve European customers. The Commission could, however, arguably be criticised for not attaching sufficient weight to the finding that significant exports were made from Europe in making inferences regarding the potential for imports into Europe in the event of a SSNIP. If transport costs are sufficiently low as to permit European production to be exported outside Europe, then this might suggest that those same transport costs would permit non-European production to be imported into Europe in the event of a SSNIP. If this were indeed the case, then the relevant market for benzoic acid may be wider than Europe.

The case law highlights a number of points to consider when undertaking a review of sales patterns.

First, there is the question, touched on in the review of precedent considered here, of what proportion of sales should be considered, that is,

---

[104] Case COMP/M.5153 – *Arsenal/DSP*, Commission decision of 9 January 2009.
[105] Ibid., paras. 49 and 50.

the threshold at which sales patterns are regarded as sufficiently substantial to demonstrate competitive interaction. In principle, it is not necessary to set any such threshold; the existence of any sales to a given point would demonstrate the feasibility of making sales to that point, and potentially to others equally distant. In practice, however, it may be imprudent to rely on the most distant shipment, which, by definition, will represent an extreme observation. In particular, the most distant shipment may have occurred in non-representative circumstances, such as a supply outage by a customer's usual supplier. In such circumstances, while the customer may have been prepared to use the more distant supplier as a short-term 'distress purchase' option, it may not be willing to use that supplier as a regular alternative in the case of a SSNIP.

The Commission's precedent appears to demonstrate implicit attempts to correct for such effects via the use of distances capturing 70–80% of sales (*Kronospan/Constantia*,[106] *Sonoco/Ahlstrom*[107]) and distances over which 'regular' sales are made (*Omya/Huber PCC*[108]). Notifying parties may wish to consider the extent to which their most distant shipments are representative by investigating the circumstances surrounding those transactions. Similarly, it may be instructive to compare the volumes sold to customers in the most distant locations with those purchased by customers located closer to the point of origin, or to check for discontinuities in the distribution of shipment distances: if the most distant supply destination is located 1,500 km from the point of origin while the second most distant is located only 1,000 km away, the absence of other customers between 1,000 km and 1,500 km might in itself provide an indication that the 1,500 km delivery distance is not representative.

The second issue to take into account in analysing sales patterns is the potential distinction between transport modes. As noted by the Commission in *Omya/Huber PCC*,[109] the economically viable delivery radius will generally differ according to the mode of transport employed. Rail and sea transportation, for instance, are typically cheaper per mile than road transportation, meaning that shipments via these two modes of transport can generally be economically made over greater distances. Where

---

[106] Case COMP/M.4525 – *Kronospan/Constantia*, Commission decision of 19 September 2007.
[107] Case COMP/M.3431 – *Sonoco/Ahlstrom*, Commission decision of 6 October 2004.
[108] Case COMP/M.3796 – *Omya/Huber PCC*, Commission decision of 19 July 2006.
[109] Ibid.

different forms of transportation are available in different locations this may therefore give rise to differences in effective delivery radii. If, for instance, the parties to a merger have a rail or seaport link adjacent to their factories the resultant delivery radii that they are able to serve may not be representative of the distances over which rivals without such facilities may be able to exert a competitive constraint (and vice versa).

The third factor to take into account is the potential impact of shipment size. In so far as there are economies of scale in transportation, such that the average cost per kilometre per unit of a large shipment is lower than for a small shipment, then the distance over which firms are able to compete for business may differ according to the scale of the customers in question. Larger customers may be able to choose from suppliers within a wider geographic area than smaller customers, such that the relevant geographic market for the former is broader than for the latter. The Commission acknowledged the difference in purchasing patterns for pan-European and local large/medium customers in *Ineos/Kerling*.[110]

### 3.5    Analysis of price levels

#### 3.5.1    Description of technique

The previous section has discussed how information on pre-merger sales patterns may be used to provide evidence on the extent to which customers and firms might be expected to respond to changes in relative prices and, therefore, on the definition of the relevant market. In this section we consider a similar approach employing information on pre-merger price levels to make inferences about likely responses to price changes. Specifically, the approach seeks to draw conclusions on market definition from comparisons of price levels across products and/or geographic regions.

The analysis of price levels as an indicator of market definition can be traced back to Antoine Cournot, who, writing in 1838, defined a market as '... the whole of any region in which buyers and sellers are in such free intercourse with one another that the prices of the same goods tend to equality easily and quickly'.[111]

---

[110] Case COMP/M.4734 – *Ineos/Kerling*, Commission decision of 30 January 2008, paras. 87 and 88.

[111] Cournot (1838), 'Recherches sur les Principes Mathématiques de la Théorie des Richesses', quoted in A. Marshall, *Principles of Economics*, 8th edn (London: Macmillan and Co., Ltd, 1920).

This is an intuitive description of a condition that might be expected to hold across a market. If prices are not able to equalise, then it may be presumed that their failure to do so is due to some impediment to free trade between buyers and sellers that delineates separate markets.

As with evidence on sales patterns, this approach has the considerable advantage of being analytically simple, and requiring only information that is generally readily available to parties (and regulators). Unfortunately, however, the theoretical basis for drawing inferences on market definition from observations of pre-merger price levels is questionable in most circumstances.

Indeed, equality of prices across a relevant market can be expected to occur only in the very special case of complete homogeneity. In reality, however, most products of interest in merger assessments are differentiated in their characteristics, while different geographic regions are necessarily differentiated from one another by virtue of their location and resultant transport costs. In these situations neither equality nor inequality of prices can be used to distinguish between alternative hypothesised market definitions.

The purpose of this section is to outline the technique as it appears to be applied by the European Commission, while also providing a critique highlighting its limitations.

In order to be a useful test for market definition equality of prices would need to be capable of distinguishing between situations in which a candidate group of goods/regions does and does not constitute a relevant market. That is, price equality would need to be necessarily associated with competition between products and regions, and price inequality necessarily associated with an absence of such competition.

This correspondence between price equality and a relevant market does not in fact apply, meaning that observations of price levels cannot allow a hypothesised market definition to be either confirmed or rejected. Price equality as a test for market definition fails in both directions. First (and somewhat trivially), an observation of price equality does not necessarily imply that two products or regions lie in the same market, as such equality may arise by coincidence. Second, and more substantively, an observation of different price levels does not necessarily imply that two products or regions lie in different markets.

This second disconnect between price equality and market definition, that prices may be unequal even within a relevant market, can be illustrated by returning to the first principles of the hypothetical monopolist test. The hypothetical monopolist test asks whether a SSNIP over a particular set of goods would be rendered unprofitable by a reduction in demand for those goods by existing customers. Demand-side substitution depends on the degree of marginality within existing customers, that is, how close those customers are to switching to an alternative.

If the products in question are identical, then price will be the only factor on which customers will make their purchase decisions. Consequently, equality of prices will arise as a result of a willingness by customers to switch between identical products. Indeed, for homogeneous products it is clear that customers will in the event of a SSNIP be willing to switch to any (identical) product whose price is less than that of the product to which the SSNIP is applied.

If the products are accepted as identical from the perspective of consumers, however, there is no need for further market definition analysis and evidence. The need for such analyses and evidence arises where products are differentiated such that there is uncertainty as to the extent of customer substitution between products. In practice, cases involving differentiated products comprise the majority of merger analyses, and the entirety of non-trivial product market definition exercises.

In the case of differentiated products, customers choose between alternatives by weighing the various characteristics of those alternatives, including price. Each customer will implicitly rank the various differentiated alternatives according to the extent to which each product's overall combination of attributes and characteristics, both the benefits conferred from consumption and the costs of doing so, meets his or her preferences. The question for market definition is whether a SSNIP for a candidate market would be sufficient to induce customers to change their subjective ranking of products, such that some customers that previously ranked the candidate good highest would now rank an alternative highest and choose to purchase that alternative.

In order to make that prediction, it is necessary to understand the distance between customers' rankings of each product, not solely on price but across the entirety of characteristics.

This can be illustrated with a simple example in which customers make a trade-off between price and quality. At prevailing price levels an individual consumer may choose to purchase a low quality product at a low price rather than a high quality product at a high price in the absence of any price differences, deciding that, while she would prefer to consume the higher quality good, the incremental benefit of that good is outweighed by its incremental cost relative to the low quality good. It is perfectly possible, however, that consumers would respond to an increase in the price of the low quality good by revisiting this trade-off between price and quality, and deciding that, given the new relative price levels, the reduced price difference between the low and high quality goods is outweighed by the difference in their quality. That is, a purchaser of the low price/low quality good may decide to respond to a SSNIP in respect of that product by switching to the high price/high quality good. This may be the case even though the prices of the two goods are unequal, both before and after the hypothesised SSNIP.

This mechanism may apply irrespective of the relative price levels of the two goods. Even if the high quality product's price is double that of the low quality good, customers may still be marginal between purchasing the two, based on a trade-off between their characteristics and prices. It should thus be apparent that an observation of price differences between differentiated products cannot be relied upon as evidence that those products do not compete within the same relevant product market. Conversely, an observation that the prices of two products are equal may represent evidence that they do in fact lie in the same market, although this evidence should not be regarded as conclusive given the possibility that equality in pricing arises by chance.

Turning to questions of geographic market definition, observations of price differences may be more dispositive. In questions of geographic market definition the options between which customers are choosing (that is, the same product supplied from different locations) may be principally or solely differentiated in only one dimension, that is location. Abstracting from any product differentiation, customers' ranking of geographic alternatives will be made solely on the basis of a comparison of transport costs. In this respect the analysis of geographic market definition is analogous to that of homogeneous products set out above. Consequently, a comparison of delivered prices may be used to identify the alternative sources of supply to which customers in a particular location may be expected to turn in the event of a localised SSNIP.

To give an example, assume that widgets produced in Spain, France and Poland are sold in those countries for €100 per unit, and that the cost of transportation is €2 per widget between France and Spain and €12 per widget between Poland and Spain. In this scenario, customers in Spain would be expected to respond to a SSNIP for Spanish widgets by beginning to source widgets from France, but would not be expected to seek to purchase widgets in Poland as the delivered cost (€112) would exceed that of Spanish widgets notwithstanding the SSNIP. Consequently, in this example, price level data may imply that the relevant geographic market for Spanish widget producers includes France, but not Poland.[112]

In the assessment of geographic market definition for similar goods produced in different regions it may therefore be appropriate to examine differences in the delivered prices of goods from different regions at a given point. If those differences are smaller than or comparable to the 5–10% SSNIP range, then those transport costs are insufficiently large to give rise to separate markets, whereas differences in delivered prices in excess of this level might suggest insulation from competitive constraints.

In summary, therefore, price differences may be relevant to the assessment of geographic market definition, but should not be considered determinative for questions of product market definition. As the discussion below will show, however, the Commission has typically focused its observations on price levels on questions of product market definition. Moreover, where it has made observations on price levels in the context of geographic market definition, it has not directly related these observations to information on transport costs but instead tended only to observe that different price levels may suggest different supply and demand conditions in different countries.

### 3.5.2   An example

Consider a proposed merger between two German car manufacturers, Hark and Rapp, each of which specialises in saloon cars. The parties have argued that their output faces competition from, *inter alia*, French saloon car manufacturer Dauphine and German manufacturers Gottleib, which manufactures luxury saloon cars, Ferry, which produces sports cars, and Dub, which produces compact cars. For simplicity, we assume that each manufacturer produces only one model.

Table 2.8 summarises the price of each of the six producers' cars in their country of manufacture.

As regards product market definition, the data in the table might suggest that the saloon cars produced by Hark and Rapp lie in a separate market from the compact, the luxury saloon and the sports car produced

---

[112] Note that this simple example does not allow for the possibility of a chain of substitution between these countries, whereby Polish widget producers constrain French producers which then constrain Spanish producers. As explained at Section 2, the extent of the geographic market may therefore be broader than the distances over which goods are or economically could be transported.

Table 2.8 *Product categories and prices by manufacturer*

| Manufacturer | Category | Country of manufacture | Price |
|---|---|---|---|
| Hark | Saloon | Germany | €26,500 |
| Rapp | Saloon | Germany | €27,000 |
| Gottleib | Luxury saloon | Germany | €35,000 |
| Dub | Compact | Germany | €19,000 |
| Ferry | Sports | Germany | €40,000 |
| Dauphine | Saloon | France | €27,000 |

by Dub, Gottleib and Ferry, respectively. The price differences between each of these categories are significantly larger than a 5% SSNIP over the merging parties' products, which equates to between €1,325 and €1,350. Even if the prices of the parties' saloon cars rose by such an amount, they would remain significantly below that of the sports and luxury saloon cars produced by Ferry and Gottleib.

This overlooks the differentiation between these products, however. A SSNIP in the parties' saloon cars may induce customers to switch to either the compact, luxury saloon or sports categories, notwithstanding the price differences between them. German consumers who chose a saloon car at the prices in Table 2.8 may have had a preference for a luxury saloon but decided that the greater attributes of a luxury saloon were not sufficient to outweigh the €8,000 to €8,500 price difference. Following a SSNIP in German saloon cars, however, which would narrow the price difference between the two categories, some of these marginal customers might decide that the smaller difference in price has been outweighed by the superior specification of a luxury saloon and switch from the parties to Gottleib.

Equally, some customers that would choose a saloon car at the prices shown in the table might respond to a SSNIP in German saloon cars by switching to a compact car. Customers that value saloon cars at €8,000 more than compact cars would, at the prices above, choose a Hark over a Dub. However, if the price of the Hark were to rise by 5%, to €27,825, €8,825 higher than the price of the Dub, then those customers would switch to the Dub.

If the proportion of saloon car customers that are marginal between saloon cars and the totality of other categories is sufficiently large, then the presence of those other categories will prevent a hypothetical saloon monopolist from profitably imposing a SSNIP. Consequently, these categories would exert a competitive constraint on suppliers of saloons, and should be included in the same relevant product market.

The information on price differences for differentiated cars does not allow this possibility to be discounted and so, without further information, provides no meaningful evidence on product market definition, notwithstanding the clear price differences observed.

As regards geographic market, the price information in Table 2.8 might provide some useful information on the scope for French imports to constrain German saloon manufacturers. If we assume that Dauphine saloons are, in the view of consumers, identical in every way to saloons manufactured by Hark and Rapp (a strong assumption that we will reconsider below), then German consumers will switch to French imports in the event that the cost of German products rises above that of French imports.

Let us assume that the cost of transporting a car between France and Germany is €500 per vehicle. In that case, the delivered cost of a Dauphine to a customer in Germany would be €27,500. At the prevailing prices shown above, this would be more expensive than either a Hark or a Rapp. A 5% SSNIP on these two models would raise their prices to €27,825 and €28,350, respectively, above the imported price of a Dauphine. On the assumption of homogeneity between all saloon cars, this would suggest that German customers would, following a SSNIP on German saloon cars, switch their demand entirely from German vehicles to Dauphine products. This suggests that a SSNIP in German saloon cars would be rendered unprofitable by switching to French imports, such that French vehicle manufacturers should be included in the same relevant geographic market as German producers.

This logic rests, however, on the assumption that all saloon cars are identical. While this may be an appropriate assumption in many cases concerning geographic market definition, where similar or identical products are produced in different regions and transportation costs are the only differentiating factor, this assumption is unlikely to be valid in the case of motor cars. The fact that Hark's and Rapp's saloon cars sell for slightly different prices in Germany would suggest that there is some differentiation in saloon cars; similarly, if Dauphine were observed to be making some sales in Germany, despite a delivered cost (€27,500) higher than the prevailing prices of Hark and Rapp shown in the table, this would also point to differentiation between saloon car models.

If there is indeed differentiation between the three saloon car manufacturers' products then this will undermine the logic above as it will not be possible to predict consumers' likely response to changes in relative prices based on price alone. If some German customers have a preference for German cars then a SSNIP in German saloon cars may not induce sufficient switching to Dauphine to undermine the SSNIP, even if the delivered price of Dauphine is lower than the price of domestic German vehicles. With differentiated products the converse situation may also arise, whereby German customers with a preference for Dauphine saloons may respond to a SSNIP in German cars by switching to French imports even if transport costs were €1,500 per unit. Although in this situation Dauphine cars would remain more expensive in Germany than Hark and Rapp cars (€28,500 versus €27,825 and €28,350, respectively), the narrowing of the price differences may induce German buyers to switch to Dauphine vehicles after the German SSNIP where they previously would have chosen a German car based on the larger premium for a French import.

This example highlights that observations of price differences will not generally permit robust conclusions on market definition to be drawn without further evidence on consumer preferences. Such evidence may be collected directly from customers, for instance via surveys as discussed at Section 3.3 above, or inferred from firms' behaviour using techniques discussed at Sections 3.6, 3.7 and 3.8 below.

### 3.5.3    Use in EU merger control

Notwithstanding the criticism set out above, the Commission has cited evidence on price levels in its market definition analyses in a surprising number of recent merger assessments.

The Commission considered price levels in its assessment of product market definition for lecithin during *Cargill/Degussa Food Ingredients*.[113] In considering whether there existed competition between genetically modified and non-genetically modified lecithin, the Commission rebutted the parties' claim that the two lay in the same relevant market on the grounds that the production processes and supply chains for the two differed and that the primary purchasers of non-GM lecithin are food producers while other customers tend to purchase GM lecithin.[114] These two forms of qualitative evidence were augmented by a review of prices

---

[113] Case COMP/M.3975 – *Cargill/Degussa Food Ingredients*, Commission decision of 29 March 2006.
[114] Ibid., paras. 50 and 51.

for the two types of lecithin, which found that non-GM lecithin commanded a premium over GM lecithin of more than 50%.

The Commission also noted a diverging trend between the prices of the two products over time, consistent with the price correlation methodology detailed at Section 3.6, although the decision presents no data or formal analysis in this regard.[115]

The Commission consequently concluded that GM and non-GM lecithin lay in separate relevant product markets. However, given the reference, albeit somewhat cursory, to divergent price patterns for the two products, it is not clear how much weight the Commission placed on the observation of differing prices in reaching this conclusion.

In *Lufthansa/Austrian Airlines*,[116] the Commission used evidence on price levels to cast doubts on the parties' claim that significant competitive interaction existed between air and train travel on the Munich–Vienna route. The decision states:[117]

> [The parties'] average fully-flexible economy and unrestricted business fares are more than three times as expensive as [rail operator] Deutsche Bahn's average fully-flexible first-class fares. [The parties'] average semi-flexible economy fares are more than twice as expensive as Deutsche Bahn's average fully-flexible second-class fares. Even [the parties'] average non-flexible economy fares are more than [50–60]% more expensive than Deutsche Bahn's average fully-flexible second-class fares. These considerable price differences suggest that train travel cannot be considered as a close competitor to air travel, particularly for time sensitive passengers.

Conversely, in the same decision, the Commission cited evidence of similarity in prices in concurring with the parties' view that the airline Niki provided a constraint on the Vienna–Zurich route. In particular, the Commission found that qualitative evidence suggesting that Niki represents a credible constraint on this route:

> … [i]s confirmed by the comparison of the average prices of the tickets bought by passengers that book close to the date of departure on the three carriers. Niki's prices seem to be more or less comparable to [Lufthansa's] prices, and, in certain months, Niki's tickets appear to be on average more expensive. Moreover, when compared with [Austrian Airlines], Niki's tickets are consistently, albeit only slightly, more expensive.[118]

---

[115] Ibid., para. 52.
[116] Case COMP/M.5440 – *Lufthansa/Austrian Airlines*, Commission decision of 28 August 2009.
[117] Ibid., para. 144.    [118] Ibid., para. 245.

The Commission reiterated its view that price levels may be relevant to product market definition in *Inco/Falconbridge*.[119] In responding to the parties' argument that plating nickel and stainless steel nickel products lay in the same relevant market, the Commission stated that 'the parties do not address the fact that [there are] significant price differences, which is in itself evidence of distinct product markets.'[120]

Similarly, in *Arjowiggins/M-real Zanders Reflex*,[121] the Commission cited differences in prices (and, given similar costs, margins) for reel and sheet paper as evidence that, in conjunction with price correlation and stationarity analysis, suggested separate product markets. It noted that costs could not be put forward to explain why Arjowiggins' sheet margins were significantly higher than its reels margins and therefore considered that these differences must be attributed to other factors such as the competitive dynamics, which would point to sheets and reels being in separate markets.[122]

Price differences are also mentioned as one of a number of factors in the Commission's delineation of separate product markets for the supply of gas to various types of customer (such as power stations, industrial users and households) in *DONG/Elsam/Energi E2*.[123]

Similarly, in *Unilever/Sara Lee Body Care*,[124] the Commission bolstered the evidence concerning market definition for male and non-male deodorants from its demand estimation analysis (see Section 3.2, above) with evidence of differences in average prices between these two products.[125] The notifying parties argued that these price differences were an artefact of product mix effects, particularly the greater prevalence of premium brands in the male segment, although the Commission argued that such differences in brand composition were, in themselves, evidence of separate markets.

As regards geographic market definition, in *ABF/GBI Business*,[126] the Commission pointed to 'a clear gap between the average price' between

---

[119] Case COMP/M.4000 – *Inco/Falconbridge*, Commission decision of 4 July 2006.

[120] Ibid., para. 112.

[121] Case COMP/M.4513 – *Arjowiggins/M-real Zanders Reflex*, Commission decision of 4 June 2008.

[122] Ibid., para. 58.

[123] Case COMP/M.3868 – *DONG/Elsam/Energi E2*, Commission decision of 14 March 2006, paras. 102 and 107.

[124] Case COMP/M.5658 – *Unilever/Sara Lee Body Care*, Commission decision of 17 November 2010.

[125] Paragraphs 71 et seq.

[126] Case COMP/M.4980 – *ABF/GBI Business*, Commission decision of 23 September 2008.

member states in its finding of national markets for yeast 'which may, to a large extent, reflect the different demand structure in each [national] market'.[127] This observation is not, however, explicitly related to the magnitude of transport costs in a manner that might demonstrate that international shipments of yeast would not be able to overcome localised SSNIPs. The Commission did, however, combine its observation of differing national price levels with an assessment of relative movements between those prices over time (in line with the price correlation technique discussed at Section 3.6). This being the case, it is not clear precisely how much weight the Commission attached to its evidence on price levels in deciding that the relevant geographic markets for yeast were narrower than the EEA.

On the basis of the above cases, it appears that the Commission has on occasion reviewed price levels when defining relevant markets, although this has typically been used as supporting, rather than determinative, evidence for its conclusions. In particular, it has on a number of occasions presented evidence on price levels together with evidence on price movements in line with the price correlation methodology discussed at Section 3.6.

Nevertheless, the Commission has, in a number of cases, correctly noted that it may be unsafe to draw conclusions on market definition based on price levels. Where it does so, it typically goes on to argue (again, correctly) that movements in prices over time (discussed at Section 3.6) are of greater evidential value.

For instance, in *JCI/VB/FIAMM*,[128] the Commission stated that it:[129]

> agrees in principle that different price levels in themselves may not always be sufficient to conclude that markets are national. In certain circumstances it may be relevant to assess the extent to which prices move in parallel and a finding of such parallel price movements could indicate a wider market.

However, the Commission went on in that case to present an analysis of cross-country price differences that sought to control for various differentiating factors identified by the parties. Indeed, the Commission held that such differentiation in product specifications between countries may in itself be evidence of the existence of separate national markets:[130]

---

[127] Ibid., paras. 73 and 74.
[128] Case COMP/M.4381 – *JCI/VB/FIAMM*, Commission decision of 10 May 2007.
[129] Ibid., para. 196.    [130] Ibid., para. 188.

> Even if (at least parts of) the existing price differences across countries
> could be explained by factors like variations in customer size, differences
> in product-mix, differences in distribution cost and/or variations in the
> relevance of brands, all these differences together indicate that the condi-
> tions of demand across the EEA are still very heterogeneous and thus
> from a qualitative point of view would indicate that the IAMs for auto-
> motive starter batteries show national characteristics.

Nonetheless, based on the parties' claims regarding factors that may give
rise to different price levels in different member states, the Commission
undertook a detailed regression analysis that sought to explain the
identified price variation with reference to factors such as customer type,
size and location, product specification and transaction size. The Commission concluded that the price differences could not be explained by
these other factors, and therefore that the relevant markets were national,
notwithstanding its recognition that price differences need not be dispositive of separate markets.

A similar analysis was undertaken by the parties in *Areva/Urenco*.[131]
In this instance the Commission criticised the range of control variables
used in that analysis as too simplistic to capture the degree of contract
variability observed in the market for the supply of low enriched uran-
ium, and consequently concluded that it was unable to place any weight
on the parties' claim that similar price levels are observed throughout the
world. Nonetheless, the Commission did not make any conceptual criticisms of the approach adopted by the parties.

The Commission made a similar point regarding the value of evidence
on price levels in dismissing a 'price dispersion' analysis in respect of
geographic market definition put forward by the parties in *Arjowiggins/
M-real Zanders*.[132] The parties claimed that the fact that differences in
prices within each member state were as great as price differences across
countries, and that there were 'significant overlaps' in countries' distribution of prices, supported broad geographic markets. This is effectively a less
onerous variation on testing for equality of prices between countries.

The Commission rejected this evidence, although not on the grounds
that price equality or inequality provides no information on the likelihood of customer switching but on the grounds that an analysis of price

---

[131] Case COMP/M.3099 – *Areva/Urenco/ETC JV*, Commission decision of 6 October 2004, paras. 91, 92 and 100.
[132] Case COMP/M.4513 – *Arjowiggins/M-real Zanders Reflex*, Commission decision of 4 June 2008.

levels is a less powerful form of evidence on market definition than the price correlation and stationarity analyses undertaken by the Commission. The decision states that:

> The Commission does not find that [the parties' evidence of price dispersal between countries] is a convincing argument for a wider geographic market. It finds that its analysis of the movement of average prices in the different countries provides more pertinent information for a market definition exercise. Even if there are similar price dispersions across the different countries, the fact that the movement of average prices in two different countries develops in different ways over time implies that these two countries are not in the same relevant geographic market ...[133]

In this case the Commission was clearly of the view that evidence on pre-merger price levels is less dispositive of market definition than evidence of price movements over time, a topic considered in the following two sections.

## 3.6    Price correlation analysis

### 3.6.1    Description of technique

Price correlation analysis is frequently used in European merger analysis, and the relevance of evidence on price movements for the purpose of market definition is explicitly acknowledged in the Market Definition Notice.[134] The technique is related to stationarity analysis, which will be described in Section 3.7 below.

Price correlation analysis is based on the principle that, where two products or regions lie in a single relevant market, demand- and/or supply-side substitution between the two will cause their prices to move together over time.

Thus, if products A and B compete in the same relevant product market, then a reduction in the price of the former will lead to a reduction in demand for the latter. This reduction in demand for B will then place pressure on its supplier to reduce its price. Similarly, if the price of product A were to increase, this would reduce the competitive pressure on producers of product B, which will then create scope for a profitable increase in the price of B. In each case, changes in the price of product A lead to similar changes in the price of product B.

---

[133] Case COMP/M.4513 – *Arjowiggins/M-real Zanders Reflex*, Commission decision of 4 June 2008, para. 86.

[134] Market Definition Notice, para. 39; see also para. 45.

The same logic applies to issues of geographic market definition regarding similar products supplied in different locations. If the price of widgets supplied in country A rises, then this will reduce competitive pressure on firms whose output competes with widgets produced in country A, which is likely to manifest itself in an increase in those companies' prices. Thus, if widgets in countries A and B lie in the same relevant geographic market, an increase in the price of widgets in A would likely be followed by an increase in the price of widgets in B. Similarly, a reduction in the price of widgets supplied in country A will place downward pressure on prices charged by widget suppliers in country B due to the scope for their existing customers to take advantage of the reduction in the price of widgets produced in A.

Conversely, if the prices of two products, or of products in different regions, are observed to develop independently over time, then this would suggest that there is an absence of competitive interaction between the two products or regions, and consequently imply the existence of separate relevant markets.

The degree of co-movement between price series can be assessed graphically, and also via the **correlation coefficient**, an easily computed statistical measure of the extent to which movements in one price series over time are accompanied by movements in another price series. A correlation coefficient can take any value between minus one and one. Correlation coefficients close to unity arise when two price series track each other very closely, while two entirely unrelated series will give a correlation coefficient of zero.[135] For the reasons explained above, the greater the degree of correlation between two price series, the more likely the products or regions are to compete within the same relevant market.

There are two fundamental issues associated with price correlation analysis that should be taken into account when employing this technique for the purpose of defining relevant markets. These are the possibility that correlation may be spurious and the fact that there is no clearly defined benchmark against which to assess whether observed correlation is sufficient to demonstrate competitive interaction between products/regions consistent with a relevant antitrust market.

---

[135] Negative correlation coefficients indicate that the price series tend to move in opposite directions.

The following two sub-sections consider the problems posed by spurious correlation and benchmarking in price correlation analyses.[136] We then discuss the use of lagged variables to capture lagged responses by competing suppliers.

**3.6.1.1 Spurious correlation**    Spurious correlation arises when two products' price series exhibit co-movement that is caused by factors other than competitive interactions. If one or more of the determinants of price for one of the products under consideration also affects the other product(s) being assessed, then changes in those determinants will affect the price of both products, and so increase the degree of correlation. This correlation, which is not due to genuine competitive interaction, will increase the degree of co-movement, and bias the results of the analysis towards suggesting that the two products lie in the same relevant market.

This problem is best illustrated by an example. Consider an analysis concerning correlation between wholesale motor fuels produced in Austria and Hungary in order to assess whether oil refineries in these two countries lie in the same geographic market. Due to the high degree of common costs present in the production of wholesale fuels, any analysis based on the simple evolution of absolute price levels over time could be expected to produce very high correlation levels, irrespective of the existence of international competitive constraints. By far the most significant cost in the production of refined fuels is the input cost of crude oil, the price of which is determined on a worldwide market. An increase in the price of crude oil at a particular point in time would be expected to feed through to an increase in the price of all wholesale fuels, irrespective of where they are produced. As such, an increase in crude prices would lead to an increase in wholesale fuel prices in both Austria and Hungary, irrespective of any competitive interaction that may exist between these countries. Similarly, reductions in the world crude oil price would be passed through to the wholesale fuels market in the form of reduced prices for refined fuels, irrespective of the degree of competition. This pattern will lead to co-movements in wholesale motor

---

[136] For a more general critique of the use of price correlation analysis, see G. J. Werden and L. M. Froeb, 'Correlation, Causality, and All That Jazz: The Inherent Shortcomings of Price Tests for Antitrust Market Delineation' (1993) 8 *Review of Industrial Organization* 329–53.

fuel prices that are due to the common input costs, and not necessarily due to competitive interaction.

The problem of spurious correlation is widely recognised. In *Friesland Foods/Campina*,[137] the Commission dismissed the price correlation analysis submitted by the parties primarily due to the presence of milk as a common input into the production of various cheeses:[138]

> Although these prices exhibit a certain level of long run co-movement, it should be recalled that milk is the most important ingredient for cheese and therefore a significant cost component. The prices of both nature and rindless cheese therefore necessarily reflect changes in the price of milk, irrespective of whether or not these cheese types are substitutable on the demand or supply side. In addition, co-movement of variables can also be caused by changes in tastes or a series of unrelated variables which affect demand for different products in the same way but do not necessarily imply that the products are in the same market. In such cases it is generally erroneous to infer causal links or to conclude that the products in question are in the same market.

The Commission noted the importance of common costs in rejecting the parties' evidence on cross-border co-movements in the prices of automotive batteries in *JCI/VB/FIAMM*:[139]

> a large fraction of production costs are raw materials (lead) [and it would] be expected that an increase in the production costs – such as an increase in the price of lead – would give the seller an incentive to increase prices generally in all countries, just as it would be likely to lead to similar price trends for all other products that use the same raw material.

In light of this observation, and of an apparent doubt concerning the parties' claims that price co-movement is actually observed between the countries in question, the Commission relied instead upon its observation of price differences (discussed at Section 3.5) to delineate separate national markets for automotive batteries.[140]

Importantly, the impact of common costs is uni-directional, in the sense that the presence of any common cost factors will serve only to increase the measured degree of correlation. As such, it is not always

---

[137] Case COMP/M.5046 – *Friesland Foods/Campina*, Commission decision of 17 December 2008.
[138] Ibid., para. 513.
[139] Case COMP/M.4381 – *JCI/VB/FIAMM*, Commission decision of 10 May 2007, para. 198.
[140] Ibid., para. 199.

necessary to control for common costs in order to reach a conclusion on market definition. For instance, in *Inco/Falconbridge*[141] the parties claimed that the Commission did not control for common cost factors when analysing the correlation between price premiums for different products.[142] In that case, however, the correlation coefficient found by the Commission was close to zero (and indeed negative), notwithstanding the potential inclusion of common costs. Exclusion of such common cost factors would have further reduced the already negligible degree of observed correlation: '... it has to be pointed out that the failure of the Commission to control for all common cost factors will result if at all in a higher positive correlation ... Hence, the Commission's approach provides a conservative, upper boundary of the actual correlation.'[143]

As such, this issue of common costs may be relevant only where a simple correlation of prices identifies a degree of co-movement sufficiently high to suggest, against either a chosen benchmark or a subjective opinion, a credible prospect that the product/regions in question compete in the same relevant market. In such circumstances it is necessary to extend the analysis to investigate whether the identified correlation is robust to the removal of common costs. However, if limited correlation is observed even before controlling for common costs, it can be concluded that the same conclusion will hold *a fortiori* if common costs were to be removed.

Where common costs are identified, their effect can be easily controlled for by stripping those costs from the price series being compared. Stripping out the common cost element produces a net price, over those common cost items. The logic of the price correlation analysis then applies directly to these net prices.

To return to the example of wholesale fuel products in different European countries, if the margin over crude oil costs that refiners are able to obtain in Austria moves together with the margin over crude oil costs that refiners are able to obtain in Hungary, then this would provide evidence suggesting that common competitive conditions are at work here, such that Austrian refiners are forced to reduce their margins over crude oil in response to price reductions implemented by Hungarian refiners, and vice versa.

---

[141] Case COMP/M.4000 – *Inco/Falconbridge*, Commission decision of 4 July 2006.
[142] Ibid., paras. 108–19.    [143] Ibid., para. 118.

Alternatively, the data might show that, although there is correlation between the absolute prices charged by Austrian and Hungarian refiners, when crude oil costs are stripped out of the prices, there is little or no correlation in net prices. This would suggest that the apparent correlation in prices is driven by changes in input costs, and that changes in pricing behaviour in Austria do not affect pricing in Hungary (and vice versa). This would in turn point to an absence of any significant competitive interaction between those countries, and would indicate that refineries in the two countries do not lie in the same relevant market.

It should be noted that, while stripping common costs from price series gives a form of margin, the analysis should nevertheless focus on the identification of correlation in prices (albeit adjusted for common input costs), rather than correlation in margins as normally defined. As such, it is only common costs that should be removed. It is not correct to investigate correlations between margins more generally, such as the margins calculated and reported by firms in the ordinary course of business. Such margins will reflect firms' production costs, which need not be correlated even where there is competition between those firms, and in so far as exogenous and unrelated cost shocks affect one or each of the products/regions in question, this will obscure competitive inter-actions that may exist.

To give an example, imagine that widgets and gadgets both sell at €7 per unit, that the margin on both is €2 per unit, and that there is competition between the two. In the event of a reduction in the unit production cost of gadgets from €5 to €3, gadget producers may choose to pass on some of the cost reduction to consumers and thereby reduce their prices from €7 to €6. This price reduction may put downward pressure on the price of widgets, causing widget pro-ducers to reduce price to €6. The margins of gadget producers have thus increased from €2 to €3 while those of widget producers have decreased from €2 to €1. The cost change specific to gadget producers has caused the margins of gadget and widget producers to move in different directions precisely because of the competition between the two products. Correlation of net margins is thus not a meaningful test of competition between products/regions. Effectively, examining margins potentially generates spurious negative correlation by intro-ducing non-common cost changes to the analysis. It is therefore only common costs that should be removed from prices series used for correlation analysis.

In *Arjowiggins/M-real Zanders Reflex*,[144] the Commission used gross margin data supplied by the parties as a means of controlling for the effect of common costs in its price correlation analysis, stating that:

> One explanation for such a finding [high correlation coefficients between the prices of paper reels in different countries] may be that the close movements in prices may be driven by common movements in input costs. Thus, the gross margin data submitted by Arjowiggins lend themselves particularly well to assessing the role of the common input cost movements. The findings [of analysis of these data] show that the correlation coefficients for prices excluding common costs (gross margins) are very low and do not by and large attain values such that the countries could be considered to be part of the same market.[145]

However, it is not clear how the gross margins provided by the parties were calculated, and whether they stripped out only common costs. In so far as these gross margin data removed non-common cost items, this may explain the lower degree of correlation than that observed for prices in absolute.

Common input costs are the most frequently observed source of spurious correlation, but other exogenous (that is, unrelated to competition) factors that may affect price include regulatory changes, exchange rate movements, demand seasonality etc. It is essential that any and all such common factors are considered and, where necessary, taken into account when conducting correlation analyses.[146]

**3.6.1.2  Benchmarking correlation**  The second frequently cited issue associated with price correlation analysis is that economic theory cannot provide any guidance as to what level of correlation is sufficient to demonstrate the existence of a single relevant market for a particular industry, or what level is dispositive of separate markets. While the directional effect is clear, specifically, that a higher degree of correlation represents stronger evidence of competition between products/regions,

---

[144] Case COMP/M.4513 – *Arjowiggins/M-real Zanders Reflex*, Commission decision of 4 June 2008.

[145] Ibid., para. 88.

[146] It should be noted that where exogenous shocks such as those identified above fall asymmetrically on products or regions (such as in the case of plant shut downs, product introductions or exchange rate movements affecting only one product) these shocks may provide a direct means of assessing the effect of one firm or a group of firms attempting to worsen their supply terms. The evidential value of such shocks for market definition is discussed at Section 3.8 below.

there is no agreement on the point at which correlation becomes sufficiently high to 'prove' that the products and regions in question belong to
the same relevant market.

Notwithstanding this absence of a clear theoretical benchmark for
correlation consistent with competition, it has been suggested, in the
context of geographic market definition, that '… in general, it is hard to
reconcile any correlation coefficient below 0.8 with the hypothesis that
two geographic areas are in the same market'.[147]

The grounds for this position are not entirely clear, as there is no
economic basis for the claim that correlation below 0.8 is inconsistent
with competition between two regions. It is worth noting, however, that
the Commission has also cited a benchmark correlation coefficient of 0.8
in its discussion of product market definition. For example, in *Arjowig-
gins/M-real Zanders Reflex*,[148] the Commission assessed the degree of
correlation between thermal and carbonless paper on the basis of a
benchmark correlation coefficient of 0.8, which was found to exist
between various types of reel paper products that were accepted as
belonging in the same relevant product market.[149]

An arguably preferable alternative to the use of arbitrary absolute
correlation coefficient benchmarks is to compare the correlation between
the products/regions of interest with the degree of price correlation
observed between two products/regions in the same industry that are
widely held to lie in the same market.

This principle was explained by the Commission in the *Arjowiggins/
M-real Zanders Reflex*[150] decision, which noted that 'in order to assess
whether the prices of two products are sufficiently correlated to be considered in the same market, it is typical to use as a benchmark the correlation
between two products that are accepted as being in the same market'.[151]

In *ABF/GBI Business*,[152] the Commission sought to benchmark the
level of correlation between yeast prices in different member states

---

[147] D. Donath, 'The Use of Pricing Analysis for Market Definition Purposes: The *Arjowig-
gins/M-real Zanders Reflex* and *Arsenal/DSP* mergers' (2009) 1 *Competition Policy
Newsletter* 41–50.

[148] Case COMP/M.4513 – *Arjowiggins/M-real Zanders Reflex*, Commission decision of
4 June 2008.

[149] Ibid., para. 403.

[150] Case COMP/M.4513 – *Arjowiggins/M-real Zanders Reflex*, Commission decision of
4 June 2008.

[151] Ibid., Annex 1, para. 27.

[152] Case COMP/M.4980 – *ABF/GBI Business*, Commission decision of 23 September 2008.

against the degree of correlation observed in intra-national regional sales data.[153] Having found that 'prices across all regions of Spain are very much correlated with the price in the region of Madrid and to a lower extent with the region[s] outside Spain', the Commission concluded that its analysis identified evidence of competition between regions within Spain and the absence of any meaningful interaction between Spain and other member states.

The use of benchmarking in this manner, that is, to demonstrate an absence of constraints according to a defined benchmark, is somewhat questionable, however. While it is legitimate to say that correlation in excess of a level found between products or regions agreed to be characterised by competition is consistent with competition (or, equivalently, that correlation less than that found between products and regions regarded as lying in separate markets is consistent with an absence of competition), it does not necessarily follow that finding correlation between the regions or products of interest below the benchmark necessarily indicates an absence of competition. Such a benchmark does not represent the minimum level of correlation consistent with competition, but simply a figure above that notional minimum.

In the context of *ABF/GBI Business*,[154] the correlation between prices in Spain and other countries may be consistent with the existence of competition, even if it is less than that observed between regions within Spain. Only if the level of inter-country correlation were higher than the intra-country level could a firm conclusion be drawn. The approach to benchmarking taken by the Commission in *ABF/GBI Business*[155] thus fails to move the issue beyond a question of judgement, namely whether the correlation of interest is insufficiently close to the identified benchmark.

An equivalent criticism can be made of the Commission's reasoning regarding product market definition in *Arjowiggins/M-real Zanders Reflex*.[156] The Commission established the degree of correlation between the prices of different types of reel paper regarded as clearly lying within the same product market and stated that this level of correlation 'is the lowest possible correlation benchmark that is indicative of reels and

[153] Case COMP/M.4980 – *ABF/GBI Business*, Commission decision of 23 September 2008, para. 77.
[154] Case COMP/M.4980 – *ABF/GBI Business*, Commission decision of 23 September 2008.
[155] Ibid.
[156] Case COMP/M.4513 – *Arjowiggins/M-real Zanders Reflex*, Commission decision of 4 June 2008.

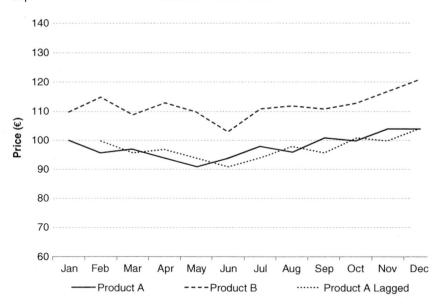

**Figure 2.9**   Hypothetical example of lagged price correlation

sheets as being in the same market'.[157] Again, this overlooks the possibility that reels and sheets could be less correlated than different types of reel, and yet still sufficiently correlated to lie in the same relevant market.

**3.6.1.3   Lagged responses**   Correlation analyses will often explore the possibility of lags in the hypothesised competitive interaction between regions/products. There may be delays in the process by which demand, and particularly supply, side responses occur, such that the price of one product/region does not respond to changes in the other within the same time period. Such delays in price responses can obscure correlation between prices. In Figure 2.9, for instance, the price of product B follows movements in the price of product A with a delay of one month. Thus, an increase in the price of product A in a particular month tends to be associated not with an increase in the price of product B in that month, but an increase in the price of product B in the following month. This can be seen in the chart, where the third series plots the price of product A shifted forward one month (that is, each month's

[157] Ibid., Annex 1, para. 27.

observation in the lagged series is the previous month's actual observation). It can be seen that changes in the lagged product A series closely reflect contemporaneous changes in the product B series.

Given this pattern, the correlation coefficient between the two unadjusted data series is relatively low, at 0.62. If, however, lags are introduced into the series, whereby the series for product A running from January to November is correlated with the time series for product B running from February to December (that is, each month for A is compared to the following month for product B), the correlation coefficient rises to 0.92, reflecting the high degree of co-movement between the lagged series.

In *Arjowiggins/M-real Zanders Reflex*,[158] the Commission acknowledged the theoretical possibility, and implications for price correlation analysis, of such lags in its comments on the parties' submissions.[159]

It should be noted that using lagged observations necessarily reduces the number of observations that can be used. As shown in the previous example, a one-month lag in monthly data will reduce the number of observations by one (that is, a series of 12 contemporaneous monthly observations produces a series of 11 observations lagged by one observation). Where lags are employed, care should be taken that sufficient data remain to provide the number and duration of observations required for meaningful results.

It is typical to investigate a range of lags in any price correlation analysis to allow for the possibility of delays in the transmission of competitive constraints. The length of such lags that may exist will vary across different industries based on the frequency with which prices are changed. Visual inspection of price series will frequently assist with identifying the existence and approximate length of lags.

### 3.6.2    An example

In this hypothetical example we consider whether price evidence supports the hypothesis that the relevant European market for wholesale fuels (i.e. refined petrol and diesel sold to retailers and to commercial users) is EEA-wide or suggests that relevant markets are national. In this example we consider two illustrative locations: the Netherlands, which is the source of refined oil imports into Europe via the Rotterdam and Antwerp sea terminals; and Germany.

---

[158] Case COMP/M.4513 – *Arjowiggins/M-real Zanders Reflex*, Commission decision of 4 June 2008.
[159] Ibid., Annex 1, paras. 10 and 11.

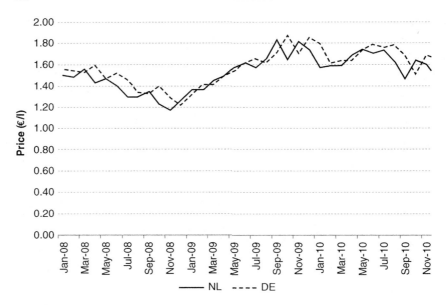

**Figure 2.10**   Wholesale petrol prices in the Netherlands and Germany, €/litre

Figure 2.10 shows average monthly data on prices in each country over the period 2008 to 2010. In order to control for product mix effects, the data relate to a particular grade of refined oil product, 97 octane petrol, and to volumes sold through the retail distribution channel only. The chart shows that there is a high degree of correlation between the prices in the Netherlands and Germany. This impression is confirmed by a correlation coefficient of 0.82 between the two.

It should be recognised, however, that the prices of refined fuel supplied in the Netherlands and Germany will contain a significant common cost in the form of the cost of crude oil. In order to control for movements in crude oil prices that affect the price of refined fuel in both the Netherlands and Germany net prices for each country can be calculated by removing the monthly cost of crude per litre of petrol from the retail price data shown in Figure 2.10.

Figure 2.11 plots these two net price series. The degree of correlation between the net prices is visibly lower than between the absolute prices shown above and, indeed, the corresponding correlation coefficient is only 0.11. This demonstrates the importance of taking into account common costs; failure to do so in this instance would erroneously increase the correlation coefficient from 0.11 to 0.82, as shown above.

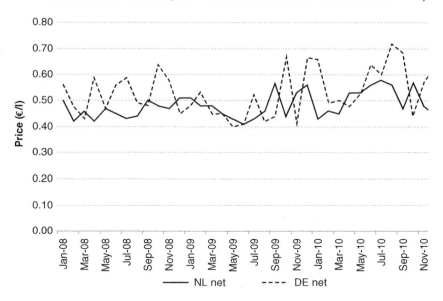

**Figure 2.11**    Net wholesale petrol prices in the Netherlands and Germany

The virtual absence of correlation between the two net price series would seem to suggest that Germany and the Netherlands do not lie in the same relevant market. Visual inspection of the chart, however, suggests that there may be a lag in the response of German prices to changes in the price of petrol in the Netherlands. This can be investigated via a correlation analysis of lagged prices, as explained above.

Figure 2.12 plots the lagged net price for the Netherlands against the net price for Germany (that is, the value of NL net lag in February 2008 corresponds to the value of NL net in January 2008, and so on). As suggested by inspection of figure 2.11, introducing the one-month lag increases the degree of correlation substantially, the coefficient between these two series being 0.73.

While this chart exhibits a reasonably high degree of correlation, the question remains of whether a correlation coefficient of 0.73 is sufficiently high to demonstrate that there is a single relevant geographic market for wholesale 97 octane petrol supplied to retailers in the Netherlands and Germany. As explained above, although there is no definitive threshold above which price correlations can be said to prove that two products/regions lie within the same market, one approach is to benchmark the estimated correlation coefficient against price series that are known to belong in the same market.

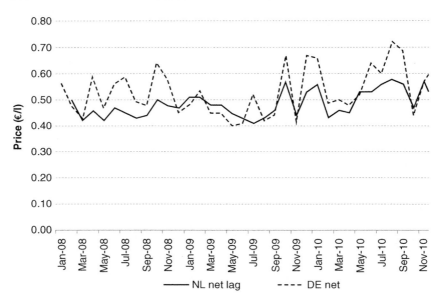

**Figure 2.12**   Lagged net wholesale petrol prices in the Netherlands and Germany

Let us assume, for this purpose, that it is generally accepted that the Netherlands represents a single relevant geographic market, for instance due to testimony from market participants and observations of trade flows across the country. On this basis, the degree of correlation observed between the prices of 97 octane petrol in different provinces within the Netherlands will provide a guide to the degree of correlation consistent with competition in the wholesale fuels industry. Let us assume that one of the merging parties has provided monthly wholesale 97 octane petrol prices in four of the twelve provinces in the Netherlands over a similar time period to the data analysed above. These data can be combined with the crude price data above to produce monthly net prices in these provinces, and correlation coefficients between these net prices produced. Table 2.9 shows illustrative inter-province correlation coefficients between net prices in the four provinces of Zeeland, Groningen, North Holland and Limburg.

The table shows that correlation may be as low as 0.69 between provinces in the Netherlands that are regarded as belonging to the same relevant geographic market. The median correlation coefficient between the four provinces is between 0.73 and 0.74.

This evidence suggests that the correlation coefficient of 0.73 observed for lagged net wholesale petrol prices in the Netherlands and Germany is

Table 2.9 *Provincial price correlation coefficients*

|  | Zeeland | Groningen | North Holland | Limburg |
|---|---|---|---|---|
| **Zeeland** | 1.00 | | | |
| **Groningen** | 0.69 | 1.00 | | |
| **North Holland** | 0.84 | 0.73 | 1.00 | |
| **Limburg** | 0.76 | 0.74 | 0.71 | 1.00 |

consistent with those regions lying in the same geographic market. Even though some province pairs in the Netherlands, such as North Holland and Zeeland, exhibit higher degrees of price correlation, it is the lowest degrees of correlation consistent with competition that should be considered the benchmark against which to test the Germany–Netherlands correlation.

### 3.6.3    Use in EU merger control

The Commission has examined price correlation with respect to product market definition in a relatively large number of recent Phase II merger investigations. Table 2.10 and Table 2.11 summarise instances in which the Commission has relied on correlation analysis for the assessment of product and geographic market definition.

The Commission's jurisprudence has noted that care must be taken in the application of price correlation analysis. It has also recognised that such evidence should not be viewed in isolation but must be viewed in the context of other forms of evidence. In *Friesland Foods/Campina*[160] for instance, the Commission stated that:

> … co-movement of prices cannot be considered as decisive evidence for market definition purposes … co-movements can be caused by factors other than competitive constraints; further information is therefore required as regards the definitions of product categories, transactions included and the methods of aggregation. Price correlations should also be balanced against other evidence such as the qualitative evidence gathered in the market investigation.[161]

[160] Case COMP/M.5046 – *Friesland Foods/Campina*, Commission decision of 17 December 2008.
[161] Ibid., para. 515.

Table 2.10 *Price correlation analysis in product market definition*

| Case | Product market | Outcome |
|------|----------------|---------|
| **UPM/Myllykoski and Rhein Papier**[1] **(2011)** | Magazine paper | The parties conducted a correlation analysis, which showed a high degree of price correlation between different grades of magazine paper that the parties submitted lay within a single relevant market. The Commission did not accept these findings. First, the Commission stated that 'price co-movements do not, in themselves, constitute sufficient evidence for market definition. Namely, price co-movement does not directly answer to whether or not a price increase of 5–10% would be profitable … Neither does finding that prices of two products move closely together provide any insights as to the causality of the relationship between the prices'.[2] Second, the Commission noted that the parties' analysis suffered from several shortcomings, in particular failing to control for common shocks and common costs. |
| **Votorantim/ Fischer/JV**[3] **(2011)** | Orange juice | In response to correlation analysis submitted by the parties the Commission again noted that price correlation does not, in itself, constitute conclusive evidence on market definition.[4] The Commission stated that such evidence should not be assessed in isolation but together with the other evidentiary material gathered during the market investigation. In light of that other |

Table 2.10 (*cont.*)

| Case | Product market | Outcome |
| --- | --- | --- |
| | | evidence, the Commission held that the levels of correlation identified by the parties (0.56 between orange juice and apple juice, 0.64 between grapefruit juice and apple juice) were too low to support a wider market than orange juice. |
| *Unilever/Sara Lee Body Care*[5] *(2010)* | Deodorant | The Commission undertook a price correlation study in a number of national markets, which showed a significant degree of co-movement of male and non-male deodorant prices.[6] However, the Commission identified a number of instances where prices did not move in the same direction. While the parties argued that these divergences were explained by the introduction of new premium male deodorants, the Commission argued that such segment-specific events supported its contention that prices are set separately in the two product segments. |
| *Lufthansa/SN Airholding*[7] *(2009)* | Airlines | The Commission's correlation analysis indicated that the price of flexible fares and non-flexible fares on five routes considered evolved independently over time, suggesting that the two lie in separate relevant product markets.[8] |
| *Friesland Foods/ Campina*[9] *(2008)* | Dairy products | The Commission rejected the parties' price correlation analysis, primarily due to the presence of a common cost (milk) resulting in spurious correlation between different dairy products.[10] |

Table 2.10 (*cont.*)

| Case | Product market | Outcome |
|------|---------|---------|
| *Arjowiggins/ M-real Zanders Reflex*[11] *(2008)* | Paper | The Commission undertook price correlation analysis to investigate whether paper sold in reels and paper sold in sheets lie in the same relevant product market. The Commission calculated correlation coefficients for prices in a number of member states, and found that the correlations observed ranged from between $-0.32$ and $0.5$. These levels were substantially below the benchmark levels of correlation found for various grades of coated paper regarded as lying within a single relevant market, indicating that reels and sheets do not lie in the same product market.[12] |
| *Ryanair/Aer Lingus*[13] *(2007)* | Airlines | The Commission put forward a correlation analysis which showed that there was substantial correlation between the prices for flights from Dublin to Stansted, Dublin to Gatwick and Dublin to Luton, suggesting that these three routes lie in the same relevant market.[14] |
| *Inco/ Falconbridge*[15] *(2006)* | Plating and stainless steel nickel products | The Commission examined correlation between the price of nickel supplied for plating and stainless steel, expressed as a premium over nickel prices to control for common input costs. The Commission found a correlation of $-0.2$ between the two products' price premiums, suggesting separate product markets.[16] |

Table 2.10 (*cont.*)

| Case | Product market | Outcome |
| --- | --- | --- |
| ***Johnson&Johnson/ Guidant***[17] ***(2005)*** | Medical equipment | A low degree of price correlation was, *inter alia*, held to indicate that bare metal stents and drug-eluting stents lie in separate relevant product markets.[18] |

[1]  Case COMP/M.6101 – *UPM/Myllykoski and Rhein Papier*, Commission decision of 13 July 2011.

[2]  Paragraph 44.

[3]  Case COMP/M.5907 – *Votorantim/Fischer/JV*, Commission decision of 4 May 2011.

[4]  Paragraphs 92 et seq.

[5]  Case COMP/M.5658 – *Unilever/Sara Lee Body Care*, Commission decision of 17 November 2010.

[6]  Ibid., paras. 75 et seq.

[7]  Case COMP/M.5335 – *Lufthansa/SN Airholding*, Commission decision of 22 June 2009.

[8]  Ibid., Annex 1, para. 4.

[9]  Case COMP/M.5046 – *Friesland Foods/Campina*, Commission decision of 17 December 2008.

[10]  Ibid., para. 513.

[11]  Case COMP/M.4513 – *Arjowiggins/M-real Zanders Reflex*, Commission decision of 4 June 2008.

[12]  Ibid., para. 54.

[13]  Case COMP/M.4439 – *Ryanair/Aer Lingus*, Commission decision of 27 June 2007.

[14]  Ibid., Annex III, para. 43.

[15]  Case COMP/M.4000 – *Inco/Falconbridge*, Commission decision of 4 July 2006.

[16]  Ibid., paras. 107 and 108.

[17]  Case COMP/M.3687 – *Johnson&Johnson/Guidant*, Commission decision of 25 August 2005.

[18]  Ibid., para. 17.

Table 2.11 *Price correlation analysis in geographic market definition*

| Case | Product Market | Outcome |
| --- | --- | --- |
| ***Arsenal/DSP*[1]** ***(2009)*** | Benzoic acid | The Commission's analysis found a divergence of prices in the EEA, Asia and North America, suggesting that the relevant geographic market was not global.[2] |
| ***Arjowiggins/M-real Zanders Reflex*[3]** ***(2008)*** | Carbonless paper | The Commission's correlation analyses were not conclusive in determining whether the relevant geographic markets were national or EEA-wide. The Commission suggested that its findings may be distorted by the presence of spurious correlation, and so augmented its correlation analysis with a stationarity analysis, which indicated that the relevant markets were national.[4] |
| ***ABF/GBI Business*[5]** ***(2008)*** | Yeast | The Commission found that compressed yeast prices in Spain, Portugal and France developed independently over time, whereas higher correlation was observed between prices in different regions of Portugal, suggesting that the relevant markets were national.[6] |
| ***Ineos/Kerling*[7]** ***(2008)*** | PVC | The parties submitted price correlation analyses that showed a high degree of co-movement (greater than 0.5) between S-PVC prices between pairs of EU member states.[8] This, combined with evidence on price stationarity and critical loss and shock analyses, led the Commission to find that the relevant geographic |

Table 2.11 (*cont.*)

| Case | Product Market | Outcome |
|------|----------------|---------|
| | | markets were broader than the UK and the Nordic region, and at least as broad as North Western Europe. |
| *JCI/VB/FIAMM*[9] *(2007)* | Automotive components | The parties submitted an analysis which showed a relatively high price correlation between EU countries. The Commission acknowledged that its evidence of price differences may not be dispositive of separate geographic markets if there were evidence of co-movement over time, but nonetheless considered that the existence of price differences in excess of transport costs outweighed such evidence.[10] The Commission also highlighted the potential role of common input costs in driving the parties' correlation analysis results, although it does not appear to have attempted to modify the analysis to control for these common costs. |
| *Inco/ Falconbridge*[11] *(2006)* | Plating and stainless steel nickel products | The Commission concluded that there was insufficient price correlation between the EU and the rest of the world to indicate a global market. The Commission used data on the parties' ten largest European and ten largest global customers to calculate a weighted average price for EU and global sales, and based its correlation analysis on these series.[12] |

Table 2.11 (cont.)

| Case | Product Market | Outcome |
|------|----------------|---------|
| **Blackstone/ Acetex**[13] **(2005)** | Acetic acid | The parties submitted a correlation analysis demonstrating a global market but this was dismissed by the Commission on grounds of spurious correlation.[14] |

[1]  Case COMP/M.5153 – *Arsenal/DSP*, Commission decision of 9 January 2009.
[2]  Ibid., para. 81.
[3]  Case COMP/M.4513 – *Arjowiggins/M-real Zanders Reflex*, Commission decision of 4 June 2008.
[4]  Ibid., paras. 69 and 70.
[5]  Case COMP/M.4980 – *ABF/GBI Business*, Commission decision of 23 September 2008.
[6]  Ibid., paras. 75–7.
[7]  Case COMP/M.4734 – *Ineos/Kerling*, Commission decision of 30 January 2008.
[8]  Ibid., para. 55.
[9]  Case COMP/M.4381 – *JCI/VB/FIAMM*, Commission decision of 10 May 2007.
[10]  Ibid., paras. 196–8.
[11]  Case COMP/M.4000 – *Inco/Falconbridge*, Commission decision of 4 July 2006.
[12]  Ibid., paras. 218–20.
[13]  Case COMP/M.3625 – *Blackstone/Acetex*, Commission decision of 13 July 2005.
[14]  Ibid., paras. 34, 35 and 57.

According to the Commission, an obvious downside of a correlation analysis is that it does not indicate how different suppliers would respond to a (future) price increase, as noted by the Commission in *Ineos/Kerling*:[162]

> However, this type of price correlation studies [*sic*] checks the price convergence, that is to say an identified relationship between prices in distinct regions. It does not provide information about the elasticity of supply of the different groups of producers. Hence, such tests alone do not provide direct decisive evidence that the producers in different regions belong to the same relevant geographic market from a competition law perspective, although it is clearly an element pointing toward this direction. However when combined with other qualitative evidences, these price correlation studies can serve the purpose of defining the antitrust markets.

[162]  Case COMP/M.4734 – *Ineos/Kerling*, Commission decision of 30 January 2008, para. 56.

Nevertheless, the Commission has recognised the value of price correlation analysis where its limitations are taken into account. The Commission's view appears to be that an absence of price correlation is dispositive of separate markets, although the presence of price correlation may not necessarily prove the opposite. In *Arjowiggins/M-real Zanders Reflex*,[163] for instance, the Commission stated that:[164]

> While the evidence that prices move together over time is not conclusive evidence of strong competitive constraints between two products, it is certainly consistent with the two being in the same market. At the same time, however, if strong price co-movements over time are not found, this suggests that the competitive relationship between the two products is not particularly strong and thus they are not in the same product market.

Similarly, in *ABF/GBI Business*[165] the Commission reported a 'striking difference' between the dynamics of prices between member states over the period 2002 to 2008, which, combined with observations of absolute price differences in 2006, was held to indicate that 'the dynamics of the market are indeed different [between member states] and that the competitive interplay between producers and demand is to a large degree independent'.[166]

## 3.7    Stationarity analysis

### 3.7.1    Description of technique

The preceding section has discussed one method by which price data can be analysed to investigate whether those prices are subject to common determinants that would suggest that the products/regions in question lie in the same relevant market. Stationarity analysis represents a further means of using price data to investigate questions of market definition. This technique has in recent years come to play an increasingly important role, with the Commission relying on it particularly to support a finding of narrow geographic markets in a number of recent cases.[167]

---

[163] Case COMP/M.4513 – *Arjowiggins/M-real Zanders Reflex*, Commission decision of 4 June 2008.

[164] Ibid., para. 52.

[165] Case COMP/M.4980 – *ABF/GBI Business*, Commission decision of 23 September 2008.

[166] Ibid., para. 76.

[167] See, for instance, Case COMP/M.4513 – *Arjowiggins/M-real Zanders Reflex*, Commission decision of 4 June 2008 and Case COMP/M.5153 – *Arsenal/DSP*, Commission decision of 9 January 2009.

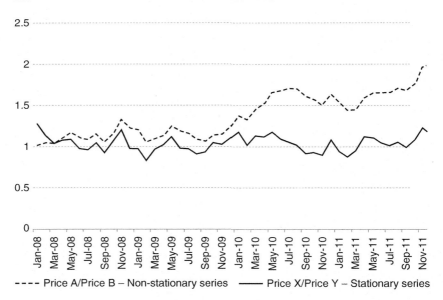

Figure 2.13   Examples of non-stationary and stationary price series

Stationarity analysis examines whether the ratio of two products' or regions' prices remain approximately constant over time. The rationale for stationarity analysis as a tool for market definition is based on the same principle as price correlation analysis. As explained in Section 3.6, where products lie in the same relevant market, their prices should not diverge significantly over time due to the possibility of demand- and/or supply-side substitution between those products.

The logic is that if there is effective competition between two products or regions then increases in the price of one will be matched by increases in the price of the other, and vice versa, such that the ratio of their prices will not change over time. Conversely, if one product or region is able to sustain an increase in price relative to the other, leading to an abiding change in their relative price ratio, then this could suggest that the two lie in separate relevant markets.

The concept of stationarity is illustrated in Figure 2.13, which shows an example of a non-stationary price ratio for two products, A and B, and an example of a stationary price ratio for two products, X and Y.

The dashed line shows that the ratio of the price of product A to the price of product B increases from around 1 at the start of 2008 to around 2 by the end of 2011. This implies that, whereas product A sold at around the same price as product B in the beginning of 2008, the price of product A by the end of 2011 was around twice that of product B. This may be due to an increase in the price of product A over this period, a reduction in the price of product B, or a combination of the two. Irrespective of the cause, the observed decline in the price ratio indicates that substitution between the two products has not been sufficient to bid up the price of product B once it started to fall or to prevent the price of product A from rising. This would create a presumption that the two products lie in separate relevant markets.

By contrast, the solid line shows that, while there are short-term fluctuations in the relative price of products X and Y, the ratio of their prices is consistently centred on a value of one. As such, the ratio of the price of product X to the price of product Y is said to be 'stationary'.[168] This indicates that the price of product X did not diverge from that of product Y on a non-transitory basis (and vice versa) over the period in question. This implies that there is sufficient competitive interaction between the two products to conclude that they lie within the same relevant market.

The European Commission has advocated this form of analysis as an alternative to price correlation analysis on the grounds that it addresses the two central problems of price correlation, namely the possible impact of common costs, which may give rise to the identification of spurious correlation, and the lack of a well-defined benchmark, which makes the identification of relevant markets on the basis of correlation coefficients alone a somewhat arbitrary exercise.[169] With regard to the former, the argument is that the effect on prices of changes in common costs will cancel out when the ratio of prices is considered, obviating the need to use net prices in order to strip out common cost items.

Regarding the latter issue, the presence of stationarity can be formally investigated using statistical hypothesis testing techniques, thus avoiding the need for arbitrary or ad hoc benchmarks. A commonly used statistical methodology for assessing stationarity is the **Dickey–Fuller** test, which uses the fact that the value of a non-stationary series will reflect its own previous values to test whether a particular set of data exhibits stationarity.[170] The Dickey–Fuller test, and other tests for stationarity,

---

[168] Note that the ratio of prices need not be centred on a value of one to be stationary; a price ratio centred on any value over time would be stationary and therefore consistent with two products or regions lying in the same relevant market.

[169] See, for instance, Case COMP/M.4513 – *Arjowiggins/M-real Zanders Reflex*, Commission decision of 4 June 2008, para. 51.

[170] Other stationarity tests include the Phillips–Perron test and the KPSS test.

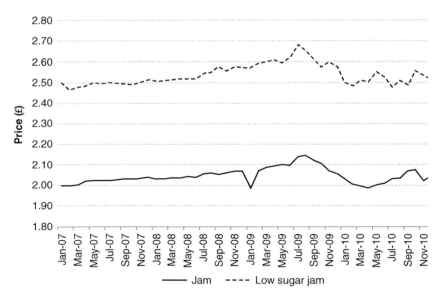

**Figure 2.14**  Wholesale UK jam and low sugar jam prices, £/jar

can be readily undertaken within statistical and econometric software packages such as Stata or E-Views.

### 3.7.2   An example

In this example we use stationarity analysis to investigate whether jam and low sugar jam sold in the UK lie in the same relevant market. Figure 2.14 shows monthly average wholesale prices of jam and low sugar jam sold by a particular producer between 2007 and 2010.

It can be seen that, while there is a significant absolute price difference between the two price series, both products follow a similar pattern, rising steadily until August 2009, and then declining to early 2010 after which both price series become relatively stable. The correlation coefficient between the two series is 0.81. This provides evidence that the two products may lie in the same relevant market, although since the price of both is significantly affected by common costs, represented by the price of fruit, there is likely an element of spurious correlation within this figure.

In order to address this potential issue, Figure 2.15 plots the ratio of the two products' prices. This figure shows that the price of jam has typically stood at around 80% of the price of low sugar jam, although it has exhibited a significant degree of fluctuation around this figure.

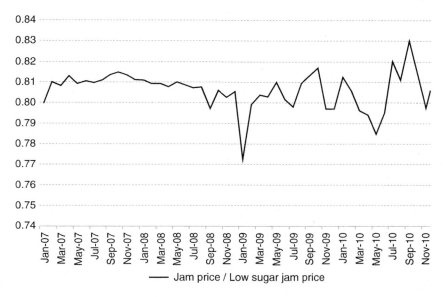

**Figure 2.15**    Relative wholesale UK prices for jam and low sugar jam

The existence of a relatively stable relationship between the two products' prices suggests that the prices of each are constrained by the possibility of substitution. This visual impression is confirmed by the application of the abovementioned Dickey–Fuller test, which rejects the hypothesis of non-stationarity at the 99% confidence level.[171]

### 3.7.3    Use in EU merger control

The Commission has undertaken stationarity analyses in two recent merger investigations: *Arjowiggins/M-real Zanders Reflex*[172] in 2008 and *Arsenal/DSP*[173] in 2009.

In both of these cases, stationarity analyses were used in conjunction with correlation analyses to investigate the definition of the relevant geographic market. The Commission explained the rationale for the use

---

[171] Note that statistical testing does not allow a hypothesis to be confirmed, only the converse hypothesis to be rejected with a given degree of confidence.

[172] Case COMP/M.4513 – *Arjowiggins/M-real Zanders Reflex*, Commission decision of 4 June 2008.

[173] Case COMP/M.5153 – *Arsenal/DSP*, Commission decision of 9 January 2009.

of stationarity analysis as a complement to correlation analysis in the following terms:[174]

> the Commission also undertook a stationarity analysis of relative prices (between different country pairs) to further strengthen its geographic market tests, as (i) there is no clear benchmark against which to assess the correlations and (ii) the relative prices reduce the role of common elements to a minimum.

In *Arjowiggins/M-real Zanders Reflex*, the Commission used the price for carbonless paper sold in reels and sheets in Germany, France, Italy, Poland, Spain and the United Kingdom to assess the parties' claim that the relevant geographic market was EEA-wide. The Commission's analysis found that 'there are significant trends in the relative prices, and there is thus no support for markets that are wider than national'.[175]

Similarly, in *Arsenal/DSP*,[176] the Commission's stationarity analysis found that the prices of benzoic acid in the EEA, Asia and North America had been diverging over time. This led the Commission to conclude that the relevant geographic markets were narrower than global.[177]

A stationarity analysis was also submitted by the parties in the *Ineos/Kerling*[178] case, in order to dispel the notion that the relevant geographic market was limited to the UK. The Commission accepted this analysis acknowledging:[179]

> relative net prices between the United Kingdom and other countries are stationary for most of the analysed countries. Accordingly, it appears that the prices in the United Kingdom move together with the prices in the rest of the EEA countries, which is indicative of a market which is wider than the United Kingdom.

More recently, however, the Commission has taken a more sceptical view of stationarity analyses submitted by the parties in *Votorantim/Fischer*[180a] and *Olympic/Aegean Airlines*.[180b] In *Votorantim/Fischer* the Commission stated that evidence of price correlation and stationarity

---

[174] Case COMP/M.4513 – *Arjowiggins/M-real Zanders Reflex*, Commission decision of 4 June 2008, para. 69.

[175] Ibid., para. 70.

[176] Case COMP/M.5153 – *Arsenal/DSP*, Commission decision of 9 January 2009.

[177] Ibid., para. 81.

[178] Case COMP/M.4734 – *Ineos/Kerling*, Commission decision of 30 January 2008.

[179] Ibid., para. 151.

[180a] Case COMP/M.5907 – *Votorantim/Fischer/JV*, Commission decision of 4 May 2011.

[180b] Case COMP/M.5830 – *Olympic/Aegean Airlines*, Commission decision of 26 January 2011.

'could be consistent with both products competing closely, but does not establish such a conclusion', going on to state that 'such evidence is not meant to be assessed in isolation, but together with the other evidentiary material gathered during the market investigation'.[180]

In *Olympic/Aegean Airlines* the parties submitted evidence that there was a stationary relationship between Aegean's prices for business and fully flexible fares, suggesting that time-sensitive and non-time-sensitive passengers lay within the same relevant market.[181] The Commission, however, rejected this evidence, on two principal grounds. First, and somewhat contrary to its position in *Ineos/Kerling*, the Commission disputed whether price stationarity was dispositive of competitive interaction, stating that:[182]

> Evidence concerning co-movements in fares, either tested via stationarity tests on the relative fare, or by other econometric means, is not a suitable instrument to prove the inclusion of one or more products into the same market, but rather to disprove the assumption that they belong to separate markets. In other terms, the stationarity in relative fare is a necessary, not a sufficient condition, for the inclusion of the products in the same market.

Second, the Commission noted that spurious stationarity may arise where the underlying price series considered are themselves stationary.[183] That is, if the prices of product A and product B are stationary, then the ratio of their prices will also be stationary, even in the absence of competitive interactions. This logic suggests that stationarity analysis can provide useful evidence for market definition only when at least one of the underlying price series can be shown to be non-stationary.

Having rejected the parties' stationarity evidence on the above grounds, the Commission provided the following general comment on the role of stationarity analysis within market definition, stating that:[184]

> Even if the conclusion of the stationarity Study were to be considered correct, [this] would not constitute sufficient evidence to conclude about

---

[180] *Votorantim/Fischer*, paras. 92 and 93. The Commission also noted that the parties' finding of stationarity was not robust to changes in the time period considered, and that prices over a longer period than that employed by the parties were not stationary. See para. 95.

[181] Case COMP/M.5830 – *Olympic/Aegean Airlines*, Commission decision of 26 January 2011, Annex I, paras. 43 et seq.

[182] Ibid., Annex I, para. 52.    [183] Ibid., Annex I, para. 60.

[184] Ibid., Annex I, para. 68.

the existence of a single market ... In order to reach such a conclusion, additional evidence pointing in the same direction would be necessary. This evidence could come from various sources, and be either of quantitative or qualitative nature. In the absence of such corroborative evidence, the sheer detection of stationarity in the relative fare could not provide meaningful insight into the question concerning the boundaries of the relevant market.

Taken together, the Commission's comments in *Votorantim/Fischer and Olympic/Aegean Airlines* suggest that it is unlikely to accept stationarity analyses as evidence on questions of market definition without further corroboration, and that it may be disinclined to accept stationarity as a basis for including, rather than excluding, alternatives from relevant markets.

### 3.8    Shock analysis

#### 3.8.1    Description of technique

Sections 3.6 and 3.7 discussed the use of price co-movements to infer competitive constraints between firms and products. The price correlation and stationarity approaches rely on observing the effect of changes in one firm's price on the pricing decision of other firms, but the price correlation and stationarity approaches are agnostic as to the source of those initial price movements.

Shock analysis represents a related form of evidence on market definition that focuses explicitly on specific events, or 'shocks', that affect firms' pricing and supply behaviour. Where such events impair the ability of one or more firms to supply a good or service, this may have an analogous effect to an attempt by a firm or group of firms to impose a price increase or equivalent worsening of supply terms. Market shocks may therefore inform the assessment of how customers and firms might respond to a SSNIP.

Intuitively, such analyses can only be employed in cases where suitable shocks have arisen. The three most common forms of shock are the entry of new suppliers or products, plant shutdowns that affect one firm's ability to supply, and changes in exchange rates or import duties that have an asymmetric effect on pricing for firms located in different regions. The logic by which such shocks may be used to investigate hypotheses regarding relevant market definition is set out below.

Regarding the first form of shock, where a new product is introduced, or a new firm commences operation, its presence would be expected to have a negative impact on the business of existing firms whose products compete in the same relevant market. The goal of an **entry analysis** is to use this shock to identify evidence of that impact by comparing the performance of incumbent firms before and after the entry event. If such an impact is identified, then this constitutes evidence that the new entrant/product lies within the same relevant market as the incumbents. If no such impact is found, this would suggest that the incumbent firms are not materially constrained by the new entrant/product, and therefore that this new entrant is unlikely to lie in the same relevant market. This logic applies equally to questions of both product and geographic market definition.

Specifically, the impact caused by entry can be investigated by examining prices and sales volumes of the incumbent firms before and after entry. Ideally, both of these variables should be examined, as incumbent firms may react to increased competition within their relevant market by reducing price in order to mitigate volume losses.[185]

The **analysis of supply outages**, for instance due to equipment failure or industrial disputes, is based on similar logic. If a particular production facility exerts a competitive constraint on a group of firms, and therefore lies within the same relevant market, then the removal of that facility's supply will reduce the competitive constraint on those firms. This should lead to an identifiable positive impact on other firms competing in the same market as the subject of the shutdown. Analysis of supply outages therefore allows the identification of the set of firms and products for which the firm suffering the outage is a constraint.[186]

Again, this logic applies to questions of both product and geographic market definition. Thus, if the closure of a widgets plant allows suppliers of gadgets to raise price, this indicates that gadgets are competitively constrained by widgets and, therefore, that widgets lie in the same relevant product market as gadgets. Equally, if widget manufacturers in the UK are observed to benefit from an outage in French widget production through an ability to increase price profitably, this would suggest

---

[185] Note that incumbents' pre- and post-entry volumes should be measured in absolute, rather than as a share of supply over a candidate set of goods. Any increase in demand for the candidate set of goods following the entry of the new firm/product will necessarily dilute the incumbents' share of supply, even in the absence of any direct substitution between them.

[186] Note that planned maintenance shutdowns are likely to have less of an impact on supply conditions than unplanned shutdowns, as suppliers and customers are more likely to have made provisions against their effect via stock building. In practice therefore, shock analysis, where feasible, must be reviewed carefully against the industry facts and circumstances in each case.

that French widget suppliers constrain, and therefore lie in the same relevant geographic market as, UK producers.

A former Chief Economist at DG COMP commented favourably on the use of this technique, explaining that:[187]

> Because negative supply shocks lead to a restriction in output, they can provide useful information about the strength of the competitive reactions of producers located in other regions … Such natural experiments can be a suitable empirical methodology to shed light on the source of existing competitive constraints that are likely to impede the exercise of market power … Unexpected outages, though short-lived, may provide some indication about the source of the competitive constraint faced by producers located in the EEA.

The positive impact of supply outages on other firms and products may manifest itself through either an increase in price for the remaining firms in the relevant market, an increase in those firms' volumes or, most likely, both.

Two potential limitations of the supply outage shock methodology should be borne in mind when applying the technique. First, plant shutdowns do not correspond to the 5%–10% SSNIP that forms the basis for the hypothetical monopolist test. Where the lost volumes represent a significant proportion of the relevant market, their withdrawal may lead to a price uplift of more than 5–10%. This in turn may lead to demand- and supply-side substitution that would not take place in response to the 5–10% SSNIP that is considered for market definition purposes. In order to avoid defining erroneously broad markets, an examination of volume changes resulting from a supply outage should be combined with an assessment of prices to ensure that the supply outage has not led to a situation outside the realms of the SSNIP test.

The second potential limitation of the supply outage shock methodology is that firms' observed response to a short-term temporary supply outage may be different to their likely response to a non-transitory price increase, such as the one required by the hypothetical monopolist test. Where rivals would need to make significant investments if they were to respond to an output withdrawal (e.g. in product repositioning, production expansion or expanding their geographic sales networks), a short-term shock may not be sufficient to justify such responses even

---

[187] L. Roeller and O. Stehmann, 'The Year 2005 at DG Competition: The trend towards a more effects-based approach' (2006) 29 *Review of Industrial Organization* 281–304.

if they would be rational following a more permanent price increase. As such, care should be taken when interpreting the consequences of short-term shocks in order to avoid the identification of erroneously narrow markets by failing to capture potential medium- and long-term effects.[188]

While the preceding forms of shock analysis have considered changes in the structure of supply, a third form of shock analysis uses **changes in exchange rates** that introduce exogenous changes (that is, changes that are not due to decisions of participants in a candidate market) in the relative prices of products in a candidate market. Where suitable exchange rate movements are observed, those movements can produce a situation analogous to the hypothetical monopolist SSNIP test. In particular, where one country's currency appreciates against another's, this reduces the cost to customers in the former of importing from producers in the latter. This is equivalent, from the perspective of those customers, to an increase in the price of domestic producers. The response of firms and customers to that increase will therefore provide an indication of what response could be expected in the case of a hypothetical domestic monopolist attempting to exercise market power. If the domestic producers that have suffered an effective worsening of their competitiveness due to the exchange rate movement are observed to reduce their price, then this would suggest that they compete with, and so lie in the same geographic market as, these other suppliers. Alternatively, if domestic producers are able to maintain their price and volume levels notwithstanding the effective reduction of the price of imports, this would suggest that international suppliers do not exert a sufficiently strong competitive constraint to justify their inclusion in the same relevant market.

This line of investigation is related to the price correlation technique outlined in Section 3.6 above. The exchange rate movement provides changes in the effective relative prices of goods produced in different regions, which, if those regions lie in the same relevant market, will be offset by price changes to maintain co-movement between the two. An application of this form of analysis is provided in the example set out in the following section.

A potentially important point to control for in undertaking such analyses is the possible effect of the exchange rate movement in question

---

[188] Intuitively, this problem will not arise in the case of entry analysis, which is concerned with permanent, rather than temporary, changes in market structure.

on input costs. If domestic producers, whose prices have been made relatively less competitive as a result of a currency appreciation, rely on imported inputs to manufacture their products then that currency appreciation will also serve to reduce the cost of those inputs. This will tend to produce an incentive for the domestic producers to cut their price even in the absence of any increased pressure caused by the availability of relatively more competitive imported finished goods. Failure to take this issue into account may lead to an erroneous impression that prices have been cut in response to increased import competition and, as a result, to an overly broad definition of the relevant geographic market.

Consequently, where imported inputs are present, the cost of those inputs should be removed from the price of finished goods before examining the impact of exchange rate movements, in the same manner that common costs should be stripped from final prices in the context of price correlation analysis.

### 3.8.2   An example

In order to demonstrate the application of the shock analysis technique, consider a hypothetical merger between two plywood producers with manufacturing facilities in Hungary. Further assume that (i) the proposed merger would result in a monopoly in this country if the relevant geographic market were considered to be national; (ii) there is a large number of plywood producers in neighbouring member states, such that the transaction would bring about a *de minimis* increase in concentration if the relevant market were found to be broader than national; and (iii) no meaningful imports of plywood into Hungary from these countries are currently observed.

In this example we will use two forms of shock analysis to investigate whether Hungary constitutes a relevant geographic market for the supply of plywood and, in particular, whether the possibility of plywood imports into Hungary is sufficient to impose a competitive constraint on the domestic producers that will persist following the proposed merger.

First, consider the consequences of a temporary plant shutdown. Assume that one of the parties, Forestry International, suffered a fire that forced it to shut down its Hungarian production plant during the second half of 2009. Assume that this plant normally produced 4 million tonnes of plywood per annum, representing 40% of Hungarian plywood production. If the relevant geographic market were national, then this reduction in supply within that market would be expected to have led to

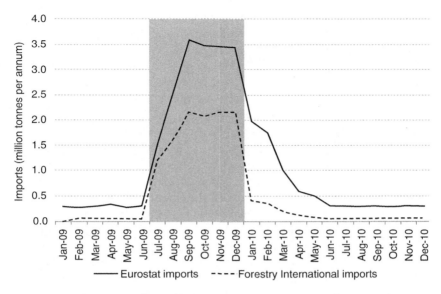

**Figure 2.16**   Hungarian plywood imports, January 2009 – December 2010

an increase in the price in that market; that is, there should be an identifiable increase in the other merging party's price during the period of the shutdown. Conversely, if the relevant market were broader than national, then the production shutdown should be observed to bring about an increase in imports as Hungarian plywood customers responded to the local supply shortage by switching to producers located outside Hungary.

Figure 2.16 shows the evolution of plywood imports into Hungary during the period 2009–2010 according to two different sources. The first is public data from Eurostat, while the second set of data is supplied by Forestry International, the plywood producer whose Hungarian plant was the subject of the shutdown, and concerns shipments that it made into Hungary from its other plants in Europe.

The public data show that imports into Hungary at the time of the fire suffered by Forestry International's Hungarian plant peaked at a little above 3.5 million tonnes per annum in September 2009, a figure representing around seven-eighths of the output lost due to the fire. This indicates that there is some considerable flexibility in plywood import volumes into Hungary, even in the very short term. While unable fully to offset the large reduction in domestic production resulting from the plant shutdown, imports replaced the majority of those volumes, suggesting that there would be scope for imports to frustrate an attempt by a monopolist of Hungarian plywood production to impose a SSNIP.[189]

Before drawing a firm conclusion on market definition, however, it is important to recognise that market responses to a temporary production shutdown may differ from the response that would be seen in the event of a SSNIP. Both firms and customers may have engaged in behaviour during the extreme circumstances of a sudden 40% reduction in domestic production that would not necessarily occur following a 5–10% increase in Hungarian prices. One way in which firms' responses may not have reflected those that would have occurred in the event of a SSNIP on Hungarian plywood is the identity of the importers.

Specifically, Figure 2.16 showed that a significant proportion of the increase in plywood imports into Hungary in 2009, around 2 million of the 3.5 million tonnes annualised increase, was attributable to Forestry International, the company whose plant suffered the shutdown. To the extent that these volumes demonstrate an ability for non-Hungarian producers in general to make imports into Hungary, they are relevant to the assessment of the scope for a hypothetical Hungarian plywood monopolist profitably to raise prices, notwithstanding the fact that Forestry International itself would clearly not make imports into Hungary to undermine a post-merger price increase. However, Forestry International's willingness to increase shipments into Hungary may simply be a result of its position as the firm that suffered the fire, in which case the observed imports might not reflect the likely behaviour that independent firms outside Hungary would choose to adopt. For instance, Forestry International may have been contractually obliged to serve its Hungarian customers, necessitating uneconomic imports that independent firms would not make; or it may have opted to make uneconomic imports in order to maintain customer goodwill prior to the Hungarian plant recommencing production. The circumstances surrounding these imports should therefore be carefully investigated.

Importantly, the observed increase in imports may not have been sufficient to prevent price increases from occurring in Hungary as a result of the shock. It is therefore useful to check the impact of a supply shutdown not only on volumes, but also on prices. Figure 2.17 shows the price charged by the remaining Hungarian producer over the period of

---

[189] A review of the countries from which these imports are being made would provide an indication of the precise extent of the relevant geographic market.

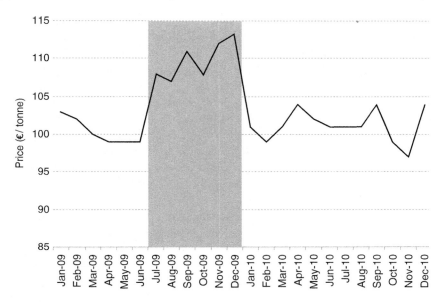

**Figure 2.17**    Hungarian plywood prices

Forestry International's plant shutdown. This will reflect the prevailing price in Hungary taking account of the constraining effect of the imports precipitated by the shutdown.

The data show that, during the period of the Hungarian plywood production shutdown, prices rose by around 10%, averaging €110 per tonne throughout the second half of 2009 and around €100 per tonne before and after. This suggests that the supply response that arose was not sufficient to prevent a SSNIP in Hungarian prices. While this does not necessarily imply that such a SSNIP would be profitable for a hypothetical monopolist of Hungarian plywood, the fact that the observed supply response was not sufficient to prevent prices from rising by almost 10% may suggest that the supply response to a SSNIP would be insufficient to render that SSNIP unprofitable.[190]

---

[190] These data could, however, be combined with margin data to establish a critical loss volume for a 10% SSNIP, which could then be compared to the 40% Hungarian output restriction that the above data indicate is required to sustain a 10% SSNIP. Using the breakeven critical loss formula set out at Section 3.1 above, it can be shown that a 15% margin would lead to a critical volume reduction of 40% for a SSNIP of 10%. Thus, if plywood margins were below 15% then a hypothetical Hungarian monopolist would be prepared to withdraw 40% of its output in order to achieve a 10% price increase.

The second shock analysis exploits the fact that Hungary is not a member of the Euro currency area, and employs changes in the Hungarian Forint:Euro exchange rate to examine the impact of exogenous changes in the price of imported plywood produced in the Eurozone on the conduct of the domestic producers.

Changes in the Forint:Euro exchange rate will replicate the effect of changes in the relative prices of plywood produced in Hungary and plywood produced by suppliers in the Eurozone. Responses to such changes in relative prices are likely to reflect the responses of firms and consumers to a geographically localised change in prices better than the more unusual circumstances of a supply shortfall such as that discussed above.

In particular, if Hungary represents a separate geographic market for the supply of plywood, we would expect to see changes in the Forint: Euro exchange rate to have no effect on locally denominated prices, as there will have been no change in the competitive conditions within Hungary. If, on the other hand, the scope for imports represents an important competitive constraint on Hungarian plywood prices, Hungarian prices would respond to exchange rate movements in order to remain competitive as regards import prices. Thus if Forint-denominated prices in Hungary are observed to increase (decrease) whenever the Forint depreciates (appreciates) relative to the Euro, then this would point to a definition of the relevant geographic market wider than Hungary.

In order to test this hypothesis, Figure 2.18 plots the monthly average sale price of plywood in Hungary, denominated in both Forints and Euros, against the Forint:Euro exchange rate.

The chart shows that there was a significant increase and subsequent decrease in the Forint:Euro exchange rate in the middle of 2006, which represents an ideal economic shock with which to examine the competitive relationship between Hungarian plywood manufacturers and manufacturers in neighbouring member states. The chart shows that the change in Forint:Euro in 2006 was around 10%, which fits within the magnitude of the price increase envisaged in the SSNIP test.

The chart also shows that the Forint denominated price of plywood sold in Hungary closely tracks the Forint:Euro exchange rate, while the Euro denominated local price remains broadly constant over time.

The implication of this pattern can be demonstrated by reference to the temporary peak in the Forint:Euro exchange rate in mid-2006. Between March and August, the number of Forints to the Euro rose by

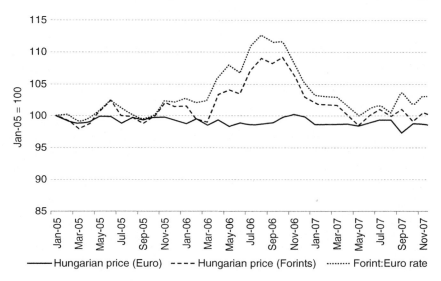

**Figure 2.18**    Hungarian plywood prices and Forint:Euro exchange rate

10%, from around 251 to 277. For Hungarian customers the price of plywood imported from Eurozone manufacturers therefore rose by a similar proportion, all else constant. This increase in the cost of imports led to an increase in the general level of Hungarian plywood prices denominated in local currency, as local producers responded to the profitable opportunity to increase price presented by a slackening of the competitive constraint provided by imports.

From the August 2006 peak, the Forint:Euro exchange rate decreased once more, the value of the Forint returning to its early 2006 level by the first quarter of 2007. This decline in value was once more closely tracked by the local price of plywood. As imports became cheaper, this effectively increased the locally denominated price of plywood produced in Hungary, relative to the price of imports. Rather than being able to maintain this high price, suppliers in Hungary reduced their prices, in recognition of the increased likelihood of domestic customers switching to foreign producers. Had imports not represented a substitute to locally produced plywood, such a price decrease would not have been necessary, and the Forint denominated price would have remained constant.

The second shock analysis thus provides strong evidence that Hungary lies within a broader geographic market for plywood, in which customers can credibly threaten to switch their demand to manufacturers located elsewhere within the Eurozone. A similar pattern is exhibited throughout the period covered by the sales data, with movements in the Forint:Euro exchange rate bringing about commensurate changes in local Hungarian plywood prices, rather than allowing the Hungarian price in Euros to diverge from that of foreign competitors.

### 3.8.3    Use in EU merger control

Although shock analyses of this sort may be somewhat anecdotal in their focus on a particular incident and mix of qualitative and quantitative assessment of the consequences, they can nonetheless represent a rich source of evidence on market definition. The European Commission has undertaken shock analyses for the purpose of market definition in a number of Phase II cases since 2004. We have classified these by the type of shock examined.

**3.8.3.1    Entry**    In *Lufthansa/SN Airholding*,[191] the Commission focused on VLM's entry on the Antwerp–Manchester route in 2006 to test the parties' claim that the airports of Brussels ('BRU') and Antwerp ('ANR') belonged to the same relevant geographic market. Specifically, it estimated the impact of VLM's entry on the Antwerp–Manchester ('MAN') route on the prices charged by SN for the route Brussels–Manchester as well as any volume impact brought about by the shock. The Commission ultimately concluded that VLM's entry had no noticeable impact on either SN's prices or volumes on the Brussels–Manchester route:[192]

> VLM's entry had no effect on either SN's flexible economy class fares or SN's non-flexible economy class fares ... In terms of passenger numbers, the number of SN's non-flexible economy class passengers was very similar in 2006 and 2007, ... although VLM transported more than ... passengers in 2007 ... Thus, it seems that VLM's entry on the ANR–MAN route has not created a significant constraint on SN's BRU–MAN service.

Likewise, the Commission argued that the entry or expansion of Eurostar train services had an impact on competitive conditions on airline routes from Brussels but not those from Antwerp, again suggesting that the Brussels and Antwerp airports did not belong to the same market. In this respect, the decision reads:[193]

---

[191]  Case COMP/M.5335 – *Lufthansa/SN Airholding*, Commission decision of 22 June 2009.
[192]  Ibid., para. 100.
[193]  Case COMP/M.5335 – *Lufthansa/SN Airholding*, Commission decision of 22 June 2009, para. 102.

While it is indeed correct that the higher impact of Eurostar on BRU–LCY fares does not rule out substitutability between ANR and BRU, it is indeed the case that this higher impact implies that both ANR and BRU are subject to different competitive conditions, which is not consistent with BRU and ANR being in the same market when interpreted along with the other evidence that is presented in the decision.

**3.8.3.2 Supply outages** In *Inco/Falconbridge*,[194] the Commission noted that plant strikes resulting in reduced supply of high purity cobalt only had an impact on the prices of these products, while the prices of lower grades were unaffected:[195]

> There is a difference in LMB prices of 99.3% cobalt and 99.8% cobalt. It is striking to note that the differential between high and low-grade cobalt widened as a result of the announcement of a strike at Inco's Sudbury operations and production difficulties on the part of two other producers in 2003. The risk of a new strike in June 2006 at Inco's Sudbury operations is also driving up prices of high purity cobalt ... This illustrates that there is a specific demand and market for high purity cobalt, which is affected strongly by events affecting the output of the suppliers of the cobalt with the highest purity cobalt such as Inco.

The Commission concluded that the available evidence pointed to a lack of substitutability between these products and, therefore, that the supply of high purity cobalt constituted a separate relevant product market.

The effects of plant outages may also provide insights into geographic market definition.[196] The Commission described the usefulness of this type of analysis in the *Ineos/Kerling* case:[197]

> Outages can offer competitors opportunities to increase sales and obtain higher margins on the additional sales, assuming they have the ability to expand output or otherwise reallocate sales to affected customers. An analysis of the evolution of volumes, prices and margins over this period can therefore provide additional evidence on the scope of the geographic market and in particular whether the geographic market is limited to the United Kingdom or rather wider than the United Kingdom.

In this case, an unexpected partial shutdown at Ineos' plant in Barry, South Wales, in June 2004 resulted in a substantial decrease of

---

[194] Case COMP/M.4000 – *Inco/Falconbridge*, Commission decision of 4 July 2006.
[195] Ibid., para. 193.
[196] Case COMP/M.4734 – *Ineos/Kerling*, Commission decision of 30 January 2008.
[197] Ibid., para. 142.

production for a period of five months. This provided a natural experiment for assessing whether Ineos and Kerling together enjoyed a monopoly over a relevant geographic market that comprised the UK. The Commission's analysis found that the volumes lost by Ineos were not 'completely captured by Kerling, as customers looking for alternative sources of supply turned to imports'.[198]

Equally, although Kerling absorbed some of the volumes that Ineos could not supply, it was not able to increase its margins to take advantage of the reduction in UK production. This provided good evidence that important competitive constraints lay outside the UK, and so that the relevant market for S-PVC was broader than national.

The *Blackstone/Acetex*[199] case, concerning the production of acetyls and plastics, turned on the question of geographic market definition, with the parties claiming that the relevant market was worldwide. The parties undertook a shock analysis for VAM, a commodity chemical derived from acetic acid, although an absence of suitable shock events prevented similar analyses being conducted for other products relevant to the transaction. The parties sought to demonstrate that the relevant market was global by showing that unexpected supply outages in Asia had an impact on prices in Western Europe. However, the Commission regarded this evidence as inconclusive for the purpose of assessing whether suppliers in Western Europe were constrained by Asian producers, pointing out that supply shortages in Europe were not found to have an impact on Asian prices.[200]

The Commission went on to examine the effect of supply shocks on VAM trade volumes. Its analysis found that supply outages in Western Europe had an identifiable impact on imports from North America, although the available data were insufficient to draw conclusions on imports from Asia.[201] This led the Commission to conclude that the relevant geographic market for Western Europe included, at minimum, North America.[202]

In *Votorantim/Fischer/JV*,[203] the Commission asked customers how they reacted following a substantial price increase of orange juice caused by hurricanes in 2004/2005 in Florida, finding that most did not switch to other juices.[204] While the magnitude of switching to other juices was

[198] Ibid., para. 145.
[199] Case COMP/M.3625 – *Blackstone/Acetex*, Commission decision of 13 July 2005.
[200] Ibid., paras. 36 and 37.     [201] Ibid., para. 40.     [202] Ibid., para. 41.
[203] Case COMP/M.5907 – *Votorantim/Fischer/JV*, Commission decision of 4 May 2011.
[204] Ibid., para. 79.

not considered in detail, this evidence was used in support of the Commission's conclusion that there existed a separate relevant product market for orange juice.

**3.8.3.3   Exchange rate fluctuations**   As explained above, changes in exchange rates effectively represent changes in the cost of imported goods. Exchange rate movements thus provide natural experiments whereby the effect of changes in the relative prices of products produced in different countries and regions can be observed, shedding light on the definition of the relevant geographic market.

The Commission undertook such an analysis in the *Arsenal/DSP*[205] case, where it found that:[206]

> under the assumption that the US and EEA markets are integrated, it would be expected that the US producers would be increasing their exports to the EEA, as the USD/EUR exchange rate decreased by more than 30% from 2001 to 2007. The US exports to the EEA, however, decreased by more than [30–40]% during that period and by over [50–60]% during the last nine years. It thus appears that the US producers do not pose a competitive constraint on the EEA producers of benzoic acid even under very favourable market conditions.

A similar analysis was undertaken in the *Ineos/Kerling*[207] case, where the parties demonstrated that a sharp Sterling depreciation did not have any long-run effect on prices of PVC in Continental Europe relative to the United Kingdom. Whilst the Commission did not accept such evidence as conclusive, not even in combination with the supportive results from price correlation and stationarity tests, it did ultimately acknowledge that the relevant market was at least North Western Europe, after considering the impact of the exchange rate shock on imports into the UK.[208]

---

[205] Case COMP/M.5153 – *Arsenal/DSP*, Commission decision of 9 January 2009.
[206] Ibid., para. 45.
[207] Case COMP/M.4734 – *Ineos/Kerling*, Commission decision of 30 January 2008.
[208] Ibid., para. 152.

# 3

# Horizontal mergers I: unilateral effects

## 1. Introduction

This chapter discusses the economics of unilateral effects concerns in horizontal mergers. A merger is said to give rise to unilateral effects where the elimination of the competitive constraint between the merging parties enables the merged entity to increase prices above their pre-merger levels. The reason why each party's price is likely to increase is that sales which would have previously been lost to rivals as a result of a price increase are partially recaptured in higher sales of the product sold by the other merging firm. The greater the propensity of customers to switch between the parties' products, the greater will be the relaxation in the pre-merger competitive constraints and the greater will be these unilateral effects. Since the incentive of the merged entity to raise price resulting from the elimination of that competitive constraint would arise even in the absence of any price increase by remaining competitors, such competition concerns are known as unilateral effects (or non-coordinated effects).

In many ways, the economic concept of unilateral effects is analogous to the legal concept of single firm dominance, since both concepts concern post-merger price increases based on the reduction in the competitive constraints on the merged entity. The traditional analysis of single firm dominance involves the definition of the relevant market and an assessment of post-merger market shares. This traditional approach implicitly assumes that the strength of the competitive constraints provided by each firm is proportional to its market share: the larger is one party's market share, the greater is the share of lost sales resulting from a price increase by the other party that it is expected to capture. Therefore, the greater the likelihood that the merged entity would be able to engage in unilateral price increases.

Importantly, whilst this assumption may be reasonable when firms' products are homogeneous, many mergers take place in markets where goods or services are differentiated. Where firms sell differentiated products, products are not perfect substitutes for one another. Importantly, in industries with differentiated products, the competitive constraints provided by different firms will vary and some firms will be 'closer' competitors to others. This variation in the 'closeness' of competition raises a number of complications for defining the relevant market and makes market shares less meaningful. For this reason, some observers have argued that the definition of the relevant market is no longer necessary or indeed appropriate in the assessment of unilateral effects in differentiated product markets.

This chapter is organised as follows.

Section 2 sets out some key economic concepts that are relevant for unilateral effects analysis and provides a brief summary of the main theoretical models of unilateral effects from the industrial economics literature. Economic theory, reflected in the EC Horizontal Merger Guidelines,[1] suggests that unilateral effects may arise if the merger would eliminate an important competitive constraint that the parties previously exerted upon one another. This is a necessary condition for a finding of unilateral effects. Important competitive constraints are considered to be more likely to exist in cases where the merging firms have large market shares, where there is a high degree of substitutability between the merging parties' products, or where one of the parties represents an 'important competitive force'.

Section 3 describes a number of empirical techniques which have been developed to test for the existence of important competitive constraints between merging parties, and applied in cases under the Merger Regulation. For each technique, we describe the data that are typically required. This is then followed by an illustrative example showing how the technique is applied in practice and by a summary of the more important EC merger cases in which that technique was relied upon by the Commission. We also present a number of case studies, which provide a detailed discussion of merger cases in which a particular technique played a key role in the competitive assessment.

Section 4 sets out some additional issues that may be relevant to the assessment of unilateral effects concerns. We first explain that, although

---

[1] Commission Guidelines on the assessment of horizontal mergers under the Council Regulation on the control of concentrations between undertakings (the 'EC Horizontal Merger Guidelines'), OJ C031/5, 5 February 2004.

unilateral effects concerns typically occur when merging parties are actual competitors, concerns may also arise due to the elimination of potential competition, that is, when the threat of entry by one party into a market served by the other party exerts an important influence on competition in that market. We then describe a further concern that may arise particularly in the presence of relatively homogeneous products. When market conditions are such that rivals are unlikely to increase their supply substantially in the event of a price increase, this may limit the constraint facing the merging firms and increase any incentive to reduce output and, thereby, raise prices. In this section, we also analyse the role that switching costs may play in the competitive assessment of mergers. Finally, we describe the conditions under which partial equity stakes amongst competing firms can dilute firms' incentives to compete with each other even if the stakes in question do not grant any form of control.

Section 5 sets out a number of countervailing factors that may materially reduce the risk of significant post-merger price increases, even where the merging parties are found to exert an important constraint on each other pre-merger. This includes the ability of large buyers to take steps to counteract the market power of the merged entity, the scope for entry, rivals' ability to reposition their products, and efficiency gains. While these more dynamic and strategic features of competition are typically not captured in the standard (static) economic models of competition, they can, as acknowledged in the EC Horizontal Merger Guidelines, have potentially significant effects on market outcomes. Finally, the section briefly sets out the conditions under which an otherwise problematic merger may ultimately not be considered to give rise to anti-competitive effects due to the fact that one of the parties is a failing firm.

## 2.    Important competitive constraints: economic theory and the EC Horizontal Merger Guidelines

### 2.1    Economic theory and key concepts

#### 2.1.1    Economic models and market concentration

There are two types of basic theoretical models which provide the cornerstones of the modern economic theory of oligopoly.[2] These are

---

[2] The defining feature of an oligopolistic market is that a small number of firms account for the majority of sales and that the suppliers recognise both their ability to affect market conditions and their strategic interdependence.

the Cournot model (1838) and the Bertrand model (1883). In the former, firms are assumed to choose the quantity of output to produce, with a single market price emerging at the level that equates market supply (i.e. the total output level chosen by firms) with market demand. In the Bertrand model, firms are assumed to choose their price. Each firm's output is then determined by the demand for its product, given its price and the prices chosen by its rivals. Both models assume that each firm chooses a quantity/price level that maximises its profit given the quantity/price level chosen by each other firm.[3]

Although the Cournot and Bertrand models are very simplistic and are consequently unlikely to provide a realistic representation of most industries, they can be used to illustrate the importance of market shares and closeness of competition for the assessment of unilateral effects concerns.

**2.1.1.1 Cournot model** A key feature of Cournot competition is that the market price, which is determined by overall market output, decreases steadily towards the marginal cost as the number of competing firms increases. This relationship is illustrated in the example in Figure 3.1, which assumes that all firms produce at a constant marginal cost equal to €2, resulting in identical individual market shares.[4]

This chart illustrates the impact of increases in market concentration (that is, reductions in the number of firms) on competitive performance. Interestingly, the price effect resulting from a change in the number of firms is very limited when the market is relatively unconcentrated but becomes very significant in the presence of a small number of firms that each has a high market share. In particular, as shown in Figure 3.1, a reduction in the number of firms from 10 to 9 in our example results in a price increase of €0.07 or 2.6% (from €2.73 to €2.80), whilst a merger that reduces the number of firms from 3 to 2 gives rise to a more significant price increase of €0.67 or 16.8% (from €4.00 to €4.67).

This feature of the Cournot model provides theoretical support to the principle that *mergers between firms with large market shares are*

---

[3] A situation in which each firm is doing the best it can given the decisions of every other firm is referred to as a Nash Equilibrium.

[4] In the example we further assume that firms produce a homogeneous product and face a linear demand function given by $p = a - Q$, where $p$ is the price and $Q$ is the total output of all firms in the market. In such circumstances it can be shown that the equilibrium Cournot price is given by $(a + nc)/(n + 1)$, where $n$ is the number of firms and $c$ is the marginal cost. In this example, the market demand curve is assumed to be $p = 10 - Q$.

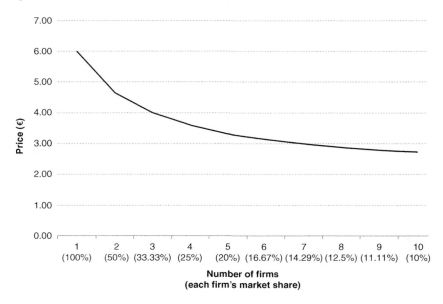

**Figure 3.1**   Cournot relationship between price and number of firms

*significantly more likely to give rise to unilateral effects than mergers between firms with low market shares.*

Another interesting feature of the Cournot model is that its predicted prices exhibit a direct relationship with the **Herfindahl–Hirschman Index**, HHI. The HHI is a measure of market concentration, defined as the sum of the squared market shares of all firms in the industry. The HHI summarises the distribution of market shares in a single measure and thereby provides a description of the degree of concentration of a market. The HHI increases as the number of firms falls and/or as the degree of market share asymmetry between firms rises. The HHI has a minimum value of zero and a maximum value of 10,000 in the extreme case of one firm with the entire market, as illustrated in Table 3.1.[5]

The relationship between the Cournot market price and the HHI can be expressed as follows:[6]

---

[5] Moreover, the HHI is higher when firms' market shares are asymmetrically distributed. For example, if there are two firms, one with a 90% share and the other with a 10% share, the HHI is 8,200, which is significantly larger than the HHI of 5,000 that is obtained if each of the two firms has a 50% share.

[6] See K. Cowling and M. Waterson, 'Price–cost Margins and Market Structure' (1976) 43 *Economica* 267–74.

Table 3.1 *Relationship between number of firms and HHI*

| Number of firms | Market share of each firm | HHI |
|---|---|---|
| 5 | 20% | $20^2 + 20^2 + 20^2 + 20^2 + 20^2 = 2{,}000$ |
| 4 | 25% | $25^2 + 25^2 + 25^2 + 25^2 = 2{,}500$ |
| 2 | 50% | $50^2 + 50^2 = 5{,}000$ |
| 1 | 100% | $100^2 = 10{,}000$ |

$$\frac{p - c}{p} = \frac{\text{HHI}}{\varepsilon}$$

where $p$ is the Cournot price, $c$ denotes firms' marginal cost and $\varepsilon$ is the market elasticity of demand.

The above relationship indicates that higher values of the HHI will be associated with higher prices and margins, and vice versa. It follows that increases in concentration, as reflected in the HHI, will give rise to higher prices. However, given that the assumptions of the Cournot model are highly stylised and therefore unlikely to reflect firms' strategic behaviour in any real life industry, the actual relationship between HHIs and market outcomes may in practice be weak.

**2.1.1.2 Bertrand model** Bertrand competition has been shown to result in lower prices and larger quantities than Cournot competition.[7] Indeed, if we assume that firms produce a homogeneous product at a common constant marginal cost, Bertrand competition will lead to a price equal to the marginal cost for any number of competitors greater than one. On this basis, all levels of market concentration short of pure monopoly will produce equally competitive outcomes.

If, however, we adopt the more realistic assumption that firms produce differentiated products then Bertrand prices will, like the Cournot price, decrease gradually as the number of firms increases.

This is illustrated in Figure 3.2, which shows the relationship between the Bertrand price equilibrium and the number of firms for different degrees of substitutability between firms' products. The degree of substitutability is expressed by parameter $d$ which varies between 0 (implying

---

[7] See, for example, X. Vives, 'On the Efficiency of Bertrand and Cournot Equilibria with Product Differentiation' (1985) 36 *Journal of Economic Theory*, 166–75; and N. Singh and X. Vives, 'Price and Quantity Competition in a Differentiated Duopoly' (1984) 15 *Rand Journal of Economics* 546–54.

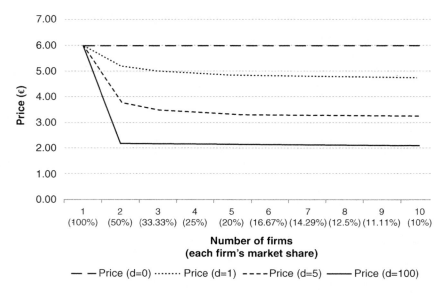

**Figure 3.2**   Bertrand relationship between price and number of symmetric firms for different degrees of substitutability between firms' products

that each firm is a monopolist supplier of its own product) and infinity (implying that firms' products are perfectly substitutable).[8] The marginal cost of production in this example is set at €2.

The chart shows that the higher the degree of substitutability between firms' products, the faster the equilibrium price will converge to the marginal cost level as the industry becomes less concentrated. In particular, if the parameter $d$ is sufficiently high, the Bertrand price falls from the monopoly level, equal to €6, to close to the marginal cost, equal to €2, as the number of firms increases from one to two, with further increases in the number of firms having a negligible impact on prices.

Importantly, the above analysis assumes that firms' products are all equally substitutable (i.e. that the degree of substitutability expressed by the parameter $d$ is identical for all products). In the presence of asymmetries in the degree of substitutability between each firm's products,

---

[8] In the example we further assume that firms face a linear demand function as in R. E. Levitan and M. Shubik, *Market Structure and Behaviour* (Cambridge, Mass.: Harvard University Press, 1980). For a more detailed discussion of the equilibrium properties arising in this setting, see M. Motta, *Competition Policy: Theory and Practice* (Cambridge University Press, 2004).

however, it can be demonstrated that a reduction in the number of firms brought about by a merger will have quite a different price impact depending on the identity of the merging firms. In particular, a merger that brings together two products that are very close substitutes will give rise to a much more significant price increase than a merger between two firms whose products are highly differentiated.

This feature of the Bertrand model provides theoretical support for the principle that *mergers between firms supplying close substitutes are significantly more likely to give rise to unilateral effects than mergers between distant competitors*. This important issue is discussed in more detail below.

### 2.1.2 Closeness of competition and diversion ratios

In any horizontal merger analysis, the object is to assess the extent to which the change in structure brought about by the merger affects the incentives of the firms involved to raise price. In a merger between Firms A and B, the potential impact on pricing incentives can be illustrated by a simplified model of the pre- and post-merger consequences of an increase in the price of a hypothetical Firm A:

- Pre-merger, Firm A is constrained from raising price by a variety of factors, most notably the likelihood that if it raises price customers will react by switching their demand to substitute products supplied by Firms B, C, D, etc.
- Post-merger, however, *to the extent that consumers who switch away from Firm A choose Firm B as their alternative*, Firm A is no longer so concerned about the consequences of a rise in its price. As a result of the merger, any customer demand that 'switches' to product B continues to fall to the post-merger firm and so no longer represents a part of the competitive constraint acting on the firm.[9]

This simple example demonstrates that the degree of demand diversion between the merging parties' products is central to an assessment of the competitive impact of a horizontal merger.

In many cases the starting point for horizontal merger assessment is a review of the merging firms' market shares. This approach can be understood in the context of the above description of how a merger may change firms' pricing incentives via demand diversion. If Firm B

---

[9] The post-merger firm continues, however, to be constrained by the customer's ability and inclination to switch to competing products supplied by firms C, D, etc.

accounts for a high share of the total market, then it may be reasonable to assume that the threat to switch to B provided a large part of the pre-merger constraint on Firm A's pricing (and vice versa). On this basis, one might be concerned about the impact of a merger between firms with high market shares on competition.

The above logic is based on the assumption that, if a high proportion of customers have chosen to purchase from Firm B, then a similarly high proportion of any customers lost by Firm A could be expected to choose to switch to Firm B. This may be a valid assumption where products are homogenous. In reality, however, most firms' products are differentiated to a greater or lesser extent. Where products are differentiated, customers cannot be assumed to switch between firms and products in proportion to their market shares. Consequently, in differentiated product markets the scope for a lessening of competition resulting from a horizontal merger cannot necessarily be inferred from the size of the merging firms, but must be assessed via direct observation of demand diversion patterns.

Economists typically investigate differentiated product mergers by calculating 'diversion ratios' between the merging parties.[10] A diversion ratio measures the proportion of customers lost by one firm following a unilateral price rise that would switch to another firm. Thus, the diversion ratio between Firms A and B would be defined as the proportion of those customers switching away from product A that would switch to product B as opposed to products C, D, etc. The diversion ratio between two merging parties reflects the proportion of the pre-merger competitive constraint facing each firm that derives from the presence of the other and will therefore be removed by the merger. The greater the diversion ratio between merging parties, the greater is the degree of competition between the parties, and therefore the greater the risk that the merger will bring about a lessening of competition. If two-thirds of the consumers who would switch away from product A would buy product B instead, the likelihood of a loss of competition from the merger of A and B would be much greater than if those who switched from product A would choose predominantly products C, D, etc.

---

[10] For a description of diversion ratios and their application to unilateral effects analysis of mergers, see C. Shapiro, former Deputy Assistant Attorney General at the US Department of Justice, 'Mergers with Differentiated Products', *Antitrust*, Spring 1996. See also RBB Brief 19, 'Lost in Translation: The use and abuse of diversion ratios in unilateral effects analysis', June 2006 and C. Walters, *Diversion Ahead! Approximating diversion ratios for retail chain mergers* (Competition Commission, Occasional Papers, November 2007).

**Figure 3.3**    Illustration of geographic differentiation: petrol stations on a motorway

### 2.1.3    An example

As an illustration of the role that diversion ratios can play in merger assessment, consider the following hypothetical example involving four independently owned petrol stations, denoted A, B, C and D, which are all located on a motorway. Assume that the distance between each petrol station is the same, as shown in Figure 3.3, and that Firms A, B and C each have a 20% market share while D's share is significantly higher at 40%.

Suppose that A is contemplating the acquisition of one of its competitors, and in particular of petrol station B or D. If the assessment is limited exclusively to an inspection of pre- and post-merger market shares, the first acquisition would seem significantly less problematic as it would lead to a combined market share of 40% as opposed to the merger between A and D, which would leave the new entity with a share of 60%.

However, drivers considering the purchase of petrol at station A are unlikely to consider petrol station B and D as equally substitutable. For example, a person contemplating a stop at petrol station A is unlikely to be willing to take the risk of running out of petrol by driving all the way to petrol station D in the event of an increase in the price charged by A.

To test this hypothesis, Firm A conducts a survey asking its customers how they would react to a hypothetical 5% price increase implemented permanently by Firm A assuming that the price at the other stations remained unchanged. Assume that the survey results indicate that 10% of customers would switch away from Firm A and that their volumes would be diverted to the other stations as follows: 60% to station B, 30% to station C and 10% to station D. Table 3.2 shows the volume distributions across the four petrol stations before and after the price increase as implied by the results of the survey.

The table shows that following the price increase, the volume of petrol sold by Firm A would decrease by 10% (from 1,000 to 900 litres). Firm B would experience an increase in its throughput of 60 litres, and as such it would be the beneficiary of the majority of the volumes diverted away from Firm A. Petrol station C would gain 30 litres while petrol station D would increase its sales by a modest 10 litres.

Table 3.2 *Volume diversions following Firm A's hypothetical price increase*

| Petrol station | Sales pre-price increase (litres per day) | Sales post-price increase (litres per day) | Actual sales gain |
|---|---|---|---|
| A | 1,000 | 900 | −100 |
| B | 1,000 | 1,060 | +60 |
| C | 1,000 | 1,030 | +30 |
| D | 2,000 | 2,010 | +10 |

It is clear from the above that the conclusion drawn from a simple review of market shares, namely that a merger between A and D would be more problematic than a merger between A and B, was incorrect. In particular, despite the lower combined market shares, the acquisition of petrol station B would be significantly more likely to allow Firm A to raise prices post-merger, given the high proportion of diverted sales that the merged entity would be able to retain. On the contrary, the acquisition of D would be unlikely to give rise to unilateral effects since it would not cause the removal of a particularly important competitive constraint.

This example serves to illustrate the principle that market shares can provide a misleading guide as to the potential competitive effects of horizontal mergers. Where products are differentiated it is important to seek evidence on the demand diversion between products in order properly to assess the degree of pre-merger competition between the parties, and therefore the likely impact of the merger.

## 2.2    Important competitive constraints in the EC Horizontal Merger Guidelines

The EC Horizontal Merger Guidelines, which set out the analytical framework that the Commission applies when assessing horizontal mergers, explain that a merger may give rise to unilateral effects if it eliminates an important competitive constraint that the parties previously exerted upon each other.[11] Consistent with the economic principles set out above, important competitive constraints are considered to be more likely to exist if:

[11] EC Horizontal Merger Guidelines, paras. 24–5.

- the merging firms have large market shares; or
- the parties' products are particularly close substitutes.

In addition, the EC Horizontal Merger Guidelines state that unilateral effects may arise if one of the parties represents an 'important competitive force'. In what follows, we discuss each of these conditions in turn.

### 2.2.1 Merging firms have large market shares

The link between market shares and the scope for unilateral price increases is set out in the EC Horizontal Merger Guidelines, which point out that the 'larger the increase in the sales base on which to enjoy higher margins after a price increase, the more likely it is that the merging firms will find such a price increase profitable despite the accompanying reduction in output'.[12] This logic derives from the central trade-off between margin and volume that underpins firms' pricing decisions (see Chapter 1). Any given price increase will be associated with a particular loss of sales. The benefit of that price increase will be enjoyed across the remainder of the firm's volumes.

Consequently, the cost to a firm of implementing a given price increase (in terms of profits that would have been earned on forgone output) do not vary with the firm's size, but the benefit of the price increase (higher margins on remaining output) will be greater for a firm with a larger sales base, all else being constant. Therefore, all else being equal, the incentive to raise price will be stronger in the case of an acquisition of a rival that greatly increases the sales base of a particular firm.

Accordingly, the EC Horizontal Merger Guidelines set out a number of market share thresholds that provide general guidance for the assessment of unilateral effects. First, the EC Horizontal Merger Guidelines establish a 'safe harbour' for smaller firms, by acknowledging that unilateral effects are unlikely to occur when combined market shares are below 25%.[13]

Second, the EC Horizontal Merger Guidelines equally state that unilateral effect concerns are particularly likely to arise if combined market shares exceed 50%. Indeed, the EC Horizontal Merger Guidelines state

---

[12] EC Horizontal Merger Guidelines, para. 27.
[13] It is worth noting that the Form CO requires parties to provide market data for affected markets where the combined market shares exceed 15%. In practice, however, the Commission typically demands more detailed information for markets where the merging firms have higher shares than 25%, typically in excess of 35% or 40%.

that '[a]ccording to well-established case law, very large market shares – 50% or more – may in themselves be evidence of the existence of a dominant market position'.[14]

These thresholds do not constitute rigid or binding rules for merger assessment, however. In particular, the EC Horizontal Merger Guidelines explicitly note that unilateral effects may arise in the case of mergers resulting in combined market shares of between 40% and 50%, and in some cases even below 40%.[15]

The EC Horizontal Merger Guidelines also define various non-binding presumptions based on the HHI. In particular:

> The Commission is unlikely to identify horizontal competition concerns in a market with a post-merger HHI below 1000. Such markets normally do not require extensive analysis;[16]
>
> The Commission is also unlikely to identify horizontal competition concerns in a merger with a post-merger HHI between 1000 and 2000 and a delta below 250, or a merger with a post-merger HHI above 2000 and a delta below 150.[17]

It is worth noting that these thresholds are extremely low, such that they tend to be of little practical relevance. An HHI of 1,000 implies a degree of concentration equivalent to a market with ten equally sized post-merger firms. Given that markets are typically more concentrated than this, few mergers can benefit from the general exception from extensive analysis provided in the EC Horizontal Merger Guidelines.

For example, any proposed merger taking place within a symmetric eight-firm market will result in a post-merger HHI in excess of 1,500 and to an increase of more than 300 HHI points, leaving the transaction outside the Guidelines' HHI safe harbour.

Given the exceptionally conservative level at which the thresholds have been set, it is unsurprising that, since the adoption of the EC Horizontal Merger Guidelines, HHI calculations have not played any meaningful role in the Commission's merger enforcement.

### 2.2.2    Merging firms are close competitors

As explained above, unilateral effects result from the elimination of important competitive constraints between the merging parties that determine their pre-merger behaviour. Such competitive constraints

---

[14] EC Horizontal Merger Guidelines, para. 17.    [15] Ibid., para. 17.
[16] Ibid., para. 19.    [17] Ibid., para. 20.

derive from the extent to which each party regards the other as a likely alternative for its existing customers.

As set out above, the likelihood of unilateral effects can in some cases be inferred from market shares. If Firms A and B both account for a high share of the total market, then it may be reasonable to assume that the threat of existing customers of Firm A to switch to B provides a significant pre-merger constraint on Firm A's pricing, and that therefore one might be concerned about the impact of a merger between Firms A and B on competition.

However, where products are differentiated, market shares may over- or under-estimate the competitive constraint between two firms. The consequences of a merger for competition will then depend on the closeness of competition between the products supplied by the merging parties. Firms are more likely to be each other's closest competitors if they are relatively more similar in their various product or geographic attributes to one another than to other products in the relevant market.

Thus, a merger between two car manufacturers of luxury models, e.g. Mercedes and BMW, is more likely to give rise to unilateral effects than a merger between a manufacturer of luxury models and one of small family cars. Similarly, as illustrated in the hypothetical example set out above, a merger bringing together two petrol station operators is more likely to give rise to unilateral effects if the parties' networks are geographically proximate than if they tend to cover different regions.

The importance of assessing the degree of substitutability between the merging parties' products is explicitly acknowledged in the EC Horizontal Merger Guidelines, which note[18] that:

> The higher the degree of substitutability between the merging firms' products, the more likely it is that the merging firms will raise prices significantly. For example, a merger between two producers offering products which a substantial number of customers regard as their first and second choices could generate a significant price increase. Thus, the fact that rivalry between the parties has been an important source of competition on the market may be a central factor in the analysis.

Crucially, showing closeness of competition is just one of a number of necessary conditions for concluding that a merger will result in unilateral effects that significantly reduce competition. Equally important is showing that remaining rivals do not provide an effective competitive

---

[18] At para. 28.

constraint (i.e. that they are *not* close substitutes to the merging parties[19]), and that those rivals would be unable to reposition their offerings in response to the hypothetical price increase so as to become close substitutes in the future.[20] In addition, it is highly unlikely that competition would be significantly impeded if only a small number of customers consider the two merging parties' products as the closest substitutes.

### 2.2.3   Merger eliminates an 'important competitive force'

The EC Horizontal Merger Guidelines also indicate that a merger may give rise to unilateral effects through the elimination of an 'important competitive force', such that the merger will 'change the competitive dynamics in a significant, anti-competitive way'.[21] By contradistinction to the elements of the EC Horizontal Merger Guidelines discussed above, this element seeks to capture competition concerns that may arise where one of the merging firms has a greater influence on the competitive process than its market share or closeness of competition with the other party would suggest. As examples of such situations the EC Horizontal Merger Guidelines suggest recent entrants that are expected to exert a significantly increased competitive constraint in the future, or firms with promising pipeline products in markets where innovation is an important aspect of competition.[22]

The EC Horizontal Merger Guidelines' reference to important competitive forces has, on occasion, been used to argue for intervention against mergers involving so-called 'maverick' firms pursuing a particularly aggressive pricing policy.[23] To the extent that a firm acts as a 'maverick', however, this should be reflected in an assessment of the closeness of competition between it and the other merging party. Any claim that a firm is an important competitive force over and above that suggested by an analysis of market shares and/or diversion ratios must therefore be carefully substantiated. Specifically, the fact that a company

---

[19] It is worth noting that in principle a merger may have negative effects on competition even if it does not remove the closest competitive constraint. Although the Commission has made it clear both in its Guidelines and its case law that the removal of a particularly close constraint may be sufficient, in practice it typically refrains from intervening where at least one rival supplier poses a closer constraint on each merging party than the parties exert on each other.

[20] This issue is discussed in further detail in Section 5 below.

[21] EC Horizontal Merger Guidelines, para. 37.     [22] Ibid., para. 38.

[23] See Section 2.3 below for details of such cases.

has adopted a different business model from the other suppliers or that it charges much lower prices does not automatically make it a 'maverick' firm.

Indeed, if one merging firm is following a different pricing policy to its rivals (for instance, a low price/low quality business model), this may suggest a degree of differentiation between it and other firms that would imply an absence of important competitive constraints between it and other suppliers. This can usefully be illustrated using an analogy from the new car market. In this market, Tata and Mercedes operate in the low-end and the high-end respectively without exerting a strong competitive constraint on each other. As such, it would not be appropriate to take evidence of low prices for Tata cars as evidence that Tata is an 'important competitive force' imposing a strong constraint on Mercedes.

Following the text of the EC Horizontal Merger Guidelines, it appears that the role of the important competitive force concept is to capture changes in competitive conditions over time. Use of the principle should therefore be restricted to cases in which there are reasonable grounds to expect that current competitive conditions will not reflect likely future circumstances. In general, there will be relatively few cases in which one of the merging parties can be anticipated to exert a greater constraint on the other in the future than currently is the case.

In short, whatever the nature of a firm's behaviour, it is always necessary to determine whether that firm exerts an important competitive constraint on the other merging party (or would be expected to do so in the absence of the merger). If it is not possible to demonstrate this on the basis of a coherent set of evidence, a unilateral effects finding cannot be sustained.

### 2.3   Commission's recent enforcement practice

During the period 2004–2011, the Commission investigated unilateral effects concerns in fifty-one Phase II merger cases. Of these,

- nineteen mergers were cleared unconditionally;[24]

---

[24] (1) Case COMP/M.4781 – *Norddeutsche Affinnerie/Cumerio*, Commission decision of 23 January 2008; (2) Case COMP/M.4647 – *AEE/Lentjes*, Commission decision of 5 December 2007; (3) Case COMP/M.4215 – *Glatfelter/Crompton Assets*, Commission decision of 20 December 2006; (4) Case COMP/M.4094 – *Ineos/BP Dormagen*, Commission decision of 10 August 2006; (5) Case COMP/M.3975 – *Cargill/Degussa Food Ingredients*, Commission decision of 29 March 2006; (6) Case COMP/M.6101 – *UPM/*

- twenty-nine mergers were cleared subject to undertakings;[25] and

---

*Myllykoski and Rhein Papier*, Commission decision of 13 July 2011; (7) Case COMP/ M.6106 – *Caterpillar/MWM*, Commission decision of 19 October 2011; (8) Case COMP/ M.6214 – *Seagate/HDD Business of Samsung*, Commission decision of 19 October 2011; (9) Case COMP/M.5907 – *Votorantim/Fischer/JV*, Commission decision of 4 May 2011; (10) Case COMP/M.5529 – *Oracle/Sun Microsystems*, Commission decision of 21 January 2010; (11) Case COMP/M.4956 – *STX/Aker Yards*, Commission decision of 5 May 2008; (12) Case COMP/M.4747 – *IBM/Telelogic*, Commission decision of 5 March 2008; (13) Case COMP/M.4734 – *Ineos/ Kerling*, Commission decision of 30 January 2008; (14) Case COMP/M.4662 – *Syniverse/BSG*, Commission decision of 4 December 2007; (15) Case COMP/M.4523 – *Travelport/Worldspan*, Commission decision of 21 August 2007; (16) Case COMP/M.3848 – *Sea-Invest/EMO-EKOM*, Commission decision of 18 August 2006; (17) Case COMP/M.3178 – *Bertelsmann/Springer/JV*, Commission decision of 3 May 2005; (18) Case COMP/M.5141 – *KLM/Martinair*, Commission decision of 17 December 2008; (19) Case COMP/M.3625 – *Blackstone/Acetex*, Commission decision of 13 July 2005.

[25] (1) Case COMP/M.5440 – *Lufthansa/Austrian Airlines*, Commission decision of 28 August 2009; (2) Case COMP/M.5335 – *Lufthansa/SN Airholding*, Commission decision of 22 June 2009; (3) Case COMP/M.5153 – *Arsenal/DSP*, Commission decision of 9 January 2009; (4) Case COMP/M.4513 – *Arjowiggins/M-real Zanders Reflex*, Commission decision of 4 June 2008; (5) Case COMP/M.5658 – *Unilever/Sara Lee Body Care*, Commission decision of 17 November 2010; (6) Case COMP/M.4187 – *Metso/Aker Kvaerner*, Commission decision of 12 December 2006; (7) Case COMP/M.4000 – *Inco/ Falconbridge*, Commission decision of 4 July 2006; (8) Case COMP/M.3653 – *Siemens/ VATech*, Commission decision of 13 July 2005; (9) Case COMP/M.5153 – *Arsenal/DSP*, Commission decision of 9 January 2009; (10) Case COMP/M.4525 – *Kronospan/ Constantia*, Commission decision of 19 September 2007; (11) Case COMP/M.3436 – *Continental/Phoenix*, Commission decision of 26 October 2004; (12) Case COMP/ M.4919 – *StatoilHydro/ConocoPhillips*, Commission decision of 21 October 2008; (13) Case COMP/M.3916 – *T-Mobile Austria/Tele.ring*, Commission decision of 26 April 2006; (14) Case COMP/M.5675 – *Syngenta/Monsanto's Sunflower Seed Business*, Commission decision of 17 November 2010; (15) Case COMP/M.4381 – *JCI/VB/FIAMM*, Commission decision of 10 May 2007; (16) Case COMP/M.4980 – *ABF/GBI Business*, Commission decision of 23 September 2008; (17) Case COMP/M.4504 – *SFR/Télé 2 France*, Commission decision of 18 July 2007; (18) Case COMP/M.4726 – *Thomson Corporation/Reuters Group*, Commission decision of 19 February 2008; (19) Case COMP/M.4381 – *JCI/VB/FIAMM*, Commission decision of 10 May 2007; (20) Case COMP/M.3868 – *DONG/Elsam/Energi E2*, Commission decision of 14 March 2006; (21) Case COMP/M.3687 – *Johnson&Johnson/Guidant*, Commission decision of 25 August 2005; (22) Case COMP/M.3696 – *E.ON/MOL*, Commission decision of 21 December 2005; (23) Case COMP/M.3796 – *Omya/Huber PCC*, Commission decision of 19 July 2006; (24) Case COMP/M.4404 – *Universal/BMG Music Publishing*, Commission decision of 22 May 2007; (25) Case COMP/M.3431 – *Sonoco/Ahlstrom*, Commission decision of 6 October 2004; (26) Case COMP/M.2978 – *Lagardère/Natexis/VUP*, Commission decision of 7 January 2004; (27) Case COMP/M.4180 – *Gaz de France/Suez*, Commission decision of 14 November 2006; (28) Case COMP/M.3216 – *Oracle/Peoplesoft*, Commission decision of 26 October 2004; (29) Case COMP/M.3099 – *Areva/ Urenco/ETC JV*, Commission decision of 6 October 2004.

- three mergers, *Ryanair/Aer Lingus*,[26] *EDP/ENI/GDP*[27] and *Olympic/ Aegean Airlines*,[28] were prohibited. More recently, the Commission also prohibited *Deutsche Börse/NYSE Euronext*[29] in February 2012.

Significantly, only in two Phase II cases (*T-Mobile Austria/Tele.ring*[30] and *JCI/VB/FIAMM*[31]) did the parties hold combined market shares below a level that might indicate single firm dominance; meanwhile, several of the cases cleared unconditionally featured post-merger market shares well above 50%. Table 3.3 summarises the Commission's rationale for clearance in a number of these cases. This table shows that evidence on lack of closeness of competition between the parties and the extent of spare capacity held by rivals are frequently cited as factors assuaging unilateral effects concerns in the presence of high market shares.

In many of the cases that were cleared subject to undertakings, the Commission concluded that the parties' products were particularly close substitutes. Table 3.4 provides details on a number of such cases.

Furthermore, in a number of cases, the Commission required undertakings as it considered that the proposed merger would give rise to unilateral effects as a result of the elimination of an important competitive force. Table 3.5 shows examples of cases in which the Commission considered that one of the merging parties was an important competitive force or 'maverick'.

Finally, two of the three cases that were ultimately prohibited between 2004 and 2011, namely *Ryanair/Aer Lingus*[32] and *Olympic/Aegean Airlines*,[33] involved the combination of airline companies which, according to the Commission, would have led to the creation of a monopoly or a dominant position on a number of routes, making unilateral effects highly likely. The other prohibited case, *ENI/EDP/GDP*,[34] involved the

---

[26] Case COMP/M.4439 – *Ryanair/Aer Lingus*, Commission decision of 27 June 2007 and Case COMP/M.5434 – *Ryanair/Aer Lingus II*, Commission decision of 23 January 2009.

[27] Case COMP/M.3440 – *ENI/EDP/GDP*, Commission decision of 9 December 2004.

[28] Case COMP/M.5830 – *Olympic/Aegean Airlines*, Commission decision of 26 January 2011.

[29] Case COMP/M.6166 – *Deutsche Börse/NYSE Euronext*, Commission decision of 1 February 2012.

[30] Case COMP/M.3916 – *T-Mobile Austria/Tele.ring*, Commission decision of 26 April 2006.

[31] Case COMP/M.4381 – *JCI/VB/FIAMM*, Commission decision of 10 May 2007.

[32] Case COMP/M.4439 – *Ryanair/Aer Lingus*, Commission decision of 27 June 2007.

[33] Case COMP/M.5830 – *Olympic/Aegean Airlines*, Commission decision of 26 January 2011.

[34] Case COMP/M.3440 – *ENI/EDP/GDP*, Commission decision of 9 December 2004.

Table 3.3 Cases cleared unconditionally despite shares indicative of dominance

| Cases | Combined market shares (increment) | Rivals' shares | Commission's conclusions |
|---|---|---|---|
| *Norddeutsche Affinerie/ Cumerio (chemicals)*[1] | 50–60% (15–20%) | One main rival with a 20–30% share, several smaller rivals with shares of 0–15% | The parties' combined share in the merchant market for copper shapes was 50–60%. The Commission accepted that the merged entity would be constrained by significant spare capacity held by rivals. The Commission also found some evidence that the parties would be constrained by the scope for customers to backward integrate into the production of copper shapes. |
| *Cargill/Degussa Food Ingredients (food)*[2] | 55–65% (0–10%) | One main rival with a 25–30% share | The parties held a combined share of 55–65% in the EEA market for non-GM deoiled lecithin and faced only one significant rival. Cargill, however, was a recent entrant, had a relatively low share of 0–10% and was found not to represent an important competitive constraint on Degussa. Furthermore, the Commission found that a number of global suppliers, who had invested in significant production capacity, were in the process of entering the EEA. |

| Case | Combined share | Rivals | Commission analysis |
|---|---|---|---|
| *UPM/Myllykoski and Rhein Papier (paper)*[3] | 50–60% (20–30%) | Two main rivals with shares of 20–30% and 10–20%, several smaller rivals with shares below 10% | Despite the parties' 50–60% combined market share, the Commission found that rivals would have both the ability and the incentive to raise output should the merged entity increase prices. In particular, the Commission noted the role of high fixed costs in giving suppliers an incentive to vigorously pursue sales. This was confirmed by an analysis using seasonal demand variations as a form of natural experiment, which found that prices were not higher in peak demand periods. |
| *Seagate/HDD Business of Samsung* (IT equipment)[4] | 40–50% (5–10%) | Two main rivals with shares of 20–30% | While the parties' combined shares on some hard-disk drive market segments were 40–50%, customer responses to the Commission's market investigation indicated that they were not close competitors. This was confirmed by bidding analyses, which suggested that customers did not obtain worse terms when three, rather than four, bidders were present. |
| *Votorantim/Fischer/JV* (beverages)[5] | 40–50% (10–20%) | Two main rivals with shares of 20–30% and 10–20% | The Commission held that orange juice was a largely homogeneous product and that all suppliers were equally close. The decisive question was thus whether |

Table 3.3 (*cont.*)

| Cases | Combined market shares (increment) | Rivals' shares | Commission's conclusions |
|---|---|---|---|
| | | | customers could switch to rivals and whether rivals had sufficient spare capacity. The Commission conducted a detailed switching and multi-sourcing analysis, which showed that most customers tended to divide their purchase requirement between at least three suppliers and that they often switched or shifted volumes between these suppliers. In addition the Commission found that rivals would readily be able to increase output in response to any unilateral price rise. |

[1] Case COMP/M.4781 – *Norddeutsche Affinerie/Cumerio*, Commission decision of 23 January 2008.
[2] Case COMP/M.3975 – *Cargill/Degussa Food Ingredients*, Commission discussion of 29 March 2006.
[3] Case COMP/M.6101 – *UPM/Myllykoski and Rhein Papier*, Commission decision of 13 July 2011.
[4] Case COMP/M.6214 – *Seagate/HDD Business of Samsung*, Commission decision of 19 October 2011.
[5] Case COMP/M. 5907 – *Votorantim/Fischer/JV*, Commission decision of 4 May 2011.

Table 3.4 *Cases cleared subject to undertakings in which the parties' products were considered particularly close substitutes*

| Cases | Combined market share (market share increment) | Rivals' shares | Short summary |
|---|---|---|---|
| *Unilever/Sara Lee* (consumer products)[1] | Higher than 50% | Several rivals with significant shares | The Commission concluded that separate national markets existed for male and non-male deodorants. The Commission identified concerns in a number of EEA countries. In several markets the parties were considered to be close, though not necessarily the closest rivals, based primarily on an analysis of customer switching. A merger simulation model supported a finding of unilateral effects with limited predicted average price increases (although significant price increases were estimated for individual brands). The Commission did not agree with the parties' argument that retailers (supermarkets) had sufficient countervailing power and did not find any evidence of significant potential entry. |
| *Kronospan/Constantia* (industrial materials)[2] | 60–80% (30–40%) | Less than 10% individually | The parties' combined market share for raw particle board was 60–80% in the affected region with an increment of 30–40%. The |

Table 3.4 (*cont.*)

| Cases | Combined market share (market share increment) | Rivals' shares | Short summary |
|---|---|---|---|
| | | | Commission concluded that customers in Austria, Hungary, Slovakia and Romania would have only limited possibilities to switch suppliers and that the main suppliers would not have significant spare capacity to increase their outputs. Expanding capacity was considered to require a considerable investment and a significant lead time. Although some capacity was expected to come on stream in the affected area within the next two years, the Commission held that this additional capacity would barely be sufficient to meet the increasing demand for raw particle board. |
| *Inco/Falconbridge* (metals)[3] | 70–100% (30–40%) | Less than 10% individually | There were several segments of nickel and cobalt applications in which the parties enjoyed combined shares well in excess of 70%. The Commission found that the parties were closest rivals based on *inter alia* a review of their internal documents and a shock analysis, which showed that Inco lost |

| | | | |
|---|---|---|---|
| | | | most sales to Falconbridge following a strike at one of its plants. The Commission also found evidence that the parties' much smaller rivals would have no ability to increase output substantially. |
| *Continental/Phoenix* (car components)[4] | 60–70% (15–20%) | Less than 10–15% individually | The merged entity would be by far the leading player for utility air spring systems in Europe with a combined share of 60–70% (Phoenix 15–20%) and no rival holding a share of more than 10–15%. The parties were deemed to be closest rivals on the basis of a ranking study conducted amongst customers and a bidding analysis. Although customers were large and sophisticated, they were held to have insufficient countervailing power to constrain the merged entity. |
| *Arjowiggins/M-real Zanders* (paper)[5] | 40–60% (10–20%) | Three significant rivals with the largest having a 20–30% share and several local niche players | The parties had a combined EEA-wide share of 40–60% for carbonless paper that could be further divided into sheets and reels (increment 10–20%). In addition, the EC found shares exceeding 50% in several countries. The Commission attached great value to the negative feedback received from many customers during the course of its market investigation. The Commission found no evidence that declining demand |

Table 3.4 (*cont.*)

| Cases | Combined market share (market share increment) | Rivals' shares | Short summary |
|---|---|---|---|
| | | | had not resulted in substantial spare capacity as suppliers had adapted capacity to changes in demand. Rivals therefore had no spare capacity to increase output and the merged entity would have an incentive to increase prices. |

[1] Case COMP/M.5658 – *Unilever/Sara Lee Body Care*, Commission decision of 17 November 2010.

[2] Case COMP/M.4525 – *Kronospan/Constantia*, Commission decision of 19 September 2007.

[3] Case COMP/M.4000 – *Inco/Falconbridge*, Commission decision of 4 July 2006.

[4] Case COMP/M.3436 – *Continental/Phoenix*, Commission decision of 26 October 2004.

[5] Case COMP/M.4513 – *Arjowiggins/M-real Zanders Reflex*, Commission decision of 4 June 2008.

Table 3.5 *Cases in which one of the parties was considered an important competitive force or maverick*

| Case | Combined market shares (increment) | Rivals' shares | Commission's conclusions |
|---|---|---|---|
| T-Mobile Austria/ Tele.ring[1] | 30–40% (10–20%) | According to the Commission the merger would result in close symmetry between the merged entity and the second largest player Mobilkom which had a slightly higher share than the merged entity, i.e. 35–45% | The Commission found that 'Tele. ring, as a maverick, has a much greater influence on the competitive process in this market than its market share would suggest'.[2] Its market share grew significantly during the years prior to the merger and it was considered to offer considerably lower prices in a highly concentrated market. |
| StatoilHydro/ ConocoPhillips[3] | 40–50% (10–20%) in Sweden 30–40% (0–5%) in Norway | In Sweden the merged entity's combined share was nearly twice that of its main rival whereas in Norway the combined share was lower than that of the main rival | JET Sweden acted as a 'pricing maverick' according to the Commission and therefore its market share did not reflect its competitive significance. The Commission conducted an extensive econometric analysis, which showed that JET Sweden's presence had the most significant impact on pricing. |

Table 3.5 (cont.)

| Case | Combined market shares (increment) | Rivals' shares | Commission's conclusions |
|---|---|---|---|
| *Oracle/Sun Microsystems*[4] | 45–55% (0–5%) | The merged entity faced two significant rivals (IBM and Microsoft), each with shares of c. 20% | The Commission held that Sun Microsystems, which offered an open source database (MySQL) with an estimated revenue share of only 0–5%, 'potentially exerts an important and growing competitive constraint on Oracle and other proprietary database vendors.'[5] The transaction was nonetheless cleared since Oracle made informal commitments that removed the need to reach a conclusion on the significance of this constraint. |
| *Syngenta/ Monsanto's Sunflower Seed Business*[6] | 40–50% (0–10%) | The market share increment was modest and there were several rivals that had much higher shares than Monsanto (between 10% and 30%) | The Commission concluded that, although Monsanto had a relatively low share of less than 10%, the proposed merger would have removed a considerable and innovative competitor to Syngenta, reinforcing the latter's market leader position. |

| JCI/VB/FIAMM[7] | 50–60% (2%) | In this case the market share increment was insignificant. The market was effectively a duopoly with the main rival holding the remaining market share (40–50%) | The Commission acknowledged that FIAMM only had a share of less than 2% for OE batteries for trucks/HCV and was not considered by customers as the closest competitor to JCI. The Commission nonetheless argued that FIAMM had, despite its financial difficulties, the ability to expand given its unused capacity. In contrast, the Commission found that whilst rivals had a similar ability to expand output, they were unlikely to have the incentive to do so. |

1 Case COMP/M.3916 – *T-Mobile Austria/Tele.ring*, Commission decision of 26 April 2006.
2 Paragraph 126.
3 Case COMP/M.4919 – *StatoilHydro/ConocoPhillips*, Commission decision of 21 October 2008.
4 Case COMP/M.5529 – *Oracle/Sun Microsystems*, Commission decision of 21 January 2010.
5 Paragraph 756.
6 Case COMP/M.5675 – *Syngenta/Monsanto's Sunflower Seed Business*, Commission decision of 17 November 2010.
7 Case COMP/M.4381 – *JCI/VB/FIAMM*, Commission decision of 10 May 2007.

proposed acquisition of Gás de Portugal (GDP), the incumbent gas company in Portugal, by both Energias de Portugal (EDP), the incumbent electricity company in that same country, and ENI, an Italian energy company. The Commission concluded that the merger would have strengthened EDP's dominant position in the Portuguese electricity wholesale and retail markets, and GDP's dominant position in the Portuguese gas markets, as a result of the elimination of potential competition.[35] This particular type of unilateral effects concern will be discussed in detail in Section 4.2 below.

In summary, the Commission's approach to unilateral effects concerns can thus be summarised as follows:

- The Commission will not normally require a substantive analysis where the merging parties' combined market share in each relevant market is not more than 25%.
- The Commission is unlikely to identify concerns where the merging parties' combined market share is between 25% and 40–50% (the dominance threshold), unless the merger is considered to eliminate a particularly close competitor or an important competitive force.
- The Commission is likely to identify concerns where the merging parties' combined market share exceeds the dominance threshold unless it can be shown that the parties are not particularly close competitors and that the merger would not eliminate an important competitive force.


### 3.  Important competitive constraints between the parties: empirical techniques

A number of empirical techniques have been developed to test for the existence of important competitive constraints between the merging parties. In this section, we discuss the following techniques, which have been relied on by the Commission in merger investigations in recent years:

---

[35] The proposed merger was blocked also on the basis of non-horizontal effects, namely input foreclosure in the wholesale electricity market and customer foreclosure in some gas markets. For a detailed summary of this case, see G. Conte, G. Loriot, F. X. Rouxel and W. Tretton, 'EDP/ENI/GDP: The Commission prohibits a merger between gas and electricity national incumbents' available on http://ec.europa.eu/competition/publications/cpn/2005_1_84.pdf.

- Survey evidence
- Customer switching analysis
- Price/concentration studies and analysis of the impact of rivals' presence
- Entry analysis
- Natural experiments
- Merger simulation
- Win/loss and bidding analysis.

The discussion of each technique is organised as follows. We first provide a brief description of the technique and of the data that are typically required to perform it. This is then followed by an illustrative example showing how the technique is applied in practice and by a summary of the more important merger cases in which the technique was relied on by the Commission. In this section, we also present a number of case studies, which provide a detailed discussion of merger cases where particular techniques played a key role in the competitive assessment.

### 3.1   Survey evidence

#### 3.1.1   Description of technique

The discussion at Section 2 has established that the scope for unilateral effects in horizontal mergers depends, to a significant effect, on customer substitution patterns. Since the issue of closeness of competition is all about customers' preferences for different products and how their purchasing patterns might change in the event of a relative price change, one obvious source of evidence on this is consumer survey evidence. Chapter 2 has already discussed, in the context of market definition, the potential problems associated with the use of customer surveys to collect information on the likely behaviour of market participants (e.g. sample selection, the weight that can be placed on responses to hypothetical questions, etc.). Nevertheless, the Commission relies heavily on survey information as a source of qualitative information on customer preferences. Moreover, surveys are also increasingly being used by competition authorities to estimate diversion ratios in order to provide a quantitative reflection of the extent to which the merging parties exert important competitive constraints on one other.

As noted in Section 3.3.1 in Chapter 2 on market definition, the content of a customer survey and the inferences that may be drawn from it will depend significantly on the nature of buyers in the market and in particular on whether buyers are firms (with extensive market knowledge) or end-consumers (who are likely to have invested significantly less time and effort to understand the characteristics and prices of the products and services in question). In the latter case, it is particularly important that surveys adhere to established principles of survey design, including ensuring that questions are easy to understand and free from any framing bias.

Customer surveys frequently play an important role in the Commission's merger assessment process and are used for a wide range of issues including the appraisal of unilateral effects. In markets characterised by business-to-business transactions, the Commission will often ask customers to give their opinion about the likely effects of the merger as part of the market investigation. Although it is not clear how much weight such qualitative evidence receives, the Commission has made it clear in past cases that any feedback should be analysed within the relevant context and should be evaluated against other evidence. For example, in *JCI/VB/FIAMM*,[36] the Commission stated that:

> As a general comment, the Commission notes that whereas subjective opinions of third parties on the general competitive situation are useful in many respects, these opinions in themselves are not sufficient to override the overall factual evidence gathered and systematically investigated in the course of the market investigation, which in turn forms the basis for the Commission's assessment. These opinions must take due account of the appropriate context, including for example the nature of the interest of the third party in question in the outcome of the proceedings, the extent of its knowledge and overview of the market situation and the degree of substantiation underpinning the opinion.[37]

Regardless of whether a case involves business-to-business or business-to-consumer transactions, the Commission may use customer surveys as a source of quantitative information on the degree of substitution between the merging firms and their competitors. The Commission will seek to collect a range of information with which to assess customer preferences. First, the Commission will typically ask customers to identify the range of credible alternative suppliers to the merging parties that they either have used in the past or would consider using. This will assist with defining the extent of the relevant market within which the parties' products are supplied.

---

[36] Case COMP/M.4381 – *JCI/VB/FIAMM*, Commission decision of 10 May 2007.

[37] Ibid., para. 428. In that case, the Commission dismissed the parties' argument that most customers had not indicated any concerns with respect to the effects of the proposed merger in the market for starter batteries whereas the Commission found unilateral effects. The Commission also noted that the parties had misinterpreted the replies.

Second, the Commission often asks customers to rank suppliers in terms of the technical features of their products and/or their pricing. However, care should be taken in drawing conclusions on the scope for unilateral effects on the basis of such evidence. Since a ranking analysis does not say anything about the distance between alternatives, it would be incorrect to claim that the merger would be likely to have anti-competitive effects solely on the basis that the two parties have ranked first and second in a customer survey. Indeed, as already explained, unilateral effects are likely to arise from a merger between close competitors only where consumers do not consider the products supplied by the remaining rivals to represent close substitutes for those of the merging parties.

Third, as shown in the hypothetical example below, the Commission may seek to calculate diversion ratios by collecting information on customers' stated responses to hypothetical price increases by one of the merging firms, or, in some cases, on customers' stated behaviour in the hypothetical scenario in which the product or service of one of the merging parties is unavailable.[38] By combining these responses with information on customers' purchase values, revenue weighted diversion ratios for the parties can be calculated. If the other party is the most significant destination for revenues lost by one or both of the merging parties then this would represent prima facie evidence that customers view the merging firms as particularly close rivals.

### 3.1.2   An example

Consider a hypothetical merger between two supermarket chains, A and B, who each own fifty stores in an EU country. The proposed merger would reduce the number of chains from four to three, with Firms C and D controlling fifty stores each throughout the country. Competition between supermarkets takes place at a local level, which implies that in order to assess the risk of unilateral effects, it is necessary to measure the closeness of competition between the parties on a store-by-store basis. Accordingly,

---

[38] Note that one problem with asking customers how they would react if one party's product or service were unavailable is that the pattern of diversion generated by such a question will be representative of the relative preferences over alternatives of *all* customers, not only *marginal* customers (i.e. those that would switch purchases in response to a small but significant increase in price by the merging party). It is the relative preferences of marginal customers over alternatives that determine the importance of those alternatives as competitive constraints. The pattern of diversion across marginal customers could in principle differ to that observed across customers on average.

the Competition Authority conducts a consumer survey, whereby twenty shoppers at each of A's and B's stores are asked the following questions:[39]

- How much did you spend in the store today?
- If this store had not been available which store would you have used instead?

The responses collected at one of A's stores are set out in Table 3.6.

The survey responses are then used to compute a revenue weighted diversion ratio relative to each store. Specifically, the diversion ratios relative to A's store above are calculated as follows:

- Diversion to B: (€20 + €30 + €50 + €40)/€1,405 = 0.10
- Diversion to C: (€130 + €70 + €150 + €30 + €90 + €120 + €30 + €80)/ €1,405 = 0.50
- Diversion to D: (€25 + €70 + €70 + €40 + €50 + €140 + €150 + €20)/ €1,405 = 0.40.

In other words, the revenue weighted diversion ratio to B's store (10%) is relatively low, and significantly lower than the diversion ratios to C (50%) and D (40%), suggesting that unilateral effects would be unlikely to arise post-merger at this particular store.

### 3.1.3    Use in EU merger control

In addition to the qualitative surveys that have traditionally been conducted as part of its market investigations, the Commission has in recent years increasingly relied on large-scale consumer surveys, particularly in mergers where the demand side is characterised by final consumers such as in retail and service markets. In this context, the best practices guidance on the submission of economic evidence, which was published by the Commission in October 2011, provides some recommendations on how surveys should be conducted in order to obtain a representative survey sample and avoid biases.[40] In particular, paragraph 30 of the document reads:

---

[39] This example is inspired by the survey conducted in 2005 by the UK Competition Commission to assess the unilateral effect concerns raised by Somerfield's proposed acquisition of 115 grocery stores from Morrisons (*Somerfield plc and Wm Morrison Supermarkets plc*, September 2005). The UK competition authorities have adopted the same survey technique in many retail mergers since then. See RBB Brief 19, 'Lost in Translation: The use and abuse of diversion ratios in unilateral effects analysis', June 2006 for a more detailed discussion.

[40] More generally, the document focuses on the presentation of economic and econometric analysis, and on the submission of economic data. See 'DG Competition – Best practices

Table 3.6 *Survey responses for one of A's stores*

|  | Expenditure | Named alternative store |
|---|---|---|
| Respondent 1 | € 130 | C |
| Respondent 2 | € 20 | B |
| Respondent 3 | € 25 | D |
| Respondent 4 | € 30 | B |
| Respondent 5 | € 70 | C |
| Respondent 6 | € 70 | D |
| Respondent 7 | € 150 | C |
| Respondent 8 | € 30 | C |
| Respondent 9 | € 50 | B |
| Respondent 10 | € 70 | D |
| Respondent 11 | € 40 | D |
| Respondent 12 | € 50 | D |
| Respondent 13 | € 40 | B |
| Respondent 14 | € 90 | C |
| Respondent 15 | € 140 | D |
| Respondent 16 | € 120 | C |
| Respondent 17 | € 150 | D |
| Respondent 18 | € 30 | C |
| Respondent 19 | € 80 | C |
| Respondent 20 | € 20 | D |
| **Total expenditure** | **€ 1,405** | |

Large-scale surveys of final consumers may usefully supplement qualitative or other documentary evidence obtained from targeted requests of information to market participants. Whilst the evidential value of replies to information requests from market participants lies in the substance of the information provided by players with intrinsic industry or market knowledge, the specific purpose of large-scale surveys of final consumers is to obtain statistically relevant data in order to estimate the characteristics, behaviour and views of a larger group of final consumers from the responses received from a smaller sample.

Recent cases in which the Commission used customer surveys to inform its competitive assessment include the following:

for the submission of economic evidence and data collection in cases concerning the application of Articles 101 and 102 TFEU and in merger cases', available at http://ec.europa.eu/competition/antitrust/legislation/best_practices_submission_en.pdf.

*Siemens/VA Tech*:[41] The parties supplied equipment used in power stations, electricity supply networks, trains, steelworks and large buildings. The Commission used surveys to investigate which purchasing factors were most important to customers and found that most customers regarded price to be less important than non-price factors (e.g. product quality). The Commission then proceeded to assess customers' views on the closeness of the parties' offers in respect of these non-price factors. The majority of customers deemed the merging firms to be their first and second choice for hydropower and metal plant construction. The Commission therefore concluded that Siemens and VA Tech were particularly close competitors for these products.

*Lufthansa/SN Airholding*:[42] In this case the Commission relied on a third party agency to undertake a survey of air passengers. Whilst an important objective of this study was to assess the extent of the relevant product and geographic markets, the survey also sought to investigate the competitive constraint exerted by other airlines, such as easyJet, on overlapping routes. For example, on the Brussels–Berlin route passengers were found to have a clear preference for the merging parties over easyJet. In particular, the survey results indicated that around 15% of the respondents who flew with the merging firms in the past would switch between these two firms in response to a small but significant change in relative prices, while only around 8% would switch to easyJet.

*Ryanair/Aer Lingus*:[43] In assessing the proposed merger, the Commission hired a third party to conduct a passenger survey at Dublin airport. Passengers were asked to list the alternative airlines they considered for their journeys, and how they would react to a small but significant change in relative prices.

The survey found that Ryanair was the most frequently considered alternative by Aer Lingus passengers, and that Aer Lingus was the most often cited alternative by Ryanair customers.

In its response to the statement of objections, Ryanair argued that the survey was potentially biased due to the way in which the questions were framed, with the merging parties being specified by name as potential

---

[41] Case COMP/M.3653 – *Siemens/VA Tech*, Commission decision of 13 July 2005.
[42] Case COMP/M.5335 – *Lufthansa/SN Airholding*, Commission decision of 22 June 2009.
[43] Case COMP/M.4439 – *Ryanair/Aer Lingus*, Commission decision of 27 June 2007 and Case COMP/M.5434 – *Ryanair/Aer Lingus II*, Commission decision of 23 January 2009.

options while other airlines were not. The parties also criticised the survey for being conducted only at Dublin airport, where both parties had an operations base, and not in airports at the other end of the various routes.

*Statoil/JET*:[44] The acquisition of JET Scandinavia by StatoilHydro raised horizontal overlaps between the two firms' retail fuel networks in Norway and Sweden. During the Phase II investigation, the Commission undertook a customer survey, which, according to a subsequent paper published by the case team, ultimately played an important role in the Commission's assessment of the scope for the transaction to give rise to unilateral effects.[45] The survey was based on 1,250 Swedish and 1,001 Norwegian motor fuels consumers who were interviewed by telephone or over the internet during a period of two months. The key findings of the survey were that Jet was perceived as a low-price supplier in both Sweden and Norway, that consumers were price-sensitive (e.g. 54% of respondents in Sweden ranked price as the most important factor when deciding where to fill up) and that roughly half of customers considered that the proposed transaction would be likely to have a negative impact on competition.

As discussed in Section 3.6 of this chapter, certain competition authorities, including those in the UK, have adopted the practice of combining evidence on diversion ratios from surveys with information on the merging firms' gross margins in simple tests that seek to characterise the potential for a merger to give rise to unilateral effects. To date, the Commission has not sought to employ survey evidence on diversion ratios in this way.

### 3.2    Customer switching analysis

#### 3.2.1    Description of technique

Evidence on customers' switching behaviour is often used to understand the extent to which merging parties compete against one another, as well as to measure the competitive constraint exerted by other competitors on the merging parties. More specifically, the aim of a switching analysis is

---

[44] Case COMP/M.4919 – *StatoilHydro/ConocoPhillips*, Commission decision of 21 October 2008.

[45] J. Cloarec, D. Johansson, P. Redondo, D. Donath, E. Glowicka and C. Hariton, 'Fuel for Thought – StatoilHydro/ConocoPhillips (Jet)' (2009) 1 *Competition Policy Newsletter* 71–6.

to obtain approximate estimates of the diversion ratios between the various suppliers' products and, therefore, to identify the extent to which each party's customers are likely to regard the other party as a substitute. If the evidence shows that customers do not switch predominantly from one party to the other, this would suggest that the parties do not represent the closest competitors for one another and that the proposed merger is not likely to eliminate an important competitive constraint.

The focus of a switching analysis is an assessment of the behaviour of customers that have previously moved their business away from each of the merging parties. Specifically, the goal is to observe the destination company to which these customers switch their purchases. This can be indicative of the proportion of any sales lost by each of the merging parties that would, pre-merger, accrue to the other as a result of a unilateral price increase, and, consequently provide a guide as to the magnitude of the competitive constraint that the parties exert on one another.

In order to undertake a switching analysis, the merging parties are typically required to collect the number of customers and value of business lost over a recent period (for instance, three years prior to the merger), and the alternative suppliers to which that business was switched.

An approximation of the diversion ratio from Firm A to Firm B is then given by the value of sales lost by Firm A to Firm B over this period divided by the total value of sales lost by Firm A over the period.[46]

As well as a customer switching analysis, it is sometimes useful to perform an analysis of the overlapping customers, i.e. an analysis of the customers that currently buy from both merging parties. Competition authorities often focus their attention on overlapping customers when assessing unilateral effects concerns. Indeed, to the extent that a significant proportion of customers purchase only from the two parties *and* they do not consider other suppliers as sufficiently valid alternatives, then the reduction in choice brought about by the merger might indeed allow the new entity to raise prices. This possibility is noted in the EC Horizontal Merger Guidelines, which state that:

---

[46] Note that, in order not to understate the diversion ratio, the total value of lost sales should exclude business lost due to customers that ceased purchasing the product in question (e.g. as a result of going out of business), as these customer losses do not reflect the competitive constraint under which firms operate. Equally, the total value of lost sales should exclude lost customers for which the destination is unknown. Importantly, however, to the extent that cases in which the destination is unknown tend to be instances of switching to smaller rivals, this could bias upwards the estimated diversion to larger rivals that are recorded in the data.

Customers of the merging parties may have difficulties switching to other suppliers because there are few alternative suppliers or because they face substantial switching costs. Such customers are particularly vulnerable to price increases. The merger may affect these customers' ability to protect themselves against price increases. In particular, this may be the case for customers that have used dual sourcing from the two merging firms as a means of obtaining competitive prices. Evidence of past customer switching patterns and reactions to price changes may provide important information in this respect.[47]

An analysis of the overlapping customers is typically done in the following way.

First, all instances of customer overlaps between the parties need to be identified.

Second, for each overlapping customer, one needs to investigate: (i) whether their purchases from the two parties are of the same type of product;[48] (ii) the role of other *current* suppliers and the spare capacity held by each of these producers; and (iii) the role of other producers as *potential* suppliers of the required type of product. The following detailed information is required for this purpose:

- the volumes bought from each supplier;
- the type of product purchased;
- indications of alternative suppliers, should the customer decide not to rely entirely on the merged entity or to keep the same number of suppliers utilised;
- evidence on the identity of the suppliers used by each overlapping customer in the recent past (e.g. three/five years).

### 3.2.2 An example

Consider a proposed merger between two Firms, A and B, who both produce an industrial product in competition with two other rivals, Firms C and D. The demand side of the market comprises only thirty customers whose purchases from each supplier in 2009 and 2010 have been estimated by the merging parties. Table 3.7 shows these estimated deliveries in value terms for both years.

---

[47] EC Horizontal Merger Guidelines, para. 31.
[48] Indeed, substantial overlap at a customer level might actually represent evidence of complementarity between the two merging parties to the extent that customers typically purchase different products from them.

Table 3.7 Firms' estimated deliveries in 2009 and 2010

| Customer | 2009 | | | | 2010 | | | |
|---|---|---|---|---|---|---|---|---|
| | Firm A | Firm B | Firm C | Firm D | Firm A | Firm B | Firm C | Firm D |
| Customer 1 | 70 | 0 | 30 | 0 | 0 | 0 | 30 | 70 |
| Customer 2 | 80 | 0 | 0 | 20 | 80 | 0 | 0 | 20 |
| Customer 3 | 70 | 0 | 30 | 0 | 70 | 0 | 30 | 0 |
| Customer 4 | 0 | 70 | 0 | 30 | 0 | 0 | 70 | 30 |
| Customer 5 | 0 | 0 | 10 | 90 | 10 | 0 | 0 | 90 |
| Customer 6 | 0 | 80 | 10 | 10 | 0 | 90 | 10 | 0 |
| Customer 7 | 40 | 0 | 0 | 60 | 0 | 0 | 40 | 60 |
| Customer 8 | 40 | 0 | 10 | 50 | 20 | 20 | 10 | 50 |
| Customer 9 | 50 | 0 | 10 | 40 | 50 | 0 | 10 | 40 |
| Customer 10 | 0 | 0 | 30 | 70 | 30 | 0 | 0 | 70 |
| Customer 11 | 0 | 20 | 20 | 60 | 0 | 40 | 20 | 40 |
| Customer 12 | 40 | 0 | 60 | 0 | 0 | 0 | 60 | 40 |
| Customer 13 | 50 | 0 | 0 | 50 | 0 | 0 | 50 | 50 |
| Customer 14 | 30 | 30 | 40 | 0 | 30 | 0 | 40 | 30 |
| Customer 15 | 80 | 0 | 20 | 0 | 100 | 0 | 0 | 0 |
| Customer 16 | 0 | 0 | 10 | 90 | 0 | 90 | 10 | 0 |
| Customer 17 | 70 | 0 | 0 | 30 | 60 | 0 | 10 | 30 |
| Customer 18 | 0 | 40 | 30 | 30 | 0 | 70 | 0 | 30 |
| Customer 19 | 0 | 30 | 50 | 20 | 0 | 0 | 80 | 20 |
| Customer 20 | 10 | 30 | 10 | 50 | 0 | 40 | 10 | 50 |
| Customer 21 | 20 | 0 | 40 | 40 | 80 | 0 | 0 | 20 |

| | | | | | | | | |
|---|---|---|---|---|---|---|---|---|
| Customer 22 | 60 | 10 | 10 | 20 | 80 | 10 | 10 | 0 |
| Customer 23 | 0 | 30 | 50 | 20 | 50 | 30 | 0 | 20 |
| Customer 24 | 0 | 50 | 0 | 50 | 0 | 0 | 50 | 50 |
| Customer 25 | 0 | 50 | 30 | 20 | 0 | 50 | 50 | 0 |
| Customer 26 | 0 | 60 | 0 | 40 | 0 | 40 | 0 | 60 |
| Customer 27 | 0 | 30 | 20 | 50 | 0 | 50 | 0 | 50 |
| Customer 28 | 40 | 30 | 30 | 0 | 40 | 30 | 10 | 20 |
| Customer 29 | 0 | 0 | 0 | 100 | 0 | 0 | 0 | 100 |
| Customer 30 | 0 | 40 | 50 | 10 | 50 | 40 | 0 | 10 |
| **Total sales** | **750** | **600** | **600** | **1,050** | **750** | **600** | **600** | **1,050** |
| **Market share** | **25%** | **20%** | **20%** | **35%** | **25%** | **20%** | **20%** | **35%** |

Table 3.8 *Value of business lost by Firm A to its rivals between 2009 and 2010*

| Firm B | Firm C | Firm D |
|---|---|---|
| 30 | 100 | 110 |

Table 3.9 *Value of business lost by Firm B to its rivals between 2009 and 2010*

| Firm A | Firm C | Firm D |
|---|---|---|
| 0 | 150 | 50 |

On the basis of these data, the parties' combined market shares are 45% in both 2009 and 2010 with an increment of 20 percentage points, which may give rise to prima facie unilateral effects concerns. However, in order to move beyond market shares to an assessment of the closeness of competition, the information collected by the parties can be used to perform a switching analysis and an analysis of overlapping customers, as set out below.

Table 3.8 and Table 3.9 show the total value of the business lost by Firm A and Firm B respectively to each of their rivals between 2009 and 2010.

Thus, Firm A lost significantly more business to Firms C and D than to Firm B, which suggests that Firm B is unlikely to represent a particularly close competitor for Firm A. Similarly, when Firm B loses business it does so most often to the benefit of Firm C, suggesting these two are particularly close substitutes, while no customer appears to have switched any of its business from Firm B to Firm A.

On the basis of this switching analysis, the proposed merger between A and B appears to create significantly less concern for competition than a simple market share analysis would suggest.

The figures in the example above are constructed so that, for each customer, it is easy to see the sales lost by each firm and the sales won by a particular rival. In particular, each customer's total demand is constant between years and in each case volumes are won by no more than one firm. In practice, the picture is unlikely to be so clear-cut. Each customer's total demand is likely to change from year to year and customers may reallocate purchases across firms in a more complex manner. In these cases, it may be necessary to construct measures of switching based on how customers have changed the relative proportions of their total purchases accounted for by various firms.

An analysis of the overlapping customers can be used to further test the closeness of competition between the merging parties. First of all, the data in Table 3.7 show that in 2010 only five customers purchased from both Firm A and Firm B. In other words, there is a low degree of customer overlap between the two merging parties. Moreover, an analysis of each of these customers' circumstances reveals the following important points:

- Customer 8 also purchased from Firm C (10% of its requirements) and Firm D (50%) in 2010 and it was not an overlapping customer in 2009, as no purchases were made from Firm B in that year.
- Customer 22 also purchased from Firm C (10%) in 2010 and from Firm D in 2009 (20%).
- Customer 23 also purchased from Firm D (20%) and it was not an overlapping customer in 2009 as it purchased 50% of its requirements from C and none from A in that year.
- Customer 28 also purchased from C (10%) and D (20%) in 2010.
- Customer 30 also purchased from Firm D (10%) in 2010. It was not an overlapping customer in 2009 as it purchased 50% of its requirements from C and none from A in that year.

In sum, the data provide support for the view that the merged entity would be unlikely to find itself in a position to raise prices to any of these overlapping customers due to the fact that they currently purchase from other suppliers and could presumably also switch back to suppliers from whom they purchased in the recent past.[49] Therefore, the concern described in the EC Horizontal Merger Guidelines, that customers that have used dual sourcing from the parties may be particularly vulnerable to price increases post-merger, does not arise in this example.

### 3.2.3   Use in EU merger control

The Commission has conducted a switching analysis in order to assess the degree of closeness of competition between the parties in a number of recent merger investigations.

---

[49] It would need to be verified, of course, that rival suppliers have sufficient spare capacity to accommodate additional volume requirements.

*Syniverse/BSG*[50] concerned the merger of two companies active in the supply of GSM wireless communication data clearing services. Within the data provided by the merging parties, which encompassed between ten and fifteen instances of switching, the Commission noted that there was only one case of a customer switching between the parties.[51] The Commission concluded that this evidence, when read in conjunction with the results of a bidding analysis (see Section 3.7 below), demonstrated that the merging parties were not one another's closest competitors and that the merged entity would be subject to strong competitive constraints from rivals, such that the merger was unlikely to result in anti-competitive unilateral effects.[52]

In *Kronospan/Constantia*,[53] the Commission investigated the scope for the transaction to give rise to unilateral effects in the market for raw particle board, a product used to make furniture. During its Phase II investigation, the Commission conducted an analysis of overlapping customers, based on the merging firms' sales data over a three-year period. This analysis showed that the merging firms made a significant proportion of their sales to common customers, which contributed to a finding that there would be a removal of an important competitive constraint.[54] Combined with the Commission's finding that rivals to the merged entity would be limited in their ability to respond to price increases due to their locations and also capacity constraints, the Commission found that the transaction as originally notified would have significantly impeded effective competition.[55] A modified version of the transaction, in which Kronospan acquired a sub-set of Constantia's wood-based boards and related products businesses and committed not to acquire the remaining assets, was accepted by the Commission.

In *T-Mobile Austria/Tele.ring*,[56] the Commission investigated the closeness of competition between the merging parties as mobile network operators (MNOs) in Austria. The Commission concluded that Tele.ring

---

[50] Case COMP/M.4662 – *Syniverse/BSG*, Commission decision of 4 December 2007.
[51] Ibid., para. 81.      [52] Ibid., para. 101.
[53] Case COMP/M.4525 – *Kronospan/Constantia*, Commission decision of 19 September 2007.
[54] Ibid., para. 46. See also Case COMP/M.4726 – *Thomson Corporation/Reuters Group*, Commission decision of 19 February 2008, para. 410, where the Commission found that 60–80% of customers source certain products only from Thomson and Reuters 'hence they heavily depend on them'.
[55] Case COMP/M.4525 – *Kronospan/Constantia*, Commission decision of 19 September 2007, para. 81.
[56] Case COMP/M.3916 – *T-Mobile Austria/Tele.ring*, Commission decision of 26 April 2006.

exercised a greater constraint on T-Mobile than would be suggested by its market share on the basis, in large part, of a switching analysis. In particular, the Commission was able to use number portability data to track the behaviour of customers switching between MNOs. The switching analysis conducted by the Commission found that:

> In 2005 more than half of all customers who switched provider and made use of number portability went to tele.ring and between 57% and 61% of those who left T-Mobile and Mobilkom with their telephone numbers switched to tele.ring. In second place behind tele.ring in 2005 was H3G, around which picked up some 20% of all customers switching provider and using number portability.[57]

According to the Commission, this evidence implied the existence of an important competitive constraint between the parties, such that the proposed merger was likely significantly to impede effective competition on the Austrian market for the provision of mobile telephony services to final consumers.[58] The transaction was ultimately cleared after the parties agreed to divest telecommunications frequencies and mobile communication sites.[59]

### 3.3   Price/concentration studies and analysis of the impact of rivals' presence

#### 3.3.1   Description of technique

Price/concentration studies seek to use existing differences in the levels of market concentration within an industry to identify the relationship between prices and the level of concentration. If it is assumed that a stable relationship exists between price and concentration across markets, estimates of that relationship may provide useful information regarding the potential impact on prices of the change in concentration resulting from a merger in one particular market. In other words, one way to evaluate the potential impact of a merger is to benchmark the prospective post-merger firm's position against existing markets in which concentration has already reached the post-merger level.

Intuitively, the most important element of a price/concentration study is the selection of suitable comparator markets used to establish a relationship between price and supply concentration. Consequently, this

---

[57] Case COMP/M.3916 – *T-Mobile Austria/Tele.ring*, Commission decision of 26 April 2006, para. 50.
[58] Ibid., para. 125.      [59] Ibid., para. 130.

kind of analysis is normally applied within industries in which there exist analogous markets where concentration is already close to post-merger levels from which to observe prices. As such, the technique is most often used in industries characterised by a multitude of local geographic markets (e.g. retailing, airlines) or in national markets where international comparisons are available and valid.

Nonetheless, different markets are, in practice, likely to differ in respects other than the level of concentration. This may potentially confound simple comparisons of concentration and performance. For example, a firm in one particular area may have developed a product of a superior quality and thus have been able to increase both its output (leading to a high market share) and its price (due to consumers' higher willingness to pay for its product). The positive relationship between price and concentration observed in this case would provide little information regarding the effect of concentration on price resulting from the intensity of competition. In addition, certain factors (e.g. cost conditions) may have an influence both on prices and on firms' entry decisions (and thus the number of firms in an industry), implying that the observed relationship between price and number of firms does not inform how changes in concentration (holding other things constant) cause changes in price.[60] Under some circumstances, however, econometric techniques may be used to control for these factors in order to attempt to isolate the impact of concentration on firm performance.[61]

### 3.3.2    An example

Suppose that two banks, A and B, are attempting to merge. The main area in which competition issues are considered potentially to arise is lending to small- and medium-sized enterprises (SMEs). Suppose further, that lending to SMEs represents a relatively small part of any individual branch's business, and that, as a result, it is reasonable to assume that firms do not make decisions regarding where to open branches on the

---

[60] This is an example of endogeneity, which is discussed further in Section 3.4.2 below and in Appendix A.

[61] Certain commentators have suggested that the difficulties that arise with the interpretation of price/concentration analysis are so serious that the technique should not be used at all. See, e.g., Newmark (2004), who concludes that 'price-concentration studies, even when employed in the latter stages of a merger investigation, must be interpreted with great care at the least and probably should not be employed at all.' C. M. Newmark, 'Price–Concentration Studies: There You Go Again', prepared for the *DOJ/FTC* Merger Workshop, 'Concentration and Market Shares' panel, revised 14 February 2004.

basis of the profitability of this part of their business.[62] In the area of lending to SMEs the two banks face varying levels of competition at a local level, in the sense that each bank faces a relatively large number of competing branches in certain areas (up to five rivals) while being a local monopolist in other areas. The existence of this variation in concentration makes it possible to analyse the difference between interest rates charged to SMEs in areas containing few rivals and interests rates in areas in which a number of rivals are present.

To the extent that interest rates tend to be higher the lower the number of suppliers, this could provide an indication that competition takes place at a local level and that unilateral effects are likely to arise in those areas that will have few rivals post-merger. Conversely, to the extent that no such relationship exists, then this would be consistent with the view that the level of concentration at a local level has no bearing on competitive outcomes, which may suggest that competitive interactions take place within a broader geographic market. In so far as the parties' combined shares at a national level are relatively modest, such a finding would imply that the proposed transaction is not likely to give rise to unilateral effects in any particular local area.

Crucially, in order to be meaningful, this type of analysis needs to take into account other factors that may affect interest rates at a local level other than the number of competing branches. The most important factor influencing the price for SME lending is likely to be the level of risk associated with the businesses that each branch typically deals with. Intuitively, the higher the level of risk faced by any given branch, the lower will be the attractiveness to that branch of lending to its customer base and, consequently, the higher will be the interest rate that the branch in question will typically charge, all else being equal.

Table 3.10 shows the average interest rate charged by bank A at each of its fifty branches in 2011. It also shows the number of rival branches within each town and the average risk category of the customers with whom the branch deals. For simplicity, we assume that there are only three discrete levels of risk: 1 (low risk), 2 (medium risk) and 3 (high risk). It also shows which of bank A's local branches face competition from bank B, the other merging party, and from bank C, the other major rival with a nationwide presence.[63]

---

[62] The relevance of this assumption will be explained below.

[63] For simplicity, we do not expressly analyse the competitive constraint exerted at a local level by rival banks, D, E, etc. Ideally, information on the location of their branches would also be required.

Table 3.10 *Average interest rates charged by bank A's branches in 2011, presence of rivals and average risk category*

| | Average interest rate | Number of rivals | B present? | C present? | Risk |
|---|---|---|---|---|---|
| Branch 1 | 8% | 5 | Yes | Yes | 1 |
| Branch 2 | 8% | 4 | Yes | Yes | 1 |
| Branch 3 | 8% | 3 | Yes | No | 1 |
| Branch 4 | 8% | 5 | No | Yes | 1 |
| Branch 5 | 8% | 4 | No | Yes | 1 |
| Branch 6 | 9% | 3 | Yes | Yes | 1 |
| Branch 7 | 9% | 5 | No | No | 1 |
| Branch 8 | 9% | 4 | No | Yes | 1 |
| Branch 9 | 9% | 3 | Yes | No | 1 |
| Branch 10 | 9% | 5 | No | No | 1 |
| Branch 11 | 10% | 4 | Yes | Yes | 1 |
| Branch 12 | 10% | 3 | Yes | No | 1 |
| Branch 13 | 10% | 5 | No | No | 1 |
| Branch 14 | 10% | 4 | No | No | 1 |
| Branch 15 | 10% | 3 | Yes | No | 1 |
| Branch 16 | 11% | 2 | No | Yes | 2 |
| Branch 17 | 11% | 4 | Yes | Yes | 2 |
| Branch 18 | 11% | 3 | No | Yes | 2 |
| Branch 19 | 11% | 2 | No | Yes | 2 |
| Branch 20 | 11% | 4 | Yes | Yes | 2 |
| Branch 21 | 12% | 3 | No | Yes | 2 |
| Branch 22 | 12% | 2 | Yes | No | 2 |
| Branch 23 | 12% | 4 | No | Yes | 2 |
| Branch 24 | 12% | 3 | No | No | 2 |
| Branch 25 | 12% | 2 | No | No | 2 |

| Branch | % | | | | |
|---|---|---|---|---|---|
| Branch 26 | 13% | 3 | Yes | Yes | 2 |
| Branch 27 | 13% | 2 | Yes | No | 2 |
| Branch 28 | 13% | 4 | Yes | No | 2 |
| Branch 29 | 13% | 3 | No | Yes | 2 |
| Branch 30 | 13% | 2 | Yes | No | 2 |
| Branch 31 | 14% | 4 | Yes | No | 2 |
| Branch 32 | 14% | 3 | No | Yes | 2 |
| Branch 33 | 14% | 2 | No | No | 2 |
| Branch 34 | 14% | 4 | No | No | 2 |
| Branch 35 | 14% | 3 | No | No | 2 |
| Branch 36 | 15% | 2 | Yes | Yes | 3 |
| Branch 37 | 15% | 1 | No | Yes | 3 |
| Branch 38 | 15% | 2 | No | Yes | 3 |
| Branch 39 | 15% | 1 | No | Yes | 3 |
| Branch 40 | 15% | 0 | No | No | 3 |
| Branch 41 | 16% | 2 | Yes | No | 3 |
| Branch 42 | 16% | 1 | No | Yes | 3 |
| Branch 43 | 16% | 0 | No | No | 3 |
| Branch 44 | 16% | 2 | Yes | No | 3 |
| Branch 45 | 16% | 1 | Yes | Yes | 3 |
| Branch 46 | 17% | 0 | No | No | 3 |
| Branch 47 | 17% | 2 | Yes | Yes | 3 |
| Branch 48 | 17% | 1 | Yes | No | 3 |
| Branch 49 | 17% | 0 | No | No | 3 |
| Branch 50 | 17% | 2 | No | No | 3 |

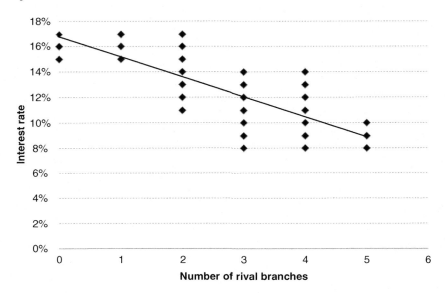

**Figure 3.4**  Interest rates against the number of rival branches, ignoring the level of risk

Figure 3.4 plots the average interest rates charged by bank A at its fifty branches against the number of rival branches. The figure highlights the existence of a negative relationship between interest rates and number of local competitors, which is confirmed by a downward sloping trendline. This simple graphical analysis might suggest that the number of local competitors matters and that, to the extent that the proposed transaction would reduce the number of competing branches in many localities, this might be expected to give rise to potentially significant unilateral effects.

However, it would be unsafe to draw such a conclusion without taking into account the potentially important factor represented by the risk faced by each of bank A's branches. To the extent that risk does indeed matter then ignoring it might give rise to misleading results. This will likely be the case if, for whatever reason, the level of risk faced by each branch happens to be correlated with the number of rivals. In other words, if the areas characterised by a large proportion of highly risky businesses (e.g. small start-up companies) – and, therefore, higher interest rates – coincide with the areas where bank A faces a small number of rivals (and vice versa), then not taking the level of risk into account would lead the analysis incorrectly to ascribe the observed high interest rates to a lack of competition at a local level.

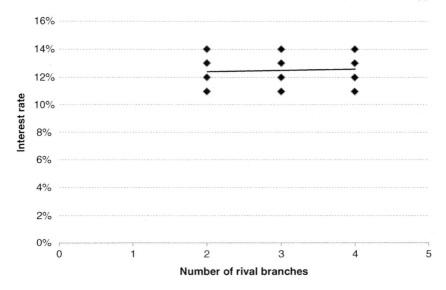

**Figure 3.5**   Interest rates against the number of rival branches, medium risk level

Indeed, it can be verified that if we appropriately incorporate the level of risk into the analysis, the picture changes dramatically. For instance, if we focus our attention only on those branches whose customers are characterised by a medium level of risk, then there is no longer a negative relationship between average interest rates and number of rival branches, as shown in Figure 3.5. Since the same is true for the other categories of risk as well (i.e. low-risk branches and high-risk branches), the appropriate conclusion is that the interest rates charged by bank A's branches do not actually depend on the number of local competitors. This supports the view that a reduction in the number of local players brought about by the proposed merger should not be expected to give rise to unilateral effects concerns.

In addition to understanding the general relationship between the number of rivals and interest rates across different local areas, it may be informative to analyse whether the presence of bank B in particular has an impact on bank A's interest rates. The results of such analyses can usually be interpreted as follows:

• If A's prices are significantly lower than on average whenever it faces B as a competitor then it may be reasonable to infer that the presence of B acts as a competitive constraint on A, preventing A from increasing

Table 3.11 *Bank A's average interest rate in areas where B is present or not present*

|              | Risk level |      |      | Average |
|              | 1          | 2    | 3    |         |
|--------------|------------|------|------|---------|
| **B not present** | 9.0   | 12.5 | 15.9 | 12.7    |
| **B present**     | 9.0   | 12.5 | 16.2 | 12.2    |

prices. A merger between A and B may in this case give rise to unilateral price increases as it would remove the competitive constraint exerted by bank B on bank A.[64]

- If, on the other hand, A's prices are not significantly influenced by B's presence, this would suggest that B does not provide a particularly important constraint on A's behaviour. In this case, a merger between A and B is unlikely to give rise to unilateral effects.

Table 3.11 compares, for each risk category, the average interest rates charged by bank A in those areas where it faces competition from bank B with those charged in areas where bank B is not present. The table shows that on average across all areas A charges slightly less when B is present. However, this may be because bank B is present relatively more frequently in regions characterised by a lower risk level. Importantly, bank A does not charge lower interest rates on average where B is present when areas in each of the three risk categories are considered separately. This supports the view that this bank does not exercise a particularly important competitive constraint on bank A.

Furthermore, Table 3.12 suggests that bank C is likely to represent bank A's closest competitor. Indeed, the table shows that, within each risk category, bank A typically charges markedly lower interest rates in those areas where C is present relative to those areas where C is not present.

The above conclusions can be further tested by undertaking an econometric analysis, aimed at explaining bank A's interest rates, the dependent variable, with the level of risk faced by each branch as well as the number and identity of local competitors. As explained in Chapter 1,

---

[64] However, as discussed in Section 5 below, it may be that other factors would prevent the merged entity from increasing prices, such as the reaction of other rivals or the prospect of entry.

Table 3.12 *Bank A's average interest rate in areas where C is present or not present*

| | Risk level | | | Average |
|---|---|---|---|---|
| | 1 | 2 | 3 | |
| C not present | 9.4 | 13.1 | 16.4 | 13.2 |
| C present | 8.6 | 11.9 | 15.2 | 11.6 |

econometric analysis is increasingly used by the Commission and by notifying parties to assess the scope for mergers to give rise to unilateral effects. In particular, regression analysis, which is discussed further in Appendix A, seeks to explain how changes in one variable (the 'dependent variable') are explained by a group of other variables (the 'explanatory variables'). This form of analysis is well suited to assess whether two parties exert an important competitive constraint on each other and whether the loss of this constraint may give rise to a price increase. By taking other important factors into account, econometric analyses are able to isolate the impact of Firm B on Firm A's prices and vice versa.

Importantly, a merger between A and B will raise concerns only if one party's prices are significantly influenced by the other party's presence both in a *statistical* and in an *economic* sense. A price difference is statistically significant if the analysis gives a high degree of confidence (typically a 95% probability or more) in the conclusion that the existence of that difference does not arise merely by chance. But a statistically significant price difference is not necessarily important from an economic point of view. For example, if A's price is 0.1% lower when B is present, this may be statistically significant but will almost always be considered as insufficient in magnitude to raise concerns. Results need to be both statistically and economically significant if they are to form a robust basis for enforcement action.

The first step in carrying out an econometric analysis is to specify a model that relates the explanatory variables to the dependent variable of interest. An example of a simple econometric model that might be specified in this case is presented below:[65]

---

[65] It should be noted that this example is highly stylised and in any practical setting the model would have to take account of a number of issues that are not addressed here.

Table 3.13 *Econometric analysis of impact of rivals' presence on bank A's interest rates*

|  | Coefficient | Standard error | P-value | 95% Confidence interval |
|---|---|---|---|---|
| **Risk** | 3.56 | 0.23 | 0.000 | [3.09, 4.02] |
| **Number of rivals** | 0.10 | 0.13 | 0.482 | [−0.18, 0.37] |
| **B present?** | −0.09 | 0.24 | 0.7818 | [−0.56, 0.39] |
| **C present?** | −1.11 | 0.25 | 0.000 | [−1.61, −0.61] |
| **Constant** | 5.65 | 0.82 | 0.000 | [3.99, −7.31] |

$$Interest\ rate_i = \alpha + \beta\ Risk_i + \gamma\ Number\ of\ rivals_i + \delta\ Bdummy_i + \eta\ Cdummy_i + \varepsilon_i$$

where

- $\alpha$ is the constant term, reflecting the average interest rate setting aside other factors
- *Risk* is the average risk associated with branch $i$'s business and can take the value 1 (low risk), 2 (medium risk) or 3 (high risk)
- *Number of rivals* is the number of rival branches faced by branch $i$
- *Bdummy* is a so-called 'dummy' variable which is set at one if branch $i$ faces local competition from bank B and at zero otherwise
- *Cdummy* is another 'dummy' variable which is set at one if branch $i$ faces local competition from bank C and at zero otherwise
- $\varepsilon_i$ is the error term.

Table 3.13 shows the results of this analysis.

The following points are worth noting. First, the coefficient associated with the variable 'risk' is statistically significant at the 5% level (since the 95% confidence interval does not include zero) and its value is

---

For example, as explained in Section 2.1.3, theory predicts that the price effect resulting from a change in the number of firms is likely to be limited when there are many firms present and greater when there are fewer firms present. As such, the effect of firm B's presence on firm A's price is likely to depend on the number of rivals present. To take account of this, it would be necessary to include additional explanatory variables that allow for the 'interactions' of the effects of the number of firms present and the presence of firm B to be estimated. In addition, any practical application would need to take the categorical nature of the risk variable into account.

equal to 3.56. This means that if the level of risk dealt with by a branch increases by one (e.g. from 1, or low risk, to 2, or medium risk), then the expected average interest rate offered by that branch increases by approximately 3.5 percentage points.

Second, consistently with the graphical analysis set out in Figure 3.5, the regression formalises the claim that there is no evidence that the variable 'number of rivals' explains variation in interest rates, given that the relevant coefficient is not statistically different from zero at the 5% level. Interestingly, should one omit the variable 'risk' from the regression, the variable 'number of rivals' would become statistically significant, erroneously suggesting as per Figure 3.4 that an increase in the number of rivals gives rise to lower interest rates.

Third, and most importantly, bank A's interest rates are markedly lower, by more than one percentage point, in those areas where bank C is also present. Conversely, bank B does not appear to have any impact on bank A's interest rates, suggesting that the two parties are not each other's closest competitors and that unilateral effects would be unlikely to arise as a result of the merger.

As a final remark, we have assumed throughout the example above that the number of firms offering loans to SMEs in each local area is exogenously determined. In other words, we have taken the number of firms in each local area as a fact of nature, rather than being a function of entry decisions made by firms on the basis of the expected profitability of operating in each area. In this case, we sought to justify this assumption on the basis that lending to SMEs represents a relatively small part of any individual branch's business, and that, as a result, it is reasonable to assume that firms do not make decisions regarding where to open branches on the basis of the profitability of this part of their business. In practice, such an assumption is only justifiable under certain special circumstances. In general, therefore, the analysis will need to take account of the endogeneity of firms' entry decisions, for instance via the use of instrumental variables. Endogeneity is discussed further in Appendix A.

### 3.3.3   Use in EU merger control

The Commission has in a number of recent cases undertaken price/ concentration analyses and/or an analysis of the effect of the presence of one merging party on the prices charged by the other merging party.

In *Sanofi-Aventis/Zentiva*,[66] the Commission stated that econometric analysis, along with other evidence, confirmed that competition concerns relating to the introduction of pipeline generic products could be excluded since it demonstrated that Zentiva did not exercise a unique competitive constraint on Sanofi-Aventis in any of the affected countries as compared to other generic producers.[67] Specifically, the Commission gathered data including sales, prices and advertising expenditure for the years 1996 to 2008 in all geographic markets in which Sanofi-Aventis faced the entry of a generic producer at the molecule level between 1998 and 2010 in ten countries.[68] The Commission performed an econometric analysis in order to test whether, as compared to an average generic producer, Zentiva exerted a stronger competitive constraint on Sanofi-Aventis.[69] The Commission found no significant evidence that Zentiva should be regarded as a special competitor for Sanofi-Aventis, either when it entered as the first 'independent' generic or when it entered at a later stage. According to the Commission, the results of the analysis therefore suggested that the competitive constraint exerted by Zentiva on Sanofi-Aventis was not stronger than that exercised by an average generic competitor.[70]

In *Ryanair/Aer Lingus*,[71] the Commission was particularly concerned about the competitive constraint that the parties exerted upon each other in routes out of Dublin. The Commission conducted various econometric analyses to assess whether in the pre-merger scenario the presence of one party had an impact on the price level set by the other party. Initially, the Commission carried out a cross-section regression analysis of price differences across different routes at a given point in time. The main purpose of this exercise was to compare the prices of one party in the routes where the other party was present to its prices on routes where the latter was not present. The econometric models used included a number of other explanatory variables to account for variation in demand and costs across routes. Ultimately, the Commission concluded that the values and statistical significance of the coefficients did not allow for definitive conclusions to be drawn due mainly to the existence of route specificities that were not being captured by the explanatory variables used.[72] The Commission decided to rely instead on an analysis that

---

[66] Case COMP/M.5253 – *Sanofi-Aventis/Zentiva*, Commission decision of 4 February 2009.
[67] Ibid., para. 510.     [68] Ibid., para. 543.     [69] Ibid., para. 545.     [70] Ibid., para. 547.
[71] Case COMP/M.4439 – *Ryanair/Aer Lingus*, Commission decision of 27 June 2007.
[72] This is known as omitted-variable bias (OVB).

sought to identify how changes in the presence of rivals over time (i.e. entry) affected pricing. This analysis is discussed further in Section 3.4.3 below.

The Commission undertook econometric analyses to assess the competitive impact of rivals' local presence during the 2008 *Statoil/JET*[73] merger investigation. This investigation, and the econometric analyses of rivalry conducted therein, are discussed in the following case study.

### 3.3.4   Case study: *Statoil/JET*

Econometric analyses of the type discussed in this section were employed by the Commission to assess the proposed acquisition by StatoilHydro ('Statoil') of ConocoPhillips' 'JET' unmanned petrol stations in Scandinavia.[74] In October 2008, after a Phase II investigation, the Commission cleared the merger subject to a number of conditions. In Sweden, the Commission found that the transaction as notified would lead to unilateral effects concerns.[75] Consequently, it required Statoil to divest a network of stations.

Statoil was a long-standing operator of mainly manned petrol stations in Sweden with a historical market share of between 30 and 40 per cent. JET entered the Swedish market in 1978 as the first unmanned, 'no frills' operator, offering petrol and diesel at a lower pump price than manned stations but without any additional services.[76] As a result of its first-mover advantage, JET had been able to obtain attractive sites, providing it with the highest efficiency (in terms of average annual sales volumes per station) of all Swedish petrol station networks. JET had a market share of between 10 and 20 per cent, leading to a combined post-merger share of between 40 and 50 per cent.

**3.3.4.1   JET's role**   In the first decade following its 1978 entry, JET played an active role in the Swedish market. It steadily increased its

---

[73] Case COMP/M.4919 – *StatoilHydro/ConocoPhillips*, Commission decision of 21 October 2008.

[74] Case COMP/M.4919 – *StatoilHydro/ConocoPhillips*, Commission decision of 21 October 2008. This case study draws on A. Lofaro and J.P. van der Veer, 'Fuelling the Debate? The role of econometrics in Statoil/JET' (2010) 31 (6) *European Competition Law Review* 222–5.

[75] The Commission also concluded that the transaction would give rise to unilateral effects in Norway.

[76] Since JET's entry, other operators (including established operators) also introduced unmanned stations such that more than half of all petrol stations in Sweden were unmanned at the time the merger was notified to the Commission.

pump price discount relative to manned stations' prices in an attempt to gain market share. However, from about 1990 onwards, JET's strategy in Sweden changed. Since that time, for a period of around 15 years, JET and other unmanned operators maintained exactly the same discount (of SEK 0.25 per litre for petrol) to manned stations. JET followed manned prices at a constant discount, but did not initiate price reductions with a view to increase its market share.

In the years immediately preceding the merger, JET's discount was on two separate occasions challenged by rivals, first by Shell and then by Statoil. Both operators had engaged in restructuring and had significantly lowered their costs. They subsequently tried to translate their reduced cost base into a higher market share and thus reduced prices at their manned stations towards the level offered by JET.[77]

On both occasions, JET feared a loss of competitiveness if the lower pump price differentials resulting from the Shell and Statoil price reductions persisted. JET thus reacted by reducing its own prices so as to restore the original differentials.[78] Shell and Statoil, however, were persistent in their attempts to cut their prices in order to reduce the differential between their and JET's prices. On both occasions, this led to a prolonged price war during which all players used exceptionally low prices as an instrument to force rivals to either accept or reject the new differentials. A critical question, as we shall see, is how to interpret pricing evidence drawn from the unstable price war periods.

### 3.3.4.2 Econometric estimates

The Commission's assessment focused on the impact of JET on competition in the Swedish market and, in particular, on Statoil's prices. Specifically, the Commission was concerned that JET, as a low-price competitor with lower pump prices than manned rivals, might exert a stronger competitive constraint than its market share would suggest.[79] The Commission characterised JET as a possible 'maverick', an important driver of price competition in the market, the elimination of which could give rise to unilateral effects. In order to determine whether JET exerted an important competitive

---

[77] This is fully consistent with economic theory, which suggests that a firm that benefits from a reduction in its unit production costs has an incentive to reduce its price to achieve extra sales volumes.

[78] Initially, some other unmanned operators also resisted Shell and Statoil's initiatives to reduce differentials. These other operators, however, tended to accept the new differentials much quicker than JET did.

[79] EC Horizontal Merger Guidelines, para. 37.

constraint on Statoil, the Commission and the parties' economists undertook econometric analyses, which made use of extremely large amounts of data on an outlet-by-outlet basis on prices, volumes, density of population, number and identity of local rivals, etc.

Despite being based on somewhat different specifications, the econometric analyses conducted by the Commission and the parties' economists produced broadly similar results. In particular, both the Commission and the parties' econometric models agreed that, *outside the price war periods*, JET's presence did not have a significant impact on Statoil's prices.[80] These results underlined the passive role played by JET outside price war periods, simply following prices set by others at a constant discount without initiating price reductions. JET thus did not exert a significant competitive constraint on Statoil in normal periods. However, *during the two price wars*, both the parties and the Commission found that Statoil stations charged significantly lower prices whenever they were in proximity to a JET station.

### 3.3.4.3  Placing econometrics in the right economic context  Although the results of the analysis of the parties and the Commission were broadly similar, there was strong disagreement on the way these results should be interpreted. The Commission relied particularly on the econometric results relating to the price war periods to argue that JET exercised a significant competitive constraint on Statoil, the elimination of which would likely have resulted in unilateral effects. The parties' response was that this interpretation was flawed.

Crucially, the parties argued that JET's impact during price wars did not in any way imply that JET was preventing Statoil from increasing prices, or that JET was trying to gain market share by initiating price reductions. Indeed, as explained earlier, the price wars were triggered by price *decreases* initiated by Shell and Statoil, not by JET. However, concerned about a loss of competitiveness, JET responded aggressively to these price reductions. But since Statoil had initiated a pricing policy designed to reduce the previously applicable price premium for its stations relative to JET, this in turn led Statoil to charge very low prices when facing a JET station as local competitor, giving rise to the result

---

[80] In particular, the influence of JET on Statoil's prices was statistically insignificant according to the model submitted by the parties, and statistically significant but economically negligible according to the Commission's model.

that Statoil's prices wherever JET was present were lower than elsewhere. Importantly, though, there was no evidence suggesting that JET had sought to increase its market share by refusing to follow price *increases* initiated by others. On this basis, the parties argued that the econometric results could not be taken to imply that JET exerted a significant competitive constraint on Statoil, preventing the latter from increasing prices.

If the Commission were to use its econometric analysis to support a theory of unilateral effects, that theory would thus have to be that the new entity might not respond as aggressively as JET did before the merger to rivals' price reductions.

While such a theory may represent a plausible story of harm, it would not be *sufficient* to conclude that the proposed transaction would be anti-competitive. The reason for this is that aggressive reactions to rivals' price reductions may have both positive *and* negative welfare implications. Positive effects clearly occur because consumers benefit in the short term from the low prices triggered by aggressive reactions. Importantly, how-ever, negative effects are also likely to arise. This is because rivals are less prone to reduce prices in the first place if they know that any such initiative is likely to be met with short-term aggression.[81] In other words, the apparently aggressive pricing response of JET to the pricing initiatives of Shell and Statoil could be seen as a defensive form of conduct that was designed to discourage price competition. Any theory of harm would need to take *both* effects into account, appropriately weighing the positive and negative impacts.

Rather than address this trade-off, however, the Commission simply relied on JET's observed impact on Statoil's prices during price wars as evidence of a significant competitive constraint.[82] In doing so, the Commission arguably ignored the economic context that gave rise to JET's impact on Statoil's prices during price wars, in particular the deterrent effect on future price reductions contemplated by rivals that arose from JET's consistent aggressive response to rivals' price cuts.

---

[81] Firms might even be deterred from investing in cost reduction programmes if they know that they would face aggressive reactions from rivals when trying to pass on these cost reductions to consumers in the form of lower prices.

[82] The subsequent article published by the case team, referred to above (see Section 3.1.3) also limits itself to stating the results of the econometric analysis without attempting to put these into the appropriate economic context.

## 3.4.  Entry analysis

### 3.4.1   Description of technique

The preceding section discussed price/concentration studies, which seek to measure the relationship between prices and the level of concentration, and analyse the impact of each party on the other party's prices. These approaches represent forms of cross-sectional analysis, meaning that in essence they seek to compare firms' performances in different markets at a particular point in time in order to make inferences as to how a change in market structure brought about by a merger might change market outcomes.

The same logic can also be applied across time, rather than across markets, by comparing the evolution of firms' performance within a particular market where changes in market structure took place. For example, if a firm entered a market relatively recently, it might be possible to compare price levels before and after in order to assess the competitive impact of the new firm's presence and, therefore, to assess the likely risk of post-merger unilateral effects from a reduction in the number of firms. As entry involves a reduction in market concentration, a merger bringing about an increase in concentration may have the opposite effect on concentration from that observed following entry. The impact of market entry may be particularly pertinent to merger assessment where the entrant in question is one of the parties to the merger, as the addition of such a firm may closely correspond to the opposite of the change brought about by the merger under investigation.

In what follows, we provide a simple example illustrating how the analysis of entry may inform merger assessment.

### 3.4.2   An example

Consider a proposed merger between two producers of branded soups, A and B. After the merger, the new entity would enjoy a market share of more than 40% and it would face only two rivals, Firms C and D, indicating that the risk of unilateral effects would need to be carefully investigated by the Commission. However, a simple analysis of the available evidence supports the view that the merging parties do not represent particularly close substitutes and that the merger would not eliminate an important competitive constraint. In particular, Figure 3.6 shows the evolution of monthly shares during January 2008–December 2010 and each firm's monthly prices during the same period.

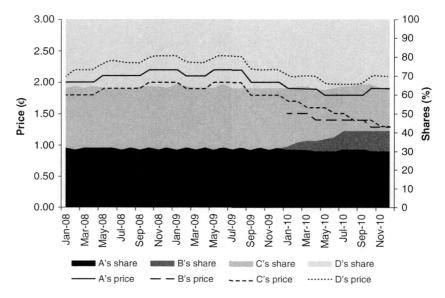

**Figure 3.6**    Monthly shares and prices during January 2008–December 2010

Two important points emerge from a graphical inspection of the figure. First, Firm B entered the market only in January 2010, and it reached a market share of 11% by December of the same year almost exclusively at the expense of Firm C. Indeed, the figure clearly shows that the market shares of both Firms A and D were virtually unaffected by Firm B's entry. Second, prior to Firm B's entry, Firm C's prices showed a high degree of parallelism with those of Firms A and D. However, following Firm B's entry, which introduced its product at a significantly lower price, Firm C's price significantly fell converging rapidly to Firm B's price.

This simple analysis therefore provides strong evidence against the view that the merger would give rise to unilateral effects. The price of product B would likely remain effectively constrained by Firm C, while the price of product A would continue to be constrained by Firm D.[83]

---

[83] As in the discussion in the preceding section, it will often be necessary to apply econometric techniques to take account of factors that may affect both firms' entry decisions and competitive outcomes (e.g. market growth and changes in cost conditions).

### 3.4.3   Use in EU cases

The Commission has considered entry in the assessment of unilateral effects in a number of Phase II merger cases in recent years.

For example, the Commission analysed the impact of rival entry in *Lufthansa/SN Airholding*,[84] *Lufthansa/Austrian Airlines*,[85] *Johnson&-Johnson/Guidant*[86] and *Ryanair/Aer Lingus*.[87] Specifically, in *Lufthansa/SN Airholding*,[88] the Commission undertook an econometric analysis that suggested that the entry of easyJet on the Brussels–Berlin route led to a significant reduction in SN's fares on that route. The Commission's analysis used changes in fares on the Brussels–Munich and Brussels–Hamburg routes to control for external factors affecting air fares, observing that SN's fares on the Berlin route fell from higher than on the Hamburg route prior to easyJet's entry to a similar or lower level after easyJet's entry. Therefore, the Commission concluded that easyJet posed a competitive constraint on SN that would remain post-merger.

Similarly, in *Lufthansa/Austrian Airlines*,[89] the Commission investigated whether the entry of rivals could shed light on the intensity of the competitive constraints that the new entity would face post-merger. In particular, analysis of the Vienna–Munich route showed that the entry of low-cost carrier Niki in 2007 had no impact on the merging parties' prices (at least when considering time-sensitive passengers). Similarly, on the Vienna–Frankfurt route, Niki's entry in October 2006 had no effect on the parties' prices for fully flexible business and economy tickets. The Commission noted that Niki's entry had an impact on the price of Lufthansa's non-flexible economy tickets, but that less of an impact was observed in relation to Austrian Airlines' non-flexible economy tickets. As such, the Commission concluded that Niki did not constitute a competitive constraint on the merging parties for time-sensitive passengers, and probably for all passengers.

In *Johnson&-Johnson/Guidant*,[90] the Commission investigated the scope for unilateral effects in the supply of cardio-vascular medical

---

[84] Case COMP/M.5335 – *Lufthansa/SN Airholding*, Commission decision of 22 June 2009.
[85] Case COMP/M.5440 – *Lufthansa/Austrian Airlines*, Commission decision of 28 August 2009.
[86] Case COMP/M.3687 – *Johnson&-Johnson/Guidant*, Commission decision of 25 August 2005.
[87] Case COMP/M.4439 – *Ryanair/Aer Lingus*, Commission decision of 27 June 2007.
[88] Case COMP/M.5335 – *Lufthansa/SN Airholding*, Commission decision of 22 June 2009.
[89] Case COMP/M.5440 – *Lufthansa/Austrian Airlines*, Commission decision of 28 August 2009.
[90] Case COMP/M.3687 – *Johnson&-Johnson/Guidant*, Commission decision of 25 August 2005.

devices. While the Commission did not conduct a detailed entry analysis, it did point out that the entry of new products had not resulted in a decrease of the parties' market shares, suggesting that entrants had not been able to impose a material competitive constraint on the merging firms.

In *Ryanair/Aer Lingus*,[91] the Commission carried out an econometric analysis that sought to identify how changes in the presence of rivals over time affected pricing.[92] The Commission conducted a before-and-after analysis, which consisted of two different specifications. The first specification was aimed at assessing the effect of one party's entry (or exit) on the other party's fares, while the second specification analysed the effects of changes in capacity (frequencies) by one party on the other party's prices. These models accounted for demand and cost variations both over time and across routes. Although the Commission's analysis was subject to some specific caveats, the primary advantage of this methodology over the analysis across routes at a given point in time (discussed in Section 3.3.3 above) was considered to be that the introduction of the time dimension mitigated the omitted-variable bias concern that cast doubt over the reliability of the cross-section analysis; the main reason for this was that most unobservable components were not likely to vary over time within a given route.[93] Given this latter point, the Commission considered this approach reliable enough so as to take its results into account in its assessment. Although the Commission did not find a statistically significant effect on Ryanair's prices in response to route entry by Aer Lingus, it found that Ryanair's presence on an Aer Lingus route was associated with Aer Lingus charging 5–10% lower prices. This finding contributed to the Commission's conclusion that the proposed merger was likely to bring about a significant impediment to effective competition.

---

[91] Case COMP/M.4439 – *Ryanair/Aer Lingus*, Commission decision of 27 June 2007.

[92] Specifically, the Commission undertook a *fixed-effects regression analysis* with panel data. 'Panel data' refers to multi-dimensional data. In the particular case at hand, it refers to data defined along two dimensions: (a) the different routes (which form a cross-section), and (b) the various points in time.

[93] For a more detailed overview of the EC's econometric analysis, see M. de la Mano, E. Pesaraesi and O. Stehman, 'Econometric and Survey Evidence in the Competitive Assessment of the Ryanair–Aer Lingus Merger' (2007) 3 *Competition Policy Newsletter* 73–81.

## 3.5    Natural experiments

### 3.5.1    Description of technique

In the preceding sections, we discussed how it may be possible to make inferences regarding the competitive constraints that firms impose on one another by considering how variations in concentration and the presence of particular rivals, either across markets or across time, affect prices. As noted above, a problem that may be encountered in these studies is that the variations in concentration that are observed (across markets or across time) may be a function of demand and cost conditions that also affect prices.[94]

Natural experiments involve studying how firms respond to changes in the market that are exogenously determined, i.e. that are not a function of firms' decisions. Under certain circumstances these exogenous changes enable one to make inferences regarding the extent to which a particular firm (or group of firms) exerts a competitive constraint on rivals. The natural experiment that is most frequently relied on in merger analysis involves making use of temporary unplanned supply disruptions.[95] Disruptions of supply may arise for a number of reasons including industrial action, a power outage or a fire at a particular firm's plant. If the supply disruption is sufficiently serious, then it may provide the basis for a natural experiment. In particular, the event may enable one to answer various questions such as: Where would customers turn in the event that a particular source of supply was unavailable? Are rivals able to expand output in response to a reduction in supply by a particular firm? How do prices charged by rivals change when a particular firm is (temporarily) no longer offering its product in competition with them? This approach is illustrated in the stylised example below.

### 3.5.2    An example

Suppose that two producers of industrial equipment, A and B, are proposing to merge. The firms have market shares of 30% and 20% respectively. The post-merger entity would face competition from two additional Firms, C and D, each enjoying a market share of 25%. Given

---

[94] This problem, known as endogeneity, is discussed further in Appendix A.
[95] Other events that could be used for the purposes of undertaking natural experiments include changes in the tax regime that affect firms in different geographic or product areas separately, and, as discussed in detail in Chapter 2 in the context of defining geographic markets, changes in exchange rates.

Table 3.14 *Firms' average monthly sales volumes in the three-month period prior to the outage and the three-month period during the outage of Firm B's plant*

|  | Three-month period prior to outage | Three-month period during outage |
|---|---|---|
| **Firm A** | 30 | 30 |
| **Firm B** | 20 | – |
| **Firm C** | 25 | 35 |
| **Firm D** | 25 | 35 |

that the post-merger firm's share would be around 50%, there is initially considered to be a risk of unilateral effects resulting from the merger.

Now suppose that over the course of the last year, Firm B underwent a three-month period in which its plant was inactive as a result of a serious fire. During this period, Firm B had to cease all production. By observing how other market participants responded to the outage of Firm B's production, it is possible to make some inference regarding the competitive constraints that each other firm would exert on Firm B under normal circumstances.

Table 3.14 shows the average monthly sales volumes of each of the four firms in the three-month period prior to the outage and the three-month period during the outage of Firm B's plant.

The table shows that during the three-month period prior to the outage of its plant, Firm B sold on average 20 units per month. During the three-month period of outage, both Firm C and Firm D experienced an increase in their average monthly sales of 10 units per month. Therefore, in the face of the absence of Firm B's product (or equivalently an infinite price increase for that product), half of Firm B's business diverted to Firm C and half diverted to Firm D, whereas none of that business diverted to Firm A. This may be taken as evidence that the most important competitive constraints on Firm B are represented by Firms C and D and that, perhaps as a result of binding capacity constraints, Firm A does not appear to exert any constraint on B.

Suppose further that no significant price increase is observed to be implemented by the remaining three suppliers during the outage period. This finding would support the view that Firm B does not represent a source of competition in the industry that is crucial for the delivery of competitive outcomes, and therefore that competition in the post-merger environment would continue to be effective.[96]

### 3.5.3   Use in EU cases

The Commission has employed natural experiments and, in particular, temporary supply disruptions to assess competitive constraints in a number of merger investigations.

In *Inco/Falconbridge*,[97] the Commission used supply disruptions resulting from industrial action at one of Inco's production plants to assess competition in the supply of nickel. The Commission noted that Falconbridge appeared to gain a significant proportion, between 25 and 35%, of the sales lost by Inco during a 13-week strike in 2003.[98] This led the Commission to conclude that Falconbridge exerted an important competitive constraint on Inco. The merger was ultimately cleared subject to the divestment of Falconbridge's Nikkelverk refinery in Norway together with related assets to LionOre, an already active player in nickel mining.

In its assessment of *Ineos/BP Dormagen*,[99] the Commission considered the parties' submission that rivals' responses to power failures at the merging firms' plants demonstrated those rivals' ability to increase ethylene oxide production to offset any potential attempt to withdraw output post-merger. It noted that while the findings regarding past ability to react to short-term outages cannot be immediately extrapolated to future ability to react to more permanent anti-competitive reductions in merchant sales by the combined entity, the studies nevertheless contributed, together with the other findings of the Commission, to the conclusion that the combined entity would be unlikely to reduce its sales to the merchant market since its competitors would have both the ability and incentive to counteract such a strategy.[100]

In *Friesland Foods/Campina*,[101] however, the Commission rejected the parties' evidence that a shutdown at one of Campina's plants resulting

---

[96] This example is clearly highly stylised. In practice, it may be necessary to use econometric techniques to control for other factors that affect firms' pricing and output decisions prior to, during and after the supply disruption.

[97] Case COMP/M.4000 – *Inco/Falconbridge*, Commission decision of 4 July 2006.

[98] Ibid., para. 373.

[99] Case COMP/M.4094 – *Ineos/BP Dormagen*, Commission decision of 10 August 2006.

[100] Ibid., para. 97.

[101] Case COMP/M.5046 – *Friesland Foods/Campina*, Commission decision of 17 December 2008.

from fires in 2004 had no impact on the overall supply of dairy products in the Netherlands. The Commission argued that temporary shutdowns do not bring about permanent changes in industry structure and so cannot be directly translated into predictions regarding post-merger pricing incentives.[102] In particular, the Commission noted that the duration of contracts in the dairy industry may have served to obscure the impact of temporary changes in industry supply; that, within the international export market the Campina plant in question accounted for a small proportion of supply; and that Campina may have outsourced production to third parties in order to mitigate the output lost at the affected plant.[103] The Commission's position here demonstrates that, in order for a supply outage natural experiment to be meaningful, it must be confirmed that the shock in question had a material impact on industry supply.

### 3.6    Merger simulation

#### 3.6.1    Description of technique

Merger simulation describes a broad category of techniques that seek to use data on existing firm behaviour to predict how that behaviour will change in response to a merger.[104] In essence, merger simulation comprises the following process. First, pre-merger market data are used to calibrate a mathematical description of competitive interactions between firms in the industry. Once this model has been established it is then modified to reflect the changes in firm ownership that will result from the proposed merger. This post-merger model will then predict how the change in ownership will alter the incentives of all firms within the industry (both the merging parties and their rivals) and, consequently, the overall effect of the merger on industry volumes and prices.

In practice, however, the use of merger simulation is a highly technical and data-intensive process, and requires the use of some strong, and, in some circumstances, questionable economic assumptions in order to render the mathematics tractable. In this section we do not attempt to provide a complete description of how merger simulation can and should

---

[102] Ibid., para. 794.    [103] Ibid., paras. 795–9.

[104] The following discussion draws in part on RBB Brief 12, 'The Emperor's New Clothes? The role of merger simulation models', January 2004. See also A. Lofaro and D. Ridyard, 'The Role of Economics in European Merger Control', in N. Levy, *European Merger Control Review – A guide to the Merger Regulation* (LexisNexis, 2011), Section 24.05.

be undertaken, but offer an introduction to merger simulation techniques and how and when they might be used.

A number of approaches have been developed to simulate the unilateral effects of mergers using econometric techniques, often in the context of mergers in branded consumer goods industries due to the availability of scanner data.[105]

The use of merger simulation models raises many methodological challenges.[106] These models also raise controversies because of the way in which they are often driven by significant assumptions about the way in which consumers make choices and in which competitors interact.

There are many variants of merger simulation models that range in sophistication. The choice between models is largely a compromise between flexibility, in the sense of imposing as few restrictions and assumptions on the model as possible, and data requirements. As a general rule, the greater the availability of data in an industry, the more flexible the modelling approach that can be employed. However, all models posit some assumptions as to the nature of competition between firms. The standard assumption made in merger simulation models in differentiated product markets is that firms compete in a manner consistent with Bertrand competition: that is, each firm chooses a price to maximise profits assuming its rivals will keep their prices constant.

The Commission has recognised that merger simulation models will necessarily abstract from reality in some way, but that the essential question is whether the simplifying assumptions made allow the model to reflect the central elements of competition in the industry in question. In *Oracle/Peoplesoft*,[107] it was stated that:

---

[105] See, e.g., J. Baker, 'Contemporary Empirical Merger Analysis', FTC Working Paper; D. Hosken, D. O'Brien, D. Scheffman and M. Vita, 'Demand System Estimation and its Application to Horizontal Merger Analysis' (DOJ Working Paper, April 2002); and J. Hausman, G. Leonard and D. Zona, 'A Proposed Method for Analyzing Competition Among Differentiated Products' (1992) 60 *Antitrust Law Journal* 889–900. In 2004, DG COMP issued a Technical Report on merger simulation methodologies: R. Epstein and D. Rubinfeld, 'Effects of Mergers Involving Differentiated Products', COMP/B1/2003/07, available at http://ec.europa.eu/competition/mergers/studies_reports/effects_mergers_involving_differentiated_products.pdf.

[106] See D. Scheffman and M. Coleman, 'FTC Perspectives on the Use of Econometrics in Antitrust Cases' (FTC Bureau of Economics Working Paper, 2002). The authors make a number of practical criticisms of econometric simulations based on structural demand estimates, arguing that these have often tended to create implausibly large predicted post-merger price effects.

[107] Case COMP/M.3216 – *Oracle/Peoplesoft*, Commission decision of 26 October 2004.

> The Commission agrees that the use of simulation models depends critically on the ability of the model to adequately capture the fundamental mechanisms that drive the behaviour of the different market participants and that, in principle, the assessment as to whether that is the case in any particular case may be a subject of debate. For models to be mathematically tractable it is necessary to make simplifying assumptions and in this process it is important to ensure that the essential mechanisms that are left in the model adequately reflect the reality.[108]

One of the main reasons for increased interest in the technique is the development of simple simulation models that require only limited data on the merging firms and their competitors. The Proportionally Calibrated Almost Ideal Demand System (PCAIDS) model, advocated by Epstein and Rubinfeld, and the Antitrust Logit Model (ALM) developed by Froeb and Werden are some of the simplest models.[109] For example, the PCAIDS model requires just three inputs – the pre-merger market shares, the aggregate elasticity of market demand and the brand level demand elasticity of one of the merging parties – in order to generate a prediction on the effect of a horizontal merger. The PCAIDS model and the ALM share a number of simplifying assumptions. In particular, both models assume that if one firm raises its price it loses demand to other brands in proportion to their market shares.[110] Assumptions about the shape of the demand curve determine the amount by which the merged entity post-merger firm will find it optimal to raise its price, and the assumption of Bertrand competition allows the model to be solved for its ultimate impact on overall market prices. However, one should bear in mind that these are extremely restrictive models in which the parties' pricing behaviour post-merger is constrained to be related directly to the market share of the merging firms. Thus, the simplicity of these models comes at a very high cost – their complete inability to explain the reality of an industry that is characterised by differentiation.

---

[108] Ibid., para. 193.

[109] R. Epstein and D. Rubinfeld, 'Merger Simulation: A Simplified Approach with New Applications' (2002) 69 *Antitrust Law Journal* 883–917; G. Werden and L. Froeb, 'The Effects of Mergers in Differentiated Products Industries: Logit Demand and Merger Policy' (1994) 10(2) *Journal of Law, Economics & Organization* 407–26.

[110] Thus, for example, in a three-firm model containing brands A, B and C where market shares are 20%, 20% and 60% respectively, it assumes that the loss of demand brand A will suffer if it raises price will be distributed between brands B and C in the ratio 25:75.

It is possible to add slightly more realism into these models through introducing 'nests' into the demand assumptions, whereby certain products are acknowledged to be closer substitutes than others. In these 'nested logit' models, the assumption that by raising price a firm will lose demand to other brands in proportion to their market shares only applies between those products that have been allocated to the same nest, but not between different nests. Crucially, however, the composition of the nests does not emerge from the data but must be imposed on the model by assumption. For further discussion of nested logit models and discrete choice more generally, see Appendix B.

With better information on the nature of inter-brand competition, a further class of more ambitious simulation models seeks to avoid potentially arbitrary assumptions on nesting by including statistical estimates of the individual own- and cross-price elasticities as inputs into the simulation. This approach was adopted by Ivaldi and Verboven in their analysis of the European truck market conducted for DG COMP on the *Volvo/Scania*[111] merger and in the study conducted by Foncel and Ivaldi, again for DG COMP, in the *Lagardère/Natexis/VUP*[112] merger.[113] Such approaches require much more in terms of data, but can claim to derive more realistic results based on the actual interaction between brands. They also allow the analysis to be unconstrained by specific market definitions, since the degree of substitutability between brands 'reveals itself' through the estimation process.

Despite the sophistication of the empirical techniques they use, the predictions generated by these models remain highly dependent on a number of key technical parameters. For example, assumptions regarding the curvature of demand can make the difference between high or low post-merger price increases, and varying assumptions about the nature of interaction between the members of an oligopoly group affect the way in which a unilateral price rise by the merging firm will translate to an

---

[111] Case COMP/M.1672 – *Volvo/Scania*, Commission decision of 15 March 2000.

[112] Case COMP/M.2978 – *Lagardère/Natexis/VUP*, Commission decision of 7 January 2004.

[113] In particular, in the *Volvo/Scania* merger investigation, the analysis conducted by Ivaldi and Verboven predicted that the merger would have led to substantial losses in consumer welfare in the Nordic countries in which the merging parties were strong, and also analysed the extent to which different scenarios of efficiency gains might mitigate those adverse effects. They also found that an alternative merger between Volvo and Renault (the transaction that did in the event take place after the Scania deal was prohibited) would not generate material adverse effects.

industry-wide outcome.[114] A more fundamental set of issues raised by these models is whether they provide a reliable guide to the actual effects of mergers. For all their sophistication in measuring the historical relationship between competing brands, the theoretical foundations of most merger simulation models are, as noted above, extremely simple Bertrand models that incorporate a built-in bias towards predicting that any horizontal merger will raise prices. Questions as to whether such models provide a valid representation of real world oligopoly interaction have led a number of critics to caution against reliance on these techniques.[115]

### 3.6.1.1   An aside on price pressure tests

We have provided an overview above of the sophisticated merger simulation tools that have been employed by the Commission in a number of in-depth merger investigations. A number of competition authorities, particularly those in the UK, have recently started to make use of simple tools that are related in spirit to merger simulation, and that may under certain circumstances provide insights into the likely effects of a merger before a more detailed investigation is initiated.

These tools are often referred to collectively as price pressure tests. As discussed above, horizontal mergers give rise to an incentive to increase prices due to the internalisation of the positive effect of a price increase by one merging party on the demand for the other merging party's product. A unifying feature of price pressure tests is that they make use of two key pieces of information – the diversion ratio between merging firms and pre-merger gross margins – to produce insights regarding the size of this incentive to increase price.

There are a number of variants of price pressure tests, and three have attracted particular attention from competition authorities: the

---

[114] For a discussion, see G. Werden, 'Simulating the Effects of Differentiated Products Mergers: A Practitioners' Guide' (June 1996) *Proceedings: Strategy and Policy in the Food System: Emerging Issues* 20–1; and G. Werden and L. Froeb, 'Calibrated Models Add Focus, Accuracy and Persuasiveness to Merger Analysis' (Discussion Paper, 2002).

[115] David Scheffman, the former Director of Economics at the FTC Bureau of Economics, has been one of the most outspoken critics. In particular, he was co-author of a paper with two of the main proponents of merger simulation techniques, Luke Froeb, his successor at the FTC, and Greg Werden, Senior Economic Counsel to the US Department of Justice Antitrust Division, which seeks to draw some practical Guidelines around the use of such techniques. See G. Werden, L. Froeb and D. Scheffmann, 'A Daubert Discipline for Merger Simulation' (Working Paper, 2004). The work of these authors represents a more balanced and critical stance on merger simulation than is found in that of many of the European economic commentators.

*Illustrative Price Rise* (IPR), *Upward Pricing Pressure* (UPP) and the *Gross Upward Pricing Pressure Index* (GUPPI).[116]

The first simple test based on pre-merger margins and diversion ratios to be considered in merger control was the illustrative price rise (IPR) approach. Its first use by a European competition authority was by the UK Competition Commission in *Somerfield/Morrisons* in 2005.[117] The IPR approach takes information on diversion ratios and pre-merger margins, along with an assumption regarding the specific shape of demand, and produces a predicted ('illustrative') price increase. Specifically, in the case of symmetric firms,[118] IPRs are calculated as $(m * d)/(1 - m - d)$ if demand is assumed to be iso-elastic and $(m * d)/2$ $(1 - d)$ if demand is assumed to be linear.[119] A significant criticism of this approach is that the predicted price increases produced by this approach are very sensitive to the choice of the demand specification. In particular, the price increases produced by an assumption of iso-elastic demand are potentially much higher than those produced by an assumption of linear demand. Furthermore, given that IPRs must always be positive, making this approach operational requires defining a threshold for the predicted percentage price increase above which IPRs give cause for concern. A number of commentators have noted that using an assumption of iso-elastic demand leads to the likelihood that concerns will be found with apparently unproblematic mergers even using relatively high thresholds for tolerable predicted price increases.[120]

More recently, two related alternative indicators, UPP and GUPPI, have been proposed. These approaches eliminate the need to make an assumption regarding the shape of demand. The basic intuition behind

---

[116] An overview of each of these tests (and some extensions) is provided in RBB Economics, 'Conjectural Variations and Competition Policy: Theory and Empirical Techniques' (A Report for the OFT, October 2011).

[117] Somerfield plc and Wm Morrison Supermarkets plc, September 2005. For a critical discussion of the use of IPRs in that case see U. Akgun and D. Ridyard, 'Lost in Translation: The use and abuse of diversion ratios in unilateral effects analysis' (2006) 27(10) *European Competition Law Review* 564–8.

[118] Analogous versions of the IPR formulae for asymmetric merging parties are more complicated, and are not presented here. These can be found in RBB Economics, 'Conjectural Variations and Competition Policy: Theory and Empirical Techniques' (A Report for the OFT by October 2011).

[119] These formulae are presented and discussed in more detail in C. Shapiro, 'Mergers with Differentiated Products' (1996) 10 *Antitrust* 23–30.

[120] See, e.g., D. Parker, 'Illustrative Price Rises from Mergers in Differentiated Products Markets', *Global Competition Policy* (April 2009) (Release 2).

these approaches is that the incentive to increase price following the merger can be conceptualised as resulting from an increase in the cost of making an extra sale for each merging firm. Consider a merger between Firm A and Firm B. Pre-merger, if Firm A makes extra sales (by reducing price), this cannibalises some of Firm B's sales and therefore comes at a cost to the profits of Firm B which Firm A is not taking into account in its pre-merger pricing decision. For each of the extra sales that Firm A makes, Firm B loses profits equal to the proportion of those sales that are won from Firm B, $DR_{AB}$,[121] multiplied by the absolute margin that Firm B would have earned on each of those sales, $M_B$. After the merger, Firm A takes account of this external cost to Firm B when making its pricing decision. The product, $DR_{AB} * M_B$, can therefore be considered as a notional increase in marginal cost of Firm A, which results from the internalisation of the cannibalisation of Firm B's sales. As with a standard increase in marginal cost, this notional cost increase leads to 'upward pressure' on Firm A's price.

The UPP approach, proposed by Joseph Farrell and Carl Shapiro,[122] compares this notional cost 'increase' to a cost decrease that can be thought to arise from merger specific efficiencies. The UPP for Firm A is given by

$$UPP_A = (DR_{AB} * M_B) - E_A C_A$$

where $DR_{AB}$ is the diversion ratio from product A to product B, $M_B$ is the gross absolute margin on the product of Firm B, and $E_A$ is the percentage reduction in Firm A's marginal cost, $C_A$. If the notional cost increase $(DR_{AB} * M_B)$ is greater than the cost decrease $E_A C_A$ then the UPP will be positive and the merger can be expected to increase prices. As such, to implement the UPP approach requires evidence or, more likely given that UPP is intended to be an initial screen, an assumption,

---

[121] Note that we assume that the proportion of extra sales that come from Firm B when Firm A *reduces* price is the same as the proportion of lost sales that divert to Firm B when Firm A *increases* price. This is a trivial assumption and is not the same as assuming that the diversion ratio from Firm A to Firm B, $DR_{AB}$, is the same as the diversion ratio from Firm B to Firm A, $DR_{BA}$, since the latter relates to changes in Firm B's price.

[122] C. Shapiro and J. Farrell, 'Antitrust Evaluation of Horizontal Mergers: An Economic Alternative to Market Definition' (Competition Policy Center UC Berkeley, November 2008).

regarding the proportionate decrease in marginal cost that is expected to arise as a result of merger specific efficiencies.[123]

The GUPPI approach, proposed by Salop and Moresi,[124] does not require such an assumption regarding efficiencies. The idea behind the GUPPI is that since the product, $DR_{AB} * M_B$, can be considered as a notional marginal cost increase for one firm arising from the merger, this value is potentially of interest in and of itself. In particular, this can in principle be combined with information on the rate of pass through of cost changes, $\rho$.[125] The change in A's price can then be predicted as the change in A's opportunity cost of increasing price multiplied by the pass through rate, $DR_{AB} * M_B * \rho$. This expression can be divided by A's price to reach a prediction of the percentage price increase of A's price. The GUPPI for Firm A is often expressed as

$$G_A = (DR_{AB} * M_B)/P_A$$

This index can be combined with information on the pass through rate, $\rho$, such that an expression for the predicted percentage price increase is simply given by

$$\text{Percentage increase in price of } A = G_A * \rho$$

A criticism of the GUPPI is that without combining this index with information on the pass through rate, it is difficult to put this value (which will always be positive) in context for the purposes of making a decision over whether the merger appears problematic.[126] At the same time, $\rho$ is extremely difficult to estimate in practice (even in the context of an in-depth investigation). Moreover, since the pass through rate for any

---

[123] Farrell and Shapiro originally proposed that mergers should be given a standard efficiency credit of $E = 10\%$ in order to operationalise this test as an initial screen.

[124] S. C. Salop and S. Moresi, 'Updating the Merger Guidelines: Comments' (2009), available at www.ftc.gov/os/comments/horizontalmergerguides/545095-00032.pdf.

[125] Note that $\rho$ is a measure of the amount by which a firm's price would increase relative to an increase in its marginal cost, holding the marginal cost of all other firms in the industry constant. For a further discussion of the relevant notion of pass through in a merger context, see S. Jaffe and E.G. Weyl, 'Price Theory and Merger Guidelines' (2011) 3(1) CPI Antitrust Chronicle.

[126] In Streetcar/Zipcar, the UK Competition Commission reached a conclusion of 'moderate' price rises from its analysis of margins and diversions ratios. However, it gave no guidance regarding the significance threshold or offsetting (efficiency) factor it used to reach this 'moderate' price rise conclusion, even though the product of diversion ratios and margins will be positive for all mergers. For a discussion of this case, see RBB Brief 36, 'Road-testing UPP: the Zipcar/Streetcar merger', available at http://www.rbbecon.com/publications/downloads/rbb_brief_36.pdf.

single firm depends on the shape of demand and rival responses, any assumption on ρ also incorporates implicit assumptions regarding the shape of demand and the nature of strategic interaction between firms.[127]

It is important to note that the original aim of pricing pressure tests was to provide an initial screen for identifying mergers that might cause competition concerns that is superior to an approach focusing on market shares.[128] Simple measures based on diversion ratios and margins do not account for a number of important factors such as supply-side responses (e.g. entry and product repositioning), multi-product pricing, pricing responses by rivals and certain demand-related factors, and as such can only form part of the overall assessment of unilateral effects. As such, and as their original proponents have noted, these simple tests should not be considered as a substitute to a more in-depth investigation.[129]

Even as a first phase screen, there is an ongoing debate over whether or not price pressure tests should form an important part of the investigation. Their main value lies in the fact that they are grounded in modern industrial economics and therefore represent an advance over traditional 'initial screening' analysis in differentiated product mergers, in so far as that analysis is restricted to an assessment of market shares.[130] Compared to merger simulation methods, these tests require very limited information, making them possible to implement during first phase investigations, in which time constraints typically do not allow for more complex exercises. Nonetheless, the use of these tests has been criticised by certain commentators. Although each of the approaches described above has its own specific shortcomings in terms of the restrictiveness of a test's assumptions or the lack of thresholds against which to judge a test's results, a criticism that applies to all of these is that they focus a

---

[127] In this respect an arbitrary assumption regarding the rate of pass through is potentially as strong as the explicit assumption regarding the shape of demand that is required to implement IPR formulae.

[128] The need for such tests is arguably greater in the US where the definition of the relevant market and the subsequent assessment of market shares is a crucial part of the courts' assessment of mergers.

[129] For example, Farrell and Shapiro introduce UPP as 'a simple, new test for making an *initial determination* of whether a proposed merger between rivals is likely to reduce competition and thus lead to higher prices'. See the article by J. Farrell and C. Shapiro cited above at n. 123.

[130] In practice, however, there is no reason to believe that Phase I in EC cases should be seen as equivalent to an 'initial screen' as the term was first used by the proponents of these tests. The Commission is in principle able to do more in Phase I than screen mergers on the basis of the results of simple pricing pressure tests or market share analyses.

great deal of attention on two numbers – diversion ratios and gross margins – at an early stage of the investigation. Gross margins, in particular, are usually difficult to measure and may become a substantial area of debate between merging parties and competition authorities, giving rise to the possible opportunity cost that other aspects of the industry, which are nonetheless extremely relevant, forgo consideration in the initial investigation.

The positive aspects of price pressure tests have resulted in some competition authorities deciding to use and refer to them in their merger decisions and EC Horizontal Merger Guidelines. However, the European Commission has neither used price pressure tests nor taken a public stand on the suitability of their use – whether the Commission will be using them or not in the future for the moment remains an open question.

### 3.6.2    An example

Consider the following simple example, with three firms producing differentiated products at a common and constant marginal cost $c$, which is estimated to be equal to €2, and facing no fixed costs or capacity constraints. The proposed merger involves Firm 1 and Firm 2. A merger simulation is being conducted in order to assess the scope for the transaction to give rise to unilateral effects.

The first step in the analysis involves estimating econometrically each of the three firms' demand functions. Although sales are typically affected by a number of price and non-price factors (e.g. advertising, weather conditions, etc.), we assume for simplicity that demand for each product depends only on the price of that product and on the prices charged by the suppliers of the other two products. As far as the demand for product 1 is concerned, this can be expressed by the following relationship:

$$q_{1,t} = \alpha + \beta\, p_{1,t} + \gamma\, p_{2,t} + \delta\, p_{3,t} + \varepsilon_t$$

where

- $q_{1,t}$ represents sales of product 1 at time $t$,
- $\alpha$ is the constant,
- $\beta$, $\gamma$ and $\delta$ are the coefficients representing the effect of the price of each product on the level of sales of product 1,
- $\varepsilon_t$ is the error term at time $t$, which reflects the fact that the prices of the three products cannot explain completely the dependent variable.

Table 3.15 *Sales of each product at various price levels*

| p1 | p2 | p3 | q1 | q2 | q3 |
|----|----|----|----|----|----|
| 10 | 10 | 10 | 80 | 80 | 80 |
| 11 | 10 | 10 | 70 | 84 | 84 |
| 12 | 10 | 10 | 60 | 88 | 88 |
| 10 | 11 | 10 | 84 | 70 | 84 |
| 10 | 12 | 10 | 88 | 60 | 88 |
| 10 | 10 | 11 | 84 | 84 | 70 |
| 10 | 10 | 12 | 88 | 88 | 60 |

The econometric analysis, based on monthly price and volume data relative to the period 2009–2011, produces the following estimated demand functions for each of the three products:[131]

$$q_1 = 100 - 10p_1 + 4p_2 + 4p_3$$
$$q_2 = 100 - 10p_2 + 4p_1 + 4p_3$$
$$q_3 = 100 - 10p_3 + 4p_1 + 4p_2$$

The above equations imply that each time Firm 1 increases the price of its product by €1, its demand can be expected to fall by 10 units, while the demand for Firm 2's and Firm 3's products can be expected to increase by 4 units each (assuming that they leave their prices unchanged). Price increases implemented by Firm 2 and Firm 3 will have analogous consequences, as illustrated in Table 3.15.

The next step in the analysis involves calculating the equilibrium price pre-merger. Each firm's profit can be obtained by multiplying the margin on each unit sold times its output. For example, Firm 1's profit can be expressed as follows:

$$\Pi_1 = (p_1 - c)q_1 = (p_1 - €2) * (100 - 10p_1 + 4p_2 + 4p_3)$$

Assuming that each firm chooses the price that maximises its profit, i.e. assuming that firms compete *à la* Bertrand, it can be verified that in equilibrium the three firms will each set a price equal to €10. For instance, as shown in Figure 3.7, assuming that Firm 2 and Firm 3 charge a price equal to €10, Firm 1's profit is maximised if it also charges a price equal to €10. Any other price would deliver lower profits. Given the

---

[131] A description of the econometric techniques required to estimate this demand system is beyond the scope of this book.

**Figure 3.7** Firm 1's profit for different price levels assuming Firms 2 and 3 set a price equal to €10

symmetry of the demand system, this implies that each firm charging €10 is indeed an equilibrium pre-merger.

The fact that a merger simulation model, once estimated, produces a forecast of pre-merger prices permits a useful cross-check in appraising the veracity of the model. If the model predicts prices in the pre-merger industry structure that diverge materially from those actually observed pre-merger, then this suggests that the model does not reflect the competitive process within the industry in question, and cannot be regarded as a reliable means by which to forecast the impact of a merger in that industry.

The final step involves estimating the impact that the proposed merger between Firm 1 and Firm 2 would have on prices. The new entity's profit can be written as follows:

$$\begin{aligned}
\Pi_{1+2} &= (p_1 - c)q_1 + (p_2 - c)q_2 \\
&= (p_1 - €2) * (100 - 10p_1 + 4p_2 + 4p_3) + (p_2 - €2) \\
&\quad * (100 - 10p_2 + 4p_1 + 4p_3)
\end{aligned}$$

Following the same logic as before, the new entity would need to find the optimal values of $p_1$ and $p_2$ that maximise its profit, given the behaviour of Firm 3.

Intuitively, the elimination of the competitive constraint that Firm 1 and Firm 2 exert on each other will give rise to higher prices post-merger. The reason for this can be seen by looking again at Table 3.15, which showed that any price increase implemented by Firm 1 would boost demand for Firm 2 and vice versa. This demand-boosting effect would be taken into account by the merged entity giving rise to higher prices in the new equilibrium.

Indeed, it can be shown that the merged entity would choose a price for each of its two products of around €13 (i.e. 30% higher than the prices charged by Firm 1 and Firm 2 pre-merger), while its rival will choose a price of around €11. In other words, our simple merger simulation model predicts that significant unilateral effects would arise post-transaction unless the new entity would be expected to benefit from a reduction in its marginal cost as a result of the merger. Any such cost reduction would be passed on, at least in part, to consumers, offsetting – albeit only partially in our example – the anti-competitive effects of the transaction.[132]

Importantly, in this type of setting, reductions in marginal costs typically represent the only countervailing factor to an increase in market power resulting from a horizontal merger. Other important factors, such as the possibility that rivals might reposition their products or extend their product portfolios, are completely ignored.[133] As the EC Horizontal Merger Guidelines explicitly acknowledge that these countervailing factors may influence the incentive of the merged entity to raise prices, it is important to recognise that even a well-specified merger simulation model can only represent a part of the overall set of evidence that sheds light on the likely impact of a proposed merger.

### 3.6.3   Use in EU cases

Merger simulation models clearly have a role to play in modern merger analysis. It is, however, very difficult in practice to fully capture all relevant aspects of competition and many models therefore suffer from highly simplified assumptions which undermine their predictive power. It might be for these reasons that DG COMP has traditionally relied on merger simulation techniques on a relatively limited number of cases in its merger decisions and relied instead on other ways to apply empirical

---

[132]   Indeed, in our example, it can be shown that even if the marginal cost $c$ of the new entity is assumed to fall to 0, post-transaction prices would still increase by almost €2 (from €10 to just below €12).

[133]   The issue of product repositioning is discussed in further detail in Section 5.3 below.

techniques in merger analysis that do not rest on such restrictive assumptions. Significant cases in which the Commission's decision discussed merger simulation analyses include the following.

In *Volvo/Scania*,[134] the Commission considered a merger simulation based on nested-logit demand and Bertrand competition that it commissioned from academics. Ultimately, however, the Commission was unwilling to rely on the merger simulation results in its assessment due to 'the novelty of the approach and the level of disagreement' between the academics and the parties.[135] The published decision did not contain any further details on the merger simulation and the sources of disagreement, but several commentaries shed light on the issues that arose. Most importantly, the model used list prices instead of actual net prices. This was a serious flaw considering the importance of discounts within the relevant markets for heavy trucks.[136] The Commission ultimately based its decision to prohibit the merger on a traditional analysis of high market shares combined with certain competitive advantages that the merging parties had in the Nordic markets for the supply of heavy trucks.

In *Phillip Morris/Papastratos*,[137] the parties put forward a merger simulation model based on nested-logit demand and Bertrand competition that suggested that the merger would provide little scope for unilateral effects, a result driven primarily by the assumption that the parties' products lay in different segments and so should be placed in separate nests. The Commission accepted that the evidence supported this product differentiation, and therefore that there was minimal scope for unilateral effects.[138] However, it is not clear what practical impact the merger simulation model had on the Commission's conclusion: the simulation's results could only be accepted once separate evidence had been collected to confirm the validity of the assumption that substitution between the parties' products was limited. It may well be the case that

---

[134] Case COMP/M.1672 – *Volvo/Scania*, Commission decision of 15 March 2000.
[135] Ibid., para. 75.
[136] The authors commissioned to perform the Volvo/Scania merger simulation discussed the limitations of the model: see M. Ivaldi and F. Verboven, 'Quantifying the Effects of Horizontal Mergers in European Competition Policy' (2005) 23 *International Journal of Industrial Organization* 669–91. See also J. Hausman and G. K. Leonard, 'Using Merger Simulation Models: Testing the Underlying Assumptions' (2005) 23 *International Journal of Industrial Organization* 693–8.
[137] Case COMP/M.3191 – *Phillip Morris/Papastratos*, Commission decision of 2 October 2003.
[138] Ibid., para. 32.

that evidence in itself would have been sufficient to rule out unilateral effects and justify a clearance decision. As such, the merger simulation exercise arguably became redundant once the cross-checks necessary to accept the simulation had been undertaken.

In *Lagardère/Natexis/VUP*,[139] a merger simulation model was conducted by external academics on behalf of the Commission.[140] This model predicted relatively modest price increases within a range from 3.74% to 5.54% for general literature books in pocket format. The model was based on list prices excluding tax to final consumers and did not therefore take into account any discounts provided to dealers. It is likely that the Commission would have identified concerns in the absence of this evidence as the merger combined the two leading suppliers resulting in a market share of more than 50%.

In *Oracle/Peoplesoft*,[141] the Commission employed a merger simulation model in order to assess the likely impact of the merger on a candidate market that encompassed only Oracle, Peoplesoft and SAP. This model found that the merger 'was likely to lead to significant harm to customers due to a combination of reduced choice and increased prices', which is perhaps unsurprising given that, on the market definition assumed by the model, the transaction would reduce the number of suppliers from three to two.[142] Having undertaken the merger simulation analysis on this basis, however, the Commission ultimately reached the view that the relevant product market was broader than assumed, such that a further four or five suppliers should be considered rivals for the parties' products. This new conclusion undermined the Commission's merger simulation model, which was then withdrawn from the assessment. It is interesting to note that the Commission did not attempt to produce a revised merger simulation model reflecting its final conclusion on market definition, possibly due to the time and data constraints that often hamper the use of merger simulation models.

Nonetheless, while recognising that its merger simulation model in this particular case was rendered inapplicable by the assumed market definition on which it was predicated, the Commission did set out its support for the technique in general. In particular, the Commission argued that the assumptions required by merger simulation models were

---

[139]    Case COMP/M.2978 – *Lagardère/Natexis/VUP*, Commission decision of 7 January 2004.
[140]    Ibid., paras. 700 et seq.
[141]    Case COMP/M.3216 – *Oracle/Peoplesoft*, Commission decision of 26 October 2004.
[142]    Ibid., para. 191.

more transparent than implicit assumptions that may underpin other forms of economic evidence:[143]

> The debate over which simplifications to accept in the model should not obscure the fact that any prospective analysis of the effect of a merger will inherently be based on assumptions. A prediction of the effect of a merger made within the framework of a model is based on a high degree of transparency regarding the logical consistency of the prediction as well as its underlying assumptions. A prospective analysis made outside the framework of an economic model based on qualitative assessment is equally, though in a less transparent and implicit way, based on a number of assumptions and may therefore equally be subject to the same kinds of criticisms.
>
> The Commission therefore maintains as a general point that this kind of simulation model can be a useful tool in assisting the Commission in making the economic assessment of the likely impact of a merger.

In *Kraft Foods/Cadbury*,[144] a merger simulation model based on Bertrand competition and employing a nested-logit demand approach was used by the parties' advisers to assess the impact of the merger on the chocolate confectionery market in the UK and Ireland.[145] The nests for the model (countlines, tablets and pralines) were defined according to the product classifications within Nielsen scanner data. The simulation model estimated that the proposed operation would lead only to very small weighted average price increases in the UK and in Ireland, even in the absence of any efficiencies. The Commission undertook a range of robustness and sensitivity tests on the parties' analysis, and found that the claimed results applied for a range of assumed inputs used to calibrate the model.[146] On the basis of this analysis, corroborated by other evidence suggesting that the parties were not particularly close competitors (in particular, the Commission acknowledged the strong preference of UK and Irish customers for traditional British chocolate varieties as distinct from 'continental' chocolate), the Commission concluded that

---

[143] Ibid., paras. 19 and 195.

[144] Case COMP/M.5644 – *Kraft Foods/Cadbury*, Commission decision of 6 January 2010.

[145] Ibid. The parties overlapped in a number of food and beverage markets. In particular, both Kraft and Cadbury were strong players in the chocolate confectionary business in the EEA, where Kraft's main chocolate brands include Milka, Côte d'Or and Toblerone, while Cadbury was the market leader in the UK and Ireland, and also owned local brands in France, Poland, Romania and Portugal.

[146] Case COMP/M.5644 – *Kraft Foods/Cadbury*, Commission decision of 6 January 2010, para. 68.

the transaction would not give rise to any competition concerns in the UK and Irish markets.[147]

The Commission undertook a merger simulation analysis in *Unilever/ Sarah Lee Body Care*,[148] which sought to predict the impact of the proposed transaction on a number of deodorant markets in which the parties' Axe, Sanex, Dove and Rexona brands would account for a high combined share of supply. In contrast to *Kraft Foods/Cadbury*,[149] where the merger simulation analysis was proposed by the parties, the merger simulation in *Unilever/Sara Lee Body Care* was initiated by the Commission, emphasising the Commission's commitment to the technique where feasible and appropriate. As in *Kraft Foods/Cadbury*, the Commission first undertook a demand estimation exercise using a nested logit model and then carried out a merger simulation to estimate the possible impact of the transaction on deodorant prices. The analysis was done at a country level and was focused exclusively on four countries – Belgium, the Netherlands, Spain and the UK.

For the demand side, two different variations of the nested logit model were used, one setting one level of nests and the other setting two levels.[150]

On the supply side, the assumptions of the model were based on standard, static Bertrand competition. The simulation exercise predicted that the transaction would result in hypothetical price increases in the range of 1–6% (the exact estimate varied by country and product type). The Commission concluded, on the basis of the predicted hypothetical price increases and a range of other indicators, that the merging parties were close competitors in the various deodorant markets. Based on the results of its investigation, the Commission reached the view that the

---

[147] However, the Commission identified competition concerns within chocolate confectionery in Poland and Romania, where the combined market share of Kraft/Cadbury was particularly high and their brands were considered to compete more closely, in particular in the chocolate tablets markets. To remedy these concerns, Kraft committed to divest Cadbury's Polish confectionery business marketed under the Wedel brand and Cadbury's domestic chocolate confectionery business in Romania.

[148] Case COMP/M.5658 – *Unilever/Sara Lee Body Care*, Commission decision of 17 November 2010.

[149] Case COMP/M.5644 – *Kraft Foods/Cadbury*, Commission decision of 6 January 2010.

[150] The one-level specification postulated that consumers perceive male deodorants to be closer to each other than to non-male deodorants (and vice versa); thus two nests (male deodorants and non-male deodorants) were defined. The two-level model was considered a refinement of the former, to which an extra layer of nests was added for skin-friendly and non-skin-friendly deodorants.

proposed transaction would give rise to competition concerns in Belgium, the Netherlands, Denmark, the United Kingdom, Ireland, Spain and Portugal. In order to remedy these concerns, Unilever offered to divest Sara Lee's Sanex brand and the merger was finally cleared.[151]

The Commission acknowledged that its simulation model suffered from several limitations, including assumptions on substitution patterns, on the absence of entry, and on fixed retailer margins. Given the sensitivity of this type of econometric analysis to the conditions imposed and the generally low price increases that the results showed, one would have expected the Commission's decision not to place too much weight on the outcome of the simulation. However, the Commission stated that the modelling exercise – along with the collection of the other qualitative and quantitative evidence available – significantly increased the overall reliability of the assessment. This suggests not only that the Commission may be increasingly willing to instigate merger simulation analyses but also that it may be willing to accord higher importance to their results in future.

Interestingly, and as already noted above, the Commission (unlike certain other competition authorities such as those in the UK) has not yet applied pricing pressure tests (such as UPP or GUPPI) or simplified merger simulation tools such as IPR.[152] It remains to be seen whether these tests will become part of the toolkit used by the Commission in future cases.

### 3.7   Win/loss and bidding analysis

#### 3.7.1   Description of technique

In markets where companies bid for contracts, historical market shares often do not give a good indication of future market power. In such markets, competition sometimes takes the form of bids 'for the market', rather than competition 'in the market', and thus actual market shares do not have much bearing on the degree of competition. Indeed, if contracts are large and infrequent, the winning or losing of one contract can

---

[151] Note that Sanex was the brand that, among other things, showed the highest hypothetical price increases in the outcome of the simulation exercise.

[152] For example, the UK Competition Commission applied the IPR framework in *Somerfield Morrisons* (2005) and applied the GUPPI framework in *Zipcar/Streetcar* (2011). The OFT applied IPRs in *ASDA/Netto* (2011) and GUPPI in *Unilever/Alberto Culver* (2011).

completely change the market share profile.[153] Firms who do not have any share of a particular market, but who bid for contracts, can influence the degree of competition, so long as their bids are credible.[154] However, it is not simply the number of credible bids that is important; in some bidding markets it is possible to have intense competition with very few bidders.

As acknowledged in the EC Horizontal Merger Guidelines, an analysis of win/loss data can be a useful way to assess the presence of important competitive constraints between firms in markets where competition between suppliers takes the form of bidding for contracts placed by customers.[155]

In particular, win/loss data can offer complementary information to that provided by market share data because they help identify the strength of the competitive constraints on each of the merging parties provided by each existing competitor. This is acknowledged by the EC Horizontal Merger Guidelines, which note that 'In bidding markets it may be possible to measure whether historically the submitted bids by

---

[153] Generally, the greater the size and the smaller the number of tenders, the more likely it is that the Commission will deem market shares to be a poor proxy of market power. For instance, in *Siemens/VA Tech* the Commission pointed out:

> It should be noted that the fact that there is bidding on a market does not in itself allow any conclusion to be drawn as to the intensity of competition to be expected, or as to the significance of market shares as an indicator of possible market power. The key factor is rather the bidding pattern in individual cases. For example, even where there is a small number of credible bidders, particularly intensive competition is to be expected if, in a bidding market, a large proportion of tenders is awarded in a few, large transactions and the products of the various competitors and their cost structure are largely homogeneous. In this and similar cases, market shares would, in practice, provide very little information on the possible market power of a bidder.

[Case COMP/M.3653 – *Siemens/VA Tech*, Commission decision of 13 July 2005, para. 39.]

[154] It may be the case that in certain situations market share may reflect a firm's ability to make a credible bid as it may indicate that the firm has the requisite experience and resources, scale economies or brand to fulfil the contract.

[155] It is worth noting that there are markets characterised by formal tender procedures (e.g. customers may be obliged to organise tenders) and markets where customers invite several suppliers to submit quotes. There is no clear-cut line between the two and most non-consumer markets with relatively high value products or contracts will display some level of tendering. The Commission has not limited the use of bid data analysis to only formal tender procedures.

one of the merging parties have been constrained by the presence of the other merging party.'[156]

Importantly, regardless of whether any such constraint is caused by a high degree of closeness of competition between the parties' products or by one of the parties being an important competitive force, this will result in the company in question showing up as bidder and/or as the 'runner-up' in a large proportion of the contracts won by the other party.[157] In particular:

- If Firm B's product is a particularly close substitute for product A, then one would expect that in a large proportion of contracts won by Firm A, customers saw Firm B as the next best alternative and, therefore, they would have used the credible threat of switching to the latter in order to extract the best possible price from Firm A. The elimination of Firm B might therefore allow Firm A to raise its price post-merger.
- If Firm B adopts a highly aggressive pricing strategy (i.e. it is a potential important competitive force), then even if its product is not a particularly close substitute for product A, it may well bid for and/or be selected as the runner-up in a significant proportion of contracts won by Firm A. Crucially, though, this will only occur if the two parties' products are not so differentiated as to make customers' threats of turning to product B not credible in the eyes of Firm A. Under these circumstances, customers would be better off relying on other firms (i.e., Firms C and/or D) to obtain a competitive price from Firm A and

---

[156] EC Horizontal Merger Guidelines, para. 29. Furthermore, in the *IBM/Telelogic* decision, the Commission states:

> 'Win/loss' data describe instances where each Party won a new contract (e.g. contract with a firm that was not yet a customer, new project of an existing customer) as well as instances where each Party lost a potential contract (e.g. renewal of an already existing contract, extension of an already existing contract, new potential business opportunity). The purpose of such a quantitative analysis is to assist in the assessment of closeness of substitution between each Party's products, e.g. by measuring 'meeting' frequencies of each Party's products in customers' procurement processes and by measuring whether the presence of each Party's offering has an influence on the outcome of customers' procurement processes.

[Case COMP/M.4747 – *IBM/Telelogic*, Commission decision of 5 March 2008, para. 186.]

[157] In fact, in many circumstances it is the second-placed bidder that effectively determines the price that is the result of a bidding contest. In order to win, a firm has in principle to set a price that is just slightly more attractive to a customer than the next-best alternative – there is no incentive for the winning firm to set the absolute lowest price its marginal cost levels allow for if a higher price would also suffice to win the deal.

a merger between Firm A and Firm B cannot be considered to eliminate an important competitive force.

To assess whether a proposed merger would bring together the best-placed bidders for any customer requirements and to evaluate the effects of the merger according to the way it would affect the intensity of the bidding between the contestants, a number of different types of analysis can in principle be undertaken, subject to the required data and information being available. Ideally, the following information on each bidding contest won and lost by each merging party during the previous three/five years would be employed:[158]

. date of the tender;
. customer name and customer location;
. key product requirements;
. contract duration and expected annual volume sales split by product;
. list price and net price offered by each merging party by product;
. incumbent supplier;[159]
. winning supplier;
. other bidders (if applicable/known);
. primary competitor/runner-up (if applicable/known).[160]

Depending on the amount of data and information that can be collected by the parties on each tender, one or more of the following forms of analysis may be feasible:

. *Participation analysis.* A participation analysis is the simplest type of bidding analysis that can be undertaken. This requires the

---

[158] Where possible the parties should check what information the Commission required in past bid data analyses in the same sector (many decisions list the exact variables included in the bid data request) or agree on the list of information with the Commission. It is also worth noting that firms normally have more information on contracts that they have won than on those they have lost. For this reason, although the parties are typically requested to provide data on both tenders won and lost, win data are often more reliable and comprehensive.

[159] The identity of the incumbent is typically required to assess the importance of switching costs in the industry and the extent to which the parties are uniquely well placed to compete for new business relative to other rivals.

[160] Note that the information on bidders and the identity of the runner-up is typically more reliable if collected by the parties during the normal course of business. If the parties do not collect such information in the normal course of business, they may be required to rely on their local sales managers to reconstruct the main sources of competition that they faced in each tender.

identification, for each tender, of the bidders that took part in the contest. To the extent that the parties are particularly close competitors, they will tend to show up as bidders against one another more frequently than other suppliers. If the parties are observed to not frequently face one another in tenders then this would suggest that they are not competing for the business of the same customers, and so that the two are not close competitors.

- *Runner-up analysis.* A runner-up analysis can be usefully undertaken in those cases in which, as well as the name of the bidders, the ranking of the losing bidders can be established. Importantly, the second-placed bidder in each bidding contest can be normally considered as the player that exercised the strongest competitive constraint on the winner of that particular contest. Therefore, if the data reveal that one of the merging parties often ranks second behind the other merging party, this may suggest that the two companies represent the closest competitors for one another and that the merger would eliminate an important constraint, which may allow the post-merger entity to raise prices.
- *Analysis of the relationship between prices and identity of runner-up/ bidders.* If data on prices and discounts offered by the parties in each tender are available, it may be possible to assess the extent to which the prices at which tenders were won are affected by the identity of the runner-up or the presence of other firms in the tendering process.[161] If a merging party is found to offer lower prices when the other merging party participates in a tender than in cases where the other is not present, then this would indicate that the proposed merger may eliminate an important competitive constraint and, therefore, that the post-merger entity may be able to raise prices unilaterally. Alternatively, if the prices offered by each merging party are unaffected (after taking into account all other relevant factors such as the size of the contract and the number of bidders) by the presence of the other merging party, this would indicate that there is nothing unique about the competitive constraint that the two parties exert on one another and, therefore, that the proposed merger would be unlikely to give rise to unilateral effects.
- *Analysis of the relationship between prices and number of bidders.* When data on the prices and/or discounts are available and there is significant variation in the number of suppliers that typically bid for

---

[161] See S. Bishop and A. Lofaro, 'Assessing Unilateral Effects in Practice: Lessons from *GE/ Instrumentarium*' (2005) 26(4) *European Competition Law Review* 205–8.

contracts, it might be possible to test for the existence of a relationship between prices (discounts) and number of bidders. To the extent that prices tend to decrease systematically as the number of bidders increases, this might suggest that a merger between two bidders might give rise to unilateral effects, even if the two parties cannot be characterised as particularly close competitors.

### 3.7.2   An example

Suppose that in a bidding market, there are currently five suppliers of a particular product, denoted A, B, C, D and E. The product is sold only in three countries, namely the UK, Germany and Italy. Even though suppliers are able to bid for tenders in any country as they wish, they might not be perceived as credible bidders by customers if they lack a significant distribution infrastructure in the country where the customer is located. The proposed merger involves Firm A, which has a physical presence in each of the three countries, and Firm B, which owns a local infrastructure only in the UK and Germany. Out of the other three firms, only Firm D is physically present in all countries, while Firm E is not present in the UK and Firm C is not present in Italy.

In the context of the proposed transaction, Firm A collected the information on bids it had won over the last 5 years as shown in Table 3.16.

In what follows we present simple examples of the types of analysis that might be undertaken in order to assess the pre-merger competitive constraint that Firm B exercises on Firm A, given the data set out above. In practice, it may be necessary to obtain information on other factors (for example, the size of each tender), and to control for the impact of these factors using econometric techniques.

**3.7.2.1   Participation analysis**   Table 3.17 shows the frequency with which each supplier was present as a bidder in the contests won by Firm A in the UK, Germany and France.

On the basis of this analysis, it appears that in the UK, Firm A faces competition most frequently from Firm C (ten tenders), followed by Firm D (nine tenders). Firm B shows up as a bidder slightly less frequently (seven tenders), whilst Firm E is present in only two tenders, most likely as a result of the fact that it does not have any infrastructure in this country. The picture in Germany is somewhat different. While Firms C and D take part in almost all tenders (nine), Firm E shows up as a bidder in seven cases and Firm B in only five of them. Finally, in Italy it

Table 3.16 *Firm A's bidding data for the UK, Germany and Italy*

| Tenders | Country | Firm A's discount | Other bidders | | | | Runner-up |
|---|---|---|---|---|---|---|---|
| | | | Firm B | Firm C | Firm D | Firm E | |
| Tender 1 | UK | 25% | X | X | X | | Firm C |
| Tender 2 | UK | 18% | X | X | X | | Firm D |
| Tender 3 | UK | 15% | X | X | X | X | Firm B |
| Tender 4 | UK | 24% | X | X | X | | Firm C |
| Tender 5 | UK | 20% | | X | X | X | Firm C |
| Tender 6 | UK | 18% | X | X | X | | Firm D |
| Tender 7 | UK | 18% | | X | X | | Firm C |
| Tender 8 | UK | 26% | X | X | X | | Firm C |
| Tender 9 | UK | 18% | X | X | X | | Firm C |
| Tender 10 | UK | 15% | | X | X | | Firm B |
| Tender 11 | Germany | 24% | X | X | X | X | Firm C |
| Tender 12 | Germany | 10% | | | X | | Firm D |
| Tender 13 | Germany | 20% | X | X | X | X | Firm E |
| Tender 14 | Germany | 16% | | X | X | X | Firm B |
| Tender 15 | Germany | 16% | X | X | X | X | Firm B |
| Tender 16 | Germany | 25% | | X | X | X | Firm C |
| Tender 17 | Germany | 24% | | X | X | X | Firm E |
| Tender 18 | Germany | 25% | | X | X | X | Firm C |
| Tender 19 | Germany | 24% | X | X | X | | Firm C |
| Tender 20 | Germany | 15% | X | X | X | X | Firm E |
| Tender 21 | Italy | 9% | | | X | | Firm D |

Table 3.16 (*cont.*)

| Tenders | Country | Firm A's discount | Other bidders | | | | Runner-up |
|---|---|---|---|---|---|---|---|
| | | | Firm B | Firm C | Firm D | Firm E | |
| Tender 22 | Italy | 10% | | | | X | Firm E |
| Tender 23 | Italy | 14% | X | | X | X | Firm E |
| Tender 24 | Italy | 5% | | | X | | Firm D |
| Tender 25 | Italy | 13% | | X | X | X | Firm E |
| Tender 26 | Italy | 5% | | | | X | Firm E |
| Tender 27 | Italy | 12% | | X | X | X | Firm D |
| Tender 28 | Italy | 4% | | | | X | Firm E |
| Tender 29 | Italy | 15% | X | | X | X | Firm D |
| Tender 30 | Italy | 8% | | | | X | Firm E |

Table 3.17 *Rivals' participation in bids won by Firm A in the UK,
Germany and Italy*

|         | Firm B | Firm C | Firm D | Firm E |
|---------|--------|--------|--------|--------|
| **UK**      | 7      | 10     | 9      | 2      |
| **Germany** | 5      | 9      | 9      | 7      |
| **Italy**   | 2      | 2      | 6      | 8      |

is Firm D and Firm E that appear to represent Firm A's typical rivals, with Firm B and Firm C showing up in only two instances, again probably due to the lack of a physical presence in this country.

**3.7.2.2  Runner-up analysis**  A runner-up analysis sheds further light on the closeness of competition between Firm A and the other suppliers. Table 3.18 shows the instances in which each supplier was identified as Firm A's primary competitor.

This further analysis suggests that Firm C represents Firm A's closest competitor in both the UK and in Germany, since it shows up as the runner-up in six and four cases respectively in these two countries. The other merging party, Firm B, does not appear to represent a particularly close competitor to Firm A in either of these two countries, being a runner-up in only two of ten cases. This conclusion holds even more strongly in Italy, where Firm B is never identified as the primary competitor, Firms D and Firm E being the primary competitors in all instances.

**3.7.2.3  Analysis of the relationship between prices and identity of the runner-up**  Since data on the discounts off the list price offered by Firm A in each contest are available, it is possible to undertake an assessment of the relationship between discounts and the identity of the primary competitor. As explained above, to the extent that a firm exercises a particularly significant competitive constraint on a rival, one would expect the latter to offer higher discounts in those instances in which the former is selected as the runner-up. Table 3.19 shows the average discount offered by Firm A across all bids in which each rival was the runner-up.

The table corroborates the results of the runner-up analysis. In the UK the average discount offered by Firm A when Firm C is the runner-up

Table 3.18 *Rivals' identification as primary competitors in bids won by Firm A*

|         | Firm B | Firm C | Firm D | Firm E |
|---------|--------|--------|--------|--------|
| UK      | 2      | 6      | 2      | 0      |
| Germany | 2      | 4      | 1      | 3      |
| Italy   | 0      | 0      | 4      | 6      |

Table 3.19 *Average discount offered by Firm A when facing individual rivals as primary competitors*

|         | Firm B | Firm C | Firm D | Firm E |
|---------|--------|--------|--------|--------|
| UK      | 15%    | 22%    | 18%    | –      |
| Germany | 16%    | 25%    | 10%    | 20%    |
| Italy   | –      | –      | 10%    | 9%     |

is 22%, significantly higher than the average discount offered when other firms, and in particular the other merging party, Firm B, is the primary competitor (only 15%). Similarly, in Germany, the presence of Firm C as a primary competitor leads Firm A to offer discounts of 25% on average, significantly higher than the 16% discount offered when Firm B is the runner-up. In Italy, it would appear that Firm A typically grants roughly similar discounts (around 10%) regardless of whether the primary competitor is Firm D or Firm E, although this is not directly relevant to the assessment of the proposed merger of Firm A and Firm B, the latter not being present as a runner-up to the former in Italy.

**3.7.2.4  Analysis of the relationship between prices and number of bidders**   Finally, the available data can also be used to assess whether, regardless of the closeness of competition between Firm A and each of the other firms, competitive concerns would arise purely as a result of the reduction in the number of bidders brought about by the proposed merger. As explained above, this could be a concern to the extent that prices typically decrease (i.e. discounts typically increase) as the number of bidders increases.

In this respect, it is worth noting that discounts in Italy, where B and C are barely present and where competition appears to take place in many

Table 3.20 *Average discounts granted by Firm A in the UK, Germany and Italy*

| UK | Germany | Italy |
|---|---|---|
| 20% | 20% | 10% |

cases between only two bidders, tend to be significantly lower than in the other two countries. This is illustrated in Table 3.20, which shows that the average discount in Italy is 10%, exactly half of the average discount in the UK and Germany.

Significantly, however, the fact that the average discount in Germany, where all five firms regularly bid for contracts, is the same as the average discount in the UK, where Firm E is only barely present, may suggest that competitive outcomes can be achieved when there are less than five bidders in the contest.

This issue can be investigated in more detail by considering all contests regardless of the country in which they took place and examining the relationship between average discounts and number of bidders. Figure 3.8 plots this relationship.

The chart shows that average discounts tend to be low (7%) when only two suppliers take part in the contest, but sharply increase, to around 19%, when there are three bidders, with additional bidders having no incremental impact on discounts. This finding suggests that competition between three bidders is sufficient to obtain competitive outcomes.

Since Firm B is virtually absent in Italy and since the data suggest that at least three credible bidders would remain both in Germany (the merged entity and Firm C, Firm D and Firm E) and in the UK (the merged entity and Firm C and Firm D), it seems reasonable to conclude that unilateral effects are unlikely to arise simply as a result of the reduction in the number of bidders caused by the proposed merger.

### 3.7.3   Use in EU merger control

Detailed bid data analysis was already a prominent feature in merger cases before the introduction of the EC Horizontal Merger Guidelines. Examples of high-profile cases before 2004 include *Bombardier/ADtranz*,[162] *Philips/*

---

[162] Case COMP/M.2139 – *Bombardier/ADtranz*, Commission decision of 3 April 2001.

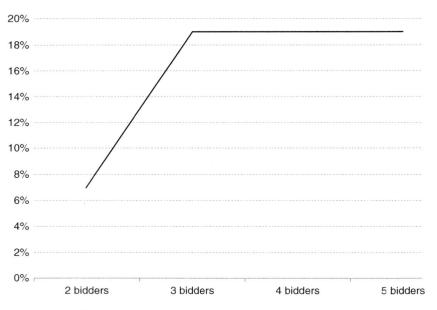

**Figure 3.8**   Relationship between average discounts and number of bidders

*Agilent Health Care Solutions*[163] and *GE/Instrumentarium*.[164] The technique was also used in *Oracle/PeopleSoft*,[165] in which an econometric analysis of the bidding data demonstrated that there was no connection between the identity or number of the competitors and the bidding behaviour of the merging parties.

The Commission appears to rely on participation analyses more frequently than other forms of bidding studies. Participation analyses have the considerable advantage of being readily undertaken, as suppliers will often be aware of the identity of the rivals faced in tenders, even when they are not aware of the identity of the second-placed bidder.[166]

In *Syniverse/BSG*,[167] the Commission cleared the merger, which reduced the number of bidders from three to two with broadly equal

---

[163] Case COMP/M.2256 – *Philips/Agilent Health Care Solutions*, Commission decision of 2 March 2001.

[164] Case COMP/M.3083 – *GE/Instrumentarium*, Commission decision of 2 September 2003.

[165] Case COMP/M.3216 – *Oracle/Peoplesoft*, Commission decision of 26 October 2004.

[166] In some cases, however, it may be possible for competition authorities to obtain information on tender rankings from customers.

[167] Case COMP/M.4662 – *Syniverse/BSG*, Commission decision of 4 December 2007.

shares of supply, on the grounds that the two bidders that would remain post-merger would be sufficient to ensure effective completion. In particular, the Commission relied upon a bidding study in reaching the view that the remaining rival, Mach, would continue to exercise a significant competitive constraint on the merged entity:[168]

> The analysis of the bidding data, gathered through the market investigation has shown that BSG and Syniverse were never the only two bidders in a tender. In fact, in the cases where only two clearing houses took part in a tender, they were either BSG and Mach or Mach and Syniverse. This means that in nearly half of the cases, the [customers] determined that the tender process was sufficiently competitive with two bidders, namely Mach and BSG or Mach and Syniverse.

In addition to the observation that the merging parties very rarely faced each other directly, it also appears to be significant in the Commission's reasoning that customers were, notwithstanding the presence of three potential suppliers pre-merger, satisfied with inviting only two firms to participate in bids. As such, even with only two bidders remaining post-merger, the Commission may find no concerns where two interrelated conditions are met: (a) customers consider a few bidders sufficient to ensure a competitive outcome; and (b) the merging firms are not considered close competitors and generally bid against another supplier who will remain an effective constraint post-merger (e.g. in *Syniverse/BSG*,[169] with the exception of one tender, Mach was apparently the runner-up in all tenders).

As pointed out in *IBM/Telelogic*,[170] focusing exclusively on the participation of firms in the final round of bidding and ignoring participation in earlier rounds may give rise to an incomplete picture of

---

[168] Ibid., para. 74. There are conflicting cases where the Commission has suggested that a reduction of (key) bidders from three to two is likely to be anti-competitive. See, e.g., Case COMP/M.3314 – *Air Liquide/Messer Targets*, Commission decision of 15 March 2004, and Case COMP/M.3512 – *VNU/WPP/JV*, Commission decision of 15 September 2004 (para. 29): 'A reduction in the number of credible competitors from three to two would be likely to raise strong competition concerns, because it would leave only one alternative bidder in cases where the customer has a preference for changing to a new supplier.' In these cases the Commission thus appears to have been unwilling to accept that two credible bidders are sufficient to ensure effective competition. In practice, the difference in approach may stem from the fact that these cases, unlike *Syniverse/BSG*, were resolved within first phase review periods.

[169] Case COMP/M.4662 – *Syniverse/BSG*, Commission decision of 4 December 2007.

[170] Case COMP/M.4747 – *IBM/Telelogic*, Commission decision of 5 March 2008.

the competitive environment in which firms operate. Specifically, the Commission noted:

> The in-depth Phase II market investigation showed that the average number of companies taking part in the first round is five. During the final round the average number of competitors left as was established in the Phase I market investigation comes to three. Focusing exclusively on the number of bidders in the final round does not, therefore, reflect the actual competitive situation as it does not take account of potential competitors.[171]

While participation studies are more easily undertaken, they may shed less light on competitive interactions than runner-up analyses. Where the latter technique captures the closeness of competition between suppliers, participation studies can only identify the range of rivals active within the same sphere of activity. As such, participation studies may be considered to some extent analogous to market definition exercises, as distinct from runner-up analyses that seek directly to measure the closeness of competition and therefore the scope for unilateral effects. Consequently, participation studies may either under- or over-state the degree of competition between merging parties.

The Commission has indicated in several decisions that a participation analysis is based on the assumption that companies only take part in those tenders which they think they have a chance of winning. Such an assumption is not unreasonable where participation involves significant costs. However, where this is not the case and most, if not all, firms within an industry take part in the vast majority of tenders, a participation study may over-state the importance of less competitively significant firms. Indeed, as the Commission indicated in the *IBM/Telelogic*[172] case, the fact that customers invite a number of suppliers to submit bids does not necessarily mean that all of them will be able to submit credible bids:[173]

> In view of the high degree of heterogeneity of the individual tools, and of the limited knowledge customers may have, in particular at the start of the evaluation process, of the tools characteristics and its performance in practice, it is necessary to be cautious in drawing conclusions from the simple fact that a specific tool is mentioned on a long list or even on a short list. As set out in the chapter on the procurement process, the

---

[171] Ibid., para. 66.
[172] Case COMP/M.4747 – *IBM/Telelogic*, Commission decision of 5 March 2008.
[173] Ibid., para. 154.

customer will often only know whether the long- and even the short-listed products were realistic substitutes to the tool eventually chosen by the end of the procurement process.

Under these circumstances, the assessment of the scope for the transaction to eliminate an important competitive constraint will be better addressed via a runner-up analysis than a simple participation analysis.

An analysis of the relationship between pricing and bidding behaviour is often more complex than a participation or runner-up analysis but, as explained above, can be extremely informative when the required data are available.

In *Oracle/PeopleSoft*,[174] the Commission carried out an econometric analysis of bidding data provided by Oracle and PeopleSoft. Its aim was to investigate the extent to which the competitive situation of a particular bid (measured by the number and identity of final-round bidders) had an impact on the discounting offered by the seller in question.[175] The Commission found that once the size of the deal was taken into account in the analysis, the number of final bidders no longer provided any additional explanatory power over the discount offered and no general pattern emerged regarding the presence of a particular competitor prompting particularly high discounts.[176] Whilst the Commission agreed that there was no evidence based on bidding data that constituted proof of an anti-competitive effect of the merger, it noted more generally that the absence of a statistically significant relationship between prices and the number/identity of bidders did not necessarily imply that the merger had no harmful effects, due for example to poor data quality or because the identity of bidders in the final round provided an incomplete picture of the actual competitive process.[177] In any event, the Commission concluded that the market after the merger would still contain more bidders than buyers usually invite to the final round and that SAP (the largest supplier) would remain a very strong competitor.

In *Syniverse/BSG*,[178] a pricing analysis supplemented the evidence from the participation analysis (discussed above) that the parties were not particularly close competitors. The Commission used econometric analysis to control for other factors during an assessment of whether BSG's

---

[174] Case COMP/M.3216 – *Oracle/Peoplesoft*, Commission decision of 26 October 2004.
[175] Ibid., para. 199.        [176] Ibid., para. 201.        [177] Ibid., paras. 202–3.
[178] Case COMP/M.4662 – *Syniverse/BSG*, Commission decision of 4 December 2007.

prices for data clearing differed according to the presence or absence of Syniverse from competitive tenders. The Commission found that:

> ... prices offered by BSG are unaffected by whether or not Syniverse participated in a tender, which implies that Syniverse does not exert a strong competitive pressure on BSG's prices. Consequently, the proposed operation would not remove a significant competitive constraint on BSG and the combined entity would not have the ability to increase prices unilaterally as a result of the proposed operation.[179]

When analysing the results of bid data, it is important to consider whether the merging firms may be close bidders in a specific identifiable market segment or niche. If so, it could be argued that such segments represent a separate relevant market. This approach was adopted by the Commission in *Oracle/PeopleSoft*,[180] where bid data formed part of the overall evidence used to define a separate market for high-end customers exceeding a certain size.[181]

The Commission considered the same point in *AEE/Lentjes*,[182] but found that:

> Detailed analysis of the projects won by different competitors showed further that these had no special features such as might suggest that firms specialised in certain types of tender. Although each firm possesses certain strengths, e.g. in the area of combustion technology, tenders are as a rule organised on a functional basis ... which means that all established competitors are able to carry out major projects. In particular, no projects could be identified in which the parties possessed a definite advantage or in which their competitors were unable to participate.[183]

The Commission reached a similar conclusion in *IBM/Telelogic*,[184] where it noted that: 'segmentation by the size of the project, the industry or the region of the customer does not seem to exhibit higher levels of interaction between the parties than between Telelogic and its main competitors.'[185]

The foregoing also means that the bid data sample needs to be comprehensive and representative of all different market segments.

---

[179] Ibid., para. 78.
[180] Case COMP/M.3216 – *Oracle/PeopleSoft*, Commission decision of 26 October 2004.
[181] Ibid., paras. 128–35.
[182] Case COMP/M.4647 – *AEE/Lentjes*, Commission decision of 5 December 2007.
[183] Ibid., para. 69.
[184] Case COMP/M.4747 – *IBM/Telelogic*, Commission decision of 5 March 2008.
[185] Ibid., para. 195.

Biased samples may arise if segments in which the merging firms are particularly close or distant rivals are under- or over-represented in the sample. In *Oracle/Sun Microsystems*,[186] the Commission and the parties argued in detail about the reliability of the two datasets that were used for the participation analysis, namely HQ Apps (an Oracle dataset that contained requests made by sales representatives for discounts exceeding a certain threshold) and CRM (overview of database sales opportunities). The parties claimed that the HQ Apps dataset was not reliable as sales representatives are likely to have a tendency to exaggerate competition when requesting exceptional discounts. The Commission dismissed this criticism, noting that even if there was such tendency 'this does not imply that the aggregate figures would bias the benchmark results in any particular direction'.[187] Furthermore, the Commission did not consider the CRM analysis, which was put forward by the parties and which showed that Sun Microsystems was only an insignificant player, to be sufficiently representative due to the existence of a number of possible sources of bias. The Commission also argued that this evidence did not outweigh the evidence obtained from other sources (HQ Apps, the Commission's own market investigation, existing customer surveys), and that in those segments of the overall database market where MySQL and Oracle competed, MySQL had the potential to impose an important competitive constraint on Oracle. However, the Commission did also acknowledge that although MySQL and Oracle competed in certain parts of the database market, they were not close competitors in others, such as the high-end segment. This, coupled with the fact that the open source nature of MySQL implied that Oracle would not have the ability to remove MySQL, and that another open source database, PostgreSQL, was considered by many database users to be a credible alternative to MySQL, led the Commission to conclude that the proposed transaction would not significantly impede effective competition.

More recently, in *Caterpillar/MWM*,[188] a bidding analysis for generator sets allowed the Commission to identify the closeness of competition between the merging parties and the other firms, and to finally conclude that the parties were not each other's closest competitors. Specifically, as far as Caterpillar bidding data is concerned, the Commission stated:

---

[186] Case COMP/M.5529 – *Oracle/Sun Microsystems*, Commission decision of 21 January 2010.

[187] Ibid., para. 279.

[188] Case COMP/M.6106 – *Caterpillar/MWM*, Commission decision of 19 October 2011.

> It should be concluded from CAT's bidding data that the Parties are not close competitors in the overall market for gas gensets and that GE is by far the most important constraint to the combined entity. Additionally, there are also other relevant competitors, such as Tognum, Cummins and Guascor among others, which are closer to CAT than MWM. Even in the power range where CAT is stronger (that is to say, 1.5–2MW), the bidding data analysis reveals that MWM and CAT are not close competitors.[189]

The Commission also made this analysis from MWM's perspective, reaching a similar conclusion: 'it should be concluded from MWM's bidding data that the Parties are not close competitors. MWM and GE are closer competitors than MWM and CAT; and Tognum and Cummins represent stronger competitive constraints to MWM than CAT.'[190]

In addition, the bidding analysis undertaken was also critical for market definition purposes since it made it clear that the proposed transaction should not be considered a 'three to two' merger as initially suggested: 'the proposed concentration cannot reasonably be characterised as a "3 to 2" transaction on any of the suggested product markets based on the quantitative analysis of the bidding data submitted by the Parties'.[191]

### 3.7.4    Case study: *Pirelli/BICC*

The Commission's decision to clear the *Pirelli/BICC*[192] merger provides a good illustration of some of the issues specific to mergers in bidding markets.[193] In this case, both Pirelli and BICC were active in the market for the production and sale of power cables to energy utilities. Although their combined market shares would have been 75–95% in the United Kingdom and Italy, the Commission held that the existence of enough credible bidders even after the merger meant that the merger would not create or strengthen a dominant position. The economic analysis employed by the parties in this case comprised two key elements that combined to overturn the initial presumption of the Commission against the case due to these high market shares. These were the transitional state of the industry and the bidding nature of competition.

---

[189] Ibid., para. 106.     [190] Ibid., para. 113.     [191] Ibid., para. 112.
[192] Case COMP/M.1882 – *Pirelli/BICC*, Commission decision of 19 July 2000.
[193] This case study draws on A. Lofaro and S. Bishop, 'Disregarding History: The EC Commission's *Pirelli/BICC* Decision' (2001) 22(7) *European Competition Law Review* 288–91.

**3.7.4.1  Transitional state of the industry**  In its decision, the Commission notes that power cable markets used to be predominantly national because of customers' preference for national suppliers and because of different national product specifications (i.e. different mains voltages and frequencies, etc.). These factors made it difficult for power cable companies to supply products outside their 'home' country and resulted in national requirements being met predominantly by domestic firms. As already noted, on a national basis, the combined market shares of the two merging parties were very high in Italy and the United Kingdom. However, several changes had over time radically affected the nature of competition.

These included the move from state-controlled to privately owned commercially run organisations. The removal of political control over the running of the company was typically followed by privatisation and, where possible, by the liberalisation of domestic markets. An important consequence of these changes was the greater focus these more commercially oriented buyers placed on reducing costs. That fact was recognised by the Commission, which noted that:

> Deregulation has increased utilities' incentives to bargain more aggressively with their cable suppliers. Most countries either have or are planning to introduce regulatory systems, whereby efficiency gains above a set level accrue to the utilities. For example, in the United Kingdom, RPI-X price controls, which are reassessed every five years, ensure that a minimum level of efficiency gains is passed on to the consumer, while setting strong incentives for utilities to perform.[194]

In particular, the liberalisation process gave privately owned utility companies an incentive to seek tenders from more than just domestically located power cable suppliers so as to secure their power cables on the most attractive terms. The ability of power cable producers located outside a domestic market to compete was also enhanced by the introduction of EC directives on public tenders and public procurement, as well as by the increasing degree of standardisation of technical specifications.

For these reasons the Commission held that the competitive constraint on domestic suppliers provided by producers located outside Italy and the United Kingdom were now significant. In a market displaying such dynamic characteristics, the Commission concluded that it would have

---

[194]  Case COMP/M.1882 – *Pirelli/BICC*, Commission decision of 19 July 2000, para. 54.

been inappropriate to base the competitive assessment of the merger simply on historical market share information. On the contrary, a forward-looking approach, which took into account the impact of the proposed transaction at a European level, was deemed necessary.

### 3.7.4.2 Bidding competition

There was, however, something of a puzzle that required explanation in this market. Despite the increasing competitive constraint posed by foreign suppliers of power cables, liberalisation, and the other changes discussed above, had yet to result in power supply producers winning substantial shares of business outside their home country at the time the merger was looked at by the Commission. On the contrary, in most countries, incumbents had managed to maintain their high market shares.

However, competition in the power cable market takes the form of bidding for contracts placed by a relatively small number of large customers. As noted above, where competition takes this form market shares do not necessarily provide a good indicator of the strength of future competition. In particular, firms without any historical sales in this type of market can be very influential in determining the prices paid by customers.

Indeed, the economic analysis submitted to the Commission by the parties demonstrated that despite maintaining a high share of domestic business, domestic power cable producers had only been able to do so by dramatically reducing their prices in the face of intensified competition from non-local bidders. That is, the evidence showed that power cable companies, although they were still relatively unsuccessful when bidding in foreign countries, were increasingly able to exercise competitive pressures and ultimately influence the price at which national incumbents were able to win the projects. In other words, the competitive benefits of a European market were being achieved with modest levels of inter-state trade. As the Commission's decision points out, 'over-capacity combined with the threat of losing out to foreign competitors at present enables utilities to achieve highly competitive bids from their incumbent domestic suppliers'.[195]

Moreover, the decision notes that 'cable suppliers have found themselves confronted over the past three years with rapidly declining prices (by up to 60%) and decreasing profit margins'.[196]

---

[195]  Case COMP/M.1882 – *Pirelli/BICC*, Commission decision of 19 July 2000, para. 47.
[196]  Ibid., para. 61.

**3.7.4.3   Analysis of credible bidders**   However, the mere existence of a bidding market does not in itself ensure that effective competition will be maintained whatever the structure on the supply side.[197] Rather, since the key determinant of a firm's competitive importance is its ability to submit a credible bid, the analysis of these markets must proceed by considering the credibility of the bidders that could be called upon to tender by customers, should they consider competition amongst their existing bidders to be insufficient.

The results of the Commission's investigation on the credibility of the remaining suppliers of power cables indicated that:

> Apart from the parties, there are a number of large European cable suppliers such as ABB, Alcatel, NKT, Brugg (and possibly Sagem and BICC General), which possess the technical capabilities, production capacity and quality certifications to supply the major European utilities with know-how intensive HV/EHV [high and extra high] voltage cables in large quantities. As such, they are credible bidders in any major European tender for HV/EHV power cables.[198]

Due to the existence of enough credible bidders even after the merger, the Commission concluded that the merger between Pirelli and BICC would not give rise to anti-competitive effects. The transaction, which was subjected to a Phase II inquiry, was therefore cleared unconditionally without the need for a statement of objections or an oral hearing.

## 4.   Further issues relevant in the assessment of unilateral effects

### 4.1   Introduction

This section sets out some additional issues that may be relevant to the assessment of unilateral effects concerns. The section is organised as follows. Section 4.2 explains that although unilateral effects concerns typically occur when merging parties are actual competitors, concerns may also arise where it is considered that the merger might eliminate potential competition. Section 4.3 describes a further concern that may arise particularly in the presence of relatively homogeneous products. When market conditions are such that rivals are unlikely to increase their supply substantially if prices increase, their ability to exert a competitive constraint may be limited, giving scope for the merging firms to reduce

---

[197] This is also explicitly recognised by the Commission at ibid., para. 79.
[198] Ibid., para. 73.

output and thereby raise prices. Section 4.4 then analyses the role that switching costs may play in the competitive assessment. Importantly, switching costs are explicitly mentioned in the EC Horizontal Merger Guidelines as a factor that may influence whether significant unilateral effects are likely to result from a merger. Finally, in Section 4.5 we describe the conditions under which partial equity stakes amongst competing firms that fall short of legal control can dilute firms' incentives to compete.

## 4.2     Elimination of potential competition

### 4.2.1     Elimination of potential competition in the EC Horizontal Merger Guidelines and EU precedents

Unilateral effects concerns typically arise when merging parties are actual competitors, whose activities overlap in one or more relevant markets. In such instances, the concern is that the two parties exert an important competitive constraint on one another, the elimination of which may allow the new entity to raise prices. However, a merger can also give rise to unilateral effects when the parties do not compete against each other in any relevant market. As set out in the EC Horizontal Merger Guidelines, such concerns arise when two conditions are fulfilled.

First, the threat of entry by one party into a market served by the other party exerts an important influence on the outcomes in that market. Thus, if Firm A sets its price taking account of the threat of Firm B entering the market were prices to rise sufficiently, a merger between A and B may be expected to lessen the constraints determining the terms of A's pre-merger offer.[199] Alternatively, if a potential competitor is not already affecting terms within that market, there must be a significant likelihood that it would enter and grow into an effective competitive force. In this regard, the EC Horizontal Merger Guidelines state that 'evidence that a potential competitor has plans to enter a market in a significant way could help the Commission to reach such a conclusion'.[200]

---

[199] The notion that the threat of entry can potentially constrain an incumbent firm's prices is associated with William J. Baumol, who introduced the concept of 'contestable markets': see W. J. Baumol, J. C. Panzar and R. D. Willig, *Contestable Markets and the Theory of Industry Structure* (San Diego: Harcourt Brace Jovanovich, 1982).

[200] EC Horizontal Merger Guidelines, para. 60.

Second, there should not be 'a sufficient number of other potential competitors, which could maintain sufficient competitive pressure after the merger'.[201] This condition serves to highlight competition concerns in situations where one of the merging parties is uniquely able (or unusually well-placed) to enter the other's market.

It is worth noting that in the majority of cases, potential competition is of second order importance to actual competition. Where actual competition in a market is effective, a merger with a potential competitor should normally be viewed as eliminating a more distant competitive constraint. As such, an absence of existing competition would normally be a prerequisite for unilateral effect theories regarding potential competition, which therefore will tend to arise only in exceptional circumstances.

There have been a number of Phase II cases since 2004 where the Commission assessed the risk that unilateral effects could materialise as a result of the elimination of potential competition.

In *STX/Aker Yards*,[202] the Commission was initially concerned that the proposed merger might remove STX as a potential new entrant into a concentrated cruise ship manufacturing market. The Commission ultimately dismissed this concern on the grounds that STX was considered to be neither a unique ('the market investigation confirmed that other shipbuilders from the Far East such as Mitsubishi from Japan and South Korean companies such as Samsung and Daewoo are at least as well placed as STX to become potential entrants into the cruise ship market'[203]) nor a likely entrant. Interestingly, while the timeliness of entry is not explicitly mentioned in the EC Horizontal Merger Guidelines, the Commission did raise the point in dismissing potential competition concerns in this case, noting that: 'during the market investigation no plans or specific evidence was [sic] found indicating a likely and timely entry by STX in the market in a significant way'.[204]

In *ENI/EDP/GDP*,[205] the Commission concluded that a merger between the Portuguese electricity (EDP) and gas (GDP) incumbents would reinforce a quasi-monopoly position through the elimination of a potential entrant into both markets. GDP, as a gas incumbent, was deemed to be uniquely well placed to enter the Portuguese electricity

[201] Ibid., paras. 59–60.
[202] Case COMP/M.4956 – *STX/Aker Yards*, Commission decision of 5 May 2008.
[203] Ibid., para. 56.    [204] Ibid., para. 55.
[205] Case COMP/M.3440 – *ENI/EDP/GDP*, Commission decision of 9 December 2004.

market due to a number of specific advantages relative to other potential entrants, such as access to gas, which is an important input for electricity generation, a local brand and an established distribution network. Similarly, EDP, as a major purchaser of gas for its wholesale electricity business, was considered as one of the most credible potential entrants into the wholesale gas supply market where GDP was the incumbent supplier.

*DONG/Elsam/Energi E2*[206] involved the acquisition of Elsam and Energi E2 ('E2'), regional electricity generation incumbents in Denmark, and of Københavns Energi Holding ('KE') and Frederiksberg Elnet ('FE'), Danish electricity suppliers, by DONG, the Danish state-owned gas incumbent. After a Phase II investigation, the Commission concluded that the deal would have reinforced DONG's dominant position due to (i) the removal of actual and potential competition from E2, Elsam, NESA and KE, as well as (ii) the ability of the merged entity to weaken its remaining competitors on the market by engaging in customer foreclosure.[207] Interestingly, although there was apparently no evidence that E2 and Elsam had concrete plans to enter, the Commission did not consider such evidence necessary in this case, noting that 'the fact that Elsam's internal papers do not explicitly mention that it had strong entry intentions, does not, while obviously being relevant evidence, eliminate the commercial incentives which Elsam would have'.[208]

In *Omya/Huber PCC*,[209] the Commission concluded that the proposed acquisition by Omya of Huber's on-site precipitated calcium carbonate business, a mineral used in paper production, would have given rise to unilateral effects as it would have removed a potential entrant capable of supplying the heartland of the paper industry in southern Finland. The Commission found evidence that Huber had concrete plans to enter this market, in which Omya enjoyed a quasi-monopoly position, and held that Huber had sufficient experience and ability to compete effectively in this market.[210] The Commission also considered 'it extremely unlikely that any other potential competitor would create or maintain sufficient competitive pressure after the merger'.[211]

---

[206] Case COMP/M.3868 – *DONG/Elsam/Energi E2*, Commission decision of 14 March 2006.
[207] Ibid., para. 455. The foreclosure concerns raised in this case are discussed in Chapter 5.
[208] Ibid., para. 461.
[209] Case COMP/M.3796 – *Omya/Huber PCC*, Commission decision of 19 July 2006.
[210] Ibid., paras. 339 et seq.        [211] Ibid., para. 429.

In *Johnson&Johnson/Guidant*,[212] both parties were active in the development, production and sale of vascular medical devices and the Commission was concerned that by eliminating Guidant as a potential competitor in the market for coronary stents, the merger would give rise to unilateral effects. After a Phase II investigation, however, the Commission concluded that, while Guidant would likely have been one of the key players in the market, other new entrants, such as Medtronic and Abbott, would also be likely to exert a significant competitive constraint, compensating for the loss of competition resulting from the proposed merger.[213] The transaction thus failed to meet the second condition required for potential competition concerns, namely an absence of other potential entrants.

### 4.2.2    Case study: Analysis of potential entry in the *UK Svitzer/Adsteam* case[214]

In what follows, we illustrate how the issue of potential competition can be addressed in practice with reference to the UK Competition Commission (CC) 2006 investigation of the acquisition of Adsteam Marine Ltd ('Adsteam') by SvitzerWijsmuller A/S ('Svitzer').[215] The CC concluded that, despite the fact that the transaction reduced the number of leading harbour towage operators in the UK from two to one, no substantial lessening of competition would arise post-merger. This is due to the fact that the two parties, each of whom was the sole operator in a number of UK ports, did not exert any appreciable competitive constraint on one another. Furthermore, neither party was considered to be uniquely placed as a likely potential entrant into the ports operated by the other. As a result, the transaction was cleared subject to the sole divestment of Adsteam's operations in the port of Liverpool, the only UK port in which the parties were both present prior to the merger.

As the proposed merger would have brought together the two leading harbour towage operators in the UK, with the post-merger entity supplying around 90% of the country's harbour towage services, clearance could only be granted if the CC could satisfy itself that harbour towage

---

[212] Case COMP/M.3687 – *Johnson&Johnson/Guidant*, Commission decision of 25 August 2005.

[213] Ibid., paras. 115 and 116.

[214] See www.competition-commission.org.uk/rep_pub/reports/2007/fulltext/523.pdf for the final report published by the UK Competition Commission on 9 February 2007.

[215] This case study draws on S. Lewis and A. Lofaro, '*Svitzer/Adsteam*: Assessing unilateral effects when monopolists merge' (2008) 29(2) *European Competition Law Review* 135–8.

services provided at different UK ports did not exercise a significant competitive constraint on one another. Despite concerns expressed by the OFT that customers might have the ability to threaten to switch ports when they negotiate their towage tariffs, the CC did indeed acknowledge that no such competitive constraints between ports existed due to an insufficient degree of both demand-side substitution[216] and supply-side substitution.[217]

The absence of any significant competitive constraint between ports implied that, with the exception of Liverpool, where both parties were present as actual competitors, the proposed transaction did not involve a structural change in the supply of harbour towage services. Therefore concerns surrounding the elimination of competitive constraints could arise only to the extent that one party was a potential entrant into a port served by the other, and that this provided an important constraint on the behaviour of the incumbent in that port. This would require that:

1. the other merging party would find entry to the port profitable at current prices; and
2. there were no other operators that could also enter profitably at current prices, which would continue to constrain prices at their current levels after the merger.

In assessing the feasibility of entry, it was important to take account of the high fixed costs that characterise the harbour towage business. Such costs imply that any entry strategy could only be viable if a sufficient number of customers could be secured so as to benefit from economies of scale. This could be achieved either by displacing the incumbent entirely or by 'cherry-picking' certain customers. The CC accepted that either strategy might involve entry being sponsored by a group of customers, since many respondents to their customer questionnaire said that the threat of sponsoring entry was an important source of bargaining

---

[216] The few instances of observed customer switching had occurred within the port of Liverpool, where the two parties were competing against each other for harbour towage business.

[217] Although it is technically possible to move tugs from port to port, commercial considerations imply that there is little or no scope for supply-side substitution in the harbour towage market. This is due to the fact that both parties were operating within each port with the minimum number of tugs required by the Port Authority to meet peak demand. This restricted their ability to engage in any strategic redeployment of tugs to rivals' ports. Indeed, tugs were never redeployed to rivals' ports in response to changes in relative prices.

power.[218] Such sponsored entry would most likely take the form of customers offering their business to the new entrant at a guaranteed price.

In order to determine whether or not the threat of customers sponsoring entry in the event of a price rise was credible, the parties undertook an in-depth investigation of the viability of entry in each port in which they operate. This was conducted both from the point of view of an entrant with similar costs to the incumbent in each port (i.e. Svitzer or Adsteam) and from the point of view of an entrant that could achieve lower costs by employing a non-unionised crew.[219] The model of entry that was submitted to the CC incorporated a detailed analysis of:

1. the cost structure of the incumbent at each port that quantified the fixed and variable costs that would be incurred at every level of supply, taking account of the minimum number of tugs that the parties considered necessary to operate at any given level of supply; and
2. the profile of customers in each port, taking account of the volume of tug jobs each demands per year, the number of tugs each requires for their vessels, and the average net prices that each obtains from the incumbent.

The model enabled the calculation of the market share an entrant would have to obtain in order to break-even by targeting individual customers, taking into account the fact that the net prices obtained by the different customers in a port vary.

The model also showed that in the event that 'cherry-picking' entry occurred, the incumbent's average unit costs would increase significantly due to the loss of economies of scale, making its business unprofitable.

This strongly indicated that the threat of losing even a relatively small portion of business was likely to provide an effective constraint on the incumbents' behaviour. Indeed, this was consistent with the available evidence that the profitability of harbour towage services in UK ports is generally low due to the effective competitive constraints posed by the threat of entry.

This analysis, along with other evidence submitted by the parties, informed the CC's conclusions regarding the feasibility of entry in each

---

[218] CC's final decision, para. 8.30.
[219] Svitzer considered that an international entrant into its ports could operate at a lower cost by avoiding the legacy costs associated with unionised wages and pension costs that it incurred.

port. The CC concluded that Adsteam could not be considered a potential entrant into Svitzer's ports, but that Svitzer could be considered a potential entrant into Adsteam's ports. However, Svitzer was by no means unique in this respect. There were a number of well-known international towage operators with existing business relationships with Adsteam's customers, and with substantial expertise in the provision of harbour towage services, that could also be considered as potential entrants to the relevant ports. The threat of entry by these operators would continue to exert a constraint on the prices and service quality of the merged entity.

In summary, the CC accepted that neither Svitzer nor Adsteam enjoyed a unique advantage over other credible potential entrants. As a consequence, the proposed transaction could not be considered to reduce the competitive constraints to which each UK 'monopoly' port was subjected pre-merger.

## 4.3   Rivals' ability to increase supply

### 4.3.1   Rivals' capacity in the EC Horizontal Merger Guidelines

At paragraph 32, the EC Horizontal Merger Guidelines set out a concern that may arise particularly in the presence of relatively homogeneous products, namely that unilateral effects are more likely when merging firms' rivals do not have enough capacity to replace any output that the new entity might withdraw. If a firm's rivals are unable to offset any reduction in its output, then that reduction will have a greater effect on market volumes and therefore price, and so make it more likely that the withdrawal would be profitable. On the contrary, where a firm anticipates that its rivals will expand their output to offset a reduction in its volumes, the firm will recognise that such a reduction will not be profitable because the firm will lose sales without enjoying any increase in price.

Specifically, the EC Horizontal Merger Guidelines point out that:

> when market conditions are such that the competitors of the merging parties are unlikely to increase their supply substantially if prices increase, the merging firms may have an incentive to reduce output below the combined pre-merger levels, thereby raising market prices. The merger increases the incentive to reduce output by giving the merged firm a larger base of sales on which to enjoy the higher margins resulting from an increase in prices induced by the output reduction.[220]

---

[220]  EC Horizontal Merger Guidelines, paragraph 32.

On the other hand, when market conditions are such that rival firms have enough capacity and would find it profitable to expand output, it is unlikely that the Commission would conclude that the proposed merger would give rise to unilateral effects. In particular, the EC Horizontal Merger Guidelines explain that in order to demonstrate that rivals would be likely to defeat an attempt by the merged entity to raise prices or withdraw output, it is necessary to show the following:[221]

- first, that competitors do not face *capacity constraints* or that their existing capacity could be expanded relatively easily and cheaply; and
- second, that existing spare capacity is not significantly more costly to operate than capacity currently in use. In other words, unilateral effects are unlikely to arise if rivals do not suffer from significant *cost disadvantages* vis-à-vis the merging parties.

### 4.3.2    An example

In the following example, we illustrate how the presence of cost disadvantages and/or capacity constraints among rival suppliers can give rise to legitimate unilateral effects concerns.

Suppose that there are four potential bidders, A to D, all bidding for a one-off project. There are no fixed costs and marginal costs do not vary with output, but the marginal costs of the bidders differ in the manner shown in Table 3.21.

If all bidders have complete and accurate information about each other's costs, the equilibrium price will be 110. This is the highest price that Firm A can bid without its closest rival, B, being able to undercut its price. A general rule of competitive auctions of this type is that the competitive price is determined by the costs of the second-highest bidder. Even if A's costs were 50, dramatically lower than B's, it would still need to bid no lower than 110 to win the contract.[222]

Assessment of unilateral effects concerns in this setting is straightforward. A merger between bidders A and C would have no effect on the

---

[221] Ibid., para. 34.

[222] Of course, the assumptions of this simple model are highly simplified and unrealistic. In particular, to the extent that the products offered by the various players are differentiated, it may be sufficient for firm A to bid, say, 112 pre-merger in order to win the bid. Similarly, if bidders do not know the costs of their rivals they may bid lower than is strictly necessary to win the bid. For example, Firm A might incorrectly believe that B's costs are 109, in which case it may choose to bid 109 instead of 110. Furthermore, when there are substantial fixed costs, firms would on average need to bid at a level that covered their average total costs, leading to bids per unit in excess of marginal costs.

Table 3.21 *Bidding competition between firms with different costs*

| Firm | Costs |
|------|-------|
| A | 100 |
| B | 110 |
| C | 115 |
| D | 120 |

competitive price level, since the combined entity, Firm A+C, still needs to outbid B in order to win the contract. Only a merger between A and B is competitively significant because in that case the combined entity, Firm A+B, will need only to beat bidder C whose costs are 115; consequently, the price could be raised to as much as 115.

Two points emerge from this simple example. These are that:

- pre-merger, the two firms with the highest costs, namely Firm C and D, play no important competitive role in this setting and competitive pressure would not be decreased if these suppliers were to disappear from the process; and
- the extent of any post-merger price rise following a merger of the two lowest cost suppliers (A and B) is determined by how similar are the costs of the second and third most efficient firms (B and C). The higher the cost disadvantage suffered by the latter, the more significant the scope for the merger to give rise to unilateral effects.

Let us now consider a slight modification of the previous example, whereby we assume that suppliers are subject to capacity constraints. Specifically, in the modified example in Table 3.22, we assume that Firms A and C both have 50 units of capacity, that the second most efficient supplier, Firm B, has only 20 units of capacity and that the least efficient firm can produce up to 30 units. Assume further that the customer's requirement is equal to 40 units.

The pre-merger price in this revised setting is 110 with Firm A supplying the entire customer's requirement. A merger between A and B (i.e. the two companies with the lowest costs) would again lead to a price increase: as in the previous example, the merged entity would now be able to charge a price of up to 115 for all 40 units.

On the other hand, the effect of a merger between Firm A and Firm C (i.e. the two companies with the largest capacities) would depend on the cost difference between Firms C and D. Post-merger, Firm A+C

Table 3.22 *Bidding competition between firms with different costs and capacity constraints*

| Firm | Costs | Capacity |
|------|-------|----------|
| A | 100 | 50 |
| B | 110 | 20 |
| C | 115 | 50 |
| D | 120 | 30 |

would now have a choice of either (i) pricing at 110 for a full 40 units, at a profit of 400; or (ii) pricing at 120 for 20 units and allowing B to undercut it to sell the remaining 20 units demanded, giving the merged firm a profit of 400.

In this example, Firm A+C is equally well off increasing its price to 120 (and serving half the customer's demand) as setting a price of 110 (and serving the whole of the customer's demand). However, if D's cost had been 119 instead of 120, the merged firm would have been constrained in charging a price no higher than 119 to sell 20 units, giving a profit of 380, which is lower than that resulting from charging the pre-merger price of 110.

In short, the effect of a merger between suppliers in the presence of cost asymmetries and capacity constraints can be quite complex and it will depend on the costs of the parties relative to those of rival suppliers, as well as on each firm's available capacity.

### 4.3.3   EU cases

The Commission has typically undertaken an assessment of rivals' capacity when assessing mergers involving homogeneous products. As is clear from the Commission's case law, in order for concerns regarding unilateral effects to be mitigated in such industries, rivals need to have both the *ability* and *incentive* to expand output in a response to a hypothetical price increase.

The assessment of rivals' ability to expand production typically requires an analysis of whether those rivals jointly possess sufficient spare capacity (i.e. total capacity minus actual production volumes) to safeguard competition and defeat a hypothetical price increase. Note that it is not necessary that rivals are capable of supplying all demand served by the merging firms. The relevant question is whether rivals, individually or combined, can supply the hypothetical volume loss that makes a given price increase unprofitable for the merging firms. As the Commission noted in the *Ineos/BP Dormagen*[223] merger, it is important to undertake a prospective analysis where possible since the capacity situation pre-merger may not prevail due to anticipated changes in capacity or demand. In addition to considering firms' physical production capabilities, such as the current stock of machinery and equipment, it may be necessary to consider the following additional factors, which may influence rivals' ability to expand output in the short term:

- *Availability of raw materials.* On the purchasing side, inputs such as raw materials may not be readily available due to shortages, exclusive contracts or vertical integration. For example, one of the merging firms may have locked up a considerable proportion of available inputs through exclusive supply contracts or vertical integration.
- *Sales and distribution capabilities.* On the sales side, extra staff may be required to expand sales. This is of particular concern where rivals do not focus on the same customers or geographical areas as the merging firms or where sales including after sales services require substantial investments at a local level.
- *Ease of adding capacity.* Even if spare capacity is limited, there may be evidence that capacity can be easily expanded on an incremental basis, for example, by adding a machine to an existing production line.

For instance, in *Glatfelter/Crompton Assets*,[224] the Commission accepted that if 'Glatfelter increased the price significantly and profitability for wet laid fibre materials for tea and coffee filtration thus possibly increased for Ahlstrom, Ahlstrom could divert capacity or could invest in adding capacity by converting an existing machine or purchasing and converting a second hand machine'.[225] In addition, in *AEE/Lentjes*,[226] the Commission noted that:

> Each competitor seems therefore to plan its capacities in the medium to long term dependent on projects: companies rank projects internally according to their own criteria and assign capacity to them accordingly. On the basis of this planning process and its timetable, projects with a

---

[223] Case COMP/M.4094 – *Ineos/BP Dormagen*, Commission decision of 10 August 2006.

[224] Case COMP/M.4215 – *Glatfelter/Crompton Assets*, Commission decision of 20 December 2006.

[225] Ibid., para. 98.

[226] Case COMP/M.4647 – *AEE/Lentjes*, Commission decision of 5 December 2007.

high likelihood of success may arouse interest among many competitors. If necessary – so the market investigation showed – new capacities can be brought on stream at short notice. One competitor mentioned the possibility, where necessary, of increasing its capacity temporarily by up to 50%.[227]

The Commission has conducted an assessment of concerns resulting from the possible lack of spare capacity in a number of cases. Some examples include the following.

In *Kronospan/Constantia*,[228] which involved the acquisition of part of the raw and coated particle board business of Constantia by Kronospan, the Commission argued that rivals held insufficient spare capacity to prevent unilateral effects in a number of countries, including Austria, Czech Republic, Hungary, Slovakia and Slovenia.[229] The parties held a combined share of 60–80% for raw particle board production in these countries. The Commission also pointed to instances of capacity shortages in the past that had resulted in price increases. Moreover, capacity expansion was considered to require substantial investment and a significant lead time (at least two years). Whilst some new capacity was expected to become available in the affected areas, the Commission argued that, due to the increasing demand for raw particle board, this would not be sufficient to defeat any attempt by the post-merger entity to increase prices. Imports from outside the affected area were feasible but, according to the Commission, would only act to constrain the parties' prices at a higher level than observed pre-merger; that is, there was competition between the parties that kept price below the level at which imports would become financially viable.

In its assessment of the *Inco/Falconbridge*[230] merger, the Commission concluded that the merging parties' most important rival had insufficient capacity (representing only 20% of the total market) to impose a competitive constraint. Moreover, the Commission found that this key rival was unable to increase output also because it did not have sufficient access to the relevant inputs. Other smaller rivals had no excess capacity either and suffered from a number of competitive disadvantages that made them less viable suppliers. Consequently, the merging parties with

---

[227] Case COMP/M.4647 – *AEE/Lentjes*, Commission decision of 5 December 2007, para. 97.
[228] Case COMP/M.4525 – *Kronospan/Constantia*, Commission decision of 19 September 2007.
[229] Ibid., paras. 59 et seq.
[230] Case COMP/M.4000 – *Inco/Falconbridge*, Commission decision of 4 July 2006.

a combined share of 75–95% for the supply of high purity nickel would not be constrained post-merger.

In *Arjowiggins/M-real Zanders Reflex*,[231] the carbonless paper market was found to exhibit no significant spare capacity despite ongoing demand decline. On the contrary, the Commission found that there was 'no indication that a demand shock has placed any of the main competitors in a situation of severe overcapacity where they would be forced to make cut-price sales and thus undermine market prices. On the contrary, manufacturers appear to be well aware that excess production would depress prices, and thus they have aligned capacity closely to demand'.[232] Consequently, competitors were considered to have little spare capacity and to be unlikely to divert capacity used for the production of other products or exports to the production of carbonless paper for supply in the EEA-market. The Commission therefore concluded that rivals would not undermine post-merger unilateral effects in the carbonless paper market.

A finding of an ability on the part of rivals to increase output in response to a hypothetical price increase post-merger has in certain cases been sufficient to dismiss concerns without an analysis of those rivals' incentives to do so. For example, in the already mentioned *Glatfelter/Crompton Assets* case,[233] the Commission held that the merged entity, which would hold a combined share of industrial fibre materials between 60 and 70%, would nonetheless be constrained by several competitors who had sufficient spare capacity and the means to swiftly increase capacity if needed. The Commission did not appear to analyse explicitly whether such expansion would require any cost that would offset the incentive to increase output when faced with a price increase.

In other cases, however, the Commission has argued that rival firms' ability to expand output is not sufficient to dismiss concerns, but that their incentive to do so must be established. These cases show that it is necessary to consider carefully rivals' costs of increasing output (such as additional labour or investments in ancillary equipment). In addition, where it is argued that firms may switch capacity from the production of other products, it is necessary to consider the opportunity costs arising from forgoing sales of those other products.

---

[231] See Case COMP/M.4513 – *Arjowiggins/M-real Zanders Reflex*, Commission decision of 4 June 2008.

[232] Ibid., para. 393.

[233] See Case COMP/M.4215 – *Glatfelter/Crompton Assets*, Commission decision of 20 December 2006.

In *JCI/VB/FIAMM*,[234] the Commission found that rivals appeared to hold around 10% spare capacity. However, it noted that there was no evidence that they would have the incentive to use that spare capacity to increase output in response to a price increase. Increased capacity utilisation through, for instance, an increased number of shifts including weekend shifts would entail significant cost. Furthermore, the Commission noted that, while there was technical scope to switch production from IAM batteries to OE batteries, the higher margins earned on IAM batteries would provide a disincentive for such supply-side substitution unless there was a substantial price increase for OE batteries. In this context, the decision reads:[235]

> ... the profitability of unilateral price increases for the merged entity largely depends on whether or not the expansion of supply is profitable for alternative suppliers, that is to say, whether the alternative suppliers not only have the ability but also the economic incentive to serve those OE-customers which would allegedly switch in the event of a unilateral price increase by the merged entity.

The Commission ultimately concluded that while the parties had demonstrated the technical ability of rivals to increase output, no evidence was provided on the incentive to do so taking into account the extra cost of expansion as well as the profits forgone as a result of not being able to use the spare capacity for the production of other products.

In *Bertelsmann/Springer/JV*,[236] the Commission considered whether rivals would be able to constrain the joint venture, which would control between 45% and 50% of installed rotogravure magazine printing capacity in Germany. The Commission considered three aspects of rival capacity: the extent of existing spare rotogravure magazine printing capacity in Germany; the scope for switching printing equipment used for advertisements and catalogues to the printing of magazines in response to a relative price increase; and the extent of planned increases in rotogravure magazine printing capacity.[237] Overall, the Commission found that, across these three forms of capacity, rivals could potentially bring to bear a combined capacity in excess of the parties' total capacity, assuaging unilateral effects concerns.[238] The Commission, in particular,

---

[234] Case COMP/M.4381 – *JCI/VB/FIAMM*, Commission decision of 10 May 2007.
[235] Ibid., para. 360.
[236] Case COMP/M.3178 – *Bertelsmann/Springer/JV*, Commission decision of 3 May 2005.
[237] Ibid., paras. 104 et seq.
[238] Ibid., para. 138.

noted that printers would be able to switch a substantial proportion of their equipment to the printing of magazines should prices increase. As part of this analysis, the Commission calculated the average contribution margins by product and found that the margins earned on the printing of magazines were sufficient to compensate for the loss of margins earned on other products.

In *Arjowiggins/M-real Zanders Reflex*,[239] the Commission concluded that, given the significant opportunity costs, rivals would not have the incentive to divert capacity from the production of thermal paper to carbonless paper where the parties held a dominant share. This finding was also confirmed by the parties' own submission that 'thermal paper capacity would constrain carbonless prices only if the latter rose by 5% to 8%.'[240] An analysis of relative margins also indicated that no significant diversion took place despite significant changes in relative margins between carbonless and thermal paper. On this specific point, the Commission points out at that:

> There were also periods where switching from thermal to carbonless paper would have been profitable for some manufacturers. However, such switching did not take place in any significant scale. This indicates that manufacturers either cannot or do not want to react relatively quickly to changes in relative margins when they decide to allocate production to either thermal paper or carbonless paper. Hence, there are no indications that competitors post-merger would be more likely to switch production to carbonless paper to an extent that would defeat a capacity reduction by a dominant supplier controlling 50% of the carbonless paper market than they are today.[241]

It may be possible, under certain circumstances, to carry out a natural experiment to test whether rivals have both the ability and incentive to increase output in response to a supply reduction or a hypothetical price increase. As already discussed in Section 3.5, natural experiments were used in *Ineos/BP Dormagen*[242] and *Inco/Falconbridge*.[243]

In *Ineos/BP Dormagen*,[244] the Commission undertook a detailed analysis to assess how rivals responded to historical capacity outages by one of the merging firms who had a combined share of around 50–60%. Whilst not determinative, this natural experiment, together with other

---

[239] Case COMP/M.4513 – *Arjowiggins/M-real Zanders Reflex*, Commission decision of 4 June 2008.
[240] Ibid., para. 401.    [241] Ibid., para. 404.
[242] Case COMP/M.4094 – *Ineos/BP Dormagen*, Commission decision of 10 August 2006.
[243] Case COMP/M.4000 – *Inco/Falconbridge*, Commission decision of 4 July 2006.
[244] Case COMP/M.4094 – *Ineos/BP Dormagen*, Commission decision of 10 August 2006.

evidence, contributed to the conclusion that rivals had both the ability and incentive to respond by increasing output.[245]

In *Inco/Falconbridge*,[246] the Commission supported its conclusion that the merging parties would not be constrained post-merger by observing that, following a strike at one of Inco's plants, customers had switched to Falconbridge and not to other rivals resulting in a temporary price hike.[247]

### 4.3.4   Assessing mergers in electricity markets

Mergers taking place in electricity markets provide a good illustration of the issues that need to be taken into account when assessing concentrations between suppliers of homogeneous products whose production facilities are characterised by cost asymmetries and capacity constraints. In what follows, we describe the type of unilateral effects concerns that typically arise from these mergers and the empirical techniques that can be used to assess these concerns.

A number of important mergers in this sector have been attempted in Europe over the last decade.[248] For example, in 2004, the European Commission decided, after a detailed Phase II investigation, to prohibit the proposed acquisition of joint control over Gás de Portugal (GDP), the incumbent gas company in Portugal, by Energias de Portugal (EDP), the incumbent electricity company in Portugal, and Italian energy company ENI. The Commission analysed the possible impact of the proposed operation on the gas and electricity supply markets in Portugal and concluded that the transaction would strengthen EDP's dominant position in the electricity wholesale and retail markets in Portugal.

In 2008, the Commission approved the merger of Gaz de France (GDF) and the Suez group[249] after an in-depth investigation, subject to a 'comprehensive and far-reaching package of remedies',[250] which were considered to address the initial finding that the deal would have anti-competitive effects in the gas and electricity wholesale and retail markets

---

[245] Case COMP/M.4094 – *Ineos/BP Dormagen*, Commission decision of 10 August 2006, para. 97.

[246] Case COMP/M.4000 – *Inco/Falconbridge*, Commission decision of 4 July 2006.

[247] Ibid., para. 373.

[248] For a survey of the recent application of merger control in the European energy sector, see G. Federico, 'The economic analysis of energy mergers in Europe and Spain' (2011) 7(3) *Journal of Competition Law & Economics* 603–29.

[249] Case COMP/M.4180 – *Gaz de France/Suez*, Commission decision of 14 November 2006.

[250] See http://europa.eu/rapid/pressReleasesAction.do?reference=MEMO/06/424&format=HTML&aged=0&language=EN&guiLanguage=fr.

in Belgium and in the gas markets in France.[251] The Commission's concerns related mainly to the removal of the increasing competitive pressure that GDF and Suez exerted on each other in both Belgium and France. Given the conditions on the markets, including the very high barriers to entry, their respective dominant positions would have been considerably strengthened by the merger, according to the Commission.

In 2009, the Commission required significant undertakings in order to clear EDF's proposed acquisition of a majority stake in SPE, the second largest electricity operator in Belgium.[252] The two parties had a combined share in the Belgian electricity wholesale market of only between 10% and 20%, a long way behind the share of around 70% enjoyed by market leader GDF Suez (Electrabel). Nevertheless, the Commission found that the proposed transaction would be likely to give rise to unilateral effects as a result of a reduction in the merged entity's incentives to invest in new capacity.

In September 2005, Gas Natural, the leading gas operator in Spain launched a €22.5 billion hostile bid for Endesa, Spain's largest electricity incumbent. Had the bid been successful, the combined company would have become the largest gas and electricity operator in Spain and Latin America, serving 16 million customers in Europe and 30 million worldwide. The *Gas Natural/Endesa*[253] case is particularly interesting because of the detailed competitive assessment that could be conducted thanks to the extremely detailed market data published daily by OMEL, the operator of the Spanish electricity market.

The remainder of this section provides a short description of the main characteristics of wholesale electricity markets which are relevant to the assessment of the competitive effects of mergers in this industry. We then set out the concerns these concentrations typically give rise to and we briefly summarise how these concerns can be assessed with reference to the *Gas Natural/Endesa* case.

### 4.3.4.1  Market characteristics

The main characteristics that are pertinent to the assessment of the competitive impact of mergers in wholesale electricity markets are as follows.[254]

---

[251] See Commission's press releases (see IP/06/802 and IP/06/1109).

[252] Case COMP/M.5549 – *EDF/Segebel*, Commission decision of 12 November 2009.

[253] See Tribunal de la Defensa de la Competencia, Expediente de Concentración Económica C94/05 Gas Natural/Endesa, 5 January 2006.

[254] The discussion here follows in part RBB Brief 17, 'The Need for Reality Checks: An example from the Netherlands', August 2005.

- *Demand for electricity fluctuates significantly over time.* In particular, consumption of electricity is particularly low during the early hours of the morning and it typically has two peaks: one at around midday and one in the early evening hours. Furthermore, daily consumption is significantly lower at weekends.
- *The elasticity of demand is relatively low.* As noted by Hope,[255] the aggregate market demand elasticity is particularly low in the short run when the flexibility of consumers to switch to other energy forms is quite limited because of past investment decisions in energy equipment. Even in the long run, empirical studies show low demand elasticities, typically in the range of $-0.15$ to $-0.25$ for household demand.
- *Electricity is non-storable.* Electricity cannot be stored and it is therefore necessary that at each point in time the total amount of electricity produced matches demand. The requirement for supply and demand to balance at all times requires an extremely careful coordination between generation and transmission. As noted by Armstrong et al.,[256] this is a major reason why the two activities have traditionally been vertically integrated.
- *Different generation technologies face different cost conditions.* On the supply side, electricity production is characterised by a number of generation units of different types (e.g. coal-fired, gas-fired, hydro, combined cycle gas turbine (CCGT) or nuclear). Due to the different technical characteristics and input costs of each type of generation unit, there are substantial differences in the marginal cost of each generator. Nuclear plants, for example, have high fixed costs but relatively low marginal costs, and cannot be switched on or off at short notice. Other types of plants have relatively higher marginal costs but are more flexible. These different characteristics give rise to a 'merit order' of plants whereby generation units with low marginal costs provide the base load electricity production and those with higher marginal costs are switched on only as demand increases during peak hours. Figure 3.9 provides a graphical representation of a hypothetical merit order,[257]

---

[255] See E. Hope, 'Market Dominance and Market Power in Electricity Power Markets' (ISSN-nr 1652–8069, Konkurrensverket, Stockholm, 2005).

[256] See M. Armstrong, S. Cowan and J. Vickers, *Regulatory Reform – Economic Analysis and British Experience* (MIT Press, 1994).

[257] In reality, the merit order may be more complicated than this. Wind energy has a very low marginal cost and so typically enters the supply curve at the bottom, but its availability is dependent on the weather. The merit order is also affected by the tax

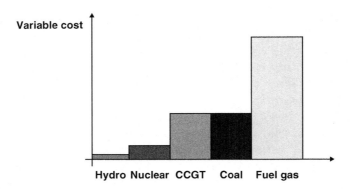

**Figure 3.9**    Hypothetical merit order of electricity generation plants

showing that nuclear and hydro plants are the generation technologies with the lowest variable costs while fuel gas plants have the highest variable costs.[258]

- *Wholesale electricity markets are typically bidding markets,* in which operators submit bids to provide particular amounts of electricity at particular prices for each hour during the following day. For each period the market is cleared at a single price determined by the generation unit with the highest bid that is required to operate at that time in order for demand to be met. That market price allows plants with lower marginal costs to earn a margin over these costs.

**4.3.4.2    Unilateral effect concerns**    In the wholesale electricity market, unilateral effects could materialise in one of the following ways.

First, the post-merger entity may have an incentive to raise its prices if the proposed transaction would bring together a number of 'marginal' generation units (i.e. units that are often the last ones to be used so that the price bid for those units subsequently determines the market price) that were previously owned by the individual parties. As the merger would relax the competitive constraint that these marginal units exert

---

regime on carbon emissions, which may make an otherwise cheap (but high emission) technology incur a higher variable cost than an otherwise costly (but low emission) technology.

[258] Note that whilst the accounting marginal cost of hydro power is close to zero, the true marginal cost of hydro is the opportunity cost of generation at another time. The willingness to supply hydro depends on factors such as precipitation and the level of water in reserves.

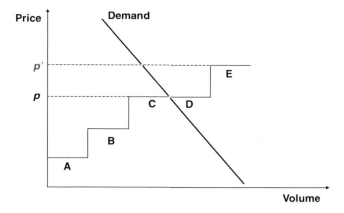

**Figure 3.10**   Unilateral effects arising from the elimination of competition between marginal generation units

on one another, this may lead to an increase in the price bid by the merged entity for these plants and thereby to higher market prices. Figure 3.10 provides a graphical illustration of this concern.

The figure shows five plants, A to E, which have been ranked according to their marginal costs of generation. Plants C and D face identical costs of generation and the bold line denotes the level of demand at different prices. In this example, the demand curve crosses the section of the supply curve where competition between plants C and D determines the price. In other words, plants C and D represent the marginal generation units and competition between these two plants delivers a pre-merger price equal to $p$, which is assumed to be equal to plant C's and plant D's marginal cost. A hypothetical merger between C and D would eliminate the competitive constraint that these two plants exerted on each other, and it would allow the new entity to raise the price to $p'$ (i.e. just below the marginal cost of Firm E).

Second, unilateral effects could also occur to the extent that the proposed transaction would bring together a number of 'infra-marginal' generation units (i.e. production units that have low marginal costs of productions and that would benefit from the higher prices) as this may give the merged entity an incentive to increase the price bid for some of its marginal units (or even withdraw the bids related to these units altogether). Such a strategy might result in higher market prices, either because one of these units is the price-setting unit, or because the strategy might change the identity of the price-setting unit to a rival plant bidding

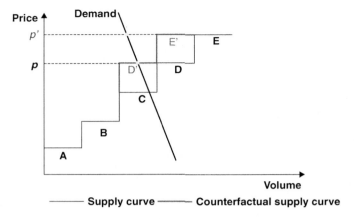

**Figure 3.11**   Unilateral effects arising from the withdrawal of marginal plants

a higher price. Even though the merged entity might lose revenues from the unit for which the high bid is submitted (since it may be priced out of the market), this loss may be more than compensated by the higher market prices it would thereby earn from its other generating units. Intuitively, the larger the number of infra-marginal plants brought together by the merger, the larger the incentive that the post-merger entity would have to increase the price bid for its marginal units. Figure 3.11 provides a graphical illustration of this concern.

The figure shows five plants, A to E, which again have been ranked according to their marginal costs of generation. In this example, the demand curve crosses the section of the supply curve where plant C determines the price. Since plant C does not face competition from rivals with the same marginal cost of production, it will charge a price equal to $p$ (i.e. just below the marginal cost of plant D). Suppose now that plant A and plant C wish to merge. Note that, unlike in the previous example, after the merger, there is no immediate prediction of a post-merger price rise. This is due to the fact that plant D, which forces plant C to bid $p$ pre-merger, would continue to constrain the post-merger Firm (A+C)'s behaviour.

However, a price increase cannot be ruled out since the new entity (A+C) may have an incentive to raise the bid for plant C above the level of prices bid by plants D and E, or even withdraw this plant altogether. Should the combined entity choose to do that, the supply curve would shift leftwards due to the disappearance of plant C (see the counterfactual supply curve highlighted in grey in Figure 3.11). In the post-merger situation, plant D, which was not producing in the pre-merger scenario due to its higher marginal cost, has become the new marginal generation unit and it will bid a price equal to $p'$ (i.e. just below the marginal cost of Firm E). Importantly, this outcome is not inevitable since the post-merger entity will have an incentive to engage in the hypothesised withdrawal strategy only if the higher margins earned from plant A at the higher price $p'$ more than compensate for the lost margins from plant C.

In what follows, we provide a brief summary of how these concerns were assessed in the *Gas Natural/Endesa* case.

**4.3.4.3 Case study: *Gas Natural/Endesa*** The proposed transaction would have combined Endesa, which at the time enjoyed a market share of around 40% in electricity, and Gas Natural, whose market share was less than 5% in the electricity market. Despite its limited share in the overall wholesale market, Gas Natural was an important competitor in the CCGT segment, with a generation capacity projected to increase from less than 2GW to 4–5GW in the near future. This coupled with the fact that Endesa owned a number of coal plants, which faced similar costs to CCGT plant (see Figure 3.11), meant that the two unilateral effects concerns set out above had to be carefully analysed.

*Concern 1: Would the new entity have an incentive to raise its prices as a result of the transaction bringing together many 'marginal' CCGT/coal generation units?* Whether the strong position the new entity would have enjoyed in the CCGT/coal segment was likely to allow it to raise prices depended on two conditions.

*Condition 1*: CCGT and coal plants should frequently represent the marginal plants, that is, they should often be the price-setting production facilities. If this is not the case, then the increase in concentration within the CCGT/coal segment brought about by the proposed transaction would be less likely to have a direct effect on prices.

*Condition 2*: Whenever a CCGT or a coal plant is a marginal plant, it should mostly compete in the auction with other CCGT and coal plants rather than with other generation technologies, such as nuclear and fuel. If this is not the case, then a high market share within the CCGT/coal segment would not give the post-merger entity the ability to increase prices, as Gas Natural would remain constrained by production plants with other technologies.

To assess whether Conditions 1 and 2 were likely to be satisfied, Endesa's economists relied on a very extensive dataset comprising the pool price in Spain for each hour during the period January 2004 – May 2005 as well as data on all winning and losing bids submitted by each Spanish generator for each individual plant during the same period. All these data were publicly available from OMEL at the time in which the transaction was assessed. These data showed that CCGT and coal were the marginal price-setting technologies in more than half of the total number of hours during the period. This indicated that the technologies controlled by the merging parties were frequently the determinant of prices and, therefore, that Condition 1 was likely to be satisfied.

Furthermore, to assess the extent to which CCGT and coal plants mostly competed with each other rather than with other generation technologies (i.e. to test Condition 2), Endesa's economists analysed the identity of infra-marginal bids (i.e. bids lower than the equilibrium price at each hour) and supra-marginal bids (i.e. bids higher than the equilibrium price at each hour) for each hour during the same period as above. This analysis found that whenever CCGT or coal were the price-setting technology, the vast majority of bids within 1% of the equilibrium price were made by other CCGT and coal plants. This finding suggested that the coal/CCGT segment was unlikely to be effectively constrained by other generation technologies and that, therefore, a significant increment in concentration in this segment had the potential of bringing about anti-competitive effects.

*Concern 2: Would the new entity have an incentive to withdraw some of its marginal plants in order to raise prices?* Endesa's economists used the OMEL price and bid data to analyse the merged entity's incentive and ability to withdraw some plants (or bids related to part of the generation capacity of those plants) in order to raise prices. This analysis proceeded by modifying the actual hourly supply curve implied by all market participants' bids to reflect a hypothetical gradual withdrawal of the merged entity's bids in order to produce a series of counterfactual supply curves. As shown in Figure 3.11, removing bids results in leftwards shifts in the supply curve and in counterfactual supply curves that become progressively steeper. These counterfactual supply curves for each hour were then compared to the actual demand curve to assess the impact of each hypothetical bid withdrawal on equilibrium prices. By calculating the resulting effect on the merged entity's profits of each bid withdrawal the merged entity's optimal bidding strategy for each hour was identified.

It is worth noting that this type of analysis, which indicated that the post-merger entity would have the incentive to withdraw some of its plants, is to some extent partial as it does not attempt to model competitors' reactions to the volume withdrawal strategy. Intuitively, a supply response could either enhance any predicted anti-competitive effect of the transaction (e.g. faced with an attempt at increasing prices by the post-merger entity, rivals may find it profitable to engage in a similar strategy) or alleviate it (e.g. rivals could replace some or all of the withdrawn bids by the post-merger entity by increasing their volumes bid).

However, despite their limitations, the analysis set out provided a useful indicator of the strength of the competitive constraint that the merging parties exerted on each other and, therefore, the risk that the transaction might give rise to unilateral effects. Based in part on these types of analyses and considerations, the Spanish Competition Tribunal recommended to block the merger in January 2006 due to its likely anti-competitive effects. The Spanish government later decided, in February 2006, to override the Tribunal by approving the concentration even though significant remedies were imposed,[259] including the divestment of electricity generation capacity well in excess of Gas Natural's portfolio at the time.[260]

## 4.4    Switching costs

In this section, we describe the role of switching costs in the appraisal of unilateral effects. The presence of switching costs is sometimes cited as a reason for challenging mergers at lower levels of market concentration than might otherwise be justified. The EC Horizontal Merger Guidelines explicitly refer to switching costs as one of the factors that are considered to influence whether significant unilateral effects are likely to result from a merger:[261]

---

[259] The Supreme Court eventually overruled the government with a transitory suspension of this decision.

[260] However, this was not the end of the story. After German E.ON made an offer for Endesa in February 2007, Acciona and Enel successfully acquired more than 92% of Endesa in October 2007 for an estimated €42.5 billion. Acciona and Enel initially jointly managed Endesa through an Acciona-controlled holding company, but in February 2009 Enel agreed to buy out Acciona's stake.

[261] EC Horizontal Merger Guidelines, para. 31.

> Customers of the merging parties may have difficulties switching to other suppliers because there are few alternative suppliers or because they face substantial switching costs. Such customers are particularly vulnerable to price increases.

Our discussion is organised as follows. We first explain the effects of switching costs on competition, before going on to consider the implications for merger assessment with reference to two high-profile banking merger decisions in the UK: *Lloyds/Abbey* and *Lloyds/HBOS*.[262]

### 4.4.1   Effects of switching costs on competition

Switching costs arise where customers who have purchased from one supplier face real or perceived obstacles impeding their ability to switch to a rival's product, even if the two firms' products are functionally identical. As such, switching costs may serve to reduce switching by existing customers. Switching costs are potentially significant in markets characterised by high information-gathering costs or transaction costs, and are most important where these costs give rise to long-term relationships and repeated transactions. Such relationships have been cited as important in service industries such as utilities, insurance and banking.[263]

Economic research has addressed the impact of switching costs on pricing and competition. One of the key papers in this area describes a model in which each firm must in every period balance the incentive to charge a high price to exploit its locked-in customers against the incentive to set a low price to attract new customers that build up the firm's current volumes and thereby increase future profits.[264] In this model, the incentive to exploit current customers generally dominates the incentive to win new customers, as firms value current profits more than future profits and so generally give a lower priority to attracting new customers than to exploiting existing customers. This finding leads to a

---

[262] This section draws on A. Lofaro and D. Ridyard, 'Switching Costs and Merger Assessment – Don't Move the Goalposts' (2003) 24(6) *European Competition Law Review* 268–71.

[263] See, e.g., S. Sharpe, 'The Effect of Consumer Switching Costs on Prices: A theory and its application to the bank deposit market' (1997) 12(1) *Review of Industrial Organization* 79–94.

[264] See P. Klemperer, 'Competition When Consumers Have Switching Costs: An overview with applications to industrial organization, macroeconomics, and international trade' (1995) 62(4) *Review of Economic Studies* 515–39.

prediction that firms' prices will be higher in the presence of switching costs, all else being constant.

A second interesting result presented in the literature is that, in the presence of switching costs, a firm with a lower market share generally has an incentive to price more aggressively than a firm with a large market share. Small firms do not have a large base of infra-marginal customers to worry about when competing for new business, and, for this reason, can afford to be more aggressive in their pricing policies than the leading players.[265]

It would, however, be simplistic to rely on such results to justify a general prediction that markets in which customers face switching costs are less competitive. Indeed, in a dynamic setting, the contest to win the right to supply locked-in customers can be all the more intense because of the benefits that those switching costs confer on suppliers. In other words, competition in the presence of switching costs is often different, but is not necessarily any less effective, than in markets where no such costs arise.

### 4.4.2    Implications of switching costs for merger assessment

In any horizontal merger analysis the fundamental object is to assess the extent to which the proposed transaction would eliminate an important competitive constraint, allowing the merged entity to raise prices. As explained in Section 2, unilateral effects are more likely to arise in the presence of a high degree of closeness of competition between the parties' products. Given this basic principle of horizontal merger analysis, what are the implications when assessing a merger in a sector, such as banking, where customers face high real or perceived switching costs?

To answer this question, consider first an extreme situation in which all consumers, due to a perception that switching costs are very high, consider themselves to be completely 'locked in' or captive to their existing bank. In such a scenario, the reduction in the number of banks arising from any merger cannot have any anti-competitive effect, since the prices consumers are charged by each bank are not in any way constrained by the existence of other banks. Such a situation is analogous to one in which merging parties are sufficiently differentiated in their offers as to lie in separate relevant markets.

---

[265] This is based on the assumption that firms are unable to engage in significant discriminatory pricing between new and old customers. If firms can discriminate, they can in principle offer lower prices to new customers and higher prices to existing customers.

In practice, banks do compete against one another for customers (or for sections of demand) that are price-sensitive and that are not 'locked in' to one provider. Therefore, it is relative to these customers that it is necessary to ensure that the merger will not reduce customer choice in a way that will allow the remaining banks to increase prices. In order to assess the degree to which competitive pressures will be relaxed by the change of ownership structures caused by the merger, this implies a need to focus on both banks' marginal business and to assess the extent to which that business is likely to switch between the two merging banks as opposed to other providers.

The extent of any customer 'lock-in' is often very difficult to assess, because the switching costs that cause inertia are dependent on the individual consumer's circumstances as well as on the nature of the product. Nevertheless, the same principle applies – competitive activity focuses on the business that is contestable, and the impact of the merger should be judged by its impact (if any) on competition for this business.

Thus, even in the presence of switching costs the same exercise as in a 'conventional' industry is required, namely to identify each of the merging parties' closest competitors. But does the presence of switching costs have any influence on the identity of the main competitive constraints? As explained above, switching costs imply that firms of different sizes will have very different incentives, with smaller firms being normally more aggressive on price than their larger rivals. This in turn implies that a merger between two firms with relatively high market shares may have less impact on competition than one in which a large bank merges with a smaller rival. Thus, normal assumptions about market shares and changes in market structure might not apply.

**4.4.2.1** *Lloyds/Abbey National*    In July 2001, the UK Competition Commission (CC) issued its recommendation to block the proposed hostile takeover of Abbey National by Lloyds TSB Group.[266] Although Abbey National accounted for just 5% of the market for personal banking, it was considered to be a 'maverick' firm, the removal of which would eliminate an important competitive force on the major UK banks (Barclays, HSBC and Royal Bank of Scotland). In motivating its decision, the CC emphasised the fact that customers perceive

---

[266] Competition Commission, 'Lloyds TSB Group plc and Abbey National plc – A report on the proposed merger', July 2001.

switching between banks as a difficult process, and that the actual rate of switching is very low.

Importantly, the abovementioned prediction from economic theory that small firms may provide the strongest competitive constraint in a market with switching costs was highlighted by the evidence provided by Abbey to the CC inquiry. The CC summarises the situation as follows:[267]

> Abbey National submitted that, in markets with switching costs, firms with low market share tended to grow (or 'sow') their share by competing aggressively and through price, while those with high market share tended to exploit (or 'harvest') theirs by preserving or increasing margins on the existing customer base. The merger, it argued, would replace a firm in sowing phase with one in harvesting phase, to the detriment of consumers and competition.

The *Lloyds/Abbey* case also illustrates how switching costs can affect the analysis in other ways. Although smaller banks might have a stronger incentive to compete on price, the CC also believed that a bank needed to achieve a certain critical scale in order to provide a viable alternative to the major suppliers. By reducing the number of new business opportunities for an emerging supplier, the CC argued that switching costs represented a barrier to growth and made it harder for another bank to replicate the competitive presence that Abbey National had achieved. The CC noted that: 'the existence of barriers to switching makes it difficult for entrants to acquire customers at a rapid rate and exacerbates the problem of diseconomies of scale in branch networks, marketing and other costs which entrants suffer in comparison with incumbents.'[268]

Thus, not only did the merger risk eliminating a player which, due to the impact of switching costs on behaviour, likely had a more important effect on competition than might be suggested by its market share, those same switching costs would also have made it harder for other banks to grow post-merger in order to achieve the kind of challenging position that Abbey National had built up. This double impact of switching costs made the facts of this transaction particularly problematic.[269]

---

[267] Lloyds/Abbey National, para. 2.79.     [268] Ibid., para. 2.111.

[269] This does not mean that the decision to block the merger was uncontroversial. For example, the CC relied on collective dominance concerns, arguing that the non-aggressive pricing behaviour of the leading banks indicated a predisposition towards cooperative behaviour. Yet the switching costs explanation for this behaviour lies in

**4.4.2.2    Lloyds/HBOS**    In October 2008, the UK Government cleared the *Lloyds/HBOS* merger despite the fact that the Office of Fair Trading (OFT) had reached the conclusion that the transaction gave rise to clear competition concerns.[270] The Government's decision was motivated by public interest issues, and, in particular, a perceived need to ensure the stability of the UK financial system.

The OFT's conclusion that the merger, which gave the new entity a combined market share in Great Britain of 30–40% (with an increment of 10–20%), would be likely to give rise to unilateral effects was based to a significant extent on an assessment of the impact of switching costs and customer inertia on the merged firm's pricing behaviour. In particular, the OFT argued that:

- by increasing Lloyds' customer base, the merger would encourage the new entity to attach (even) more weight to the enhancement of margins than to the growth of market share. In other words, Lloyds was expected to be a less aggressive competitor following the merger, even if it is accepted that it must compete, to a certain extent, to maintain its market share levels; [271]
- more importantly, since HBOS was considered a leader of the competitive fringe and, other than Grupo Santander (who acquired Abbey National in 2004), the only player that came close to the major UK banks in terms of number of branches, its removal as a 'prime challenger' to the leading banks was considered to be detrimental to the level of actual and potential competition.[272]

The OFT's overall conclusion is summarised as follows:[273]

> The combined effect of increasing Lloyds' market share significantly and of removing an important challenger is expected to be the dampening of competitive conditions in the market as a whole, and the associated unilateral effects. As a result, the value for money of PCA propositions

---

unilateral incentives, not coordination or collusion, so arguably one of the main planks of the CC's reasoning in the *Lloyds/Abbey* case was defective.

[270] Office of Fair Trading, 'Anticipated acquisition by Lloyds TSB plc of HBOS plc – Report to the Secretary of State for Business Enterprise and Regulatory Reform', 24 October 2008. This document is referred to henceforth as the 'OFT decision'.

[271] OFT decision, para. 124.

[272] Ibid., para. 129. In particular the decision points out that 'several competitors who responded to the OFT identified HBOS as the bank to whom they tend to lose the most PCA customers'.

[273] Ibid., para. 133.

is expected to worsen not only for the merged entity but for the industry as a whole because the merger may change the incentives of all firms present in the market to compete by worsening value for money in equilibrium.

Given this analysis, it is interesting to speculate on how the OFT might have evaluated a merger between two of the big four UK clearing banks – a merger between Lloyds and HSBC, for example. In terms of market shares alone, such a merger looks much more problematic, yet the logic of the switching costs arguments might actually lead to fewer competitive concerns for such a merger. A merger between two of the major players, each of whom on the OFT's analysis is content to 'harvest' its stock of existing customers rather than seeking to win share from rivals, could not realistically be argued to eliminate either bank's main constraint. To the extent that customers of either bank choose to switch accounts, the likelihood is that they would change to one of the smaller challenging banks and not to one of the other majors.[274]

### 4.4.3    Conclusions

It is a well accepted idea in the economic literature that the presence of switching costs can affect the way in which competition works. This explains, and may sometimes justify, the efforts by competition and regulatory authorities to intervene to reduce switching costs in sectors such as banking and utilities. When it comes to merger appraisal, there is sometimes a tendency to infer from this that the presence of switching costs automatically justifies greater intervention.

However, this is not the case. The assessment of a proposed merger in a market characterised by switching costs requires an analysis of which rivals each of the merging parties would lose their (price-sensitive) customers to, should they increase prices above their current level. This is no different from the types of issue that should be addressed in the assessment of mergers in 'conventional' markets. The EC Horizontal Merger Guidelines appear to agree with this principle, and point out that post-merger price increases in markets characterised by switching costs may be more likely to arise 'for customers that have used dual sourcing from the two

---

[274] A scenario not dissimilar to this did emerge in the *SEB/FSB* merger (Case COMP/ M.2380, Commission decision of 19 September 2001), which involved a proposed merger between two of the four major domestic banks in Sweden. That merger was subjected to a Phase II investigation in July 2001, but was abandoned by the parties prior to completion of the inquiry.

merging firms as a means of obtaining competitive prices'.[275] In other words, if customers face lower costs to switch volumes between the parties than from the parties to rival suppliers, then unilateral effects would be more likely to arise as a result of the merger.

Moreover, the economic theory of switching costs can have some important and counter-intuitive implications for merger assessment. Switching costs can imply that smaller firms are generally more price aggressive than larger firms because they have more to gain and less to lose by undercutting their larger rivals.[276] Consequently, a merger between two firms with relatively high market shares may well have less impact on competition than a merger that eliminated rivalry from a smaller player.

## 4.5   Partial ownership

Competition law is usually only concerned with control or de facto control. For this reason little attention has traditionally been given to the impact on competition of transactions in which one party acquires a financial interest in, but no ability to exert control over, another party.[277] In this context, it is worth noting that in the absence of control, minority shareholdings will not even fall under merger control rules but can only be investigated under Articles 101 and 102 of the TFEU.[278]

However, partial ownership is becoming an increasingly prominent issue in competition cases. For example, in October 2010, the UK Office of Fair Trading started an investigation into Ryanair's acquisition of a minority shareholding of 29.8% in Aer Lingus. In June 2012, the OFT decided to refer the acquisition to the Competition Commission on the grounds that the stake 'has resulted or will result in a substantial lessening of competition on a number of Ryanair and/or Aer Lingus routes between the UK and Ireland.'[279]

---

[275] EC Horizontal Merger Guidelines, para. 31.

[276] The incentive for mobile network operators with relatively small shares of supply to compete more vigorously than firms with larger customer bases was considered by the Commission in Case COMP/M.3916 – *T-Mobile Austria/Tele.ring*, Commission decision of 26 April 2006, paras. 74–81.

[277] In practice, the issue of whether the firm acquiring partial ownership gains any control may not be straightforward. In this section we consider partial ownership not to confer any ability to influence the decision of the target firm.

[278] See O. Koch, 'Yes, We Can (Prohibit) – The *Ryanair/Aer Lingus* merger before the Court' (2010) 3 *Competition Policy Newsletter* 41–5.

[279] 'OFT refers Ryanair's minority stake in Aer Lingus to Competition Commission', press release 47/12, 15 June 2012, available at www.oft.gov.uk/news-and-updates/

One of the concerns raised by the OFT is that, as a result of its shareholding, Ryanair's incentives to compete with Aer Lingus may be softened since it would be able to raise prices knowing that a proportion of any profits lost as a result of passengers switching to Aer Lingus would be recaptured through its stake in Aer Lingus.[280]

In what follows, we present economic intuitions as to why, and how, minority share ownership can in principle have effects on competitive behaviour and market outcomes of the type predicted by the OFT. Although these intuitions are based on formal models of competitive behaviour from the industrial organisation literature, for didactic purposes, we illustrate these results through the use of a simple example.[281]

Consider an industry in which there are three firms, denoted as A, B and C, and assume the following:

- Firm A has a 20% market share, Firm B has 20% and Firm C has 60%.
- If Firm A raises price unilaterally by 10%, it will lose 20 units of sales as consumers switch those units of consumption to other suppliers.
- Diversion ratios are proportionate to market shares.

We can infer that even though a 10% price rise would allow Firm A to earn a higher profit on the units that it would retain, such a price rise would not be profitable pre-merger due to the prospect of losing 20 units of volume. If it were profitable, Firm A would already have implemented the price rise.

Suppose now that Firm A acquires a 20% stake in Firm B, but that this stake does not provide any form of control whatsoever over Firm B.

The question we need to ask is: What are the unilateral effects of Firm A's partial ownership of Firm B? To answer this question it is necessary

---

press/2012/47–12. The press release points out that its investigation was suspended on two occasions: once by the OFT itself because it had insufficient information with which to proceed; and once due to a legal challenge by Ryanair, which was dismissed by the Court of Appeal in May 2012.

[280] In its press release, the OFT also raised the concerns that the minority stake may give Ryanair the ability to weaken Aer Lingus as a competitor through use of its voting power at Aer Lingus shareholder meetings and that it may restrict Aer Lingus' options to benefit from investment by other airlines which may, in turn, weaken the competitive position of Aer Lingus over time.

[281] In the economic literature there are numerous theoretical models which analyse the competitive effects of partial ownership. The seminal contribution is that of T. F. Bresnahan and S. C. Salop, 'Quantifying the Competitive Effects of Production Joint Ventures' (1986) 4(2) *International Journal of Industrial Organization* 155–75. See also D. P. O'Brien and S. C. Salop, 'Competitive Effects of Partial Ownership: Financial and corporate control' (2000) 67 *Antitrust Law Journal* 559–614.

to analyse how the existence of partial ownership of Firm B affects Firm A's incentives to raise prices. Firm A might have an incentive to increase its price because it knows that by doing so it will gain higher margins from its own sales *and* will capture some of the value from any sales diverted from Firm A to Firm B following the price rise. Clearly, the higher the percentage of customers that, following Firm A's price rise, would switch to Firm B, the higher is Firm A's incentive to increase its price.

From the assumptions above, we can estimate that the 20 units of lost Firm A sales that would result from a 10% price increase will be distributed amongst competing firms in proportion to their shares of the rest of the market. Since Firm B's share is a third of Firm C's share, this implies that:

- 5 units will go to Firm B; and
- 15 units will go to Firm C.

Since Firm A has a 20% stake in Firm B, the 5 units that are lost to Firm B are now in effect partially recouped by Firm A via its equity stake. The question then becomes how far this extra factor – the incremental profit attributable to the 20% equity stake in the 5 units, which corresponds to just one unit – cushions the impact of the postulated price rise and makes Firm A more inclined to increase price.

Two diluting factors serve to lessen the scope for unilateral effects in a partial ownership transaction, relative to an equivalent full merger between the same firms:

- Only a fraction of the financial benefit to Firm B of gaining sales from Firm A accrues to Firm A.
- Unlike a standard unilateral effect, the incentive to increase price is asymmetric; whereas, under a full merger of Firms A and B, both may be expected to respond to demand diversion between them by increasing price, in this partial ownership scenario, only Firm A has an incentive to increase price. This is due to the fact that Firm B receives no benefit from sales diverted to Firm A.

These factors indicate that the scope for unilateral effects due to minority ownership will tend to be significantly smaller than in the case of full mergers.[282] Nonetheless, significant unilateral effects might arise if the acquirer and the target enjoy particularly high market shares and/or their

---

[282] Note that *any* horizontal merger – even between two firms each with 5% shares – will generate a unilateral effects prediction of a post-merger price rise. But merger policy blocks only those extreme cases where the post-merger impact is large.

products are very close substitutes. Equally, the risk of unilateral effects will rise with the size of the minority shareholding in question.

A modified HHI has been proposed in the literature as a way to take into account the changes in incentives brought about by minority shareholdings.[283] The modified HHI is mentioned in the EC Horizontal Merger Guidelines, which state that 'in markets with cross-shareholdings or joint ventures the Commission may use a modified HHI, which takes into account such share-holdings (see, e.g. Case IV/M.1383 – Exxon/Mobil, point 256)'.[284]

Recall that the standard HHI is defined as the sum of the squares of each firm's share (see Section 2.1.1.1). The modified post-merger HHI is calculated by adding to the standard pre-merger HHI an additional term, as follows:[285]

*Modified HHI = Standard HHI+[stake * Market share of acquirer*
*\* Market share of target]*

In our example with three firms and Firm A purchasing a 20% stake in Firm B, this is equivalent to:

$$Modified\ HHI\ =\ Standard\ HHI + [0.20\ *\ Market\ share\ of\ Firm\ A$$
$$*\ Market\ share\ of\ Firm\ B] = 20^2 + 20^2 + 60^2 + [0.20\ *\ 20\ *\ 20]$$
$$= 4,400 + [80] = 4,480$$

The modified HHI represents the post-merger level of concentration, and the change in concentration ('delta') is simply the difference between the post-merger modified HHI and the pre-merger standard HHI.

---

[283] See T. Bresnahan and S. Salop, 'Quantifying the Competitive Effects of Production Joint Ventures' (1986) 4(2) *International Journal of Industrial Organization* 155–75; R. J. Reynolds and B. R. Snapp, 'The Competitive Effects of Partial Equity Interests and Joint Ventures' (1986) 4(2) *International Journal of Industrial Organization* 141–53.

Note that these unilateral effects models simply capture the immediate incentive effects of owning a stake in a competitor. They do not measure the separate phenomenon of joint equity interests that create points of contact that might facilitate coordinated behaviour. See, e.g., D. Malueg, 'Collusive Behavior and Partial Ownership of Rivals' (1992) 10(1) *International Journal of Industrial Organization* 27–34.

[284] EC Horizontal Merger Guidelines, footnote 25.

[285] Note that this formula assumes that Firm A acquires a share of Firm B but no ability to control B. This assumption is clearly not plausible in instances where the acquired stake is high. O'Brien and Salop (2000) present variants of the modified HHI formula for different assumptions regarding the impact of partial ownership on control including 'silent financial interest' (the case we consider here), 'proportional control' and 'one-way control'. See D. P. O'Brien and S. C. Salop, 'Competitive Effects of Partial Ownership: Financial and corporate control' (2000) 67 *Antitrust Law Journal* 559–614.

These modified HHIs have been used in a number of merger cases, including *Exxon/Mobil*[286] and *Alcan/Pechiney*,[287] in which a series of equity cross-holdings between the parties and their competitors affected the competition analysis.[288] Their relevance should not be overstated, however. In particular, the modified HHI is useful in assessing the impact of minority shareholding only in so far as the standard HHI is regarded as a reliable guide to unilateral effects. As explained above, however, HHIs do not take account of product differentiation, which, in most markets, will be the crucial issue. It is for this reason that the EC Horizontal Merger Guidelines acknowledge that 'HHI levels ... do not give rise to a presumption of either the existence or the absence of [competition] concerns'.[289] Indeed, mergers with high HHIs (and significant increments in the HHI) have been cleared unconditionally in the past. To the extent that standard HHIs are of limited value, the same considerations must apply to modified HHIs too.

The latter point is precisely the conclusion reached in a 2008 OECD Policy Roundtables paper on minority shareholdings, which notes:[290]

> The analysis of the variation of the [modified HHI] index pre- and post-transaction can offer some guidance as to whether a partial ownership acquisition may have an impact on the firm's incentives to compete, given a certain market structure and a certain corporate structure. However, this methodology is predictive in nature and cannot be relied upon to assert that a certain transaction will necessarily result in a significant lessening of competition. ... Therefore, the [modified HHI] index, just like the HHI index, can be no more than a screening device.

As discussed in Section 3.6 of this chapter, in recent years various indices have been proposed that seek to capture the effects of mergers on unilateral pricing incentives of firms selling differentiated products.

---

[286] Case COMP/M.1383 – *Exxon/Mobil*, Commission decision of 29 September 1999.

[287] Case COMP/M.1715 – *Alcan/Pechiney*, withdrawn on 14 March 2000.

[288] Similar considerations were also integral to the Commission's analysis in *E.ON/MOL*, which concerned vertical integration in the Hungarian gas supply where MOL, an integrated oil and gas group primarily active in Hungary on the markets for natural gas, oils, fuels and chemicals, still retained a minority stake of 25% (plus one share) post-merger. See Case COMP/M.3696 – *E.ON/MOL*, Commission decision of 21 December 2005.

[289] EC Horizontal Merger Guidelines, para. 21.

[290] 'Minority Shareholdings', OECD Policy Roundtables, 2008, available at www.oecd.org/dataoecd/40/38/41774055.pdf.

The 'gross upward pricing pressure index' or GUPPI,[291] can be modified for use in partial ownership cases. In a full merger between two single product Firms A and B, the absolute gross upward pressure on the price of the product produced by Firm A as a result of the loss of the constraint exerted by Firm B is given by

$$G_A = DR_{AB} * M_B$$

where $DR_{AB}$ is the diversion ratio from product A to product B, and $M_B$ is the gross absolute margin on the product of Firm B (i.e. B's price minus its marginal cost). As explained above, the product, $DR_{AB} * M_B$, can be considered as a notional marginal cost increase for Firm A arising from the merger.[292]

O'Brien and Salop have considered how this intuition can be extended to mergers involving an acquisition of partial ownership.[293] All else being equal, the larger the ownership stake in Firm B purchased by Firm A, the greater the profit recaptured by Firm A on sales diverted to Firm B, and hence the greater the reduction in the opportunity cost to Firm A of raising price. Hence, a modified measure of gross upward pricing pressure where Firm A only acquires an ownership stake of Firm B of proportion S is given by

$$G_A = DR_{AB} * M_B * S$$

Intuitively, Firm A only recuperates a proportion S of the margin earned on each diverted sale so that the effective gross margin recuperated from A's perspective is lower by this proportion.

As noted previously, simple measures based on diversion ratios and margins do not account for a number of important factors such as supply-side responses (e.g. entry and product repositioning), multi-product pricing, pricing responses by rivals and certain demand-related factors, and as such can only form part of the overall assessment of unilateral effects.

---

[291] S. C. Salop and S. Moresi, 'Updating the Merger Guidelines: Comments' (2009), available at www.ftc.gov/os/comments/horizontalmergerguides/545095-00032.pdf.

[292] If information on the rate of pass through of cost changes to price changes, $\rho$, is known, then the change in A's price is equal to the notional change in A's marginal cost multiplied by the pass through rate, $DR_{AB} * M_B * \rho$. This expression can be divided by A's price to reach a prediction of the percentage price increase of A's price.

[293] See D. P. O'Brien and S. C. Salop, 'Competitive Effects of Partial Ownership: Financial and corporate control' (2000) 67 Antitrust Law Journal 559–614.

## 5.    Countervailing factors

### 5.1    Introduction

As discussed in Section 2, most theoretical models of firm behaviour predict that increases in market concentration will relax competitive constraints between suppliers and hence result in higher prices. However, in order to reach the conclusion that significant unilateral effects would be likely to result from a proposed transaction it is necessary to take into account other factors that can affect market outcomes. This principle is set out very clearly in the EC Horizontal Merger Guidelines, which establish the need for merger review to consider:[294]

- The likelihood that buyer power would act as a countervailing factor to an increase in market power resulting from the merger.
- The likelihood that entry would maintain effective competition in the relevant market.
- The likelihood that efficiencies would act as a factor counteracting the harmful effects on competition which might otherwise result from the merger.
- The conditions for a failing firm defence.

This section explains the conditions under which these countervailing factors may significantly reduce the risk of post-merger price increases, even where the parties may have been found to exert an important competitive constraint on each other pre-merger. We discuss in turn the ability of large buyers to take steps to countervail the market power of the merged entity (Section 5.2); rivals' ability to reposition their products and the likelihood of new entry (Section 5.3), efficiency gains (Section 5.4) and the failing firm defence (Section 5.5). For each factor, we provide a brief summary of the key principles as set out in the EC Horizontal Merger Guidelines, an example or case study illustrating how its relevance can be assessed in practice, and a brief account of previous merger cases in which each countervailing factor was successfully invoked.

### 5.2.    Buyer power

#### 5.2.1    Buyer power in the EC Horizontal Merger Guidelines

Unilateral effects concern the exercise of pricing power by suppliers, which may arise from a dearth of suitable alternatives and rivals. Buyer

---

[294] EC Horizontal Merger Guidelines, para. 11.

power refers to an equivalent measure of negotiating strength that purchasers may enjoy if there are sufficiently few customers in a market. The presence of buyer power may serve to counter the exercise of pricing power by suppliers, and thereby mitigate unilateral price rises that may otherwise occur following a merger. This is explicitly recognised by the EC Horizontal Merger Guidelines, which state: 'The competitive pressure on a supplier is not only exercised by competitors but can also come from its customers. Even firms with very high market shares may not be in a position, post-merger, to significantly impede effective competition, in particular by acting to an appreciable extent independently of their customers, if the latter possess countervailing buyer power.'[295]

Countervailing buyer power is defined in the EC Horizontal Merger Guidelines as the bargaining strength that the buyer has vis-à-vis the seller in commercial negotiations due to its size, its commercial significance to the seller and its ability to switch to alternative suppliers.[296]

As illustrated in detail in the case study in Section 5.2.3 below, customers enjoying buyer power may be able to prevent an existing supplier from increasing prices by engaging in a variety of different strategies, such as sponsoring new entry, facilitating brand repositioning,[297] threatening to switch large volumes to a competitor or entering the market themselves.

If buyer power is to be effective, the buyer must usually be of considerable size. It is important to note, however, that size is not the only important factor; in arguing that a merger will not generate unilateral effects it is not sufficient simply to observe that the parties' customers are large. It must be demonstrated that there are existing alternative or potential suppliers to which buyers can credibly threaten to transfer their purchases, and that the loss of sales to such alternatives would have a material impact on suppliers' profitability.

It should also be noted that, as well as countervailing the creation of market power, buyer power may actually be created by a merger. This can represent an efficiency gain where it allows the merged entity to negotiate lower prices from its suppliers and to pass on at least some of the resulting cost savings to final consumers in terms of lower prices for its final goods. Furthermore, the EC Horizontal Merger Guidelines note the possibility that a merger through the creation of buyer power in

---

[295] EC Horizontal Merger Guidelines, para. 64.    [296] Ibid., para. 64.
[297] For retailers, this could take the form of commissioning an own-brand product, or promoting or committing to buy an alternative branded good.

upstream markets actually harms downstream competition by giving the merged entity an incentive to reduce its purchases of an input and reduce output downstream.[298]

### 5.2.2   Relevance in EU cases

Recent Phase II cases where the Commission considered buyer power as a countervailing factor include the following.

In *Cargill/Degussa Food Ingredients*,[299] evidence that larger customers (food manufacturers) and distributors actually encouraged new entry contributed to a finding of no concerns.

In *Friesland Foods/Campina*,[300] while the Commission conceded that certain retailers (the largest Dutch supermarket chains) could exercise countervailing power, it argued that smaller retailers and 'out of home' wholesalers did not have such power. The Commission further pointed out that buyer power exists only if buyers can effectively threaten to switch to rivals or stop purchasing the products from the merged entity.[301] If such alternatives are unavailable or their credibility would be significantly diminished by the proposed transaction, buyers would not be able to provide a countervailing force post-merger. This point was stressed by the Commission at paragraph 967, which reads:

> Furthermore, even if buyer power existed prior to the merger, it must also exist and remain effective following the merger. This is because the merger of two suppliers may reduce the buyer power if it thereby removes a credible alternative.

Similarly, in *Syngenta/Monsanto's Sunflower Seed Business*,[302] the Commission rejected the argument that customers had bargaining power since in certain market segments 'no significant substitute to Syngenta and Monsanto exists besides Pioneer [which] explains why various customers in the market investigation indicated that the new entity would be able to raise prices in Spain'.[303]

---

[298]  EC Horizontal Merger Guidelines, para. 61.

[299]  Case COMP/M.3975 – *Cargill/Degussa Food Ingredients*, Commission decision of 29 March 2006.

[300]  Case COMP/M.5046 – *Friesland Foods/Campina*, Commission decision of 17 December 2008.

[301]  Ibid., paras. 761, 762 and 967.

[302]  Case COMP/M.5675 – *Syngenta/Monsanto's Sunflower Seed Business*, Commission decision of 17 November 2010.

[303]  Ibid., para. 256.

COUNTERVAILING FACTORS                                    291

More recently, in *Western Digital Ireland/Viviti Technologies*,[304] the Commission examined a 3-to-2 merger in the markets for 3.5-inch hard disk drives (HDDs), as the proposed transaction was assessed on the basis that the *Seagate/HDD Business of Samsung*[305] merger had already taken place. In previous cases in the HDD industry, the Commission had considered the countervailing constraint exerted by buyers via the so-called 'Conner effect'.[306] Specifically, the Commission had accepted the argument that combined market shares would likely be lower than the simple addition of the parties' market shares due to the multi-sourcing strategy adopted by customers and the fact that many customers purchasing from both companies would in all likelihood add a new supplier to keep the number of competing suppliers constant. However, in *Western Digital Ireland/Viviti Technologies*,[307] the Commission found no evidence of countervailing buyer power, and, in particular, it argued that the market investigation revealed that customers were generally unwilling to alter their procurement strategies by allocating a very high proportion of sales to any single supplier or switching to single sourcing. On these bases, the Commission considered that the merger would compromise the ability of buyers to multi-source effectively.

Importantly, whilst large customers may be able to exercise the necessary countervailing power to undermine a price increase post-merger, smaller customers may lack such power and may therefore be more vulnerable.[308] If no price discrimination is feasible against these smaller customers, the latter may be protected under the umbrella of larger customers. However, many markets for intermediate products are characterised by some degree of price discrimination or differentiation,

---

[304] Case COMP/M.6203 – *Western Digital Ireland/Viviti Technologies*, Commission decision of 23 November 2011.

[305] Case COMP/M.6214 – *Seagate/HDD Business of Samsung*, Commission decision of 19 October 2011.

[306] See, e.g., Case COMP/ M. 5483 – *Toshiba/Fujitsu HDD Business*, Commission decision of 11 May 2009, para. 33 and footnote 6; and Case COMP/M. 6214 – *Seagate/HDD Business of Samsung*, Commission decision of 19 October 2011, para. 434.

[307] Case COMP/M.6203 – *Western Digital Ireland/Viviti Technologies*, Commission decision of 23 November 2011.

[308] This does not necessarily mean that these smaller customers cannot switch suppliers post-merger. Indeed, with smaller requirements, it may even be easier to switch, or there may be a wider set of alternative suppliers capable of serving their requirements. Nonetheless, where there is a fixed cost of switching supplier, the average cost of switching (per unit of output) may be proportionally higher for smaller customers.

implying that smaller customers will obtain different terms and conditions to larger customers.

It is for this reason that in *Friesland Foods/Campina*,[309] the Commission concluded that smaller retailers were not protected despite larger retailers having considerable buyer power:[310]

> [E]ven if a large retailer were to derive some degree of bargaining power from their large size or a sophisticated purchasing strategy, there is no generally convincing reason why other retailers should also be positively affected. The merged entity would not have to grant smaller buyers similar discounts as those offered to larger buyers to prevent them from switching. In fact, the market investigation suggested that the retail market for fresh milk is relatively competitive. This competition would induce larger retailers to take steps that protect only themselves, if such a possibility existed, from a lessening of competition between suppliers, as these firms may stand to gain from an increase in their rivals' costs after the merger.

A case that is frequently cited, including in the EC Horizontal Merger Guidelines, is *Enso/Stora*,[311] which concerned the merger of two leading European producers of pulp, paper and packaging board. In what follows, we discuss this case in some detail.

### 5.2.3    Case study: the *Enso/Stora* decision[312]

The merger between Enso and Stora created the largest paper and board manufacturing company in the world.[313] The main markets affected by this transaction were newsprint, magazine paper and, more acutely, liquid packaging board (LPB), where the post-merger firm's share was some 60%.[314]

Within the market for LPB the only other players, Korsnas and Assidoman, accounted for 10–20% of EEA sales each. Moreover, concerns over the very high post-merger market share were heightened by apparently high barriers to entry, very modest demand growth and the

---

[309] Case COMP/M.5046 – *Friesland Foods/Campina*, Commission decision of 17 December 2008.

[310] Ibid., para. 276.

[311] Case COMP/M.1225 – *Enso/Stora*, Commission decision of 25 November 1998.

[312] Ibid.

[313] This case study draws on A. Lofaro and S. Baker, 'Buyer Power and the *Enso/Stora* Decision' (2000) 21 *European Competition Law Review* 187–90.

[314] LPB is the board routinely used for the packaging of liquid goods such as milk and fruit juice. The decision cites a post-merger market share of 50–70%.

absence of effective potential competition from EEA-based producers of other board products, such as MoDo and Metsa-Serla, and non-EEA producers.[315] In short, this was a merger that on a formalistic analysis of market structure would undoubtedly have been blocked.

However, the Commission recognised that the buying-side of this market was also extremely concentrated. In particular, Tetra Pak accounted for 60–80% of total demand, the remainder being purchased by Elopak and SIG Combibloc, representing 10–20% each. In recognition of the degree of concentration amongst the customers, the Commission extended the analysis to explore whether purchasers might be able to exert countervailing buyer power on the merged entity.

The term 'buyer power' is often used wherever the demand side is concentrated. As noted above, however, it is not mere size or concentration per se that is relevant, but rather the ability of buyers to take actions that undermine any attempt by suppliers to increase prices. This can be done by, *inter alia*, inducing or threatening to induce changes to the structure of the market in the medium term. In the *Enso/Stora*[316] case, the Commission's analysis shows that buyers had at least two strategies that could be used to thwart any attempted post-merger price rise.

### 5.2.3.1 Small losses in volume have significant impact on suppliers' average costs   The first strategy is the threat of buyers to switch their demand or part of it to other suppliers. The effectiveness of this threat was recognised by the Commission, as follows:[317]

> the production of liquid packaging board is a high fixed-cost industry, where high rates of capacity utilization are necessary in order to achieve satisfactory levels of profitability. To lose the large volumes purchased by Tetra Pak would therefore mean that the parties would have to find other customers in order to fill the capacity. This would not be an easy task in the short term.

Importantly, since the costs of LPB suppliers are sensitive to the level of capacity utilisation, the ability of buyers to discipline suppliers does not

---

[315] At paragraph 77, the Commission notes that no entry into the liquid packaging board had taken place over the last ten years.

[316] Case COMP/M.1225 – *Enso/Stora*, Commission decision of 25 November 1998.

[317] Ibid., para. 90. Moreover, at para. 94, the Commission makes a similar point when it assesses the impact of a loss of Elopak and SIG Combibloc's volumes on Stora Enso's profitability.

Table 3.23 *Firms' volume of sales to each customer*

|  | Firm A | Firm B | Firm C | Firm D | Total |
|---|---|---|---|---|---|
| Customer 1 | 70 | 10 | 15 | 5 | 100 |
| Customer 2 | 50 | 50 | 0 | 0 | 100 |
| Customer 3 | 0 | 0 | 45 | 55 | 100 |
| *Total sales* | *120* | *60* | *60* | *60* | *300* |
| *Market share* | *40%* | *20%* | *20%* | *20%* | *100%* |

require that all demand is switched. Instead, the ability of even the smaller buyers to shift volumes away from existing suppliers imposes a significant competitive constraint. The decision states that: 'a large shift of volumes to alternative suppliers such as AssiDoman and Korsnas, who could in principle switch WTL [another board category] capacity to the production of liquid packaging board, could hurt Stora Enso significantly, should the parties attempt to exercise market power.'[318]

Since unit costs are adversely affected by a drop in capacity utilisation, the impact on the merged entity of losing even a portion of the business of one of its major customers would be significant.

To see this, consider the numerical example in Table 3.23, with four suppliers, A, B, C and D, and only three buyers. For simplicity, we assume that the three customers are equally sized and split their purchases as set out in the table.

The four suppliers produce at identically sized plants, each of which has a maximum capacity of 75 units, has a fixed cost of €50, and a variable cost per unit of €1. This gives the relationship between output and average unit costs set out in Table 3.24.

Assume that Firm A owns two such plants, whilst Firms B, C and D have one plant each. Figure 3.12 shows how the average unit cost of production decreases as the total volume produced increases, due to the decreasing relative importance of fixed costs. The square in the figure represents the current level of production of each plant (60 units) and the horizontal line shows the pre-merger price, which is assumed to be equal to €2. At this level of production and prices, each plant makes a net margin equal to €0.17 per unit (equal to €2 minus average unit costs of €1.83).

---

[318] Ibid., para. 94.

Table 3.24 *Average unit cost at plant level for different levels of output*

| Units produced | Fixed costs | Variable costs | Total costs | Average unit cost |
|---|---|---|---|---|
| 15 | € 50 | € 15 | € 65 | € 4.33 |
| 30 | € 50 | € 30 | € 80 | € 2.67 |
| 45 | € 50 | € 45 | € 95 | € 2.11 |
| 60 | € 50 | € 60 | € 110 | € 1.83 |
| 75 | € 50 | € 75 | € 125 | € 1.67 |

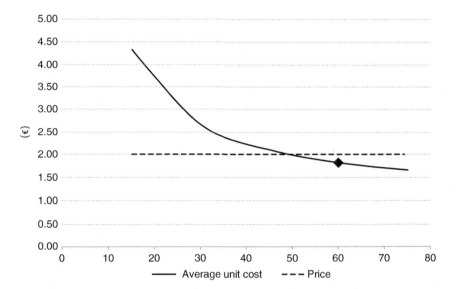

Figure 3.12    Average unit cost of production for different levels of output

Suppose that the proposed transaction involves Firms A and B. The new entity would have a market share of 60%, similar to the *Enso/Stora* case. However, unilateral effects would be unlikely to arise post-merger since customers would be able to defeat any attempt by the new entity to raise prices by switching volumes to one or more of their rivals. For instance, customer 1 would be able to prevent its price from increasing by 5% to €2.10 by threatening to switch 15 units from any of the post-merger firm's plants to Firm C or D. As shown in Figure 3.13, the loss of these units would raise the plant's average unit cost to €2.11 and, therefore, make the plant loss-making even at the higher hypothetical post-merger price level.

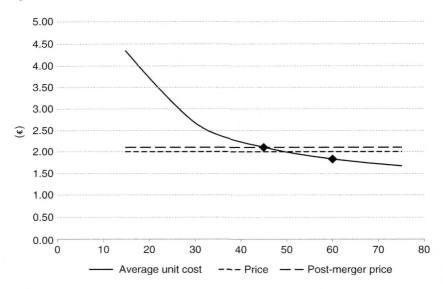

**Figure 3.13**   Average unit cost of production after post-merger price increase

**5.2.3.2   Sponsoring new entry**   The second strategy identified by the Commission in *Enso/Stora*[319] relates to Tetra Pak, which, it was argued, 'buys such large volumes of liquid packaging board that it would have the option of developing new capacity with other existing or new suppliers, should the parties attempt to exercise market power'.[320]

Hence, even when suppliers of LPB may need to expand or build completely new capacity to supply significant volumes of LPB, the ability of customers such as Tetra Pak to underwrite such capacity expansion with committed orders dramatically reduces the risk of making such investments. Irrecoverable investments, or sunk costs, that would be considered too risky if the suppliers faced a fragmented demand side are made much less risky when they can be made in effective collaboration with a large customer.

Returning to our hypothetical example, both customers 1 and 2 would be able individually to underwrite existing or new suppliers' investment in the construction of a new plant, for example by signing a long-term supply contract, should the merged entity attempt to raise prices. So long

[319] Case COMP/M.1225 – *Enso/Stora*, Commission decision of 25 November 1998.
[320] Ibid., para. 91.

as the customer could guarantee to purchase at least 50 units from the new plant at the pre-merger price level of €2, the new entrant would cover its total costs.[321] Both customers of Firms A and B (customers 1 and 2) have sufficient volume requirements to threaten credibly to sponsor entry (i.e. to justify the investment in capacity expansion from the entrant's point of view).

### 5.2.4   Conclusions

There are a number of reasons why the *Enso/Stora*[322] case is often referred to as an important decision and explicitly mentioned in the EC Horizontal Merger Guidelines.

First, the Commission acknowledged, perhaps for the first time, that a pure supply-side approach is not valid when customers are more than the small and essentially passive recipients of a take-it-or-leave-it offer from suppliers. A more careful analysis of the buying side of the market is needed when the customers themselves can play an active role in influencing the structure of the supply-side of the market.

Second, the decision recognises that in some circumstances even mergers that lead to high shares in markets protected by what would conventionally be regarded as substantial barriers to entry do not necessarily give rise to competition concerns.

Third, the decision acknowledges that buyer power is not merely equated with a high level of concentration on the buyer side of the market. In any case where 'buyer power' arguments are advanced as a counterbalance to market power, the question to ask is 'power to do what?' This requires the identification of those mechanisms that may allow buyers to inflict, or threaten to inflict, substantial damage on existing suppliers. In its decision, the Commission identifies two such mechanisms: the strategic switching of some purchases from one supplier to another, and the underwriting of entry that might otherwise be too costly or risky.[323]

---

[321] To see that the new plant would just break even with sales of 50 units at a price of €2, note that at this output and price level total costs (€50 in fixed costs + 50€ in variable costs) would equal revenue (50 * €2).

[322] Case COMP/M.1225 – *Enso/Stora*, Commission decision of 25 November 1998.

[323] Importantly, the Commission followed the same reasoning in its more recent decision *Korsnäs/AD Cartonboard*, which further reduced the number of liquid packaging board producers from three to two. See Case COMP/M.4057 – *Korsnäs/AD Cartonboard*, Commission decision of 12 May 2006.

### 5.3  Product repositioning and new entry

#### 5.3.1  Product repositioning and new entry in the EC Horizontal Merger Guidelines

Unilateral effects are most likely to occur when a merger brings together two products that consumers consider to be particularly close substitutes, and for which rivals' products are regarded as more distant alternatives. An assessment of differentiation between the merging and rival brands is normally based upon firms' pre-merger product portfolios, with the implicit assumption that the pre-merger situation will reflect the range of brands that will be available post-merger. In some cases, however, this approach may give an overly static view of the market. Following a merger, it may be possible for existing, non-merging competitors to reposition their brands to appeal to customers of the merged entity. If a non-merging firm repositions its brand in such a way that it is a closer substitute to the brands of the merging firms the competitive constraint on the merging firms will be increased, and any assessment based on pre-merger diversion ratios will overstate the scope for the merger to give rise to unilateral effects. Moreover, there is a clear incentive for non-merging firms to reposition their brands closer to the merging parties': if there is any prospect of those firms raising their price post-merger, then this will increase the number of customers seeking a similar alternative to the merged entity's brands, and thereby increase the potential sales to be made by rivals offering similar brands.

The scope for product repositioning may therefore reduce any incentive for unilateral increases in price. Significantly, this supply-side dynamic is not generally anticipated by theoretical unilateral effects models or in simulations based on historical market data.

The possibility that product repositioning may act as an effective countervailing factor to an increase in market power resulting from the merger is acknowledged in the EC Horizontal Merger Guidelines, which reads:

> In some markets it may be relatively easy and not too costly for the active firms to reposition their products or extend their product portfolio. In particular, the Commission examines whether the possibility of repositioning or product line extension by competitors or the merging parties may influence the incentive of the merged entity to raise prices.[324]

---

[324] EC Horizontal Merger Guidelines, para. 30.

For example, consider a scenario in which two 'deluxe' range companies facing suppliers of 'economy' products merge, and a static model of competition predicts a unilateral incentive to raise the price of both brands post-merger. Although the proposed transaction would eliminate an important competitive constraint, anti-competitive effects may ultimately be unlikely to arise if there is a realistic prospect that an existing economy brand would be able to reposition itself at the top end of the market, or launch a new luxury brand. Indeed, such repositioning would make the rival a close substitute to the products produced by the merging parties, and thus increase the losses that would be incurred by the merged firm should it attempt to increase prices. This would decrease the incentive of the merged firm to increase prices through an effect that could not be measured by historical patterns of demand switching, since the hypothesised repositioned brand did not exist pre-merger.

Brand repositioning can involve either changes in the fundamental product characteristics or changes in the way the good is marketed. Either way, the extent to which this will restrain any unilateral price increase depends upon the speed and cost involved in repositioning. Large customers, such as grocery retailers, can facilitate brand repositioning by accepting and promoting new brands.

Concerns over unilateral price increases may similarly be lessened if the possibility exists for new entry to the market. As with repositioning, attempts by the merged entity to implement unilateral price increases may serve to increase the incentive for firms outside the market to enter, thereby placing downward pressure on prices. In this respect, the EC Horizontal Merger Guidelines note: 'The Commission examines whether entry is likely or whether potential entry is likely to constrain the behaviour of incumbents post-merger. For entry to be likely, it must be sufficiently profitable taking into account the price effects of injecting additional output into the market and the potential responses of the incumbents.'[325]

There are sometimes disagreements between competition authorities and parties over the price benchmark that is relevant for assessing the viability of entry for the purpose of understanding the competitive constraints that the merged entity would face. For example, in the above mentioned *Svitzer/Adsteam* case,[326] the UK Competition Commission ('CC') argued that the threat of sponsored entry could only be considered

---

[325] EC Horizontal Merger Guidelines, para. 69.
[326] See Section 4.2.2.

to provide a constraint on the behaviour of an incumbent towage operator if an entrant could remain profitable at prices 10% below current
prices (or maybe even lower). This is because it considered that after
entry, increased competition would drive prices to 10% below their
current levels. Therefore, the CC concluded that a towage operator
considering entry into a monopoly port would be unlikely to enter unless
it could profitably do so at prices 10% below their current levels.

However, this reasoning is flawed in the context of assessing
the potential for a horizontal merger to give rise to anti-competitive
effects where new entrants are able to sign relatively long contracts that
guarantee the new supplier business at a specific price. The relevant
benchmark for assessing horizontal mergers is the *prevailing price level*:
the concern is whether the elimination of a competitor (or a potential
competitor) will permit the merged entity to increase prices above that
benchmark.

As noted above, in *Svitzer/Adsteam* the CC agreed that the main
competitive constraint in each monopoly port was the threat of potential
entry and that, *currently*, any attempt to increase prices above prevailing
levels would not be profitable (by definition). In order to assess the likely
competitive effects of the merger it is necessary to understand how other
firms would respond to any attempt to increase prices above prevailing
levels. For the merged entity to be subject to effective competitive
constraints post-merger only requires that a number of customers would
be able to sponsor entry by guaranteeing their business at current prices
to alternative towage operators, and that these operators would be able to
profitably supply them at current prices.

For example, any attempt by Svitzer to raise prices at any port
from 100 to 110, say, would be unprofitable provided that a group of
customers could respond by guaranteeing their business at a price of
100 to another towage operator, and that the 'cherry-picking' strategy
of entering that port and supplying that group of customers at a
price of 100 would be viable for the towage operator. Contrary to
the CC's argument, a new entrant would therefore not need to offer a
significant discount over pre-merger prices in order for customers to
find it profitable to react to a post-merger price increase by sponsoring
entry.

As with product repositioning, new entry is considered to be more
effective if it can be done relatively quickly and cheaply. On this point,
the EC Horizontal Merger Guidelines state: 'For entry to be considered a
sufficient competitive constraint on the merging parties, it must be

shown to be likely, timely and sufficient to deter or defeat any potential anti-competitive effects of the merger.'[327]

The rationale for this requirement is that if there are significant lags between deciding to enter the market and becoming operational, existing firms will have more time to respond to the entry, as well as a longer period in which to reap the benefits of higher prices. The EC Horizontal Merger Guidelines make clear that the Commission will normally consider entry to be timely only if it occurs within two years.[328] The EC Horizontal Merger Guidelines also stress that entry is likely to be less effective if there are high sunk costs in the industry:[329]

> entry is likely to be more difficult if the incumbents are able to protect their market shares by offering long-term contracts or giving targeted preemptive price reductions to those customers that the entrant is trying to acquire. Furthermore, high risk and costs of failed entry may make entry less likely. The costs of failed entry will be higher, the higher is the level of sunk cost associated with entry.

However, it would be incorrect to consider that the threat of entry necessarily lacks credibility when it can only take place with a potentially significant delay and in the presence of significant sunk costs. Specifically, in some markets, particularly those characterised by large buyers and significant sunk costs, the timescales that are appropriate to evaluate responses may be rather different to those applied routinely in other markets. Indeed, in such markets, despite the lag between commissioning new capacity and the onset of production, the threat to do so may well have *immediate* constraining effects on pricing.

To understand why this is so, one needs to consider the risks from the perspective of the buyers and the merging parties. In particular, the merging parties will typically have made sizeable sunk investments in their capacity in contemplation of supplying the market for many years. The prospect of earning excess profits for one or two years after the merger, whilst large customers underwrite and assist the product development or entry of others will often be unlikely to outweigh the long-term damage to their sales that would follow once that entry occurred. Under these circumstances, the post-merger entity would know that the new entrant's investment would also be sunk and hence committed to the market for many years to come. In short, the size and length of time

---

[327] EC Horizontal Merger Guidelines, para. 69.     [328] Ibid., para. 74.
[329] Ibid., para. 69.

needed to make the investments required for entry are counterbalanced by the length of time that the capacity would subsequently be in competition with the merged entity.

The knowledge that customers have the ability to switch strategic volumes or induce entry, and of the damage that such actions would have on the merged entity in the medium and long term, may well be sufficient to dissuade the parties from exercising any perceived short-run market power. Even though it would take time to be carried out, the mere threat of exercising buyer power can therefore be sufficient to constrain post-merger prices.

Finally, the threat of entry is more likely to be credible and, therefore, to defeat any attempt by the post-merger entity at increasing prices under the following circumstances:[330]

- when customers do not face significant costs in switching suppliers;
- when potential new entrants do not face supply or demand disadvantages vis-à-vis the incumbents, such as access to patents or other scarce inputs;
- when there are no significant network effects that limit the extent to which a smaller player can compete effectively; and
- when the market is expected to experience growth in the future.

### 5.3.2    Relevance in EU cases

Supply-side response arguments are normally put forward in cases where there is evidence that the proposed transaction would leave the merged entity with a very high share or would be likely to eliminate a particularly close constraint, such that there is a need for the parties to establish countervailing factors to mitigate unilateral effects concerns. As indicated by the case review below, the assessment of supply-side responses typically focuses on the likelihood of entry rather than repositioning.

In *Cargill/Degussa Food Ingredients*,[331] the Commission concluded that entry barriers were relatively low in the EEA market for non-GM fluid lecithin, in which the merged entity had a combined share of 30–50%.[332] In particular, there was evidence that large customers had successfully sponsored entry in the past and that Brazilian and Asian suppliers were increasingly present in Europe. The Commission

---

[330] Ibid., para. 72.
[331] Case COMP/M.3975 – *Cargill/Degussa Food Ingredients*, Commission decision of 29 March 2006.
[332] Ibid., paras. 101–9.

therefore held that unilateral effects were not likely to arise, notwithstanding the merged entity's high share of EEA sales.

In *Syngenta/Monsanto's Sunflower Seed Business*,[333] the Commission's
market investigation established that various suppliers with strong positions outside the EU had plans to enter the European market for
sunflower seed, including those national markets where unilateral effects
concerns had been identified. The Commission, however, argued that 'it
is unlikely that those seed producers would be able to gain a significant
market share in the short to medium term allowing them to exert a
competitive constraint on other relevant players.'[334] Such a conclusion
was based on the observation that previous instances of entry had not
resulted in market shares exceeding 5%.[335]

A detailed analysis of entry barriers was conducted in both *Ryanair/Aer
Lingus*[336] cases. The parties argued that entry was common within the
airline industry, as confirmed by previous merger investigations in the UK
(*BA Connect/Fly BE*) and Germany (*Air Berlin/LTU*) as well as over sixty
examples of entry on routes served by Ryanair. The reason why entry was
deemed to be relatively straightforward is that airlines can reallocate
aircraft capacity within their existing organisations without the need for
significant investment. However, the Commission considered that the
merging parties' position at the Irish airports was somewhat protected,
since they enjoyed greater scale economies and flexibility than potential
rivals that were based elsewhere. Ryanair's response was that any cost
advantage it enjoyed related mainly to scale economies at the network
rather than airport level (noting, for instance, that its operational costs were
not higher in Cork than in Dublin even though nineteen aircraft were based
in Dublin as compared to only one in Cork) and that marketing economies
were insignificant, with most sales and promotions being done through the
internet. In the end, although some airlines contacted during the market
investigation did not rule out entry, the Commission did not view them
as credible entrants since they were considered to lack the airport base
advantages described above. The Commission also noted airport conges-
tion and slot constraints as an entry barrier that might impede the scope for
rivals to constrain the new entity at Irish airports post-merger.

---

[333] Case COMP/M.5675 – *Syngenta/Monsanto's Sunflower Seed Business*, Commission
decision of 17 November 2010.
[334] Ibid., para. 260.    [335] Ibid., para. 263.
[336] Case COMP/M.4439 – *Ryanair/Aer Lingus*, Commission decision of 27 June 2007; Case
COMP/M. 5434 – *Ryanair/Aer Lingus II*, Commission decision of 23 January 2009.

In *Western Digital Ireland/Viviti Technologies*,[337] the Commission found that Toshiba, a recent entrant in 3.5-inch Business Critical HDDs, had the technical capability to enter the 3.5-inch segments of concern (i.e. Desktop and Consumer Electronics) but would be unlikely to do so in a timely manner. In addition, the Commission stated that even if entry were to take place in a reasonable time horizon, customers would not, at least in the short term, be able credibly to threaten to switch a significant portion of their supply requirements to Toshiba. The Commission therefore concluded that the hypothetical constraint imposed by Toshiba after entering the market would not be sufficient to replace the role played by Viviti in the pre-merger scenario.

Finally, in *Johnson&Johnson/Synthes*,[338] the Commission found that an exclusive relationship between the AO Foundation, a highly reputed Swiss-based surgeon-led organisation, and Synthes resulted in a general reluctance amongst surgeons to switch to alternative suppliers of trauma devices. These barriers to switching were considered to make entry less attractive and therefore less likely.

In sum, the Commission views low entry barriers or the threat of entry as a sufficient countervailing factor against a finding of unilateral effects concerns only under exceptional circumstances.

The mere possibility of entry will typically not meet the relevant threshold, namely that entry would be likely, timely and sufficient, unless the relevant markets are truly contestable as evidenced by actual instances of significant entry. In addition to identifying instances of entry, it may be necessary for the parties to demonstrate that such entry had an impact on market outcomes, which may require an analysis of the effect of entry similar to that discussed in Section 3.4.

## 5.4   Efficiency analysis

### 5.4.1   Efficiency analysis in the EC Horizontal Merger Guidelines

Normal profit-maximisation implies that firms will pass on some portion of any variable cost reduction to customers via lower prices.[339] Consequently,

---

[337] Case COMP/M.6203 – *Western Digital Ireland/Viviti Technologies*, Commission decision of 23 November 2011.

[338] Case COMP/M.6266 – *Johnson&Johnson/Synthes*, Commission decision of 18 April 2012.

[339] See J. Stennek and F. Verboven, 'Merger Control and Enterprise Competitiveness: Empirical analysis and policy recommendations' (2001) 5 *European Economy* 130–94,

if a merger leads to a reduction in the merged firm's variable costs, this will create an incentive to reduce price that may partly or entirely offset any incentive to raise price due to the lessening of pre-merger competitive constraints. A merger that would otherwise have given rise to price increases may nonetheless lead to no detrimental impact on consumers if there is a simultaneous reduction in variable costs arising from the merger.

As described in the EC Horizontal Merger Guidelines, however, a number of practical problems arise in converting this theory into a robust efficiency defence. In particular, the EC Horizontal Merger Guidelines note that each of the following must be demonstrated in order to sustain an efficiency defence:[340]

- merger specificity
- consumer benefit
- verifiability.

We consider each of these three points in turn below.

First, in order to be accepted as a countervailing efficiency, cost reductions must be shown to be *merger-specific*; that is, it must be the case that the efficiencies could not be achieved without the merger. If the claimed efficiencies could in fact be realised without the reduction in competition associated with the concentration, then the Commission will consider the relevant counterfactual to the merger to incorporate those same efficiencies without the lessening of competition, in which case the latter represents the net impact of the merger.[341]

Second, the Commission will ascertain whether claimed cost reductions will indeed affect the merging firms' pricing decisions and thereby lead to *consumer benefits*. The simplest economic models of pricing behaviour distinguish fixed and variable costs (see Chapter 1). In such models, reductions in fixed costs (e.g. from the post-merger elimination of head office buildings and staff) will not have any impact on pricing, whereas efficiencies that reduce unit production costs will increase margins and thereby provide an incentive to reduce price to achieve additional sales volumes.[342] Accordingly, the EC Horizontal Merger Guidelines state that:

---

for a detailed description of factors that impact upon the extent to which cost savings will be passed on to consumers.

[340] EC Horizontal Merger Guidelines, paras. 78–88.

[341] See, e.g., ibid., para. 85.

[342] The intuition here is simply explained. Consider a situation where a pre-merger margin of 30% is doubled to 60% as a result of marginal cost reductions following a merger.

> In line with the need to ascertain whether efficiencies will lead to a net
> benefit to consumers, cost efficiencies that lead to reductions in variable
> or marginal costs are more likely to be relevant to the assessment of
> efficiencies than reductions in fixed costs; the former are, in principle,
> more likely to result in lower prices for consumers.[343]

In practice, however, the distinction between costs that will affect pricing
and those that will not is more complex, and often some costs that in
accounting terms are deemed 'fixed' can affect pricing decisions. For
example, suppose that a merger gives the new entity improved technical
knowledge that allows it to build a new production plant at a lower capital
cost than either merging party could have done beforehand. Even though
capital costs of the new plant will typically be placed in the 'fixed' category,
the greater efficiency in this cost element could allow the post-merger
firm to embark on investments in capacity and output expansion that
would not otherwise have been viable, and as such the cost reductions
should truly fall in the 'marginal' category for the purposes of the
assessment of the firms' pricing and output behaviour decisions.

Even where marginal cost reductions are identified, the parties still face the
task of verifying to the satisfaction of the Commission that the efficiencies
both exist and will lead to price reductions that will more than outweigh the
reduction in competition. This is a complex empirical task, and one which,
given the parties' incentives to claim efficiencies and the asymmetry of
information between the parties and the Commission, will never be straightforward. In this respect the EC Horizontal Merger Guidelines note that:

> When the necessary data are not available to allow for a precise quantita-
> tive analysis, it must be possible to foresee a clearly identifiable positive
> impact on consumers, not a marginal one. In general, the longer the start
> of the efficiencies is projected into the future, the less probability the
> Commission may be able to assign to the efficiencies actually being
> brought about.[344]

---

Assume also that the firm has an opportunity to increase sales by 10% if it concedes a
price reduction of 5%. At the pre-merger profit margin of 30%, that opportunity would
not be attractive, since the 5% price cut would mean an effective reduction in per-unit
margins (from 30% to around 26%) of more than 12%. The profit on the higher sales
volumes would not be enough to outweigh this gross margin reduction. Post-merger,
however, the calculation is changed since the 5% price reduction now involves a
reduction in gross margin of only around 4%, which is more than compensated by the
prospective volume gain of 10%.

[343] EC Horizontal Merger Guidelines, para. 80.
[344] EC Horizontal Merger Guidelines, para. 86.

As well as confirming the existence of efficiencies, the Commission will also seek to confirm that the claimed efficiencies will be sufficient in magnitude to offset the identified lessening of competition. As such, the scope for successful invocation of the efficiency defence will decline with the impact of the merger on competition, all else being constant. The EC Horizontal Merger Guidelines point out that: 'It is highly unlikely that a merger leading to a market position approaching that of a monopoly, or leading to a similar level of market power, can be declared compatible with the common market on the ground that efficiency gains would be sufficient to counteract its potential anti-competitive effects.'[345]

In the context of a merger that creates or strengthens a position of market leadership, increasing the efficiency of the market leader could give that firm such a lead over its rivals that the long-run vitality of competition is endangered.[346] This kind of argumentation is found in decisions such as *Aerospatiale-Alenia/de Havilland*,[347] the first merger to be prohibited under the Merger Regulation, in which arguments of post-merger efficiencies appeared to exacerbate the Commission's concerns. Critics of the Commission have often argued that this translates to an 'efficiency offence' under EU merger control, and that the Commission's intentions in such cases amount to protection of competitors, not competition.[348] However, despite the concerns raised in the past, it seems clear from the discussion of efficiencies in the EC Horizontal Merger Guidelines that efficiencies are unlikely to be considered a negative aspect of any horizontal merger.[349]

---

[345] EC Horizontal Merger Guidelines, para. 84.

[346] Efficiencies based on scale advantages can also have an impact on arguments about the ease of entry. Arguments that the merging firms need to acquire scale equivalent to a substantial portion of the market in order to compete effectively will normally undermine claims that entry represents a credible competitive constraint, unless entrants are able to achieve their required scale in some adjacent market or product area.

[347] Case COMP/M.053 – *Aerospatiale-Alenia/de Havilland*, Commission decision of 2 October 1991.

[348] Note that efficiency offence considerations can arise also in the context of exclusionary effects (see Chapter 5). See A. Papanikolaou and M. Rosenthal, 'Merger Efficiencies and Remedies', published in *The European Antitrust Review 2012*, Global Competition Review.

[349] In any event, in the face of any concern regarding the negative impact of efficiencies on competition, it should be incumbent upon the regulator to show how competition is likely to be harmed and how consumer welfare will be reduced in the long-run.

### 5.4.2    Relevance in EU cases

Given the height of the hurdles that the parties face when putting forward an efficiency defence, it is questionable whether efficiencies will ever play an important role in decisions under the Merger Regulation in any but the most exceptional cases. Indeed, a review of Phase II merger cases since 2004 reveals that the Commission has always rejected efficiency defences put forward by the parties once it has reached the conclusion that the proposed transaction would remove an important competitive constraint. Some examples include the following.

In *Ryanair/Aer Lingus*,[350] the Commission noted that, even if the criteria for an efficiency defence were met, 'the claimed efficiency gains would in all likelihood be insufficient in magnitude to reverse the anti-competitive effects identified'.[351]

In *Arjowiggins/M-real Zanders Reflex*[352] the Commission argued that 'claimed efficiencies from "R&D, sales and other corporate functions" are not specified in any detail and are anyway likely to be savings in fixed costs that are less likely to bring about consumer benefits'.[353] This confirms the Commission's reluctance to put weight on fixed cost savings, due to the uncertainty that any such savings would be passed on to consumers. This case also serves to illustrate the difficulty in convincing the Commission to accept cost savings resulting from capacity reduction or rationalisation through, for instance, plant closures. On this point the decision reads:[354]

> Unless a convincing argument for merger specificity is presented, it is not obvious that a merger is necessary to allocate production capacity efficiently. In a competitive market, it would be expected that the least efficient machines exit the market once their marginal cost of production exceeds market prices. Especially if the rationalisation of production capacity is due to an anticompetitive output reduction, a merger decreases, rather than enhances, allocative efficiency. Likewise, a merger is not necessary for companies to reach efficient scale; on the contrary, the incentives to reach efficient scale would normally be greater the more competitive a market is.

---

[350] Case COMP/M.4439 – *Ryanair/Aer Lingus*, Commission decision of 27 June 2007.
[351] Ibid., para. 626.
[352] Case COMP/M.4513 – *Arjowiggins/M-real Zanders Reflex*, Commission decision of 4 June 2008.
[353] Ibid., para. 445.    [354] Ibid., para. 447.

In *Lufthansa/SN Airholding*,[355] the parties argued that lower fixed costs on a route lower the yield levels at which entry becomes profitable, thereby increasing potential competition. However, the Commission indicated that benefits arising from increases in frequencies on existing routes or services on new routes 'would not be immediate but conditional on a chain of events and thus considerably less certain than the price effect of a marginal cost reduction (which would create immediate incentives for price reductions)'.[356] The Commission also argued that the parties could, and likely would, have implemented the projected cost savings through 'a very low level of cooperation between airlines, which does not even require that the airlines are members of the same alliance'.[357] Again, this illustrates how difficult it can be to convince the Commission that claimed efficiencies are merger specific and could not be achieved unilaterally or through less restrictive means, such as partial JVs or cooperative arrangements.

In *T-Mobile Austria/Tele.ring*,[358] the parties sought to argue that the merger would allow better utilisation of capacity across their mobile networks, leading to reductions in average fixed costs per customer. The Commission rejected this argument, however, noting that 'it cannot be assumed that this kind of [fixed] cost saving will be passed on to consumers'.[359]

In *UPM/Myllykoski and Rhein Papier*,[360] the Commission acknowledged the substantial efforts undertaken by the Parties to demonstrate the efficiencies arising from the transaction, and in particular the supporting evidence used to demonstrate the expected reductions in variable costs. However, although the Commission found that the lack of competition concerns meant it was not necessary to assess potential efficiencies, it nevertheless criticised the parties for not attempting to show what percentage, if any, of the synergies would be passed on to customers beyond observing that a considerable proportion of the synergies would result from variable cost savings.

---

[355] Case COMP/M.5335 – *Lufthansa/SN Airholding*, Commission decision of 22 June 2009.
[356] Ibid., para. 426.      [357] Ibid., para. 417.
[358] Case COMP/M.3916 – *T-Mobile Austria/Tele.ring*, Commission decision of 26 April 2006.
[359] Ibid., para. 47.
[360] Case COMP/M.6101 – *UPM/Myllykoski and Rhein Papier*, Commission decision of 13 July 2011.

In *Deutsche Börse/NYSE Euronext*,[361] the parties submitted a detailed efficiency defence.[362] One of their major claims was that the merger would benefit customers through greater liquidity. The Commission conducted a detailed analysis of various academic studies, and rejected the parties' argument by concluding that competition has far more potential to generate liquidity gains than consolidation. Another major efficiency claim put forward by the parties was that, as a result of the merger of Eurex (owned by Deutsche Börse) and Liffe (owned by NYSE Euronext), customers would benefit from having to post less collateral for security. The Commission's analysis did confirm that the proposed transaction was likely to lead to collateral savings due to increased cross-margining opportunities. However, the Commission indicated that the potential savings were much smaller than what the parties had estimated – in particular, that they were in the range of tens of millions instead of 3.1 billion Euros. In addition, the Commission also found that some of these benefits were not merger-specific, and that the merged entity would be likely to capture a considerable portion of these savings, thereby reducing the consumer-benefit of the efficiencies in question. The Commission finally concluded that, in any event, the claimed efficiencies would not be substantial enough to counteract the harm to consumers brought about by the merger.

## 5.5    Failing firm defence

### 5.5.1    Failing firm defence in the EC Horizontal Merger Guidelines

In principle, the Commission's framework for merger assessment recognises a so-called 'failing firm defence', whereby a transaction that would otherwise be prohibited may be cleared where it involves a firm that would most likely otherwise have exited the market. The EC Horizontal Merger Guidelines state that:

---

[361] Case COMP/M.6166 – *Deutsche Börse/NYSE Euronext*, Commission decision of 1 February 2012.

[362] Case COMP/M.6166 – *Deutsche Börse/NYSE Euronext*, Commission press release 'Mergers: Commission blocks proposed merger between Deutsche Börse and NYSE Euronext' of 1 February 2012. See also Mlex article, 'Commission Prohibits Proposed Merger between Deutsche Börse and NYSE Euronext – frequently asked questions' of 1 February 2012.

the Commission may decide that an otherwise problematic merger is nevertheless compatible with the common market if one of the merging parties is a failing firm. The basic requirement is that the deterioration of the competitive structure that follows the merger cannot be said to be caused by the merger. This will arise where the competitive structure of the market would deteriorate to at least the same extent in the absence of the merger.[363]

As such, the failing firm defence can be viewed as a special case of the general question of the relevant counterfactual for competitive assessment. When a transaction involves a failing firm, the counterfactual to the merger may be, rather than a situation in which the merging parties remain competitors, a situation in which any existing competition between the parties is eliminated. If it can be demonstrated that the appropriate counterfactual to a merger involves an absence of competition between the parties due to exit by one of them, then it follows that the merger will not serve to reduce competition relative to the situation that would arise absent the merger.[364]

In practice, however, the Commission has established an extremely high hurdle for the failing firm defence, such that it has very rarely been successfully raised. The EC Horizontal Merger Guidelines set out the following three conditions for the use of the failing firm defence:[365]

- the allegedly failing firm would in the near future be forced out of the market because of financial difficulties if not taken over by another undertaking;
- there is no less anti-competitive alternative purchase than the notified merger;
- in the absence of a merger, the assets of the failing firm would inevitably exit the market.

The first of these conditions requires the parties to demonstrate that the business in question is not financially viable as currently operated. The Commission has not provided guidance on what is sufficient to meet this requirement, but has in the past pointed to sustained losses and has accepted that businesses that have entered administration or bankruptcy procedures represent failing firms.

---

[363] EC Horizontal Merger Guidelines, para. 89.     [364] See ibid., para. 9.
[365] Ibid., para. 90.

There is some overlap between the second and third conditions, each of which concern the possibility that there may be a counterfactual to the merger that does not involve the complete exit of a failing firm. The second condition is a factual one, requiring that the parties demonstrate that there is no alternative transaction in contemplation that would raise less serious competition concerns. In practice, the Commission has also considered the efforts made by parties to find alternative buyers in assessing this condition, and appears to require evidence that good endeavours were made to find an alternative buyer before proceeding with the transaction for which the failing firm defence is claimed.

These two conditions will frequently be met; it is not unusual for a firm in financial difficulties to be sold, nor for there to be only a single party seeking to acquire it. It is, however, the third condition required for the failing firm defence that is the most onerous. The third condition requires that there be no realistic prospect that *any* party other than the proposed acquirer would be willing to acquire and operate the firm in question (or its assets). That is, it must be demonstrated that the financial position of the firm and its assets is such that no investor would be willing to acquire those assets (for use rather than disposal) at any price. If financial investors would be willing to acquire and operate the business at a nominal (or even zero) value, then the third element of the failing firm defence will fail. The Commission would instead assess the transaction against the counterfactual of a third party operating the failing firm and/or its assets as an independent source of competition within the market.

The purpose of these tests is to ensure that the failing firm defence is permitted not simply where a competitor represents the most willing buyer for a firm in difficulties, but represents the only means by which the firm's assets will remain active within the market. Consequently, the failing firm defence will apply in situations in which a firm is in such a straitened position that an investor without pre-existing activities in the industry would not choose to purchase and operate the business for zero consideration, but where that firm is nonetheless an attractive proposition to a rival due to the scope for synergies with that rival's existing activities. Such situations will arise only rarely, with the result that the failing firm defence is accepted only in exceptional circumstances.

## 5.5.2   Relevance in EU cases

As noted above, due to the onerous conditions established by the Commission, the failing firm defence has been accepted in European merger notifications on very few occasions.[366] Indeed, the Commission has cleared only two mergers on such grounds: *Kali+Salz/MdK/Treuhand*[367] in 1993 and *BASF/Eurodiol/Pantochim*[368] in 2001. These two cases provide the foundation for the three criteria for the failing firm defence set out in the EC Horizontal Merger Guidelines.

The first case, *Kali+Salz/MdK/Treuhand*,[369] brought together the salt and potash activities of Kali+Salz and MdK, a company owned by the former German Democratic Republic and under the control of Treu-hand, a state trustee. The merger would give rise to a monopoly in potash fertilisers, a market characterised by significant barriers to entry. The transaction was nevertheless cleared on the grounds of it being a 'rescue merger', that is, that MdK was a failing firm.

In reaching this conclusion, the Commission noted the following three points. First, the Commission recognised that MdK was loss making and that the state trustee was unlikely to be willing to continue to inject any further capital into the business.[370] Second, the parties were able to demonstrate that, despite significant efforts to divest the business, no third party had made an offer for the company.[371] The potash market was in a state of over-capacity and there was limited or no scope for efficiencies among companies other than Kali+Salz. Third, the Commission held that it could be reasonably expected that, even in the absence of the proposed merger, MdK's market share would, upon exit, ultimately divert to Kali+Salz.[372]

*BASF/Eurodiol/Pantochim*[373] concerned the acquisition by BASF of two subsidiaries of the SISAS group, Eurodiol and Patoch, active in the production of various specialty chemicals. The Commission found that the merger would give rise to combined market shares well above 40%,

---

[366] Interestingly, the UK competition authorities, while employing conditions for the failing firm defence similar to those set out in the Guidelines, have permitted a number of mergers under the failing firm defence since the start of the recent economic downturn. See: *Long Clawson Dairy Limited/Millway* merger inquiry, Competition Commission, 14 January 2009; *Anticipated acquisition by HMV of 15 Zavvi stores*, Office of Fair Trading, 14 May 2009; *Anticipated acquisition by Kingfisher plc of 30 stores from Focus*, Office of Fair Trading, 24 August 2011.

[367] Case COMP/M.308 – *Kali+Salz/MDK/Treuhand*, Commission decision of 14 December 1993.

[368] Case COMP/M.2314 – *BASF/Eurodiol/Pantochim*, Commission decision of 11 July 2001.

[369] Case COMP/M.308 – *Kali+Salz/MDK/Treuhand*, Commission decision of 14 December 1993.

[370] Ibid., paras. 73 et seq.     [371] Ibid., paras. 80 et seq.     [372] Ibid., paras. 78 et seq.

[373] Case COMP/M.2314 – *BASF/Eurodiol/Pantochim*, Commission decision of 11 July 2001.

that there were high barriers to entry, and that rivals were capacity constrained. As regards the failing firm defence, the Commission found that the SISAS group was in financial difficulties and that the target businesses had been placed under pre-bankruptcy proceedings in Belgium.[374] The Commission further found that there was no less anticompetitive solution as no company other than BASF was willing to make an offer for the business.[375]

As regards the third element of the *Kali+Salz/MdK/Treuhand*[376] analysis, the Commission noted that, unlike that case, BASF, Eurodiol and Pantochim were not the only firms in the market, and so that there would likely be some diversion to third parties following the exit of Eurodiol and Pantochim.[377] Nonetheless, the Commission recognised that such exit would 'most probably lead to a considerable deterioration of market conditions, to the disadvantage of the customers'.[378] Consequently, the Commission established the condition, now reflected in the Guidelines, that in order to invoke the failing firm defence, it was necessary to show that absent the merger the target firms' capacity would exit the market.[379]

Due to the particular circumstances of the target's plants and Belgian bankruptcy proceedings, the Commission found that another buyer would be unlikely to take over the assets post-bankruptcy.[380] The Commission noted that the target's plants were characterised by high costs and frequent production shutdowns, that there were material environmental risks associated with the production process, and that parts of the qualified workforce required to run the plants had left the business. The Commission also recognised that a buyer purchasing the assets within six months of bankruptcy would be obliged to take over the entire workforce, while restarting production more than six months after bankruptcy would create its own technical problems.

Finally, the Commission considered how market conditions in the event of the merger would compare to those in the event of exit by the target business.[381] It noted that the parties' rivals faced severe capacity constraints and would be unlikely to expand supply to offset the removal

---

[374] Ibid., paras. 144 et seq.    [375] Ibid., paras. 146 et seq.
[376] Case COMP/M.308 – *Kali+Salz/MDK/Treuhand*, Commission decision of 14 December 1993.
[377] Case COMP/M.2314 – *BASF/Eurodiol/Pantochim*, Commission decision of 11 July 2001, para. 150.
[378] Ibid., para. 151.    [379] Ibid., para. 152.    [380] Ibid., paras. 152 et seq.
[381] Ibid., paras. 157 et seq.

of the Eurodiol and Pantochim capacity from the market, while the high fixed costs of the target business meant that BASF would need to operate these plants at close to capacity to achieve profitability. As such, it found that market conditions could be expected to be more favourable to customers in the event of the merger than in the event of the targets exiting the market.

Consequently, following this detailed review of the failing firm claim, the Commission found that 'under the particular and exceptional circumstances of the case at this specific moment in time … the deterioration of the competitive structure resulting from the notified operation will be less significant than in the absence of the merger'.[382]

The Commission has considered, but rejected, the failing firm defence in a number of recent investigations. The parties sought to invoke the failing firm defence during *JCI/VB/FIAMM*.[383] This transaction, which was ultimately cleared subject to remedies, would have given JCI's VB Autobatterie business a dominant share of supply in the market for car and truck batteries. The parties sought to argue that, absent the transaction, FIAMM's poor financial health would have forced it to exit the market.[384]

The parties were successful in establishing that the company was in financial difficulties and that there was no other less anti-competitive solution available, such that liquidation was likely to occur.[385] However, as regards the third criterion set out in the EC Horizontal Merger Guidelines, the Commission was unable to conclude that in the absence of the merger '**all of the assets** of FIAMM SBB would **inevitably** exit the market' due to the scope for third parties to purchase FIAMM's assets following liquidation.[386]

The Commission went on to undertake a detailed review of the liquidation counterfactual in order to assess whether and to what extent the 'merger scenario' might bring about a lessening of competition relative to the 'failed firm scenario'. Ultimately, the Commission found that the liquidation scenario would lead to a 'capacity gap' that would encourage future entry, while the 'merger scenario' would deter entry and expansion by rivals, and that the FIAMM brands would not necessarily be acquired by the dominant player JCI in the event of

---

[382] Case COMP/M.2314 – *BASF/Eurodiol/Pantochim*, Commission decision of 11 July 2001, para. 163.
[383] Case COMP/M.4381 – *JCI/VB/FIAMM*, Commission decision of 10 May 2007.
[384] Ibid., para. 238. [385] Ibid., paras. 712–36.
[386] Ibid., para. 750 (emphasis in original text).

liquidation.[387] Consequently, the Commission concluded that 'the effects of the merger are likely to be significantly worse than the effects of the non-merger scenario (that is to say, liquidation)', and rejected the failing firm defence.[388]

The Commission also set out a detailed assessment of the failing firm defence in the *Olympic/Aegean Airlines*[389] prohibition decision, finding that the transaction failed to meet each of the three criteria set out in the Guidelines. As regards the first condition, the Commission not only found that the parties were unable to demonstrate that Olympic Air's financial position would necessarily force it into bankruptcy, but also that there was a range of potential restructuring options, including switching to a mid-low-cost carrier business model or joining a global air alliance, that might improve that financial position.[390]

The Commission was unable to exclude the possibility of a less anti-competitive alternative to the transaction, finding that several bidders were interested in Olympic's assets, and concluding that internal emails demonstrated that the parties did not give serious consideration to alternative purchasers.[391]

Finally, the Commission found that Olympic's assets would not exit the market in the event of bankruptcy. Its brand and logo, and its route/traffic rights would revert to the Greek government, which expected to allocate them to other airlines, while Olympic's leased aircraft, which were particularly suited to operation in Greece, would be expected to be taken up by other Greek airline operators.[392]

A concept that has been considered in a number of the Commission's decisions is that of the 'failing division', an argument that a particular unit within a broader business would exit the market in the absence of an acquisition. The Commission has considered such arguments in a number of cases and, while allowing the possibility that a failing division might permit clearance of an otherwise problematic transaction, has on each occasion rejected the argument.[393] In *Newscorp/Telepiù*,[394] the

---

[387] Ibid., paras. 795 and 814.    [388] Ibid., para. 815.
[389] Case COMP/M.5830 – *Olympic/Aegean Airlines*, Commission decision of 26 January 2011.
[390] Ibid., paras. 1991–2070.    [391] Ibid., paras. 2071–87.    [392] Ibid., paras. 2088–119.
[393] See Case COMP/M.993 – *Bertelsmann/Kirch/Premiere*, Commission decision of 27 May 1998; Case COMP/M.1221 – *Rewe/Meinl*, Commission decision of 3 February 1999; and Case COMP/M.2876 – *Newscorp/Telepiù*, Commission decision of 2 April 2003.
[394] Case COMP/M.2876 – *Newscorp/Telepiù*, Commission decision of 2 April 2003.

Commission set out its thinking on the issue, stating that in the case of the failing division argument:

> the burden of proving that the defence ... is valid must be especially heavy. Otherwise, every merger involving the sale of an allegedly unprofitable division could be justified under merger control law by the seller's declaring that, without the merger, the division would cease trading.[395]

In summary, therefore, the Commission's approach to the failing firm defence demonstrates that such arguments will be accepted only in exceptional circumstances, and will require detailed factual evidence concerning the particular circumstances of the businesses and assets in question to demonstrate that a transaction represents the only means by which a failing firm's assets will remain within a market.

---

[395] Case COMP/M.2876 – *Newscorp/Telepiù*, Commission decision of 2 April 2003, para. 212.

# 4

# Horizontal mergers II: coordinated effects

## 1. Introduction

Coordinated effects arise when a merger creates conditions that make tacit coordination (or tacit collusion) more likely or more effective.[1] Tacit coordination is a situation in which firms' prices are higher than some competitive benchmark.[2] Firms engaging in tacit coordination collectively gain relative to the situation in which they compete against one another, as total industry profits are higher than would be the case under competition. However, tacit coordination creates a temptation for each firm involved to 'cheat' on the collusive agreement by setting a lower price or producing a higher output. By cheating in this way, each firm can increase its own profits at the expense of those firms that adhere to the collusive agreement.

The fact that tacit coordination involves such a temptation implies that a number of elements are required for tacit coordination to arise and be sustained:

- Firms must be able to coordinate their decisions over the setting of a competitive variable such as price or quantity sold.
- Firms must be able to detect in a timely way that a deviation from the agreement has occurred.
- Firms must be able to punish a cheater by increasing output or reducing price for a period after a deviation so as to depress the profits of the deviating firm in a way that makes deviation unattractive.

---

[1] The terms 'collusion', 'collusive agreement' and 'coordination' are used in a broad sense and include behaviour based on a tacit understanding between firms. The terms should not be considered synonymous with 'illegal collusive agreement' such as is prohibited under the Article 101 TFEU competition rules. From an economic perspective the terms 'collusion' and 'coordination' are synonymous. Similarly, the terms 'collusive agreement' and 'collusive understanding' are used interchangeably.

[2] In technical terms, the benchmark is usually the equilibrium price of a game in which firms meet only once in the marketplace.

If these necessary conditions are met, there is scope for firms to reach a collusive agreement that is *internally sustainable* (i.e. the coordinating firms themselves have the incentive to adhere to the collusive agreement).

In addition, it is necessary for coordination to be *externally sustainable* (i.e. the coordinating firms must not be constrained by factors such as an actual competitive fringe or potential competitors that prevent the coordinating firms from exercising collective market power).

All else being equal, collusive outcomes are considered to be easier to achieve and sustain in more concentrated markets. First, it may be easier in practice to establish and monitor collusive conduct with fewer parties. Second, the gain from deviating is likely to be greater when there is a large number of firms, each with a small market share. Each party to a collusive agreement in a fragmented market has a small share in the collusive profits but could potentially achieve a large increase in market share as a result of cheating. On the other hand, the relative gains from deviation are likely to be lower for firms holding a large proportion of the market.

As a result, a merger that reduces the number of players in a market and thereby increases market concentration can, under certain circumstances, give rise to an increased risk that sustainable tacit coordination will arise or may make pre-existing tacit coordination more robust.

The economic concept of tacit coordination can be equated with the legal concept of collective dominance. The EC Horizontal Merger Guidelines note that:

> A merger in a concentrated market may significantly impede effective competition, through the creation or the strengthening of a collective dominant position, because it increases the likelihood that firms are able to coordinate their behaviour in this way and raise prices, even without entering into an agreement or resorting to a concerted practice within the meaning of Article 81 of the Treaty. A merger may also make coordination easier, more stable or more effective for firms that were already coordinating before the merger, either by making the coordination more robust or by permitting firms to coordinate on even higher prices.[3]

Increased prices that follow a shift to a more collusive market situation are termed 'coordinated effects' since they do not result from the individual actions of the merged firm, but from the realisation amongst the main firms in the market that they are now better placed to come to a

---

[3] See EC Horizontal Merger Guidelines, para. 39.

tacitly collusive arrangement. Importantly, coordinated effects rely on other firms, as well as the merged entity, modifying their behaviour following the merger. Coordinated effects are therefore distinct from unilateral effects, discussed in Chapter 3, where the incentive of the merged firm to increase its price arises without the need for any accommodating response from the other firms remaining in the industry. Moreover, under unilateral effects the higher post-merger price results from a short-term profit-maximising strategy (i.e. the firm could not obtain higher profits in the short run by cutting its price and increasing market share at the expense of its competitors). This difference implies that the framework adopted by the Commission for the assessment of coordinated effects is different in character to that adopted for the assessment of unilateral effects.[4]

The remainder of this chapter discusses the economic theory of tacit coordination and how the potential for a horizontal merger to give rise to consumer harm through coordinated effects may be assessed in practice. Section 2 presents the theoretical background that forms the basis for much of the Commission's policy regarding the assessment of coordinated effects. First, we present a version of the 'textbook' economic model of tacit coordination and explain the important notion of the critical discount factor. Second, we discuss the factors that, according to the economic literature, affect the critical discount factor and therefore the likelihood that firms would be able to sustain tacit coordination.

Section 3 discusses how the insights of economic theory can be applied in a practical framework for assessing coordinated effects. We briefly discuss the traditional 'checklist' approach and its shortcomings. We then present the prevailing framework for the assessment of coordinated effects, which is consistent with that set out in the EC Horizontal Merger Guidelines and that essentially requires consideration of the following three questions:

---

[4] It should be noted that a merger that gives rise to a price increase due to the elimination of competition between the merging parties may relax the competitive constraints exerted on rivals and thereby allow those rivals to raise their prices. However, rival responses of this kind do not imply that the merger should be considered to have given rise to coordinated effects. Even though both the merged entity and its rivals have increased their prices relative to the pre-merger situation, their decisions to do so do not rely on any form of tacit coordination. The merged entity's decision to raise price is optimal given the elimination of a direct competitive constraint. Each rival's higher post-merger price level is simply a best response to the higher price level chosen by the merged entity.

- Will the merged entity and remaining competitors be able to reach a tacit understanding?
- Are market characteristics such that any tacit understanding would likely be sustained?
- Will the proposed transaction make it significantly more likely that tacit coordination will occur or make tacit coordination more effective?

We discuss the issues that must be considered in answering each of these questions and consider how these issues have been approached by the Commission in past cases.

## 2. Economic concepts

### 2.1 Textbook tacit coordination

The theoretical background to tacit coordination is provided by non-cooperative game theory, and specifically, the theory of repeated games.[5]

In what follows we present a version of the 'textbook' model of coordination, using the example of two independent widget producers that each seek to maximise their own profit.[6] Whilst, in this example, we consider two firms that sustain coordination by setting 'high' prices, the model discussed here can be adapted to consider an analogous situation in which the firms collude by setting 'low' quantities or capacities.

Suppose that the two widget producers, Firms A and B, have a choice of whether to set a high price, H, or a low price, L. Suppose first that the firms have only one opportunity to set their prices and that, once set, prices cannot be changed. Let us assume that if both firms choose the high price then they will each obtain a profit of 30. If both firms choose the low price, then they will each earn profits of only 20. However, suppose further that if one firm were to choose H while the other

---

[5] Game theory is the branch of mathematics that models strategic interaction among agents. The analysis of firms' behaviour in oligopolistic markets relies heavily on game theory, and in particular on non-cooperative game theory. A game is said to be non-cooperative if the players are assumed to act independently to maximise their own payoffs (in the case of firms, profits) and are not able to make binding promises to one another. For collusion to arise within a non-cooperative game, collusion must be in each firm's individual interest given the conduct of other firms.

[6] This textbook model follows Friedman (1971), which provides an early example of the study of equilibria in repeated games where players use simple strategies. See J. Friedman, 'A Non-cooperative Equilibrium for Supergames' (1971) 38 *Review of Economic Studies* 1–12.

Firm B's price

|  | H | L |
|---|---|---|
| **H** | Collusion<br><br>30 , 30 | Deviation<br><br>0 , 40 |
| **L** | Deviation<br><br>40 , 0 | Competition<br><br>20 , 20 |

Firm A's price

**Figure 4.1**    Payoffs of different strategies

chose L, the firm that chose L would obtain profits of 40, while the other would obtain profits of 0. This information can be represented as shown in Figure 4.1.

In the diagram, each cell represents a pair of choices, one for Firm A and one for Firm B. For example, the top right-hand cell represents the situation in which Firm A chooses price H but Firm B chooses price L. The first of the two numbers in each cell indicates the profits that will be received by Firm A if the combination of prices represented by that cell is chosen, while the second number indicates the profit that will be received by Firm B for that combination of prices.

It is clear that each firm is better off when both firms choose H (the top left-hand cell) compared to the situation in which both firms choose L (the bottom right-hand cell). Imagine that the firms had a chance to talk to each other before setting price but that while each firm could propose to set prices at H, neither firm can make a binding commitment to do so. An important insight from game theory is that we should not expect this discussion to result in either firm setting its price at H in these circumstances. To see why this is the case, note that while both firms are better off when they each charge high prices than when they each charge low prices, each firm can obtain higher profits still by deviating from (or cheating on) an agreement to set price at H by choosing price L. In fact, irrespective of what the other firm chooses, each firm can improve its own profits by choosing the low price. Consider the situation facing Firm B. If Firm A chooses price H (top row of the diagram), Firm B is best served by choosing price L, as this would give profits of 40 rather than 30. If, on the other hand, Firm A chooses price L (bottom row), Firm B is again better off choosing price L, as this gives profits of 20 rather than 0.

Thus, even without knowing which strategy Firm A will choose, Firm B will always prefer to choose price L.

As Firm A has symmetric preferences, both firms will choose L, giving each a profit of 20, notwithstanding the possibility of greater profits available if they each set price H. In technical terms, each firm choosing H does not constitute a Nash Equilibrium.[7] It is therefore apparent that if these firms meet only once in the market, then they will not be able to make an effective collusive agreement. The temptation to cheat on an agreement to price at H is too great to allow such an agreement to be sustained in this framework.

However, a modification to this textbook model of pricing interactions may allow tacit coordination to arise. If, instead of meeting only once in the market, firms interact with one another on a repeated basis then coordination may constitute a Nash Equilibrium. Suppose that the widget producers set their prices once a month and expect to do so for an indefinite period of time. Each month the profits depend on the prices they choose as set out in Figure 4.1. Importantly, each firm applies a discount factor of d (a positive number less than one) to profits earned one period in the future. For example, a profit of 10 earned one period in the future is worth $10*d$ today (which is less than 10).[8] A profit of 10 earned two periods in the future is worth $10*d$ one period in the future and so only $(10*d)*d$ today (which equals $10d^2$). Suppose now that firms agree on the following: each firm will price at H in each period so long as the other firm priced at H in each prior period, and will price at L otherwise. Will such an agreement enable the firms to collude on price H in each period?

Consider Firm A's decision regarding its price today. It is possible to observe that whether it can achieve higher profits from adhering to coordination (pricing at H) or deviating from coordination (pricing at L) will depend on its discount factor, d. If Firm A decides to adhere to coordination, the value of its profits today will be the sum of the per-period collusive profits discounted at the appropriate discount factor

---

[7] See Section 2.1.3 in Chapter 3 on unilateral effects for a brief discussion of Nash Equilibrium.

[8] For example, a discount factor of 0.9 would imply that a profit of 10 earned next period is only worth 9 today. The discount factor of 0.9 would arise if it were possible for a firm to invest profits today at an effective per period interest rate of 11.11%. This is because if profits of 9 had been earned today and invested at this interest rate, in the next period the investment would have a value of 10 (equal to 9 + (0.1111 * 9)). The firm is therefore indifferent between a profit of 9 today and a profit of 10 next period.

reflecting how far into the future they are earned: ($30 + 30d + 30d^2 + 30d^3 +\ldots$ ). The present value of this infinite sequence of (ever decreasing) profits is equal to $30/(1 - d)$.[9]

If Firm A decides to deviate from coordination, it will earn the 'deviation' profits of 40 for one period, and the competitive profits of 20 in every subsequent period given that coordination will have broken down. This implies that the present value of profits from deviation will be ($40 + 20d + 20d^2 + 20d^3 +\ldots$), which can be shown to be equal to $40 + 20d/(1 - d)$.

By finding the value of d at which the present values of profit from adherence ($30/(1 - d)$) and the present value of profit from deviation ($40 + 20d/(1 - d)$) are equal, it is possible to determine the critical discount factor, $d^*$, at which firms will be indifferent between colluding and deviating. It follows that for any value of d above the critical discount factor $d^*$, firms will have an incentive to maintain price H in each period and coordination will be sustainable.

In this example it can be shown that the critical discount factor is 0.5.[10] To verify this, note that if Firm A has a discount factor at this critical level, the present value of its profits under adherence will be 60 (equal to $30/(1 - 0.5)$) and the present value of its profits under deviation will also be 60 (equal to $40 + (20^*0.5)/(1 - 0.5)$). In other words, if the firm has a discount factor of 0.5, it is indifferent between adhering to coordination and deviating. If Firm A had a discount factor below this critical level, however, it would obtain higher profits from deviating than from adhering to coordination. For example, if Firm A's discount factor were equal to 0.4, then the present value of profits from coordination will be 50 (equal to $30/(1 - 0.4)$), whereas the present value of profits from deviation will be 53.33 (equal to $40 + (20^*0.4)/(1 - 0.4)$).

The insight from the textbook model is that coordination may be sustainable if firms are sufficiently 'patient' in the sense that they place considerable weight on profits earned in the future (i.e. have sufficiently high discount factors). It follows that anything that reduces the level of 'patience' required of firms for coordination to be sustainable (i.e. reduces the critical discount factor), in some sense makes coordination

---

[9] The sum of an infinite geometric sequence $a + ad + ad^2 + ad^3 + \ldots$ is equal to $a/(1 - d)$ if d is less than one.

[10] The critical discount factor in the simple setting presented here can be calculated as (deviation profit – collusion profit)/(deviation profit – competition profit), which is equal to $(40 - 30)/(40 - 20) = 0.5$.

'easier' to sustain. Economic theory has identified a number of elements that have an influence on the critical discount factor. This body of theory therefore provides insight into the likelihood that firms will be able to *sustain* coordination and forms the basis for much of the Commission's policy regarding the assessment of coordinated effects. In Section 2.2 below we discuss a number of elements that influence the critical discount factor.

One might observe that this example has focused heavily on the question of whether firms can *sustain* coordination, and has said nothing about how firms will *reach* an agreement to coordinate. Here, we have crudely assumed that firms are able to understand that each is playing a particular strategy (price at H if the rival has colluded in previous periods and L otherwise), without saying much about how the firms come to this understanding. This, unfortunately, is symptomatic of the economic literature on coordination. The typical assumption in the economic literature on tacit coordination is that firms can easily reach coordination on their contingent strategies leaving the sustainability of the coordination as the only question to be examined. Whilst a great deal of attention has been focused on showing the conditions under which collusion can be sustained in equilibrium under the assumption that each firm has knowledge of the strategy of every other firm, economic theory has had much less to say about how firms might in practice acquire this knowledge (and in particular whether it must arise through communication or whether it can arise through observation of market outcomes).[11] In essence, this implies that the economic theory of repeated games is silent on how firms *reach* a collusive agreement.[12] This has led some to state

[11] There is a great deal of evidence from experimental economics that shows that communication between players increases the likelihood of collusion. See, e.g., C. Holt and D. Douglas, 'The Effects of Non-binding Price Announcements on Posted Offer Markets' (1990) 34 *Economics Letters* 307–10. A recent paper by D. J. Cooper and K. U. Kühn explores different explanations for how communication might foster collusion through a series of experiments that vary the type of communication available. They consider that the persistence of collusion depends significantly on how rich the message space is within which subjects can communicate with each other: see D. J. Cooper and K. U. Kühn, 'Communication, Renegotiation and the Scope for Collusion' (Florida State University Working Paper, 2010).

[12] This is problematic because tacit coordination always involves a problem of choosing amongst multiple equilibria. In particular, the Nash Equilibrium of the one-shot game repeated every period is always a (subgame perfect) Nash Equilibrium of a repeated game. That is, the Nash Equilibrium in the one-shot game of deviation by both parties will remain valid in addition to any collusive equilibria that become feasible in the repeated game.

that the economic theory of collusion is really a theory of explicit collusion (in which firms can communicate their strategies to one another) rather than one of tacit collusion (in which firms cannot); or that economic theory provides only 'half' a theory of tacit coordination.[13]

Importantly, the literature on coordinated effects in merger control has also been criticised on the grounds that it has not been able to set out a precise framework for identifying the point at which the change in market structure brought about by a merger 'tips' behaviour from being competitive to collusive in nature. This is in stark contrast to the theory of unilateral effects, where there is broad consensus among economists on the framework that should be used for the analysis.[14] Whereas unilateral effects analysis is concerned with the effect of changes in industry structure holding the form of interaction between firms constant, coordinated effects theories conjecture a change in the very nature of that interaction. Economic theory is unable to identify a deterministic mechanism by which changes in industry structure will lead to a switch from competitive to collusive interactions between firms.

## 2.2   Factors that affect the critical discount factor

As noted above, economic theory's primary contribution to the assessment of whether coordination is more or less 'likely' to arise is insight into factors that affect the critical discount factor – and through this the *existence* of collusive equilibria. In this section we discuss a number of factors that influence the critical discount factor.[15] Since the critical discount factor is the discount factor below which firms' will be unable

---

[13] For example, at the OFT and CC Joint Review of Substantive Merger Guidelines Roundtable to discuss coordinated effects, Professor Kai-Uwe Kuhn noted: '... if you take the theory seriously, everyone who is playing the game and is playing the equilibrium, knows exactly what the other person is playing. In that sense, it is really the theory of explicit collusion. It is not the theory of tacit collusion, because in tacit collusion we somehow think that people are not talking in the first place.' He also noted: 'I think that some of the work ... suggests that the difficulties of achieving an agreement may be just as important for determining whether we can achieve collusion or not as satisfying the incentive compatibility constraints that is in our theory'. See transcript of 'Coordinated Effects: What is the right analytical threshold?' at the UK Competition Commission, Thursday 2 October 2008.

[14] See A. Lofaro and D. Ridyard, 'The Economic Analysis of Joint Dominance under the EC Merger Regulation' (2000) 1 *European Business Organization Law Review* 539–59.

[15] For further discussion of the relevant factors for collusion, see M. Ivaldi, B. Jullien, P. Rey, P. Seabright and J. Tirole, 'The Economics of Tacit Collusion' (Report for DG Competition, European Commission, 2003).

to sustain coordination, anything that increases the critical discount factor 'raises the bar' for the minimum level of 'patience' required if coordination is to be sustainable and hence can be considered to make coordination harder to sustain.

All else equal, the critical discount factor will be increased by anything that:[16]

- increases the profits available from deviation;
- reduces the profits available from adhering to coordination; or
- increases the profits available after other firms have reacted by punishing the deviation (i.e. makes punishment less severe).

For each market characteristic identified below, we use (+) in the subheading to indicate that the critical discount factor is increasing in that characteristic and (−) to indicate that the critical discount factor is decreasing in that characteristic.[17] While theory informs us that certain factors may influence the critical discount factor and, therefore, the *sustainability* of coordination, some of these factors might also be expected to influence the ability of firms to *reach* terms of coordination. The ability of firms to reach terms of coordination is discussed in detail in Section 3.1. Importantly, some of the factors considered below (in particular, the number of competitors, asymmetry and multi-market contact) could be changed by a merger, implying that a merger may influence the likelihood that coordination can be sustained.

### 2.2.1 Number of competitors (+)

All else being equal, the higher the number of competitors in a market, the higher will be the critical discount factor. This is because the relative gain from deviating from rather than adhering to a collusive agreement is likely to be greater when there is a large number of firms, each with a small market share. Each party to a collusive agreement in a fragmented market has a small share in the collusive profits but could potentially achieve a large increase in market share as a result of cheating.[18]

---

[16] These propositions can be verified by reference to the formula for the critical discount factor in the simple game set out above: (deviation profit − collusion profit)/(deviation profit − competition profit).

[17] As discussed further below, it is not possible to 'net off' plus factors and minus factors against one another to determine the overall likelihood of coordination.

[18] On the other hand, the relative gains from deviation are likely to be lower for firms holding a large proportion of the market.

To see this, suppose that the maximum profit that could be achieved by a monopolist in an industry is €100. If, instead of a monopolist, there are two identical firms in the market, then the maximum profit that each of them can earn under perfect coordination is half of the monopoly profit, €50, with the short-term payoff to deviation equal to €100.[19] As the number of identical firms increases, each firm's maximum collusive profit decreases (i.e. with three firms it is €33.3, with four firms €25, etc.), while the short-term payoff to unilateral deviation remains at €100 for each firm. Therefore, increasing the number of firms gives each firm increasingly strong incentives to deviate from the understanding to secure market share gains at the expense of its rivals.

### 2.2.2    Ease of entry (+)

Greater ease of entry serves to increase the critical discount factor, all else being constant, making coordination less sustainable. This is because the prospect of entry reduces the expectation of future collusive profits, which makes deviation relatively more attractive.[20] Similarly, the threat of entry may constrain current profits available from coordination.

### 2.2.3    Frequency of interaction/price adjustments (−)

More frequent interaction between firms or more frequent price adjustments will tend to lower the critical discount factor. This is because deviating firms will have less time to enjoy the benefit from higher deviation profits before facing retaliation from rivals. If, on the other hand, firms can enjoy the benefits of deviation for a substantial length of time before punishment occurs (e.g. because customers only issue tenders every few years) then this is likely to give rise to a high critical discount factor and make coordination less sustainable all else being constant.

### 2.2.4    Transparency (−)

A greater degree of transparency over the parameters on which firms are coordinating will tend to reduce the critical discount factor. Transparency makes it more likely that deviations will be recognised and so that punishment will follow. In particular, greater transparency will increase

---

[19] In practice, profits from deviation would be very slightly lower than monopoly profits due to the need to set a price slightly below the monopoly level in order to undercut the rival firm.

[20] Even if all firms adhere to collusion, they will end up being retaliated against by the new entrant.

the extent to which firms can distinguish between a reduction in their own demand caused by a reduction in overall market demand and a reduction in their own demand caused by deviation by a rival. With greater transparency firms may have less incentive to deviate as such deviation is less likely to be mistaken for a market-wide demand shock and therefore go unpunished.[21]

### 2.2.5 Demand growth (−)

All else being equal, demand growth will reduce the critical discount factor and make coordination more sustainable. This is because demand growth increases the expected volume of future sales and therefore increases the value of future profits resulting from coordination relative to the value of profits available from deviation given current sales. Importantly, however, industries with rapidly growing demand are frequently susceptible to future entry, the prospect of which, as noted above, may serve to undermine coordination.

### 2.2.6 Demand fluctuations/lumpiness of demand (+)

If market demand fluctuates significantly over time, this will tend to increase the critical discount factor and make coordination less sustainable, all else being constant.[22] When firms find themselves facing higher than average market demand at any point in time, they will have an increased short-term incentive to deviate from coordination to capture a large share of that transient demand. Therefore, when demand fluctuates

---

[21] An important result from the economic literature is that collusion cannot necessarily be ruled out in the presence of a lack of transparency, though firms may have to satisfy themselves with less ambitious collusive outcomes in order to eliminate their incentives to deviate from the tacit agreement. The stability of collusion in the absence of transparency was first analysed formally by Green and Porter: see E. J. Green and R. Porter, 'Noncooperative Collusion Under Imperfect Price Information' (1984) 52(1) *Econometrica* 87–100. In their model, Green and Porter assume that demand at every period fluctuates in a random fashion. Firms can only observe the market price but have imperfect information about their rivals' output. An observed price reduction may then be caused either by a negative demand shock or by the cheating of a player who has produced more than the tacitly agreed amount of output. Under these assumptions, the equilibrium price is found to be below the monopoly level and to tend towards this level as the variance of the demand shock goes to zero. An important feature of the Green and Porter model is that, although no firm has an incentive to deviate from the collusive strategy in equilibrium, temporary price wars will periodically occur when negative demand shocks lead to price reductions.

[22] See J. Rotemberg and G. Saloner, 'A Supergame-theoretic Model of Business Cycle and Price Wars during Booms' (1986) 76 *American Economic Review* 390–407.

greatly in a market, it will be particularly difficult for firms to sustain coordination during periods of high demand.

A similar effect arises where a large buyer, whose requirements account for a significant proportion of total demand, invites coordinating firms to compete for its business. Intuitively, the incentive to deviate from the understanding will be great in these circumstances, since the immediate reward from securing the large customer's business may outweigh the long-term benefit of adhering to the collusive agreement. For this reason large buyers can, in principle, destabilise attempts by firms to collude through their procurement practices.

### 2.2.7 Asymmetry (+)

Asymmetry between firms may take a number of different forms. For example, firms may be asymmetric with respect to the range of products they sell, with respect to their levels of capacity or with respect to their costs of production. A number of different economic models show that collusion is more difficult to sustain with asymmetric firms. To the extent that differences between firms cause them to have different critical discount factors (which may be due to differences in their profits from deviation, their profits under collusion, and/or their profits when punished), then these differences will make collusion harder to sustain.

This is because, where firms have different critical discount factors, the relevant critical discount factor for understanding the sustainability of collusion is the *highest* amongst the colluding firms. The sustainability of collusion requires that each firm has an actual discount factor above its own critical discount factor (i.e. all firms in the group must find it profitable to adhere to collusion over the long term).[23] If asymmetry causes the critical discount factor to be high (close to 1) for one particular firm, then sustainability of collusion for the group as a whole is likely to rest on whether that firm's discount factor is above its (high) critical discount factor.

A number of different forms of asymmetry may make collusion harder to sustain and, with respect to each form of asymmetry, economic theory

---

[23] Although, in principle, where firms have different discount factors it may be possible for firms to collude in more complicated ways by allocating asymmetric output quotas so that firms with relatively low discount factors receive a disproportionate share of market demand under collusion to keep them from deviating. See J. Harrington, 'Collusion Among Asymmetric Firms: The case of different discount factors' (1989) *International Journal of Industrial Organization* 289–307.

provides insight into the characteristics of firms that will have relatively low incentives to collude.

- Under asymmetry in costs, low-cost firms will tend to have a higher critical discount factor and will therefore be less inclined to participate in collusion than higher-cost rivals. Low-cost firms have more to gain from deviating than high-cost firms due to the higher margins that they can earn on additional volumes gained from a reduction in price. At the same time, it may be difficult for high-cost firms to punish low-cost firms for deviation if effective punishment would require them to price below cost.[24]

- Under asymmetry in the number of substitutable product varieties sold by firms, 'small' firms (i.e. those with narrow product ranges) will have a higher critical discount factor than 'large' firms (i.e. those with broader ranges), and may therefore be less inclined to participate in collusion.[25] Smaller firms will likely have a greater willingness to cheat on a collusive agreement by cutting price both because they receive a smaller share of the collusive profits and because the resulting increase in sales will largely comprise diversion from the products of larger firms. In addition, the 'large' firm may have a limited incentive to punish the smaller firm because doing so will harm its profitability across its entire range of products. Similar intuition implies that firms with small market shares may have a greater willingness to cheat. Smaller firms benefit less from adherence and have more to gain from deviation than larger firms.

- Under asymmetry in capacity, 'large' firms (i.e. those with greater capacity) will have a higher critical discount factor and may therefore be less inclined to participate in collusion than 'small' firms.[26] A firm

---

[24] Note, however, that in Vasconcelos (2005) it is smaller high-cost firms that are the most difficult to induce to coordinate. In this setting, high-cost firms are allocated a small share of the market under collusion. which makes it harder to make collusion, incentive compatible for these firms (in the absence of side payments). See H. Vasconcelos, 'Tacit Collusion, Cost Asymmetries, and Mergers' (2005) 36 *RAND Journal of Economics* 39–62.

[25] The intuition set out here is based on K.U. Kühn, 'The Coordinated Effects of Mergers in Differentiated Products Markets' (CEPR Discussion Paper No. 4769).

[26] The intuition here is based on O. Compte, F. Jenny and P. Rey, 'Capacity Constraints, Mergers and Collusion' 2002 46 *European Economic Review* 1–29. A finding in this paper is that the main problem for collusion is to prevent the large firm from deviating. Collusion is easier to sustain when the large firm's capacity decreases (reducing its incentive to deviate) and when the small firm's capacity increases (increasing its power to retaliate).

with larger capacity may benefit from cheating as doing so allows it to increase output significantly. At the same time, firms with smaller capacities will not pose a significant retaliatory threat in the event of deviation. On the other hand, firms with smaller capacities will stand to gain less from deviation as the potential increase in output from the collusive level will be smaller.

Importantly, firms could appear symmetric along a number of dimensions (including market share) but differ significantly along an important dimension that implies that coordination is difficult to sustain.

### 2.2.8   Multi-market contact (−)

If firms interact with each other across a number of different geographic or product markets, then this may, under certain circumstances, reduce the critical discount factor and make coordination more sustainable.[27]

As noted above, if there is significant asymmetry between firms in a particular product of geographic market, this may undermine their ability to sustain coordination in that market. However, if firms interact with one another across a number of markets, then this may counterbalance asymmetry within individual markets, allowing coordination to be sustained across all markets. For example, if Firm 1 has low costs in geographic market A but Firm 2 has high costs in this market, it may be difficult to induce Firm 1 to adhere to coordination. However, if the firms also interact in geographic market B, in which Firm 2 has low costs and Firm 1 has high costs, it might be possible to sustain coordination in *both* markets. Firm 1 may fear retaliation in market B if it were to cut price to increase sales in market A, whereas Firm 2 may fear retaliation in market A if it were to cut price in market B. In addition, multi-market contact can increase the frequency with which firms interact with one another, which will reduce the time period over which the profits from deviation can be enjoyed before retaliation takes place.

### 2.2.9   Innovation (+)

Where innovation is an important feature of competition between firms, this will tend to increase the critical discount factor and, therefore, make coordination less sustainable. Innovation may give one firm a significant

---

[27] The implications for collusion of multi-market contact were first investigated in B. D. Bernheim and M. D. Whinston, 'Multimarket Contact and Collusive Behavior' (1990) 21 *RAND Journal of Economics* 1–26.

advantage over its rivals (e.g. in terms of its marginal cost of production or the quality of its product). If firms recognise that there is some material probability that a significant asymmetry will develop between them in the future as a result of an innovation then, for the reasons discussed above in relation to the discussion of the implications of cost asymmetry, they may recognise that coordination will become impossible to sustain at some point in the future. The reduction in the future value of coordination will make adherence to coordination today less attractive relative to the alternative of deviation, and thereby imply that coordination is sustainable only if firms place greater weight on future profits.

### 2.2.10 Degree of substitutability (?)

The impact of the degree of substitutability between firms' products on their critical discount factors is typically ambiguous. A significant degree of differentiation between firms' products will imply that each firm's demand will be less sensitive to price changes by other firms than under the case of homogeneous products. This has implications for both the benefits of deviation from coordination and the extent to which it is possible for firms to punish one another severely. On the one hand, product differentiation will reduce the increase in sales that a deviating firm will gain since many consumers will continue to prefer other products despite the change in their relative prices. This will tend to limit the incentive to cheat on a collusive agreement. On the other hand, to the extent that each firm's demand is relatively insensitive to the price set by other firms, this will also limit the ability of firms to punish one another severely and so reduce the potential cost of deviation.[28]

### 2.2.11 Excess industry capacity (?)

It was noted above that asymmetry in capacity could make collusion harder to sustain. However, excess capacity in an industry will, absent asymmetry, normally have an ambiguous effect on firms' critical discount factors. On the one hand, excess capacity increases the benefits from deviating because firms will be better able to serve increased demand resulting from a price reduction. On the other hand, firms will be able to

---

[28] While the effect of product differentiation on the ability to sustain collusion is ambiguous, it may be the case that product differentiation decreases the feasibility of coordination by increasing the difficulty of *reaching* coordination. This issue is discussed further in Section 3.1.

punish any deviation more severely and more rapidly where they are able to draw upon spare capacity.

### 2.2.12    Market demand elasticity (?)

The elasticity of market demand potentially affects both the benefits of adherence to and deviation from collusion and has no clear impact on the critical discount factor. In particular, more inelastic market demand will tend to increase the profits available from adhering to collusion (since the collusive price will not bring about a significant reduction in the level of sales) but also increase the benefit of deviating from collusion.

To see why this is the case, consider a simple setting where two firms selling perfectly substitutable products engage in collusion by charging the monopoly price and sharing half the monopoly profits.[29] Due to perfect substitutability, a firm needs only slightly to undercut the monopoly price in order to win the entirety of market demand and therefore earn (slightly less than) the entire monopoly profit. As market demand elasticity decreases, the profit-maximising price of a monopolist and the profits that will be earned by a monopolist both increase. Therefore, in this simple setting, both the benefit of colluding (i.e. half the monopoly profit) and the benefit of deviating (i.e. slightly less than the whole of monopoly profit) increase as the elasticity of market demand decreases. The overall effect on the attractiveness of adhering to coordination is ambiguous.[30] However, the lower the elasticity of market demand, the greater will be the price that maximises profits under collusion relative to the competitive price. This implies that, at least as far as consumer welfare is concerned, collusion may be more of a concern in markets with low elasticity of demand, although it should be noted that where market demand is inelastic a given price increase will result in a smaller

---

[29] Suppose that after one firm is observed to deviate, both firms charge the competitive price in each period following deviation. In this case, due to the fact that the products are perfectly substitutable, competition implies zero profits.

[30] In the simple case set out here, the two effects actually cancel out exactly. Recall that the critical discount factor in the simple setting presented here can be calculated as (deviation profit – collusion profit)/(deviation profit – competition profit). Deviation profit is equal to the whole of the monopoly profit, $\pi_m$, collusion profit is equal to half the monopoly profit, $\pi_m/2$, and competition profit is equal to zero due to Bertrand competition with perfect substitutability. Therefore the critical discount factor is $(\pi_m - \pi_m/2)/\pi_m$, which equals 0.5 for all values of $\pi_m$. That is, market demand elasticity, which affects $\pi_m$, has no impact on the critical discount factor in this example.

reduction in quantity demanded, which will serve to reduce the negative impact on total welfare.

## 3. Framework for the assessment of coordinated effects

As noted in the introduction to this chapter, coordinated effects are said to arise if a merger makes it easier for the merged firm and at least one rival to reach and sustain an agreement to coordinate that causes consumer harm. The previous section presented the key insights from economic theory regarding the sustainability of tacit coordination. The underlying economic motivation for coordinated effects concerns is that a merger can influence the *critical* discount factor and thus potentially have an influence on the existence of collusive equilibria given firms' *actual* discount factors. In this section we discuss how the insights from economic theory can be organised into a coherent framework for assessing coordinated effects and discuss a number of cases in which coordinated effects concerns have been considered.

The traditional approach to the assessment of coordinated effects adopted by the Commission in early cases involving the assessment of collective dominance is often labelled the 'checklist approach'.[31]

The 'checklist approach' is based on a consideration of whether the industry under investigation exhibits characteristics that are likely to be conducive to tacit coordination, such as symmetry between post-merger firms, buyers with little influence over the process of competition and barriers to entry. However, an approach that mechanically considers each 'checklist' factor in turn and attempts to weigh factors that tend to make coordination more likely against factors that tend to make coordination less likely is unsatisfactory. The 'checklist' by itself provides no basis for assessing industries in which factors that (all else being equal) facilitate coordination and factors that (all else being equal) undermine coordination are present. Many industries will exhibit some of the characteristics identified in the 'checklist' and few will exhibit all. Moreover, even where an industry exhibits a number of facilitating factors (e.g. lack of innovation, small buyers, transparency and stable demand), the presence of a single countervailing factor (e.g. low barriers to entry) may render coordination impossible.

---

[31] This approach was first applied in 1992 in Case COMP/M.190 – *Nestlé/Perrier*, Commission decision of 22 July 1992 and later in 1996 in Case COMP/M.619 – *Gencor/Lonrho*, Commission decision of 24 April 1996.

The Commission was criticised in the CFI *Airtours* judgment for its mechanical application of the 'checklist approach' in *Airtours/First Choice*.[32] The Commission has subsequently set out in its EC Horizontal Merger Guidelines a more systematic approach to the assessment of coordinated effects.[33]

Essentially, an assessment of coordinated effects requires consideration of three questions, each of which must be answered in the affirmative for concerns to arise.[34] These are:

- Will the merged entity and remaining competitors be able to reach a tacit understanding?
- Are market characteristics such that any tacit understanding would likely be sustained?
- Will the proposed transaction make it significantly more likely that tacit coordination will occur or make tacit coordination more effective?[35]

For the first question to be answered in the affirmative, it is necessary to identify a plausible mechanism that firms would be likely to adopt in order to reach an understanding on the terms of coordination.

For the second question to be answered in the affirmative, it is necessary that three further sub-conditions are satisfied, which are themselves cumulative.[36] First, firms must be able to monitor deviations from the collusive understanding. Second, firms must be able to deter deviations through credible punishments. These two conditions are often said to be required for 'internal stability'. Third, there must not be an ability

---

[32] The Commission had blocked the proposed acquisition of First Choice by Airtours in September 1999 (Case COMP/M. 1524 – *Airtours/First Choice*, Commission decision of 22 September 1999) on the grounds that the merger would have created collective dominance between the three largest suppliers of short-haul package holidays in the UK. The CFI issued its judgment annulling the Commission's decision in June 2002.

[33] EC Horizontal Merger Guidelines, paras. 39 et seq.        [34] Ibid., para. 42.

[35] In Case COMP/M. 4980 – *ABF/GBI Business*, Commission decision of 23 September 2008, the Commission followed a similar approach although the organisation of its assessment overlaps these three questions somewhat. In that case the Commission organised its assessment into three parts: an assessment of the presence of market conditions conducive to tacit coordination; the identification of a likely mechanism for tacit coordination (which included both the notions of reaching and sustaining tacit coordination) along with identification of the resulting degree of tacit coordination that could be expected in the absence of the merger; and an assessment of the effect of the merger in making coordination easier, more stable or more effective.

[36] EC Horizontal Merger Guidelines, para. 41. These three conditions reflect the CFI's analysis in the 2002 *Airtours* judgment.

or incentive for outsiders to destabilise coordination. Potential outside destabilising influences may include expansion by smaller firms that are already active in the market (the 'competitive fringe'), entry by potential competitors and the exertion of buyer power by large customers. This last condition is required to guarantee 'external stability' to the coordinating group.

For the third question to be answered in the affirmative, it is necessary to identify a particular change that is *specific* to the merger itself and that increases the likelihood or effectiveness of tacit coordination.

The following subsections consider each of the three questions posed above in turn.

It should be noted at the outset that the EC Horizontal Merger Guidelines state that the Commission will take account of evidence of past coordination.[37] The existence of pre-merger coordination has important implications for each of the three questions posed above. In particular, if the Commission can point to the existence of pre-merger coordination, its theory of harm need only be that the merger makes that pre-existing coordination more robust or more effective. In such a case, the threshold for showing that a merger harms competition through coordinated effects is typically considered to be lower than where the theory of harm involves the industry 'switching' from competitive to collusive interaction. This is consistent with economic theory's inability to provide a clear framework for identifying the point at which a change in market structure leads to an expected change towards coordinated behaviour by the remaining participants. Establishing pre-merger coordination was a crucial issue in ABF/GBI Business, elements of which are discussed in detail in each of the following subsections.

### 3.1 Will the merged entity and remaining competitors be able to reach a tacit understanding?

In order for tacit coordination to arise, firms must be able to reach an understanding of the terms of coordination. The parameters over which firms are most likely to agree to coordinate are set out in the EC Horizontal Merger Guidelines and include:[38]

---

[37] See EC Horizontal Merger Guidelines, para. 43. The Guidelines also note that the Commission will take into account evidence of coordination in similar markets.

[38] Ibid., para. 40.

- **Coordination on price**. The most direct way in which firms can adjust their competitive behaviour so as to lead to an increase in price above the level that would prevail under conditions of effective competition is for firms to adjust their pricing strategies. If firms can coordinate their pricing strategies then the intensity of competition can be reduced.
- **Coordination on non-price parameters of competition**. The scope for coordination on non-price parameters of competition arises where the outcome of price competition is affected by previous strategic decisions, e.g. regarding the level of investment in capacity. In such circumstances, it is not necessary for firms to coordinate all strategic decisions in order to reduce the effectiveness of competition. In particular, by restricting production capacity, prices can be expected to increase even if firms continue to compete vigorously on price.
- **Customer/market sharing**. The effectiveness of competition can also be reduced if firms are able to agree tacitly not to target each other's customers. By effectively allocating customers amongst the various coordinating firms, each firm is able to charge higher than competitive prices to its customers. Similarly, firms may tacitly divide the market, for instance by geographic region or customer category, and agree not to enter or expand within rivals' 'home' areas. By separating the market into areas of influence, each firm will be able to charge higher than competitive prices in its area with the risk of entry controlled via the threat of retaliation in the entrant's own 'home' market segment.

The EC Horizontal Merger Guidelines note that the ability of firms to reach the terms of coordination is affected by a number of factors.[39]

Coordination is considered easier to achieve among fewer players.[40] This is because the number of interrelations between firms increases rapidly with the number of firms in a market. For example, with two firms in a market there is only one interrelation between competitors and, therefore, only one 'agreement' that needs to be reached. However, with three firms in a market there are three interrelations between competitors and, therefore, three tacit 'agreements' that potentially need to be reached. With four firms, there are six interrelations between competitors, whereas with five firms there are ten.

The EC Horizontal Merger Guidelines also note that the ability of firms to establish terms for coordination is likely to be affected by the complexity of the market. Factors that affect the degree of complexity

---

[39] Ibid., paras. 44 et seq.    [40] Ibid., para. 45.

include the number and heterogeneity of the products that are the subject of coordination, the volatility of demand and production costs, and the importance of innovation. Specifically, the EC Horizontal Merger Guidelines note that it is easier to sustain coordination on a price for a single homogeneous product than on hundreds of prices in a market with many differentiated products.[41] Product differentiation can make reaching the terms of coordination difficult since this may require firms to agree on collusive price differentials rather than collusive prices.

In addition, the EC Horizontal Merger Guidelines note that it is easier to reach coordination when supply and demand conditions are relatively stable rather than changing continuously.[42] In markets with fluctuating demand or cost conditions, reaching terms of coordination may require firms frequently to come to new (tacit) agreements on which price (or quantity) levels constitute adherence to coordination and what conduct constitutes deviation requiring punishment. For example, it might not be clear whether a firm that increases its price only slightly after a significant cost or demand increase affecting all firms should be punished for deviating from coordination.

Further, the EC Horizontal Merger Guidelines note that it may be easier to reach a tacit understanding if firms are relatively symmetric in terms of market shares, capacity levels and levels of vertical integration, or are linked by cross-shareholdings or participation in joint ventures.[43] Asymmetry between firms may render agreement on the terms of coordination particularly difficult as each firm may prefer a different price increase (or quantity reduction) to emerge through coordination.

The Commission will also give consideration to the institutional features of the market that may play a role in facilitating coordination, such as industry bodies that publish sales and/or price information, trade associations that share information between members, or linkages between firms themselves (including cross-shareholdings and joint ventures).[44]

Importantly, the EC Horizontal Merger Guidelines note that even in complex environments firms may be able to reach terms of coordination.[45] They note in particular that where firms produce a large number of products, it may be possible for firms to reduce the complexity of coordination by implementing simple pricing rules such as defining a small number of pricing points or establishing a fixed relationship

---

[41] EC Horizontal Merger Guidelines, para. 45.   [42] Ibid.
[43] EC Horizontal Merger Guidelines, para. 48.   [44] Ibid., para. 47.   [45] Ibid.

between certain base prices and a number of other prices. This implies that firms that compete across a diverse range of differentiated products may still be able to reach terms of coordination on price across their entire portfolios. To take a stylised example, consider two firms that provide courier services. A delivery for each pairing of an origin with a destination constitutes a distinct service with a distinct price. It might appear that the firms would find it hard to reach terms on how to coordinate prices for courier services for each of the thousands of origin–destination pairs that they serve. Nonetheless, it may be sufficient for the firms to simply agree on two pricing components – a fixed fee and a per-kilometre fee – in order to effectively coordinate prices across their entire portfolio of 'products'. However, where the products in firms' portfolios are differentiated along many dimensions, and in particular along dimensions that are less easy to codify (e.g. quality or branding), it may not be possible for firms to reduce the complexity of their pricing in this way.

Even if market complexity makes coordination on price infeasible, it may be possible for firms to reduce the effectiveness of competition by coordinating on non-price variables. In particular, where the outcome of price competition is affected by non-price variables set by previous strategic decisions (such as capacity levels), it may be possible for firms to raise prices across a range of products by reaching terms of coordination over those non-price variables. For example, rather than attempting to coordinate on the price of each origin–destination pair, the two courier firms considered above might be able to coordinate on the size of their fleets. The effect of this coordination may be higher prices as a result of the firms subsequently competing against each other to fill a lower overall capacity than may have resulted from firms' decisions absent coordination.[46]

Firms may also be able to eliminate the need to reach terms over price coordination in complex markets by agreeing simple rules regarding market or customer segmentation. For example, the courier firms could reach a tacit agreement whereby each firm refrains from offering its rivals' customers a low price, allowing each to raise prices to its own customer base. Alternatively, each firm may tacitly agree to refrain from encroaching on a geographic area served by its rival, allowing each firm to charge a higher price in its 'home' territory. The EC Horizontal Merger

---

[46] A concern of this type was raised by the Commission in Case COMP/M.1524 – *Airtours/ First Choice*, Commission decision of 22 September 1999.

Guidelines note that terms of market segmentation are easier to reach if customers have simple characteristics based on geography or customer type and if it is easy to identify each customer's supplier.[47]

The EC Horizontal Merger Guidelines recognise that coordination may be harder to achieve in markets in which innovation is important.[48] In particular, innovation may change firms' relative production costs or product quality, thereby requiring frequent (tacit) renegotiation of coordination terms. There is a theoretical possibility that innovation itself may form part of a tacit collusive agreement. Such an agreement might conceivably involve firms collusively under-investing in R&D or otherwise holding back on product improvement. However, this is generally unlikely due to the time period over which R&D typically takes place, the fact that R&D can be carried out covertly, the high potential gains from successful research and the potential difficulty of punishing a firm with a successful innovation.

Where underlying market conditions are complex or non-transparent, it is crucial that any theory of tacit coordination clearly articulates the parameters that are hypothesised to form the basis of coordination, and that the alleged means of reaching agreement is plausible in view of market conditions.

In past cases, the Commission has not always articulated which pricing parameters might form the basis of a hypothesised tacit understanding, or clearly set out how firms are considered to be able to reach agreement on those terms.[49]

More recently, however, the Commission has placed emphasis on articulating coherent theories of coordination and testing these against the available evidence. The Commission considered this issue in detail in its second decision regarding the *Sony/BMG* merger (in 2007), which is discussed in detail below.

### 3.1.1   Theory of coordination in *Sony/BMG*

The Sony BMG Music Entertainment joint venture brought together recorded music businesses Sony Music and Bertelsmann Music Group. The deal was initially cleared in 2004 after a Phase II investigation, during which the Commission had issued a Statement of Objections

---

[47] EC Horizontal Merger Guidelines, para. 46.     [48] Ibid., para. 45.
[49] See discussion of the *Sony/BMG* (2004) decision below.

('SO').[50] However, after an appeal to the CFI by the Independent Music Companies Association, IMPALA, the Commission's clearance decision was annulled in 2006.[51] The parties appealed the CFI judgment to the ECJ,[52] while the Commission initiated a second Phase II investigation of the JV, which resulted in a new unconditional clearance in 2007.[53]

The *Sony/BMG* merger reduced the number of major recording companies ('majors') in the EEA from five to four.[54] In both the first (2004) and second (2007) merger investigations the principal theory of harm considered by the Commission was that the merger would give rise to coordinated effects.[55]

Before considering the theories of coordination addressed by the Commission it is important to note the salient features of pricing of recorded music. The net wholesale price of CDs (i.e. the net price at which record companies sell albums to retailers) depends on two main factors: (i) the Published Prices to Dealers (PPDs, also known as list prices); and (ii) discounts granted against PPDs.[56] Each album is allocated a PPD, which applies to all customers. Conversely, discounts differ from one customer to another.[57] The Commission found that several types of discounts were used by record companies, all of which were negotiated separately with individual customers. The types of discounts varied according to the set of albums to which they applied and the time over which they applied.[58]

---

[50]  Case COMP/M.3333 – *Sony/BMG*, Commission decision of 19 July 2004 (the '*Sony/BMG* 2004 decision').

[51]  See Case T-464/04 *Impala* v. *Commission* [2006] ECR II-2289.

[52]  See C-413/06P *Bertelsmann and Sony Corporation of America* v. *Impala* [2008] ECR II-4951.

[53]  See Case COMP/M.3333 – *Sony/BMG*, Commission decision of 3 October 2007 (the '*Sony/BMG* 2007 decision').

[54]  The Commission defined a market for physical recorded music, including all physical CD albums, irrespective of their genre or their compilation/single artist status and distinguished this from the digital market. The Commission concluded that the relevant geographic markets for physical and digital recorded music are national, but that the licensing of digital music could develop into a multi-territorial market in the future. See *Sony/BMG* 2004 decision, paras. 17, 27, 37 and 41.

[55]  Since the Commission's second investigation related to a completed merger, the Commission was in the unusual position of being able to assess the effect of the merger on the basis of observed market outcomes.

[56]  This net wholesale price itself ultimately impacts the retail price to end-customers.

[57]  See *Sony/BMG* 2007 decision, para. 457.

[58]  For example, file discounts were general discounts negotiated annually that affected all albums sold to a particular customer, though these could differ by category of album; campaign discounts were offered in relation to particular promotional campaigns, were negotiated on an ad hoc basis and applied for a short period; retrospective discounts were

The Commission's theory of harm in the 2004 investigation, which provided the basis for its SO, focused on whether there was evidence of pre-merger coordination. In particular, the Commission examined whether average wholesale net prices (i.e. list prices less discounts) exhibited a high degree of parallelism, whether list prices were aligned and whether there was close correlation between average net prices and average list prices. Crucially, however, the Commission did not articulate whether the hypothesised coordination would involve discounts applied at the album level (which showed a high degree of variation) and, if so, how firms would agree on the appropriate discount for each album. Furthermore, it did not explain how firms would agree on how to allocate albums to different list price points. As such, the theory of harm was silent on a number of important questions surrounding the practical operation of coordination.

In the 2007 investigation the Commission considered in detail how majors might have been able to reach a tacit understanding on recorded music pricing. It set out a number of theories of tacit coordination and assessed these against market facts.[59]

In doing so, the Commission benefited from the fact that, since the parties had already implemented the transaction following the clearance obtained in 2004, the competitive assessment could be conducted against a counterfactual in which the deal had not occurred.

The Commission focused its assessment on a theory of harm whereby tacit coordination on prices would occur at and shortly after the release date.[60]

---

principally end-of-year bonuses, where rebates were negotiated with customers, for example, on the basis of turnover in the previous year. See *Sony/BMG* 2007 decision, para. 471.

[59] The scope of the data analysed was also significantly widened compared to the original examination of the merger, in which only data related to the top 100 sales of each major was collected and in which attention focused on the alignment of net and gross prices on average. In *Sony/BMG* 2007 decision, the Commission analysed transaction data, the most disaggregated level of information available.

[60] The Commission dismissed three other theories of price-based tacit coordination relatively swiftly: coordination on the level of budgets established by record companies to forecast sales volumes, prices, discounts, costs and profits, at album/project, or country level; coordination on the price of each title; and coordination of general 'pricing policy'. The Commission also dismissed non-price-based tacit coordination concerning access to retailer shelf space, access to radio airplay, influence over chart rules, coordination on release dates, or coordination on publishing and recording activities.

At the outset, the Commission noted that chart albums account for approximately 60–70% of Sony BMG gross sales at the EEA level and the majority of chart album sales are achieved within the first 20 weeks following release.[61] Coordination amongst majors covering chart album prices during the early post-release period would therefore cover a significant part of the majors' activity and revenue. After a detailed investigation, however, the Commission dismissed this theory for a number of reasons.

In particular, the Commission considered whether the net wholesale prices charged to retailers by each major followed commonly agreed rules. The Commission grouped transactions of single-pocket CDs along with information that it argued was observable to industry participants such as the country in which the product is sold, the identity of the major that sells it, the identity of the retailer that buys it, the presence of the CD in the charts at the time of the transaction, whether or not it is the first week of transaction of the CD, and its PPD at the time of the transaction.[62] For example, a distinct group would be formed by all transactions of single-pocket CDs sold by Sony to MediaMarkt in Germany at a particular PPD in the first week of transaction that were in the charts at the time of the transaction.[63] For each group, the Commission measured the variation of total discount levels, weighted by sales volume. It noted that if this variation were small for a particular group then it may be the case that the group was subject to a common discount policy.[64]

The Commission considered for each country the percentage of units sold by each major that belonged to a group with a 'small' variation of total discount level and the percentage that belonged to a group with a 'large' variation, and considered whether these percentages had changed post-merger.[65] The Commission found that for the vast majority of

---

[61] See *Sony/BMG* 2007 decision, para. 563.

[62] The analysis assumed PPDs were fully observable. This was a conservative assumption because, as noted below, the Commission found that PPDs were only partially transparent.

[63] See *Sony/BMG* 2007 decision, para. 575.    [64] See ibid., para. 577.

[65] The Commission used a cut-off point of 2 for the standard deviation weighted by transaction size to determine whether dispersion of discounts around the average was small or large. If one group of transactions had an average discount of 10% and a weighted standard deviation around this average of 1.5 percentage points, the transactions of this specific group are considered to be close enough to each other so that the group exhibits a stable discount policy common to all transactions. If, however, the weighted standard deviation was 3 percentage points then the transactions of this group would have discount levels that are too different for this group to share a

countries less than 60% of transactions were in 'small' variation groups for at least three of the five majors.[66] It also found that the impact of the merger on this statistic had generally been limited. The Commission concluded that the segmentation of transactions it studied did not exhibit sufficient evidence of recurrent discount patterns in the early life of albums to support a finding of coordination.[67]

The Commission further considered the transparency of the parameters that gave rise to these segmentations of transactions. It concluded that PPDs could not be considered a reliable focal point for a theory of coordination in most countries and ruled out transparency over discounts due to the fact that they were negotiated privately by each major with each customer on a bilateral basis.[68]

The Commission also considered whether the net wholesale price of CD albums could be reverse engineered from their retail prices. Intuitively, if there were a fixed and known relationship between wholesale prices and net prices over time (i.e. reductions in wholesale prices always result in lower retail prices), then adherence to the understanding could in principle be verified by monitoring the behaviour of retail prices. However, the Commission's and the parties' analysis supported the view that reverse engineering wholesale prices from retail prices is very difficult for albums in general. This issue is discussed further in Section 3.2.1.1 below.

To summarise, the Commission found that there was no coordination at the level of the selection of list prices. Even based on the conservative assumption of full transparency of PPDs, a significant number of sales transactions did not follow a simple and stable discount pattern that could be inferred by a knowledgeable market participant based on public information. Moreover, PPDs were only partially transparent. Finally, as discussed in more detail in Section 3.2.1.1 on monitoring, it was deemed impossible to reverse engineer net wholesale prices from retail prices with the necessary level of certainty. The Commission was therefore able to dismiss the theory of tacit coordination on single-pocket album prices at and shortly following their release date.[69]

---

common discount scheme. See Case COMP/M.3333 – *Sony/BMG*, Commission decision of 3 October 2007, para. 578.

[66] Case COMP/M.3333 - *Sony/BMG*, Commission decision of 3 October 2007, para. 581.

[67] Ibid., para. 587.     [68] Ibid., para. 594.

[69] *Sony/BMG* 2007 decision, para. 602.

### 3.1.2    Theory of coordination in *ABF/GBI Business*

In September 2008, the Commission issued its decision on the acquisition by Associated British Foods (ABF) of several subsidiaries and assets involved in the yeast business from Gilde (henceforth 'the GBI Business' or 'GBI').[70] The decision is an important one as it came soon after the ruling of the ECJ in *Sony/BMG* v. *IMPALA*[71] and demonstrates that the Commission is still willing to rule against mergers on coordinated effects grounds. The main theory of harm in this case related to the likelihood that the merger would strengthen existing tacit coordination. While the Commission's decision arguably represents evidence that it has adopted the economic approach set out in the EC Horizontal Merger Guidelines, it still leaves open some important questions over the circumstances in which the Commission may consider there to be evidence of pre-merger coordination and, as discussed further in Section 3.3, conclude that a merger gives rise to coordinated effects.

The Commission's analysis focused on the Spanish and Portuguese markets for compressed yeast.[72] Before assessing the likely competitive effects of the proposed merger in each geographic market, the decision provides a general background of the supply and demand conditions common to France, Portugal and Spain. It highlights the stable or slightly declining demand for compressed yeast and notes that demand is, subject to moderate seasonality, largely determined by factors that change only slowly over time (such as population size).[73] The Commission found that

---

[70] Case COMP/M.4980 – *ABF/GBI Business*, Commission decision of 23 September 2008. The remainder of the seller's European yeast business was acquired by the French company Lesaffre. See Case COMP/M.5020 – *Lesaffre/GBI UK*, Commission decision of 11 July 2008. That case was cleared subject to commitments after a Phase I investigation.

[71] Case C-413/06P *Bertelsmann and Sony Corporation of America* v. *Impala* [2008] ECR II-4951.

[72] Compressed yeast was one of three separate product markets identified by the Commission (the others being dry and liquid yeast). The Commission's investigation found that customers would be unlikely to switch to other forms of yeast in response to small but significant increases in the price of compressed yeast, and, despite recognising there to be a degree of supply-side substitutability between different forms of yeast, it found that this was insufficient to justify a broad market. Separate geographic markets for compressed yeast were defined in France, Portugal and Spain on the basis of considerable differences in demand and distribution systems amongst nations, the importance of local sales and distribution networks, local branding and differences in price levels and price dynamics. See Case COMP/M.4980 – *ABF/GBI Business*, Commission decision of 23 September 2008, paras. 31, 40 and 84.

[73] Ibid., paras. 114–17.

in a number of member states, the two largest producers post-merger (the merged entity and its largest competitor, Lesaffre) would together account for 90–100% of the market.[74] In particular, it found that the merged entity would have a market share of 70–80% in Portugal with Lesaffre having a share of 20–30%, while in Spain both the merged entity and Lesaffre would have shares of 40–50%. In France the merged entity would be the second largest producer, with a share of 30–40% against Lesaffre's share of 60–70%. Regarding technological innovation, the Commission noted that whilst there may be scope for incremental process innovation, there was no expectation that technological leap-frogging could threaten the large established producers.[75]

The Commission's competitive assessment attributed an important role to distributors, which provide yeast producers with access to artisan bakeries. These customers require regular small deliveries and were found to consider personal contact and stable relationships with distributors to be important.[76] The Commission further noted a number of market characteristics specific to Portugal and Spain. It found that the relationships between both yeast producers and distributors on the one hand and distributors and artisan bakeries on the other hand tend to be long term and that distributors rarely switch between producers.[77] Moreover, in Portugal, all distribution agreements were found to be exclusive, specifying that distributors could not distribute competitors' yeast and could only distribute in a particular geographic area.[78] In Spain, the Commission found de facto exclusivity, with very few exceptions to the rule that distributors procure yeast from one supplier only.[79] In addition, the Commission found that artisan bakers tend to develop long-term relationships with a single distributor based on past experience, proven reliability, ongoing direct contacts, knowledge of the bakery's requirements and ability to supply other products.[80]

The Commission explicitly identified a number of characteristics of the compressed yeast market that it held were conducive to tacit coordination and that were relevant for its assessment of the ability of firms to reach an understanding of the terms of coordination. In addition to highlighting the high supplier concentration, the Commission noted that the market was characterised by a high degree of product homogeneity

---

[74] See Case COMP/M.4980 – *ABF/GBI Business*, Commission decision of 23 September 2008, para. 119.

[75] Ibid., para. 121.  [76] Ibid., para. 123.  [77] Ibid., paras. 126 and 127.

[78] Ibid., para. 128.  [79] Ibid., para. 129.  [80] Ibid., para. 134.

(despite considering that brand was important in terms of being recognised for quality) and transparency in competitors' final prices, volumes and capacity.[81]

Having assessed the characteristics of the compressed yeast market in Spain, the Commission considered yeast producers' ability to reach an understanding of the terms of coordination.[82] Crucially, it argued that the Spanish compressed yeast market already exhibited a degree of tacit coordination.[83] The Commission highlighted transparency in prices, sales and capacity levels and concluded that transparency in prices was enhanced by the homogeneity of the product, the actions of customers reporting competitors' prices to distributors and by the role played by distributors themselves. It found that exclusive territories facilitated understanding of the terms of coordination by reducing competition between distributors outside their assigned territories, reducing competition between distributors of different suppliers and enhancing transparency by ensuring that in each region there was one distributor for each supplier.[84]

In support of the view that the market already exhibited tacit coordination, the Commission cited data showing that prices had remained stable in the years prior to 2006 but had been increasing for each of the three main players subsequently.[85] The Commission noted that input costs had risen from 2005 onwards and that, whilst input cost changes can sometimes disrupt tacit coordination, in this case the common technology of the three main players implied that each was similarly affected.[86]

The Commission's interpretation of these price developments as evidence of pre-merger tacit coordination can be criticised in this case. An increase in costs that affected each of the three players equally would also be expected to cause each firm to increase its price if those three firms were behaving as a non-coordinating oligopoly. It is not clear how, having identified common cost increases that coincided with observed price increases, the Commission was able to distinguish the firms' pricing behaviour from that which would have been expected in the absence of tacit coordination.[87] In general, the observation that firms' prices move

---

[81] Ibid., paras. 191 and 193.

[82] The Commission's assessment in Portugal proceeded along similar lines.

[83] Case COMP/M.4980 – *ABF/GBI Business*, Commission decision of 23 September 2008, para. 206.

[84] Ibid., para. 221.     [85] Ibid., para. 223.     [86] Ibid., para. 224.

[87] In particular, it is not clear whether or not similar pricing behaviour was observed in France, where the Commission considered that concerns over tacit coordination were

in parallel with one another is consistent with those firms competing against one another and, indeed, as discussed in Chapter 2, the absence of co-moving prices is often held as evidence that firms are not competing in the same relevant market. In the specific instance in which the cause of parallel price increases is identified as a common cost increase, it may be considered particularly dangerous to conclude that those price increases are evidence of tacit coordination.[88]

As discussed in Section 3.3 below, the position taken by the Commission with respect to the *current* degree of tacit coordination had significant implications for its assessment of the *effect* of the merger.

### 3.2 Are market characteristics such that any tacit understanding would likely be sustained?

The preceding section has considered the factors relevant to assessing whether firms might be able to identify a mutually beneficial form of collusive behaviour. The next consideration in the assessment of coordinated effects is whether firms would have an ability and incentive to sustain such behaviour.

In order for coordination to be sustainable, a number of conditions must be met. First, it must be the case that the firms that form the collusive group themselves have the incentive to pursue coordination. This condition, often referred to as the internal stability condition, requires that firms are able to monitor deviations from coordination and have the ability and incentive to punish firms that deviate. Second, it must be the case that firms outside the collusive group do not have the ability and incentive to undermine the sustainability of coordination. This condition, often referred to as the external stability condition, requires that expansion by smaller firms, entry by potential competitors

---

mitigated by lower market transparency, lower entry barriers and greater buyer power due to the absence of the (de facto) exclusive distribution structure found in Portugal and Spain.

[88] It is possible to show that under both competitive and cooperative scenarios, firms react to increases (decreases) in their costs by decreasing (respectively, increasing) their outputs and thereby increasing (respectively, decreasing) the market price. Without a full knowledge of all demand and costs parameters, it is not possible to establish whether an observed price pattern is the outcome of collusive rather than competitive behaviour. In other words, if some of the parameters are unknown, the collusive and competitive equilibria are indistinguishable.

and/or the exercise of buyer power by large customers would not undermine coordination.

The following is a detailed discussion of the factors that affect the internal and external stability of coordination.

### 3.2.1   Internal stability

**3.2.1.1   Monitoring deviations**   The EC Horizontal Merger Guidelines note that, in order for coordination to be sustainable, markets need to be sufficiently transparent to allow coordinating firms to monitor whether other firms are deviating.[89]

When assessing the degree of transparency in a market the key consideration is the extent to which firms can infer the actions of their rivals from the information available to them.[90] Even if firms cannot observe the actions directly, they may be able to impute those actions indirectly from other information available. For example, if market demand conditions are stable, a firm may be able to infer that a decrease in its own demand is due to a decrease in a rival's price. In this instance, the firm may ascertain that its rival has deviated from coordination by decreasing price without observing its rival's price directly.

The EC Horizontal Merger Guidelines note that transparency may be higher when there are fewer firms active in the market.[91] The number of rivals will affect the scope for both direct and indirect monitoring. In terms of direct monitoring, it is reasonable to expect that tracking the behaviour of a small number of rivals will be easier than tracking a large number of competitors. In the case of indirect monitoring, it will be easier to make inferences regarding the actions of rivals when there are fewer active firms because individual suppliers' actions will have a larger impact on market outcomes. For example, with two firms in a market, each firm may recognise that any price cut it implements will have a large impact on the demand of its rival and thus be detected relatively easily. However, with many active firms, a firm may recognise that a price cut will have a relatively small impact on each of its rivals' demand and may thus remain undetected.

Transparency is affected by the way in which transactions take place in the market. Where transactions are confidentially negotiated between buyers and sellers on a bilateral basis, transparency may be low.[92]

---

[89] EC Horizontal Merger Guidelines, para. 49.     [90] Ibid., para. 50.
[91] Ibid.     [92] Ibid.

In any assessment of the degree of transparency in a market it is necessary to consider carefully the information that each firm has on its rival's business decisions. For example, it may be possible to observe that firms can determine each other's prices through features of the industry such as information exchanges, clauses in contracts with customers (particularly meet-the-competition and most-favoured-customer clauses) or through the actions of distributors or retailers.[93] To the extent that capacity is supposed to represent the parameter over which firms coordinate, it may be possible to determine the degree of market transparency by reference to publicly available information on plant capacity or announced capacity expansion projects. Similarly, if customer segmentation is hypothesised to represent the mechanism for coordination, it will be instructive to investigate whether supplier–customer relationships are generally common knowledge amongst industry participants. The Commission may also consider the extent to which the parties' internal documents suggest they are able to determine the capacities of their rivals or the identities of (and/or the quantities supplied to) their rivals' customers.

The mechanism of monitoring deviations envisaged by the Commission in the *ABF/GBI Business*[94] decision was fairly straightforward and involved suppliers directly observing one another's prices, customers and capacities. However, the Commission has also had to consider how firms might be able to monitor deviations in far more complex settings. In particular, in the past the Commission has considered whether firms might be able to deduce prices charged at the wholesale level (over which coordination is supposed to take place) by monitoring prices at the retail level. This form of monitoring was considered in Sony/BMG (2007). The assessment of monitoring in the *ABF/GBI Business* decision and the *Sony/BMG* (2007) decision are discussed in turn below.

*Monitoring in* ABF/GBI Business    The *ABF/GBI Business*[95] case illustrates how in the course of assessing firms' abilities to monitor deviations the Commission will consider information that firms have on their rivals' decisions and how this information is gathered. In its assessment of

---

[93] Distributors played an important role in the assessment of monitoring in the case of *ABF/ GBI Business*, discussed in detail below.

[94] Case COMP/M.4980 – *ABF/GBI Business*, Commission decision of 23 September 2008.

[95] Case COMP/M.4980 – *ABF/GBI Business*, Commission decision of 23 September 2008.

firms' incentives to deviate from tacit coordination, the Commission emphasised the high degree of transparency of the compressed yeast market. As noted in Section 3.1.2 above, the Commission found that the compressed yeast market could be considered relatively transparent as far as competitors' prices were concerned.[96] The Commission also noted a high degree of transparency regarding competitors' capacities and specifically noted the precision and detail of rivals' capacity estimates submitted by the parties.[97] The Commission also found that it took less than two months to identify the competitor to which a customer had switched and identified reporting practices by distributors as important in this regard.[98] It noted that, given the stable market demand, it would be easy to infer deviations from collusive conduct via decreases in their own sales.[99] Moreover, the Commission held that, due to the role played by distributors in facilitating the flow of information, yeast producers would also be able to monitor rivals' prices for deviation. The time lag to detect deviations was considered to be short due to the fact that deliveries were made weekly.[100]

*Monitoring in* Sony/BMG *(2007)*   In *Sony/BMG*[101] (2007) the Commission considered whether it might be possible for the majors to monitor the terms of coordination over net prices charged to their customers by monitoring the retail prices charged by those customers. The theory was that if there were a fixed or predictable relationship between retail prices and net prices, then net prices could be inferred from retail prices.

In responding to this theory, the parties submitted a survey of retail prices in various different countries at different points in time for each of their top ten customers.[102] Since Sony BMG did not collect retail prices, these were collected by an independent research consultancy. Six waves of data collection took place at fortnightly intervals in the top ten recorded music retailers in the capital cities of the five largest European recorded music markets, leading to more than 1,000 observations for each country. Each retail price observation was matched to the last invoice price charged by Sony BMG for the same album to the same

---

[96] Ibid., para. 193.      [97] Ibid., para. 194.      [98] Ibid., para. 197.
[99] Ibid., para. 231.      [100] Ibid., para. 236.
[101] Case COMP/M.3333 – *Sony/BMG*, Commission decision of 3 October 2007.
[102] The survey covered all Sony BMG albums that were listed in the official album charts in the week before each data collection.

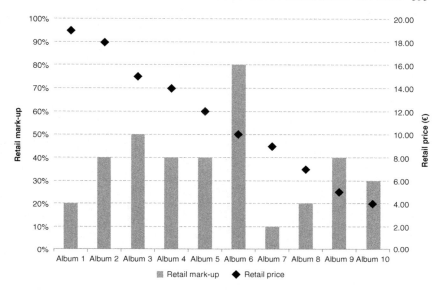

**Figure 4.2**   Retail price and retail mark-up, Retailer A, 10 albums

retailer. The analysis of these data showed that there was no stable relationship between retail prices and invoice prices.

First, there was no evidence of a standard mark-up being used by individual retailers. Figure 4.2 shows, as an illustrative example, the retail prices and retail mark-ups over net wholesale price for a single retailer ('Retailer A') in a single country during the first survey wave across a range of ten albums (ordered by retail price).

This chart shows that there was no relationship between the Retailer A's price for individual albums and the mark-up over wholesale price for those albums. This would preclude the use of retail prices as a means of monitoring publishing companies' wholesale prices to retailers.

Second, there was no evidence of a standard mark-up for the same album across retailers. Figure 4.3 shows the retail prices and retail mark-ups for a single album ('Album 1') in the first wave of data collection across a range of ten retailers in a single country, ranked in descending order by retail price.

Again, there is no relationship between each retailer's retail price and mark-up that would allow the latter to be inferred from observations of the former.

Third, changes in retail prices over time were not systematically related to changes in invoice prices. Figure 4.4 shows the retail price and invoice

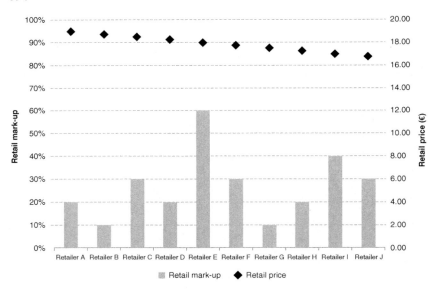

**Figure 4.3**   Retail price and retail mark-up, Album 1

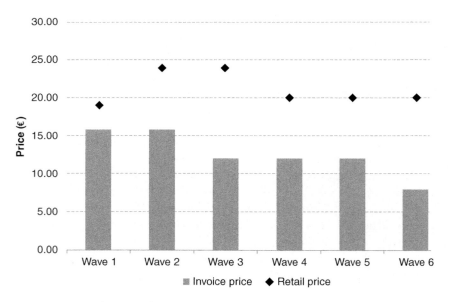

**Figure 4.4**   Retail price and invoice price, Album 1, Retailer A, Germany, Wave 1 to Wave 6

price relative to Album 1 for the same retailer ('Retailer A') in each of the six survey waves. It can be seen that in wave 1, the album had an invoice price of €15.83, and was sold by Retailer A at €19 (which corresponds to the 20% mark-up highlighted in the two previous figures). In wave 2, there was no change in invoice price, but the retailer increased the retail price by €5 to €24. In wave 3, the invoice price was lowered to €12 but the retail price remained at €24. Finally, in wave 6, a further invoice price drop to €8 did not result in a decrease of the retail price.

Overall, analysis of the survey data found that each retailer applied non-standardised mark-ups to Sony BMG chart albums, that for any given Sony BMG chart album retailers applied different mark-ups and that mark-ups varied over time. This implied that the pricing complexity present at the wholesale level was mirrored at the retail level. The analysis therefore showed that inference of wholesale prices from retail prices would be very difficult in the recorded music industry, such that retail prices could not be used as a monitoring mechanism. Although there were some disagreements between the parties and the Commission over the parties' survey of retail prices, the market investigation confirmed that wholesale price monitoring via retail prices is very difficult for albums in general.[103] The Commission further noted that even when looking at the first week following release only, where mark-ups applied by retailers were more uniform, the level of transparency would not allow the net wholesale prices of competitors' albums to be deduced with a sufficient degree of precision.[104] Finally, the Commission noted that it did not find any evidence that major record companies were engaged in systematic monitoring of competitors' retail prices.[105]

#### 3.2.1.2 Retaliation

The EC Horizontal Merger Guidelines recognise that coordination must be sustained by the threat of future retaliations.[106] The importance of establishing that it is possible for firms to punish a deviator is clear from the CFI's assessment of the Commission's decision in *Airtours/First Choice*.[107] The CFI noted that the Commission must establish that 'deterrents exist which are such that it is not worth the while of any member of the dominant oligopoly to depart from the common course of conduct'.[108]

---

[103] Case COMP/M.3333 – *Sony/BMG*, Commission decision of 3 October 2007, para. 599.
[104] Ibid., para. 600.   [105] Ibid.   [106] EC Horizontal Merger Guidelines, para. 52.
[107] See Case T-342/99, *Airtours plc* v. *Commission of the European Communities*, 6 June 2002.
[108] Ibid., paras. 194–5.

In order for coordination to be sustained, retaliation must be both *effective* and *credible*. In the following subsections we discuss these two interrelated concepts.

*Effective punishment may not be credible*    In principle, the more severe the retaliation, the more *effective* it is likely to be in ensuring the stability of coordination. Hypothetically, a very severe (and thus very *effective*) retaliation strategy might be for a firm to start giving its products away for free in the event that a rival deviates from a collusive agreement. However, whilst such a retaliation strategy would certainly hurt rivals, it would also give rise to substantial losses for the retaliating firm itself. Consequently, such a threat to punish deviation by pricing at zero may not be *credible*, in the sense that, once a rival had deviated, there would be no incentive for rivals to implement the punishment. The EC Horizontal Merger Guidelines acknowledge the importance of considering firms' incentives to retaliate and recognise that punishment may entail short-term losses for the firm carrying out the retaliation.[109] The Commission has dismissed coordination concerns in merger cases on the basis that threats to punish deviation would lack credibility. Two notable examples are *Norske Skog/Parenco/Walsum* and *UPM-Kymmene/Haindl*, discussed below.

Assessment of credibility of punishment in *Norske Skog/Parenco/ Walsum* and *UPM-Kymmene/Haindl*
In both *Norske Skog/Parenco/Walsum*[110] and *UPM-Kymmene/Haindl*,[111] two mergers involving producers of newsprint and magazine paper, the Commission dismissed a theory of coordination of investment in new capacity after consideration of the credibility of punishment. One of the theories of harm set out in the Commission's Statement of Objections in both cases was that, post-merger, firms would refrain from investing in new production plants in order to limit capacity and raise prices in the long run.[112] The Commission considered that coordination would be

---

[109] EC Horizontal Merger Guidelines, para. 54.

[110] Case COMP/M.2499 – *Norske Skog/Parenco/Walsum*, Commission decision of 21 November 2001.

[111] Case COMP/M.2498 – *UPM-Kymmene/Haindl*, Commission decision of 21 November 2001.

[112] Case COMP/M.2499 – *Norske Skog/Parenco/Walsum*, Commission decision of 21 November 2001, para. 129. An additional theory of harm considered by the Commission involved coordination of output downtime during periods of low demand. As discussed

sustained by the threat that firms would, in the event of a deviation, engage in an 'investment race', which would result in over-capacity, leading to lower prices and reduced profitability.[113] However, after examining the parties' arguments, the Commission decided that it was unlikely that firms would be able to sustain coordination on new investment.

The Commission noted that to prevent any firm from investing too much or too soon, the coordinating firms would need to be able to detect any potential deviation and to restrain deviation through some credible punishment threat. However, once investment was committed by one firm, any punishment threat based on the commitment of further investment would lose its credibility, because it would be too costly to pursue.

In other words, the Commission recognised that after deviation had in fact occurred, rivals would be better off refraining from costly punishment. Appreciating this, firms would not be dissuaded from deviating by investing in new capacity in the first place.[114]

*Credible punishment may not be effective*   As in the theoretical example in Section 2.1 above, retaliation may simply take the form of reversion to 'normal' competitive behaviour.[115] While the threat to revert to competitive behaviour is *credible*, there is no guarantee that it will be sufficiently severe to be effective in deterring deviation.[116] As explained in

further below, this theory was dismissed on the basis that coordination would likely be undermined by the action of fringe players.

[113] Ibid., para. 131.

[114] The Commission found that it was unlikely that firms could become aware of an investment project by a deviating firm before the investment became irreversible. That being the case, any retaliatory announcement to invest would not succeed in discouraging unwanted investments. The lack of visibility implied that by the time a commitment to invest is made by a rival, responding to it is not a credible step. See Case COMP/ M.2499 – *Norske Skog/Parenco/Walsum*, Commission decision of 21 November 2001, para. 135.

[115] Technically, the notion of 'normal' competitive behaviour here corresponds to behaviour consistent with the Nash Equilibrium of a one-shot game in which firms meet once in the market.

[116] In theory, it is possible for more extreme forms of punishment to be credible (or, in technical terms, to form part of a subgame perfect Nash Equilibrium). This may be the case when firms agree to revert back to collusion only if all firms participate in costly punishment and not if one or more firms 'deviate' by not participating in the punishment. Firms must then be sufficiently patient that it is attractive to endure the painful punishment period in order to obtain future collusive profits. A formal treatment is provided in D. Abreu, 'Extremal Equilibria of Oligopolistic Supergames' (1986) 39(1) *Journal of Economic Theory* 191–225.

Section 2.1, whether retaliation is effective in sustaining coordination depends not only on the profits of the deviator under punishment but also the profits available from maintaining coordination, the profits available from deviation before punishment and the rate at which firms discount future profits. All else being equal, if the profits available from deviation are high then a more severe punishment will be required to make deviation unattractive. Similarly, all else being equal, if the profits available from maintaining coordination are high (e.g. because there is expected to be significant demand growth in the industry) then a less severe form of punishment may be sufficient to deter deviation.

In what follows we discuss a number of other factors that are relevant for the assessment of the effectiveness of retaliation.

*The timing of retaliation*   The time lag over which retaliation can take place is an important part of the assessment of the deterrent to deviation. The EC Horizontal Merger Guidelines note that retaliation that manifests itself after some significant time lag, or that is not certain to be activated, is less likely to be sufficient to offset the benefits from deviating.[117]

This time lag may be related to the degree of transparency in the market. For example, if the hypothesised monitoring mechanism relies on the use of an industry body to exchange information on firms' past prices or sales then it will be necessary to consider how timely the information is exchanged in any assessment of the timeliness of retaliation. Where the information available corresponds to prices set or quantities sold some time ago, firms may take account of the fact that they will be able to enjoy the benefits of deviating for a significant period of time before facing retaliation from rivals.

The time lag may also be related to the nature of competition in the market. If firms interact with one another relatively infrequently in competition for large orders then punishment may be insufficiently timely to discipline deviation, even if that deviation can be detected immediately.

The Commission has considered the timeliness of retaliation in a number of cases. In *ABF/GBI Business*,[118] the Commission found that the compressed yeast market was characterised by a high frequency of interaction since all three players supplied customers or distributors on a regular basis, and that distributors supplied artisan bakeries (and

---

[117] EC Horizontal Merger Guidelines, para. 53.
[118] Case COMPM.4980 – *ABF/GBI Business*, Commission decision of 23 September 2008.

reported back to their suppliers) on a weekly or even bi-weekly basis.[119] In its discussion of the severity of deterrence, the Commission noted that retaliation would be timely due to the frequency of transactions in the yeast market and that it would be possible to determine rapidly the identity of a deviating player.[120]

Lag in retaliation was one consideration that led the CFI to reverse the Commission's decision to block the *Airtours/First Choice* merger.[121] The Commission had maintained that the possibility of increasing capacity in the following holiday season would allow firms to deter deviations from rivals in choosing capacity for the current holiday season.[122] In assessing this retaliation mechanism, the CFI first noted that, given lack of transparency, it would be difficult for a rival to detect a deviation at the capacity planning stage.[123] The CFI further noted that the characteristics of the relevant market and the way that it functions made it difficult for retaliatory measures to be implemented 'quickly and effectively enough for them to act as adequate deterrents'.[124] In particular, it rejected the notion that increasing capacity in the following season would act as an effective deterrent to deviation in the current season.[125] With regard to other deterrence mechanisms considered by the Commission, the CFI noted that the Commission was wrong to conclude that the mere threat of reverting to a situation of oversupply would provide an effective deterrent, or that increasing capacity in the selling season period or de-listing rivals' brochures would be sufficient.[126]

*Multi-market contact* Retaliation need not be restricted to the market in which the deviation occurred. Where firms meet in multiple markets, punishment can extend to all the markets in which firms interact, thus

---

[119] Case COMPM.4980 – *ABF/GBI Business*, Commission decision of 23 September 2008, para. 155.

[120] Ibid., para. 243.

[121] Case COMP/M.1524 – *Airtours/First Choice*, Commission decision of 22 September 1999.

[122] Ibid., para. 152.

[123] *Airtours plc v. Commission of the European Communities*, 6 June 2002, para. 198.

[124] Ibid., para. 197.

[125] Specifically, it stated that 'it is appropriate to observe that increasing capacity in that way is unlikely to be effective as a retaliatory measure, given the unpredictable way in which demand evolves from one year to the next and the time needed to implement such a measure'. See *Airtours plc v. Commission of the European Communities*, 6 June 2002, para. 205.

[126] Ibid., paras. 200–6.

increasing the overall severity of the punishment. It is important to bear in mind, however, that multi-market contact does not in and of itself necessarily increase the likelihood that coordination will be sustainable. In particular, if it is not possible for two firms to sustain coordination in a particular market, it will not be possible for them to sustain coordination in multiple markets where each market simply mirrors the conditions of the first. While the ability to *punish* in multiple markets tends to reduce the critical discount factor (making coordination easier to sustain), the ability to *deviate* simultaneously in multiple markets will tend to increase the critical discount factor (making coordination harder to sustain). Where the markets in which firms meet are mere replicas of one another, these two effects will tend to offset one another.[127]

For multi-market contact to increase the stability of coordination, it must be the case that there is some asymmetry in each individual market or that multi-market contact allows for more timely retaliation. In particular, if firms interact with one another in multiple product or geographic markets, it may be possible for a firm to punish a deviator in a timely way even if firms do not interact frequently in any single market or if it has high costs of expanding production in the particular market in which the deviation occurred.

The Commission has considered the implications of multi-market contact in a number of cases including *Air Liquide/BOC*,[128] and *Solvay/Montedison-Ausimont*.[129] In the former case, the Commission argued that the transaction would have led to the strengthening of already existing dominant positions in the markets for bulk and cylinder gases in the United Kingdom, Ireland and France. These dominant positions would have allegedly been reinforced due to the elimination of the potential competition exerted by the two parties on one another, and also by the increased scope for retaliation in other producers' home markets. With regard to the latter concern, the Commission pointed out that:

> In assessing the competitive force that Linde/AGA would exercise, the fact that Linde/AGA would have certain regional strengths should be taken into account. Like Air Liquide/BOC, although on a smaller scale, Linde/

---

[127] This result is set out in B. D. Bernheim and M. D. Whinston, 'Multimarket Contact and Collusive Behavior' (1990) 21 *RAND Journal of Economics* 1–26.

[128] Case COMP/M.1630 – *Air Liquide/BOC*, Commission decision of 18 January 2000, para. 102.

[129] Case COMP/M.2690 – *Solvay/Montedison-Ausimont*, Commission decision of 9 April 2002, para. 53.

AGA would have a strong position in certain 'home' territories (Austria, Scandinavia and certain regions within Germany). There is a risk that Linde/AGA would concentrate on those regions where it enjoys specific competitive advantages and lower risk, thereby reducing the overall level of competition.[130]

The decision goes on to describe how the proposed transaction would have affected strategic behaviour by comparing suppliers' retaliation possibilities before and after the merger. Before the merger, a producer contemplating an aggressive expansion strategy in the UK (i.e. BOC's 'home' traditional territory), would likely face the possibility of a counter-reaction by BOC within the UK only; BOC's ability to threaten credibly to retaliate outside its home market was considered to be limited since it lacked a suitable production and distribution infrastructure in many continental European markets.[131]

Following the merger, the combined Air Liquide/BOC would have enjoyed a very strong position in the UK and in France. This, according to the Commission, implied that aggressive competitive initiatives within the UK could have been discouraged by the threat of retaliation not only within the UK but also in France. Moreover, following the merger, the new entity would also have gained the possibility to retaliate in any entrant's own home market using Air Liquide's strong position and established infrastructure across continental Europe. According to the Commission, Air Liquide/BOC would, for instance, have been in a position to use its presence in Germany to deter German firms Linde and Messer, which had recently entered the UK, from pursuing aggressive competition in the UK.

The Commission's assessment in this case can arguably be criticised for emphasising the effect of multi-market contact on increasing retaliatory power without carrying out a more detailed assessment that took account of its effect on the incentives to deviate. In particular, even though it may be true that a German supplier who undercut prices in the UK could be punished post-merger in both the UK and France, it is also true that the same supplier, knowing this, would probably undercut prices in both countries to start with. The resulting effect on the stability of coordination cannot be known a priori and it would have required a

---

[130] Case COMP/M.1630 – *Air Liquide/BOC*, Commission decision of 18 January 2000, para. 112.
[131] Ibid., para. 193.

specific and detailed analysis by the Commission. Such an analysis is, however, not present in the decision.[132]

Finally, the Commission highlighted multi-market contact as a factor that would increase the credibility of deterrence in *ABF/GBI Business*.[133] It noted that ABF, GBI and Lesaffre interacted in a number of markets besides compressed yeast in Portugal and Spain and also met across a number of other geographic markets inside and outside Europe in the supply of a number of different bakery products. It noted further that the sale of the assets in question would lead to a more symmetric position of ABF and Lesaffre worldwide.[134]

*Excess capacity*    Retaliation is likely to be more severe when firms have significant excess capacity. If firms are capacity constrained, then they will not be able to punish deviators by expanding output. As noted at Section 2.2 above, however, since firms must have excess capacity in order to benefit from deviation, there is no clear relationship between the level of excess capacity in an industry and the sustainability of tacit coordination in general.

In *ABF/GBI Business*[135] the Commission noted that a return to fully competitive interaction would represent an effective deterrent mechanism due to the significant impact on prices that would result from any increase in output (due to the low elasticity of demand) and the fact that each of the three main players held significant excess capacity.[136] It therefore appears that in this case excess capacity was considered to be a factor that would serve to increase the sustainability of coordination by exacerbating the consequences of a return to competition.

### 3.2.2    External stability

The EC Horizontal Merger Guidelines note that for coordination to be sustainable the behaviour of the colluding firms must not be undermined or frustrated by the actions of other agents, be they non-coordinating rivals, potential competitors or customers.[137]

---

[132] For a more detailed discussion of this case, see A. Lofaro and S. Bishop, 'A Legal and Economic Consensus? The theory and practice of coordinated effects in EC merger control' (2004) *The Antitrust Bulletin*, Spring/Summer, 195–242.

[133] Case COMP/M.4980 – *ABF/GBI Business*, Commission decision of 23 September 2008, para. 244.

[134] Ibid., para. 203.

[135] Case COMP/M.4980 – *ABF/GBI Business*, Commission decision of 23 September 2008.

[136] Ibid., paras. 240–2.    [137] EC Horizontal Merger Guidelines, para. 56.

The importance of assessing the constraints on market power arising from buyer power and potential competition is discussed further in relation to the assessment of unilateral effects.[138] It is important to recognise, however, that buyer power and potential competition have an even greater potential to mitigate competition concerns in the context of assessing coordinated effects.

This is because not only may buyer power and potential competition place constraints on the extent to which firms acting as a unified collusive group can exert market power, but they may also have a significant impact on the cohesiveness of the collusive group itself.

In the following sections we consider the role of non-colluding rivals (both current and potential) and buyer power in the assessment of coordinated effects in mergers.

**3.2.2.1 Non-colluding rivals** Colluding firms may be constrained by the possibility of expansion by current suppliers that are not party to the collusive agreement (often referred to as a 'competitive fringe' or 'fringe'), and/or by the scope for entry in response to higher prices brought about by coordination.

The prospect of entry or expansion by fringe firms will reduce firms' expectations of collusive profits in the future and thereby reduce the present value of profits from adhering to coordination today. If firms consider that there is a significant prospect that coordination will break down in the future as a result of entry or expansion then they will behave in a more myopic way, taking commercial decisions that will maximise short-term, rather than long-term, profits. If firms pay less attention to the future, this reduces the potential cost of deviation in terms of forgone future profits. Therefore, the threat of entry or expansion by fringe players can have serious implications for the sustainability of coordination.

*Assessment of the role of the fringe in* Airtours/First Choice    The CFI's reversal of the Commission's decision in *Airtours/First Choice*[139] shows the importance of considering the impact of fringe players in any assessment of coordinated effects. The Commission was of the opinion that barriers to market entry and to growth beyond a certain size would

---

[138] See Section 5 on countervailing factors in Chapter 3 on Unilateral Effects.

[139] Case COMP/M.1524 – *Airtours/First Choice*, Commission decision of 22 September 1999.

prevent smaller operators from supplying adequate extra capacity to compensate for the reduction in capacity arising from coordination between the larger players. The CFI investigated the Commission's position by considering the possible responses of smaller tour operators and potential competitors. It found that the Commission underestimated the reactions of these players.[140]

The CFI noted that the relevant issue to consider was not whether a single smaller tour operator could reach the size necessary to compete effectively with integrated tour operators but whether the several hundred smaller operators taken as a whole could respond effectively to the hypothesised reduction in capacity.[141] It examined in some detail the ability of smaller tour operators to put on extra capacity, noting several examples of small tour operators that had expanded in the past in response to supply shortages and operators that had stated their intention to expand in future.[142]

The Commission also examined whether the ability of smaller operators to expand capacity would be undermined by inadequate access to airline seats and travel agencies.

With regard to airline capacity, the CFI found that smaller tour operators' airline seat requirements would continue to be met by players that are independent of the large tour operators.[143] In particular, the CFI criticised the Commission for failing to recognise that reduction in larger tour operators' use of third-party airline capacity would increase the capacity available to the smaller operators.[144] The CFI found that, contrary to the Commission's contention, several alternative sources of supply existed for airline capacity, including overseas carriers based at the destination airport, scheduled airlines and low-cost carriers, as well as independent charter airlines in the UK.

With regard to distribution, the CFI found that the Commission was wrong to conclude that smaller tour operators would not have access to a channel through which to distribute their products on favourable enough conditions to enable them to expand their capacity. It noted, in particular, that nearly 40% of all foreign package holidays sold through travel agencies were sold through independent agencies, and that other methods of distribution, such as direct sales by telephone or the internet, existed and accounted for a material proportion of package holiday sales.[145]

---

[140] *Airtours plc v. Commission of the European Communities*, 6 June 2002, para. 277.
[141] Ibid., para. 213.    [142] Ibid., paras. 217–27.    [143] Ibid., para. 231.
[144] Ibid., para. 232.    [145] Ibid., para. 257.

*Assessment of the role of the fringe in* Norske Skog/Parenco/Walsum *and* UPM-Kymmene/Haindl  In *Norske Skog/Parenco/Walsum*[146] and *UPM-Kymmene/Haindl*[147] the Commission dismissed a theory whereby firms would coordinate 'downtimes' – temporary closure of paper machines – to support prices during periods of low demand after considering the role of smaller fringe players. In its SO, the Commission suggested that it may be possible to coordinate downtimes through public announcements and that coordination could be sustained by a simple retaliation mechanism whereby other firms would target a deviator's customers with low prices.[148]

However, the Commission found that tacit coordination via this mechanism would likely be undermined by the actions of fringe players.[149]

The Commission found that Norske Skog itself exemplified how a relatively small paper producer could increase its market share and become a leading worldwide player.[150] As such, it considered that the remaining fringe players (SCA, Myllykoski, Palm and Abitibi/Bridgewater in the market for newsprint and Norske Skog, Burgo and SCA in the market for wood containing magazine paper) would be able to increase production in the event of coordinated production downtimes, rendering such coordination unsustainable.[151]

The Commission estimated that a significant volume of spare capacity would be in the hands of fringe players in a period of low demand on the basis of information on current installed capacity and historic utilisation rates during periods of low demand.[152] The Commission found that, given its estimates of the elasticity of industry demand, attempting to raise price by a significant amount through output restrictions would not be possible in view of the possibilities for the fringe to increase production almost immediately through higher capacity utilisation rates. The Commission found that over a longer period the fringe would be able to increase capacity.[153]

---

[146] Case COMP/M.2499 – *Norske Skog/Parenco/Walsum*, Commission decision of 21 November 2001.

[147] Case COMP/M.2498 – *UPM-Kymmene/Haindl*, Commission decision of 21 November 2001.

[148] See Case COMP/M.2499 – *Norske Skog/Parenco/Walsum*, Commission decision of 21 November 2001, para. 132.

[149] Ibid., para. 139.    [150] Ibid., para. 141.    [151] Ibid., para. 142.

[152] Ibid., para. 147.    [153] See ibid., para. 147.

It should be noted that in this case the Commission was able to satisfy itself that the fringe would be able to counteract reductions in output, and therefore increases in price, by the larger firms acting as a cohesive group. However, the Commission did not explicitly consider the extent to which the presence of the fringe might have affected the colluding firms' ability to act as a cohesive group in the first place. In particular, it did not consider that the ability of the fringe to expand output may have reduced the attractiveness for the coordinating firms of adhering to coordination rather than deviating by expanding output themselves. On this basis, fringe firms may have been effective in mitigating competition concerns even if they could not replace all of the output that the Commission hypothesised might be removed by coordinating firms. That is, having satisfied itself that the fringe would offset the effect of any coordinated effects, it was not necessary for the Commission to consider how the fringe would impact the sustainability of post-merger tacit coordination.

*Assessment of the role of the fringe in* ABF/GBI Business    In *ABF/GBI Business*,[154] the Commission judged the reactions of 'outsiders' to the collusive agreement to be insufficient to mitigate its concerns regarding tacit coordination. The Commission noted that barriers to entry and expansion were significant in yeast production due to the importance of branding, the need for an established local sales force and the need to develop a network of distributors in the face of distributors' de facto or formal exclusive relationships with existing suppliers.[155] It considered that no *de novo* entry could be expected in the foreseeable future and that there was limited ability for actual or potential competitors in neighbouring markets to expand capacity into supplying Spain or Portugal. In particular, it found that successful entry or expansion would require a local distribution system, local sales personnel, recognised brands and the establishment of a reputation for quality and consistency of supply.[156] It found that these factors represented significant barriers to entry that would impact the ability and incentives for current marginal players such as Lallemand and Zeus, as well as possible new entrants, such as Turkish yeast producers, to discipline tacit coordination.[157]

The Commission also noted the role that spare capacity currently held by the major players could play in deterring new entry. It noted that new entrants could be dissuaded by the prospect of aggressive and targeted

[154] Case COMP/M.4980 – *ABF/GBI Business*, Commission decision of 23 September 2008.
[155] Ibid., para. 166.     [156] Ibid., para. 248.     [157] Ibid., para. 255.

pricing behaviour by the established major players once entry had been detected. Certain potential entrants might also be wary of retaliation in other geographic markets as a response to entry in Spain.[158]

#### 3.2.2.2   Buyer power
Under certain circumstances buyers can protect themselves from higher prices by taking actions that destabilise coordination or constrain the prices that can be sustained by colluding firms.

As noted in Section 2.2 above, both the frequency with which competing firms interact with one another and the lumpiness of demand affect the critical discount factor and thus the sustainability of coordination. Sophisticated buyers may be able to influence both of these features of the market by concentrating their demand in fewer orders.[159]

By choosing to purchase in bulk, buyers both increase the value to sellers of individual transactions and make transactions less frequent. Increasing the order size implies that firms have more to gain in the short term from undercutting rivals in order to obtain the order. Reducing the frequency of interactions implies that retaliation can occur less rapidly. Both of these factors tend to reduce the stability of coordination by increasing the incentive on the part of suppliers to cheat on the collusive understanding.

In addition, important buyers can potentially undermine the stability of coordination among suppliers through the threat of sponsoring new entry or sponsoring the growth of smaller players. As noted above, the threat of entry or fringe expansion may not only mitigate market power exerted by suppliers acting as a collusive group but also reduce the incentives of suppliers to adhere to coordination.

*Assessment of the role of buyers in* Pirelli/BICC   In *Pirelli/BICC*,[160] the Commission was able to dismiss concerns surrounding coordination in the markets for extra-high voltage ('EHV') and high voltage ('HV') power cables used for the transmission of electrical power after considering the bidding structure of competition and the strength of buyers. The Commission observed that in the HV/EHV market, the two leading firms, Pirelli/BICC and Alcatel, would achieve a combined market share

---

[158] Ibid., para. 262.
[159] For a formal treatment of the role that buyer power can play in undermining the extent of collusion, see C. Snyder, 'A Dynamic Theory of Countervailing Power' (1996) 27 *RAND Journal of Economics* 747–69.
[160] Case COMP/M.1882 – *Pirelli/BICC*, Commission decision of 19 July 2000.

of 55–65% and considered whether these firms might be able to sustain coordination by bidding less aggressively than under competitive conditions or by tacitly allocating markets geographically (for example, by avoiding one another's traditional home markets).[161]

The Commission noted that in the HV/EHV market, bidding transactions took place infrequently, with only a few, high value, contracts placed each year in each country. It found that the 'winner takes all' nature of competition for these large contracts gave rise to strong incentives to bid aggressively for each contract, thus undermining the sustainability of coordination.[162] In addition, it found that the main customers of HV/EHV power cables typically purchase large quantities and would consequently have the possibility actively to develop new supply sources through strategic allocation of orders to selected cable producers.[163]

In relation to the separate market for low voltage ('LV') and medium voltage ('MV') power cables, the Commission found that LV/MV transactions tended to take place more frequently (and have lower value) than in the HV/EHV market. This suggested that individual suppliers might be more inclined to abstain from aggressive bidding. However, the Commission recognised the presence of sophisticated buyers that could undermine coordination by altering the nature of interaction between suppliers to their advantage. In particular, the Commission noted that buyers could aggregate their demand over a period of time (up to two years) and hence create less frequent and more valuable transactions, in order to increase bidders' incentives to compete aggressively.[164] It also found that, by offering a higher allocation to smaller (second-tier) players and thus reducing existing suppliers' volumes, buyers could exert pressure on suppliers with a significant fixed cost base and that such strategies were indeed employed by a number of large utility customers.[165]

### 3.3    Will the proposed transaction make it significantly more likely that tacit coordination will occur or make tacit coordination more effective?

Coordinated effects arise if a merger brings about some structural change to the market that makes it more likely that coordination will occur or makes tacit coordination more effective. Assessing the specific industry changes that will result from a merger is therefore a crucial element of

---

[161] Ibid., para. 81.    [162] Ibid., para. 82.    [163] Ibid., para. 84.
[164] Ibid., para. 90.    [165] Ibid.

any assessment of coordinated effects, albeit one that arguably does not always receive sufficient attention.[166]

The EC Horizontal Merger Guidelines note that coordinated effects concerns may arise either where a merger increases the likelihood that firms will be able to coordinate their behaviour and thereby raise prices or where a merger makes 'coordination easier, more stable or more effective for firms, that were already coordinating before the merger, either by making the coordination more robust or by permitting firms to coordinate on even higher prices'.[167]

As noted in Section 2, the economic theory of tacit coordination has focused to a large extent on the existence of collusive equilibria, which is closely associated with the issue of sustainability. The key insight of this theory is that a merger may bring about a change that reduces the critical discount factor by increasing the profits from coordination, reducing the profits from deviation or reducing the profits of firms under punishment. A change that reduces the *critical* discount factor in turn increases the range of *actual* discount factors for which collusive equilibria exist and so in some sense makes it easier for coordination to be sustained.

It is important to emphasise, however, that the standard economic theory of tacit coordination is essentially silent on how firms select between equilibria. This means that the theory has very little to say about the circumstances under which a merger that reduces the requirement on how patient firms have to be to sustain coordination will in fact give rise to a switch in the mode of interaction between firms from one of competition to one of coordination. As such, it is difficult to predict the circumstances in which a particular merger may be expected to give rise to such a switch in firm behaviour.

The conceptual difficulties that arise in showing that a market that is currently characterised by competition will switch to one characterised by coordination following a merger suggest that it is far more likely that the Commission will pursue a coordinated effects case on the basis of the concern that *existing* tacit coordination will be facilitated, strengthened or exacerbated than the concern that a competitive market will become collusive.

---

[166] For example, in *Sony/BMG* (the 2004 decision), the question of the effect the JV would be likely to have on coordination received surprisingly little attention. The Commission dismissed relatively briefly the prospect that the transaction could cause the mode of competition to switch from competitive to collusive interaction. See Case COMP/M. 3333 – *Sony/BMG*, Commission decision of 19 July 2004, paras. 155–8.

[167] EC Horizontal Merger Guidelines, para. 39.

Somewhat surprisingly, the EC Horizontal Merger Guidelines do not discuss separately the issue of how the effect of the merger on coordination will be assessed. It can be seen, however, that structural market features that change as a result of mergers (particularly, the number and symmetry of firms) enter the EC Horizontal Merger Guidelines' discussion of reaching a tacit agreement, monitoring rivals and deterring deviations.[168] As such, it follows that the Commission will consider whether changes in market structure brought about by a merger may impact the extent to which firms may be able to both reach and sustain coordination.

### 3.3.1   Merger specific factors affecting the likelihood and effectiveness of tacit coordination

A merger can influence the extent to which coordination can be reached and sustained by market participants in a number of ways. In particular, it can do so through reducing the number of market participants, increasing symmetry, removing a 'maverick' or increasing market segmentation and retaliation possibilities. We consider each of these in turn below.

**3.3.1.1   Reducing the number of market participants**   The most obvious way in which a merger affects the ability of firms to reach and sustain tacit coordination is by reducing the number of players in the market. A reduction in the number of players in the market can make tacit coordination easier to achieve and sustain for a number of reasons.

First, as noted in Section 2.2, a reduction in the number of competitors in the market will reduce the critical discount factor. The gain from deviation (relative to earnings under coordination) is likely to be smaller when there are fewer firms each with a larger market share.

Second, a reduction in the number of competitors in the market may make it easier to reach the terms of coordination. As explained in Section 3.1, the number of interrelations between firms increases disproportionately with the number of suppliers in a market. A merger that reduces the number of firms in a market from three to two reduces the number of interrelations between competitors from three to one, which in effect reduces the number of 'agreements' that need to be reached from three to one.[169]

---

[168]   Along with the various other factors discussed above, such as product characteristics and the nature of demand, that are effectively 'held constant' pre- and post-merger.

[169]   With three firms A, B and C, there are three interrelations between competitors (A–B; A–C and B–C). After a merger between firms A and B, there is only one interrelation

Third, monitoring of deviations may be made easier by a reduction in the number of competitors. With fewer firms in a market, deviation by one firm may be easier to notice as the impact of the deviation on rivals (in terms of lost demand) may be more severe and more clearly distinguishable from a fluctuation in market demand. Knowing that any deviation will be easily detected by rivals may reduce the incentives for both the post-merger entity and its rivals to deviate.

Fourth, a reduction in the number of competitors may make it easier for firms to agree upon which of them should bear the cost of punishing a deviator (e.g. through lower prices).

Consideration of these factors might suggest that horizontal mergers, by reducing the number of competitors in a market, always increase (at least to some extent) the risk that tacit coordination will be reached and sustained. However, as noted below, a reduction in the number of firms might actually *reduce* coordination concerns, if it causes incentives for the remaining players to diverge.

### 3.3.1.2 Increasing symmetry

Symmetry amongst firms may make it easier for them to reach an understanding and to sustain that understanding over time.

First, as noted in Section 2.2, asymmetry in costs, number of product varieties or capacity may imply that at least one firm has a high critical discount factor and is thus in some sense difficult to induce to coordinate. Second, symmetry between firms may facilitate the process of agreeing terms for coordination by aligning their views on what would constitute an attractive collusive agreement.[170]

It is important to recognise that where a merger reduces symmetry it can make tacit coordination less easy to sustain, notwithstanding the reduction in the number of firms in the market. In a recent UK Competition Commission working paper, Davis and Huse present an empirical coordinated effects merger simulation model in a differentiated product market and apply this framework to the network server market.[171] They find that the incentives to coordinate actually *fell* as a result of the merger

---

between competitors (AB–C). In a similar way, the Commission noted in *Sony/BMG* that a reduction in the number of firms from five to four would imply that the number of 'bilateral competitive relationships' would fall from ten to six: see Case COMP/M.3333 – *Sony/BMG*, Commission decision of 3 October 2007, para. 157.

[170] EC Horizontal Merger Guidelines, para. 48.

[171] See P. J. Davis and C. Huse, 'Estimating the Coordinated Effects of Mergers', UK Competition Commission working paper, 2010.

between Hewlett Packard (HP) and Compaq and argue that, contrary to conventional logic, incentives to coordinate will *ceteris paribus* often fall in this way after a merger.[172]

An interesting feature of the Davis and Huse modelling framework is that whilst merging parties may find that coordination is 'easier' to sustain post-merger non-merging parties' critical discount factors may increase as a result of the merger (i.e. they become less inclined to coordinate). This result emerges because whilst the non-merging firms' collusive and defection payoffs do not change, the payoffs they receive under punishment (which the authors assume to be reversion to normal competition) increase as a result of the merger. In other words, unilateral effects following a merger make the prospect of 'normal' competition between post-merger firms less mutually destructive and so, by reducing the severity of punishment, make deviation from tacit coordination relatively more attractive. In practice, however, it is not wholly clear that an increase in the prevailing competitive price would preclude firms from implementing retaliation as severe as would have been the case pre-merger, for instance by using prices below the post-merger competitive level. Nonetheless, it is clear that mergers may be disruptive events and may reduce, rather than increase, the likelihood that coordination will be sustained.

**3.3.1.3    Removing a 'maverick'**    It is often noted that coordination is made more difficult to sustain by the presence of a 'maverick' firm. Indeed, the EC Horizontal Merger Guidelines mention explicitly the circumstance in which 'one of the merging firms is a maverick firm with a high likelihood of disrupting coordinated conduct' as one of the special cases where horizontal competition concerns might be identified with merger in relatively unconcentrated markets.[173]

---

[172]  This paper follows Kühn (2004) by studying Bertrand differentiated products. See K. U. Kühn, 'The Coordinated Effects of Mergers in Differentiated Products Markets' (CEPR Discussion Paper No. 4769, 2004). An observation in that paper is that, as noted in Section 2.2 above, asymmetry in the number of (substitutable) product varieties sold may imply that a 'small' firm (i.e. with a lesser range) will have a greater willingness to cheat on the collusive agreement by cutting price than a large firm because it receives a smaller share of the collusive profits and because the resulting increase in sales for its products will largely represent diversion from the products of the larger firm. In addition, the large firm may have a limited incentive to punish the smaller firm because doing so will harm its profitability across its entire range of products.

[173]  EC Horizontal Merger Guidelines, para. 20. The EC Horizontal Merger Guidelines specifically highlight the elimination of a maverick as one of the circumstances in which

The term 'maverick' is generally understood to refer to a firm whose incentives to adhere to a collusive agreement are lower than those of other firms, such that the firm is likely to be a source of instability for coordination.[174] Broadly, there are two ways in which a difference in incentives between firms could arise:

- A maverick could be a firm with a high *critical* discount factor. As discussed in Section 2.2 above, asymmetry between firms (with respect to costs, capacities and product portfolios) could give rise to differences in their critical discount factors. For example, a firm with lower costs than others might have a higher critical discount factor, and thus be less likely to be patient enough to adhere to coordination.

- A maverick could be a firm with a low *actual* discount factor (i.e. a firm that places little weight on future profits relative to current profits). This will mean that even if there is no asymmetry that leads that firm to have a higher critical discount factor than any other firm, it will nonetheless be less willing to adhere to coordination than other firms. There are a number of reasons why a firm might have a lower actual discount factor than other firms. For example, a firm's management compensation may be based on short-term profits and may be myopic with respect to profits over the longer term.

The notion of a maverick in the EC Horizontal Merger Guidelines is sufficiently broad to encompass both of these ideas. In particular, when discussing how a merger may affect the likelihood or significance of coordination beyond reducing the number of players in a market, the EC Horizontal Merger Guidelines note:

> For instance, a merger may involve a 'maverick' firm that has a history of preventing or disrupting coordination, for example by failing to follow price increases by its competitors, or has characteristics that give it an incentive to favour different strategic choices than its coordinating competitors would prefer. If the merged firm were to adopt strategies similar to those of other competitors, the remaining firms would find it easier to coordinate, and the merger would increase the likelihood, stability or effectiveness of coordination.[175]

the Commission might identify horizontal competition concerns in a merger with a post-merger HHI between 1,000 and 2,000 and a delta below 250, or a merger with a post-merger HHI above 2,000 and a delta below 150.

[174] The term 'maverick' is also sometimes used in the context of unilateral effects analysis to refer to a firm that is a particularly important competitive force in the market.

[175] See EC Horizontal Merger Guidelines, para. 42.

Given that the notion of a maverick is relatively vague, there is generally no clear basis for determining which firms should be considered mavericks. In addition, where a firm is characterised as a maverick as a result of past aggressive behaviour by its managers or as a result of a history of introducing disruptive innovations, it may not be obvious whether a merger involving that firm should be considered to eliminate the maverick 'gene' or whether the maverick 'gene' should be considered to be preserved in the merged entity.[176]

Moreover, it is important to recognise that a merger may give rise to changes that *create* a maverick. For example, a merger may give rise to efficiencies that reduce the merging firms' marginal costs, which could reduce the extent to which firms in the post-merger environment could both reach and sustain tacit coordination.

### 3.3.1.4    Increasing market segmentation and retaliation possibilities

A merger may alter the set of product and geographic markets in which firms are present. This may improve the ability of firms to reach and sustain tacit coordination by allowing them to engage in market segmentation or by enhancing their abilities to retaliate against one another.

For example, a merger may increase the sustainability of a market-sharing agreement in which firms tacitly agree not to compete aggressively in each other's 'home' markets by giving the merged entity a small presence in its main rival's home market. This small presence may facilitate further expansion in the rival's home market and thereby enhance the threat of punishment in the event that the rival deviates from the tacit agreement by attempting to expand in the merged entity's home market.

As noted in Section 2.2 and Section 3.2.1.2 above, multi-market contact can under certain circumstances increase the stability of tacit coordination by balancing asymmetry across individual markets and thereby allowing tacit coordination to be sustained across all markets. As such, a merger that increases the extent of multi-market contacts may in principle enhance the sustainability of coordination. It is important to

---

[176] In practice, if a smaller firm that is characterised as having 'maverick' management is being acquired by a larger firm that is characterised as having 'conformist' management, the Commission will likely presume that the management of the post-merger entity will more closely resemble that of the larger acquiring firm unless there are convincing reasons to believe otherwise.

recognise, however, that an increase in the number of markets in which firms interact cannot be taken definitively to increase the sustainability of coordination. Any theory of harm due to coordinated effects based on greater multi-market contact must be carefully articulated to identify why multi-market contact in that particular case might improve the scope for coordination.

### 3.3.2 Assessment of the effect of the merger in *ABF/GBI Business*

In *ABF/GBI Business*,[177] the Commission placed particular emphasis on the question of whether and how the merger would make tacit coordination easier, more stable or more effective. With regard to Spanish compressed yeast, it noted at the outset that there was evidence that the market already exhibited some degree of tacit coordination.[178] It was therefore only necessary for the Commission to show that the merger would exacerbate tacit coordination concerns and not that the market would 'flip' from one currently characterised by non-coordinated competition to one characterised by coordination.

First, the Commission discussed the effect that the reduction of the number of players from three to two would have on the market. It noted that this reduction would make tacit coordination easier for four primary reasons:[179]

- The merged entity and Lesaffre would face a higher incentive to coordinate since the short-run gain from aggressive behaviour would be lower (with a smaller base of rival's customers from which the merged entity could attract new sales) and the long-run gains from preserving tacit coordination would be higher (with a larger base of customers over which the merged entity would enjoy supra-competitive margins).
- The merged entity and Lesaffre would be better able to agree on the terms of coordination since the merger would reduce the number of competitors that need to be party to the tacit agreement.
- Monitoring, whilst already possible, would be facilitated by the reduction of players. In particular, the Commission considered that time lags necessary to detect deviation would be reduced and the identity of the deviating firm would be even more obvious.

---

[177] Case COMP/M.4980 – *ABF/GBI Business*, Commission decision of 23 September 2008.
[178] Ibid., para. 274.    [179] Ibid., paras. 285–9.

- Punishments would gain further credibility and effectiveness since there would be no need to agree amongst third parties which firm is best suited to punish a deviator and no issue of firms free-riding on punishment carried out by other suppliers.

Second, the Commission discussed the specific effect of eliminating GBI as a potential force for destabilising tacit coordination. There was a number of reasons why the removal of GBI in particular gave the Commission concerns over tacit coordination:[180]

- The size and location of GBI's plant suggested that it might be affected differently by future unanticipated demand and supply shocks. In particular, the single plant GBI used to supply Spain and Portugal was also used to supply other markets. Changes in demand conditions in those other markets could have affected its incentives with respect to the supply of Spain and Portugal.
- The potential for the merged entity to rationalise production across certain of its plants was deemed to increase cost symmetry between the merged entity and Lesaffre.
- The transfer of assets to ABF and removal of GBI as an independent player would have left two firms with identical spare capacities and symmetric market shares of 40–50% each.
- GBI had in the past invested in R&D leading to some innovation. The Commission also noted that the merger rested on an IP-sharing agreement between Lesaffre and ABF. It considered that in addition to eliminating GBI as a source of potentially destabilising innovation, the patent-sharing agreement would ensure that neither of the two remaining firms would inherit a competitive advantage that could destabilise coordination. Furthermore, it noted that the sharing of IP rights would enhance transparency and homogeneity of the features of the remaining firms' products.
- GBI did not serve the liquid yeast market in Spain, which, in the absence of the merger, could have resulted in misaligned incentives. In particular, GBI would have been immune from any attempt to punish deviation with retaliation in the liquid yeast market, unlike ABF and Lesaffre.
- GBI had a somewhat different customer mix to the other two players as it had limited direct sales to industrial customers. The Commission

---

[180] Ibid., paras. 290–303.

noted that the remaining firms post-merger would have had more symmetric customer bases.

In sum, the Commission found that the merger was likely to make tacit coordination more robust than it would have been absent the merger.

While the *ABF/GBI Business*[181] decision shows that the Commission will consider not only the factors that make an industry conducive to coordination, but also how coordination would work in practice and how the merger could change the effectiveness or sustainability of coordination, it leaves some important questions unanswered. It is unclear how much weight the Commission placed on various factors in its decision and therefore how the Commission would have reacted if one of the conditions that gave rise to its concerns had not been present. For example, it is not clear whether had the merged entity faced a rival with more limited spare capacity this would have been enough to overturn coordination concerns on the basis of an inability to punish deviations. In addition, whilst the decision highlights post-merger symmetry in shares and spare capacity in Spain as a source of concern, the presence of a significantly more asymmetric situation in Portugal (where the merged entity would have had a market share of 70–80%, with Lesaffre having a share of 20–30%) was not enough to dispel concerns regarding coordinated effects in that market. This raises questions over the importance of symmetry in supporting the Commission's conclusions in Spain.

Importantly, and probably critically, the Commission held that there was sufficient evidence to conclude that the compressed yeast markets in Spain and Portugal were already subject to tacit coordination.[182] As a result, it needed only to consider whether the merger would have exacerbated existing coordination. It remains unclear how the Commission will assess coordinated effects cases in circumstances where the theory of harm necessitates a 'flip' from competitive to coordinated conduct as a result of a merger.

---

[181] Case COMP/M.4980 – *ABF/GBI Business*, Commission decision of 23 September 2008.
[182] As noted in Section 3.1.2 the evidence regarding price increases that was used to support this conclusion was arguably consistent also with non-coordinated oligopoly behaviour.

# 5

# Non-horizontal mergers

## 1. Introduction

The term 'non-horizontal merger' describes a broad class of mergers in which the parties are active in different relevant markets and as such do not exert a direct competitive constraint on one another. The absence of a direct competitive constraint is the key feature that distinguishes non-horizontal mergers from horizontal mergers.[1]

Non-horizontal mergers typically fall into one of two categories. In a vertical merger the parties are each active at different levels of the same supply chain. An example of a vertical merger is a manufacturer (the 'upstream' firm) merging with one of its distributors (the 'downstream' firm). There is a direct commercial relationship between the downstream firm and the upstream firm, with the downstream firm a customer of the upstream firm.

In a conglomerate merger, the parties are neither direct horizontal competitors nor active at different levels of the same vertical supply chain. In principle, this definition of a conglomerate merger leaves open a wide range of potential cases. The products provided by the merging parties may be complementary in nature (i.e. a fall in the price in one of the products increases demand for the other products), related on the supply side on account of being sold to the same consumers via the same distribution channels, or entirely unrelated by either demand or supply factors.

The unifying feature of all the types of merger described above is that the standard concern regarding the potential for a horizontal merger to give rise to anti-competitive effects does not apply due to the absence of

---

[1] In practice, a non-horizontal merger may also require consideration of horizontal effects. For example, one of the merging parties may be a particularly credible potential entrant into a related market served by the other merging party. For a discussion of the assessment of mergers between potential competitors see Chapter 3, Section 4.2.

substitutability between the products of the merging parties. Indeed, in a vertical merger or a conglomerate merger involving complementary products, the ability to maximise joint profits post-merger gives rise to an incentive to lower prices rather than raise prices as it does for a merger between substitutable products. These considerations give rise to the widely held view that non-horizontal mergers are less likely to be anti-competitive than horizontal mergers.

It is also generally recognised, however, that non-horizontal mergers can, in some cases, give rise to competitive harm. This harm can arise as a result of the merger reducing the extent to which competitors of the merged entity, at some level of a supply chain at which it is active, offer effective competition, with the result that consumers are harmed. Mergers that result in this kind of harm to consumers are said to give rise to 'anti-competitive foreclosure'.

This chapter discusses how the potential for a non-horizontal merger to give rise to consumer harm can be assessed in practice. Section 2 presents a number of economic concepts that are central to the assessment of non-horizontal mergers. First, it discusses the pro-competitive effects that are considered to be associated with many non-horizontal mergers. Second, it introduces the concept of anti-competitive foreclosure, which is the most common concern associated with non-horizontal mergers. Finally, it discusses briefly other competition concerns that may arise.

Section 3 discusses the scope for vertical mergers to give rise to input foreclosure, a situation in which the merged entity, by leveraging its market power upstream, increases the cost incurred by its downstream competitors in procuring an important input. The increase in the costs of rivals to the merged entity may reduce the competitive pressure that the merged entity faces downstream. Unless outweighed by efficiency gains resulting from the merger, the relaxation of this downstream constraint may allow the merged entity (profitably) to increase the prices charged to final consumers.

Section 4 discusses the scope for vertical mergers to give rise to customer foreclosure, a situation in which the merger reduces the ability of the merged entity's upstream competitors to make sales by restricting access to a significant part of the downstream customer base. To the extent that this restriction reduces the ability or incentive of upstream rivals to compete, this may lead to an increase in the costs of downstream rivals that in turn reduces the competitive pressure that the merged entity faces downstream. As with input foreclosure, in the absence of offsetting efficiency gains, the relaxation of this constraint may lead to higher prices for final consumers.

Section 5 discusses the scope for a conglomerate merger to allow the merged entity to lessen the competitive constraints that it faces, thereby giving rise to a unilateral incentive to increase prices to the detriment of consumers. Generally this action must involve the conditioning of sales in a market currently served by one merging party on sales in another market currently served by the other merging party. Tying and bundling are two broad ways in which this might be done.

Section 6 discusses a particular kind of conglomerate merger, known as a diagonal merger, in which the merging parties are an upstream supplier and a downstream competitor of the firms for which the upstream supplier's good is an input. While diagonal mergers involve upstream and downstream firms, they are distinguished from vertical mergers by the absence of a direct supply relationship between the parties. In some cases diagonal mergers may give rise to a unilateral incentive to increase price that is similar to the standard unilateral effect concern that arises in the context of a horizontal merger.

## 2.   Economic concepts

### 2.1   Pro-competitive effects

The defining characteristic of a horizontal merger is that the merging parties supply substitutable goods or services. Chapter 3 described how, by bringing these substitutable products under common control, a horizontal merger may give rise to a unilateral incentive for the merged entity to raise price due to the internalisation of the positive effect that an increase in each product's price has on the demand for the other.

By contrast, non-horizontal mergers often concern complementary, rather than substitutable, products. When the price of one complementary product falls, so demand for the other product will rise (and vice versa). Consequently, by logic related to that underpinning the theory of unilateral effects, a vertical merger or a conglomerate merger involving complementary products may give rise to an incentive for the merged entity to *reduce* its prices, even without any reduction in marginal costs due to the merger.[2]

---

[2] Although as noted below, supply-side efficiencies of this type could also arise as a result of a non-horizontal merger.

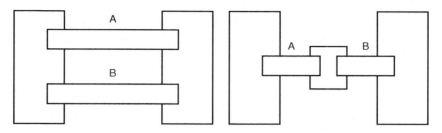

**Figure 5.1**  Illustration of substitutability and complementarity

To see how the incentives arising from mergers of substitutable and complementary goods differ, consider the following hypothetical scenarios involving mergers between two operators of toll bridges, A and B, that connect two islands. In case 1, the bridges are arranged in parallel. A consumer wishing to travel between the two islands therefore has a choice of using either A or B. In case 2, the bridges are arranged in series. A consumer wishing to travel between the two islands must make use of both bridges. These cases are illustrated in Figure 5.1. In both cases, prior to a merger, each bridge operator sets its price by maximising its short-run profit, without taking into account the effect of its pricing decision on the other operator's profits. After the merger, a single decision maker sets the price of both bridges so as to maximise the joint profit of the two operating units (the physical layout of the bridges is not changed by the merger). As explained below, whether a merger results in higher or lower prices depends on the arrangement of the bridges.

In case 1, operators A and B supply substitutable products. A small increase in the price of A will cause some 'marginal' consumers to switch from using bridge A to using bridge B. Similarly, a small decrease in the price of A will cause some 'marginal' consumers to switch from using bridge B to using bridge A. When setting its price independently, the operator of bridge A will continue to lower its price until the increase in its profits resulting from serving the 'marginal' consumers it steals from operator B is just offset by the reduction in its profits resulting from a lower price being charged to all the consumers it serves. Operator A will not take into account the harm to operator B's profits in any decision over whether to lower its price (and vice versa). A merger between the two operators allows this negative effect from reducing price (on the profits of the other firm) to be internalised. As a result, the merged entity will choose *higher* prices for each bridge than the two firms would choose when setting prices independently.[3]

In case 2, operators A and B supply complementary products. A small increase in the price of A will cause some 'marginal' consumers not to travel between the two islands. Therefore, a small increase in the price of A will reduce the demand both for A's and for B's services. When setting its price independently, operator A will continue to lower its price until the increase in its profits resulting from serving the 'marginal' consumers that it induces to make the journey between the islands is just offset by the reduction in its profits resulting from a lower price being charged to all the consumers it serves. Operator A will not take into account that a *further* reduction in its price below the price that maximises its own profit will boost not only demand for its own service but also that provided by operator B. A merger between the two firms allows this positive effect from reducing price (on the profits of the other firm) to be internalised. As a result, the merged entity will choose *lower* prices for each bridge than the two firms would when setting prices independently.

The possibility for a merger between complementary products to give rise to price reductions through the mechanism described above is often referred to as the elimination of double marginalisation or as the Cournot effect.[4] This mechanism can also potentially give rise to a post-merger incentive to increase quality. If an increase in the quality of one party's product has a beneficial effect on the other party's profits, this effect will be taken into account when the merged entity decides on the level of quality to provide.

---

[3] Of course, as described in detail in Chapter 3, whether a merger of substitutes does in practice lead to incentives to increase price will require a detailed assessment of the constraint each merging party imposes on the other, the constraints imposed by other providers in the market and the potential for counterbalancing efficiencies.

[4] Note that the mechanism is equivalent for a vertical merger and a conglomerate merger involving complementary projects. In both cases a reduction in the price of one party's product generates a positive external benefit for the profits of the other party that is taken into account in the pricing decisions of the merged entity, leading to lower prices post-merger. Typically, in the context of a vertical merger, this effect is known as the elimination of double marginalisation or double mark-up. In the context, of a conglomerate merger it is known as the Cournot effect, Cournot (1838) generally being considered to be the first author to observe that coordinated pricing amongst monopoly producers of complementary goods would tend to reduce prices. Specifically, Cournot presented an example of the complementary goods copper and zinc, which are combined to make brass. See A. Cournot, *Recherches sur les Principes Mathématiques de la Théorie des Richesses* (Paris, France: L. Hachette, 1838; English translation by N. T. Bacon in *Economic Classics*, New York, NY: Macmillan, 1897; reprinted by Augustus M. Kelly, 1960).

In addition to benefits relating to the internalisation of effects of each party's decisions on the other's demand, non-horizontal mergers often provide substantial scope for supply-side efficiencies.

In particular, non-horizontal mergers may potentially eliminate a 'hold-up' problem, whereby an investment that benefits both parties does not take place. For example, suppose that a Firm A produces a good that is an input for Firm B. Suppose that, currently, the input is generic, in the sense that it can be used in the production process of any firm that competes with Firm B. Firm A and Firm B regularly negotiate short-term contracts that specify the price that Firm B must pay for the input. Now suppose that if Firm A were to invest in a particular piece of equipment that improved its input this would greatly improve the quality of Firm B's product and increase the profits that Firm B could earn downstream. However, the benefits from the improvement of the input are specific to Firm B. In other words, once the investment is made the input produced by Firm A is only improved in so far as it is used by Firm B and not in so far as it is used by any other firm. Firm B encourages Firm A to invest in the piece of equipment and states that if Firm A does so, it will pay double for the input in future. Let us assume that, at this higher price, Firm A would be better off making the investment and Firm B is better off because the improvement in quality of its product (and the effect of that quality improvement on downstream demand and profits) justifies the higher input cost.[5]

However, Firm A will be aware that once it has made the investment Firm B could renege on its promise to pay double for the input. Given the specificity of benefits generated by the investment to Firm B, Firm A knows that in future contract negotiations Firm B will have significant bargaining power and may try to appropriate the entire surplus generated by the investment. Firm A could therefore be reluctant to make the investment in the first place. One possible way in which Firm B may try to induce Firm A to make the investment is to sign a long-term contract that guarantees Firm A a high price for the input. However, such a contract may be unattractive, for example, because variations in cost and demand conditions imply that the parties prefer short-term contracts that allow for more regular price negotiations. A merger between

---

[5] The investment represents a so-called 'Pareto' improvement in the sense that given an appropriate distribution of the benefits of the investment both parties can be made better off.

Firm A and Firm B could eliminate the hold-up problem and imply that a beneficial investment is made when absent the merger it would not have been.[6]

In addition, conglomerate mergers may give rise to economies of scope that reduce the costs of one or both of the merging parties or enable them to supply products of a higher quality.[7] Economies of scope arise where costs can be shared across the production of separate goods or services where they are produced within the same firm.[8] They can arise from a variety of sources such as: sales and distribution efficiencies (different products can rely on the same basic sales and distribution infrastructure); common assets (different products can be produced from a single piece of equipment); or from know-how (the efficiency of the production process for one product may be improved by experience in a similar production process).

A vertical merger may generate supply chain efficiencies such as guaranteed supply or better supply chain management. The merger may allow for better coordination and planning of procurement, production and distribution and may allow the merged entity to reduce costs (e.g. by reducing inventories) and become more responsive to consumer needs.[9]

---

[6] This example is similar to the case of GM and Fisher Body, as it is reported by B. Klein, R. G. Crawford and A. A. Alchian, 'Vertical Integration, Appropriable Rents, and the Competitive Contracting Process' (1978) 21 *Journal of Law & Economics* 297. Fisher Body produced wooden bodies for cars for GM. When metal bodies replaced wooden bodies, it became necessary for Fisher Body to make investments that were specific to GM and it did so after GM entered into a 10-year contractual relationship in 1919. Eventually, strains in the relationship (including GM's desire for Fisher Body to make further specific investments such as locating its plant next to GM's plant) gave rise to a merger between GM and Fisher Body between 1924 and 1926. Note, however, that this interpretation of the rationale for the merger is disputed by some. See R. Casadesus-Masanell and D. F. Spulber, 'The Fable of Fisher Body' (2000) 43 *Journal of Law & Economics* 67–104.

[7] Teece argues that if economies of scope are based on the common and recurrent use of proprietary know-how or the common and recurrent use of a specialised and indivisible physical asset, then multi-product enterprise (diversification) is an efficient way of organising economic activity. See D. J. Teece, 'Economies of Scope and the Scope of the Enterprise' (1980) 1(3) *Journal of Economic Behavior & Organization* 223–47.

[8] The term 'economies of scope' was coined by John Panzar and Robert Willlig. They define economies of scope as a situation where it is less costly to combine two or more product lines in one firm than to produce them separately. See J. C. Panzar and R. D. Willig, 'Economies of Scale in Multi-Output Production' (1977) 91(3) *Quarterly Journal of Economics* 481–93 and J. C. Panzar and R. D. Willig, 'Economies of Scope' (1981) 71(2) *American Economic Review* 268–72.

[9] See D. Thomas and P. Griffin, 'Coordinated Supply Chain Management' (1996) 94 *European Journal of Operational Research* 1–15.

To summarise, unlike horizontal mergers, non-horizontal mergers may give rise to pro-competitive effects even without a change in the production technology that allows the merged firm to produce at lower marginal costs than either party could independently. Importantly, however, supply-side efficiencies may be an important rationale for many non-horizontal mergers.

As discussed in the remainder of this chapter, whilst non-horizontal mergers are generally presumed to be pro-competitive, they can under certain circumstances give rise to anti-competitive effects.

Before considering the potential anti-competitive effect of non-horizontal mergers it should be clarified that efficiencies, which are often an important feature of such mergers, should not be considered a source of potential harm. In some cases it has been argued that reductions in prices expected to result from non-horizontal mergers may be anti-competitive where these low prices make it difficult for rivals to compete over the long term. This argument is often referred to as the 'efficiency offence'.

Whilst, in principle, long-run harm to competition (and consumers) could come about as a result of lower prices arising from merger efficiencies, in practice such arguments are unlikely to be accepted unless there is compelling evidence that the benefit to consumers in the short term is small and the long-term harm is large and relatively certain.[10] The Commission's Guidelines on the assessment of non-horizontal mergers (referred to henceforth in this chapter as the 'EC Non-horizontal Merger Guidelines') note explicitly that 'the fact that rivals may be harmed because a merger creates efficiencies cannot in itself give rise to competition concerns'.[11]

## 2.2   Foreclosure and anti-competitive foreclosure

As noted above, non-horizontal mergers can in some circumstances give rise to anti-competitive effects. The most common competition concern

[10] Comparing this short-term benefit and long-term harm would require long-term harm to be discounted at an appropriate rate. To see the importance of discounting the future if a comparison of short-term benefits and long-term harm is to be made, note that if consumers can invest at a real annual rate of 4% (say) then €1 saved as a result of lower prices today can compensate them for prices that are €1.20 higher than they would otherwise have been in 5 years' time.

[11] See Guidelines on the assessment of non-horizontal mergers under the Council Regulation on the control of concentrations between undertakings ([2008] OJ C265/07) (the 'EC Non-horizontal Merger Guidelines'), para. 16.

in these cases is that the non-horizontal merger is considered to give rise to 'anti-competitive foreclosure'.

The EC Non-horizontal Merger Guidelines explicitly distinguish between the concepts of 'foreclosure' and 'anti-competitive foreclosure'. Foreclosure refers to 'any instance where actual or potential rivals' access to supplies or markets is hampered or eliminated as a result of the merger, thereby reducing these companies' ability and/or incentive to compete.'[12] The concept of foreclosure is therefore a broad one that effectively includes any instance in which the merger gives rise to out-comes that harm the merged entity's rivals. Interpreted broadly, a price reduction that reduced rivals' ability to make sales could be encompassed by this definition of foreclosure.

However, foreclosure as defined in the Guidelines need not give rise to harm to consumers. Indeed, most pro-competitive actions (e.g. price reductions, quality improvements) make competition more difficult for a firm's rivals in the sense of placing pressure on rivals' volumes and/or margins. Importantly, such price decreases do not generally harm com-petition and will in fact benefit customers. Although a decrease in any given firm's price will always have the effect of increasing the competitive pressure on rival firms, such increases in competitive pressure are in all but exceptional circumstances welcomed, reflecting the beneficial effects of the competitive process and the efficiencies typically arising from non-horizontal mergers. As such, the mere fact of foreclosure does not necessarily give rise to legitimate competition concerns.

Nevertheless, in certain instances where rivals' access to supplies or markets is hampered as a result of a merger, the result may be a lessening of competitive pressure on the merged entity that enables it to increase the price it charges (or reduce the quality it offers) consumers. Those instances in which foreclosure results in harm to end-consumers are termed 'anti-competitive foreclosure'.

Anti-competitive foreclosure can only be said to arise if the competi-tive constraint currently provided by rivals were to be significantly reduced following a merger.[13] In order for foreclosure to give rise to

---

[12] See Non-horizontal Merger Guidelines, para. 18.

[13] The Commission notes that, in most cases, the competitive conditions existing at the time of the merger constitute the relevant comparison for evaluating the effects of a merger. However, it notes that in some circumstances, the Commission will take into account future changes to the market that can 'reasonably be predicted'. It states that 'it may take account of the likely entry or exit of firms if the merger did not take place when considering what constitutes the relevant comparison': see Guidelines, para. 20.

consumer harm, however, it is not necessary that any competitor of the merged entity actually leaves the market.[14] It is only necessary that the merged entity's competitors are no longer in the aggregate able to exert a sufficiently potent competitive constraint to discipline price increases that harm consumers.[15] This reduced competitive constraint may then provide scope for the merged entity to increase its prices.

The causes and consequences of potential anti-competitive foreclosure vary according to the type of merger under consideration.

Vertical mergers may give rise to anti-competitive foreclosure concerns of two main forms: input foreclosure (in which the merged entity leverages upstream market power to augment downstream market power) and customer foreclosure (in which the merged entity leverages downstream market power to augment upstream market power). The scope for anti-competitive foreclosure to arise through these two mechanisms is discussed at Sections 3 and 4 below.

Anti-competitive foreclosure concerns arising in the case of conglomerate mergers, on the other hand, typically relate to the leveraging of market power from one market to another through the tying or bundling of the merged entity's products.[16] An alternative concern is that through tying or bundling, the merged entity can *protect* market power (e.g. by raising entry barriers).[17] The scope for anti-competitive foreclosure in conglomerate mergers is discussed in detail at Section 5 below.

---

[14] This is noted explicitly by the Non-horizontal Merger Guidelines at para. 29:

> Foreclosure thus can be found even if the foreclosed rivals are not forced to exit the market: It is sufficient that the rivals are disadvantaged and consequently led to compete less effectively. Such foreclosure is regarded as anti-competitive where the merging companies – and, possibly, some of its competitors as well – are as a result able to profitably increase the price charged to consumers.

[15] As discussed further below, this reduced constraint could come about as a result of competitors experiencing increases in their variable costs of production.

[16] As explained further in Section 5, the term 'pure bundling' is used to describe a situation in which products are sold together in fixed proportions and are not available independently of one another. 'Mixed bundling', on the other hand, describes a more general situation in which goods are sold together in fixed proportions but are, in addition, available independently of one another. The term 'tying' is generally used to describe a situation in which customers that purchase a particular good (the tying good) are also required to purchase another good (the tied good).

[17] Whilst the Non-horizontal Merger Guidelines specifically discuss bundling and tying, the Commission does not exclude the possibility of finding concerns with other exclusionary practices. Other types of exclusionary behaviour, including cross-subsidies and predatory pricing, were alleged in GE/Honeywell (Case COMP/M.2220 – *GE/Honeywell*, Commission

For a significant period of time the mainstream view, associated with the Chicago School, held that non-horizontal mergers would not be used to leverage market power.

The argument known as the 'one monopoly profit' critique states that an integrated firm that is active in a market in which it has a monopoly and a related market that is perfectly competitive can do no better than earn monopoly rents in its monopoly market, an objective it can achieve through setting the monopoly price in that market.[18]

Consider the simple case of a vertical merger between an upstream monopolist and a downstream firm that participates in a perfectly competitive market. Pre-merger the upstream firm maximises its profits by setting a wholesale price to downstream firms that results in them charging a final price to consumers which is the same as would have been charged by a vertically integrated monopolist. Since the downstream market is competitive, it makes zero profits and the whole monopoly profit is passed back to the upstream firm. Post-merger, the firm would charge the same downstream price and earn the same level of profits, assuming that downstream firms continue to behave competitively.

A similar result holds for the case of a conglomerate merger, where a firm with monopoly power over one product cannot increase its profits by bundling the monopoly good with the good supplied in the competitive market. Indeed, if some consumers only want to purchase the monopoly good and are not interested in purchasing the competitively supplied good, then bundling can only serve to lower the firm's profits as some consumers choose to forgo consumption of the monopoly good if it can only be purchased as part of a bundle.

While the one monopoly profit principle is a useful reminder that leveraging market power into competitive markets is not necessarily a profit improving strategy, the argument is derived within a somewhat stylised theoretical framework and does not apply in all circumstances. A number of exceptions to the one monopoly profit principle have been identified within the literature. In particular, the one monopoly profit

---

decision of 3 July 2001). In *GE/Amersham* (Case COMP/M.3304 – *GE/Amersham*, Commission decision of 21 January 2004), discussed in Section 5.5.2 below, the Commission also examined whether the merged entity would gain an advantage over its rivals as it would be in a better position to match the technical development of its medical equipment and contrast media products.

[18] See R. H. Bork, *The Antitrust Paradox*, 2nd edn (New York: Free Press, 1993).

principle is based on the assumption that the downstream market is characterised by perfect competition, such as that downstream firms all charge a price equal to their marginal cost and, therefore, that all available profits can be successfully extracted by the monopolist upstream. Furthermore, it crucially does not take into account the possibility that the merged entity can change the market structure through its actions, for example, by denying scale economies to its rivals. In a dynamic setting, these actions can reduce the competitive constraints that the firm faces over the longer term and thus allow it to increase prices.[19] Modern economic theory shows that non-horizontal mergers can in certain circumstances be used to leverage market power across markets. The various ways in which anti-competitive foreclosure can arise in vertical and conglomerate mergers are discussed in detail in the remainder of this chapter.

## 2.3   Other anti-competitive effects

As noted above, anti-competitive foreclosure, a type of non-coordinated effect, represents the most common cause for competitive concern in the context of non-horizontal mergers.

However, non-horizontal mergers can also give rise to both non-coordinated effects of a somewhat different nature to those brought about by anti-competitive foreclosure, and coordinated effects.[20]

### 2.3.1   Other non-coordinated effects

A non-coordinated incentive to increase price might result from a firm gaining commercially sensitive information about a rival as a result of a non-horizontal merger.[21] This commercially sensitive information may allow the merged entity to price less aggressively than it would have done in certain circumstances (harming consumers in the short term). Given that the circumstances in which this form of non-coordinated incentive

---

[19] For a further explanation of the Chicago School argument and an overview of the scenarios in which it does not hold, see B. Nalebuff, 'Bundling, Tying, and Portfolio Effects' (DTI Economics Paper No. 1, 2003).

[20] For a comprehensive overview of the economic literature on vertical and conglomerate mergers, see J. Church, 'The Impact of Vertical and Conglomerate Mergers on Competition' Report for the Directorate General for Competition, Directorate B Merger Task Force, European Commission, 2004).

[21] See Non-horizontal Merger Guidelines, para. 78.

to increase price might arise are likely to be particular to the case at hand, we do not discuss this concern in detail.

A further form of non-coordinated effects concern may arise in a particular type of non-horizontal merger, known as a 'diagonal merger', in which the merging parties are an upstream supplier and a downstream competitor of the firms for which the upstream supplier's good is an input.[22] A diagonal merger can in principle give rise to a unilateral incentive to increase price that is similar in some sense to the standard unilateral effect that arises in the context of a horizontal merger.[23] This incentive arises on account of the fact that an increase in the price the upstream supplier charges to rivals of the other merging party will increase the costs of those rivals and may therefore cause them to increase their prices. The increase in the prices of rivals will cause some diversion of demand to the merging party that competes with those rivals downstream. Diagonal mergers are discussed further at Section 6.

### 2.3.2  Coordinated effects

As discussed in Chapter 4, coordinated effects arise when a merger creates conditions that make tacit coordination (or tacit collusion) more likely or more effective. Whilst coordinated effects concerns are more common in the context of horizontal mergers, such concerns can also arise in the case of non-horizontal mergers.[24]

In principle, a non-horizontal merger leading to foreclosure that reduces the number of players in a market could make coordination amongst remaining players more likely.[25] As discussed in Chapter 4, a reduction in the number of players in a market could make a collusive outcome easier to reach (e.g. by reducing the number of tacit agreements that need to be made) and sustain (e.g. by reducing the number of firms whose actions need to be monitored). Typically, however, if a

---

[22] The term 'diagonal merger' was first used by Higgins: see R. S. Higgins, 'Diagonal Merger' (1997) 12 *Review of Industrial Organization* 609–23.

[23] Indeed, in *Google/DoubleClick*, the Commission discusses the potential for unilateral effects arising from the diagonal relationship between Google and DoubleClick in the 'Horizontal effects' section of the competitive assessment, under the subheading 'Actual competition'. See Case COMP/M.4731 – *Google/DoubleClick*, Commission decision of 11 March 2008, para. 192.

[24] Coordinated effects have only been modelled in the context of a vertical merger in the economics literature relatively recently: see Nocke, Volker and L. White. 'Do Vertical Mergers Facilitate Upstream Collusion?' (Penn University Working Paper, 2005).

[25] See Non-horizontal Merger Guidelines, para. 120.

non-horizontal merger were expected to give rise to the exit of a significant rival, it would be more natural to assess the effects of this exit on remaining firms' unilateral incentives to increase price rather than on the likelihood that remaining firms will engage in tacit coordination.

Alternatively, a non-horizontal merger could in some circumstances facilitate coordination by increasing transparency in the market in some way (thereby making it easier to reach and monitor tacit agreements) without any rival exiting or being marginalised. External stability of a coordination agreement (see Chapter 4, Section 3.2.2) could also be increased by reducing the ability of outsiders to compete effectively or by eliminating a buyer that played a role in disrupting coordination.

Finally, a non-horizontal merger could in principle increase the scope for coordination by increasing multi-market contacts.[26] As discussed in Chapter 4, Sections 2.2 and 3.2.1, if firms interact with one another across several (product or geographic) markets, this may, under certain circumstances, increase the scope for punishment of deviations from terms of coordination and thereby make coordination more effective.

Given that coordinated effects concerns are less common in the context of non-horizontal mergers, and the fact that many of the issues that would need to be considered in the event that coordinated effects were raised as a theory of harm in a non-horizontal merger setting are the same as those discussed in Chapter 4, we do not discuss these further in this chapter.

### 3.   Vertical mergers: input foreclosure

Input foreclosure refers to a situation in which a merger leads to an increase in the cost incurred by the merged entity's downstream competitors in procuring an important input. The increase in the costs of rivals to the merged entity may reduce the competitive pressure that the merged entity faces downstream. The relaxation of this constraint may allow the merged entity to (profitably) increase the price it charges final consumers.

Figure 5.2 illustrates a merger scenario in which input foreclosure might be a concern. The chart shows a merger between an upstream

---

[26] See Non-horizontal Merger Guidelines, para. 121.

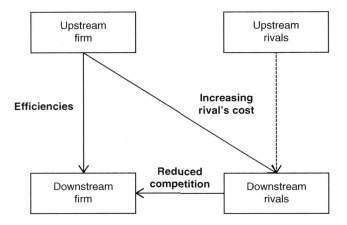

**Figure 5.2**   Illustration of input foreclosure concern

firm (for instance, a manufacturer) and a downstream firm (for instance, a distributor). As the upstream firm is, along with upstream rivals, a potential source of input supply for the downstream firm's rivals, the merged entity may potentially be able to increase those downstream rivals' costs with the goal of benefiting the downstream firm.

In discussing input foreclosure, it is common to distinguish between total and partial foreclosure. Total input foreclosure occurs when the merged entity's upstream division ceases to supply its downstream division's (actual or potential) competitors. Whilst total input foreclosure could take the form of a simple refusal to supply on the part of the merged firm, it could also be brought into effect by the upstream division switching to a new version of its product that is not compatible with the technology used by rivals to its downstream division.[27]

Partial input foreclosure occurs when the merged entity's upstream division takes some action that falls short of an outright refusal to supply, but that nonetheless results in a worsening of the terms on offer to rivals of its downstream division. In practice, there is a wide range of actions that might be taken in order to engage in partial foreclosure, depending on the nature of the markets in question. For example, partial input foreclosure could take the form of:

[27] See Non-horizontal Merger Guidelines, para. 33.

- an increase in prices charged to some or all downstream rivals;
- a reduction in the output of the input supplied to some or all downstream rivals;
- a reduction in the quality of the input supplied to some or all downstream rivals;
- a worsening of the contractual terms on which the input is supplied to some or all downstream rivals.

For the analysis of input foreclosure theories within merger assessment, the critical questions are whether the merged firm would in fact have both the ability and the incentive to increase downstream rivals' costs, and whether that would have a detrimental effect on competition. Only if all three of these conditions hold can it be concluded that 'anti-competitive foreclosure' may arise.

The remainder of Section 3 discusses the analysis of these conditions. Section 3.1 considers the ability of a merged firm to engage in input foreclosure. Section 3.2 then goes on to consider the analysis of merged firms' incentives to engage in input foreclosure. The issues relevant to the assessment of the ability and incentive to foreclose are illustrated with simple numerical examples and with a review of recent merger investigations conducted by the European Commission, including a detailed review of the Commission's decision in *Nokia/Navteq*.[28] Finally, Section 3.3 describes the circumstances under which a foreclosure strategy can be considered to give rise to consumer harm.

### 3.1 Ability to engage in input foreclosure

The first stage in any assessment of whether a merger is likely to give rise to anti-competitive input foreclosure is a consideration of whether the merged entity would have the ability to foreclose, that is the ability to increase the cost incurred by downstream rivals in the procurement of an important input.

The ability to engage in foreclosure arises only when the merged entity can affect the terms available on the market as a whole (e.g. with respect to price or quality) on which downstream rivals may purchase the input in a way that significantly impacts on the downstream rivals' costs. If in response to an increase in the price of the input the merged entity's customers could simply switch to an alternative supplier offering a

---

[28] See Case COMP/M.4942 – *Nokia/Navteq*, Commission decision of 2 July 2008.

similar product on only marginally inferior terms to those initially offered by the merged entity, then the merged entity clearly does not have the ability to materially raise the cost of its downstream rivals. Moreover, even if the merged entity can substantially increase the price its downstream rivals must pay for an input, this will not necessarily have a material impact on downstream rivals' costs of production, if the input in question represents a minor part of the downstream firms' overall costs.

These considerations give rise to a number of necessary conditions for an ability to engage in input foreclosure to exist.

First, the merged entity must have significant market power in the upstream market. If the merged entity did not have significant market power then it would not be able to affect the terms on which its downstream rivals obtain the input. The extent to which an upstream firm can be held to have the ability to affect the terms of supply to downstream firms will depend upon the degree of competition in the upstream market, which will require an analysis of competition similar to that required in analyses of unilateral effect concerns. In particular, it will normally be necessary to consider the degree of competition between the merged entity's upstream operations and those of upstream rivals. Similarly, the presence or absence of capacity constraints or expansion costs faced by rivals may affect the extent to which the merged entity would be able to raise downstream rivals' costs by increasing price or restricting access to the input.

Second, the input supplied by the merged entity must in some sense represent an important component within the downstream product.[29] If the input is not an important element of the downstream product then a worsening of the terms on which it is supplied will not materially affect competition in the downstream market. This importance might derive from the fact that the input accounts for a large percentage of the total cost of production for downstream firms. Alternatively, the input may be critical to the production process in the sense that without access to it the downstream product could not be produced (although if the input is not a significant cost factor the critical nature of the input would qualify it as meeting the 'important input' condition only in cases of total, rather than partial, foreclosure).

Both of the above conditions must hold in order for an ability to foreclose to exist. Importantly, this means that even a firm that has market power (or even dominance) in an appropriately defined market

---

[29] See Non-horizontal Merger Guidelines, para. 34.

for supply of an input to its downstream rivals does not necessarily have the ability to foreclose. For instance, an upstream firm that has the ability to substantially increase the cost at which downstream rivals procure an input that represents a relatively trivial part of their costs of production cannot be said to have an ability to foreclose.

In any assessment of a merged entity's ability to engage in input foreclosure, it is necessary to consider how third party suppliers of the upstream product will react to the foreclosure strategy. If the merged entity either refuses to supply or increases the price of an input to its rivals, this will relax a competitive constraint on remaining third party providers. This may allow third party providers to increase the price they charge independent downstream firms. The extent of this effect will depend on a number of factors.

First, if there is a low degree of product differentiation upstream between the merged entity and remaining suppliers, then this will imply (all else being equal) that the merged entity had previously imposed a strong constraint on the prices charged by third party suppliers. In this case, the removal of this constraint (as a result of total foreclosure) or the reduction of this constraint (as a result of partial foreclosure) may give rival third parties significant scope to increase their prices.

Second, the less concentrated is the supply of the input to unintegrated downstream firms amongst the remaining third party suppliers, the lower will be the scope for the merged entity's foreclosure strategy to give rise to higher prices for the unintegrated downstream firms. If remaining suppliers to the unintegrated downstream firms impose strong competitive constraints on one another, then even the removal of the upstream merged entity as an alternative input supplier (as occurs in the case of total foreclosure) will not expose downstream unintegrated firms to suppliers with a high degree of market power.

As discussed in Section 3.2 below, an important question in the overall assessment of input foreclosure is whether the merged entity can commit to the foreclosure strategy in question. While the commitment issue could be considered a factor that undermines the merged entity's ability to foreclose, we discuss this in the section on incentive to foreclose as it relates to the merged entity's incentives with respect to the supply of its downstream rivals.[30]

---

[30] Indeed, in *Nokia/Navteq*, the Commission noted the problem of commitment in the context of its discussion of the merged entity's incentive to foreclose. See Case COMP/ M.4942 – *Nokia/Navteq*, Commission decision of 2 July 2008, para. 346.

Table 5.1 *Marginal costs of suppliers*

| Supplier | Marginal cost |
|----------|---------------|
| A | 10 |
| B | 20 |
| C | 30 |

Finally, it should be noted that the ability of the merged entity to foreclose will in practice depend on a rich set of considerations that vary from case to case. These considerations relate to the counterstrategies available to downstream rivals, which may include sponsoring new entry, integrating backwards into the production of the input themselves or investing in alternative technologies that make them less reliant on the input in question.

### 3.1.1    Ability to engage in input foreclosure: an example

The following stylised example shows how an input provider's ability to foreclose depends crucially on (i) competition between third party providers of the input, and (ii) the importance of the input in the production process.

Suppose that three Firms, A, B and C, produce an input which is a component to a gadget produced by two downstream Firms, 1 and 2. Suppose that the component is extremely important in the production of the gadget and (for simplicity) represents 100% of its marginal cost of production. The component produced by A, B and C is homogeneous and none of these firms faces capacity constraints. The three upstream suppliers incur no fixed costs but differ with respect to the marginal cost they incur in the production of the component as set out in Table 5.1.

The three suppliers are engaged in a bidding contest to supply downstream Firms 1 and 2. Given the absence of capacity constraints, Firm A is able to win the business to supply both Firm 1 and Firm 2 by offering a price of 20 (as illustrated in Figure 5.3).[31] Its price is

---

[31] It should be noted that Firm B would be able to match Firm A's offer of 20 and at this price the customer would be indifferent between purchasing from Firm A or Firm B. However, we can make the assumption that Firm A wins when each offers a price of 20. Although in order to make the customer prefer its offer outright Firm A might have to offer 19.9999 (a price that Firm B cannot profitably match), we proceed with the

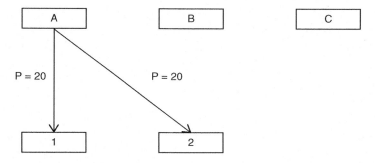

**Figure 5.3**   Illustration of pre-merger scenario

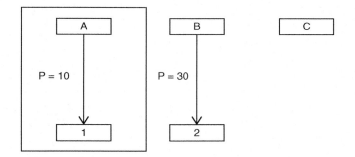

**Figure 5.4**   Illustration of post-merger scenario with input foreclosure

constrained by the presence of Firm B, which would be willing to supply at a price at least as high as 20.

Now suppose that Firm A vertically integrates with the downstream Firm 1 to create Firm A1. We refer to the upstream division of the merged entity, Firm A1, as Division A and to the downstream division as Division 1. Division A supplies Division 1 at cost but refuses to supply Firm 2. Firm B is now able to win the bidding contest to supply Firm 2 by offering a price of 30 (as illustrated in Figure 5.4).[32]

The result of Firm A1's refusal to supply Firm 2 results in the price that Firm 2 pays for the component rising from 20 to 30 (an increase of

---

convention that Firm A wins at a price of 20 because the price that makes the customer *strictly* prefer Firm A's offer is in fact 'very close' to 20.

[32] Its price is constrained by the presence of C, which would be willing to supply at a price at least as high as 30.

50%).[33] Given that the component represents 100% of its marginal cost, its overall marginal cost of supply has been increased by 50%. As such, this example suggests that Firm A1 has the ability to materially affect the terms on which Firm 2 obtains the input, and therefore the ability to engage in foreclosure.

We now consider in turn two changes to the assumptions, each of which eliminates Firm A1's ability to foreclose Firm B:

- *Firm C's marginal cost is 20 rather than 30.* If Firm C's marginal cost were the same as Firm B's at 20, the effect of Firm A1's refusal to supply Firm 2 would be to enable Firm B to win Firm 2's business only if it offered a price no higher than 20. In this case Firm A1's refusal to supply Firm 2 no longer has an effect on the price at which Firm 2 is able to obtain the input as Firm B's price is constrained by the presence of Firm C. As a result, Firm A1 no longer has the ability to foreclose Firm 2 by its refusal to supply.

- *The input is one of many components used by Firm 1 and Firm 2 and represents only 10% of the total marginal cost of producing a gadget.* If the input represented only 10% of the marginal cost that Firm 2 incurred, then even the 50% increase in the price of that particular component that results from Firm A1's refusal to supply would increase Firm 2's overall marginal cost by only 5%. In this case, even though Firm A1 can substantially increase the price at which Firm 2 purchases the input, it does not necessarily follow that it can substantially affect Firm 2's overall cost of supply.

This example highlights the importance of assessing fully the nature of competition in the upstream market (including consideration of relevant constraints on the behaviour of third parties to the merger), as well as assessing the importance of the inputs supplied by the merged entity, when considering whether an ability to foreclose exists.

### 3.1.2    Ability to engage in input foreclosure: EU case law

This section provides an overview of how the concepts discussed above have been applied in EU case law. First, we discuss the Commission's assessment of upstream market power and the importance of the input to downstream firms. We then discuss a variety of foreclosure strategies

---

[33] A similar effect on the price Firm 2 pays for components would be brought about by a partial foreclosure strategy whereby Firm A1 increased the price it charges Firm 2 for components from 20 to 30.

considered by the Commission that fall short of an outright refusal to supply. Finally, we discuss other factors that might affect the ability of the merged entity to foreclose in practice. Section 3.1.3 below discusses in detail how these concepts were applied to one particular case, *Nokia/ Navteq*.

### 3.1.2.1 Market power

As noted above, significant market power upstream is a necessary condition for the merged entity to have the ability to foreclose. In the majority of Phase II cases since 2004 in which the Commission examined vertical issues, the Commission found no concerns due to the absence of significant upstream market power.[34]

Table 5.2 shows cases since 2004 in which the Commission raised input foreclosure concerns. In almost all cases the merged entity had a leading market share upstream of more than 50%.

In those cases where the upstream market is characterised by more than one firm that is considered to have significant market power, the Commission will analyse whether important rivals are likely to either exacerbate or undermine the strategy of raising the costs of downstream rivals to the merged entity. In doing so, the Commission will consider the effectiveness of competition between leading upstream suppliers.

For example, in *Itema/Barcovision*,[35] which brought together Itema, a producer of textile machinery, and BarcoVision, which manufactured sensors and other inputs for the textiles industry, the Commission concluded that while the merged entity and its main upstream rival, Uster, each had significant market power (despite falling prices and some competition from smaller rivals), Uster would have only limited incentives to exploit its increased market power if the merged entity were to stop supplying downstream rivals. In particular, the Commission found that, 'Although it could be argued that Uster's market power could

---

[34] See, e.g., Case COMP/M.4734 – *Ineos/Kerling*, Commission decision of 30 January 2008, paras. 205–7; Case COMP/M.4781 – *Norddeutsche Affinnerie/Cumerio*, Commission decision of 23 January 2008, para. 175; Case COMP/M.4956 – *STX/Aker Yards*, Commission decision of 5 May 2008, paras. 148 and 193; Case COMP/M.4187 – *Metso/Aker Kvaerner*, Commission decision of 12 December 2006, paras. 120–3; Case COMP/M.3975 – *Cargill/Degussa Food Ingredients*, Commission decision of 29 March 2006, paras. 163–6; Case COMP/M. 3653 – *Siemens/VA Tech*, Commission decision of 13 July 2005, para. 420; Case COMP/M.3625 – *Blackstone/Acetex*, Commission decision of 13 July 2005, paras. 144 and 151; Case COMP/M.4513 – *Arjowiggins/M-real Zanders Reflex*, Commission decision of 4 June 2008, para. 514.

[35] Case COMP/M.4874 – *Itema/Barcovision*, Commission decision of 4 August 2008, paras. 47–70.

Table 5.2 *Upstream market share levels that triggered a detailed examination of input foreclosure concerns in Phase II cases 2004–2011*

| Case | Merged entity's upstream market shares[1] | Input foreclosure concerns |
|---|---|---|
| *DONG/Elsam/Energi E2*[2] | 90–100% (Gas storage)[3] | The transaction was considered to be likely to confer on DONG the ability and incentive to raise rival's costs by increasing gas storage tariffs in Denmark. |
| *E.ON/MOL*[4] | >50% (Wholesale gas)[5] 90–100% (Gas storage)[6] 70–75% (Wholesale and retail electricity)[7] | The Commission considered that the new entity would have the ability and incentive to foreclose access to wholesale gas to its competitors in the gas retail market, as well as to discriminate against its competitors in granting access to gas storage. Foreclosure concerns were also considered to arise in the wholesale and retail electricity markets. |
| *ENI/EDP/GDP*[8] | >50% (Wholesale gas)[9] | The Commission concluded that the merged entity would likely have an incentive to foreclose its downstream competitors by raising the price (or lowering the quality) of their gas supplies. |
| *Gaz de France/Suez*[10] | 80–100% (Various markets for gas[11]) | The merged entity was deemed to have greater opportunities and incentives to increase its downstream competitors' costs for ancillary services and balancing power. |
| *SFR/Télé 2 France*[12] | >50%[13] | The Commission concluded that the merged entity would have both the ability and incentive to disadvantage downstream pay TV rivals through a range of discriminatory measures notwithstanding the minimal additional share of Télé 2 for pay TV distribution (<5%). |

Table 5.2 (*cont.*)

| Case | Merged entity's upstream market shares | Input foreclosure concerns |
|---|---|---|
| *Thomson Corporation/ Reuters Group*[14] | 60–70% [15] | The merged entity was considered to have the ability and the incentive to foreclose competitors in the Aftermarket Research, Earning Estimates, Fundamentals, and TS/E markets. |
| *Syngenta/Monsanto's Sunflower Seed Business*[16] | 45–55% (Combined share of hybrids commercialised during the period 2000–2010[17]) | The merger, as initially notified, would have increased the ability and incentives for the merged entity to significantly reduce its activities of exchange and licensing of sunflower varieties in the EU, leading notably to a reduction in innovation, a foreclosure of competitors in the markets for the commercialisation of sunflower seeds and ultimately to a reduction of choice of sunflower seed hybrids for customers. |

[1] The table shows '>50%' in those instances where the EC did not provide a specific estimate but its explanations (i.e. 'clearly dominant', 'quasi-monopoly', etc.) or figures were suggesting that the share in question was well above 50%. The market share of the main rival is provided when available and relevant.

[2] Case COMP/M.3868 – *DONG/Elsam/Energi E2*, Commission decision of 14 March 2006.

[3] 'DONG's overall dominance in the Danish gas sector is partly due to its storage monopoly in Denmark': see ibid., para. 298.

[4] Case COMP/M.3696 – *E.ON/MOL*, Commission decision of 21 December 2005.

[5] 'MOL WMT is currently dominant on all the markets for the wholesale supply of gas in Hungary (gas traders and large power plants) and its dominant position is not likely to be threatened in the short to medium term': see ibid., para. 284.

[6] 'MOL Storage is the only company owning gas storage facilities in Hungary and therefore the only one able to offer gas storage services': see ibid., para. 479.

7 See ibid., paras. 629–30.

8 Case COMP/M.3440 – *ENI/EDP/GDP*, Commission decision of 9 December 2004.

9 'By allowing EDP to acquire the supplier of the main input used for the production of electricity, and hence to integrate upstream with the only supplier of natural gas in Portugal, the operation is likely to change immediately and in the near future, the conditions of competition on the wholesale market and to result in the strengthening of EDPs dominant position.' See ibid., para. 366.

10 Case COMP/M.4180 – *Gaz de France/Suez*, Commission decision of 14 November 2006.

11 See ibid., paras. 134, 139, 144, 145, 148, 157, 159 and 160.

12 Case COMP/M.4504 – *SFR/Télé 2 France*, Commission decision of 18 July 2007.

13 'Vivendi's very substantial position on the upstream and intermediate markets would enable it to boost the proprietary package of SFR/Télé 2 considerably by giving it attractive or differentiated content (channels or broadcasting rights) which is not accessible to other DSL operators or which is available to them only on terms less advantageous than those given to SFR/Télé 2': see ibid., para. 91.

14 Case COMP/M.4726 – *Thomson Corporation/Reuters Group*, Commission decision of 19 February 2008.

15 The Commission assessed shares in the four segments – Fundamentals, Estimates, Broker Research or Economic Time Series – separately but dedicated a section of the decision to the combined foreclosure concerns of the four abovementioned services. It noted that '[60–70]% of the competitors specifically redistribute Fundamentals, Estimates, Broker Research or Economic Time Series from Thomson or Reuters. It should be noted that the largest competitors, but Bloomberg, all redistribute one or several of these four specific content sets from the notifying parties.' See ibid., para. 423.

16 Case COMP/M.5675 – *Syngenta/Monsanto's Sunflower Seed Business*, Commission decision of 17 November 2010.

17 See ibid., para. 164.

increase following the merger, the prospect of further downstream integration and therefore of the loss of a sizeable, if not total, sensor sales for Uster will limit its incentive to exploit it by raising prices.[*sic*][36]

In *Nokia/Navteq*,[37] discussed in more detail in Section 3.1.3 below, the Commission considered whether competition from Tele Atlas (and Garmin) would undermine any attempt by Navteq to raise downstream rivals' costs by increasing upstream market power.[38]

**3.1.2.2   The importance of the input**   As discussed above, anticompetitive input foreclosure will be feasible only if the input in question is important for the production of the relevant product(s) downstream, either because it represents a substantial proportion of costs or is in some sense essential to the downstream activity.

If the price of the input represents only a small part of total variable costs, even a substantial price increase is unlikely to have a significant impact on the rival's ability to compete. In *Nokia/Navteq*,[39] the Commission found that the importance of the input (navigable digital maps) varied between the downstream markets to which it was supplied (see Section 3.1.3 for further discussion). In *Thomson Corporation/Reuters Group*,[40] the Commission measured the dependency of competitors on Thomson/Reuters upstream content via the share of downstream competitors' desktop workstations that carried the parties' content. In some segments, these shares were substantial, contributing to the Commission's conclusion that foreclosure strategies would be viable post-merger.

**3.1.2.3   Potential foreclosure strategies**   In most cases, the focus of the Commission has been on pricing strategies, whereby the merged entity charges higher prices to downstream rivals. Nonetheless, there is in principle a wide array of strategies beyond simple refusal to supply and increases in upstream prices that vertically integrated firms may potentially employ to undermine downstream competition. Such strategies include the following.

---

[36] Ibid., para. 69.
[37] Case COMP/M.4942 – *Nokia/Navteq*, Commission decision of 2 July 2008.
[38] A similar issue was considered in *TomTom/Tele Atlas*. See Case COMP/M.4854 – *TomTom/Tele Atlas*, Commission decision of 14 May 2008.
[39] Case COMP/M.4942 – *Nokia/Navteq*, Commission decision of 2 July 2008.
[40] Case COMP/M.4726 – *Thomson Corporation/Reuters Group*, Commission decision of 19 February 2008.

- **Sales limitation**: in *Arsenal/DSP*,[41] the Commission argued that the merged entity could increase prices and restrict the amount of benzoic acid supplied to rivals downstream, forcing downstream rivals to purchase their remaining requirements from distributors or non-EEA producers at higher prices.

- **Quality degradation**: the Commission held in *Nokia/Navteq*[42] that the merged entity would have the ability not only to increase prices but also to degrade the quality of maps supplied to downstream rivals, delay rivals' access to updated maps, or reserve innovative features for Nokia.[43] Similarly, in *SFR/Télé 2 France*[44] the Commission's market investigation suggested that the merged entity may be able to weaken the competitive pressure exerted by rivals in the downstream market for the distribution of pay TV by offering exclusive or preferential broadcasting rights to its own downstream channels.[45] In *Nokia/Navteq* the Commission also argued that the merged entity may engage in other tactics, such as delaying responses to requests for price quotations or important technical information.[46] This approach demonstrates that quality degradation need not apply to the product itself but may occur in respect of related products or services such as after-sales services, add-ons, or optional features.

**3.1.2.4  Other factors that may affect the ability to foreclose**  In addition to considerations relating to the upstream firm's market power and the importance of the input, there may be other case-specific factors affecting an integrated firm's ability to pursue foreclosure strategies post-merger.

The Commission has accepted in several cases that long-term contractual obligations may prevent a merged firm from raising prices or modifying other terms and conditions at least within the next few years following the merger. Whilst such inability may not be permanent, it may provide rivals with sufficient time to find or develop alternative sources

---

[41] Case COMP/M.5153 – *Arsenal/DSP*, Commission decision of 9 January 2009, para. 283.
[42] Case COMP/M.4942 – *Nokia/Navteq*, Commission decision of 2 July 2008.
[43] Ibid., para. 264.
[44] Case COMP/M.4504 – *SFR/Télé 2 France*, Commission decision of 18 July 2007.
[45] Ibid., para. 92.
[46] Case COMP/M.4942 – *Nokia/Navteq*, Commission decision of 2 July 2008; see also Case COMP/M.4403 – *Thales/Finmeccanica/Alcatel Alenia Space & Telespazio*, Commission decision of 4 April 2007, para. 256, where the Commission discussed several delaying tactics.

of supply. The Commission has noted the use of long-term contracts as a potential impediment to input foreclosure on several occasions. For instance, in *TomTom/Tele Atlas*,[47] the Commission noted: 'Tele Atlas's ability to foreclose its downstream competitors is limited by the long term contract that Garmin has concluded with NAVTEQ, which protects Garmin against price increases and guarantees yearly price decreases at least until 2015.'[48]

Nevertheless, the existence of such contracts is typically not regarded by the Commission as sufficient in and of itself to allay foreclosure concerns.[49]

Conversely, the existence of short-term contracts or contracts that are close to renewal may be regarded as a factor potentially increasing an integrated firm's ability to foreclose. In *Thomson Corporation/Reuters Group*[50] the Commission held that: 'contracts generally cover a short period ... and most renegotiations are already under way ... Therefore, the notifying parties will have the ability to foreclose competitors in this market.'[51]

A vertically integrated firm may be unable to reduce supply where it is already economically or legally committed to a certain level of capacity utilisation, or where the products in question are already in development. In *Thales/Finmeccanica/Alcatel Alenia Space & Telespazio*,[52] the Commission's analysis of input foreclosure focused on the pre-award stage of bidding competitions for satellite and satellite subsystems since '[p]ost award input foreclosure strategies (essentially delays in the implementation of TWT supply agreements) appear less likely, as they would be more easily detectable (in particular, customers can require a contractual right to send resident experts to follow the production process at their supplier) and would trigger pre-defined penalty payments.'[53]

---

[47] Case COMP/M.4854 – *TomTom/Tele Atlas*, Commission decision of 14 May 2008.
[48] Ibid., para. 208.
[49] See, for instance, Case COMP/M.5153 – *Arsenal/DSP*, Commission decision of 9 January 2009, paras. 286–8, or Case COMP/M.4942 – *Nokia/Navteq*, Commission decision of 2 July 2008, para. 329.
[50] Case COMP/M.4726 – *Thomson Corporation/Reuters Group*, Commission decision of 19 February 2008.
[51] Ibid., para. 372.
[52] Case COMP/M.4403 – *Thales/Finmeccanica/Alcatel Alenia Space & Telespazio*, Commission decision of 4 April 2007.
[53] Ibid., para. 255.

Apart from these contractual obligations towards customers, a merged entity's ability to engage in foreclosure strategies may be undermined by its own suppliers or its JV partners. In *Thomson Corporation/Reuters Group*,[54] the parties submitted that broker companies that provide the necessary contents for some of the merged entity's services would not agree to any foreclosure strategy that would reduce their output or exposure.[55] The Commission rejected this argument, however, as it was unclear whether broker companies had the means and incentives to oppose a foreclosure strategy.

Finally, regulatory intervention can also play an important role and affect the ability of the merged entity to engage in input foreclosure. In *E.ON/MOL*,[56] the Commission considered the pricing conditions imposed by energy regulators to be an important factor determining the ability of the merged entity to engage in input foreclosure practices. The Commission took into consideration expected changes in the regulatory framework (regulated prices were expected to be suppressed in July 2007), and concluded that these would ease the implementation of a foreclosure strategy by the merged entity.[57]

### 3.1.3   Case study: *Nokia/Navteq* – assessment of ability to engage in input foreclosure

During the *Nokia/Navteq*[58] merger investigation, the Commission undertook a detailed assessment of whether the merged entity might have the ability to engage in input foreclosure. Navteq supplied digital maps that are used in Personal Navigation Devices (PNDs), particularly mobile phone handsets that offer navigation services. The Commission considered whether the merged entity would be able to foreclose firms active in a number of downstream markets either by increasing the price and/or reducing the quality of maps supplied to rival mobile phone handset manufacturers.[59]

The Commission considered three conditions that are necessary for the merged entity to have the ability to engage in foreclosure.

---

[54] Case COMP/M.4726 – *Thomson Corporation/Reuters Group*, Commission decision of 19 February 2008.
[55] Ibid., paras. 224–5.
[56] Case COMP/M.3696 – *E.ON/MOL*, Commission decision of 21 December 2005.
[57] Ibid., para. 363.
[58] Case COMP/M.4942 – *Nokia/Navteq*, Commission decision of 2 July 2008.
[59] Ibid., para. 270.

First, the Commission considered whether the merged entity would have market power in the upstream market for navigable digital maps. In reaching its view that the merged entity did indeed have market power, the Commission highlighted structural features of the market for navigable digital maps. Specifically, it noted that Navteq had a market share of around 50% and faced only one competitor, Tele Atlas, whose navigable digital map databases had a similar coverage and quality level.[60] The Commission also noted the high gross margins earned by Navteq. Whilst accepting that high gross margins do not necessarily indicate prices in excess of the competitive level in an industry with high fixed costs and low marginal costs, the Commission stated that Navteq's 'ability to price well above marginal cost is indicative of market power.'[61]

Furthermore, it pointed out that non-navigable digital map databases would be only imperfectly substitutable to navigable digital map databases for downstream competitors, and these services would be imperfect substitutes to navigation services based on navigable maps.[62]

Second, the Commission considered the importance of the input for downstream competitors, noting that, irrespective of its share of downstream cost, an input may be important on account of being a critical component. The Commission found that the importance of the input varied across the downstream markets to which navigable digital maps were provided and considered each in turn.

Regarding the market for mobile handsets, the Commission found that digital maps accounted for a relatively small share (0–15%) of the total costs of producing mobile handsets with navigation functionality, but that, where navigation services were provided on a particular handset, digital maps constituted a critical component.[63] Given that navigation services are only one feature among others that determine a customer's choice of handset (such as the handset's music or video player), the Commission regarded it as unclear whether navigable digital map databases represented a critical input in the market for mobile handsets. As noted in our example above, if an input represents only 10% of downstream firms' production costs then even a 50% increase in the price of that input would only increase downstream costs by 5%.

Regarding the market for navigation applications on mobile handsets, the Commission found that digital maps accounted for a significant share of the costs of navigation software providers (whether these were selling

---

[60] Case COMP/M.4942 – *Nokia/Navteq*, Commission decision of 2 July 2008, para. 273.
[61] Ibid., para. 275.     [62] Ibid., para. 295.     [63] Ibid., para. 285.

to mobile network operators or commercialising them directly) and that digital maps were a critical input.[64]

Third, the Commission considered whether timely and effective counterstrategies would be available to downstream rivals.[65]

The first such counterstrategy that the Commission considered was the scope for entry in the upstream market for provision of navigable digital map databases. The Commission considered that entry was unlikely to occur and dismissed this as a potential constraint on the merged entity's ability to foreclose.[66]

The Commission also considered the role of intermediaries that hold map database and navigation software licences from Tele Atlas or Navteq to constrain the merged entity's ability to foreclose.[67] Garmin, a PND manufacturer and software developer, had concluded a long-term contract with Navteq (until 2015 with the option for Garmin to extend until 2019). Under the terms of its contract, Garmin could embed Navteq maps in its own PNDs or integrate them into navigation software that it could sell to any type of user, including for navigation services on mobile handsets.[68] The Commission concluded that Garmin could represent, to a certain extent, a credible supplier of navigable digital map databases for handset manufacturers or mobile network operators (at least in the short term).[69] In terms of the example illustrated in Section 3.1.1 above, Garmin could be considered to play a similar role to Firm C. Correspondingly, if Garmin's offer of navigation software were sufficiently attractive to rival mobile handset manufacturers, this could undermine the ability of Tele Atlas to exert market power even if Navteq had engaged in a strategy of total foreclosure.

Furthermore, the Commission assessed the degree of buyer power enjoyed by mobile network operators, and found that whilst they exerted a degree of power on Nokia, it was unclear whether they would be able to counter any strategy of Navteq aimed at foreclosing Nokia's downstream competitors.[70]

Ultimately, the Commission's findings regarding the incentive to foreclose (discussed in Section 3.2.3) enabled it to leave open its assessment

---

[64] Ibid., para. 290.

[65] In practice, it will be apparent that the factors considered by the Commission under the heading of counterstrategies could perhaps be considered within the assessment of Navteq's upstream market power.

[66] Case COMP/M.4942 – *Nokia/Navteq*, Commission decision of 2 July 2008, para. 300.

[67] Ibid., para. 306.     [68] Ibid., para. 306.     [69] Ibid., para. 315.     [70] Ibid., para. 325.

of whether the merged entity would have the ability to foreclose. In particular, the Commission concluded that it was unclear whether the merged entity would have the ability to engage in input foreclosure given the uncertainty over whether navigable digital map databases are a critical input in the market for handsets and the potential for timely and effective counterstrategies (particularly relating to the role that Garmin might play).[71]

Also left open in the Commission's assessment is an important question regarding whether the merged entity could credibly commit to a strategy of foreclosure.[72] The parties argued that Navteq could not commit to foreclose Nokia's downstream competitors since Navteq would have an incentive to undercut Tele Atlas slightly to make a profitable sale without impacting its downstream sales. Since Tele Atlas would be aware of this possibility, and it could do nothing to prevent it from occurring, it would refrain from raising its price in the first place.[73] This commitment problem is examined in the next subsection as part of our discussion of the assessment of the incentive to engage in input foreclosure.

### 3.2   Incentive to engage in input foreclosure

The preceding subsection established the factors that will determine whether a vertically integrated firm will have the ability to implement a strategy of anti-competitive foreclosure against unintegrated downstream rivals. In this subsection we consider under what conditions, even where that ability exists, an integrated firm will have an incentive to pursue such a strategy.

A vertical merger alters the incentives of the upstream division because it will now take account of the impact of its pricing decisions on its downstream division. This may give rise in some circumstances to an incentive to engage in input foreclosure to benefit the merged entity's downstream division even if this comes at some cost to the upstream division. In short, the incentive to engage in input foreclosure depends on the effect of the hypothesised foreclosure strategy on the profits of the merged entity as a whole.

An assessment of a firm's incentive to foreclose therefore requires a separate evaluation of the negative effect on profits of the upstream

---

[71] Case COMP/M.4942 – *Nokia/Navteq*, Commission decision of 2 July 2008, para. 329.
[72] Ibid., para. 271.          [73] Ibid., para. 299.

division of the firm and the positive effect on profits of the downstream division resulting from the foreclosure strategy.[74]

The negative effect on upstream profits results from the fact that input foreclosure involves the sacrifice of sales to downstream rivals.[75] The positive effect on downstream profits arises indirectly as a result of the impact of foreclosure on the price charged by downstream rivals. To the extent that downstream rivals increase their prices, this may either cause some sales to divert to the downstream division of the merged firm or allow it to raise the price it charges final consumers (or some combination of the two).

A number of interrelated factors determine whether the positive effect on downstream profits will outweigh the negative effect on upstream profits leading to an incentive to foreclose.

First, this balance depends on the relative sizes of the margin earned on forgone upstream sales and the margin earned on incremental downstream sales. If the margin on upstream sales is relatively high, this will imply that the opportunity cost of forgoing upstream sales is relatively high. A larger increase in downstream sales will therefore be required to compensate for the lost upstream sales in order for the foreclosure strategy to be incrementally profitable. Conversely, if the margin on downstream sales is relatively high, this will imply that fewer incremental downstream sales are required to justify any sacrifice of upstream sales. In the example set out in Section 3.2.1 below we consider further how relative margins earned on upstream and downstream sales affect the *critical* increase in demand for the downstream division required to make a foreclosure strategy incrementally profitable.

Second, for any given ratio of upstream margin to downstream margin, the incentive to engage in input foreclosure will depend on the increase in demand it delivers to the downstream division. This will depend on the effect of the foreclosure strategy on the costs of

---

[74] See EC Non-horizontal Merger Guidelines, para. 40: 'Essentially, the merged entity faces a trade-off between the profit lost in the upstream market due to a reduction of input sales to (actual or potential) rivals and the profit gain, in the short or longer term, from expanding sales downstream or, as the case may be, being able to raise prices to consumers.'

[75] In this case of total foreclosure all sales to unintegrated rivals are lost. In the case of partial foreclosure, fewer sales are made to unintegrated rivals at a higher price. However, assuming that the upstream firm was profit-maximising pre-merger, the total profits of the upstream division (viewed in isolation) will necessarily be lower if it increases its price as part of a partial foreclosure strategy.

downstream rivals (which in turn depends on the factors affecting the ability to foreclose, discussed in Section 3.1 above, such as the importance of the input); the extent to which any cost increase is passed on to consumers by downstream rivals in the form of higher prices; and the extent to which those downstream consumers react by substituting to the products of the merged entity's downstream division (i.e. the extent to which the merged entity's products are substitutable for those of the firms that are the subject of the foreclosure strategy).[76] In the example below we consider further how these considerations are taken into account in assessing the *actual* increase in downstream demand that a merged entity could expect to result from input foreclosure.

In principle, both the *critical* increase in downstream demand required to make a foreclosure strategy profitable and the *actual* increase in demand resulting from that strategy will also depend on (i) any increase in downstream margins due to the relaxation of the constraint imposed by downstream competitors or (ii) any increase in downstream margins due to efficiencies. We consider how these factors affect the analysis of the incentive to foreclose in the example below.

Finally, an important issue that will be considered below is whether the merged entity can credibly commit to a strategy of foreclosure.

### 3.2.1  Incentive to engage in input foreclosure: an example

In Section 3.1.1 we considered a stylised example in which a merger between an upstream component producer (Firm A) and a downstream gadget producer (Firm 1) gave rise to an *ability* on the part of the merged entity (Firm A1) to engage in total foreclosure. In what follows, we use the same illustrative example to examine the *incentive* the merged entity may have to engage in such a strategy.

We assume again that three Firms, A, B and C, produce an input that is a component to a gadget produced by two downstream Firms, 1 and 2, and that the component represents 100% of the gadget's marginal cost of production.[77] As before, the three upstream suppliers incur no fixed costs but differ with respect to the marginal cost they incur in the production of the component as set out in Table 5.1 in Section 3.1.1 above.

---

[76] The profitability of this strategy is also contingent on the downstream division having the necessary spare capacity to meet any increase in demand the foreclosure strategy generates.

[77] We refer to 'Firm A' and 'Firm 1' when they are unintegrated. Post-merger these entities are referred to as 'Division A' and 'Division 1' of the merged entity 'Firm A1'.

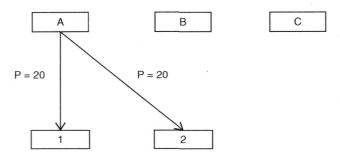

**Figure 5.5**   Illustration of pre-merger scenario

We now assume that the gadgets produced by downstream firms are differentiated, so that even if Firm 2's price is higher than Firm 1's price, some consumers may prefer Firm 2's gadget.

As in our previous example, pre-merger Firm A is able to win the business to supply both Firm 1 and Firm 2 by offering a price of 20. (See Figure 5.5.)[78]

Suppose that, at this price, Firm A sells 100 units to Firm 1 and 100 units to Firm 2. Further assume that Firm 1 and Firm 2 each sell 100 gadgets at a unit price of 40.

It is now possible to obtain the pre-merger profits of both Firm A and Firm 1. Firm A sells a total of 200 units and earns a margin of 10 on each unit (the price of 20 less its marginal cost of 10) for a total profit of 2,000. Firm 1 sells a total of 100 units and earns a margin of 20 on each unit (the price of 40 less its marginal cost of 20) for a total profit of 2,000.

We now consider the post-merger profits of both Division A and Division 1 on the assumption that the merged entity continues to supply Firm 2 at a price of 20 but now supplies Division 1 at a price of 10 (equal to its marginal cost). This situation is illustrated in Figure 5.6.

We further assume that both Division 1 and Firm 2 maintain their price of gadgets at 40.[79] Division A now sells 100 units to Firm 2 at a

---

[78]  Its price is constrained by the presence of B, which would be willing to supply at a price at least as high as 20. As explained above, we assume that Firm A wins the business at a price of 20 even though it has to offer a price an arbitrarily small amount below 20 in order to make its offer strictly preferred to Firm B's offer.

[79]  It is important to note that, in line with the discussion of the pro-competitive effect of vertical mergers at Section 2.1 above, the effect of the reduction in Division 1's marginal cost will be to provide an incentive to reduce the price of gadgets and sell a greater volume but we abstract away from this effect at this stage. The effect of taking this into account is discussed below.

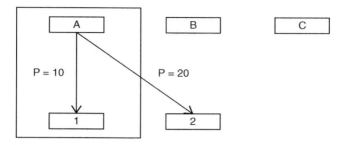

**Figure 5.6** Illustration of post-merger scenario without input foreclosure

margin of 10 per unit and 100 units to its downstream Division 1 at zero margin for a total profit of 1,000. Division 1 now sells 100 units and earns a margin of 30 on each unit (the price of 40 less its marginal cost of 10) for a total profit of 3,000. The combined profit of the merged entity Firm A1 is therefore equal to 4,000.[80]

Having established the profit that the merged entity can earn *without* foreclosure, we can now consider the merged entity's profit if it were to engage in foreclosure. To the extent that the profits for the merged entity from engaging in foreclosure are greater than 4,000, the merged entity would have an incentive to foreclose.

First note that the profits of Division A as a result of engaging in total foreclosure drop to zero. It makes no sales to Firm 2 and makes sales to Division 1 at marginal cost. The profits earned by Division 1 are less straightforward to calculate.

As noted in Section 3.1.1, the strategy of total foreclosure will increase Firm 2's cost from 20 to 30, the price at which it is supplied by Firm B.[81]

The increase in Firm 2's marginal cost will cause it to increase the price it charges consumers for gadgets by some amount. Assuming (for the time being) that division 1's price for gadgets remains at 40, the increase in Firm 2's price will cause some of its consumers to purchase from Division 1 instead. This situation is illustrated in Figure 5.7.

---

[80] Note that this is equal to the combined pre-merger profit of Firm A and Firm 1; the reduction in the component price to 10 is offset by resultant wider margins in the sale of gadgets, leaving overall profitability, absent foreclosure, unchanged.

[81] Firm B is now able to win the bidding contest to supply Firm 2 by offering a price of 30. Its price is constrained by the presence of Firm C, which would be willing to supply at a price at least as high as 30.

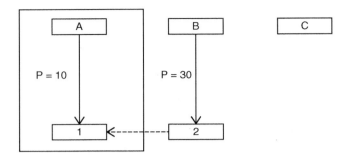

**Figure 5.7**   Illustration of post-merger scenario with input foreclosure

We now consider the critical increase in Division 1's demand required to ensure that the profits of Firm A1 are at least as high as 4,000, the merged entity's profit supposing that it does not engage in foreclosure. Recall that the margin earned on each sale by Division 1 is 30. In order to generate profits of 4,000, its sales will need to be at least as high as 134 units (since if its sales were only 133 units, its profits would be equal to 3,990 or 133 * 30). The *critical* increase in Division 1's sales is therefore equal to 34 units.[82] In short, the loss of upstream profits of 1,000 requires the downstream firm to increase sales by 34 units given its margin of 30 (since 34 * 30 = 1,020).

It can be seen that the critical increase in Division 1's sales depends on the ratio of the margin earned by Division A on forgone component sales to the margin earned by Division 1 on incremental gadget sales. Division A would have earned a margin of 10 on each forgone component sale to Firm 2 but earns a margin of 30 on each incremental gadget sale made by Division 1. Therefore the overall effect on the merged entity's profits is positive if, for each incremental gadget sale, the upstream division has had to forgo no more than 3 component sales. Given that in this example total foreclosure implies the loss of 100 component sales, the strategy is profitable so long as more than 33 (≈ 100 component sales * 10 upstream margin/30 downstream margin) incremental gadget sales are made. Had the margin on the forgone component sales been higher, the critical increase in gadget sales required to make the foreclosure strategy profitable would also have been higher.

---

[82] If it were possible to produce a fraction of a gadget, it could generate profits of exactly 4,000 by selling 33 and one-third of a gadget.

Whether the total foreclosure strategy is incrementally profitable depends on whether the actual increase in Division 1's sales is greater than this critical value. This will depend on:

- the extent to which the increase in Firm 2's marginal cost of 20 to 30 is passed on to end-consumers of gadgets; and
- the extent to which consumers of gadgets faced with an increase in Firm 2's price switch to gadgets supplied by Firm 1 (i.e. the degree of substitutability between Firm 1's and Firm 2's gadgets).

The higher the proportion of the component cost increase that is passed on to consumers in the form of higher gadget prices, the lower the substitutability between the downstream firms' gadgets required for the actual increase in Division 1's demand to exceed the critical amount.

Conversely, the higher the substitutability between the downstream products, the lower the proportion of the cost increase that is passed on by Firm 2 required for the actual demand increase to exceed the critical demand increase.[83]

In Section 3.1.1 we noted that the extent to which Firm 2's cost is increased by the total foreclosure strategy would depend on the increase in the component price faced by Firm 2 and the importance of the component in the overall marginal cost of producing gadgets. Specifically, the greater the competitive constraint imposed by Firm C on Firm B's price after Division A's refusal to supply, the lower will be the price increase brought about by the foreclosure strategy. The lower the proportion of the marginal cost represented by the component, the lower will be the effect on marginal cost of any given price increase. If it were the case that foreclosure would only increase the marginal cost of Firm 2 from 20 to 25 (rather than to 30) then this would increase either the substitutability between the downstream products or the proportion of the cost increase passed on (or some combination of the two) required in order for the actual increase in Division 1's demand to exceed the critical increase.

**3.2.1.1  Downstream price increases**  So far we have assumed that Division 1's gadget price remains constant at 40 post-merger. The benefit from foreclosure therefore derives purely from an increase in the volume

---

[83] It should be noted that these factors are themselves interrelated since the extent to which an increase in Firm 2's costs will lead it to increase price will partly depend on the extent to which any price increase will cause it to lose sales to Firm A1.

of gadgets sold by Division 1. However, any increase in the price of Firm 2's gadgets brought about by the foreclosure strategy may in fact give rise to an incentive for Firm 1 to increase its price due to the relaxation of the competitive constraint imposed by Firm 2. To the extent that Division 1 is able to increase its margin on gadget sales, this will reduce the critical increase in downstream demand required to make the foreclosure strategy profitable.

For example, suppose that due to the relaxation of the constraint imposed by Firm 2 the merged entity finds it profitable to set a price of 50 for gadgets and hence earns a margin per sale of 40. Given that Division A would have earned a margin of 10 on each forgone component sale, the loss in profits for the upstream division is 1,000. However, even if Division 1 gains no incremental sales, the increase in downstream profits resulting from the higher margin is 1,000. This is because the margin is increased by 10 (from 30 to 40) across 100 unit sales resulting in an increase in profit of 1,000, which just offsets the profits lost upstream as a result of the foreclosure strategy. This means that if the foreclosure strategy increases the price from 40 to 50, the critical increase in demand required to make the foreclosure strategy profitable is zero.

Importantly, while an increase in Division 1's gadget price will reduce the critical increase in demand required to render foreclosure profitable, any such increase will also reduce the actual increase in demand observed compared to a situation in which it held its price constant. This is because some consumers of Firm 2's gadget that might otherwise have switched following Firm 2's price increase may in the face of higher prices for the merged entity's gadgets remain with Firm 2 rather than switching.

It should be noted that the result that the critical increase in demand is zero in this example, arises because we have supposed that the merged entity's downstream price increases substantially (by 25%). This demonstrates the principle that the critical increase in downstream demand required to make foreclosure profitable depends on downstream price increases. However, as noted below, the assessment of the critical increase in demand will often necessarily be carried out on the basis of pre-merger margins, in which case the critical increase is necessarily greater than zero.

**3.2.1.2   Efficiencies**   So far this example has not considered the role of efficiencies. Recall that pre-merger, Firm 1 faced a component cost of 20 and sold gadgets for 40. The merger reduces the (internal) component cost faced by Division 1 to 10 (Division A's marginal cost of supply). Division 1 will use this input cost reduction in part to reduce its downstream gadget price and in part to increase its margins. This will have two effects, each of which may serve to increase the incentive to foreclose: first, the increase in downstream margins will reduce the *critical* increase in demand required for foreclosure to be profitable (fewer gadget sales are now required to compensate for a given loss of component sales); and, second, Division 1's lower price will raise the *actual* increase in demand observed via switching from Firm 2.

### 3.2.1.3 Use of pre-merger margin information

Attempting to take account of how an input foreclosure strategy and efficiencies may interact to affect the post-merger downstream margin greatly complicates any assessment of both the critical and actual increase in the downstream unit's demand.

As was the case in *Nokia/Navteq*,[84] which is discussed further at Section 3.2.3 below, it is typically necessary to rely on pre-merger margin information to assess the critical increase in the downstream unit's demand and to assume the downstream unit will hold prices constant when assessing the actual increase in demand it would enjoy.

Whilst an assumption that margins remain the same in the downstream market post-merger greatly simplifies the assessment of both the critical and actual increase in demand, and therefore the assessment of the overall incentive to foreclose, this assumption comes with a cost. This approach abstracts from the question that is ultimately of interest for the competitive assessment: what effect will foreclosure have on the downstream price for gadgets that consumers ultimately pay? Nonetheless, by making this assumption, it is often possible to gain significant insights into the profitability of a hypothesised foreclosure strategy for the purpose of assessing a firm's incentive to engage in foreclosure. Indeed, consideration of pre-merger margins in the upstream and downstream markets along with estimates of the degree of switching between the downstream firms that would be induced by a change in relative prices may be sufficient to rule out the incentive to foreclose in many cases.[85] For example, if downstream margins are very low compared to upstream

---

[84] Case COMP/M.4942 – *Nokia/Navteq*, Commission decision of 2 July 2008.
[85] See Chapter 3 for a discussion of the techniques for assessing substitutability, which include the use of survey analysis, customer switching analysis and econometric estimation of demand.

margins, this may give significant comfort that it is not worth sacrificing valuable upstream sales in the hope of gaining incremental downstream sales given a reasonable upper bound estimate of the substitutability of the downstream products. In that case, it might be concluded that foreclosure would not be profitable even if it were successful in raising downstream prices to some extent.

As noted above, the relative size of upstream and downstream margins can provide insights into the critical increase in downstream demand for the merged firm that is required to make input foreclosure profitable. This needs to be compared to some measure of the actual increase in demand that would result from input foreclosure in order to determine whether foreclosure would be profitable. It is generally not possible to conclude on the profitability of input foreclosure solely by comparing upstream and downstream margins. Indeed, if downstream firms produce goods that are undifferentiated, this may imply that downstream margins are relatively low (due to intense competition) and therefore that the critical increase in downstream demand is relatively high. However, with limited differentiation amongst downstream products consumers are likely to be more sensitive to small increases in rivals' prices brought about by the foreclosure strategy, implying that the actual increase in demand from a given foreclosure strategy would also be relatively high. This implies that there is no clear-cut relationship between the relative sizes of upstream and downstream margins and the incentive of a merged firm to engage in input foreclosure.[86]

### 3.2.1.4 The commitment problem
The stylised example set out above has considered the incentives of a vertically integrated firm to raise rivals' costs via a strategy of total foreclosure. However, we have not yet considered an important question about the incentive of a firm to engage in total foreclosure. Suppose that we assume as before that downstream margins will be unchanged by the merger (i.e. will remain at 30 per unit), giving rise to a critical increase in demand for Division 1 of 34 units. Suppose further that survey evidence of a high degree of substitutability between Firm 1's and Firm 2's gadgets leads to the

---

[86] See R. Inderst and T. Valletti, 'Incentives for Input Foreclosure' (2011) 55(6) *European Economic Review* 820–31. This paper considers the incentives for a vertically integrated firm to foreclose downstream rivals and notes that pre-merger margins on the up- and downstream markets are not necessarily good predictors of the incentives for subsequent (i.e. post-merger) foreclosure.

conclusion that the actual increase in demand resulting from total fore-closure is likely to exceed 34 units (e.g. most respondents state that even a small increase in the price of Firm 2's gadgets would cause them to switch to Division 1). We would then conclude that total foreclosure leads to higher profits than the benchmark case in which there is no foreclosure. However, can the merged entity credibly commit not to supply Firm 2?

Consider that in this example A's refusal to supply implies that Firm 2 must accept Firm B's price of 30 (the price that just keeps Firm C from being able to profitably undercut Firm B). However, if Firm B offers a price of 30 to Firm 2, Firm A has an incentive to undercut this price by offering a price of 29. To see why this is the case, note that undercutting Firm B by offering to supply Firm 2 at a price of 29 only marginally undermines the total foreclosure strategy. In effect, relative to a situation in which it faces total foreclosure, Firm 2's input price has fallen from 30 to 29. This will only have a 'small' impact on the price Firm 2 charges downstream and thus only a 'small' impact on the effectiveness of the merged entity's foreclosure strategy in terms of generating incremental downstream profits for Division 1. However, undercutting Firm B in this way generates a 'large' increase in profits for Division A, equal to the margin it earns per component sale ($19 = 29-10$) multiplied by the number of units that Firm 2 is willing to buy at the price of 29.[87] On this basis, it follows that the total foreclosure strategy does not constitute a Nash Equilibrium (see Chapter 3, Section 2 for an explanation of Nash Equilibrium) as there exists a profitable deviation from the strategy of refusing to supply Firm 2 in the form of marginally undercutting Firm B's price.

However, Division A securing the business of Firm 2 at a price of 29 is also not an equilibrium. This is because Firm B will have an incentive to undercut Division A by offering Firm 2 a price of 28 (since this would result in it making sales at a price above its marginal cost). This process of undercutting will continue until Firm A is forced to supply Firm 2 at a price of 20, equal to Firm B's marginal cost, in order to prevent Firm B from supplying Firm 2. This is the pre-merger price set by Firm A. Consequently, this logic implies that, unless Firm A can find some way of credibly committing not to supply Firm 2, it will not be able to engage in foreclosure.[88]

---

[87] Note that this quantity will be lower than 100, the quantity that it purchased when the price was 20.

[88] The seminal paper by Ordover, Saloner and Salop that investigated the incentive for a merged entity to foreclose in a theoretical setting similar to our example was criticised in

One response to this argument is that a forward-looking merged entity
will realise that entering into the price competition of the kind discussed
above will lower the unintegrated downstream firm's input price, which,
in turn, will lead to lower downstream prices.[89] However, this justifica-
tion involves a conjecture that considerations that may apply in a
dynamic framework are equivalent to the commitment assumption in
the static framework.[90]

One way in which Division A may be able to commit not to supply
Firm 2 is to take some action that makes its component incompatible
with the gadget produced by Firm 2.[91] In order to be effective, this
strategy requires that the compatibility decision taken by the merged
entity is not easily reversible (i.e. the cost of re-establishing compatibility
between Division A's components and Firm 2's gadgets is reasonably
large).

The economic literature highlights that the ability of the merged entity
to be able to commit not to supply its unintegrated downstream rivals, or
to supply only at a certain price, is an important consideration for
understanding how input foreclosure can arise.

### 3.2.2   Incentive to engage in input foreclosure: EU case law

The Commission has conducted a detailed examination of the merged
entity's incentives to engage in input foreclosure strategies in a number of
cases. This examination is usually based on economic evidence pertain-
ing to the relevant factors that determine the trade-off between the
profits lost in the upstream market(s) and the potential profits gained

---

a number of subsequent papers on the grounds that the model's results are driven by the
assumption that the merged entity would be able to commit not to supply. See J. Ordover,
G. Saloner and S. C. Salop, 'Equilibrium Vertical Foreclosure' (1990) 80 *American
Economic Review* 127–42. For a critique regarding commitment, see D. Reiffen, 'Equilib-
rium Vertical Foreclosure, Comment' (1992) 82 *American Economic Review* 694–7 and
O. Hart and J. Tirole, 'Vertical Integration and Market Foreclosure', Brookings Papers on
Economic Activity: Microeconomics (1990), 205–86. For discussion, see J. Church, 'The
Impact of Vertical and Conglomerate Mergers on Competition' (Report for the Director-
ate General for Competition, Directorate B Merger Task Force, European Commission,
2004).

[89] See J. Ordover, G. Saloner and S. C. Salop, 'Equilibrium Vertical Foreclosure, "Reply"'
(1992) 82 *American Economic Review* 693–704.

[90] See D. Reiffen and M. Vita, 'Comment: Is There New Thinking on Vertical Mergers?'
(1995) 63 *Antitrust Law Journal* 917–41.

[91] See J. Church and N. Gandal, 'Systems Competition, Vertical Merger and Foreclosure'
(2000) 9 *Journal of Economics Management and Strategy* 25–51.

in the downstream market(s). In *Nokia/Navteq*[92] (see Section 3.2.3, below) and *TomTom/Tele Atlas*,[93] the Commission sought to quantify the overall effect in a more comprehensive manner using econometric analysis to assess the actual diversion of demand downstream that could be expected to occur as a result of foreclosure.

The Commission typically assesses the average gross margins (i.e. prices minus variable costs) of the relevant products upstream and downstream. If gross margins are considerably higher for upstream products than for downstream products, any given loss of sales upstream will need to be compensated by a greater increase in volumes downstream.

For example, in *Itema/Barcovision*,[94] the Commission noted, 'The percentage margins are relatively small downstream and much higher upstream, which, all other things being equal, makes any extra revenues in the downstream winders market less likely to compensate for upstream losses than in a situation where downstream margins are high and upstream margins are small.'[95]

Similarly, in *Thales/Finmeccanica/Alcatel Alenia Space & Telespazio*,[96] the Commission considered the merging parties' margins at each level of the supply chain. The Commission found that margins for satellites (downstream) were significantly lower than margins for satellite components (upstream). The main source of this difference was that the downstream market was particularly competitive. This contributed to the conclusion that the incentives of the merged entity to forgo units sold upstream in order to win units sold downstream would be very limited.[97]

As noted above, given information on pre-merger margins it is in principle possible to calculate the critical increase in downstream sales needed to recoup the profit loss upstream, under the assumption that pre-merger margins are a good proxy for post-merger margins. Such a calculation was performed in *Arsenal/DSP*,[98] where the Commission noted:

---

[92] Case COMP/M.4942 – *Nokia/Navteq*, Commission decision of 2 July 2008.
[93] Case COMP/M.4854 – *TomTom/Tele Atlas*, Commission decision of 14 May 2008.
[94] Case COMP/M.4874 – *Itema/Barcovision*, Commission decision of 4 August 2008.
[95] Ibid., para. 74.
[96] Case COMP/M.4403 – *Thales/Finmeccanica/Alcatel Alenia Space & Telespazio*, Commission decision of 4 April 2007.
[97] Ibid., para. 267.
[98] Case COMP/M.5153 – *Arsenal/DSP*, Commission decision of 9 January 2009.

As the gross margin obtained by Velsicol/DSP in selling one tonne of di-benzoate plasticizer is approximately more than the gross margin it obtains when selling the quantity of benzoic acid necessary to make one tonne of di-benzoate plasticizers, the foreclosure strategy would be profitable if Velsicol/DSP could capture more than [50–60]% of the sales lost by a di-benzoate competitor. In other words, the new entity could afford to lose all sales of benzoic acid to a particular downstream competitor producing di-benzoate plasticizers, if it captures more than [50–60]% of the sales of di-benzoate plasticizers of this competitor. On the contrary, if Velsicol/DSP cannot capture more than [50–60]% of the sales of this competitor, it is unlikely that the foreclosure strategy would be profitable.[99]

Intuitively, the merged entity will find it more costly to engage in input foreclosure where it is unable to target the foreclosure strategy at competing products downstream. In *Arsenal/DSP*, one rival (Caffaro) purchased benzoic acid to produce both ketones and di-benzoate plasticisers and used more than 50% of this benzoic acid for the production of ketones. The merged entity was only active downstream in the production of di-benzoate plasticisers but could not discriminate between these two usages. The Commission therefore concluded on this basis, and also considering that Caffaro did not impose a strong constraint on Arsenal pre-merger, that the new entity would have little incentive to raise prices or restrict sales of di-benzoate plasticisers to this particular rival.[100]

The Commission has also considered the importance of each market's contribution to the merged entity's total revenues. For instance, in *DONG/Elsam/Energi E2*,[101] one of the main reasons contributing to the Commission's finding of an incentive to foreclose was the weight of each of the two activities (upstream and downstream) within total company sales. In particular, the Commission highlighted that 'while the revenues from storage contribute only 5% of the DONG group's EBITDA, its gas-trading activities contribute 39%'.[102]

Assuming that the merged entity is able to increase costs for rivals downstream, the Commission will analyse to what extent such cost increases will give rise to price increases that result in customers switching to the downstream division of the merged entity. In its case law, the

---

[99] Ibid., para. 295.     [100] Ibid., paras. 301–6.

[101] Case COMP/M.3868 – *DONG/Elsam/Energi E2*, Commission decision of 14 March 2006.

[102] Ibid., para. 363.

Commission has identified a number of factors that are relevant to this analysis such as the pass-through of costs to end-customers in the form of price increases, the elasticity of the end-demand and cross elasticity with respect to the merged entity, efficiencies and the size of the existing customer base of the merging parties.

As explained above, the less important the input is to the final product, the more substantial the price increase needs to be to have an impact on prices of the relevant downstream products. Indeed, where the input only represents a minor part of the variable cost of downstream products, even a significant increase in the price of the input does not lead to an appreciable impact on variable costs downstream. Moreover, downstream rivals are unlikely to pass on the entire cost increase, especially when they face greater competition from the merged entity that may be in a position to offer lower prices due to efficiencies. The Commission made such a point in, for instance, *Itema/Barcovision*:[103]

> indeed, most market participants have mentioned during the market investigation that the merger is likely to lead to a decrease in prices for Itema winders equipped with BarcoVision sensors. To continue competing with Itema, downstream competitors are therefore unlikely to pass on the entirety of their cost increase, which further limits the downstream effects of an input foreclosure scenario.[104]

In *Nokia/Navteq*,[105] where the map databases accounted for only a small share of the mobile handsets' wholesale prices, the Commission applied a scenario-analysis using different input price increases as well as pass-on rates, which showed that 'under any reasonable own-price elasticity and diversion rate to the merged entity, such a small price increase would lead to very few additional sales for the merged firm'.[106] Similarly, in *TomTom/Tele Atlas*,[107] the Commission reached the same conclusion and noted:

> since map databases account on average for less than 10% of the PND wholesale price, map database prices would have to increase substantially to have an effect on downstream PND market prices and allow the merged entity to capture a significant amount of sales on the downstream market. Moreover, the impact of the foreclosure strategy depends on the

---

[103] Case COMP/M.4874 – *Itema/Barcovision*, Commission decision of 4 August 2008.
[104] Ibid., para. 75.
[105] Case COMP/M.4942 – *Nokia/Navteq*, Commission decision of 2 July 2008.
[106] Ibid., para. 336.
[107] Case COMP/M.4854 – *TomTom/Tele Atlas*, Commission decision of 14 May 2008.

extent to which TomTom's competitors would pass on the map database
price increase to end-consumers. For example, a 10% price increase of the
map would only lead to a 0.5% price increase for the PND if the price of
the map represents 10% of the price of a PND and PND manufacturers
pass on 50% of the change in their cost.[108]

Even if all downstream rivals were to increase prices as a result of the
foreclosure strategy, this might give rise to a limited increase in sales for
the downstream division of the merged entity if customers would switch
to other substitutable products in response to such a price rise. The
Commission concluded in *Arsenal/DSP*[109] that an input foreclosure
strategy aimed at downstream mono-benzoate plasticiser producers was
unlikely to be profitable since a large proportion of customers would
prefer to replace mono-benzoate plasticisers by substitutable phthalate
plasticisers rather than testing a new formula containing di-benzoate
plasticisers.[110] This meant that the merged entity's downstream di-
benzoate plasticisers business was unlikely to capture the necessary
amount of sales to compensate for the upstream losses.

In *E.ON/MOL*,[111] the Commission highlighted the potential cost
savings upstream that the merged entity would experience following
non-pricing input foreclosure (i.e. lowering the quality of the service).[112]
The Commission also affirmed that economies of scale were contributing
to increase the merged entity's incentives to foreclose. In particular, the
Commission noted:

> when the marginal cost of downstream gas supply is increasing, then it
> becomes progressively more costly for the integrated firm to replace its
> rivals' sales with its own. Hence the integrated firm may find it profitable
> to engage in some nonprice discrimination, but not to raise its rivals' costs
> so high that they exit the market. An extreme form of this occurs when
> the integrated firm has a capacity constraint on its downstream produc-
> tion. In contrast, in this case, it appears that there exist economies of scale
> in the retail supply of gas to small industrial and commercial customers.
> This is due to fixed costs in developing a sales network able to induce
> consumers under the regulated segment to switch to the open segment of
> the market.[113]

---

[108] Ibid., para. 216.
[109] Case COMP/M.5153 – *Arsenal/DSP*, Commission decision of 9 January 2009.
[110] Ibid., paras. 297–300.
[111] Case COMP/M.3696 – *E.ON/MOL*, Commission decision of 21 December 2005.
[112] Ibid., para. 430.      [113] Ibid., para. 431.

Moreover, the Commission stated that the little differentiation in the retail supply of gas contributed to consumers' readiness to switch between downstream suppliers, and therefore gave rise in turn to a higher likelihood of success for an input foreclosure strategy.[114]

Low switching costs in the upstream market have the opposite effect. In *TomTom/Tele Atlas*,[115] the Commission found that given that switching costs were surmountable, in the event of an increase of the input price by the merged entity, Tele Atlas (upstream) would lose a significant amount of sales to Navteq, which would hamper the ability of the merged entity to raise downstream rivals' costs and limit the incentive to engage in the strategy.[116] In *Thales/Finmeccanica/Alcatel Alenia Space & Telespazio*,[117] the uncertainty on whether a TWT (input) foreclosure strategy would result in an increase of the merged entity's likelihood of winning satellite bids (downstream) was considered to contribute to undermine the merged entity's incentives to engage in such a strategy.[118]

### 3.2.3 Case study: *Nokia/Navteq* – assessment of incentive to engage in input foreclosure

As part of its assessment of the *Nokia/Navteq*[119] merger, the Commission carried out a detailed analysis of the merged entity's incentive to engage in input foreclosure. Specifically, it considered the trade-off between profits lost in the upstream market for digital maps due to a reduction of input sales and the profit earned on the downstream market as a result of increases in the costs of rival mobile handsets producers.[120]

The Commission noted that the gross margin obtained on the sale of a mobile handset was much higher than the gross margin obtained on the sale of a map database. Whilst the margins themselves are redacted, the Commission's decision suggests that the gross margins per handset

---

[114] Case COMP/M.3696 – *E.ON/MOL*, Commission decision of 21 December 2005, para. 429.
[115] Case COMP/M.4854 – *TomTom/Tele Atlas*, Commission decision of 14 May 2008.
[116] Ibid., para. 219.
[117] Case COMP/M.4403 – *Thales/Finmeccanica/Alcatel Alenia Space & Telespazio*, Commission decision of 4 April 2007.
[118] Ibid., para. 307.
[119] Case COMP/M.4942 – *Nokia/Navteq*, Commission decision of 2 July 2008.
[120] The Commission focused on assessing the incentive to foreclose rival producers of mobile handsets rather than the market for navigation applications on mobile handsets, in part due to data availability and in part because it considered that any incentive for the merged entity to engage in input foreclosure with regard to firms active in the market for navigation applications on mobile handsets would be weaker given Nokia's more limited presence.

earned on the sale of digital maps to mobile handset manufacturers are many times smaller than the gross margins generated by the sale of a mobile handset.[121] As explained in the example above, all else being equal, this would suggest that the critical increase in mobile handset demand required for foreclosure to be profitable might be relatively low: winning an incremental mobile handset sale could compensate for the loss of a number of digital maps sales.

In *Nokia/Navteq* the question of which costs should be considered variable for the purposes of calculating gross margins was apparently uncontroversial. It should be noted, however, that in certain cases the assessment of which costs would be avoided upstream if the firm reduced sales as part of a foreclosure strategy and which costs would be incurred regardless of foreclosure is more complex. In some cases, it may be necessary to undertake a detailed examination of the firms' cost structures, focusing particularly on the extent to which each cost item would be saved if the upstream firm reduced sales and to which each cost item would be increased if the downstream firm made additional sales.

Having established that the critical increase in downstream demand for mobile handsets might be relatively low in *Nokia/Navteq*, the Commission's analysis focused on whether the actual increase in downstream demand resulting from any foreclosure strategy would be sufficiently low to imply that foreclosure would not be profitable. The Commission identified a number of factors that suggested that the actual increase would indeed be low.

First, the Commission noted that, since map databases account for a small proportion of mobile handset costs, map database prices would have to increase substantially to have an effect on mobile handset prices. Assuming that map databases represent 10% of mobile handset costs (the actual percentage is redacted) then a 10% increase in the price of map databases would increase mobile handset costs by 1%. If mobile handset manufacturers were to pass on 50% of this cost increase to consumers in the form of higher prices, the overall increase in downstream prices would be only 0.5%. The Commission concluded that under any reasonable assumption regarding own-price elasticity and diversion ratios between downstream firms and Nokia, such a small price increase would lead to very few additional sales for the merged entity.[122]

---

[121] Case COMP/M.4942 – *Nokia/Navteq*, Commission decision of 2 July 2008, para. 334.
[122] Ibid., para. 336.

Second, navigation services are only one feature among many that determine customers' handset choices (such as the handset's music or video player). Faced with a degradation of quality or increase in price for digital maps, Nokia's rivals could enhance other features of their handsets in order to win customers.[123]

Third, the Commission considered the role played by Garmin and, in particular, Garmin's agreement with Samsung to offer a navigation solution on mobile handsets. It considered that this protection from foreclosure would limit the profits that Nokia could capture on the downstream market.[124] In the context of our example above, if there were a third downstream firm (Firm 3) that were insulated from the effect of any foreclosure strategy, this would reduce the share of the benefits from the increase in Firm 2's costs that are appropriated by Division 1.

The Commission also noted a number of factors that it considered would imply that Navteq could lose a significant amount of upstream sales to Tele Atlas if it increased price or degraded map database quality. These factors included relatively limited switching costs and the view that Tele Atlas would continue to provide good-quality map databases to all mobile handset manufacturers in a non-discriminatory manner.[125] It is arguably the case that these factors should have been considered as part of the Commission's assessment of the merged entity's *ability* to engage in foreclosure. If customers could switch easily to a product that was of equally high quality in response to a degradation of the quality of the product offered by the merged entity, then this would undermine the ability of the merged entity to affect the terms available on the market as a whole (with regard to quality) on which downstream rivals could purchase the input. In any event, the Commission's consideration of these factors at the stage of assessing the merged entity's *incentive* to foreclose highlights the blurred boundaries of the various stages of the competitive assessment of input foreclosure.

The Commission's analysis of the extent to which the merged entity could capture sales on the mobile handset market was supported by an econometric estimation of the demand for mobile handsets. Its estimate of downstream price elasticities implied, consistent with the above factors, that the merged entity would capture only a relatively limited volume of downstream sales following an increase in map database prices

[123] Case COMP/M.4942 – *Nokia/Navteq*, Commission decision of 2 July 2008, para. 337.
[124] Ibid., para. 338.      [125] Ibid., paras. 339 and 340.

charged for Nokia's competitors. The Commission concluded that since map database prices represent a relatively minor proportion of the price of mobile handsets, the elasticity estimates it obtained coupled with conservative assumptions regarding the degree of cost pass-through by rivals, implied that a strategy of total foreclosure would not be profitable for the merged entity unless Tele Atlas increased its own upstream price by more than two hundred per cent (a scenario that it considered unlikely).[126]

The Commission also sensitivity-tested its analysis to take account of the possibility that map databases would represent a more important cost in the future, given that the price of other mobile components (such as hardware) might fall relative to map database prices. The Commission found that its conclusions were robust to variations in this assumption.[127]

Furthermore, the Commission noted the problem of commitment in its assessment. In particular, it pointed out that a strategy of total foreclosure that allowed Tele Atlas to increase prices by such a substantial amount might not be credible, as the merged entity would have an incentive to undercut any higher price offered by Tele Atlas.[128] Since Tele Atlas would be able to predict this reaction from the merged entity, it would refrain from attempting to increase its prices in the first place.

With regard to partial foreclosure, the Commission found that any price increase that would have a non-negligible impact on the downstream market would not be profitable for the merged entity as the downstream gains would not be sufficient to compensate upstream losses. This conclusion was robust to a range of alternative assumptions concerning the pass-through rate, elasticities and the relative importance of map databases as a cost.

### 3.3   Effect of input foreclosure

Input foreclosure can be considered 'anti-competitive foreclosure' only in so far as it brings about higher prices in the downstream market as a result of a lessening of competition.

---

[126] See ibid., para. 346.     [127] See ibid., para. 347.

[128] See ibid., para. 346. As discussed in our example, this incentive to undercut arises because it generates a significant increase in upstream profits but need not materially reduce the price at which downstream rivals can purchase the input.

The extent to which the increase in rivals' costs caused by input foreclosure can be expected to give rise to higher downstream prices will depend significantly on whether the firms whose input costs have increased form a significant part of the market and in the aggregate represent a significant source of competition. Moreover, if the firms that are the subject of foreclosure are particularly close competitors for the downstream firm, this will increase the scope for the merged entity to increase price.

On the other hand, if foreclosure only affects a small part of the downstream market (e.g. because certain downstream players rely less on the input whose price has increased), or there are potential entrants that are unaffected by the foreclosure strategy, then the merged entity is less likely to increase prices downstream.

Any assessment of the effect of foreclosure should also take into account that over the longer term any increase in upstream prices may invite entry by new unintegrated firms at the upstream level, or may encourage downstream firms to vertically integrate upstream.[129]

Finally, as noted in Section 2.1, above, efficiencies can play an import-ant role in the assessment of vertical mergers. A vertical merger, through the elimination of double marginalisation, may give rise to an incentive for the downstream division to lower its price relative to its pre-merger level. This may occur even if the merger simultaneously gives rise to input foreclosure that raises the costs and prices of rivals and that causes them to lose sales to the merged entity. Whilst competitors may be significantly harmed by the foreclosure strategy, the overall effect on consumers may be positive as a result of the lower prices offered by the merged entity.

The Commission's discussion of the effect of foreclosure in *Nokia/ Navteq*[130] highlights the overlap between the various stages of assessment. The Commission noted that the same factors that explained the lack of any incentive to engage in partial foreclosure also implied that any

---

[129] Note that one might consider that new entry at the upstream level that defeats any attempt to increase upstream prices should already have been taken into account at the stage of assessing the ability to foreclose. This reflects the somewhat blurred nature of the boundaries between the various stages of assessment. It might be that factors that affect the scope for the merged entity to raise rivals' costs in the short term are considered at the ability to foreclose stage, whereas factors that affect the scope for the merged entity to do so over the longer term (e.g. new entry or vertical integration by downstream rivals) are considered at the stage of assessing the effect of foreclosure.

[130] Case COMP/M.4942 – *Nokia/Navteq*, Commission decision of 2 July 2008.

hypothetical foreclosure would not have a material effect in the down-stream markets. In particular, it stated that 'the low percentage of the map database in the mobile handset costs, the limited switching costs and the competition with Tele Atlas all tend to limit the price increase that could be imposed by Navteq on Nokia's competitors.'[131]

This conclusion is interesting in so far as it suggests that the Commission essentially found that the merged entity would not have the *ability* to engage in partial foreclosure, despite the fact that earlier in its decision it had left open the question of whether the merged entity would have the ability to engage in foreclosure (see discussion at Section 3.1.3 above).

Despite the lack of a finding of any anti-competitive effect arising from foreclosure, the Commission considered efficiencies that might result from the merger. It gave particular consideration to the potential for the merger to give rise to an elimination of double marginalisation given that the gross margins on map databases are high. The Commission set out the logic that post-merger the integrated company would realise that the true cost it faces for an additional map database is not 0–15% of the handset price but a small fraction of this amount. The Commission stated that if it is assumed that 30–60% of the cost decrease is passed on, the price of Nokia's handsets would decrease by some small amount (less than 5%).[132] The Commission also found that the elimination of double marginalisation would be merger specific to a large extent, since it did not observe contractual provisions in the market that served to eliminate double marginalisation.[133]

### 4.   Vertical mergers: customer foreclosure

Customer foreclosure refers to a situation in which a merger reduces the ability of the merged entity's upstream competitors to make sales by restricting access to a significant part of the downstream customer base. To the extent that this restriction reduces the ability or incentive of upstream rivals to compete, this may lead to an increase in the costs of downstream rivals that in turn reduces the competitive pressure that the merged entity faces downstream. As with input foreclosure, if efficiency gains are not sufficient, the relaxation of this constraint

---

[131] Ibid., para. 356. The Commission also took account of the ability of handset manufacturers and mobile network operators to source from Garmin, which was protected from price increases through its long-term contract with Navteq. See ibid., para. 361.
[132] Ibid., para. 366.     [133] Ibid., para. 368.

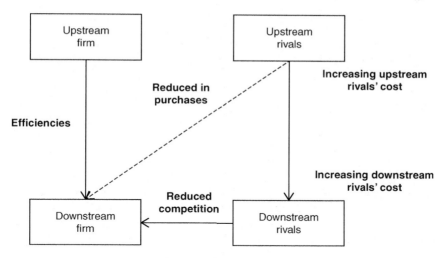

**Figure 5.8**    Illustration of customer foreclosure concern

may lead to higher prices for final consumers. Figure 5.8 provides an illustration of these effects.

Again, it must be stressed that 'anti-competitive foreclosure' is said to arise only in instances in which the result of foreclosure is a lessening of the effectiveness of competition faced by the merged entity that gives rise to consumer harm.

Importantly, there is a close conceptual link between the logic of input and customer foreclosure theories. While the mechanisms in question differ, both forms of conduct represent means by which an integrated firm may seek to bring about a lessening in downstream competition via a worsening in the terms on which unintegrated downstream rivals obtain inputs. Customer foreclosure could thus be considered an indirect means by which integrated firms may bring about input foreclosure: rather than directly worsening the terms on which downstream rivals obtain inputs, customer foreclosure involves an integrated firm using its downstream position to worsen the terms on which independent upstream firms are able to supply downstream rivals. As a result, there is a high degree of overlap between the considerations relevant to the assessment of input and customer foreclosure concerns.[134]

---

[134] In practice, however, the Commission has historically placed less emphasis on customer foreclosure concerns in merger assessment than input foreclosure theories. This may reflect the necessarily somewhat more contrived nature of customer foreclosure theories,

## 4.1   Ability to engage in customer foreclosure

The first step in any assessment of whether a merger is likely to give rise to customer foreclosure is an analysis of the merged entity's *ability* to engage in foreclosure. The ability to engage in customer foreclosure depends on the importance of the merged entity's downstream business as a buyer of inputs sold by the merged entity's upstream competitors. If as a result of reducing (or ceasing) purchases of inputs produced by third party suppliers the merged entity is able to restrict their access to market in a way that makes them less competitive in the upstream market, the merged entity is said to have the ability to engage in customer foreclosure. On the other hand, if the merged entity is not a significant buyer of the input compared to other buyers and as a result cannot influence the competitiveness of third party upstream competitors, the merged entity cannot be said to have the ability to engage in customer foreclosure.

In practice, customer foreclosure may take the form of the downstream division of the merged entity refusing to source from upstream rivals, reducing its purchases from upstream rivals or only purchasing from third parties at terms that are less favourable for them.

A key question in assessing the merged entity's ability to foreclose is whether there are alternative sources of demand for the merged entity's upstream rivals. If the pre-merger purchases of the downstream division from third party upstream suppliers are relatively small compared to the total sales made by those firms, then it is unlikely that even a complete refusal to source would have much of an impact on the ability of those upstream suppliers to continue to compete effectively. On the other hand, if the downstream division's purchases from third parties represent a substantial part of their overall sales the withdrawal of those purchases could under some circumstances adversely affect their ability to compete. Consequently, as recognised by the EC Non-horizontal Merger Guidelines, market power in the downstream market is a necessary condition for customer foreclosure to arise.[135]

The extent to which a reduction in purchases by the merged entity will affect the competitiveness of third party upstream suppliers, and thus the prices faced by unintegrated buyers of the input, will typically depend on the cost conditions of those suppliers. There are two mechanisms by

which involve an additional step in the chain of logic before anti-competitive effect can be established.
[135] EC Non-horizontal Merger Guidelines, para. 61.

which a reduction in sales could impair an upstream supplier's ability to compete. First, and most obviously, upstream rivals could simply be forced to exit due to a lack of sales rendering their activities unviable. Second, where an upstream supplier's unit production costs decline with the level of output, a reduction in sales will result in an increase in its marginal costs, thereby reducing its ability to compete on price.

Thus, where the merged entity's demand is an important factor in enabling a third party upstream supplier to achieve scale economies that ensure that it is attractive to remain in the market,[136] or where the inability to serve the merged entity implies that unintegrated downstream firms can only be supplied at a higher incremental cost, this may imply that the ability of unintegrated firms to offer effective competition to the merged entity's upstream division is reduced by the foreclosure strategy.[137] This can lead to an increase in the input prices faced by rivals to the merged entity's downstream division.

In addition, if the reduction of expected revenues resulting from customer foreclosure is sufficient to deter upstream rivals from investing in R&D that might have reduced their incremental costs of supply or increased the quality of their products, this may adversely affect their ability to compete with the upstream firm over the longer term relative to the situation in which foreclosure had not taken place.

Alternatively, even where a merged firm is able to withdraw significant · purchases from third parties, this may not result in foreclosure if it does not affect the attractiveness to third parties of remaining in the market, nor their cost of making incremental sales to unintegrated downstream firms. This could be the case if many of the costs that would have been incurred in serving the merged entity's downstream division can be avoided over the relatively short term, so that costs fall in line with any reduction in output, such that rivals' incentive to remain active in the market is not reduced. Similarly, if incremental costs are unrelated to

---

[136] Equivalently, where the merged entity's demand is an important factor in enabling a third party potential entrant to the upstream market to achieve scale economies that ensure that it is attractive to enter the market.

[137] Note, the merged entity might be a substantial buyer in a particular market in which the unintegrated upstream supplier sells, but a relatively small buyer in relation to the entire base of sales over which the upstream supplier achieves economies of scale. These economies of scale could derive, for example, from sales across a range of different geographic markets. Even if the merged entity has a significant position in one of those markets, its purchases may not be a material determinant of the upstream firm's costs of supply.

volumes sold then, as long as foreclosure does not induce exit, upstream rivals will not become any less competitive.[138]

In order for customer foreclosure to give rise to a significant increase in the costs of downstream rivals, it is necessary that the input supplied by the upstream firms that are the target of foreclosure must in some sense be important for those downstream rivals. If the cost increase caused by customer foreclosure relates to an input that represents a relatively trivial part of the costs of supply of downstream rivals, then the merged entity is likely to be unable to affect the costs of downstream rivals through customer foreclosure.[139]

In any particular case, the ability of the merged entity to foreclose may depend on a range of factors specific to the case at hand. For example, there may be factors that make it difficult for the downstream division of the merged entity to suddenly switch its demand away from competitors of the upstream division. This may be the case if there are barriers to switching large volumes of demand. In addition, as discussed further below, the merged entity's upstream rivals may engage in counterstrategies (or even counter-mergers) that undermine the ability of the merged firm to engage in customer foreclosure.

### 4.1.1   Ability to engage in customer foreclosure: an example

The following is a highly stylised example of how a firm that merges with a downstream customer, and then refuses to source from its upstream rivals, can increase its market power upstream and thereby raise the input costs of rivals to its downstream division. In this example, the goal of customer foreclosure is to create market power upstream by preventing the entry of an international potential entrant.

Suppose Firm A and Firm B are producers of a component, which is an input to the production of a gadget produced by Firm 1 and Firm 2. Firm A is relatively inefficient with a marginal cost of production of 140. Firm B, on the other hand, is relatively efficient with a marginal cost of only 50. Importantly, however, whilst Firm A faces no fixed costs, Firm B faces a fixed cost of 10,000 if it is to serve Firms 1 and 2. This is because

---

[138] It should be noted in this regard that increases in average costs arising from the spreading of fixed costs over a smaller sales base will not impact the pricing incentives of third party rivals.

[139] In practice, the importance of the cost of the input as a proportion of downstream rivals' total costs may be taken into account at the stage of assessing ability to foreclose (as it is in the case of input foreclosure) or at a later stage of the overall assessment.

Firm B currently produces components for a different geographic market in which the gadgets are somewhat different to those produced by Firms 1 and 2. The fixed cost faced by Firm B represents a one-off investment in R&D required to make its components compatible with gadgets produced by Firms 1 and 2. We assume that having made this R&D investment the components produced by Firms A and B are homogeneous.

Suppose that the downstream market for gadgets is of a fixed size of 200 units and that one component is required to produce each gadget.

To understand how a merger between Firm A and Firm 1 could give rise to customer foreclosure resulting in higher input prices for the merged entity's downstream competitor, Firm 2, we first consider market outcomes absent any merger.

First, we calculate the price that enables Firm B to break-even if it were to enter and then supply the entire market (200 units). This is the price that ensures that revenues are equal to costs. The total cost of entering and supplying 200 units is equal to the unit cost (50) multiplied by the number of units supplied (200) plus the one-off fixed cost (10,000), which is equal to 20,000. Given that supplying the market results in 200 gadget sales, the price that allows Firm B to break-even with this strategy is 100 (since 100 * 200 = 20,000). Importantly, this price is below the marginal cost of Firm A.

Absent any merger, we might therefore expect Firm B to offer to supply the entire market at a price of 140. This strategy is profitable for Firm B because it serves the market at a price higher than the break-even price of 100. Given that Firm A has a marginal cost of 140 (and therefore cannot profitably offer a lower price than this), Firms 1 and 2 can do no better than to accept Firm B's offer. This situation is illustrated in Figure 5.9.

We now suppose that Firm A merges with Firm 1 to create Firm A1.[140] We suppose that Division 1 engages in a strategy of only sourcing from Division A (at cost), regardless of the price that Firm B offers. This implies that Firm B can now only bid for the business of Firm 2 and must make its entry decision based on whether the revenues from serving Firm 2 will cover its total costs (including the fixed R&D cost of 10,000).

Suppose (for the time being) that Firm 2's demand amounts to half of the market demand (i.e. 100 components). We now calculate the price that enables Firm B to break-even if it were to win Firm 2's business.

---

[140] As above, we refer to the upstream division of the merged entity, Firm A1, as Division A and to the downstream division as Division 1.

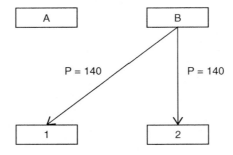

**Figure 5.9**   Illustration of pre-merger scenario

The total cost of entering and supplying 100 units is equal to the unit cost (50) multiplied by the number of units supplied (100) plus the one-off fixed cost (10,000), which is equal to 15,000. The price that allows Firm B to cover this cost from 100 gadget sales is 150 (since 100 * 150 = 15,000). Therefore, Firm B will not find it profitable to agree to supply Firm 2 at any price lower than 150.

This enables Division A to offer to supply Firm 2 at a price of 150. This strategy is profitable for Firm A because this price is above its marginal cost of supply of 140. Moreover, given that Firm B cannot profitably offer to serve Firm 2 at a price lower than this, Firm 2 can do no better than to accept Firm A's offer. This situation is illustrated in Figure 5.10.

In this example, customer foreclosure via Division 1 withdrawing its purchases from Firm B has thus raised the price at which the unintegrated firm purchases components from 140 to 150.[141]

We now consider a number of factors that affect the extent to which Division 1's refusal to source from Firm B gives rise to customer foreclosure that increases Firm 2's costs.

First, the size of the contestable downstream demand that is unaffected by the merged entity's refusal to source is a crucial determinant of the merged entity's ability to foreclose. If instead of having a demand of

---

[141] To the extent that Firm 2's demand for components is in fact lower than 100 at the higher price of 150 (because it loses some gadget sales to Firm 1 as a result of passing through some of this cost increase in the form of higher gadget prices), then the price that enables Firm B to break-even by serving Firm 2 may be somewhat higher than 150. For example, at price of 150, Firm 2's demand for components may now only be 95 units. Firm B can only profitably supply 95 components at a price of 155.26, which allows Firm A some further scope to increase its price.

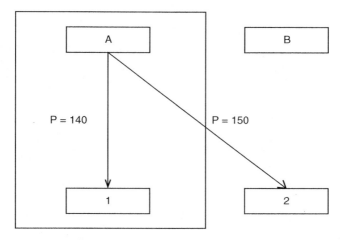

**Figure 5.10**   Illustration of post-merger scenario with customer foreclosure

100 units, Firm 2 had a demand of 110 units, the merged entity would no longer have the ability, through refusing to source from Firm B, to charge a price significantly higher than its marginal cost of 140 to Firm 2. This is because the price that would allow Firm B to enter and profitably serve Firm 2's demand of 110 is now around 141. At a price of 141, Firm B's revenues from serving Firm 2 would be 15,510 (equal to 141 * 110 units), which is just higher than its total cost of 15,500 (equal to 50 * 110 + 10,000). Therefore, any attempt to offer a price of 141 to Firm 2 would be undermined by entry by Firm B.

Second, the size of the fixed cost of entry faced by Firm B in this example is an important determinant of the merged entity's ability to engage in foreclosure. Assuming again that Firm 2's demand is for 100 units, if the fixed cost of entry were only 9,000 rather than 10,000, this would eliminate the scope for Division A to increase the input price faced by Firm 2 above its marginal cost of 140. This is because if the fixed cost of entry were only 9,000 this would imply that the price at which Firm B can just break-even and serve Firm 2 is 140. To see this, consider that at the price of 140, its revenues (14,000 = 100 * 140) are just sufficient to enable it to cover its costs (14,000 = 100 * 50 + 9,000). Therefore, given the lower fixed cost faced by Firm B of 9,000, Firm A would have no ability to raise the price above its marginal cost of 140. Any attempt to do so would allow Firm B to enter and serve Firm 2 at a lower price.

Third, the effect of any increase in the price of the input on the cost of downstream firms will depend on the importance of the component as a proportion of total costs. If components represent 100% of gadget producers' marginal costs, then an increase in component prices due to customer foreclosure would likely undermine Firm 2's ability to constrain the merged entity. Alternatively, if components only represent 10% of Firm 2's marginal cost, then an increase in the price of the component of 7% (i.e. from 140 to 150) would only cause its marginal cost of producing gadgets to increase by 0.7%.[142]

It should be noted that the example above is highly stylised. The results are driven by the specific assumptions and in particular by the fact that average costs of supply for the potential entrant vary significantly with the volume it sells due to the large fixed cost of entry it faces. Hence, its decision to enter is heavily dependent on the volume of demand that is contestable.

The example is also somewhat limited by the assumption that the demand of Firm 2 is given. If Firm 2 were able to expand sales substantially by offering a lower downstream price (both through taking sales away from Firm 1 and through expanding the market) then this could enable Firm B to counter the merged entity's foreclosure strategy by selling components at a low price to Firm 2 that enables it to expand its volume of sales. Through expanding the contestable base in this way, Firm B reduces the minimum price at which it can profitably enter. It could be that a profitable counterstrategy for Firm B exists that involves helping Firm 2 achieve a large sales volume by offering it a low input price. For example, if, by undercutting Firm 1, Firm 2 could achieve sales of 200, then the price that would allow Firm B to break-even on sales to Firm 2 would fall to only 100. The counterstrategy of offering Firm 2 a price of 100 could in this case defeat any ability of the merged entity to engage in customer foreclosure. Firm B could even merge with Firm 2 as part of its entry strategy to ensure it priced aggressively downstream and secured a demand base sufficient to render its R&D investment worthwhile.[143]

---

[142] As noted above, the importance of the cost of the input as a proportion of downstream rivals' total costs may be taken into account at the stage of assessing ability to foreclose (as it normally is in the case of input foreclosure) or at a later stage of the overall assessment.

[143] In practice, the ability of a merged entity to engage in customer foreclosure depends on a rich set of considerations. These include the ability of upstream rivals to engage in counterstrategies, which may include vertical mergers of their own.

## 4.2   Incentive to engage in customer foreclosure

A vertical merger alters the incentives of the downstream division because it will now take account of the impact of its purchasing decisions on its upstream division. This may give rise to an incentive to engage in customer foreclosure.

Whether a firm has an incentive to engage in customer foreclosure depends on whether the benefits of customer foreclosure outweigh the costs to the merged entity as a whole.

The costs associated with customer foreclosure stem from the fact that it involves the downstream division reducing or ceasing its purchases from certain upstream suppliers, which, absent the foreclosure strategy, would have been purchases it preferred to undertake. For example, the foreclosure strategy may involve the downstream division switching purchases from a more efficient upstream supplier to the upstream division of the merged entity. Therefore, the downstream division may have achieved lower input costs if it sourced from third party upstream firms rather than its own upstream division.[144] Alternatively, it may have procured a higher quality input absent the foreclosure strategy.

The benefit from engaging in customer foreclosure may stem from two factors. First, if the customer foreclosure strategy makes upstream rivals less competitive, this may enable the merged entity's upstream division to increase its margins on sales to rivals of its downstream division (or increase sales to downstream firms). Second, if the input costs of downstream rivals are increased as a result of the foreclosure strategy, this may relax the competitive constraints faced by the downstream division, enabling it to increase price and/or increase its volumes.

A number of factors determine whether the overall impact on profits will be positive leading to an incentive to foreclose. As with our discussion of the incentive to engage in input foreclosure, we consider the incentive to engage in customer foreclosure by reference to two concepts: the critical increase in downstream demand required to make the foreclosure strategy profitable; and the actual increase in downstream demand that occurs as a result of the customer foreclosure strategy. As discussed in more detail in the following subsection, the critical increase in downstream demand required to make foreclosure profitable will

---

[144] EC Non-horizontal Merger Guidelines, para. 69.

depend on the relative margins in upstream and downstream activities both in the presence of and absence of foreclosure.[145]

The actual increase in downstream demand that results from the foreclosure strategy will depend on the effect of the foreclosure strategy on the costs of downstream rivals;[146] the extent to which any given cost increase is passed on to consumers by downstream rivals in the form of higher prices; and the extent to which those downstream consumers react by substituting to the products of the merged entity's downstream division.[147]

### 4.2.1   Incentive to engage in customer foreclosure: an example

In the example set out in Section 4.1.1, the merged entity had the ability to refuse to source from B and thereby to increase its rival's input price from 140 to 150. We now use a slightly modified version of the same example to illustrate the assessment of whether a vertically integrated firm might have an incentive to engage in customer foreclosure.

Suppose that Firm B offers to supply the entire market at a price of 100, for instance due to the presence of a third potential upstream supplier, Firm C, with the same cost structure as Firm B. A price of 100 is just profitable for B in the event that it sells 200 units since revenue (100 * 200 = 20,000) equals cost (200 * 50 + 10,000 = 20,000). Suppose further that in the event that Firm 1 refuses this offer, Firm B offers to supply Firm 2 at a price of 150. This price is just profitable for Firm B in the event that it sells 100 units since revenue (150 * 100 = 15,000) equals cost (100 * 50 + 10,000 = 15,000).

We assume that the gadgets produced by Firms 1 and 2 are differentiated, but that, as before, the components produced by Firm A and Firm B are homogeneous. We assume that if the merged entity accepts Firm B's offer, both Firm 1 and Firm 2 have a unit cost of 100 and sell 100 gadgets each at a price of 200.

---

[145] The critical increase in demand for the downstream division could be zero if the increase in margin upstream due to the foreclosure strategy is equal to the reduction in margin downstream resulting from sourcing the input internally at a higher cost to that available for sourcing from third parties.

[146] This in turn depends on the factors discussed in Section 4.1 above, such as the importance of upstream scale economies and the importance of the input as a cost factor.

[147] The profitability of this strategy is also contingent on the downstream division having the necessary spare capacity to meet any increase in demand the foreclosure strategy generates.

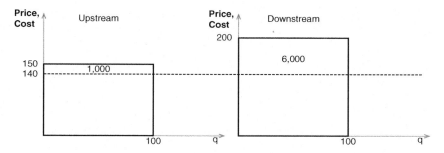

**Figure 5.11** Upstream and downstream profits of merged entity under customer foreclosure absent changes in prices and output downstream

First we consider Firm A1's profit if it accepts Firm B's offer to supply Division 1. Both Division 1 and Firm 2 accept Firm B's offer to supply the entire market at a price of 100. In this case, the profits of Division A are zero. The profits of Division 1 on the other hand are equal to the price it charges for gadgets (200) less the marginal cost (100) multiplied by the number of gadgets it sells (100), which equals 10,000. Thus, in the event that it accepts B's offer, Firm A1's profits are 10,000.

We now consider Firm A1's profits if it refuses Firm B's offer to supply Division 1. In this case, as we noted in Section 4.1.1, Division A will be able to offer a price of 150 to supply Firm 2.[148] The upstream division's profits are therefore equal to the unit price (150) less the marginal cost (140) multiplied by the number of components sold to Firm 2 (100), which equal 1,000.

The downstream division is supplied by the upstream division at marginal cost (140). For the time being, we assume that Division 1 will price at 200 even at this higher cost and even though Firm 2's costs have increased (although we will see the implications of relaxing this assumption later). Division 1's profits are equal to the price it charges for gadgets (200) less the marginal cost (140) multiplied by the number of gadgets sold to consumers (100), which equal 6,000.

The total profit of the merged entity Firm A1 in the event that it refuses to source from Firm B is therefore equal to 7,000 (as illustrated in Figure 5.11).

It is therefore apparent that absent any change in the prices and outputs of the downstream Firms 1 and 2, the merged entity can obtain

---

[148] Given that Firm B cannot profitably offer to serve Firm 2 at a price lower than this, Firm 2 can do no better than to accept Firm A's offer.

higher profits by accepting the offer of Firm B to supply its downstream division. The cost of refusing to source components from Firm B arises from the fact that it involves forgoing procurement of the component at a price that is lower than its own marginal cost of supply.

However, given that the foreclosure strategy has increased the input cost of Firm 2 from 140 to 150, this might be expected to cause it to increase the price it charges final consumers for gadgets. To the extent that this increase in input price causes some consumers to switch from Firm 2's gadgets to Division 1's gadgets, this increase in downstream demand may be sufficient to render the foreclosure strategy profitable overall.

It is now possible to calculate, holding prices in the downstream market constant at 200, how many units would need to switch from Firm 2 to Division 1 in order to justify the cost of refusing to source from Firm B. In other words, we can calculate the critical increase in Division 1's demand that is required to make this strategy profitable.[149] We also assume for the time being that Division 1's downstream price does not change as a result of the foreclosure strategy so that the benefits of foreclosure are down purely to an increase in its volume.[150]

First recall that the shortfall in profit resulting from the refusal to source case compared to the alternative was 3,000 (equal to 10,000 – 7,000). Note that every unit that shifts from Firm 2 to Division 1 as a result of the higher downstream price charged by Firm 2 adds 50 to the merged entity's profits. This is because each incremental unit sold allows the downstream division to earn a margin of 60 (equal to 200 – 140) but at the same time each incremental unit switched also represents a lost sale for the upstream division to Firm 2, on which it would have earned a margin of 10 (equal to 150 – 140). The net effect on profit of a unit switched is therefore 50. It can then be seen that the number of units that must be switched in order to increase the merged entity's profit from 7,000 to 10,000 (the profit that can be earned by sourcing from Firm B) is 60, since a net margin of 50 per unit multiplied by 60 units equals 3,000. The switch of 60 units reduces the upstream division's profit from 1,000

---

[149] In what follows we abstract away from the issue that any decrease in Firm 2's demand will mean that Firm B's price offer of 150 to serve Firm 2 will no longer be profitable, and that this might enable Division A to further increase the price of the component to Firm 2 above 150.

[150] We will later come on to see how an increase in Division 1's price due to the relaxation of competition downstream affects the *critical* increase in downstream demand.

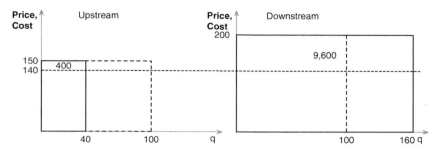

**Figure 5.12**  Upstream and downstream profits of merged entity under customer foreclosure assuming 60 units switched to downstream division

to 400 (since it now sells 40 rather than 100 units at a margin of 10 per unit). But it increases the downstream division's profit from 6,000 to 9,600 (since it now sells 160 rather than 100 units at a margin of 60 per unit). The combined entity therefore obtains profits of 10,000 (as illustrated in Figure 5.12).

The critical increase of 60 units calculated above depends on the upstream margin lost on incremental sales to Firm 2, the margin earned on downstream sales given the refusal to source *and* the margin that would have been earned on downstream sales had the merged entity accepted Firm B's offer to supply Division 1 at a price below Division A's marginal cost.

The critical increase required to make the strategy profitable would be smaller than 60 units if:

• *The margins earned on upstream sales to Firm 2 given foreclosure were higher.* Suppose that as a result of foreclosure, the upstream division could raise the price it charges Firm 2 to 160 rather than 150.[151] This would imply that the margin earned on upstream sales is now 20 (160 − 140) and that profits from the sale of 100 units to Firm 2 now earn the upstream division 2,000. In the absence of any increase in downstream volume, the profits of the downstream division would be 6,000 (since it makes 100 gadget sales at a margin of 60). The total profit of the merged entity given foreclosure would therefore be 8,000 in the absence of any increase in downstream demand. Given that, as

---

[151] This might be possible, for example, if the fixed cost of entry were 11,000, rather than 10,000. A fixed cost of entry of 11,000 would imply that the price required to break-even on sales of 1,000 units would be 160, since at this price revenues (100 * 160) would equal cost (11,000 + 50 * 100) for Firm B.

calculated previously, the merged entity will generate profits of 10,000 if it instead accepts Firm B's offer, the net effect on profits resulting from taking volumes from Firm 2 must amount to at least 2,000 in order for the foreclosure strategy to be profitable. Every unit that shifts from Firm 2 to Division 1 as a result of the higher downstream price charged by Firm 2 adds 40 to the merged entity's profits.[152] Therefore the critical increase in demand is now 50 (since 40 * 50 = 2,000).[153]

- *The margins earned on downstream sales to consumers given foreclosure were higher.* Suppose that as a result of the relaxation of competition downstream caused by the foreclosure strategy, Division 1 were able to increase its gadget price from 200 to 210.[154] This would imply that the margin earned on downstream sales is now 70 (210 – 140) and that, absent any shift in purchasing by consumers, downstream profits from the sale of 100 units are 7,000. The upstream division makes profits of 1,000 from the sale of 100 units to Firm 2 at a margin of 10 (150 – 140). The total profit of the merged entity given foreclosure would therefore be 8,000. Given that the merged entity will generate profits of 10,000 if it instead accepts Firm B's offer, the net effect on profits resulting from taking volumes from Firm 2 must amount to at least 2,000 (10,000 – 8,000) if foreclosure is to be profitable. Every unit that shifts from Firm 2 to Division 1 as a result of the higher downstream price charged by Firm 2 adds 60 to the merged entity's profits.[155] Therefore, the critical increase in demand is now 33.33 (since 60 * 33.33 = 2,000).[156]

---

[152] This is because each incremental unit sold allows the downstream division to earn a margin of 60 (equal to 200 – 140) but at the same time each incremental unit switched also represents a lost sale for the upstream division to Firm 2, on which it would have earned a margin of 20 (equal to 160 – 140). The net effect on profit of a unit switched is therefore 40.

[153] Note that if the upstream price could have been raised to 180 rather than 150, then the critical increase would be zero. The profit from foreclosure would equal the profit from accepting Firm 2's offer even if there were no shift of demand downstream to the merged entity.

[154] Note that the downstream price might also be expected to be higher than 200 due to the fact that the downstream firm's marginal cost is higher under the foreclosure strategy (140) than under the absence of foreclosure (100).

[155] This is because each incremental unit sold allows the downstream division to earn a margin of 70 (equal to 210 – 140) but at the same time each incremental unit switched also represents a lost sale for the upstream division to Firm 2, on which it would have earned a margin of 10 (equal to 150 – 140). The net effect on profit of a unit switched is therefore 60.

[156] Note that if the downstream price could have been raised to 230 rather than 210, then the *critical* increase would be zero. The profit from foreclosure would equal the profit

- *The margins earned on downstream sales to consumers absent foreclosure were lower.* Suppose that instead of making an offer to supply the entire market at a price of 100, Firm B offered to do so at a price of 110. This would imply that absent foreclosure, the merged entity's downstream margin would now be 90 rather than 100, and it would earn profits of 9,000 from 100 gadget sales. Given that profits for the merged entity from engaging in foreclosure are 7,000 absent any downstream demand shift, the net effect on profits resulting from taking volumes from Firm 2 must amount to at least 2,000 (9,000 – 7,000) if foreclosure is to be profitable. Every unit that shifts from Firm 2 to Division 1 as a result of the higher downstream price charged by Firm 2 adds 50 to the merged entity's profits.[157] Therefore, the critical increase in demand is now 40 (since 50 * 40 = 2,000).[158]

Whether the customer foreclosure strategy is profitable depends on whether the actual increase in Division 1's sales is greater than the critical value. The extent to which the actual increase in Division 1's demand will exceed the critical value will depend on:

- the extent to which the increase in Firm 2's marginal cost of 100 to 150 is passed on to end-consumers of gadgets; and
- the extent to which consumers of gadgets faced with an increase in Firm 2's price switch to gadgets supplied by Division 1 (i.e. the degree of substitutability between Firms 1 and 2's gadgets).

The higher the proportion of the component cost increase that is passed on to consumers in the form of higher gadget prices, the lower need be the substitutability between the gadgets produced by Firm 2 and Division 1 in order for the actual increase in Division 1's demand to exceed the critical amount.

Conversely, the higher the substitutability between the downstream products, the lower need be the proportion of the cost increase that is

---

from accepting Firm 2's offer even if there were no shift of demand downstream to the merged entity.

[157] This is because each incremental unit sold allows the downstream division to earn a margin of 60 (equal to 200 – 140) but at the same time each incremental unit switched also represents a lost sale for the upstream division to Firm 2, on which it would have earned a margin of 10 (equal to 150 – 140). The net effect on profit of a unit switched is therefore 50.

[158] Note that if Firm B offered a price of 130 rather than 100, then the *critical* increase would be zero. The profit from foreclosure would equal the profit from accepting Firm 2's offer even if there were no shift of demand downstream to the merged entity.

passed on in order for the *actual* demand increase to exceed the *critical* demand increase.[159]

We noted above that if customer foreclosure enabled Division 1 to increase its margin, then this would reduce the critical demand increase required to make the foreclosure strategy profitable. It should be noted that any increase in Division 1's price would also reduce the actual increase in demand it obtains due to the foreclosure strategy compared to the situation in which it held its price constant.[160]

As with the assessment of the incentive to engage in input foreclosure, it greatly simplifies the analysis of both the critical increase in demand and actual increase in demand if pre-merger downstream margins are used as a proxy for post-merger downstream margins. By making this assumption, it is often possible to gain significant insights into the profitability of a hypothesised foreclosure strategy for the purpose of assessing a firm's incentive to engage in foreclosure.

### 4.3    Effect of customer foreclosure

As with input foreclosure, customer foreclosure is only labelled 'anti-competitive foreclosure' if it results in higher prices in the downstream market as a result of a lessening of competition.

Customer foreclosure can only give rise to harm to consumers if, by reducing the sales of rival upstream firms, it decreases competitiveness upstream causing the costs of downstream rivals that procure the input to increase and this in turn leads to higher prices in the downstream market.

The extent to which upstream competitiveness is affected by the foreclosure strategy will depend significantly on the factors discussed under the assessment of the ability to engage in customer foreclosure such as the importance of scale economies and the size of the contestable downstream demand (i.e. demand that is unaffected by the foreclosure strategy). It will also depend on the extent to which the upstream firms affected by the foreclosure strategy represent an important source of

[159] It should be noted that these factors are themselves interrelated since the extent to which an increase in Firm 2's costs will lead it to increase price will partly depend on the extent to which any price increase will cause it to lose sales to Division 1.

[160] This is because some consumers of Firm 2's gadget that might otherwise have switched following Firm 2's price increase may in the face of higher prices for the merged entity's gadgets remain with Firm 2 rather than switching.

competition in the upstream market. If the foreclosure strategy only affects a small part of the upstream market (e.g. because certain important upstream players achieve minimum efficient scale through sales they make in other geographic markets), then the foreclosure strategy is less likely to reduce competition upstream.

Even if the customer foreclosure strategy causes a reduction in competition upstream, and thereby increases the prices faced by certain downstream rivals, this does not imply that it will give rise to harm to consumers.

The extent to which an increase in downstream rivals' input costs caused by customer foreclosure can be expected to give rise to higher downstream prices will depend significantly on whether the firms whose input costs have increased form a significant part of the market and in the aggregate represent a significant source of competition. Moreover, if the firms that are affected by the reduction in upstream competition are particularly close competitors for the downstream firm, this will increase the scope for the merged entity to increase price.

On the other hand, if foreclosure only affects a small part of the downstream market (e.g. because certain downstream players rely less on the input whose price has increased), or there are potential entrants that are unaffected by the foreclosure strategy, then the merged entity is less likely to increase prices downstream.

Any assessment of the effect of foreclosure should also take into account that over the longer term any increase in upstream prices may invite entry by new unintegrated firms at the upstream level. As discussed in Section 4.1, upstream firms may be able to counter any customer foreclosure strategy by merging with a downstream firm and pricing aggressively to expand the base of sales over which it can achieve scale economies.[161]

Finally, any assessment of a vertical merger must take into account the potentially important role played by efficiencies (see Section 2.1). Through the elimination of double marginalisation, a vertical merger will often give rise to an incentive for the downstream division to lower

---

[161] As with assessment of the effect of input foreclosure, the boundaries between the various stages of assessment are blurred. It might be that factors that affect the scope for the merged entity to raise upstream rivals' costs in the short term are considered at the ability to foreclose stage, whereas factors that affect the scope for the merged entity to do so over the longer term (e.g. new entry or countervailing mergers with downstream firms) are considered at the stage of assessing the effect of foreclosure.

its price relative to its pre-merger level. This may occur even if the merger simultaneously gives rise to customer foreclosure that raises the costs and prices of downstream rivals and that causes them to lose sales to the merged entity. While competitors, both upstream and downstream, may be significantly harmed by the foreclosure strategy, the overall effect on consumers may be positive as a result of the lower prices offered by the merged entity.

### 4.4    Customer foreclosure: EU case law

Although customer foreclosure is not often raised in vertical merger cases, the Commission identified this type of concern in a number of energy mergers that combined the incumbent suppliers in vertically related markets. For instance, in *ENI/EDP/GDP*,[162] the Commission advanced customer foreclosure concerns in the wholesale gas market. The proposed transaction, which was ultimately prohibited after a Phase II investigation, would have brought under common ownership the monopoly supplier of wholesale gas in Portugal and the only supplier active in the downstream markets for gas-fired power electricity generation and retail distribution of gas and electricity. The Commission concluded that the merger as notified would have foreclosed potential rivals from gaining access to sufficient demand for gas to make entry viable in the upstream wholesale gas market. According to the Commission, the proposed transaction would have therefore reinforced GDP's dominant position upstream.[163]

Similarly, in *DONG/Elsam/Energi E2*,[164] the Commission assessed the likelihood of customer foreclosure in the wholesale gas market. DONG was a quasi-monopolistic company upstream, while Elsam and E2, the Danish electricity generation incumbents in West Denmark and East Denmark respectively, were by far the most important Danish purchasers of natural gas. After analysing the long-term contracts between each of the downstream parties and DONG, the Commission concluded that a foreclosure effect would likely occur for short-term volumes, and would cover all Elsam and E2 sales following the long-term contracts' expiry. The Commission concluded that this customer foreclosure effect would

---

[162] Case COMP/M.3440 – *ENI/EDP/GDP*, Commission decision of 9 December 2004.
[163] See ibid., Section V.B.2.
[164] Case COMP/M.3868 – *DONG/Elsam/Energi E2*, Commission decision of 14 March 2006.

constitute a significant strengthening of DONG's dominant position upstream, and that this would create further disincentives for potential entrants. In particular, the decision reads: 'the foreclosure of this demand after the merger will make it more difficult for competitors to DONG to enter the Danish natural gas sector, whether as wholesale suppliers or as suppliers of final customers, thereby raising barriers to entry to all of these markets.'[165]

In *Syngenta/Monsanto's Sunflower Seed Business*,[166] competitors and potential entrants in the markets for flower seed treatment (upstream) indicated that the merger would prevent them from reaching the necessary customer base to compete effectively. In particular, customer foreclosure concerns were put forward for two different upstream markets: the market for sunflower seed treatment fungicides and the market for sunflower seed treatment insecticides. Ultimately, the Commission concluded that the merged entity would not have the ability to foreclose current competitors or potential entrants in these markets, since the proposed transaction would lead to a combined market share of [40–50%] in the market for the commercialisation of sunflower seed (downstream), leaving at least [50–60%] of the demand available for other seed treatment producers (upstream).[167]

In a number of other cases, the Commission was able to dismiss customer foreclosure concerns without the need to undertake a detailed empirical analysis. For example, in *Itema/Barcovision*,[168] the Commission readily excluded the possibility that the transaction could give rise to customer foreclosure by pointing out that: 'Uster [Barcovision's main rival]'s sales of winder sensors to Itema represent only [10–20]% of its total sales and less than 10% of the total winder sensors market. Should Itema stop buying sensors from Uster, this would have limited effects on the upstream markets, making a customer foreclosure strategy clearly unprofitable.'[169]

Finally, the Commission considered the potential for anti-competitive customer foreclosure during its investigation of the acquisition of BST, a company active in the production of technical fabrics, by WLR, a private

---

[165] Case COMP/M.3868 – *DONG/Elsam/Energi E2*, Commission decision of 14 March 2006, para. 504.
[166] Case COMP/M.5675 – *Syngenta/Monsanto's Sunflower Seed Business*, Commission decision of 17 November 2010.
[167] See ibid., Sections IX.4.1.2, IX.4.2.2 and IX.4.2.4.
[168] Case COMP/M.4874 – *Itema/Barcovision*, Commission decision of 4 August 2008.
[169] See ibid., para. 91.

equity firm that owned Safety Components International 'SCI', a company active in the manufacture of components for automotive airbag modules.[170] The assessment of customer foreclosure concerns conducted by the Commission in this case is discussed in some detail below.

### 4.4.1   Case Study: *WLR/BST*

In *WLR/BST*,[171] the Commission established that there was no horizontal overlap between the merging parties. However, BST produced a particular product, flat airbag fabric, which was an input to a product produced by SCI, cut and sewn airbag cushions (CSCs). Its competitive assessment therefore addressed whether this vertical relationship could give rise to customer foreclosure, a concern that was raised by a number of competitors of BST in the supply of flat airbag fabric.[172]

The Commission found that in the upstream market for flat airbag fabrics, BST was the EEA-wide market leader with a market share in 2005 of 45–50%.[173]

On the downstream market for CSCs, there were two main 'independent' suppliers, SCI and Aerazur, with market shares in 'independent' sales of 40–45% and 35–40% respectively. However, in addition to these 'independent' suppliers, there were producers of CSCs that were vertically integrated in the production of airbag modules and that supplied CSCs exclusively to their own in-house operations.[174] The Commission noted that 'independent' CSC producers were subject to strong competitive pressure from airbag module suppliers' own in-house production of CSCs, and that on the basis of total CSC production the share of SCI was 15–20%.[175]

The Commission considered a theory of harm in which the merged entity would foreclose rival flat airbag fabric suppliers' access to a substantial CSC customer base, and thereby reduce the ability of rival fabric producers to compete.

The Commission noted a number of factors that undermined the merged entity's *ability* to engage in customer foreclosure. The Commission found that it was difficult for a CSC producer to switch fabric

---

[170] See Case COMP/M.4389 – *WLR/BST*, Commission decision of 5 December 2006.
[171] Case COMP/M.4389 – *WLR/BST*, Commission decision of 5 December 2006.
[172] The Commission also considered and dismissed possible competitive concerns arising from input foreclosure, although it did not receive any complaints from third parties with concerns related to input foreclosure. See ibid., para. 30.
[173] Ibid., para. 24.      [174] See ibid., para. 10.      [175] See ibid., para. 23.

supplier quickly. This difficulty arose from ongoing production program commitments on both sides and the need for certain certification procedures to be followed if switching was to occur.[176]

The Commission nevertheless considered the consequences of a decision by the merged entity's downstream division to source flat fabric exclusively from its upstream division. The Commission found that only one competitor of BST currently depended on SCI for more than 10% of its flat fabric turnover.[177] It also found that most of BST's main competitors were large diversified companies that also produced a range of technical fabrics for applications other than airbag modules, and that could be expected to withstand a sudden drop in flat fabric sales without undergoing severe financial difficulties.

The Commission noted that if SCI sourced exclusively from BST, this would bring only about 10–20% of the total EEA flat fabric production in-house. The Commission recognised that given that BST's capacity was fully utilised, and could not be increased economically in the short term, a consequence of this demand being switched to BST would be that it would have to reduce sales to SCI's competitors. This displaced supply would leave unsatisfied demand for fabric from SCI's competitors, which could only be met by BST's competitors.

Moreover, the Commission found that, given that SCI's purchases of flat airbag fabrics represented only 15–25% of total EEA demand for flat airbag fabrics, BST's competitors would still have access to a substantial customer base and noted in this context that overall EEA demand for airbag products was growing at around 5% per annum.[178]

The Commission also considered the role played by customers of CSCs, airbag module manufacturers. It found that airbag module manufacturers exercised considerable influence on the choice of fabric supplier even when outsourcing CSC production, and that they had a preference for multiple sourcing of fabric in order to maintain sufficient competitive alternative suppliers.[179]

Given that the Commission did not find the merged entity to have the ability to foreclose, it did not need to carry out a detailed analysis of the merged entity's incentives in WLR/BST.

However, a particular concern raised by one of BST's fabric competitors was that the merged entity, which controlled its major cost input (i.e. fabric), would opt to cut prices of CSC in order to expand its share of the

[176] Case COMP/M.4389 – WLR/BST, Commission decision of 5 December 2006, para. 33.
[177] See ibid., para. 33. [178] See ibid., para. 35. [179] See ibid., para. 36.

CSC market; and that this would create a 'backlash' demand for cheaper fabric from other CSC's producers. This would allegedly squeeze BST's fabric competitor's margins, perhaps causing some to exit the market.[180]

Interestingly, rather than responding to such concerns by noting that to the extent the merger gave rise to downward pressure on both CSC and fabric prices, this should be welcomed as a benefit of the merger, the Commission dismissed the concern by stating that the merged entity would not have an *incentive* to adopt such a strategy. It countered this concern by noting that if airbag module producers saw that SCI was enjoying a lower fabric transfer price from BST post-merger, they would themselves request a corresponding price cut from BST for their fabric prices for in-house production. The Commission then reasoned that since fabric margins are much higher than CSC margins, the overall trade-off of a low-price CSC strategy would be negative for the merged entity. This is because any profits from increased volumes of CSC sales resulting from lower prices for the 10–30% of BST output that goes to SCI would have been outweighed by lower margins on the 70–90% of BST output sold to third parties.

It should be noted that this analysis is somewhat unconventional. It relies on BST having to lower its prices to rivals to its downstream division as a result of its downstream division becoming more aggressive in competition with those rivals. The Commission did not carry out a more conventional analysis of the incentives of the merged entity to engage in customer foreclosure that would have needed to take account of the costs of reducing purchases from certain upstream suppliers, which, absent the foreclosure strategy, would have been purchases the downstream division preferred to undertake.

## 5.   Conglomerate mergers

The term 'conglomerate merger' refers to any merger that is neither horizontal (i.e. between actual or potential competitors) nor vertical (i.e. between a supplier and a customer). Conglomerate mergers therefore include mergers between suppliers of complementary products and mergers in which the parties supply products that are neither complementary nor substitutable.[181] In most circumstances, such mergers will

---

[180]  Case ibid., para. 37.
[181]  In other words, an increase or decrease in the price of one product does not change the demand for the other product.

not raise competition concerns.[182] However, it is possible that under certain circumstances a merger between producers of complementary products or related products that are purchased by the same set of customers could give rise to anti-competitive effects.

The principal theory of harm applicable to conglomerate mergers is that the merger would allow for market power in one activity to be used as a means of reducing competition in a related market. This is often referred to as 'leveraging' of market power. It could also be the case, however, that a merger raises the possibility that the merged entity could pursue conduct that allows it to protect existing market power that, absent the merger, might have become subject to more effective competition.

In both cases, the concern is that an increase in product range allows the merged entity to take some action that lessens the competitive constraints that it faces, thereby giving rise to a unilateral incentive to increase prices to the detriment of consumers. Generally, this action will involve the conditioning of sales in a market currently served by one merging party on sales in another market currently served by the other merging party via tying and/or bundling.[183]

The term 'pure bundling' is used to describe a situation in which products are sold together in fixed proportions and are not available independently of one another. For example, a pure bundle of good A and good B implies that a customer can buy good A and good B together, but cannot buy either good A or good B on its own. 'Mixed bundling', on the other hand, describes a more general situation in which goods are sold together in fixed proportions but are, in addition, available independently of one another. Foreclosure concerns may arise where a bundle is sold for a price lower than the sum of the prices of the individual goods in question. Pure bundling can be considered as a special case of mixed bundling whereby the prices of the individual goods in the package are so high that no customer would purchase the products separately.

The term 'tying' is used to describe a situation in which customers that purchase a particular good (the tying good) are also required to purchase another good (the tied good). For example, tying of good B to good A implies that if a customer purchases good A, they must purchase good B rather than good C, which might otherwise have been an alternative to good B. Unlike the case of a pure bundle, the consumer need not

---

[182] See EC Non-horizontal Merger Guidelines, para. 92.
[183] See ibid., para. 93.

purchase good A and good B in fixed proportions but may choose the volume of B they purchase.[184] Tying can be achieved through designing the tying good so that it does not work when used with products competing with the tied good (technical tying) or through contracting such that a customer purchasing the tying good must agree to purchase the tied good and not products competing with the tied good (commercial tying).

The general concern in relation to each of these practices is that the merged entity will reduce rivals' profits to such an extent that they are no longer able to exert an effective competitive constraint on the merged entity, with the result that consumers are harmed.

As with vertical mergers, the EC Non-horizontal Merger Guidelines put forward a three-stage approach for the assessment of whether a conglomerate merger could be considered to give rise to anti-competitive foreclosure.[185] These stages relate to the questions of whether a merged entity would have the ability to foreclose its rivals, whether it would have the incentive to do so and whether foreclosure would have a detrimental effect on competition that gives rise to consumer harm. In what follows we consider in turn the factors relevant to these three analytical elements. As with the discussion of vertical mergers, it should be noted that these stages are closely interrelated and in practice a single factor, such as the likely responses by rivals or the existence of economies of scale, may be relevant to the consideration of each of these questions.

Having considered the factors relevant to the Commission's three-stage assessment, we then provide a hypothetical example that explains in more detail how a merged entity's ability and incentive to foreclose, and the likelihood that foreclosure leads to consumer harm, depends on these factors.

Finally, we present case studies of the *Intel/McAfee*,[186] *GE/Amersham*[187] and *Google/DoubleClick*[188] mergers and comment on a number of additional cases in which the Commission considered conglomerate concerns.

---

[184] Under some definitions of tying, a customer purchasing the tying good (product A) may be permitted to choose a zero volume of the tied good (product B), but is nonetheless prevented from purchasing alternatives to the tied good (product C).

[185] See EC Non-horizontal Merger Guidelines, para. 94.

[186] Case COMP/M.5984 – *Intel/McAfee*, Commission decision of 26 January 2011.

[187] Case COMP/M.3304 – *GE/Amersham*, Commission decision of 21 January 2004.

[188] Case COMP/M.4731 – *Google/DoubleClick*, Commission decision of 11 March 2008.

### 5.1 Ability to foreclose in conglomerate mergers

The first step in the assessment of whether the merged entity has the ability to foreclose through any action (such as tying or bundling) is consideration of whether it is actually *feasible* in practical terms for the merged entity to undertake the action in question. In many cases, an examination of the features of a market reveals that a particular strategy, such as pure bundling, would not be a practical option for the merged entity.

It may be that two goods have different procurement procedures, different supply chains or different procurement timelines. For example, one good may represent a one-off purchase that is undertaken only once in a decade, whereas the other good may be purchased regularly over the course of the lifetime of the first good. This might make it much more difficult to engage in any form of commercial tying of the second good to the first good. In particular, it may be the case that the products are purchased by different customers, even if at first sight this is not obvious given that the products in question are components that end up in the same system. This may be because different companies make decisions over which products to purchase for different elements of a single system. For example, it may be that an aircraft manufacturer chooses one component for the aircraft but an airline chooses the engine at a later stage via separate competitions that take place each time an airline places an order for the aircraft. Selling to different customers often makes it impossible to engage in tying or bundling.[189]

Alternatively, there may be different buying groups within a single company that are responsible for buying the different products. Whilst this may not make tying or bundling impossible, it could in practice make it significantly more difficult since it may require the seller to effect changes to the procurement procedures currently in place.

In many cases the technical tying of one product to another will not be an option. In some cases this will be obvious (e.g. in the case of a merger between a producer of tea bags and tea cups) but in other cases involving products of a more technical nature this will be a more complex question. Moreover, rather than eliminating compatibility with rival products outright, the merged entity might be able to merely diminish the compatibility of its products with that of its rivals such that their functionality

---

[189] It may still be possible to engage in technical tying with separate buyers through the implementation of compatibility standards.

is degraded when used with rival products instead of with other products produced by the merged entity.[190]

One factor that may in certain cases influence the assessment of whether bundling or tying of one product to another is feasible is whether there is evidence that these practices have been carried out in the past by companies whose range includes the products in question.

There is an important distinction between the question of whether the merged entity has the ability to engage in bundling and tying and the question of whether the merged entity has the ability to foreclose. A firm may face no material impediments to linking sales of one of their products to sales of another (e.g. offering a discount on one product in their product line to any customer that purchases another of its products). Importantly, however, such a firm will not necessarily have the ability to foreclose. Specifically, it will not necessarily be able to materially reduce the revenues or increase the costs of rivals in a way that undermines their competitiveness. For that to be the case a number of further conditions must hold.[191]

First, the merged entity must have a significant degree of market power in at least one of the markets in which it is active. Market power could arise as a result of the merged entity offering a highly differentiated product for which rival products are not considered a good substitute or as a result of rivals facing significant capacity constraints. Absent market power, it is not clear how any action undertaken by the merged entity could materially affect the extent to which its rivals can offer effective competition. If the firm is subject to effective competition for each of its products then it will be able to induce customers to choose a bundle of its products only via lower prices, which is the essence of competition and not a cause for concern. Only where a firm attempts to use pre-existing market power in one area to harm rivals and thereby lessen competition in another activity can anti-competitive foreclosure potentially arise. It is interesting to note that bundling and tying may be observed in markets in which firms do not have a significant degree of market power and in cases where the profitability of these strategies clearly does not derive from foreclosure of rivals. This leads to the important observation, discussed in relation to the example below, that a merger could give rise

---

[190] This could be considered as a case of mixed bundling, whereby quality is increased, rather than price lowered, when the merged entity's products are purchased together rather than separately.
[191] Each of these is discussed further in the example in Section 5.4 below.

to the ability and incentive to bundle products in cases where this strategy is profitable even absent any foreclosure of rivals.

Second, there must be a large common pool of customers for the products that are the subject of the leverage theory.[192] If the products in question are consumed alone by many customers, then the merged entity will be less able to affect the demand of individual products produced by its rivals through any strategy that links the sales of its products to one another.

In addition to these conditions, a number of other factors are relevant for the questions of whether the merged entity has the ability to foreclose.

First, it is relevant to consider whether, by reducing the demand for its rivals' products, the merged entity can materially affect their costs (or alternatively, the quality of their products) such that rivals are less able to offer effective competition or are even forced to exit the market entirely. A particular action may reduce a rival's sales significantly. However, if there are no significant economies of scale, for example, this reduction in demand may have no impact on the rival's incentive to remain in the market and to try to win incremental business at a similar price to that which it would have offered absent the action in question. Given that foreclosure, as defined in the EC Non-horizontal Merger Guidelines, incorporates the notion of rivals' 'ability and/or incentive to compete',[193] it is important to take into account rivals' cost structures at the stage of assessing the merged entity's *ability* to engage in foreclosure as well as at the stage of assessing its *incentive* to foreclose and the *effect* of foreclosure.[194]

Second, it is relevant to consider whether there are counterstrategies available to rivals that might be expected to undermine the merged entity's ability to foreclose. For example, it may be possible for rivals whose product ranges mirror that of the merged entity to replicate the bundling or tying strategy of the merged entity. If none of the merged entity's rivals presently produce all the goods that form part of the merged entity's tie or bundle, then it may be necessary for them to merge with one another or enter 'teaming arrangements', whereby they jointly supply a particular customer that demands both elements of the bundle. By offering a similar bundle, the merged entity's rivals may be able to neutralise any competitive advantage that might otherwise have arisen.

---

[192] EC Non-horizontal Merger Guidelines, para. 100.
[193] Ibid., para. 18.    [194] Ibid., para. 101.

## 5.2   Incentive to foreclose in conglomerate mergers

Even if the merged entity has the ability to foreclose through a strategy of bundling or tying, it will not necessarily find it profitable to do so. This is because tying and bundling can give rise to immediate costs to the merged entity that may not outweigh their benefits in terms of generating greater sales volumes or allowing higher prices in the market into which it is attempting to leverage market power.

### 5.2.1   Costs of bundling and tying

The costs of bundling and tying will depend on the extent to which the customer base for each of the products in question is interested in also purchasing the other product. In the extreme scenario when there are no common customers for the products in question (as would be the case, for example, with respect to GE's jet engines and its medical diagnostic products), pure bundling will likely give rise to significant losses as many customers that would otherwise have chosen to purchase one of the products in the pure bundle prefer to forgo consumption of that product rather than purchase the pure bundle. With regard to mixed bundling, the absence of common customers will imply that demand for this mixed bundle will be low. Moreover, it will eliminate the incentive to charge higher prices for the products when purchased in isolation because doing so will only cause customers to switch to rival stand-alone products rather than to the mixed bundle.

Even in the case where there are common customers for the products in question (as may be the case, for example, with respect to two products within GE's medical diagnostic product range), bundling can entail significant losses. A pure bundle may cause certain customers that previously purchased one of the products from the merged entity and one of the products from a rival to purchase both products from the merged entity's rivals rather than purchase the pure bundle. In addition, if the merged entity can only successfully foreclose its rivals by offering a very low price for the pure or mixed bundle, then it may be that the profits sacrificed to implement the foreclosure strategy are substantial.

### 5.2.2   Benefits of bundling and tying

Tying and bundling may lead to certain benefits to the merged entity. Importantly, whilst the benefits of tying and bundling may depend on the effect of foreclosure (discussed further below), in principle there may be instances where tying or bundling that leads to the foreclosure of rivals would have been profitable *absent any foreclosure effect*. In this case, to the extent that the bundling gives rise to foreclosure that subsequently allows the merged entity to increase price, this will constitute an additional benefit to the merged entity arising from the bundling strategy. Mixed bundling in particular, may be profitable for the merged entity even absent foreclosure if there is a significant degree of complementarity between the products of the merging parties or if mixed bundling increases the scope for the merged entity to engage in price discrimination.

If the products of the merging parties are complementary then, as discussed in Section 2.1, the merged entity will take account of the fact that a reduction in the price of one good will boost demand for the other good and vice versa (the so-called Cournot effect). The extent to which a given price reduction will be profitable will depend both on the extent to which it boosts demand for the complementary product and the margin earned on the incremental sales of the product whose demand is boosted by the price reduction. The greater the increase in demand for the other good (that is, the higher degree of complementarity) and the greater the margin earned on incremental sales of the other good, the greater will be the incentive to cut the price of the first good.[195] In order to ensure that any increase in demand for complementary goods is captured by the merged entity and not by competitors, the merged entity may have an incentive to make the reduction in the price conditional on the purchase of the complementary products from the merged entity (i.e. offer the complementary products in a mixed bundle).

Even if the products sold by the merged entity are not complementary, an incentive to engage in mixed bundling to a pool of common customers may arise due to the increased scope for price discrimination it can offer. It has been shown that offering a mixed bundle is in theory profitable for a monopolist of multiple products under surprisingly general demand conditions, if the firm can otherwise only charge a single price for each product.[196] Indeed, it can be shown that for any two goods, A and B, that have independent distributions of values (i.e. a consumer

---

[195] This is analogous to the case of a merger between substitutes, in which the incentive to increase the price of one product is affected by both the increase in demand for the other product and the margin earned on incremental sales of the other product.

[196] See R. P. McAFee, J. McMillan and M. Whinston, 'Multiproduct Monopoly, Commodity Bundling, and the Correlation of Values' (1989) 103 *Quarterly Journal of Economics* 371–83.

with a high willingness to pay for A relative to other consumers will not necessarily have a high willingness to pay for B relative to other consumers) a monopolist can obtain higher profits by offering a mixed bundle of A and B at a discount to the sum of the optimal monopoly prices of the two products.[197]

To see why this is the case, suppose the monopolist sets the price of A and B optimally, i.e. at the level for which marginal revenue equals marginal cost. At these price levels a marginal reduction in the price of either good has no impact on profits (the reduction in margin on sales to existing customers is just offset by the incremental sales made). Now suppose the monopolist offers a marginal price reduction for good B that is conditional on the purchase of A. This means the firm earns a lower margin on sales to consumers that would have bought B anyway, but it also gives rise to an increase in demand for B. These two effects just offset one another. This is because the price of B was previously set optimally and, importantly, those customers that obtain the discount (i.e. only those that purchase A) are representative of the overall demand for B – they are no more or less likely to have a high willingness to pay for B than other consumers due to the independence of the demand for A and B. Crucially, however, the conditional discount will *also* cause an increase in demand for A. This is because certain customers that did not buy A previously, will do so now that it enables them to purchase B at a marginally lower price. Since we noted that the effect on profits was neutral before taking into account the increased sales of A, these extra sales of A must increase profits over and above the profit levels obtainable absent the mixed bundle.[198]

Importantly, however, if firms are already engaging in price discrimination pre-merger, both the Cournot effect and any benefit related to further prospects for price discrimination disappear. In the case that each customer is charged its willingness to pay for each unit produced by the merging parties, the merged entity will not be able to boost sales by decreasing the price it charges to any individual customer implying that no Cournot effect can arise post-merger. Moreover, to the extent

---

[197] The result is surprisingly general because the condition that two goods have independent distributions of valuations is likely to be satisfied for the vast majority of pairs of unrelated goods chosen at random, such as apples and pens.

[198] For a further explanation of this result and an interesting discussion of why we do not in practice see a plethora of mixed bundles containing unrelated goods, see B. Nalebuff, 'Bundling, Tying, and Portfolio Effects' (DTI Economics Paper No. 1, 2003).

that each merging party is already able to price discriminate effectively through its individual price negotiations with customers, mixed bundling will offer no further scope for price discrimination.

The discussion above illustrates that tying and bundling can be profitable absent a foreclosure motive, and indeed may lead to price reductions that benefit consumers. Often, however, the benefits of tying and bundling against which the costs of these strategies must be compared may depend to a significant extent on the effect of foreclosure. If tying and bundling is very effective at causing foreclosure, and foreclosure gives rise to an opportunity for the merged entity to significantly increase its prices and/ or sales volumes, then the merged entity may have an incentive to foreclose even if it is not profitable in the short run. Whether the foreclosure strategy is profitable over the long term will then depend on whether the benefits from foreclosure outweigh the costs. The factors that influence the effect of foreclosure are discussed further below in Section 5.3.

As a final remark, if bundling involves a sacrifice of profit to drive out competitors, then it becomes similar in character to predatory pricing. As discussed in more detail in the example below at Section 5.4, any theory of harm involving short-term profit sacrifice must specify why such a strategy would become attractive or feasible post-merger given that we did not previously observe the merging parties engaging in predatory pricing pre-merger. Thus, while it could be alleged that a merged firm could offer a reduction in the price of good A to induce customers to choose good B over rivals' substitutes for B, the supplier of B could, pre-merger, offer an equivalent price cut on B to win sales from rivals. In this regard, it may be relevant to consider whether the merger makes the strategy significantly less costly (due to the demand boosting effect caused by the complementarity of the products, which is not taken into account by either party pre-merger) and, therefore, whether tying and bundling enables the merged entity to commit to more aggressive pricing behaviour in a particular market than it could have done absent the ability to link sales in that market to sales in another market.

## 5.3   Effects of foreclosure in conglomerate mergers

Bundling and tying by a merged entity may result in significant harm to its competitors by reducing demand for those rivals' products. However, it is important to recognise that all competitive conduct is intended to win share from rivals, and so anti-competitive foreclosure must be distinguished from ordinary competition on the merits. Anti-competitive foreclosure is said to arise only when harm to competitors directly gives rise to harm to consumers. The merged entity's rivals may experience a significant reduction in revenues without having their ability or incentive to compete with the merged entity for incremental business materially affected. Moreover, even if the competition exerted by the merged entity's rivals is adversely affected, consumers may gain overall as a result of lower prices arising from efficiencies generated by the merger. As with theories of harm based on customer foreclosure, a link must be established between rivals' reduced demand and a reduced ability to compete.

Nevertheless, in certain circumstances foreclosure may allow the merged entity to increase or protect market power in one of its markets via either exclusion or marginalisation of rivals. Increases in market power may come about if rivals are no longer viable as a result of the foreclosure strategy and are forced to exit. Similarly, the protection of market power may result from entry that would have otherwise occurred being deterred. More generally, increases in or the protection of market power may result from important rivals to the merged entity being marginalised. Absent countervailing factors such as buyer power or new entry (or indeed re-entry by previously marginalised rivals) that disciplines the merged entity's pricing decisions over the longer term, consumers may be harmed overall by higher prices than would have otherwise prevailed.

The marginalisation of rivals could occur if variable costs fall significantly with the level of output produced. In that case a strategy that reduces the output of rivals may increase their variable costs. This in turn could make them unwilling to offer low prices in competition with the merged entity for incremental customers.

Alternatively, if rivals expect to earn lower revenues in the future as a result of the merged entity's foreclosure strategy, they may be deterred from investing in R&D that they might otherwise have found attractive. This may imply that in future their products will be less attractive to customers than they would have been absent foreclosure, and that as such they exert a less significant constraint on the merged entity's prices. It is often difficult in practice to assess how foreclosure will affect the incentives of rivals to invest in R&D. It will sometimes be relatively clear, however, that a reduction in revenues in a particular product or geographic market is unlikely to affect the incentives of a rival that is active across multiple product or geographic markets to invest in R&D.

Even if certain competitors are marginalised (or even exit the market) as a result of foreclosure, this will not necessarily have a material impact on the competitive constraints remaining on the merged entity. It is only if a set of rivals that together represent an important competitive constraint on the merged entity are marginalised that foreclosure could give rise to concerns regarding a lessening of effective competition. It may be that firms offering single products in each of the markets served by the merged entity continue to offer effective competition even if certain rivals are marginalised, particularly if the rivals that are marginalised have higher costs or offer less attractive products.

As noted above, rivals may have the ability and incentive to respond to any attempt by the merged entity to engage in foreclosure by employing counterstrategies (or even counter-mergers) that undermine the ability of the merged entity to foreclose. Such strategies are also relevant to consider at the stage of assessing the effect of foreclosure. In certain cases sophisticated customers who have a clear interest in ensuring that they are served by competitive markets may play an important role in mitigating the anti-competitive effects of foreclosure. In addition to strategies such as threatening to sponsor entry, customers may exert buyer power through effectively sponsoring actions on the part of the merged entity's rivals, such as encouraging them to offer competing bundles through teaming arrangements, which serve the long-term interests of the buyer in terms of maintaining competition. The role that may be played by large customers who can strategically condition their purchasing decisions on their long-term interests is overlooked in much of the economic literature concerning bundling and tying. This factor, however, may be a very important consideration in many conglomerate merger cases involving industrial products.

Importantly, even if rivals are deemed unable to propose a competitive response that undermines the merged entity's foreclosure strategy and are forced to exit as a result, competition is only harmed if the exit enables the merged entity to implement sustainable increases in its prices. In certain cases, such price increases will be rendered unattractive by the prospect of inviting re-entry by rivals that previously exited due to foreclosure. For example, a rival that is induced to exit from a particular geographic market due to foreclosure, but remains active in other geographic markets, may find re-entry relatively easy and profitable if the merged entity attempts to exploit market power by charging high prices.

Finally, the assessment of efficiencies may form an important part of the assessment of the overall effect of a conglomerate merger. Efficiencies might arise from economies of scope whereby the merged entity can reduce their costs by selling a wider range of products. Alternatively, customers may gain significantly from being able to purchase multiple products from a single supplier. Moreover, the internalisation of any pricing externality due to the bringing together of sales of complementary goods may represent an efficiency that directly benefits consumers.

The source of competitive concern (e.g. low priced mixed bundles that give rise to foreclosure of rivals) may be closely related to efficiencies that lead to consumer benefits in the short term. If an investigation suggests that consumers will generally gain in the short term as a result of lower prices, then only in exceptional circumstances should the merger be prohibited on the basis that they might be harmed in the long run due to the marginalisation of rivals. Although these circumstances might in principle arise if the benefits to consumers in the short term were shown to be small and the long-term harm was shown to be large and relatively certain, such circumstances are likely to be rare in practice.

### 5.4   Foreclosure in conglomerate mergers: an example

In this section we consider a highly stylised example that highlights a number of features relevant to the assessment of the ability and incentive to engage in foreclosure through bundling.[199]

Suppose that consumers buy systems that are made up of two types of component, A and B. A consumer derives no value from either component A or component B on its own but derives some value from consuming them together. Component A is produced by two competing Firms, $A_1$ and $A_2$, whilst component B is produced independently by two competing Firms, $B_1$ and $B_2$. In this example, we consider the implications of a merger between $A_1$ and $B_1$. Pre-merger, consumers can choose to purchase one of four systems as follows: $A_1B_1$; $A_1B_2$; $A_2B_1$; or $A_2B_2$, where $A_1B_1$ denotes a system that comprises an A component from Firm $A_1$ and a B component from Firm $B_1$. Suppose that the systems are differentiated so that at equal prices for each system as a whole, some consumers will prefer one system whilst others will prefer another.

---

[199] This example is in the spirit of Choi (2008) (below). While we make use of some key intuitive results from Choi, we do not provide a detailed explanation of the assumptions behind these results here. See J. P. Choi, 'Mergers with Bundling in Complementary Markets' (2008) 3 *Journal of Industrial Economics* 553–77.

Suppose that each of the four components is produced at zero marginal cost. However, suppose that each component producer has to pay a one-off fixed cost of 8,000 every year to stay in the market.[200] Pre-merger, each component is priced at 50 and the demand for each of the four systems is 100 units (implying that total demand for each component is 200 units). The total revenues of each component producer is 10,000 (since each sells 200 units at a price of 50), which is sufficient to justify the fixed cost of staying in the market of 8,000.

Post-merger, the choice set of the consumer depends on whether the merged entity decides to engage in some form of bundling.

If the merged entity decides not to engage in any form of bundling, all four system choices will remain available post-merger.

If the merged entity decides to engage in mixed bundling, then all four system choices will continue to be available but the price of $A_1$ will be lower when it is bought together with $B_1$ than when it is bought on its own to be assembled by the consumer with a B component produced by the merged entity's rival, $B_2$. Similarly, the price of $B_1$ will be lower when it is bought together with $A_1$ than when it is bought on its own to be assembled by the consumer with an A component produced by the merged entity's rival, $A_2$.

If the merged entity decides to engage in pure bundling, then it will now not be possible for a consumer to purchase $A_1$ and assemble it with $B_2$, or for a consumer to purchase $B_1$ and assemble it with $A_2$. Therefore there will only be two systems available for consumers to choose: $A_1B_1$ or $A_2B_2$.

We consider the merged entity's ability and incentive to pursue strategies of mixed and pure bundling in turn.

### 5.4.1   Mixed bundling

Let us assume that the merged entity offers a mixed bundle of $A_1$ and $B_1$, such that whereas the total price of the system $A_1B_1$ was previously 100 (since each component was priced at 50), this system is now priced at 80. Prior to the merger, each producer does not take into account the fact that a reduction in price of its component will boost demand for complementary components. The merger allows this effect to be taken into consideration (i.e. the pricing externality is internalised), allowing the

---

[200] This could relate to the costs of maintaining the plants in which each component is produced.

price of the mixed bundle to be lower than the combined price of the individual components if they were priced independently.

However, the merged entity decides to increase the prices of the stand-alone products to 60. It takes account of the fact that if it increases the prices of the stand-alone products, some of the lost demand for systems $A_1B_2$ and $A_2B_1$, which are now more expensive due to the higher prices of both $A_1$ and $B_1$, will be recaptured by its low priced system $A_1B_1$.

In response to this, suppose that producers of the rival components, $A_2$ and $B_2$, decide to reduce the price of their components from 50 to 45. This price reduction comes about for two reasons. First, the lower price for the mixed bundle implies that the stand-alone providers have an incentive to reduce their prices so that each of the systems that contain one of their own components remains competitive with the merged entity's mixed bundle. Second, the higher price for the individual components $A_1$ and $B_1$ implies that each of the stand-alone producers has an incentive to reduce price in order to reduce switching from the 'mix and match' systems, $A_2B_1$ and $A_1B_2$, to the mixed bundle offered by the merged entity. For example, there is an incentive to reduce the price of $A_2$ to minimise the loss of switching from the system $A_2B_2$, since the substitutable product $A_1B_1$ is cheaper, and a further incentive to reduce the price of $A_2$ to minimise the loss of switching from the system $A_2B_1$, which, absent a reduction in the price of $A_2$, will seem particularly unattractive given the higher price of the stand-alone component $B_1$. However, they do not reduce their prices to as low as 40 (i.e. the implicit price of each component within the merged entity's mixed bundle) as each stand-alone firm does not take account of the fact that a small reduction in the price of its component boosts demand for the component of the other firm.[201]

As a result of these pricing decisions, each of the 'mix and match' systems, $A_2B_1$ and $A_1B_2$, now has a total price of 105. This is because they include an individual component from the merged entity, priced at 60, and an individual component from a stand-alone producer, priced at 45.

---

[201] These pricing movements are directionally the same as those found in Choi (2008). Specifically, Choi's model shows (given the assumptions regarding demand and cost conditions) that mixed bundling following the merger would have the following implications for prices: first, the price of the bundle post-merger is lower than the sum of the pre-merger component prices; second, the merged firm's prices for individual components are higher with mixed bundling; and third, the independent firms also cut their prices. See J. P. Choi, 'Mergers with Bundling in Complementary Markets' (2008) 3 *Journal of Industrial Economics* 553–77.

Table 5.3 *System prices pre-merger and post-merger under mixed bundling*

| System | Pre-merger price | Post-merger price |
|--------|------------------|-------------------|
| $A_1B_1$ | 100 | 80 |
| $A_2B_2$ | 100 | 90 |
| $A_1B_2$ | 100 | 105 |
| $A_2B_1$ | 100 | 105 |

The system comprising components from each of the stand-alone producers, $A_2B_2$, has a total price of 90, because each component has a price of 45. The system comprising components from the merged entity, $A_1B_1$, has a total price of 80, the price of the mixed bundle.

Table 5.3 summarises the total prices of each of the four systems pre-merger and in the post-merger scenario in which mixed bundling is adopted.

We now consider how the volume demanded for each system might change from the pre-merger situation in which demand for each system was 100. Since the systems are differentiated, some consumers will prefer a more expensive system to a cheaper one, and, indeed, some still prefer a 'mix and match' system. Let us assume that demand for the mixed bundle increases significantly to 170 units, as certain consumers switch from each of the other systems to the cheapest system available. The price reduction in the $A_2B_2$ system causes it to retain some customers that might otherwise have switched to the mixed bundle and also to win some sales from the higher priced 'mix and match' systems, and as a result experiences a more modest increase in demand to 110 units. The demands for the mix and match systems, $A_2B_1$ and $A_1B_2$, fall to 60 units as many consumers switch to either $A_1B_1$ or $A_2B_2$. Table 5.4 summarises the total demand for each of the four systems pre-merger and in the post-merger scenario in which mixed bundling is adopted.[202]

It is worth noting at this stage that the short-term welfare implications of the above vary across the heterogeneous consumers. It is clear that those who preferred system $A_1B_1$ at pre-merger price levels benefit since they can now buy the same system at a lower price. Similarly, those who preferred system $A_2B_2$ are better off since this system has also reduced in

---

[202] Directionally, these changes in demand are similar to those found in equilibrium in Choi: see J. P. Choi, 'Mergers with Bundling in Complementary Markets' (2008) 3 *Journal of Industrial Economics* 553–77.

Table 5.4 *System demand pre-merger and post-merger under mixed bundling*

| System | Pre-merger demand | Post-merger demand |
|---|---|---|
| $A_1B_1$ | 100 | 170 |
| $A_2B_2$ | 100 | 110 |
| $A_1B_2$ | 100 | 60 |
| $A_2B_1$ | 100 | 60 |

price. However, those that purchased a mix and match bundle, and continue to do so despite the new higher price, are worse off. The overall welfare effect is therefore ambiguous.[203]

It is now possible to determine the revenues of each firm. The revenue earned by the merged firm derives from three sources. First, revenues from sales of system $A_1B_1$ are equal to 13,600 (170 units at a price of 80 each). Second, the revenues from sales of $A_1$ components as part of the demand for the system $A_1B_2$ are equal to 3,600 (60 units at a price of 60 each). Third, and symmetrically, the revenues from sales of $B_1$ components as part of the demand for the system $A_2B_1$ are equal to 3,600 (60 units at a price of 60 each). The total revenue of the merged entity is therefore equal to 20,800.

The total revenue of each stand-alone component provider can also be calculated. Revenues for the producer of $A_2$ components come from two sources. First, revenues from the sales of $A_2$ components as part of the demand for the system $A_2B_2$ are 4,950 (110 units at a price of 45 each). Secondly, revenues from the sales of $A_2$ components as part of the demand for the system $A_2B_1$ are 2,700 (60 units at a price of 45 each). The total revenues of the producer of $A_2$ components is therefore 7,650 (4,950 + 2,700). Since the producer of $B_2$ components is in a symmetrical position, its revenues are also 7,650.

The revenues of the stand-alone providers have therefore fallen from pre-merger levels of 10,000, to 7,650 as a result of the merger and mixed bundling strategy. Recall, that we assumed that there was a fixed cost of 8,000 of maintaining the plants for producing each component. On this basis, the producers of the stand-alone components would prefer to exit

---

[203] Although a key result of Choi (ibid.) is that the overall consumer welfare effect can be negative if substitutability of different systems is sufficiently high. The price of the stand-alone products is raised to a greater extent in this case: see ibid.

the market as a result of the merger and mixed bundling strategy rather than pay the fixed cost of 8,000. If the producers of the stand-alone components exit, then the merged entity will face a reduced competitive constraint for each of its components and will find it profitable to increase prices, thus harming all consumers.

In this stylised example, the presence of the fixed cost implies that mixed bundling gives rise to the exit of the merged entity's rivals, and a lessening of competition in the longer term, despite the possible benefits to consumers in the short term from lower prices (recall that both systems $A_1B_1$ and $A_2B_2$ fell in price).

Note that, in this case, the profits of the merged entity in the short term (i.e. prior to any exit) are higher than the pre-merger profits of $A_1$ and $B_1$ combined. Pre-merger, producers of $A_1$ and $B_1$ each had revenues of 10,000. Post-merger, the merged entity earns revenues of 20,800 (implying that each division can earn a revenue share of 10,400). The firms have an incentive to merge and engage in mixed bundling even in the absence of any motive to cause the exit of rivals (e.g. they would have this incentive even if the fixed cost were only 6,000 rather than 8,000, implying that rivals would remain in the market). The fact that the mixed bundling will lower rivals' revenues to such an extent that they exit is a 'bonus' in this example, which may enable the merged entity to increase profits to an even greater extent over the longer term. Some authors refer to a situation in which bundling would be profitable in the short term even absent a foreclosure motive as non-strategic bundling and to one in which bundling is only profitable given foreclosure as strategic bundling.[204] In practice, however, the distinction between strategic and non-strategic bundling is not clear-cut.

The ability and incentive to foreclose stem from a number of features of the example.[205]

First, there is a common pool of customers for A-components and B-components. In fact, every consumer of an A-component is also a consumer of a B-component. If the components were consumed alone by many consumers (e.g. certain consumers demand an A-component

---

[204] See, e.g., B. H. Kobayashi, 'Does Economics Provide a Reliable Guide to Regulating Commodity Bundling by Firms? A survey of the economic literature' (2005) 1(4) *Journal of Competition Law & Economics* 707–46.

[205] As noted above, it is difficult to isolate factors that give rise to an ability to foreclose from factors that give rise to an incentive to foreclose in this example, because a factor that affects the extent to which there exists an ability to foreclose may simultaneously affect the extent to which there is an incentive to foreclose.

but have no interest in consuming a B-component) then there would be a reduced incentive to increase the individual component prices for $A_1$ and $B_1$, since these face competition from individual components $A_2$ and $B_2$, and the stand-alone providers would have a lower incentive to reduce their prices. Moreover, with a smaller common pool of customers for the A-component and the B-component, the ability of the merged entity to engage in foreclosure will be reduced since it will be less able to affect the demand for the individual components $A_2$ and $B_2$ through mixed bundling. Certain consumers that purchase $A_2$ but no B-component will not be persuaded to switch to $A_1$ if they have no need for $B_1$, because the stand-alone $A_2$ component is cheaper than the $A_1B_1$ system as a whole.

Second, we have implicitly assumed that the merged entity has some degree of market power. When increasing the prices of stand-alone components $A_1$ and $B_1$, it need only worry about the diversion of demand that this might cause to the single system that contains none of the merged entity's components, $A_2B_2$. If however, the merged entity faces competition from a number of producers of A-components and B-components it may be less inclined to increase the price of its individual components since this may cause diversion to a variety of different systems. For example, with a third pair of components, $A_3$ and $B_3$, rather than there being one system containing none of the merged entity's components, $A_2B_2$, there are now four, $A_2B_2$, $A_2B_3$, $A_3B_2$ and $A_3B_3$. To the extent that $A_3$ is a close substitute for $A_1$, a customer that previously purchased system $A_1B_2$ may switch to system $A_3B_2$ rather than system $A_1B_1$ following an increase in the price of the stand-alone component $A_1$ (even given the reduction in price of system $A_1B_1$). In addition, the existence of many producers of A-components may imply that $B_2$ has a reduced incentive to decrease its price in response to an increase in the price of the stand-alone $A_1$ component. One way to see why this might be the case is to consider that there is less need to reduce price to remain competitive since whereas before $B_2$ was only part of one system that had not become more expensive, $A_2B_2$, it is now part of two such systems, $A_2B_2$, and $A_3B_2$. Therefore, when the merged entity faces more competition for its products, it will generally have a lower ability to reduce the revenues of rivals through any mixed bundling strategy.

Third, there is an extreme form of economy of scale driven by the existence of the fixed cost. If rivals cannot cover the fixed cost they are induced to exit. More generally, the foreclosure effects of mixed bundling could still be a concern if there were a less extreme form of scale economies. For example, if firms faced incremental costs that reduced as output increased then a reduction in rivals' demand due to mixed bundling could give rise to an increase in their incremental costs and thus a reduction in the extent to which they constrain the prices of the merged entity. It could also be that the mixed bundling strategy reduces rivals' incentives to invest in cost-reducing R&D.[206] However, in instances where the demand for rivals' products and their profits today do not affect their ability and incentive to compete in the future it is not clear why mixed bundling should be viewed to give rise to marginalisation of rivals and less effective competition in future. Specifically, in our stylised example, with a lower fixed cost (e.g. of 6,000), there would be no exit and therefore no loss of competition in the market (subject to the caveat that some consumers may be worse off in our example due to the higher prices of systems $A_1B_2$ and $A_2B_1$). The existence and nature of scale economies is a highly relevant factor in the analysis of firms' ability and incentive to foreclose, and the ultimate effect of foreclosure.

Fourth, we have assumed that the systems required by end-users comprise only two components, both of which are produced by the merged entity. Suppose that instead of consisting of an A-component and a B-component, a system also has a C-component, which is not produced by either of the merging parties. Suppose that the C-component represents the vast majority of the total price of a system, with A- and B-components representing only a small fraction of the total price. This will, in effect, limit the extent to which A-components and B-components are complementary. It would take a very large reduction in the price of an A-component to materially reduce the price of the system, and thereby increase the demand for systems and, consequently, increase the demand for extra B-components. This will therefore reduce the extent to which there is a Cournot effect in which there is a significant incentive to sell the bundle of A- and B-components at a low price. Benefits from cutting price will exist in so far as this gives rise to stealing of market share from rival suppliers of A- and B-components but not in terms of increasing the overall market size (which is the only benefit originally identified by Cournot, who considered a merger between monopoly providers).

Fifth, we have assumed that pre-merger the producers of $A_1$ and $B_1$ had to set a single price to all customers. Suppose instead that component prices are negotiated on a customer-by-customer basis. In the extreme

---

[206] See J. P. Choi, 'Mergers with Bundling in Complementary Markets' (2008) 3 *Journal of Industrial Economics* 553–77.

case where firms negotiate prices with perfect information and are able to negotiate the division of any surplus, the Cournot effect discussed above disappears.[207] Suppose that a particular customer is willing to pay up to 60 for component $A_1$ and 55 for component $B_1$. If each component producer can perfectly price discriminate, then they will charge prices of 60 and 55 respectively for components $A_1$ and $B_1$ to that particular customer. If the two firms merge, they would set the price of the system $A_1B_1$ equal to 115 (the sum of the customer's willingness to pay for each component). There would be no incentive to reduce the price to this customer given that the customer is willing to pay this price.[208]

Sixth, we have not considered the possibility of counterstrategies on the part of the stand-alone component providers. For example, they could invest in product improvements or cost reductions to make systems containing their components more competitive with the mixed bundle offered by the merged entity. Another possible counterstrategy available to producers of $A_2$ and $B_2$ is that they engage in a merger themselves and offer a competing mixed bundle. This would restore symmetry in terms of the demand for each system. However, it is important to consider whether a counter-merger would be profitable. It could be that a counter-merger by the stand-alone providers is not immediately profitable because internalisation of the Cournot effect creates an intense form of competition between the rival systems that reduces profits for the producers of $A_2$ and $B_2$ relative to the situation in which they remain separate.[209] Nonetheless, whilst the counter-merger might reduce the short-term profits of $A_2$ and $B_2$ it would also reduce the profits of the merged entity producing $A_1$ and $B_1$. To the extent that over the longer term this would mean that they are less likely to fall behind in R&D, the rival stand-alone providers may prefer to merge.[210] Moreover,

---

[207] Perfect information is an extreme assumption. However, this case clearly shows the effect of relaxing the assumption of 'one price for all' when products are sold individually.

[208] The point that individual negotiation with customers can make the benefits of bundling disappear was raised by economists advising GE in the *GE/Honeywell* merger (see, e.g., B. J. Nalebuff, 'Bundling and the GE–Honeywell Merger' (Yale SOM Working Paper No. ES-22, September 2002) and, as discussed further in Section 5.5.3 below, was recognised by the Commission in *Google/DoubleClick* (See Case COMP/M.4731 – *Google/Double-Click*, Commission decision of 11 March 2008, para. 353).

[209] See J. Church, 'Conglomerate Mergers', in *Issues in Competition Law and Policy* (American Bar Association Section of Antitrust Law, 2008), vol. II, pp. 1503–22.

[210] See B. J. Nalebuff, 'Bundling and the GE–Honeywell Merger' (Yale SOM Working Paper No. ES-22, September 2002).

even if producers of components $A_2$ and $B_2$ did not want to offer a competing bundle, powerful customers, who would stand to gain if they did, may try to force them to do so.[211] Counterstrategies, such as a merger by stand-alone providers, could seriously undermine the ability of the merged entity to foreclose, the incentive to foreclose and any adverse effect of mixed bundling on end consumers.

Seventh, it is possible that a profitable opportunity would exist for a company to purchase the mixed bundle and sell the components unbundled at a profit. For example, it could purchase the mixed bundle at a price of 80 and sell each component at a price of 50, effectively neutralising the mixed bundling strategy. Unless the merged firm can ensure that this type of arbitrage does not take place, then it will find it impossible to engage in mixed bundling.[212]

### 5.4.2 Pure bundling

As noted above, if the merged entity decides to engage in pure bundling, then it will now not be possible for a consumer to purchase $A_1$ and assemble it with $B_2$, or for a consumer to purchase $B_1$ and assemble it with $A_2$. Therefore, there will be only two systems available for consumers to choose: $A_1B_1$ or $A_2B_2$. In particular, suppose that the merged entity can commit to the pure bundling strategy by making its products available only as an integrated system, with the components technically incompatible with those offered by other suppliers.[213]

Note that at pre-bundling prices, the aggregate demand for all four components must fall. This is because the effect of bundling is to make the systems $A_1B_2$ and $A_2B_1$ unavailable and certain consumers that purchased these systems will prefer to purchase no system rather than either of the two that remain available.

The merged entity has an incentive to lower the price of the pure bundle for two reasons. First, it has fewer infra-marginal units due to the loss of demand for $A_1$ components that formed part of the demand for the system $A_1B_2$ and the loss of demand for $B_1$ components that formed

---

[211] See ibid.

[212] This is similar to the condition that for a firm to engage in price discrimination, e.g. by selling to some consumers at a high price and to some consumers at a low price, it must be able to stop the consumers that purchase at a low price from re-selling to the high price consumers at a price that undercuts the firm.

[213] The importance of being able to commit to a strategy of pure bundling is discussed in Whinston (1990), and is also discussed further below. See M. D. Whinston, 'Tying Foreclosure, and Exclusion' (1990) 80 *American Economic Review* 837–59.

Table 5.5 *System prices pre-merger and post-merger under pure bundling*

| System | Pre-merger price | Post-merger price |
|---|---|---|
| $A_1B_1$ | 100 | 90 |
| $A_2B_2$ | 100 | 110 |

part of the system $A_2B_1$. This means that a price reduction is less costly since it will lower margins on a smaller number of units than previously. Second, it has an incentive to reduce price due to the Cournot effect given that $A_1$ and $B_1$ are complementary products. Suppose that absent any reaction by rivals the merged entity chooses to set a price for the pure bundle of 80.

However, the effect of pure bundling may cause the stand-alone providers to increase their prices.[214] Previously, any decrease in the price of $A_2$ would have boosted its demand as consumers purchased more $A_2B_1$ systems and $A_2B_2$ systems. However, under pure bundling any price decrease will give rise to a smaller increase in demand since consumers cannot purchase $A_2$ as part of the $A_2B_1$ system any more. Put differently, the upside of competing aggressively (in terms of additional sales that can be made) has become less pronounced due to the presence of the pure bundle. Given that it faces less elastic demand, the producer of $A_2$ components has, therefore, an incentive to increase its price. A similar situation applies to the producer of $B_2$. Suppose that both producers of $A_2$ and $B_2$ components choose to increase their price from 50 to 55.

Given the price increase by rivals, the merged entity may be expected to choose further to increase its prices in response to the lessened competitive constraint that it faces. We suppose that given the responses of its rivals the merged entity settles on a price for the pure bundle of 90.

Table 5.5 summarises the total prices of each of the $A_1B_1$ and $A_2B_2$ systems pre-merger and in the post-merger scenario in which pure bundling is adopted.

We now consider how the volume demanded for each system changes from the pre-merger situation in which demand for each of the four systems was 100. Given that $A_2B_1$ systems and $A_1B_2$ systems are no

[214] See J. Church, 'Conglomerate Mergers', in *Issues in Competition Law and Policy* (American Bar Association Section of Antitrust Law, 2008), vol. II, pp. 1503–22.

Table 5.6 *System demand pre-merger and post-merger under pure bundling*

| System | Pre-merger demand | Post-merger demand |
|--------|-------------------|--------------------|
| $A_1B_1$ | 100 | 180 |
| $A_2B_2$ | 100 | 110 |

longer available, some previous consumers of these systems will switch to the pure bundle offered by the merged entity and some (smaller number) will switch to the alternative system available, $A_2B_2$. Importantly, however, some consumers will no longer choose to purchase any of the systems at the prices on offer. The total demand for components will fall as a result of the number of systems available reducing from four to two. Suppose the demand for the pure bundle increases from 100 to 180 and the demand for the alternative system offered by the stand-alone providers increases from 100 to 110.

Table 5.6 summarises the total demands for each of the two systems pre-merger and in the post-merger scenario in which pure bundling is adopted.

The revenues earned by the merged entity now derive solely from the sale of the pure bundle. It sells 180 systems at a price of 90 each and therefore earns revenues of 16,200.

The total revenues of each stand-alone component provider derive solely from the sale of their components as part of the demand for one system, $A_2B_2$. Each stand-alone component provider sells 110 components at a price of 55 each and therefore earns revenues of 6,050.

The revenues of the stand-alone providers have therefore fallen from pre-merger levels of 10,000 to 6,050. This is in large part due to the fact that many consumers simply leave the market given the inability to mix and match $A_2$ with $B_1$ and $A_1$ with $B_2$.

As in the case of mixed bundling, the producers of the stand-alone components would prefer to exit rather than pay the fixed cost of 8,000. If the producers of the stand-alone components exit, then the merged entity will face a reduced competitive constraint for each of its components and will find it profitable to increase prices, thus harming all consumers.

Note that in this case, the profits of the merged entity in the short term (i.e. prior to any exit) are lower than the pre-merger profits of $A_1$ and $B_1$ combined. Pre-merger, producers of $A_1$ and $B_1$ each had revenues of

10,000. Post-merger, the merged entity earns revenues of 16,200 (implying that each division can earn a revenue share of 8,100).

The attractiveness of the pure bundling strategy in this particular example therefore relies on the exit of rivals, which enables the merged entity to increase profits over the long term. The merged entity would not engage in pure bundling absent this foreclosure motive.

If bundling involves a sacrifice of short-term profit to drive out competitors, it becomes similar in character to predatory pricing. If we do not observe predatory pricing with respect to the merging parties' products pre-merger, any theory of harm involving short-term profit sacrifice must explain why this sacrifice becomes profitable post-merger. The argument that the merged entity will be able to 'cross-subsidise' the losses on one product with profits gained as a result of market power on another product is not satisfactory in this regard. If forcing the exit of rivals through predatory conduct were profitable in the long run (noting, of course, that this could be illegal under Article 102),[215] then it is not clear why it would only be undertaken if there were cross-subsidisation from another product. To the extent that the strategy represents an attractive use of profits earned on the other good, so it would also have been an attractive use of funds (retained profits or borrowing) pre-merger.

Note, however, that there may indeed be a reason why the merger creates an opportunity to force the exit of rivals that did not exist pre-merger. Suppose that the producers of $A_2$ and $B_2$ components are just about to decide whether to incur the fixed cost of staying in the market. Suppose further that if the producers of $A_1$ and $B_1$ components could make a binding commitment to charging 'low' prices next period, the producers of $A_2$ and $B_2$ components would choose to exit rather than incur the fixed cost. However, the producers of $A_1$ and $B_1$ components

---

[215] The CFI criticised the Commission for its failure to take due account of the deterrent effect of Article 102 TFEU on the merged entity's incentives to engage in bundling post-merger in the *GE/Honeywell* judgment: 'Given the extreme nature, from a commercial perspective, of the behavior, it was incumbent on the Commission to take into account the effect which the Community-law prohibition on abuses of a dominant position might have had on the merged entity's incentive to implement such practices. Since the Commission failed to do that, it made an error of law.' See Case T-210/01, *General Electric* v. *Commission* [2005] ECR II-5575, para. 425. More generally, the 'Article 102 defence' may not be effective. The Commission has subsequently held that not all foreclosure strategies can be easily or swiftly detected and that in any event intervention can take place only after the negative effects have materialised: see Case COMP/M.3440 – *ENI/EDP/GDP*, Commission decision of 9 December 2004.

cannot make such a commitment. If the producers of $A_2$ and $B_2$ components choose to stay in the market by incurring the fixed cost, it will then be more profitable for the producers of $A_1$ and $B_1$ to renege on any threat to set 'low' prices and accommodate their rivals' decisions to stay in the market through higher prices. Pure bundling can, however, remedy this commitment problem under certain circumstances.

Suppose that whilst the producers of $A_1$ and $B_1$ cannot commit to low prices pre-merger (given that price decisions are easily reversible), the merged entity can take some irreversible action that commits it to offering the pure bundle. In particular, suppose it makes $A_1$ and $B_1$ components technically compatible only with one another and not with the complementary components offered by the merged entity's rivals. Suppose further that it would be very costly to reverse this decision. The irreversibility of this decision means that the rivals will now exit rather than pay the fixed cost because they know that unlike the threat of low prices, the merged entity cannot undo the decision to pure bundle even if to do so would be profitable in the event that the rivals did in fact stay in the market. *Ex ante*, the decision to pure bundle is not short-run profit maximising. However, the short-run profit-maximising decisions of the merged entity *given that it has committed to offer the pure bundle* will result in revenues for the rivals that are insufficient to cover the fixed costs of staying in the market. This induces rivals to exit and therefore leads to potentially higher profits for the merged entity over the long term. A forward-looking merged entity may find the decision to offer the pure bundle profitable overall.[216]

It should be noted that the attractiveness of the pure bundling strategy need not rely on the exit of rivals, as it did in the example above if systems are relatively homogeneous. If systems are relatively homogeneous the loss of demand as a result of consumers leaving the market will be smaller (i.e. there will be more switching to the bundles that remain available) and so pure bundling could in fact be profitable in the short term, to the extent that it causes rivals to increase their prices, even absent the exit of rivals.[217]

[216] Whinston was the first to point out that bundling can be used as a device to enable a monopolist to commit to more aggressive behaviour against an entrant and that this commitment can deter entry: see M. D. Whinston, 'Tying Foreclosure, and Exclusion' (1990) 80 *American Economic Review* 837–59.

[217] If systems are relatively homogeneous the loss of demand is less severe from pure bundling as consumers will substitute to the pure systems rather than leave the market altogether. Moreover, under mixed bundling independent firms lower their

As with mixed bundling the ability and incentive to foreclose stem from certain features of this example.

First, there is a common pool of customers for A-components and B-components. If the components were consumed alone by many consumers (e.g. certain consumers demand an A-component but have no interest in consuming a B-component) then the pure bundling strategy could cause a substantial loss of demand for the merged entity as a result of the elimination of the stand-alone product. Moreover, the effect of pure bundling may be to drive consumers to the stand-alone products produced by rivals, undermining the ability of the merged entity to foreclose rivals through this strategy.

Second, the exit of rivals is contingent on the fixed cost of remaining in the market. As noted above in the discussion of mixed bundling, with a lower fixed cost (e.g. of 6,000), there would be no exit and therefore no loss of competition in the market. The merged entity would no longer have the ability to marginalise its rivals. Moreover, since pure bundling is only profitable in this example in so far as it causes rivals to exit (and competition to subsequently be reduced), the merged entity will no longer have the incentive to pure bundle given the lower fixed cost. As in the case of mixed bundling, rivals' scale economies will be a relevant factor in the consideration of the merged entity's ability and incentive to foreclose and in the ultimate effect of foreclosure.

Third, we have ignored practical considerations that may undermine the ability of the merged entity to engage in pure bundling. As noted above, these practical considerations include the possibility that different components have different procurement procedures, different supply chains or different procurement timelines. In addition, there may be technical barriers to making the components incompatible with those offered by rivals (such as sophisticated customers that can adapt or modify products to restore compatibility).

---

component prices but under pure bundling they raise them. Pure bundling therefore leads to higher prices when systems are homogeneous. This also means that the profits of the independent firms are greater under pure bundling relative to mixed bundling when the systems are relatively undifferentiated. In any event, even where systems are more differentiated so that the short-term profits from mixed bundling are higher than those from pure bundling, the merged firm may still prefer to engage in pure bundling because the negative impact on independent firms' profits is greater under pure bundling than mixed bundling when systems are relatively differentiated. J. Church, 'Conglomerate Mergers', in *Issues in Competition Law and Policy* (American Bar Association Section of Antitrust Law 2008), vol. II, pp. 1503–22.

Fourth, suppose that, pre-merger, component prices are negotiated on a customer-by-customer basis. This can have significant implications for the extent to which pure bundling increases the ability and incentive of the merging parties to foreclose competitors relative to the pre-merger situation. Suppose that a particular customer prefers component $A_1$ to component $A_2$ and will choose $A_1$ over component $A_2$ as long as the price differential between the two components is not greater than 5. On the other hand, suppose that the customer prefers component $B_2$ to component $B_1$ and will choose $B_2$ over component $B_1$ as long as the price differential between the two components is not greater than 5. Pre-merger, suppose that the outcome of negotiations are such that the customer chooses $A_1$ and $B_2$ because neither the producer of $A_2$ nor that of $B_1$ is willing to undercut the prices of its rivals by 5 (which would enable it to win the customer's business) but rather it is only willing to undercut by marginally less than 5. Post-merger, the merged entity considers trying to switch the customer's demand from $B_2$ to $B_1$ by pure bundling $A_1$ and $B_1$. Note, however, that if the merged entity is to induce the customer to purchase the pure bundle, it will need to price the pure bundle at a level below the sum of the pre-merger prices it offered for the individual components. Given that pre-merger the producer of $B_1$ had no incentive to reduce its price a small amount to win this business, it is not clear why the merged entity should have an incentive to lower the implicit price of $B_1$ in order to make the customer accept the bundle. As put by Barry Nalebuff:[218]

> If customers would prefer some products from A and others from B, then the combined firm will continue to offer the individual goods at their pre-merged prices. Forcing a bundle on the consumer can only lower firm A's profits. In effect, it would have to subsidize its disadvantage using profits it could have earned from products where it is strongest. This is no different from selling individual components at a loss – a strategy it can do but would choose not to, even without bundling.

Fifth, as discussed above in relation to mixed bundling, counterstrategies may be available to the merged entity's rivals that undermine the exclusionary effects of pure bundling.

---

[218] Barry Nalebuff is Milton Steinbach Professor of Management at the Yale School of Management and was an economic adviser to GE during the Commission's investigation in the *GE/Honeywell* merger. See B. J. Nalebuff, 'Bundling and the GE–Honeywell Merger' (Yale SOM Working Paper No. ES-22, September 2002).

## 5.5    Assessment of foreclosure in conglomerate mergers: EU case law

There has been only one case in the relevant period 2004–2010 where the Commission identified conglomerate concerns leading to remedies: *Intel/McAfee*.[219] This is discussed in Section 5.5.1. Nonetheless, there are a number of cases in which the Commission has considered conglomerate theories of harm. Two of these, *GE/Amersham*[220] and *Google/Double-Click*,[221] are discussed in detail in Sections 5.5.2 and 5.5.3 below, respectively. We also make a number of references (without providing detailed discussion) to some additional cases in which the Commission has considered conglomerate concerns, including *Johnson&Johnson/Guidant*,[222] *IBM/Telelogic*,[223] *Thomson Corporation/Reuters Group*,[224] *Omya/Huber PCC*[225] and *Siemens/VATech*.[226]

As noted above, although conglomerate overlaps encompass all markets that are not horizontally or vertically related, the Commission's practice shows that the focus is on those mergers that bring together economic complements or products that are sold to the same set of customers. As with vertical foreclosure concerns, significant market power pre-merger is a necessary condition for a finding of harm.

Before considering the Commission's analysis in recent cases it is worth commenting briefly on the *GE/Honeywell* merger.[227] A great deal had been written on the economic issues in this case and as such we do not discuss this case in detail here.[228] The case was an important one because it represented a major divergence in policy with respect to non-horizontal

---

[219]  Case COMP/M.5984 – *Intel/McAfee*, Commission decision of 26 January 2011.
[220]  Case COMP/M.3304 – *GE/Amersham*, Commission decision of 21 January 2004.
[221]  Case COMP/M.4731 – *Google/DoubleClick*, Commission decision of 11 March 2008.
[222]  Case COMP/M.3687 – *Johnson&Johnson/Guidant*, Commission decision of 25 August 2005.
[223]  Case COMP/M.4747 – *IBM/Telelogic*, Commission decision of 5 March 2008.
[224]  Case COMP/M. 4726 – *Thomson Corporation/Reuters Group*, Commission decision of 19 February 2008.
[225]  Case COMP/M.3796 – *Omya/Huber PCC*, Commission decision of 19 July 2006.
[226]  Case COMP/M.3653 – *Siemens/VATech*, Commission decision of 13 July 2005.
[227]  Case COMP/M.2220 – *GE/Honeywell*, Commission decision of 3 July 2001.
[228]  The following represents a sample of the commentaries on the economics of this case: B. J. Nalebuff, 'Bundling and the GE–Honeywell Merger' (Yale SOM Working Paper No. ES-22, September 2002); D. S. Evans, and M. Salinger, 'Competition Thinking at the European Commission: Lessons from the aborted GE–Honeywell merger,' *George Mason Law Review* (May 2002), 489–532; J. P. Choi, 'The Economics and Politics of International Merger Enforcement: A case study of GE/Honeywell Merger', in V. Ghosal and J. Stennek (eds.), *Political Economy of Antitrust* (Emerald Group Publishing, 10 Apr 2007); X. Vives and G. Staffiero, 'The GE–Honeywell Merger in the EU', in B. Lyons

mergers between the US Department of Justice, which cleared the deal, and the European Commission, which prohibited it. Moreover, on appeal of the Commission's decision to the CFI,[229] the Commission was heavily criticised by the court for its analysis of the conglomerate effects, which was found to be 'vitiated by manifest errors'.[230]

During the Commission's investigation economists on both sides argued at length over the short-term incentive to engage in mixed bundling (particularly on account of the Cournot effect, see Section 5.4 above). However, the Commission concluded that this issue could be left open since the merged entity would in any event have an incentive to engage in bundling in order to marginalise its rivals. The Commission did not deem it necessary to rely on any specific economic model or analysis to support its bundling theories, explaining that it had:

> evaluated the theoretical premises of mixed bundling as presented to it in the economic analyses submitted by the parties and third parties. The various economic analyses have been subject to theoretical controversy, in particular as far as the economic model of mixed bundling, prepared by one of the third parties, is concerned. However, the Commission does not consider reliance on one or the other model necessary for the conclusion that the packaged deals that the merged entity will be in a position to offer will foreclose competitors from the engines and avionics/non-avionics markets.[231]

The Commission did not specify how the incentive to engage in fore-closure would arise post-merger when prices are set through individual negotiation and an incentive to marginalise rivals by predatory pricing had not existed pre-merger (see the Nalebuff critique noted in Section 5.4 above). The Commission emphasised that '[t]he ability of the merged entity to cross-subsidise its various complementary activities and to engage in profitable forms of packaged sales will have an adverse effect on the profitability of competing producers of avionics and non-avionics products, as a result of market share erosion.'[232]

Subsequent to the CFI's critique of its analysis in *GE/Honeywell*, and the publishing of the EC Non-horizontal Merger Guidelines, the

---

(ed.), *Cases in European Competition Policy, The Economic Analysis* (Cambridge University Press, 2008).

[229] Case T-210/01, *General Electric* v. *Commission* [2005] ECR II-5575.

[230] The CFI upheld the prohibition decision only in so far as it agreed with parts of the analysis concerning horizontal aspects of the merger.

[231] Case COMP/M.2220 – *GE/Honeywell*, Commission decision of 3 July 2001, para. 352.

[232] Ibid., para. 398.

Commission has adopted a more evidence-based approach to conglomerate issues. Where the Commission has considered the merged entity's incentive to engage in foreclosure in cases since 2004, it has recognised that tying and bundling may result in significant costs. The Commission has also placed emphasis on the question of whether rivals would continue to pose an effective competitive constraint even if the merged entity engaged in tying or bundling.

### 5.5.1   Intel/McAfee

In January 2011, the Commission conditionally cleared the merger between Intel, the leading producer of central processing units (CPUs) and chipsets, and McAfee, a provider of IT security solutions. The Commission required remedies to allay its concerns regarding non-horizontal relationships between the parties' products, and specifically, its concern that the merger would give rise to anti-competitive foreclosure of rival providers of security solutions.

At the outset, the Commission noted that there were important linkages between computer hardware (CPUs and chipsets) and security solutions. First, there was a technological link. The Commission noted that security software interacts to a greater extent than other software directly with the hardware level. This implied that security software vendors ('SSVs') needed access to up-to-date, accurate and complete interface information on new CPUs and chipsets in order to be able to develop new security software.[233]

Second, the Commission noted the commercial link between the parties' products. In particular, it noted that every device running using Intel hardware would in principle need some form of security software and that the same intermediaries, for example, Original Equipment Manufacturers ('OEMs') would be involved in the decisions over which CPUs to use and which security to install.[234]

---

[233] Interface information was also required to optimise the software with regard to performance and power consumption since the running of security processes may significantly increase the workload on the CPU and affect the available performance of the computer. In addition, the Commission noted that certain features of IT security could be more effectively enabled in hardware than in software and that the partial embedding of security solutions in hardware may lead to more robust and/or faster security solutions. See Case COMP/M.5984 – *Intel/McAfee*, Commission decision of 26 January 2011, paras. 18 and 19.

[234] See ibid., para. 21.

As a result of these linkages, the Commission considered whether Intel would have the ability and incentive to bundle or tie Intel CPU chipsets and McAfee security solutions; and/or to degrade the interoperability between Intel's hardware and security solutions on the one hand and the products of competing providers of security solutions on the other.

The Commission found that its conclusion from its 2009 Intel anti-trust decision regarding Intel's dominance continued to hold.[235] This conclusion was based on persistently high market shares, which for CPUs were higher than [70–80]% in each of the desktop, notebook and netbook sub segments and which for chipsets were higher than [70–80]% in a general chipset market and higher than [90–100%] in the possible 'after-market' of chipsets for Intel-compatible CPUs. In addition, the Commission considered that these markets were subject to very high barriers to entry and expansion.[236] The Commission noted that Intel faced one competitor in CPUs, AMD, with a share of [10–20%] and another, Via, whose position was insignificant in terms of volume shipped.[237] In particular, the Commission referred to its 2009 Intel antitrust decision, which had found that a potential entrant faces significant intellectual property barriers and has to engage in substantial initial research and development and production investment to be able to start production of x86 CPUs.[238]

The Commission noted that McAfee was one of the few security technology companies active in practically all areas of the security technology spectrum, serving end-consumers, SMEs, and large private corporations and governmental organisations.[239] In particular, it had a share of [10–20%] in end point security, in which it was the second largest worldwide player behind Symantec [30–40%]. The Commission noted that barriers to expansion in the enterprise segment were significant due to the need for brand recognition, a range of products, services and support, and trust that the company will continue to innovate.[240] In the consumer segment, the Commission found a clear division between the players with access to the OEM channel (Symantec, McAfee and Trend Micro) and the other players without such access.[241] The Commission also noted that the three largest players benefited from network

---

[235] COMP/C-3 /37.990 – Intel, ('the 2009 Intel antitrust decision').
[236] See Case COMP/M.5984 – *Intel/McAfee*, Commission decision of 26 January 2011, para. 62.
[237] See ibid., para. 72.      [238] See ibid., para. 91.      [239] See ibid., para. 63.
[240] See ibid., para. 102.      [241] See ibid., para. 104.

effects since the more users an SSV has, the higher its chances to detect new malware, in particular when those users are distributed evenly across different geographic areas.[242]

Complainants to the merger raised three forms of foreclosure concerns, namely degradation of interoperability between Intel's hardware and security solutions on the one hand and the products of competitors on the other, technical bundling/tying ('technical tying') and commercial bundling strategies. The degradation of interoperability and commercial bundling concerns are discussed in turn below,[243] followed by a brief summary of the remedies implemented to allay these concerns.

**5.5.1.1  Degradation of interoperability**  The Commission found that Intel would have the ability to degrade the interoperability of its hardware with security solutions provided by McAfee's rivals.[244] It found that developers need a range of information and a number of tools from the CPU manufacturers to develop and optimise their software for a given CPU.[245] The Commission focused on 'positive discrimination', whereby McAfee would be given preferential access to the procedures of the

---

[242] See ibid., para. 106.

[243] Refusal to provide interoperability information to third parties that enables rivals to link their products to the merged entity's products is sometimes considered as a special case of technical tying, although in Intel/McAfee the Commission considered these concerns separately. The Commission's findings with respect to technical tying (integrating McAfee technology into Intel's hardware) were similar to those in the discussion of degraded interoperability and we therefore do not discuss these separately. As with degradation of interoperability, the Commission concluded that Intel would have the ability and incentive to engage in technical tying and that this practice would likely result in harm to consumers. The Commission's discussion of technical tying can be found at Case COMP/M.5984 – *Intel/McAfee*, Commission decision of 26 January 2011, paras. 175–221.

[244] The Commission has considered interoperability issues in a number of cases. In *IBM/Telelogic* the Commission examined whether the merged entity would have the ability to refuse to provide interoperability information and found that it would have such ability. Indeed, it considered that 'any software vendor whose product's output must somehow become the input for other software products in principle has this ability' although it noted that the ability to withhold interoperability information applied to only new software projects and not existing ones. See Case COMP/M.4747 – *IBM/Telelogic*, Commission decision of 5 March 2008, para. 255. Other cases in which interoperability has been considered include Case COMP/M.3083 – *GE/Instrumentarium*, Commission decision of 2 September 2003, and Case COMP/M.2861 – *Siemens/Drägerwerk/JV*, Commission decision of 30 April 2003.

[245] See Case COMP/M.5984 – *Intel/McAfee*, Commission decision of 26 January 2011, para. 140.

CPU.[246] It considered that this form of discrimination would be difficult to detect and that it would not be possible for McAfee's rivals to react to discrimination by 'reverse engineering' Intel's hardware components.[247]

Regarding the incentive to degrade interoperability, the complainants pointed to a specific statement by Intel CEO Paul Otellini, which was interpreted as Intel's explicit intention to favour McAfee by granting it better access to Intel features or technologies than its competitors.[248] The Commission also highlighted internal documents relating to the integration of McAfee products.[249]

Critically, the Commission found that Intel could implement the hypothesised strategy without losing CPU revenues. Specifically, it noted that the only way CPU revenues would decrease would be if end-users show such a loyalty to an SSV other than McAfee that they would switch their demand to an alternative CPU supplier, which the Commission found unlikely.[250]

Finally, the Commission found regarding the effect of foreclosure that the strategy would result in the exclusion of McAfee's competitors from Intel's platform, as a result of security software from other vendors being perceived as less effective. [251] The Commission noted that innovation incentives of rivals would be impacted with a likely reduction in consumer choice. The Commission also suggested that a degradation of McAfee's interoperability with other chipsets or CPUs could further protect Intel in the CPU and chipset markets by increasing barriers to entry.[252]

**5.5.1.2  Commercial bundling**  The Commission considered whether the merged entity would have the ability and incentive to engage in pure commercial bundling (whereby CPUs and security software are sold exclusively together) and mixed commercial bundling (whereby the security software would be offered at a discount when customers buy both products from *Intel/McAfee*). Intel raised a number of practical difficulties that it would face in implementing a bundling strategy, including that CPUs for consumer PCs are typically negotiated on a

---

[246]  See ibid., para. 142.     [247]  See ibid., para. 145.

[248]  'While we'll still work with the Symantecs and Microsofts and Nortons of the world, we're also going to make sure that the best possible solution is Intel on Intel or Intel on McAfee in this case and that it's architected to run best together.' See Case COMP/ M.5984 – *Intel/McAfee*, Commission decision of 26 January 2011, para. 154.

[249]  See ibid., para. 161.     [250]  See ibid., para. 159.     [251]  See ibid., para. 166.

[252]  See ibid., para. 172.

quarterly basis while security software contracts typically cover multiple years and that the pricing terms for security software are complex.[253] However, while the Commission noted that contract cycles and durations for CPUs and security solutions are currently different and that negotiations are currently also often led by different teams for each of these products, it found that given Intel's power over OEMs it could change negotiation and contract formats.[254] The Commission found likely that Intel has the ability to enter into a foreclosure strategy through a commercial bundling between its chipsets/CPUs and McAfee's endpoint security.[255]

Regarding the incentive to engage in the hypothesised strategies, the Commission placed some emphasis on economic analysis submitted by Intel. First, this analysis claimed that the share of sales of all endpoint security software which could be shifted to McAfee by a tying or bundling strategy is low (less than 1%). The analysis took account of the relatively low proportion of PCs that both ship with an Intel processor and ship with preloaded security software trials provided by McAfee competitors (5–10%), took account of the fact that only 0–5% of these trials actually result in a security software subscription, and that some software sales are due to subscription renewals rather than new subscriptions.[256] Second, the analysis considered the critical loss accrued by Intel which would render commercial bundling unprofitable.[257] The analysis compared Intel's average profit on CPUs and chipsets that would be lost on each computer for which the OEM switches away from Intel, with the McAfee's expected lifetime profit on an incremental trial, which would be won on every PC with an incremental trial. The analysis found that bundling would be unprofitable if [less than 1%] of Intel's hardware sales were switched away from Intel.[258]

The Commission adopted a similar framework as Intel and maintained a number of the analysis' assumptions. It found that for a reasonable range of such assumptions, the critical loss stemming was higher than the critical loss submitted by Intel, but remained limited nonetheless. It therefore concluded that the incentives of Intel to engage in a commercial

---

[253] See Case COMP/M.5984 – *Intel/McAfee*, Commission decision of 26 January 2011, para. 229.

[254] See ibid., para. 237.    [255] See ibid., para. 238.    [256] See ibid., para. 268.

[257] The critical loss was defined as the share of lost hardware sales that would result in a loss of profit to the merged firm that exactly offsets the profit gained by it from incremental security software trials. See ibid., para. 269.

[258] See ibid., para. 270.

bundling might indeed be weakened by the risk of losing CPU sales to OEMs.[259] The Commission concluded that Intel would have limited incentives to engage in such a strategy if pursued in isolation.[260]

Finally, regarding the effect of foreclosure, the Commission found that a commercial bundling strategy would be unlikely to give rise to anti-competitive foreclosure of rivals. In contrast to the other strategies that the Commission considered, commercial bundling could only affect sales to consumers through Original Equipment Manufacturers (OEMs).[261] The Commission noted, however, that rivals would be able to reach customers in other ways, for example by focusing on direct sales or on the enterprise segment.

**5.5.1.3   Remedies**   In order to address the Commission's concerns regarding the degradation of interoperability and technical tying, Intel offered a set of behavioural remedies. The Commission accepted that these were best suited to remedy its concerns in the present case and set out the conditions that the remedy would need to comply with in order to be effective. Regarding interoperability, Intel's main commitment was to disclose instructions and interoperability information on a royalty free basis.[262] Regarding tying, Intel would be able to provide bundled solutions, but OEMs would be able to effectively disable any bundled Intel security functions without this degrading the quality or performance of rival security solutions.[263] The commitments would be valid for a period of 5 years, would be monitored by a trustee and would be accompanied by a dispute settlement mechanism including a fast track arbitration procedure.

### 5.5.2   GE/Amersham

The Commission had to consider a number of issues related to the ability and incentive to engage in tying and bundling during its investigation of the *GE/Amersham*[264] merger.

The products produced by the parties that were sufficiently closely related to trigger potential conglomerate concerns were GE's diagnostic imaging (DI) equipment, used to generate images of the human body for

---

[259] See ibid., para. 276.      [260] See ibid., para. 289.      [261] See ibid., para. 285.

[262] See Case COMP/M.5984 – *Intel/McAfee*, Commission decision of 26 January 2011, paras. 289 and 337–40.

[263] See ibid., paras. 341 and 342.

[264] Case COMP/M.3304 – *GE/Amersham*, Commission decision of 21 January 2004.

medical diagnosis, and Amersham's diagnostic pharmaceuticals (DPs), used to enable or enhance the clarity of the image produced by DI equipment. The products were related in the sense that they had common customers (hospitals) and formed complementary components in systems used by hospitals for diagnosis.

The Commission defined a number of different relevant product markets for DI equipment that related to the five main DI modalities of imaging equipment (X-ray, Computed tomography (CT), Magnetic resonance (MR), Ultrasound (U/S) and Nuclear imaging (NI)), but left open whether these could be further subdivided.[265] The Commission left open the exact scope of the DP markets although it considered that the parties' proposed delineation, between contrast agents and radioactive pharmaceuticals, would be too broad. This is because it considered that there was limited demand-side and supply-side substitutability between contrast agents used with certain different DI modalities and, moreover, for certain procedures involving NI, organ specific DPs were required that could each constitute a separate market.[266] Regarding the geographic market, the Commission left open whether markets could be considered national or EEA-wide but considered the possibility that markets should be defined narrowly in its competitive assessment by considering the parties' positions in various national markets.[267]

Whilst the Commission noted that GE had a high market share in certain product areas and in certain national markets, it noted that the market investigation did not attribute to GE any specific characteristics that would provide it with an important economic advantage over competitors.[268] The Commission noted that Amersham held very high market shares in certain DPs but also that, given the importance of R&D in the markets concerned, high market shares might only be temporary due to the potential for leapfrogging by competitors introducing new products.[269]

The Commission considered whether the merged entity would have the ability and incentive to foreclose competition by leveraging any pre-merger market power from one market to another. It considered two strategies in particular. First, it considered mixed (commercial) bundling of DI equipment and DPs, whereby the merged entity would offer discounts on these products when purchased together.[270] Second, it

---

[265] Ibid., para. 9.     [266] Ibid., paras. 13–14.     [267] Ibid., para. 18.
[268] Ibid., para. 23.     [269] Ibid., para. 28.
[270] The Commission also considered pure bundling (or what it termed 'forced bundling') of DI equipment and DPs, whereby the merged entity would no longer make its products

considered technical tying (whereby its products would work optimally or exclusively with one another). The Commission focused on those procedures where there was significant complementarity between DI equipment and DPs.

### 5.5.2.1 Mixed bundling

The Commission considered a theory of harm in which the merged entity would offer a bundle of DI equipment and DPs at a lower price than the sum of the individual components when purchased alone with the aim of excluding competitors. Third parties alleged that, as a result, they would face reduced revenue streams and a reduced ability and incentive to invest in R&D, which might gradually lead to their marginalisation and exit.[271]

The parties pointed to a number of factors that raised questions about the feasibility of such a strategy. They noted that there were significant differences in the procurement procedures and supply chains for DI equipment and DPs and that the products also had different procurement timelines.[272] DI equipment represents a one-off major capital expenditure that is made infrequently given its minimum lifecycle of 10 years, while DPs are purchased on an ongoing basis throughout the lifecycle of the DI equipment. The Commission noted that, whilst these considerations did not necessarily preclude commercial bundling, they would complicate its successful implementation.[273]

The Commission noted that, whilst the parties had high market shares in some product markets in certain member states, it considered that these did not in themselves indicate dominance in the context of these

available on a stand-alone basis but only as a bundle. It was quick to dismiss this possibility, however, given that the merged entity would lack an incentive to engage in such a practice since it would deny it significant sales of DPs to current users of non-GE equipment and significant sales of DI equipment to users that would prefer to continue using non-Amersham DPs. See ibid., para. 43.

[271] Case COMP/M.3304 – *GE/Amersham*, Commission decision of 21 January 2004, para. 34.

[272] In a number of cases, the Commission has determined that a particular bundling strategy would not be feasible because the customers purchasing the products in question are not the same. For example, in *Johnson&Johnson/Guidant*, the Commission noted with respect to a bundling strategy involving different areas, such as endovascular, interventional cardiology, and Cardiac management system devices (defibrillators and pacemakers), that 'a broader bundling involving products of different areas is hardly feasible as customers are generally not the same'. See Case COMP/M.3687 – *Johnson&-Johnson/Guidant*, Commission decision of 25 August 2005, para. 342.

[273] Case COMP/M.3304 – *GE/Amersham*, Commission decision of 21 January 2004, para. 35.

markets and highlighted features such as the bidding nature of the markets, the lumpy and infrequent procurement of equipment, existence of credible alternative suppliers, leapfrogging through innovation, absence of switching costs and countervailing power of hospitals.[274]

There were found to be a number of rivals in DI equipment and DPs that could undermine the ability of the merged entity to engage in foreclosure by employing counterstrategies such as price reductions, similar bundles (through teaming or counter-mergers) and technological leapfrogging as a result of innovation.[275]

As regards the incentive to engage in and effect of foreclosure, the parties put forward a number of arguments as to why marginalisation of rivals was unlikely with respect to both DI equipment and DPs.

Before considering the specifics of this assessment in *GE/Amersham*, it should be noted that in many cases in which an analysis of the likelihood of foreclosure is required, a conceptual distinction can be made between foreclosure of *existing* and *future* products. Foreclosure of *existing* products occurs if, through reducing rivals' sales, these rivals become marginalised and cease to exercise an effective competitive constraint with their existing or current product offering. For example, rivals may decide to withdraw from a market with their current product offering or find that their variable costs have increased, causing them to increase prices. Foreclosure of *future* products occurs if, through reduction in investments such as R&D or capacity, rivals become less able to exercise a competitive constraint with their future products than would otherwise have been the case. If there is no evidence that foreclosure will reduce the competitiveness of rivals with respect to their current products, the analysis inevitably becomes more speculative in nature, as it seeks to predict the effect on the competitiveness of rivals within the medium to long-term future.

In *GE/Amersham* there was an important distinction to be made between existing and future products. With respect to existing products, the parties first noted that products would only be withdrawn from a member state if the costs that would be saved exceeded the expected forgone revenue. The production of both DI equipment and DPs was characterised by significant fixed costs, many of which (e.g. sunk R&D expenditure at a global level) would not be recovered or avoided even if production within a given member state were to cease entirely. Given the

---

[274] Ibid., para. 38.    [275] Ibid., para. 39.

high contribution margins on sales of these products, the impact of any bundling strategy would have to reduce rivals' margins significantly before they found it unattractive to remain present in a particular member state due to an inability to make incremental sales that contributed to overall profits.

Second, unit variable costs were relatively constant and independent of the level of output produced, providing production did not become capacity constrained. This implied that even if rivals experienced a significant reduction in volumes, there would be no reason to believe that the competitive constraint they exerted on the merged entity for incremental business would be diminished.

Third, with respect to DI equipment there was an ongoing requirement to service the existing installed base in each member state. To earn revenues from upgrades and servicing imaging equipment that had already been sold to customers would require a presence at the national level. Since the merged entity could not affect this source of revenue, it would be difficult to induce the exit of rivals from a particular country. Moreover, with respect to DPs, the merged entity would be unable to affect rivals' sales to hospitals that already have in place DI equipment that they were not considering replacing in the near future since these customers would not consider the commercial bundle of the merged entity.

Fourth, re-entering a particular member state would be both easy and timely as the costs of re-establishing a distribution network were low. This implied that even if rivals were to exit a particular member state, the merged entity would nonetheless remain unable to exploit a position of market power.

With respect to future products, the parties noted that the incentives of rivals to invest in R&D would not be adversely affected, mainly because these incentives were not related to revenues generated in particular member states but to worldwide sales prospects.

The Commission considered that anti-competitive foreclosure could arise only if rivals were forced to exit the DP and DI markets at a global level, and that any erosion of market share in certain member states would be unlikely to lead to such global exit. It also excluded the possibility that rivals would significantly reduce their global R&D expenditure. Finally the Commission accepted that barriers to entry or re-entry in a particular member state are not significant.[276] As a result,

---

[276] See Case COMP/M.3304 – *GE/Amersham*, Commission decision of 21 January 2004, paras. 40 and 41.

the Commission concluded that whilst the commercial bundling of DI equipment and DPs may occur post-merger, it would not lead to competitive concerns.

**5.5.2.2 Technical tying** As noted above, technical tying refers to a situation in which the post-merger entity's products would work optimally or exclusively when used in conjunction with one another.

At the time of transaction, all DI equipment worked with all available DPs. The Commission investigated the hypothetical concern, raised by a third party, that the merged entity would engage in technical tying that would ultimately foreclose rivals by denying them interconnectivity with the merged entity's products.[277]

The Commission recognised that this concern could only be relevant in principle to new products since current products worked optimally with each other and no action could undo this compatibility.

The Commission considered the technical links between the manufacturing of DI equipment and the development of DPs to investigate whether new Amersham DPs could be tailored to function exclusively or optimally with GE equipment.[278] Its market investigation found that both customers and competitors found no interoperability issues with existing products. It found that to the extent that Amersham could develop breakthrough DP products that no other competitor could replicate and that could not be used with non-GE DI equipment, this would most likely take place in the field of nuclear imaging.[279] However, after a detailed investigation it concluded that Amersham's development plans in DPs, and in nuclear imaging DPs, did not raise concerns regarding the possibility that any product would work most effectively with future GE equipment to the exclusion of rival DI equipment.[280]

---

[277] The Commission also considered a second related concern that the merged entity would acquire a 'time-to-market advantage' by internalising the knowledge on development plans in DI equipment and DPs carried out by each of the merging parties. However, it dismissed this concern on the basis of serious questions regarding the feasibility of such a practice and on the basis that any such advantage could only be short-lived. See ibid., paras. 56 and 57.

[278] Another case in which the Commission considered surrounding the practical ability to engage in technical tying is *Saint Gobain/BPB*. See Case COMP/M.3943 – *Saint-Gobain/BPB*, Commission decision of 9 November 2005, para. 61.

[279] Case COMP/M.3304 – *GE/Amersham*, Commission decision of 21 January 2004, para. 49.

[280] Ibid., para. 54.

The Commission also considered the *incentive* to engage in technical tying. It considered that the hypothesised strategy would deny the merged entity significant sales of Amersham's products to the installed base of competing DI equipment. Given that rival DI equipment represented a substantial part of the nuclear imaging market due to GE's relatively modest market shares in this area, the Commission concluded that there would be no incentive to pursue technical tying in the area in which it was considered most feasible.[281]

As a result of the above, the Commission dismissed the possibility of competitive concerns related to technical tying of DI equipment and DPs.

### 5.5.3 Google/DoubleClick

In March 2008, the Commission cleared Google's proposed acquisition of DoubleClick, a leading online advertising technology company.[282]

The main actors in the online advertising industry are publishers, who sell advertising space on their websites, and advertisers, who buy advertising space in order to reach internet users.

Defining the relevant product market in which online ad space is sold is a complex task. First, online advertising appears in a variety of different formats. Google predominantly sold simple text ads, but the industry also includes static graphic ads and more advanced rich media ads (collectively referred to as display ads).[283] Second, online advertising can either

---

[281] See Case COMP/M.3304 – *GE/Amersham*, Commission decision of 21 January 2004, para. 59. Similarly, in *IBM/Telelogic*, the Commission considered whether the merged entity would have an incentive to engage in technical tying by withholding interoperability information, in order to leverage its market power in the markets for Modelling and Requirements Management tools into adjacent markets. It noted that the merged entity would incur substantial losses if it were to make its products incompatible with competing products. By comparison, it considered the benefits to the merger in terms of increased sales of tied products to be limited. See Case COMP/M.4747 – *IBM/Telelogic*, Commission decision of 5 March 2008, para. 268.

[282] See Case COMP/M.4731 – *Google/DoubleClick*, Commission decision of 11 March 2008. In addition to exclusionary concerns the Commission also considered 'diagonal effects' concerns put forward by third parties. Diagonal mergers are discussed in Section 6 below. Much of the discussion of this case is based on S. Lewis and A. Lofaro, 'Google/DoubleClick: The search for a theory of harm' (2008) 29(12) *European Competition Law Review* 717.

[283] Online ads are also differentiated by the way in which they are targeted. For example, an ad can be targeted according to a search query entered by a user (search ads), according to the content on the page on which it appears (contextual targeting), according to the user's past viewing behaviour (behavioural targeting) or according to various other

be sold directly by a publisher to an advertiser or indirectly through ad networks or ad exchanges, which act as two-sided intermediation platforms matching advertisers with publishers providing suitable ad space. For example, Google sells ad space on the websites of third party publishers that make use of its ad network, AdSense.

The parties were of the opinion, as were most of the complainants to the merger, that ads appearing in different formats, targeted by different methods and sold through different channels are all substitutable and therefore that the relevant market should at least comprise the sale of all online ad space. The Commission agreed that different types of online advertising are substitutable to a certain extent although it did not reach a firm conclusion as to whether the substitutability was sufficient to justify a single relevant market for all types of online advertising.[284]

Once a publisher has agreed to sell advertising space on its website to an advertiser (either directly or indirectly), ad serving technology is used to deliver an ad from the advertiser to the ad space, as well as playing various other important supporting roles on behalf of both advertisers and publishers.[285] Since ad serving is an input into the provision of ad space, suppliers of advertising space and suppliers of ad serving solutions sell complementary products and therefore do not compete in the same relevant markets.

Importantly, although all online ads, of any format, require some ad serving technology to place them on a website, the basic technology used to serve text ads is not substitutable for the more advanced technology, such as that provided by DoubleClick, used to serve display ads. This implies that there was no straightforward horizontal overlap between Google – a seller of ad space along with integrated (basic) ad serving for text ads, and DoubleClick – a seller of stand-alone display ad serving solutions.

Complainants raised a number of non-horizontal theories of harm, including an allegation that the merged entity would leverage Double-Click's market position in ad display serving to foreclose ad intermediaries that compete with Google's ad network (discussed in Section 5.5.3.1

---

indicators such as the user's geographic location or the time of day the user is viewing the website.

[284] The Commission did conclude, however, that a separate market could be defined for the provision of ad intermediation.

[285] DoubleClick provides services to advertisers via its advertiser-side ad serving solution (DFA) and to publishers through its publisher-side ad serving solution (DFP).

below). Another allegation was that the merged entity would leverage Google's position in advertising and ad intermediation markets to foreclose display ad serving providers that compete with DoubleClick (discussed in Section 5.5.3.2 below). A further allegation was that a 'diagonal relationship' between Google and DoubleClick would make unilateral price increases profitable for the combined entity (discussed in Section 6 below).

### 5.5.3.1 Allegations regarding foreclosure of ad intermediation providers

Complainants alleged that the merged entity would leverage DoubleClick's market position in ad serving to foreclose ad intermediaries that compete with Google's ad network. Whilst a wide range of concerns were put forward, they all involved the merged entity taking some action, such as increasing the price of display ad serving when used with competing networks, that would make DoubleClick's advertiser and publisher customers favour Google's ad networks over others.[286] It was alleged that this would lead to the marginalisation of competing ad networks and that the competitive harm would be exacerbated by the existence of network effects arising from the two-sided nature of ad intermediation.

The analysis of DoubleClick's market power was an important part of the Commission's assessment of these theories. The Commission confirmed the position set out in the Non-horizontal Merger Guidelines that substantial market power (but not necessarily dominance) is required for foreclosure concerns to arise. Specifically, the Commission stated: 'As recognised by the Non-Horizontal Merger Guidelines, in order to be able to foreclose competitors, the new entity must have a significant degree of market power (which does not necessarily amount to dominance) in one of the markets concerned.'[287]

Importantly, the Commission's decision makes clear that any assessment of the ability of a firm to foreclose its rivals will need to consider the extent to which the merged entity is constrained by rivals, and will need to go beyond a simple assessment of market shares in this regard.

---

[286] In addition, the Commission considered a hypothetical strategy whereby DoubleClick would technically 'tweak' the ad arbitration mechanism to favour Google's ad network, AdSense. See Case COMP/M.4731 – *Google/DoubleClick*, Commission decision of 11 March 2008, para. 289.

[287] Ibid., para. 333.

Despite finding that DoubleClick had market shares of 30–40% in advertiser side ad serving and 40–50% in publisher side ad serving, the Commission recognised that DoubleClick was subject to substantial competitive constraints from rival ad serving providers that would undermine its ability to foreclose rivals. The Commission found that ad serving markets were competitive, on account of the fact that there was significant evidence of customer switching, evidence that DoubleClick's customers were able to negotiate significant price (cost-per-thousand impressions or CPM) reductions at the point of renewing their contracts and evidence that prices for customers of all sizes were declining significantly over time despite increasing demand.[288] For example, the Commission stated:

> The Commission considers that the evidence provided by the parties is convincing in showing that DoubleClick has had to reduce prices in response to competitive constraints by its rivals. As explained below, the parties' data shows that CPMs have decreased within volume-tiers (and hence the fall in average CPM is not primarily driven by increases in volumes) and data on price reductions offered during renegotiations with specific customers at the time of contract renewals suggests that Double-Click has responded to competitive pressures.[289]

The analysis submitted by the parties led the Commission to state in the context of assessing the merged entity's ability to engage in foreclosure strategies based on DoubleClick's position in ad serving that: '... the market investigation has revealed that DoubleClick faces a number of competitive constraints and is not able to exercise any significant market power.'[290]

The Commission's conclusion on the absence of an ability to foreclose rival ad intermediation providers was further based on its view that DoubleClick's customers did not face substantial switching costs.[291]

A key argument put forward by complainants was that DoubleClick's ad serving price constituted a sufficiently high proportion of the cost of using an ad network that variation in this price could affect the relative attractiveness (to advertisers and publishers) of competing ad networks. However, as recognised by the Commission, the proportion of intermediation costs that ad serving represents is not a particularly relevant consideration for either publishers or advertisers when choosing between ad networks.

---

[288] See ibid., para. 168.     [289] Ibid., para. 169.     [290] See ibid., para. 296.
[291] See ibid., para. 297.

The relevant consideration for advertisers is the total cost of purchasing the ad space, and for publishers it is the total profit from selling such space. Even a relatively large increase in the price of ad serving when used with a competing ad network could not have a significant impact on these values and would therefore be very unlikely to influence advertisers' or publishers' choice of ad network.[292] Moreover, competition within the markets for display ad serving would make any substantial price increase impossible.

An important additional ingredient to the alleged foreclosure concern was that ad intermediation was prone to 'tipping' due to the existence of network effects that are often present in two-sided markets.[293] In choosing to use a particular ad network, an advertiser may take into account the number of publishers using the same network, in addition to the price the advertiser must pay to use the network. Similarly, a publisher's decision to join an ad network may be influenced by the number of advertisers using the network, as well as by the price it must pay to use the network (or its share in the advertising revenue generated).

Complainants alleged that, using the various leveraging strategies available, the merged entity would attract so many advertisers and publishers to its ad network that other ad networks with fewer members would be marginalised. The merged entity would subsequently be able to raise prices without the constraints imposed by rival networks making such a price rise unprofitable, because other networks would be of lower 'quality' from the perspective of advertisers (publishers) due to a lack of publishers (advertisers) on the other side of the market.

The concern that network effects may lead to tipping/monopolisation has been raised in other cases, most notably in relation to Microsoft's Windows operating system, but such allegations must be carefully tested in each market context where they are made. The risk of tipping is

---

[292] For example, suppose that a publisher opts for a non-AdSense network and sells a $2 per-thousand-impression ad, pays 40 cents to the ad network, and pays 5 cents to the publisher-side ad serving provider. The publisher's net profits are $1.55 per thousand impressions. Now assume the price of publisher-side ad serving were to increase by 10% from 5 cents to 5.5 cents. If the publisher were to continue using the rival network to sell the ad space, its net profits would fall by only around 0.3%, from $1.55 to $1.545 per thousand impressions.

[293] Network effects may arise when consumer utility in a certain market depends on consumption of the same good or service by other agents. Two-sided markets are characterised by a particular type of network externality whereby the externality depends on consumption of 'compatible' agents on the opposite side of the market.

greater when customers typically use only one platform, and when network effects are not exhausted at a low level of usage.

The market evidence supplied by the parties convinced the Commission that neither of these elements was present in the online advertising industry. First, advertisers and publishers frequently use more than one platform (i.e. they 'multi-home'). Given that multi-homing is attractive and costless, it is unlikely that any network effects that may exist could give rise to anti-competitive effects in the form of foreclosure of rival ad networks. This is because the attraction of an advertiser or publisher to an ad network does not make that advertiser or publisher unavailable to other networks.

Second, the evidence suggested that beyond a certain number of publishers an additional publisher joining the network provides no further benefit to advertisers already on the network. This is suggested by the observation that surveyed advertisers did not see reach (the number of unique monthly visitors to ad networks' sites as a percentage of the online population) as a key differentiating factor between ad networks despite significant variation in reach across the various alternative ad networks in the market. Hence, a rival ad network may continue to exert a competitive constraint with a relatively small number of partners on the publisher side as long as it is attractive in terms of the various other dimensions along which ad networks are judged (e.g. the targeting method used).

The Commission concluded that given the presence of credible alternatives to which DoubleClick's customers can switch and the evidence that network effects are not strong enough to induce tipping, any strategy to attract publishers/advertisers to AdSense was unlikely to be able to foreclose rivals in intermediation markets.[294]

Regarding the incentive to foreclose, the Commission considered that pure bundling of ad serving with ad intermediation would be likely to be unprofitable.[295] It noted that while the margins earned on additional sales of the bundle would exceed those lost on sales of the ad serving tools, the strategy was likely to be unprofitable in view of the switching it would entail to rival ad serving products.[296] The Commission also considered the incentive of the merged entity to engage in mixed

---

[294] See Case COMP/M.4731 – *Google/DoubleClick*, Commission decision of 11 March 2008, para. 310.
[295] See ibid., para. 315.    [296] See ibid., para. 315.

bundling (rendering ad serving products more expensive or lower quality when used with other ad networks). The Commission noted that publishers that were customers of DoubleClick's ad serving products spend relatively limited amounts on Google's non-search platform and that incentives to offer a mixed bundle might be limited as margins earned on additional sales through AdSense would merely (if at all) compensate the opportunity cost of reducing the price of DoubleClick tools.[297]

Finally, regarding the effect of foreclosure, the Commission noted that anti-competitive foreclosure was unlikely to arise because the new entity would continue to compete with a number of platforms offering the same product combination. Specifically it noted that:

> As a result of a recent wave of acquisitions, the market has evolved to a situation where 'bundled' platforms (intermediation + ad serving tools) now coexist with independent suppliers of inputs for online advertising (ad networks and ad exchange offering intermediation only and suppliers of standalone ad serving tools). In response to bundling strategies by the new entity, the competing platforms could respond by offering similar bundles.[298]

The ability of rivals to match a bundling strategy by the merged entity has been seen as an important factor that undermines the potential for anti-competitive foreclosure to arise in a number of other cases, including *Johnson&Johnson/Guidant*,[299] *GE/Smiths Aerospace*,[300] and *Procter&Gamble/Gillette*.[301]

---

[297] See Case COMP/M.4731 – *Google/DoubleClick*, Commission decision of 11 March 2008, para. 314.

[298] Ibid., para. 327.

[299] In *Johnson&Johnson/Guidant*, the Commission was satisfied that bundling would not give rise to anti-competitive foreclosure of rivals, because a bundling strategy could be matched by a number of competitors: Case COMP/M.3687 – *Johnson&Johnson/Guidant*, Commission decision of 25 August 2005, para. 341.

[300] In *GE/Smiths Aerospace*, the Commission noted that a competitor of Smiths Aerospace, UTC, was able to offer engines and power generation systems so that it would be able to replicate any bundling of these products by the merged entity and that Smiths Aerospace's other competitors would be able to respond to the tying behaviour of the new entity by teaming up with another engine manufacturer: Case COMP/M.4561 – *GE/Smiths/Aerospace*, Commission decision of 23 April 2007, para. 124.

[301] In *Procter&Gamble/Gillette*, although the merger would create greater opportunities for bundling, anti-competitive foreclosure was considered unlikely to arise given the presence of strong rivals with similar portfolios and powerful buyers. Importantly, the Commission accepted that Procter&Gamble/Gillette's enlarged product range may lead to efficiencies from one-stop-shopping and economies of scope (e.g. lower logistic costs). See Case COMP/M.3732 – *Procter&Gamble/Gillette*, Commission decision of 15 July 2005, paras. 121–2 and 131.

**5.5.3.2  Allegations regarding foreclosure of ad serving providers**
Complainants alleged that the merged entity might use Google's market
position in search advertising and (search) ad intermediation to foreclose
DoubleClick's rivals by bundling its sales of search ads or its intermedi-
ation services for the sale of search and/or non-search ads with Double-
Click's ad serving technology.

The Commission considered both pure bundling and mixed bundling strategies. Under pure bundling, advertisers wanting to place
search ads via Google's search advertising solution (AdWords) would
be (contractually) required to make a certain minimum use of DFA,
and/or publishers wanting to use Google's (search) ad intermediation
solution (AdSense) would be obliged to use DFP, either on a contractual basis or by means of a technological tie. Under mixed bundling,
Google would offer conditional discounts to induce advertisers and
publishers who utilise AdWords or AdSense to (voluntarily) utilise
DFA or DFP.

The Commission concluded that while the ability to engage in these
forms of foreclosure could not be entirely excluded, the merged entity
would be unlikely to have the incentive to engage in foreclosure and that,
in any event, such a strategy would not have a significant detrimental
effect on competition because a number of financially strong, vertically
integrated competitors would not be foreclosed.[302]

Regarding ability to foreclose, the Commission noted in particular that
there would be practical difficulties in requiring advertisers that want to
place search ads via Google's AdWords product to use DoubleClick's ad
serving product DFA. This is because prices for search advertising are
determined by an auction on a continuous basis (every time a user enters
a search query) whereas the terms according to which DoubleClick
provides display ad serving are set by contracts that typically have a
duration of one to two years, making it difficult to set the terms for these
products simultaneously.[303] These practical difficulties effectively
enabled the Commission to rule out bundling on the advertiser side.
Nonetheless, the Commission found that on the publisher side, the
practical difficulties in bundling Google's (search) ad intermediation with
DFP appeared to be more limited because for the provision of both

---

[302] See Case COMP/M.4731 – *Google/DoubleClick*, Commission decision of 11 March 2008,
     para. 332.
[303] See ibid., para. 340.

display ad serving and (search) ad intermediation for (larger) publishers, contractual arrangements of a similar nature and duration applied.[304] However, the Commission noted that the common pool of customers of Google and DoubleClick is currently fairly limited, reducing the ability of the merged entity to foreclose.[305]

Regarding the incentive to foreclose, the Commission found that bundling Google's sales of search ads and (search) intermediation services with DFA and/or DFP would not be profitable. It noted that as margins on DFA and DFP are low compared to margins on Google's direct sales of search ads and intermediated sales of (search) ads, even small volume losses in search advertising and (search) intermediation (due to customers rejecting the bundle) would outweigh the gain in profits from customers taking up DFA or DFP.[306]

The Commission also recognised that, as discussed in Section 5.4.2 above, an important benefit to bundling disappears if prices are individualised, rather than uniform across customers. In particular, the Commission noted:

> [I]n the online advertising environment transactions often involve customised solutions or services that are uniquely priced. Bundling is usually an attractive and profitable strategy in order to discern customer's willingness to pay in a context where prices are posted and uniform across customers. In the online advertising industry, bundling would not enable the new entity to increase profits because prices are highly individualized. On the advertiser side, both Google through its auction mechanism for keywords and DoubleClick through its direct negotiation with customers have the ability to vary the price of their products according to customers' willingness to pay. Similarly, on the publisher side, both Google through its negotiations with its direct partners (which account for around [>80%] of its AFS revenue) and DoubleClick through its direct negotiation with publishers, have the ability to vary the price of their products according to publishers' preferences. In such context, one of the attractions of bundling usually disappears.[307]

Finally, regarding the effect of foreclosure, the Commission reiterated that the merged entity would be very unlikely to marginalise competitors such as Microsoft, Yahoo! and AOL, noting that each of these competitors was vertically integrated and had access to considerable financial resources.[308]

---

[304] See ibid., para. 341.    [305] See ibid., para. 343.    [306] See ibid., para. 348.
[307] Ibid., para. 353.    [308] See ibid., para. 357.

## 6.   Diagonal mergers

The term 'diagonal merger' refers to a particular type of non-horizontal merger in which the merging parties are an upstream supplier and a downstream competitor of the firms for which the upstream supplier's good is an input.[309] The merger is not horizontal because the merging parties are not active in the same relevant market. Moreover, the merger is not vertical because the good produced by the upstream supplier is not an input as far as the downstream firm is concerned, despite it being an input for some of the downstream firm's competitors.

Whilst there is no customer that would switch from the good produced by one merging party to a good produced by the other merging party in response to a price increase, the two products may be substitutable in an indirect sense. This indirect substitutability arises because an increase in the price the upstream supplier charges to rivals of the other merging party will increase the costs of those rivals, potentially causing them to increase their prices, diverting downstream demand to the other merging party. A diagonal merger can therefore in principle give rise to a unilateral incentive to increase price.

Equally, a diagonal merger may give the downstream firm an incentive to increase its price if such a price increase would increase its rivals' sales and hence increase demand for the input supplied by the upstream merging party.

In assessing the extent to which a diagonal merger could give rise to an incentive to increase price it is necessary to consider:

- whether the input produced by the upstream firm is an important input for rivals of the downstream merging party;
- whether the upstream firm faces effective competition from other firms producing the input; and
- whether the products produced by downstream rivals are close substitutes for the products produced by the downstream merging party.

To understand further the unilateral effects concerns associated with diagonal mergers and the importance of each of the above considerations it is instructive to consider a stylised example in which a diagonal relationship could be said to arise.

---

[309]  This is equivalent in economic terms to a merger between a Firm A and a competitor of Firm B, whereby Firm A supplies a product that is a *complement* to the product supplied by Firm B.

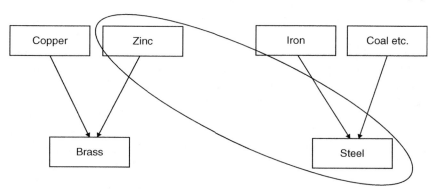

**Figure 5.13**   Illustration of a diagonal merger

### 6.1   Diagonal mergers: an example

This section presents a hypothetical example of a diagonal relationship between a supplier of zinc and a supplier of steel.[310] Zinc and copper are complementary inputs to the production of brass. Brass is a substitute for steel in certain applications. There are no customers that would consider switching from zinc to steel in the event of an increase in the price of zinc. However, these two products may nonetheless be indirectly substitutable: an increase in the price of zinc that results in an increase in the price of brass would cause an increase in the demand for steel; and an increase in the price of steel would cause an increase in the demand for brass, and therefore for zinc. A merger between a steel provider and a zinc provider would internalise this relationship, potentially giving rise to an incentive to increase the price of zinc and/or steel. Figure 5.13 illustrates the diagonal relationship between zinc and steel.

The following three conditions would need to be satisfied in order for the unilateral effects concern discussed above to materialise:

- *Zinc must represent an important cost in the production of brass.* To see why this is the case, suppose that zinc represented only 10% of the cost of producing any given volume of brass. In that case, a 10% increase in price by the zinc supplier would give rise to only a 1% increase in the production cost of brass. This would be unlikely to give rise to a

---

[310]   Higgins puts forward the example of a merger between a zinc supplier and steel supplier in the article that introduced the term 'diagonal merger'. See R. S. Higgins, 'Diagonal Merger' (1997) 12 *Review of Industrial Organization* 609–23.

significant increase in the price of brass and thus would be unlikely to give rise to a significant increase in the demand for steel. In effect, the low proportion of the cost of zinc in the overall cost of producing brass serves to lower the cross-price elasticity of demand for steel with respect to the price of zinc.

• *The zinc provider should not face effective competition from other zinc providers.* Suppose instead that the zinc supplier faced many competitors in the supply of zinc to brass suppliers. In that case, any increase in price by the zinc supplier will give rise to substitution to rival zinc suppliers by brass-producing customers, rather than any increase in the production cost of brass.

• *Brass and steel should be close substitutes.* If brass and steel were not close substitutes, then even a significant increase in the price of brass would not cause much of an increase in the demand for steel produced by the other merging party. In effect, the low degree of substitutability between brass and steel serves to lower the cross-price elasticity of demand for steel with respect to the price of zinc.

Each of these conditions must be considered simultaneously. In particular, the higher the degree of substitutability between brass and steel, the lower in principle need be the importance of zinc as a proportion of the cost of producing brass for a significant substitutability relationship to exist.

### 6.2   Case study: Google/Doubleclick – *assessment of diagonal effects*

The Commission had to consider the potential for a diagonal relationship to give rise to unilateral effects concerns during its investigation into the merger between Google and DoubleClick.[311]

As discussed in Section 5.5.3 above, there was no straightforward horizontal overlap between Google – a seller of ad space along with integrated (basic) ad serving for text ads, and DoubleClick – a seller of stand-alone display ad serving solutions.

The absence of horizontal overlaps between the parties' operations did not, however, rule out the possibility that the post-merger entity could have an immediate incentive to raise prices unilaterally.

Both the parties and complainants to the merger agreed that advertisers and publishers see text advertising and display advertising as

---

[311] See Case COMP/M.4731 – *Google/DoubleClick*, Commission decision of 11 March 2008.

substitutes. Complainants alleged that this created a diagonal relationship between Google and DoubleClick of the form described in the example above that would make unilateral price increases profitable for a combined entity.

Complainants alleged that an increase in the price of DoubleClick's advertiser-side ad serving solution (zinc in the example above) would increase the total cost to an advertiser of purchasing display advertising space (brass) in the unintegrated channel, to which DoubleClick's product is an input. Since the unintegrated channel is viewed as substitutable for the integrated channel in which Google sells text advertising (steel), there would be some diversion of demand to this channel, and some diversion of demand to Google. This diversion would be internalised by a combined entity, leading to an incentive to increase the price of the display ad serving solution.[312]

Whilst this concern makes sense in theory, analysis conducted by the parties revealed that none of the three conditions described in the context of our stylised example was present.

First, in choosing between different forms of advertising (e.g. text and display), advertisers consider the total cost of one form versus the total cost of another. Advertisers might well respond to a small but significant (5–10%) increase in the total cost of display advertising, for example, by re-allocating expenditure to text advertising. However, since display ad serving constitutes a small proportion of the total cost to the advertiser of display advertising, small but significant changes in the price of display ad serving can cause only tiny changes in the total cost of display advertising relative to the total cost of text advertising. To take a concrete example, suppose an advertiser pays 5 cents per thousand impressions in display ad serving fees to DoubleClick and pays $2 per thousand impressions to the publisher for the purchase of the ad space on the website. The total cost of advertising is therefore $2.05. If the price of the advertiser tool increases by 10% (from 5 cents to 5.5 cents), this would raise the total cost of advertising by only around 0.2% (from $2.05 to $2.055). As pointed out by the Commission, such price changes are therefore very unlikely to precipitate much (if any) switching from display advertising to text advertising.

---

[312] Similarly, an increase in the price of DoubleClick's publisher-side ad serving solution (DFP) would reduce the profits to a publisher from selling ad space in the unintegrated channel, leading to an increase in the amount of ad space sold in the integrated channel – an effect that would also be internalised by the combined entity.

Second, DoubleClick faced strong competition within the markets for display ad serving. As noted in Section 5.5.3.1, for some time, Double-Click had been forced to offer advertisers and publishers large price reductions at the point of renewing their contracts and, in addition, had lost a significant number of customers to rival display ad serving providers despite offering equally large price reductions. Competition within display ad serving implied that DoubleClick could not bring about a small increase in the price of ad serving, let alone one sufficient in size to cause any material switching to text advertising.

Third, Google supplies text ads whereas DoubleClick is an input provider to the supply of display ads. While these forms of advertising are substitutable, they are clearly differentiated to some extent. Therefore, it is unlikely that Google's integrated solution and an unintegrated solution that included DoubleClick's display ad serving technology as a component could be considered as particularly close substitutes.

The considerations set out above convinced the Commission that Google and DoubleClick did not exert a significant competitive con-straint on one another and therefore that no unilateral price increase would be profitable post-merger.

# Appendix A

## Regression analysis and econometrics

This Appendix provides a brief explanation of linear regression analysis and its use in econometrics. The goal of Section 1 is to allow the reader to gain a basic understanding of the output of regression analyses. In Section 2, we provide a brief introduction to a fundamental topic in econometrics: the identification of economically meaningful relationships. It is not our intention to provide a detailed guide to carrying out regression analysis in practice, a topic that is beyond the scope of this book. Moreover, we do not discuss the myriad of issues and complications that will often arise in regression analysis. A more detailed treatment of this topic can be found in any standard econometrics textbook.[1]

### 1. Regression analysis and statistical inference

Regression analysis is a tool for identifying a mathematical description reflecting an observed relationship between two or more variables. Regression analysis can allow a researcher to understand how the value of one variable tends to change when one or more other variables change.

To give a simplified example, consider the pricing of television sets. Let us imagine that a TV producer uses a 'rule of thumb' to set prices for its 3D ready, LED flat screen TVs. This pricing rule is based on only one aspect of the TV: its screen size. The rule can be expressed as a mathematical formula that will provide the price of a TV of any given screen size. Specifically, the TV price is given by the following equation, where P is price, and SCR is screen size in inches, minus 26 (26 inches being the minimum screen size available):

$$P = 200 + 68SCR$$

This expression tells us that the price, in Euros, will be equal to the screen size over and above the minimum 26 inches multiplied by €68, plus €200.

[1] See, e.g., J. M. Wooldridge, *Introductory Econometrics: A Modern Approach*, 4th edn (Mason, OH: Cengage Learning, 2009).

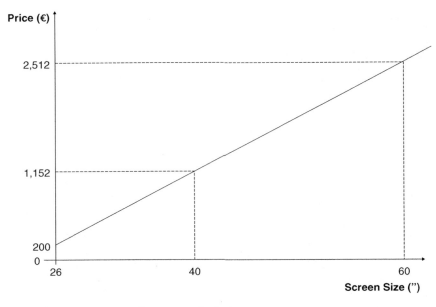

**Appendix A – Figure 1**    Illustration of rule for setting price given screen size

Thus, for any given screen size, the TV producer uses this equation to set the price. A 26-inch TV will have a price of €200, equal to 200 + 68*(26 – 26). A 40-inch TV will have a price of €1,152, equal to 200 + 68*(40–26). A 60-inch TV will have a price of €2,512, equal to 200 + 68*(60–26).

The relationship between screen size and price embodied in this equation can also be expressed graphically, as shown in Figure 1. For any given screen size, the line plotted in the figure shows the price in Euros.

In this example, the producer is using a known value of one variable (screen size) to set the value of another (price). Regression analysis reverses this process: rather than starting with the formula describing the relationship between variables to predict the value of one variable from the other, regression analysis starts with observed values for the variables and attempts to predict the formula that governs their relationship.

Suppose now that we, as researchers, hypothesise that the TV producer uses a fixed rule to set TV prices but that the specification of that pricing formula is not known to us. Note that we are not interested in understanding the economic mechanisms that cause the producer to set higher

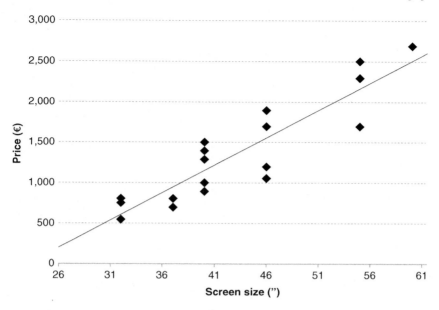

**Appendix A – Figure 2**   Illustrative regression – predicting prices from screen size

prices for larger TVs (such as the possibility that larger TVs have higher marginal costs of production, or that consumers are willing to pay more for larger TVs). We are only interested in uncovering the rule that the producer uses to set price.

Suppose that we have data showing the price and screen size of eighteen television sets sold by the producer, all with the same specification other than size (i.e. they are all 3D ready, flat screen with LED technology). The price and screen size of these eighteen observations are plotted in Figure 2.

Looking at these eighteen observations, the relationship between price and screen size for this product is relatively clear. While it is not possible to draw a straight line that goes through all the observations, the line shown on the chart can be seen to be a good reflection of the relationship. Regression analysis is a mathematical tool for identifying the equation that describes the so-called 'line of best fit' for a particular set of observations.

In most economic applications, we are interested in the effect of a change in an **explanatory variable** (here, screen size) on a **dependent variable** (here, price). That is what regression **coefficients** provide.

In this case, the regression coefficient represents an estimate of how much we can expect the producer to increase the price of a 3D ready, LED flat screen TV if the TV has a one inch bigger screen. Running a regression on the above data finds a coefficient for screen size of 68, which corresponds to the TV pricing formula described above.

The dotted line above is an attempt to describe the effect of screen size on the price of a TV, but none of the observations actually lies on that line. So we could depict the real relationship (the one we actually observe) as:

$$P = 200 + 68SCR + SOMETHING\,ELSE$$

This 'something else' is referred to as the unobservable or the **error term**; it is something that affects the economic process that we as researchers cannot see and therefore cannot incorporate into our model. In Figure 2, this error represents the distance between the dotted line and the data point, and is called the residual error, or **residual** for short.

We often have an idea, whether through application of economic theory or industry knowledge, of what factors might lie within the error term. For instance, one thing that we did not account for in our analysis was the 'newness' of the television set; each year when a new design of television sets comes out, older versions may still be sold, but at a lower price. It is likely that newer models look more stylish, are thinner and lighter or have a smaller stand. These things will affect the price of the set but are not included in our model. As discussed further below, we can include additional variables in a regression that explain some of the variance in price and thus allow us to identify the effect of screen size more accurately.

There are various forms of regression procedure for identifying the equation of a line that best fits the observed data. The most common technique is **ordinary least squares** ('OLS', the technique used here), which operates by minimising the sum of the squared residuals.

The above example is a very specific regression, in which we ask 'for 3D ready, LED flat screen TVs, what is the relationship between screen size and the price the producer sets?' If we were interested instead in the effect of screen size on the price of flat screen TVs more generally, then we would need to include more observations to account for the fact that TVs are also differentiated according to their screen technology (e.g. LED or Plasma) and other variables.

In practice, regression analyses can readily be expanded to account for multiple explanatory variables. Thus, in the context of the example above, the dependent variable of TV price might be explained not only by screen size, but also by screen type (LED or Plasma technology), whether it is '3D ready', whether it has Wi-Fi built in, its release date and other factors. Although such multi-dimensional relationships cannot be drawn graphically as in the two variable cases discussed above (such a chart would need to contain one dimension for each explanatory variable plus one for the dependent variable), the principle remains the same. Thus, a multivariate regression analysis will produce an equation that minimises the sum of square residuals from the observed combinations of the various variables included in the regression.

Suppose we applied the simple regression above (price on screen size) to a larger, more varied, sample that included TVs of various different specifications. This sample has forty-two observations and includes TVs that differ in terms of their screen technology, series model age, whether the TV is 3D ready and whether the TV is Wi-Fi enabled, as well as their screen size.

Table 1 shows the illustrative output from multivariate regression analysis that includes a number of explanatory variables in addition to screen size. While the format of the output will vary according to the software used, the key elements for the interpretation of the regression results will be common to all software packages.[2]

Table 1 presents the results for a regression that relates observations on the price of TVs to the following variables: the screen size in inches; a so-called **dummy variable**, 'LED', that takes the value 1 if the TV has an LED screen and 0 if it has a Plasma screen; a dummy variable, '3D', that takes the value 1 if the TV is 3D ready and 0 otherwise; a dummy variable, 'Wi-Fi', that takes the value 1 if the TV is Wi-Fi enabled and 0 otherwise; and a dummy for each of the model series available (if all are zero then the TV is the most recent model). These variables have been chosen on the hypothesis that the price of a television will increase with higher specifications and newer models.

The core element of any regression results is the set of **coefficients**. These are the estimated values of the gradient of the regression equation relating each explanatory variable (screen size, screen technology, series

---

[2] The process of using regression analysis to calculate coefficient estimates can be arithmetically burdensome, but can readily be performed by statistical analysis software packages, such as Stata, E-Views or SAS. Indeed, Microsoft Excel is capable of performing multivariate OLS regression analysis, albeit in a slightly cumbersome fashion, using the 'linest' command.

Table 1 *Illustrative OLS regression, dependent variable shipment price (€)*

|  | Coefficient | Standard error | t-statistic | p-value | 95% confidence interval | |
|---|---|---|---|---|---|---|
| **Screen size** | 56.13 | 5.56 | 10.10 | 0.000 | 44.82 | 67.43 |
| **LED** | 427.02 | 127.54 | 3.35 | 0.002 | 167.54 | 686.51 |
| **3D** | −50.03 | 136.12 | −0.37 | 0.716 | −326.97 | 226.91 |
| **Wi-Fi** | 145.51 | 113.17 | 1.29 | 0.207 | −84.74 | 375.77 |
| **Last model** | −244.71 | 165.58 | −1.48 | 0.149 | −581.59 | 92.16 |
| **2 models ago** | −592.35 | 115.44 | −5.13 | 0.000 | −827.21 | −357.48 |
| **3 models ago** | −953.20 | 157.39 | −6.06 | 0.000 | −1273.42 | −632.98 |
| **4 models ago** | −804.39 | 179.91 | −4.47 | 0.000 | −1170.41 | −438.37 |
| **Constant** | 309.2334 | 271.7705 | 1.14 | 0.263 | −243.69 | 862.15 |
| **n** | 42 | | | | | |
| **$R^2$** | 0.907 | | | | | |

age, etc.) to the dependent variable (price). The coefficient on each variable tells us how the average value of the dependent variable changes with a unit change in that explanatory variable. The coefficient on screen size is 56.13, meaning that each increase in screen size of one inch is on average associated with a €56.13 increase in the price of a TV, all else being equal.

The first point to review with a set of regression results is the **sign**, or direction, of the coefficients. In Table 1, the regression results show that the estimated coefficient on the LED dummy is positive. This indicates that, for a TV of a given screen size and model age, if the screen uses LED technology as opposed to Plasma we can expect the TV to be more expensive. The negative coefficient on the '3 models ago' dummy indicates that we can expect to pay a lower price for a TV of a given size and technology three releases old than an equivalent TV of the most recent model.

The sign or direction of coefficients must be interpreted in light of the question of **statistical significance**. Recall that we hypothesised that there is a 'true' underlying pricing rule that the producer employs to set prices for TVs. We are trying to identify that rule using a sample of forty-two observations of TV prices and characteristics. We observe that TVs that are Wi-Fi enabled have higher prices, on average, than those that are not (the sign of the coefficient on Wi-Fi is positive). However, this may just be an artefact of the forty-two TVs we happen to have sampled and may not be a feature of the 'true' underlying pricing rule. The concept of statistical significance relates to the confidence with which we can say that an observed effect has not arisen purely by chance. A particular coefficient on an explanatory variable (e.g. screen technology) is said to be 'statistically significant' if we can say that there is a low probability that the coefficient on that variable is different from zero by chance and we are hence able to reject the hypothesis that the variable has 'no effect' with a certain degree of confidence.[3]

The statistical significance of reported coefficient estimates may be presented in one or more of four ways: standard errors, confidence intervals, t-statistics, and/or p-values. The example above presents all four of these.

The extent to which we can be confident that there is a 'true' underlying effect will depend on the size of the effect we observe (i.e. the size of the coefficient) and on the degree of variation around that average effect we observe in the data. The smaller the variance around the average effect, the more likely that coefficient is to be an accurate reflection of the 'true' underlying effect of that variable. This variance is quantified via the **standard error** associated with each coefficient.

Whatever our chosen model, the coefficient we arrive at is always an estimate of the true parameter of interest. There will therefore be a range of alternative values surrounding our coefficient that could feasibly be the true value. If our estimator is unbiased then, given our data set, the probability of a given value being the true value declines the farther away it is from the estimate. If the estimate of a coefficient is 427.02, as for the LED screen dummy in the example above, the true value is more likely to be 427.02 than 450, which in turn is more likely to be the correct value than 375.

Once we know the standard error of an estimated coefficient, probability theory allows us to calculate the likelihood that the true value of the coefficient lies a particular distance from the estimate, given the data that we have in our sample. It is a standard result that there is a 95% probability that the true value of the coefficient lies within approximately two (1.96) standard errors of the estimated coefficient.

Thus, in Table 1, there is a 95% probability that the coefficient on the screen being LED as opposed to plasma lies within the range from 427.02 plus and minus 1.96 times the standard error (i.e. 167.54 to

---

[3] Often, in short hand, the explanatory variable itself is referred to as 'statistically significant'.

686.51). This range is called the **confidence interval**, and is shown in the final two columns of the table.

In regression analysis, we are often concerned with the direction of relationships. The principal use of standard errors and confidence intervals is to determine the likelihood that an estimated coefficient is statistically different from zero. A coefficient is said to be statistically significant at the 5% level (or significantly different from zero at the 5% level) if there is a 95% probability that the true value lies on the same side of zero as the estimated coefficient. This is equivalent to examining whether the 95% confidence interval includes only numbers of the same sign as the estimated coefficient or crosses the value of zero to include values of the opposite sign.

The standard approach in econometrics is to reject the hypothesis that a coefficient is zero (i.e. that the explanatory variable has no effect on the dependent variable) if the coefficient is statistically significant at the 5% level.[4] For those coefficients that do not meet the specified level of statistical significance we cannot reject the hypothesis that they are equal to zero at the 5% level. For example, from the output above, we can reject the hypothesis that the effect of TV screen size on its price is zero at the 5% significance level, since the 95% confidence interval does not include zero. However, we cannot reject the hypothesis that the effect of the TV being 3D ready on its price is zero at the 5% significance level, since the 95% confidence interval does include zero.[5]

The t-statistic and the p-value are alternative ways of summarising the significance of regression coefficients. The **t-statistic** represents the ratio of the coefficient to the standard error. As such, the absolute value of the t-statistic reflects the number of standard errors each coefficient lies away from zero. As per the discussion above, probability theory tells us the coefficients within 1.96 standard errors of zero are insignificant at the 5% level; an absolute t-statistic of more than 1.96 therefore indicates that a coefficient is significant at the 5% significance level.[6]

---

[4] The 5% threshold is arbitrary. Sometimes a significance level of 1% or 10% may be chosen, depending on our degree of aversion to the prospect of erroneously rejecting the 'no effect' hypothesis.

[5] We use the term 'do not reject', rather than 'accept', in hypothesis testing because the results of the test necessarily point towards the variable's significance, but do not rule out all other possibilities the way that 'to accept' indicates. The fact that we cannot rule out that the size of an effect is zero, does not mean we can 'accept' that the size of an effect is (exactly) zero.

[6] The equivalent values for the 1% and 10% significance levels are 2.58 and 1.65, respectively.

The **p-value** is related to the t-statistic, and represents the probability of observing a t-statistic that is as extreme as or more extreme than the one observed assuming that the hypothesis of 'no effect' is true. A p-value of less than 0.05 indicates that the coefficient is significant at the 5% level, and vice versa. Thus, while the t-statistic allows a coefficient to be evaluated against a specified significance level, the p-value identifies the critical significance level at which the coefficient would become statistically insignificant.

The remaining elements of the regression output are the constant, the number of observations, and the coefficient of variation. The constant represents the intercept for the regression equation; that is, the value of the price when the value of the screen size variable is 26 inches (since we defined the variable as the size of the screen minus 26 inches) and each of the other variables included in the regression is equal to zero. In many cases, the constant term is of limited interest. The analyst is often interested in the extent of the relationship between the explanatory and dependent variables; that is, the effect of a change in an explanatory variable on the dependent variable, rather than the level of the dependent variable in and of itself.

The **number of observations**, frequently denoted by the letter 'n', simply reflects the number of observed combinations of values used to estimate the regression equation. As noted above, this will affect the reliability of the estimates via their statistical significance.

The **coefficient of determination (or $R^2$)** is a statistic reflecting the 'goodness of fit' for the regression. The $R^2$ statistic lies between 0 and 1 and measures the proportion of the variation in the dependent variable that is explained by the explanatory variables. An $R^2$ of 1 means that the explanatory variables explain 100% of the variation in the dependent variable. An $R^2$ of 0 means that the explanatory variables explain none of the variation in the dependent variable. However, while it can be a useful indicator of the goodness of fit of a regression, the $R^2$ may not be of particular interest if our main concern is whether a particular variable (e.g. whether the TV is LED or Plasma) affects price holding other variables constant.

## 2. Regression analysis, endogeneity and the identification of economic effects

The preceding discussion has introduced the concept of regression analysis, which provides a tool for identifying the mathematical

relationship between observed variables. Regression analysis is a frequently used technique in the field of econometrics, which aims to link
real-world data to economic theory in order to empirically identify
economically meaningful relationships. In many cases, however, the
identification of a *statistical* relationship between variables will fail correctly to represent the underlying *economic* process governing those
variables that is of interest to the researcher due to the issue of
**endogeneity**.

In very loose terms, endogeneity can be defined as an issue which stops
us inferring that an apparent *statistical* relationship between two variables can be equated with any meaningful *economic* relationship between
those variables. In this section, we provide an illustration of endogeneity
in order to demonstrate its potential scope to lead to regression results
that give a distorted view of the true economic relationship of interest.

Our example concerns a study of the effect of education on a person's
salary.[7] We might observe that people with more years of education on
average earn higher salaries. In particular, a regression analysis might
find that, on average, one more year of education is associated with x
more Euros per year of salary. This might suggest the conclusion that one
more year of education will on average enable an individual to achieve a
higher salary of x Euros per year.

This approach, however, does not take account of the fact that individuals *choose* how many years of education to obtain. Many of the
factors that influence that choice, such as individuals' innate ability and
work ethic are unobservable to the econometrician. Critically, some of
the unobservable variables that influence educational choice are also
likely to affect how much an individual earns independently of the
amount of education they obtain. Therefore, the finding that people with
more years of education earn more might be explained (at least in part)
by the fact that individuals with a higher ability tend to choose more
years of education.

In this case the *statistical* relationship between years of education and
salary does not tell us about the incremental effect of education on salary,
which is the relationship of *economic* interest. Figure 3 is an illustration
of how the statistical relationship between education and salary may lead

---

[7] This is a well-known area of economic research in which endogeneity problems arise. See,
e.g., Z. Griliches, 'Estimating the Returns to Schooling: Some econometric problems'
(1977) 45 *Econometrica* 1–22.

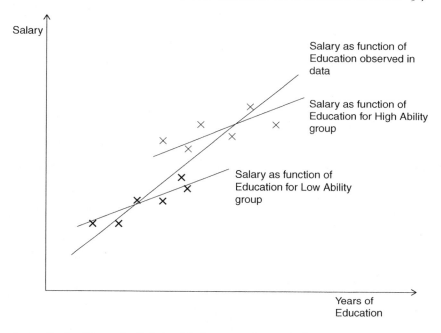

**Appendix A – Figure 3**   Relationship between salary and education

us to overstate the economically meaningful relationship that describes the additional impact on salary of an additional year of education.

Figure 3 shows a number of observations of years of education and salary for individuals with 'low ability' (denoted by bold crosses) and a number of observations of years of education and salary for individuals with 'high ability' (denoted by light crosses). It can be seen that 'low ability' individuals on average choose lower levels of education than 'high ability' individuals and for any given level of education earn a lower salary. The 'true' underlying impact of an additional year of education on salary for each group is shown by the slope of a line of best fit through each of these sets of points. However, it is not possible in practice to observe which points are associated with 'low ability' individuals and which points are associated with 'high ability' individuals. Drawing an 'observed' line of best fit through all the points as a whole leads to a line that is steeper than the 'true' relationship between education and salary within either group. The slope of the 'observed' line of best fit does not therefore reveal the true impact of an additional year of education on salary.

The problem of endogeneity discussed above would disappear entirely if any of the following were true:

- we could clone individuals and send them off to work while keeping their clones in education another year. By construction, the only difference between each individual and his or her clone would be the amount of education they receive. In this way we could directly infer the incremental economic effect of a year of schooling simply by considering the average difference in salary between each individual and his or her clone;
- a 'mad dictator' decided how much education each individual should obtain on a completely randomised basis. Recall that the endogeneity problem arises because the finding that people with more years of education earn more might be explained (at least in part) by the fact that individuals with a higher ability tend both to earn more for any given level of education and to choose to obtain more education. If educational choice is removed from the individuals, then the endo-geneity problem disappears. This is the basis for randomised trials in medical research, which are organised such that the only difference between treatment and control groups is whether or not they receive the treatment, allowing any systematic difference in medical outcomes between the groups to be attributed purely to the treatment;
- we could observe 'innate ability' directly. If we could observe 'ability' directly, we could simply divide all individuals into a 'high ability group' and a 'low ability group' and find the relationship between education and salary for each group.

Unfortunately for economic researchers none of these solutions is realis-tic. In particular, econometricians rarely have the ability to carry out experiments under controlled conditions. As such, the field of economet-rics has devoted particular attention to developing techniques to circum-vent endogeneity. A common approach is to employ **instrumental variables**. A working definition of an instrumental variable is a variable that affects one part of a system but not another, thereby enabling the researcher to identify a relationship of interest.[8] While the use of

---

[8] More precisely, the main requirements for using an instrumental variable are that the instrumental variable must be correlated with the endogenous explanatory variables, conditional on the other covariates; and the instrument cannot be correlated with the error term in the explanatory equation.

instrumental variables is beyond the scope of this book, a more detailed treatment of this technique can be found in any standard econometrics textbook.[9]

[9] For a further discussion of endogeneity and instrumental variables, see J. M. Wooldridge, *Introductory Econometrics: A Modern Approach*, 4th edn (Mason, OH: Cengage Learning, 2009).

# Appendix B

## Models for demand estimation

### 1. Introduction

In Chapter 2 we considered a simple form of demand estimation based on linear demand. This appendix provides some further background on different forms of demand estimation that are applied in the context of merger investigations.

### 1.1 Alternative models for continuous demand estimation

Consider the linear illustrative demand curve for Jaffa orange juice presented in Chapter 2, Section 3.2.1.1 at Figure 2.6. From this demand curve we can see that a one unit increase in price will lead to a fall in demand of 10 units, a relationship that holds true at all prices. Consequently, in using a linear demand system we have imposed the restriction that if the price falls from £10 to £0, for example, we will have the same increase in demand as if the price had fallen from £150 to £140. Intuitively this does not seem like a desirable attribute for a demand curve to have.

It is possible to specify a demand relationship that does not have this property. Consider a demand function that is described by the following equation:

$$quantity_j = \alpha price_j^\beta$$

This demand curve is shaped as shown in Figure 1.

The curvature and placement of the demand curve are determined by the parameters $\alpha$ and $\beta$, where $\beta$ is negative.

If we take natural logarithms of this equation (a simple transformation) the resulting relationship is linear and therefore easy to estimate using the same methods as in the simple linear model:

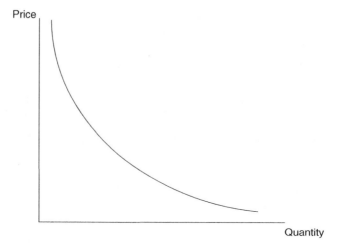

**Appendix B – Figure 1**    Non-linear demand curve

$$\text{In}(quantity_j) \;=\; \text{In}(\alpha) + \beta \text{In}\,(price_j)$$

As a technical point, the use of natural logarithms means that the coefficient $\beta$ can be interpreted as the price elasticity of demand – as such this demand curve exhibits constant elasticity at any price.

The constant elasticity demand curve is just one form of non-linear demand function that can be empirically identified. However, while the assumption of constant elasticity allows a demand curve to be identified relatively easily, the assumption of this functional form imposes restrictions on the shape of the demand curve.

The challenge in empirical analysis is to find a modelling framework that balances ease of computation (which generally requires the imposition of more assumptions regarding consumer behaviour) and flexibility (for which fewer assumptions are preferable). A popular demand model frequently used in empirical research is the **Almost Ideal Demand System (AIDS)**.[1] The AIDS model makes use of well-grounded assumptions from individual level microeconomic theory: namely, that consumers have a utility function that they maximise subject to a budget constraint. This is an important assumption that allows us to use price and quantity data, in addition to individuals' expenditure, to derive a demand function. A convenient property of the AIDS model is that if

---

[1]  A. Deaton and J. Muellbauer, (1980) 70(3) *The American Economic Review* 312–26.

all individuals in a given multi-product market conform to the restrictions imposed by the demand equation then so does the aggregate. The AIDS model yields a demand curve that provides numerous parameters of interest, including own- and cross-price elasticities, from a model with strong foundations in fundamental microeconomic theory. Nonetheless, while the AIDS model is relatively parsimonious in its data requirements, the number of parameters to be estimated increases rapidly with the number of products analysed. In a market featuring 50 differentiated products, for instance, it would be necessary to estimate $50^2$, that is, 2,500 different parameters.

### 1.2   Models for discrete demand estimation

The AIDS model is based on the assumption that consumers make purchasing decisions in order to maximise some utility function. This function is likely, in its most complete form, to include prices and other product characteristics that are both observable and unobservable to the econometrician. **Discrete choice analysis** is used to characterise the choice made by a consumer when choosing a single product from a number of options. For example, when considering how to travel from London to Brussels a consumer would not be considering *how much* of a particular mode of transport she should buy given prevailing prices, but *which* mode of transport she should buy given prevailing prices. When she chooses to travel by aeroplane she makes a discrete choice that, in theory, has maximised her utility subject to a budget constraint.

A fundamental assumption is that agents choose the alternative which provides them with the highest utility. The utility derived from a particular choice is often assumed to be a linear function of a set of choice-specific observable variables, a set of individual-specific observable variables and an unobservable random error term. For example, a consumer's utility from choosing a particular car may be related to a number of car-specific variables (size, fuel efficiency, etc.), a number of variables specific to the individual (number of family members, income, age) and some components that we cannot observe.

A complication of this approach is that we must make assumptions about what we cannot observe in the model. The assumptions we choose to make will affect the results of our analysis. A popular assumption for discrete choice analysis is that the unobserved variable follows a 'type 1 extreme value distribution' (the details of which are not important for this brief treatment), which gives the **conditional logit** demand model.[2] This model provides, for each good, the conditional probability that an individual selects that good above all others. If one has data on individual characteristics such as income or number of family members then these data can be taken into account to produce an estimate of the probability that an individual selects a particular good above all others given that individual's characteristics. Multiplication of these probabilities by the total number of consumers in the market therefore describes the total quantity demanded for each product.

Often, particularly during merger simulation, we are interested in the **odds-ratio**. This is the probability that one good, $i$, is chosen relative to the probability that another good, $j$, is chosen. Thus, for example, if the odds-ratio between $i$ and $j$ is 2, this implies that a new consumer entering the market is twice as likely to select good $i$ than $j$.

The assumptions of the conditional logit model allow the odds-ratio between products to be readily calculated in terms of observed variables. However, these assumptions also imply that the odds-ratio between goods $i$ and $j$ is independent of (a) any good other than $i$ or $j$, and (b) the number of alternative products in the market.

This property is termed the **independence of irrelevant alternatives (IIA)**. IIA implies that the probability that one good is chosen relative to the probability that another good is chosen does not change if a third alternative is added (or has its characteristics changed). Unfortunately this attribute is counterintuitive in many cases. For example, consider the following classic example (from McFadden in 1973) of a commuter's transport market, in which there are two possible methods of getting to work: by red bus or by car.[3] Suppose that a consumer chooses each of these options with probability 1/2 (implying an odds-ratio of 1). Suppose now that another option, a blue bus, is added to the set of alternative means of transport and that consumers that choose to travel by bus are completely indifferent as regards its colour (red buses and blue buses are perfect substitutes). Intuitively, one might expect that consumers would still choose 'car' with probability 1/2, and 'bus' with probability 1/2, implying that red bus and blue bus are each chosen with probability of

---

[2] See D. McFadden, 'Conditional Logit Analysis of Qualitative Choice Behaviour', in P. Zaermbka (ed.), *Frontiers in Econometrics* (New York: Academic Press, 1973).

[3] McFadden was not the first to point out the problem with IIA. This was Gérard Debreu in 1960, who used the slightly more highbrow example of the market for the music of Ludwig van Beethoven and Claude Debussy.

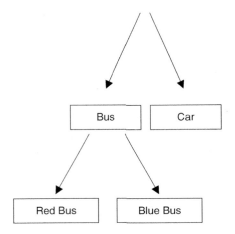

**Appendix B – Figure 2**   Structure of consumer's decision-making process

1/4. However, this would violate IIA. This is because, if IIA holds, the odds-ratio for car/red bus (previously 1) should not be changed following the addition of blue bus as an additional alternative. Indeed, in this situation IIA would require that car, red bus and blue bus are each chosen with probability 1/3. IIA fails to take into account that red bus and blue bus are closer substitutes to one another than either is to car.

The IIA assumption is the source of the criticism that logit demand models assume that switching to alternative brands is in proportion to each brand's share of supply amongst the set of alternatives. Common sense tells us that switching from a given brand need not be in proportion to brand share and that certain brands may be 'closer' to one another.

The conditional logit method can be adjusted to account for this problem via the use of nests, which cluster goods together based upon their attributes. In the above example, for instance, we might place the red bus and blue bus together in the same nest, such that the first decision made by the commuter is bus versus car, and the second decision (where bus is chosen) is red bus versus blue bus. The structure of the consumer's decision-making process in this framework is represented graphically in Figure 2.

This method of estimating a demand framework is known as the **nested logit model**. It is essentially a logit as described above applied to each stage of the decision process. It enables researchers to specify groups of alternatives that are similar to each other (allowing for some correlation of consumer tastes across products). By grouping alternatives within a particular nest into sub-nests, this can be generalised so that there are multiple nesting levels.

The nested logit model is often used in economic research and was recently used in *Kraft Foods/Cadbury* (put forward in evidence by the parties as a part of their merger simulation) and in *Unilever/Sara Lee Body Care*.

As always this estimation method has its pros and cons. One clear advantage it has is that the number of parameters to be estimated is vastly smaller than with the AIDS model described above. However, this comes at a cost. The (relative) ease with which the model is estimated is a consequence of the rigid structure on substitution patterns imposed by the choice of nests and the allocation of products between those nests. These choices, which are crucial in determining the outcome of the model, must be made *a priori* by the econometrician on the basis of other evidence or intuition. Consequently, to a large extent, the outcome of nested logit models may derive not from the econometric analysis of the data but from somewhat arbitrary decisions made by the researcher. As such, the nested logit model's inability to provide objective guidance on substitution patterns between products may in some cases make it an unattractive approach in the context of merger assessment.

For a more detailed discussion of discrete choice and demand estimation more generally, see, for example, Davis and Garcés.[4]

---

[4] P. Davis and E. Garcés, *Quantitative Techniques for Competition and Antitrust Analysis* (Princeton University Press, 2009).

# INDEX

Printed in Great Britain
by Amazon

18951325R00319